France

Red Bor[deaux]

Vintage	Médoc/Graves				
2024	6–7				
2023	7–8				
2022	7–8	7–8	7–9	6–7	7–8
2021	5–7	5–7	7–8	7–9	6–8
2020	7–8	7–9	7–8	7–8	8–9
2019	7–9	6–9	7–8	7–9	6–8
2018	8–9	8–9	7–9	7–8	7–8
2017	6–8	6–7	8–9	7–8	9–10
2016	8–9	8–9	8–10	7–9	7–8
2015	7–9	8–10	8–10	7–9	7–9
2014	7–8	6–8	8–9	8–9	7–8
2013	4–7	4–7	8–9	7–8	8–9
2012	6–8	6–8	5–6	7–9	8–9
2011	7–8	7–8	8–10	7–8	5–7
2010	8–10	7–10	7–8	7–9	8–9
2009	7–10	7–10	8–10	7–9	8–9
2008	6–8	6–9	6–7	7–8	7–8
2007	5–7	6–7	8–9	8–9	6–8
2006	7–8	7–8	7–8	8–9	6–8

France, continued

Vintage	Burgundy			Rhône	
	Côte d'Or red	Côte d'Or white	Chablis	North	South
2024	6–8	7–8	6–8	7–8	7–8
2023	7–9	6–8	7–8	6–8	6–8
2022	7–9	7–9	7–8	7–8	6–8
2021	6–8	7–8	7–8	6–8	6–8
2020	6–8	7–9	6–8	7–8	6–8
2019	7–9	7–10	7–9	8–9	7–9
2018	6–9	7–8	7–9	7–9	6–8
2017	6–9	8–9	8–9	7–9	7–9
2016	7–8	6–8	5–7	7–9	8–9
2015	7–9	6–8	7–8	8–9	8–9
2014	6–8	8–9	7–9	7–8	6–8
2013	5–7	6–7	6–8	7–9	7–8
2012	8–9	7–8	7–8	7–9	7–9
2011	7–8	7–8	7–8	7–8	6–8

Beaujolais 23 22 21 20 19 18 17 15 14, crus will keep. **Mâcon-Villages** white 23 22 21 20 19 18 17 15. **Loire** sweet Anjou, Touraine 23 22 21 20 19 18 15 10 09 07 05 02 97 96 93 90; Bourgueil, Chinon, Saumur-Champigny 23 22 21 20 19 18 17 15 14 10 09 06 05 04; Sancerre, Pouilly-Fumé 23 22 21 20 19 18 17 15 14; Muscadet 23 22 21 20 19 18 17 16 15 14.

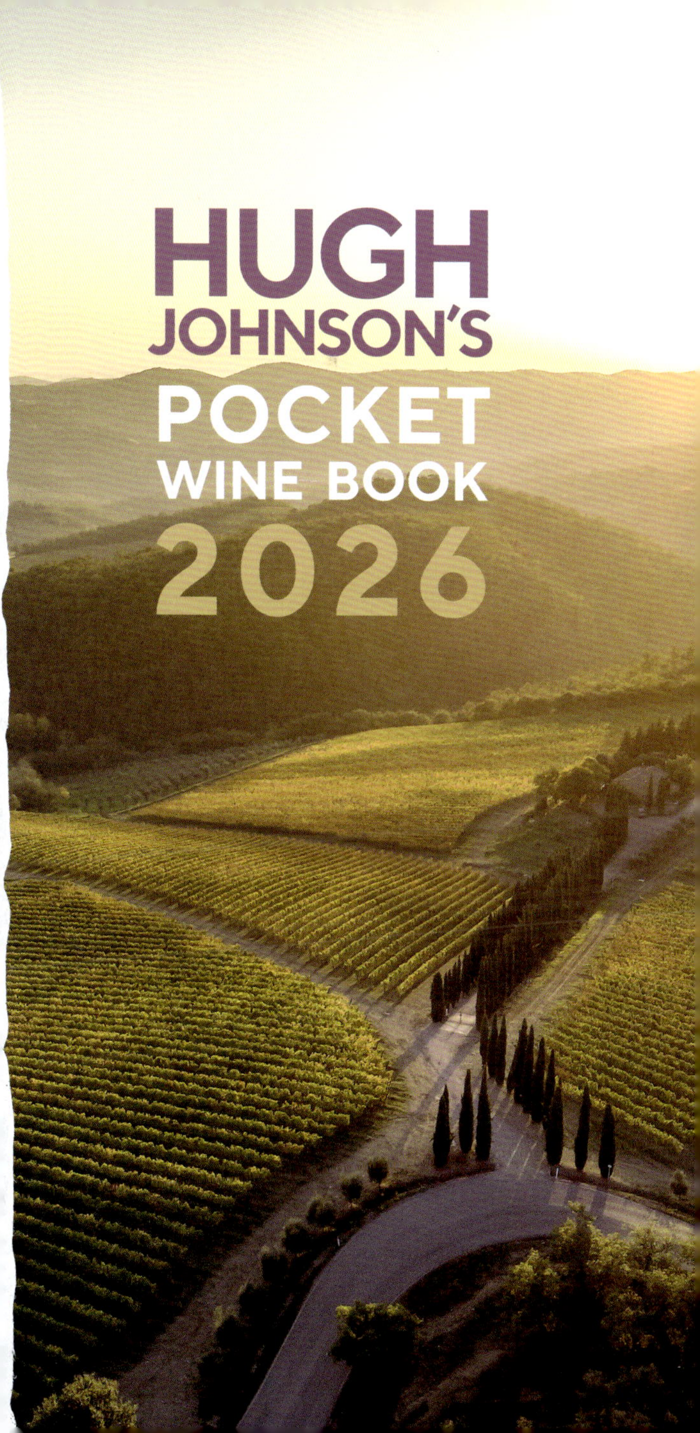
HUGH
JOHNSON'S
POCKET
WINE BOOK
2026

Hugh Johnson's Pocket Wine Book 2026

First published in Great Britain in 2025 by Mitchell Beazley, an imprint of
Octopus Publishing Group Limited,
Carmelite House, 50 Victoria Embankment,
London EC4Y 0DZ
www.octopusbooks.co.uk

An Hachette UK Company
www.hachette.co.uk

The authorized representative in the EEA is Hachette Ireland,
8 Castlecourt Centre, Dublin 15, D15 XTP3, Ireland (email: info@hbgi.ie)

Copyright © Octopus Publishing Group Ltd 2025
Illustrations copyright © Hilary Fitzgerald Campbell 2025

First edition published 1977

Revised editions published 1978, 1979, 1980, 1981, 1982, 1983, 1984, 1985,
1986, 1987, 1988, 1989, 1990, 1991, 1992, 1993, 1994, 1995, 1996, 1997,
1998, 1999, 2000, 2001, 2002 (twice), 2003, 2004, 2005, 2006 (twice), 2007,
2008, 2009, 2010, 2011, 2012, 2013, 2014, 2015, 2016, 2017, 2018, 2019,
2020, 2021, 2022, 2023, 2024, 2025

Distributed in the US by Hachette Book Group
1290 Avenue of the Americas, 4th and 5th Floors,
New York, NY 10104

Distributed in Canada by Canadian Manda Group
664 Annette St, Toronto, Ontario, Canada M6S 2C8

A CIP record for this book is available from
the British Library.

ISBN: 978-1-78472-872-4

The author and publishers will be grateful for any information that will
assist them in keeping future editions up to date. Although all reasonable
care has been taken in preparing this book, neither the publishers nor the
author can accept any liability for any consequences arising from the use
thereof, or from the information contained herein.

General Editor **Margaret Rand**
Commissioning Editor **Hilary Lumsden**
Publishing Director **Alison Starling**
Senior Developmental Editor **Pauline Bache**
Proofreader **David Tombesi-Walton**
Art Director **Yasia Williams-Leedham**
Designer **Jeremy Tilston**
Picture Research Manager **Jennifer Veall**
Senior Production Manager **Katherine Hockley**

Printed and bound in China

Mitchell Beazley would like to acknowledge and thank the following
for supplying photographs for use in this book:

Alamy Stock Photo: Paolo Bona 7; **iStock:** Fani Kurti 1, MarkSwallow 11;
Unsplash: Bernard Hermant 12

Illustrations (pp.353–68) by Hilary Fitzgerald Campbell

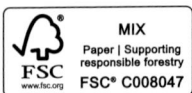

HUGH JOHNSON'S

POCKET
WINE BOOK
2026

GENERAL EDITOR

MARGARET RAND

Contributors

To demonstrate that no one person can be up to date with the vinous affairs of every wine-producing country in the world, this is the book's team of contributors:

Key: ❶ Facebook; **❷** Instagram; **❸** X (Twitter); **❹** website; **❺** book/press; **❻** blog/other media

Helena Baker DipWSET, Czechia, Slovakia: **❶** helena.baker.73; **❷** @bakerwine837; **❸** @HelenaB62554469; **❹** bakerwine.cz

Kristel Balcaen DipWSET, Belgium: **❶** kristel.balcaen.1; **❷** @kristel_balcaen; **❹** wineandwords.be; **❻** *Wijnboek voor Foodies*

Amanda Barnes MW, S America: **❶** SouthAmericaWineGuide; **❷** @southamericawineguide; **❸** @amanda_tweeter; **❺** *South America Wine Guide*

Raymond Blake, Burgundy: **❷**+**❸** @blakeonwine; **❹** blakeonwine.com; **❺** Côte d'Or

Juliet Bruce Jones MW, Midi, Provence, Corsica: **❶** latasque; **❷** @domainelatasque; **❹** domainelatasque.com

Ch'ng Poh Tiong, Asia: **❷** @Chngpohtiong; **❹** Top30.com.sg, Chngpohtiong.com; **❺** *A Primer on Pairing*; **❻** Chngpohtiong (Little Red Book "Xiao Hong Shu")

Samantha Cole-Johnson, Oregon: **❷** @samanthacolejohnson; **❹** jancisrobinson.com

Ian D'Agata, Alsace, Italy, Malta: **❷** @ian_dagata; **❹** iandagata.com, terroirsense.com/en; **❻** *Italy's Native Wine Grape Terroirs; Native Wine Grapes of Italy*

Sarah Jane Evans MW, Spain: **❶** Sarah Jane Evans MW; **❷**+**❸** @sjevansmw; **❹** sarahjaneevans.com; **❺** *The Wines of Northern Spain, The Wines of Central and Southern Spain*

Jane Faulkner, Australia: **❶**+**❷**+**❸** @winematters; **❺** *Halliday Wine Companion*

Simon Field MW, Champagne: **❻** *World of Fine Wine*

Caroline Gilby MW, E Europe, Cyprus: **❶** Caroline Gilby MW; **❷** @Caroline Gilby; **❺** *The Wines of Bulgaria, Romania and Moldova, Wines of Serbia: A New Chapter*

Susan H Gordon PhD MFA, US E States: **❷** @drsusanhillaryg; **❺** *ForbesLife, Gastronomica, The Story of Prosecco Superiore*

Michael Karam, Lebanon: **❺** *Wines of Lebanon, Arak and Mezze, Tears of Bacchus, Lebanese Wine: A Complete Guide*; **❻** *Wine and War* (Amazon Prime)

Chris Kissack, Loire **❶** drchriskissack; **❷**+**❸** @chriswinedoctor; **❹** thewinedoctor.com

James Lawther MW, Bordeaux: **❹** jancisrobinson.com; **❺** *The Finest Wines of Bordeaux, On Bordeaux*

Konstantinos Lazarakis MW, Greece: **❶** Konstantinos Lazarakis II; **❷** @Konstantinos Lazarakis MW; **❸** @Lazarakis; **❹** wspc.gr, aioloswines.gr; **❺** *The Wines of Greece*

John Livingstone-Learmonth, Rhône: **❸** @drinkrhone; **❹** drinkrhone.com; **❻** *The Wines of the Northern Rhône*

Michele Longo, Italy: **❷** @michele_nebbiolo; **❹** iandagata.com; **❻** *Italian Wine Terroirs, The Grapes and Wines of Italy, Barolo Terroir, Barolo & Co*

Wink Lorch, Bugey, Jura, Savoie: **❶**+**❷**+**❸** @WinkLorch; **❹** winetravelmedia.com; **❻** *Jura Wine, Jura Wine Ten Years On, Wines of the French Alps*; **❻** jurawine.co.uk

Adam Sebag Montefiore, Israel, Turkey, N Africa: **❹** adammontefiore.com, wines-israel.com; **❺** *Jerusalem Post, The Wine Route of Israel, Wines of Israel*

Rod Phillips, Canada **❷** @rodphillipswine; **❹** rodphillipsonwine.com; **❻** *Wines of Canada, French Wine: A History, 9000 Years of Wine*

Margaret Rand, General Editor, England: *see back flap of book*

Christina Rasmussen, Scandinavia: **❷** @christinarasmussen_; **❸** @Christina_SvR; **❹** littlewine.io, christinarasmussen.co

André Ribeirinho, Portugal: **❶**+**❷**+**❸** @andrerib; **❹** andrerib.co

John Saker, NZ: **❷** @john_saker_wine; **❹** johnsaker.com; **❺** *Pinot Noir: The New Zealand Story, How To Drink A Glass Of Wine*; **❻** Te Whenua

Ulrich Sautter, Germany, Switzerland, Luxembourg: **❹** falstaff.com, weinverstand.com

Luzia Schrampf, Austria: **❶**+**❷** @Luzia Schrampf; **❺** *111 Austrian Wines You Must Not Miss, 111 Sparkling Wines Worldwide You Must Not Miss* (with D Dejnega)

Eleonora Scholes, Black Sea & Caucasus: **❷** @spaziovino; **❹** spaziovino.com

Matthew Stubbs MW, SW France: **❷** @vinecole_wine_education; **❹** vinecole.com

Sean P Sullivan, Washington State & Idaho: **❶**+**❷** @northwestwinereport; **❸** @nwwinereport; **❹** northwestwinereport.com; **❺** *Seattle Metropolitan*

Tim Teichgraeber, California: **❷** @timskyscraper; **❻** modernwine.blogspot.com

James Tidwell MS, US SW&SE States, Wisconsin, Mexico: **❶** JamesTidwellMS; **❷**+**❸** @winejames; **❹** texsom.com

Philip van Zyl, S Africa: **❺** *Platter's by Diners Club South African Wine Guide*

Contents

How to use this book

—

The top line of most entries consists of the following information:

1. **Aglianico del Vulture** Bas

2. ★★★

3. 17' 18 19 20 21' 22 (23)

1. **Aglianico del Vulture** Bas

Wine name and region. Abbreviations of regions are listed in each section.

2. ★★★

Indication of quality – a necessarily rough-and-ready guide:

★	reliable, everyday quality
★★	very good quality
★★★	excellent
★★★★	outstanding, compelling
★ etc.	Stars are coloured for any wine that, in our experience, is usually especially good within its price range. There are good everyday wines, as well as good luxury wines. This system helps you find them.

We try to be objective, but no wine rating can ever be wholly objective.

3. 17' 18 19 20 21' 22 (23)

Vintage information: those recent vintages that are outstanding, and of these, which are ready to drink this year and which will probably improve with keeping. Your choice for current drinking should be one of the vintage years printed in **bold** type. Buy light-type years for further maturing.

22 etc.	recommended years that may be currently available
21' etc.	vintage regarded as particularly successful for the property in question
18 etc.	years in bold should be ready for drinking (those not in bold will benefit from keeping)
20 etc.	vintages in colour are those recommended as first choice for drinking in 2026. (*See also* Bordeaux introduction, p.105)
(23) etc.	provisional rating

The German vintages work on a different principle again: *see* p.178.

Abbreviations

Style references appear in brackets where required:

r	red
w	white
dr	dry
sw	sweet
s/sw	semi-sweet
sp	sparkling

DYA	drink the youngest available
NV	Non Vintage; in Champagne this means a blend of several vintages for continuity
CHABLIS	properties, areas or terms cross-referenced within the section; all grapes cross-ref to Grape Varieties chapter on pp.12–22
Foradori	entries styled this way indicate wine especially enjoyed by Margaret Rand and/or the author of that section (mid-2024–25)

For help in sourcing wines in this book we recommend winesearcher.com

If you have any feedback, please contact us on pocketwine@octopusbooks.co.uk

Agenda 2026

—

The theme of this edition is value – and honestly, you might think, does it take a whole book to talk about value in wine? The more you know and love wine, and the more you want to enjoy good wine, the more you appreciate its complexities. If value was a question of buying the cheapest available, you wouldn't bother with a book for that. But if you've got this far, you're well aware that there are few universal rules in choosing wine: what applies in one country, one region, might not apply in another.

So, here's a universal rule that applies to every region, every country: choose your wine by the producer. The appellation (the legally defined region of origin), however it's expressed, will give you a broad guide to style but not to quality, and in some of the most famous – Chablis is a good example, Rioja is another – you should only buy from a good producer. Any appellation famous enough to be a lifebelt for those grasping for a familiar name has a proportion of producers who don't try too hard. They mop up the least good grapes, make them to a price and a profit margin and sell them, often under a variety of labels, to those who don't want to try too hard to look for something better. They fulfil a function, certainly, but let's not be the ones who buy the wine.

We've added extra pages to the *Pocket Wine Book* this year – you need a bigger pocket now – and we've filled them with more growers, all of them names that our contributors rate highly. For stockists, check out winesearcher.com, because a simpler wine from a great producer will beat a more prestigious wine from a run-of-the-mill producer, and probably won't cost more. For example, at a tasting recently I gasped at the price of an Hautes-Côtes de Nuits from a leading grower. (It sometimes doesn't pay to remember what Burgundy used to cost back in the day; it only makes one sound like one's mother.) Hautes-Côtes! Really? And then I tasted it. And in the context of wines worldwide of that price or more, did it seem overpriced? No: it was a beauty. The wine was what mattered, not the appellation.

Was it a wine to keep? No; the same producer's *vins de garde* cost much, much more. It was a wine of seductive elegance, pure joy to drink now. And you know, I'm increasingly unconvinced a great wine is one that will age 30 years or more. The longer the ageing period, the less the accountability, in a sense: if it's disappointing, all you can do is shrug. The longer you age wine, the truer it is that there are no great wines, only great bottles.

Yet you expect a good return in terms of quality and complexity after all that time. You expect it to be superb, not merely as good as it was when you bought it. Of course it will have changed; but it should change for the better, not just for the older. And chances are that that producer is making better wines now than they were then. Perhaps a younger wine would have been nicer.

Nigel Greening (Felton Road, NZ) said recently that quality is not a matter of how long a wine ages, but how good it is at its peak. That sums it up perfectly. Modern winemaking and modern viticulture are better. They produce wines that are good much, much younger. Will they live as long? Possibly not. But how much does it matter if they won't see out five decades, when they are so delicious at five years or ten?

Most of us, if we have (or can organize) a place to store wine, buy far more than we can drink. My contemporaries are now selling off their cellars, realizing that they'll never get through it all and that there are other wines they want to try. They're often pleasantly surprised by the financial return, so it's win-win; they had the pleasure of buying the wine in the first place too, because buying wine, like buying cheese or buying books, is a thing that makes any day better.

Which brings me to the other universal rule: trust your wine merchant. Good independent wine merchants are gems; they love what they do, they love hunting down good wines and they don't want to take advantage of customers because they want to keep them. They are the lifeblood of wine. Supermarkets buy wine that will sell easily, at a margin that will please the bean-counters. Independents buy, in much smaller quantities, wines that they think you will love once you get the chance to taste them; so, they'll open bottles on a Saturday, or a Friday night, and they'll tell you all about them, and what happened when they went to visit the producers.

You probably won't find the very cheapest wines at an independent merchant. Which is where we came in: value in wine is not about cheapness. Our focus this year is on that sweet spot where price meets quality. At the bottom end, the price is largely tax. At the very top end, it's largely a premium paid for rarity or prestige. I'm not saying that very expensive wines are not "worth" it; but "worth" is subjective and depends on what you want. If you want to impress someone who is impressed by price, it's worth it. If you want to taste the very finest, the very rarest, it's worth it.

Quality is related to price in wine, but it's not a steady line on a graph. Quality rises very steeply in relation to price to begin with, and above a certain point (which varies with every wine, unfortunately) quality rises slowly while the price rockets. The sweet spot of value we seek is just below that point at which price starts to rise faster than quality.

People sometimes (quite often, in fact) ask me, "What's a good wine?" To which I say, "Do you only want one? We have a whole book of them."

Margaret Rand
General Editor

12 wines to try in 2026

—

Twelve wines this year, all exceptional, all remarkable for quality and value. All of these come into our sweet spot for pricing.

Red wines

Vieilles Vignes Carignan, Domaine des Tourelles, Lebanon

This is a longstanding favourite of mine, and I still don't understand how something so silky, savoury, herbal and layered can be so inexpensive. The vines are over 50 years old, and old-vine Carignan has enormous character and depth. Tourelles makes wines of poise and freshness, utterly modern, fine and long-lived.

Yallingup Cabernet Sauvignon, Nocturne, Margaret River, Australia

Minimum-intervention, indigenous-yeast Cabernet: winemaker Julian Langworthy calls it "careful neglection". A classic tobacco nose, very elegant, and a fine, detailed and subtle palate – what claret-lovers used to call "breed". Margaret River is one of the finest places in the world for Cabernet Sauvignon, and this has delicacy and weightless concentration.

Chianti Classico Riserva, Castello di Volpaia, Tuscany, Italy

This wine is rich, with dark fruit and some density at its heart, but it's transparent and bright as well, with violets and blackberry on the palate. It's 100% Sangiovese so has good acidity; you could drink it with something meaty now or put it away for a few years.

Cliff Edge Shiraz, Mount Langi Ghiran, Victoria, Australia

This Shiraz is always elegant and tense and has everything lovers of the Northern Rhône could want: it's flowery, spicy, vigorous, utterly alive and vivid, savoury and saline, and comes from granitic soils in a cool spot. The top wine is single-vineyard Langi Shiraz, and this is its lighter sibling, from various vineyards in the estate. It is exceptionally good value. And I might also mention Billi Billi, which is Shiraz from across Victoria, somewhat cheaper again, and like this wine, it tastes far more expensive than it is.

Psi, Bodegas y Viñedos Alnardo, Ribero del Duero, Spain

Peter Sisseck's entry-level wine; his Pingus sells for a great deal more. Psi is from various old-vine parcels across the region, fermented in large old oak vats and with absolutely none of the overextraction and general too-much-ness that has marred Ribera del Duero in the past. This is fresh and subtle, with notes of wild herbs and flowers, very long and compelling, helped by around 8% of Garnacha in the Tempranillo. Unusual and beautiful.

Dry Creek Valley Zinfandel, Peterson Winery, Sonoma, US

The delightful Fred Peterson does not find it insulting to have his wine described as "poor man's Ridge". Like Ridge, it's not just Zin: the complexity and the freshness that makes it compelling come from the blend. Dry Creek gutsiness but subtlety and depth too.

Quinta de Vargellas, Taylor's, Douro, Portugal
Single-quinta Vintage Port is a huge bargain: roughly half the price of classic Vintage, and the product of some of the world's best vineyards. Vargellas is always redolent of violets: aromatic, bright, super-elegant. You can drink it when it's first released and go on drinking it for well over ten years. (Not the same bottle, obviously.) You can drink it with food: cheese, of course, but also chocolate or chicken liver pâté. It's versatile, not overwhelmingly sweet and utterly moreish.

White wines

Scharzhofberger Riesling GG 2018, von Hövel, Saar, Germany
Earth, salt and spice woven into a crystalline structure with a touch of smoke: distinctive, supremely elegant and with great length. All this, and just 10.5% alcohol. German Riesling proving yet again that when it comes to tension and poise, it has no equals.

Preknadi, Diamantakos, Macedonia, Greece
Sappy green nuts and lovely bitterness all wrapped in cream and velvet, with a very long finish and terrific freshness. Preknadi is a grape I confess I had not come across before: it's almost extinct and is found in Naoussa; it was very popular before phylloxera. This small family-owned artisan winery has just 1.1 ha of it. This is a gem.

Marinič Zala, Dom Vicomte de Noüe-Marinič, Primorje, Slovenia
Slovenia is one of the places to look for value. This is made by the nephew of Burgundy legend Anne-Claude Leflaive, and it's 100% Malvasia d'Istria grown on schist and fermented with natural yeasts and no wood ageing. Think of sap and salt and green herbs with a touch of cream, a note of fennel seed and lovely acidity and structure. Characterful and unusual.

Grüner Veltliner Lössterrassen, J&P Bründlmayer, Kremstal, Austria
I was severely tempted to list one of Philipp Bründlmayer's entry-level GVs: a pure, effortless, subtle example of what the grape can do in good hands and on good terroir. Loess is the soil type that GV seems to like best, and *terrassen* are terraces. If you feel like trading up to one of Philipp B's single-vineyard wines you will, I think, be pleasantly surprised by the combination of price, concentration and tension. Even the sublime Riesling Steingraben Gedersdorf fits in our sweet spot.

Breaky Bottom, East Sussex, England
No, I haven't specified a cuvée, partly because they're all brilliant, and partly because this is a tiny vineyard tucked into the South Downs, and quantities of everything are quite small. Peter Hall is as far as you can get from the standard city/tech billionaire start-up of today: he planted his first vines in 1974 and has fought every inch of the way. But gosh, can he make wine. You don't know English sparkling until you've tasted Breaky Bottom.

Grape varieties

—

This is where the most fundamental changes in wine are appearing. No longer are half a dozen international grape varieties worshipped around the globe to the exclusion of all else: now it's all about old indigenous varieties. Everybody wants a point of difference, and that's difficult if you're making Merlot or Sauvignon Blanc.

In Europe, there are hundreds of varieties that were once grown but fell from favour, perhaps because of climate change or shifting trade patterns. Grapes that wouldn't ripen in the cooler past but ripened in the warmer further-past might be promising in a warmer future – and they might not present the problems of ever-higher alcohol and ever-lower acidity with which growers are currently grappling. Even different clones of popular vines can be interesting: centenarian vineyards across the world are being studied to see if individual vines might ripen later, keep their acidity better; everybody is scrabbling to see what we might still have.

Then there are Piwi varieties. The name (which is a brand) stands for Pilzwiderstandsfähig. They are crossings, often over several generations, of *Vitis vinifera*, the European wine vine, with American fungus- and disease-resistant *Vitis* species. They require less spraying and make organic and bio viticulture more possible in awkward climates. You might come across Solaris or Souvignier Gris; there are many others. And then there are the familiar international grapes. They're not going away. They have forged superb reputations in many countries, and they give many of the greatest wines in the world. But now they're not the only choice.

All grapes and synonyms are cross-referenced in SMALL CAPITALS throughout every section of this book.

Grapes for red wine

Agiorgitiko Greek; the grape of Nemea, now planted all over Greece. Versatile and delicious, from soft and charming to dense and age-worthy. A must-try.

Aglianico S Italy's best red, the grape of Taurasi; dark, deep and fashionable.

Alfrocheiro Portuguese; A Preto is same grape. Lovely aromas: blackberry, strawberry, plus freshness, dark colour, fine tannins. Can be v.gd, esp in Dão.

Alicante Bouschet Used to be shunned, now stylish in Alentejo, Chile, esp old vines.

Aragonêz *See* TEMPRANILLO.

Auxerrois *See* MALBEC, if red. White Auxerrois has its own entry in White Grapes.

Băbească Neagră Moldovan trad "black grandmother grape"; light body and ruby-red colour.

Babić Dark grape from Dalmatia, grown in stony seaside vyds around Šibenik. Exceptional quality potential.

Baga Portugal. Bairrada grape. Dark, tannic, fashionable. Needs a gd grower.

Barbera Widely grown in Italy, best in Piedmont: high acidity, low tannin, cherry fruit. Ranges from serious and age-worthy to semi-sweet and frothy. Fashionable in California and Australia; promising in Argentina.

Bastardo Iberian TROUSSEAU.

Blauburger Austrian cross of BLAUER PORTUGIESER, BLAUFRÄNKISCH. Simple wines.

Blauburgunder *See* PINOT N.

Blauer Portugieser Central European, esp Germany (Rheinhessen, Pfalz, mostly for rosé), Austria, Hungary. Light, fruity reds: drink young, slightly chilled.

Blaufränkisch (Kékfrankos, Lemberger, Modra Frankinja) Widely planted in Austria's Mittelburgenland: medium-bodied, peppery acidity, fresh, berry aromas, eucalyptus. Can be top quality: Austria's star red. Often blended with CAB SAUV or ZWEIGELT. Lemberger in Germany (esp Württemberg), Kékfrankos in Hungary, Modra Frankinja in Slovenia.

Bobal Spain. Can be rustic; best at high altitude; gd acidity.

Boğaskere Tannic and Turkish. Produces full-bodied wines.

Bonarda Ambiguous name. In Oltrepò Pavese, an alias for Croatina, soft fresh *frizzante* and still red. In Lombardy and Emilia-Romagna, an alias for Uva Rara. Different in Piedmont. Argentina's Bonarda can be any of these, or something else. None is great.

Bouchet St-Émilion alias for CAB FR.

Brunello SANGIOVESE, splendid at Montalcino.

Cabernet Franc [Cab Fr] In Bx: more important than CAB SAUV in St-Émilion. Outperforms Cab Sauv in Loire (Chinon, Saumur-Champigny, rosé), in Hungary (depth and complexity in Villány and Szekszárd) and often in Italy. Much of NE Italy's Cab Fr turned out to be CARMENÈRE. Used in Bx blends of Cab Sauv/MERLOT across the world.

Cabernet Sauvignon [Cab Sauv] Characterful: slow-ripening, spicy, herby, tannic, with blackcurrant aroma. Main grape of the Médoc; also makes some of the best California, S American, E European reds. Vies with SHIRAZ in Australia. Grown almost everywhere, but few places make great varietal Cab Sauv: usually benefits from blending with eg. MERLOT, CAB FR, SYRAH, TEMPRANILLO, SANGIOVESE, etc. Makes aromatic rosé. Top wines need ageing.

Cannonau GRENACHE in its Sardinian manifestation; can be v. fine, potent.

Carignan (Carignane, Carignano, Cariñena) Low-yielding old vines, fashionable now everywhere from S France to Chile, via S Africa. Lots of depth, vibrancy, but must never be overcropped. Found esp in California, Israel, N Africa, Spain (as Cariñena).

Carignano *See* CARIGNAN.

Cariñena *See* CARIGNAN.

Carmenère An old Bx variety now a star, rich and deep, in Chile (where it's pronounced "carmeneary"); Bx is looking at it again.

Castelão *See* PERIQUITA.

Cencibel *See* TEMPRANILLO.

Chiavennasca *See* NEBBIOLO.

Cinsault (Cinsaut) A staple of S France, v.gd if low-yielding, hopeless if not. Makes gd rosé. One of parents of PINOTAGE.

Cornalin du Valais Swiss speciality with high potential, esp in Valais.

Corvina Dark and spicy; one of best grapes in Valpolicella blend. Corvinone, even darker, is a separate variety.

Côt *See* MALBEC.

Dolcetto Source of relatively light red in Piedmont. Now high fashion.

Dornfelder Gives deliciously light reds, straightforward, often rustic, and well coloured in Germany, parts of the US, even England.

Duras Spicy, peppery and structured; Gaillac and parts of Tarn V, SW France.

Fer Servadou Exclusive to SW France, aka Mansois in Marcillac, Braucol in Gaillac and Pinenc in St-Mont. Redolent of red summer fruits and spice.

Fetească Neagră Romania: "black maiden grape" with potential as showpiece variety; can give deep, full-bodied wines with character.

Freisa Old Piedmontese vine, related to NEBBIOLO. Acidic, tannic, strawberry fruit, quite aromatic. Can be sparkling or semi-sparkling; gd, can be acquired taste.

Frühburgunder Old German mutation of PINOT N: Ahr but also Franken, Württemberg, where it is aka Clevner. Lower acidity than Pinot N.

Gamay The Beaujolais grape: light, fragrant wines, best young, except in Beaujolais crus (*see* France), where quality can be high, wines for 2–10 yrs. Grown in Loire Valley, Central France, Switzerland, Savoie, Canada. California's Napa Gamay is Valdiguié.

Gamza *See* KADARKA.

Garnacha (Cannonau, Garnatxa, Grenache) Important pale, potent grape for warm climates, fashionable with *terroiristes* because it expresses its site. Usually quite high alc, but much more delicate than of yore, even in Priorat. The base of Châteauneuf-du-Pape. Rosé and *vin doux naturel* in S France, Spain, California. Old-vine versions prized in S Australia. Often blended. Cannonau in Sardinia, Grenache in France.

Garnatxa *See* GARNACHA.

Graciano Spanish; part of Rioja blend. Aroma of violets, tannic, lean structure, a bit like PETIT VERDOT. Difficult to grow but increasingly fashionable.

Grenache *See* GARNACHA. **GSM:** GRENACHE/SHIRAZ/MOURVÈDRE blend.

Grignolino Italy: gd everyday table wine in Piedmont.

Kadarka (Gamza) Spicy, light reds in E Europe. In Hungary revived, esp for Bikavér.

Kalecik Karasi Turkish: sour-cherry fruit, fresh, supple. Bit like GAMAY. Drink young.

Kékfrankos Hungarian BLAUFRÄNKISCH.

Lagrein N Italian, dark, bitter finish, rich, plummy. DOC in Alto Adige (*see* Italy).

Lambrusco Productive grape of lower Po Valley; cheerful, sweet, fizzy, can be v.gd.

Lefkada In Cyprus, higher quality than MAVRO. Usually blended, as tannins can be aggressive. Called Vertzami in its Greek homeland.

Lemberger *See* BLAUFRÄNKISCH.

Limniona Greek, medium colour, gd weight, acidity, spicy red fruit. Think MENCÍA.

Listán Prieto See PAÍS.

Malbec (Auxerrois, Côt) Minor in Bx, major in Cahors (alias Auxerrois) and the star in Argentina. Dark, dense, tannic but fleshy wine capable of real quality. High-altitude versions in Argentina best.

Manseng Noir SW Fr Basque origin. Deep colour, tannic; interesting for lowish alc.

Maratheftiko Deep-coloured Cypriot grape with quality potential.

Marselan CAB SAUV X GRENACHE, 1961; gd colour, structure, supple tannins, ages well. A success in China.

Mataro *See* MOURVÈDRE.

Mavro Most planted black grape of Cyprus but only moderate quality. Best for rosé.

Mavrodaphne Greek; means "black laurel". Sweet fortifieds, speciality of Patras, also in Cephalonia. Dry versions too, great promise.

Mavrotragano Greek, almost extinct; now revived; found on Santorini. Top quality.

Mavrud Probably Bulgaria's best. Spicy, dark, plummy late-ripener native to Thrace. Ages well.

Melnik Bulgarian; from region of same name. There are two Melniks: Shiroka (Broadleafed) M and its offspring, Early M. Both have dark colour, nice dense, tart-cherry character and age well.

Mencía Making waves in Bierzo, N Spain. Aromatic, steely tannins, lots of acidity.

Merlot The grape behind the great fragrant and plummy wines of Pomerol and (with CAB FR) St-Émilion; a vital element in the Médoc, soft and strong in California, Washington, Chile, Australia. Lighter, often gd in N Italy (can be world-class in Tuscany), Italian Switzerland, Slovenia, Argentina, S Africa, NZ, etc. More often dull than great. Much planted in E Europe, esp Romania.

Meunier *See* PINOT M.

Mission *See* PAÍS.

Modra Frankinja *See* BLAUFRÄNKISCH.

Modri Pinot *See* PINOT N.

Monastrell *See* MOURVÈDRE.

Mondeuse In Savoie; the skier's red; deep-coloured, gd acidity. Related to SYRAH.

Montepulciano Deep-coloured, dominant in Italy's Abruzzo and important along Adriatic coast from Marches to S Puglia. Also name of a Tuscan town, unrelated.

Morellino SANGIOVESE in Maremma, S Tuscany; esp Scansano.

Mourvèdre (Mataro, Monastrell) A star of S France (eg. Bandol, growing influence Châteauneuf), Australia (aka Mataro) and Spain (aka Monastrell). Excellent dark, aromatic, tannic; gd for blending. Also S Australia, California, S Africa.

Napa Gamay Identical to Valdiguié (S France). Nothing to get excited about.

Nebbiolo (Chiavennasca, Spanna) One of Italy's best; makes Barolo, Barbaresco, Gattinara and Valtellina. Intense, nobly fruity, perfumed wine; tannins now better managed, still improves for yrs.

Négrette SW France; Fronton. Blends with SYRAH: purply black, fruity, sappy wines.

Negroamaro Puglian "black bitter" red grape with potential for either high quality or high volume.

Nerello Mascalese Sicilian red grape, esp Etna; characterful, best v. elegant, fine.

Nero d'Avola Dark-red grape of Sicily, quality levels from sublime to industrial.

Nielluccio Corsican; plenty of acidity and tannin, gd for rosé.

Öküzgözü Soft, fruity Turkish grape, usually blended with BOĞASKERE, rather as MERLOT in Bx is blended with CAB SAUV.

País (Listán Prieto, Mission) Trendy/trad in Chile, rustic. Listán Prieto in Canaries, Mission in CA.

Pamid Bulgarian: light, soft, everyday red.

Periquita (Castelão) Common in Portugal, esp around Setúbal. Firm-flavoured, raspberryish reds develop a figgish, tar-like quality.

Petite Sirah Nothing to do with SYRAH; gives rustic, tannic, dark wine. Brilliant blended with ZIN in California; also found in S America, Mexico, Australia.

Petit Verdot Excellent but awkward Médoc grape, now increasingly planted in CAB areas worldwide for extra fragrance. Mostly blended but some gd varietals, esp in Virginia (US).

Pinotage Singular S African cross (PINOT N x CINSAULT). Has had a rocky ride; getting better from top producers. Rosé gd too. "Coffee Pinotage" is espresso-flavoured, sweetish, aimed at youth.

Pinot Crni *See* PINOT N.

Pinot Meunier (Schwarzriesling) [Pinot M] The 3rd grape of Champagne, better known as Meunier, great for blending but occasionally fine in its own right. Best on chalky sites (Damery, Leuvigny, Festigny) nr Épernay.

Pinot Noir (Blauburgunder, Modri Pinot, Pinot Crni, Spätburgunder) [Pinot N] On a roll; Burgundy no longer has monopoly of great wines. Germany, California, Australia and NZ can be outstanding. PINOTS BL/GR mutations of Pinot N. Important in fizz.

Plavac Mali (Crljenak) Croatian, and offspring of ZIN, aka PRIMITIVO, Crljenak, Kratosija. Lots of quality potential, can be alcoholic, dull.

Primitivo S Italian grape, originally from Croatia, making big, dark, rustic wines, now fashionable because genetically identical to ZIN. Early ripening, hence the name. The original name for both seems to be Tribidrag.

Refosco (Refošk) Various DOCs in Italy, esp Colli Orientali. Deep, flavoursome, age-worthy, esp in warmer climates. Dark, high acidity. Refošk in Slovenia and points e, genetically different, tastes similar. On limestone karst in Slovenia takes PDO of Teran, which otherwise is a grape. Got it?

Rubin Bulgarian cross, NEBBIOLO x SYRAH. Peppery, full-bodied.

Sagrantino Italian grape grown in Umbria for powerful, cherry-flavoured wines.

St-Laurent Dark, smooth, full-flavoured Austrian speciality, tricky to grow and make. Can be light and juicy or deep and structured. Also in Pfalz.

Sangiovese (Brunello, Morellino, Sangioveto) Principal red grape of Tuscany and central Italy. At best, sublime and long-lasting; richness balances tea-scented astringency. Dominant in Chianti, Vino Nobile, Brunello di Montalcino, Morellino di Scansano and various fine IGT offerings. Also in Umbria (eg. Montefalco and Torgiano) and across the Apennines in Romagna and Marches. Not so clever in the warmer, lower-altitude vyds of the Tuscan coast, nor in other parts of Italy despite its nr-ubiquity. Interesting in Australia.

Sangioveto *See* SANGIOVESE.

Saperavi The main red of Georgia, Ukraine, etc. Blends well with CAB SAUV (eg. in Moldova). Huge potential, some gd winemaking.

Schiava *See* TROLLINGER.

Schioppettino NE Italian, high acidity, high quality. Elegant, refined, can age.

Schwarzriesling PINOT M in Württemberg.

Sciacarello Corsican, herby and peppery. Not v. tannic.

Shiraz *See* SYRAH.

Spanna *See* NEBBIOLO.

Spätburgunder German for PINOT N.

Syrah (Shiraz) The great Rhône red grape: tannic, purple, peppery, matures superbly. Important as Shiraz in Australia. Widely grown and a gd traveller.

Tannat Raspberry-perfumed, highly tannic force behind Madiran, Tursan and other firm reds from SW France. Also rosé. The star of Uruguay.

Tempranillo (Aragonêz, Cencibel, Tinto Fino, Tinta del País, Tinta Roriz, Ull de Llebre) Aromatic, fine Rioja grape, called Ull de Llebre in Catalonia, Cencibel in La Mancha, Tinto Fino in Ribera del Duero, Tinta Roriz in Douro, Tinta del País in Castile, Aragonêz in S Portugal. Now Australia too. It's v. fashionable; elegant in cool climates, beefy in warm. Early ripening, long-maturing.

Teran (Terrano) Close cousin of REFOSCO.

Teroldego Rotaliano Trentino's best indigenous variety; serious, full-flavoured, esp on the flat Campo Rotaliano.

Tinta Amarela *See* TRINCADEIRA.

Tinta del País *See* TEMPRANILLO.

Tinta Negra (Negramoll) Used to be Tinta Negra Mole. Madeira's most planted, mainstay of cheaper Madeira. Now too in Colheita wines (*see* Portugal).

Tinta Roriz *See* TEMPRANILLO.

Tinto Fino *See* TEMPRANILLO.

Touriga Nacional [Touriga N] The top Port grape, now widely used in the Douro for floral, stylish table wines. Australian Touriga is usually this; California's Touriga can be either this or Touriga Franca.

Trincadeira (Tinta Amarela) Portuguese; v.gd in Alentejo for spicy wines. Tinta Amarela in the Douro.

Trollinger (Schiava, Vernatsch) Popular pale red in Württemberg; aka Vernatsch and Schiava. Covers group of vines, not necessarily related. In Italy, snappy, brisk.

Trousseau (Bastardo) Jura. Robust, age-worthy. Bastardo in Iberia. Also found in California and Oregon.

Ull de Llebre *See* TEMPRANILLO.

Vernatsch *See* TROLLINGER.

Vranac W Balkans, old and varied. Related to ZINFANDEL – they're all connected around there. Soft, high tannin, colour, alc, can age.

Xinomavro Greece's answer to NEBBIOLO. "Sharp-black"; the basis for Naoussa, Rapsani, Goumenissa, Amindeo. Some rosé, still or sparkling. Top quality, can age for decades. Being tried in China.

Zinfandel [Zin] California. Blackberry-like, sometimes metallic flavour. Love it or hate it. Can be serious, structured, long-ageing, or simple. Pink too. Same as S Italian PRIMITIVO.

Zweigelt (Blauer Zweigelt) BLAUFRÄNKISCH x ST-LAURENT, popular in Austria for aromatic, dark, supple wines. Underrated. Also in Hungary, Germany.

Grapes for white wine

Airén Bland workhorse of La Mancha, Spain: fresh if made well. Old-vine versions can surprise.

Albariño (Alvarinho) Fashionable, expensive in Spain: apricot-scented, gd acidity. Superb in Rías Baixas; shaping up elsewhere, but not all live up to the hype. Alvarinho in Portugal just as gd: aromatic Vinho Verde, esp in Monção, Melgaço.

Aligoté Burgundy's 2nd white grape, now trendy and often serious. Widely planted in E Europe, Russia.

Alvarinho *See* ALBARIÑO.

Amigne One of Switzerland's speciality grapes, trad in Valais, esp Vétroz. Full-bodied, tasty; often sweet but also bone-dry.

Ansonica *See* INSOLIA.

Arinto Portuguese, rather gd; mainstay of aromatic, citrus Bucelas; also adds welcome zip to blends, esp in Alentejo.

Arneis Fine, aromatic, appley-peachy, high-priced NW Italian grape, DOCG in Roero, DOC in Langhe, Piedmont.

Arvine Rare but excellent Swiss *spécialité*, from Valais. Also Petite Arvine. Dry or sweet, fresh, long-lasting wines with salty finish.

Assyrtiko Greek, esp Santorini; one of best grapes of Med, balancing power, minerality, extract and high acid. Built to age. Could conquer the world...

Auxerrois Red Auxerrois is a synonym for MALBEC, but white Auxerrois is like a fatter, spicier PINOT BL. Found in Alsace; much used in Crémant; also Germany.

Bacchus German-bred crossing, England's answer to NZ SAUV BL. Can be shrill; makes gd orange.

Beli Pinot *See* PINOT BL.

Blanc Fumé *See* SAUV BL.

Boal *See* BUAL.

Bourboulenc This and the rare Rolle make some of the Midi's best whites.

Bouvier Indigenous aromatic Austrian grape, esp gd for BA, TBA, rarely dry.

Bual (Boal) Makes top-quality sweet Madeira wines, not quite so rich as MALMSEY.

Cabernet Blanc [Cab Bl] German Piwi (*see* p.12) with SAUV BL-like flavours.

Camaralet Jurançon. Aromatic; adds complexity to GROS MANSENG-led dry wines.

Carricante Superb grape of Etna Bianco; lemon and herbs, acidity, ages 20 yrs.

Catarratto Prolific white grape found all over Sicily, esp in w in DOC Alcamo.

Cerceal *See* SERCIAL.

Chardonnay (Morillon) [Chard] Grape of Burgundy and Champagne, ubiquitous worldwide, easy to grow and vinify. Reflects terroir but also winemaker's intentions: often a fashion victim. Can be steely or fat. Also the name of a Mâcon-Villages commune. Morillon in Styria, Austria.

Chasselas (Fendant, Gutedel) Swiss. Neutral, can be elegant (Geneva); refined, full (Vaud); exotic, racy (Valais). Fendant in Valais. Also in France, esp Savoie. Gutedel in Germany, esp S Baden. Elsewhere usually a table grape.

Chenin Blanc [Chenin Bl] Wonderful white grape of the middle Loire (Vouvray, Layon, etc). Wine can be dry or sweet (or v. sweet), but with plenty of acidity. Superb old-vine versions in S Africa, esp Swartland.

Cirfandl *See* ZIERFANDLER.

Clairette Important Rhône/Midi grape, white and rosé versions, gives freshness, restrained degree, part of many blends, incl Tavel rosé.

Colombard Slightly fruity, nicely sharp grape, makes everyday wine in S Africa, California and SW France. Often blended.

Cortese Italian; grape of Gavi. Fairly neutral, pleasant, fresh.

Dimiat (Dimyat) Perfumed Bulgarian grape, made dry or off-dry, or distilled. Far more synonyms than any grape needs.

Encruzado Portuguese, serious; fresh, versatile, ages well; esp gd in Dão.

Ermitage Swiss for MARSANNE.

Esgana Cão *See* Sercial.

Ezerjó Hungarian, with sharp acidity. Name means "thousand blessings".

Falanghina Ancient grape of Campanian hills (Italy); gd dense, aromatic dry whites.

Fendant *See* CHASSELAS.

Fernão Pires *See* MARIA GOMES.

Fetească Albă / Regală (Királyleanyka, Leanyka) Romania has two Fetească grapes, both with slight MUSCAT aroma. F Regală is a cross of F Albă and Frâncuşă; more finesse, gd for late-harvest wines. F NEAGRĂ (unrelated) is dark-skinned.

Fiano High quality, giving peachy, spicy wine in Campania, S Italy.

Folle Blanche (Gros Plant) High acid/little flavour make this ideal for brandy. Gros Plant in Brittany, Picpoul in Armagnac, but unrelated to true PICPOUL. Also respectable in California.

Friulano (Sauvignonasse, Sauvignon Vert) N Italian: fresh, pungent, subtly floral. Best in Collio, Isonzo, Colli Orientali. Found in nearby Slovenia, where it is Sauvignonasse; also in Chile.

Fumé Blanc *See* SAUV BL.

Furmint (Šipon) Superb, characterful. Trademark of Hungary: both principal grape in Tokaji and vivid, vigorous dry wine, mineral, apricot-flavoured. Šipon in Slovenia. Some grown in Rust (Austria) for sweet and dry.

Garganega Best grape in Soave blend; also in Gambellara. Top, esp sweet, age well.

Garnacha Blanca (Grenache Blanc) White version of GARNACHA/Grenache, much used in Spain and S France. Low acidity. Can be innocuous or surprisingly gd.

Gewurztraminer (Traminac, Traminec, Traminer, Tramini) [Gewurz] A v. pungent grape, spicy with rose petal, face cream, lychee, grapefruit aromas. Often rich and soft, even when fully dry. Best in Alsace; gd elsewhere. Relatively unaromatic if just labelled Traminer (or variants). In Italy, Traminer Aromatico for (dr) "Gewurz" versions. (Note umlaut in German.) Non-aromatic version is SAVAGNIN.

Glera Uncharismatic new name for Prosecco vine: Prosecco is now wine only in the EU but still a grape name in Australia.

Godello Top quality (intense, mineral) in nw Spain. Called Verdelho in Dão, Portugal, but unrelated to true VERDELHO.

Grasǎ (Kövérszőlő) Romanian; name means "fat". Prone to botrytis; important in Cotnari, potentially superb sweet wines. Kövérszőlő in Hungary's Tokaj region.

Graševina *See* WELSCHRIESLING.

Grauburgunder *See* PINOT GR.

Grechetto Ancient grape of central/S Italy: vitality, style. Blended or solo in Orvieto.

Greco S Italian: there are various Grecos, probably unrelated, perhaps of Greek origin. Brisk, peachy flavour, most famous as Greco di Tufo. Greco di Bianco is from semi-dried grapes. Greco Nero is a black version.

Grenache Blanc *See* GARNACHA BLANCA.

Grillo Italy: main grape of Marsala. Also v.gd full-bodied dry table wine.

Gros Plant *See* FOLLE BLANCHE.

Grüner Veltliner [Grüner V] Austria's fashionable flagship white; v. diverse – from simple, peppery, everyday, to great complexity, ageing potential. Useful because gd at all levels. Found elsewhere in Central Europe and outside.

Gutedel *See* CHASSELAS.

Hárslevelű Other main grape of Tokaji, but softer, peachier than FURMINT. Name means "linden-leaved"; gd in Somló, Eger as well.

Heida Swiss for SAVAGNIN.

Humagne Swiss speciality, older than CHASSELAS. Fresh, plump, not v. aromatic. Humagne Rouge is not related but increasingly popular: same as Cornalin d'Aosta. Cornalin du Valais is different. (Keep up at the back, there.)

Insolia (Ansonica, Inzolia) Sicilian; Ansonica on Tuscan coast. Fresh, racy wine at best. May be semi-dried for sweet wine.

Irsai Olivér Hungarian cross; aromatic, MUSCAT-like wine for drinking young.

Johannisberg Swiss for SILVANER.

Kéknyelű Low-yielding, flavourful grape giving one of Hungary's best whites. Has the potential for fieriness and spice. To be watched.

Kerner Quite successful German cross. Early ripening; flowery (but often too blatant) wine with gd acidity.

Királyleanyka *See* FETEASCǍ ALBǍ/REGALǍ.

Koshu More or less indigenous Japanese table-turned-wine grape, much hyped. Fresh, tannic. Orange versions gd.

Kövérszőlő *See* GRASǍ.

L'Acadie Blanc Cold-climate Canadian hybrid; some weight, honeyed; gd fizz.

Laški Rizling *See* WELSCHRIESLING.

Leányka *See* FETEASCǍ ALBǍ.

Len de l'El Gaillac; aka Loin de l'Oeuil. Versatile; usually blended, gd dessert wines.

Listán *See* PALOMINO.

Longyan (Dragon Eye) Chinese original; gd substantial, aromatic wine.

Loureiro Best Vinho Verde grape after ALVARINHO: delicate, floral. Also in Spain.

Macabeo *See* VIURA.

Maccabeu *See* VIURA.

Malagousia Rediscovered Greek grape for gloriously rose-scented wines.

Malmsey *See* MALVASIA. The sweetest style of Madeira.

Malvasia (Malmsey, Malvazija, Malvoisie, Marastina) Italy, France and Iberia. Not a single variety but a whole stable, not necessarily related or even alike. Can be white or red, sparkling or still, strong or mild, sweet or dry, aromatic or neutral. Slovenia's and Croatia's version is Malvazija Istarka, crisp and light, or rich, oak-aged. Sometimes called Marastina in Croatia. Malmsey (as in the sweetest style of Madeira) is a corruption of Malvasia.

Malvoisie See MALVASIA. Name used for several varieties in France, incl BOURBOULENC, Torbato, VERMENTINO. Also PINOT GR in Switzerland's Valais.

Manseng, Gros / Petit Exuberantly fruity whites from SW France, esp Jurançon, Pacherenc and Irouléguy. Gros Manseng is picked earlier and tends to be made dry. Petit Manseng is picked later, often sweet.

Maria Gomes (Fernão Pires) Portuguese; aromatic, ripe-flavoured, slightly spicy whites in Barraida and Tejo.

Marsanne (Ermitage Blanc) Principal white grape (with ROUSSANNE) of N Rhône; gd in Australia, California, Valais (Ermitage Bl). Soft, full wines, age v. well.

Mauzac SW France. Aromatic, note of apples. Best known for sparkling.

Melon de Bourgogne See MUSCADET.

Misket, Red Bulgarian. Pink-skinned, mildly aromatic; the basis of most country whites. There are many other Miskets, all recent crosses and less planted.

Morillon CHARD in parts of Austria.

Moscatel / Moscato See MUSCAT.

Moschofilero Pink-skinned, rose-scented, high-quality, high-acid, low-alcohol Greek grape. Makes white, some pink, some sparkling.

Müller-Thurgau [Müller-T] Aromatic wines to drink young. Makes gd sweet wines but usually dull, often coarse, dry ones. In Germany, most common in Pfalz, Rheinhessen, Nahe, Baden, Franken. Has some merit in Italy's Trentino-Alto Adige, Friuli. Sometimes called RIES X SYLVANER (incorrectly) in Switzerland.

Muscadelle Adds aroma to white Bx, esp Sauternes. In Victoria used (with MUSCAT, to which it is unrelated) for Rutherglen Muscat.

Muscadet (Melon de Bourgogne) Light, refreshing, dry wines with seaside tang, plus serious ageable ones. Also found (as Melon) in parts of Burgundy.

Muscat (Moscatel, Moscato, Muskateller) Many varieties; the best is Muscat Blanc à Petits Grains (alias Gelber Muskateller, Rumeni Muškat, Sarga Muskotály, Yellow Muscat, Tămâioasă Românească). Widely grown, easily recognized, pungent grapes, mostly made into perfumed sweet wines, often fortified, as in France's *vin doux naturel*. Superb, dark and sweet in Australia. Sweet, sometimes v.gd in Spain. Most Hungarian Muskotály is Muscat Ottonel except in Tokaj, where Sarga Muskotály rules, adding perfume (in small amounts) to blends. Occasionally (eg. Alsace, Austria, parts of S Germany) made dry. Sweet Cap Corse Muscats often superb. Light Moscato fizz in N Italy.

Muskateller See MUSCAT.

Narince Turkish; fresh and fruity wines.

Neuburger Austrian, rather neglected; mainly in the Wachau (elegant, flowery), Thermenregion (mellow, ample-bodied) and n Burgenland (strong, full).

Olaszrizling See WELSCHRIESLING.

Païen See SAVAGNIN.

Pálava Czech, rather gd. Pink-skinned, rose aromas, gd freshness.

Palomino (Listán) Great grape of Sherry; little intrinsic character, gains all from production method. Now table wine too. As Listán, makes dry white in Canaries.

Pansa Blanca See XAREL·LO.

Pecorino Italian: not a cheese but alluring dry white from a revived variety.

Pedro Ximénez [PX] Makes sweet brown Sherry under its own name, and used in Montilla, Málaga. Also in Argentina, Australia, California, Canaries, S Africa.

Petit Courbu SW France. Age-worthy, some distinction.

Picolit NE Italian, used for late-harvest (sw); grapes dried on mats or left on vine, with botrytis or not. Delicate wine, should be v.gd, sometimes is.

Picpoul (Piquepoul) S French, best known in Picpoul de Pinet. Should have high acidity. Picpoul N is black-skinned.

Pinela Local to Slovenia. Subtle, lowish acidity; drink young.

Pinot Bianco *See* PINOT BL.

Pinot Blanc (Beli Pinot, Pinot Bianco, Weissburgunder) [Pinot Bl] Mutation of PINOT N, similar to but milder than CHARD. Light, fresh, fruity, not aromatic, to drink young; gd for Italian *spumante*, and potentially excellent in the ne, esp high sites in Alto Adige. Widely grown, not esp fashionable. Weissburgunder in Germany and best in s: often racier than Chard.

Pinot Gris (Pinot Grigio, Grauburgunder, Ruländer, Sivi Pinot, Szürkebarát) [Pinot Gr] Popular as Pinot Grigio in N Italy, even for rosé, but top, characterful versions can be excellent (Alto Adige, Friuli); trad *ramato* is skin-contact. Cheap versions are just that. Terrific in Alsace for full, spicy whites. Once important in Champagne. In Germany can be alias Ruländer (sw) or Grauburgunder (dr): best in Baden (esp Kaiserstuhl) and S Pfalz. Szürkebarát in Hungary, Sivi P in Slovenia (characterful, aromatic).

Pošip Croatian; mostly on Korčula. Quite characterful and citrus; high-yielding.

Prosecco Old name for grape that makes Prosecco. Now you have to call it GLERA.

Renski Rizling Rhine RIES.

Rèze Super-rare ancestral Valais grape used for *vin de glacier*.

Ribolla Gialla / Rebula Acidic but characterful. In Italy, best in Collio. In Slovenia, trad in Brda. Can be v.gd. Favourite of amphora users.

Rieslaner Rare German cross (SILVANER X RIES); fine Auslesen in Franken and Pfalz.

Riesling Italico *See* WELSCHRIESLING.

Riesling (Renski Rizling, Rhine Riesling) [Ries] The greatest, most versatile white grape, diametrically opposite in style to CHARD. From steely to voluptuous, always perfumed, far more ageing potential than Chard. Great in all styles in Germany; forceful, steely in Austria; lime-cordial fruit, toast in S Australia; rich, spicy in Alsace; often v.gd elsewhere.

Rkatsiteli Found widely in E Europe, Russia, Georgia. Can stand cold winters and has high acidity; protects to a degree from poor winemaking. Also in NE US.

Robola In Greece (Cephalonia) a top-quality, floral grape, unrelated to RIBOLLA GIALLA but related to Rebula.

Roditis Pink grape, all over Greece, usually making whites. Gd when yields low.

Roter Veltliner Austrian; unrelated to GRÜNER V. There is also a Frühroter and an (unrelated) Brauner Veltliner.

Rotgipfler Austrian; indigenous to Thermenregion. With ZIERFANDLER, makes lively, lush, aromatic blends.

Roussanne (Bergeron) Rhône grape of real finesse, called Bergeron in Savoie. Now popping up in California and Australia. Can age many yrs.

Ruländer *See* PINOT GR.

Sauvignonasse *See* FRIULANO.

Sauvignon Blanc [Sauv Bl] Distinctive aromatic, grassy to tropical wines. Grassy, pungent NZ style taken over world; trad blackcurrant-leaf Sancerre-style more rewarding. Blended with SÉM in Bx. Sauv Gr is pink-skinned, less aromatic version with untapped potential.

Sauvignon Vert *See* FRIULANO.

Savagnin (Heida, Païen) Grape for VIN JAUNE from Jura: aromatic form is GEWURZ. In Switzerland known as Heida, Païen or Traminer. Full-bodied, high acidity. Savagnin Rose (Roter Traminer) is pink-skinned; can be outstanding in Alsace.

Savatiano Greek; much used for Retsina, much improved: herbal, fresh.

Scheurebe (Sämling) Grapefruit-scented German RIES x SILVANER (possibly), esp successful in Pfalz (Auslese and up). Can be weedy: must be v. ripe to be gd.

Sémillon [Sém] Gives lusciousness to Sauternes, but less important for dry white Bx. Superb in Australia, S Africa, beeswax richness with age (e, not é).

Sercial (Cerceal, Esgana Cão) Portuguese: makes the driest Madeira. Cerceal, also Portuguese, seems to be this plus any of several others.

Seyval Blanc [Seyval Bl] French hybrid of French and American vines; v. hardy, attractively fruity. Popular and reasonably successful in E US and England.

Silvaner (Johannisberg, Sylvaner) Can be excellent in Germany's Rheinhessen, Pfalz, esp Franken, plant/earth flavours and mineral notes. As Johannisberg in Valais (Switzerland) v.gd (and powerful). Lightest of Alsace grapes, but can be concentrated, textured.

Šipon *See* FURMINT.

Sivi Pinot *See* PINOT GR.

Spätrot *See* ZIERFANDLER.

Sylvaner *See* SILVANER.

Tămâioasă Românească *See* MUSCAT.

Torrontés Name given to a number of grapes, mostly with an aromatic, floral character, sometimes soapy. A speciality of Argentina; also in Spain. DYA.

Traminac Or Traminec. *See* GEWURZ.

Traminer Or Tramini (Hungary). *See* GEWURZ.

Trebbiano (Ugni Blanc) Principal white grape of Tuscany, but all over Italy in many guises. Rarely rises above the plebeian except in Tuscany's Vin Santo. Some gd dry whites under DOCs Romagna or Abruzzo. Trebbiano di Soave, aka VERDICCHIO, only distantly related; T di Lugana now called Turbiana. Grown in S France as Ugni Bl, and Cognac as St-Émilion. Mostly thin, bland wine; needs blending (and better growing).

Ugni Blanc [Ugni Bl] *See* TREBBIANO.

Verdejo The grape of Rueda in Castile, potentially fine and long-lived.

Verdelho Great quality in Australia (pungent, full-bodied); rare but gd (and medium-sweet) in Madeira.

Verdicchio Potentially v.gd, muscular, dry; central-E Italy. Wine of same name.

Vermentino Italian, sprightly with satisfying texture; ageing capacity.

Vernaccia Name given to many unrelated grapes in Italy. Vernaccia di San Gimignano is crisp, lively; Vernaccia di Oristano is Sherry-like.

Vidal French hybrid much grown in Canada for Icewine.

Vidiano Cretan producers love this. Powerful, stylish. Lime/apricot and gd acidity; gd fizz too.

Viognier Ultra-fashionable Rhône grape, finest in Condrieu, less fine but still aromatic in the Midi. Often gd to v.gd elsewhere.

Viura (Macabeo, Maccabéo, Maccabeu) Workhorse white grape of N Spain, widespread in Rioja, Cava country, over border in SW France; gd quality potential.

Weissburgunder PINOT BL in Germany.

Welschriesling (Graševina, Laški Rizling, Olaszrizling, Riesling Italico) Not related to RIES. Light and fresh to sweet and rich in Austria; ubiquitous in Central Europe, where it can be remarkably gd for dry and sweet wines.

Xarel·lo (Pansa Blanca) A trad Catalan grape, for Cava (with Parellada, MACABEO). Tannic, can age, can be superb. Lime-cordial character in Alella, as Pansa Blanca.

Xynisteri Cyprus's most planted white grape. Can be simple and is usually DYA; but when grown at altitude makes appealing, mineral whites.

Zéta Hungarian; BOUVIER x FURMINT used by some in Tokaji Aszú production.

Zierfandler (Spätrot, Cirfandl) Found in Austria's Thermenregion; often blended with ROTGIPFLER for aromatic, orange-peel-scented, weighty wines.

Wine & food

Food evolves; wine evolves. The soft, tucked-in tannins of lots of red wines now mean that those reds will sometimes happily match fish; in any case, the way we eat now means that the protein on the plate is not the only factor, or even the main factor, in choosing a wine. Orange wines give us extra choices; rosé is year-round. Treat the suggestions in these pages as directions of travel rather than rules: ideas to spark other ideas as you survey your wine rack or your merchant's shelves. Choosing the wine is part of the fun – too much fun not to take seriously.

On p.37 you'll find a box of can't-go-wrong favourites with food; the entries below give lots of specific matches enjoyed over the years.

Before the meal –apéritifs

Don't be tempted by quantity over quality here. The best value is Fino Sherry, the most expensive is gd fizz – but if you're going for fizz, make sure it's gd. Or how about a magnum of rosé?

First courses

Aïoli Chances are you're on holiday, and cold Provence rosé is ideal. Or anything cold, fresh and neutral.

Antipasti / tapas / mezze You can be in Italy, Spain, Greece or Edinburgh: a selection of savoury, salty, meaty, cheesy, fishy, veggie bits and pieces works perfectly with Fino Sherry, XYNISTERI, orange wines. Roasted peppers, aubergines suit young fruity reds: CAB FR, KADARKA. In emergencies, gd Prosecco.

Burrata Richness in excelsis. Worth top Italian white: FIANO or Cusumano's GRILLO. Or mature SÉM.

Carpaccio, beef or fish Beef version works well with most wines, incl reds. Tuscan is appropriate, but fine CHARDS are gd. So are pink and Vintage Champagnes. Give Amontillado a try. **Salmon** Chard or Champagne. **Tuna** VIOGNIER, California Chard, Sancerre. Or sake.

Charcuterie / prosciutto / salami High-acid, unoaked red works better than white. Simple Beaujolais, BARBERA, Etna, REFOSCO, SCHIOPPETTINO, TEROLDEGO, Valpolicella. If you must have white, it needs acidity. Chorizo makes wines taste metallic. Prosciutto with melon or figs needs full dry or medium white: CHENIN BL, FIANO, MUSCAT, VIOGNIER.

Dim sum Classically, China tea. Alsace PINOT GR or German dry RIES; light PINOT N. For reds, soft tannins, freshness are key. Bardolino, GARNACHA, Rioja; Côtes du Rhône. Also NV Champagne or English fizz.

Eggs See also SOUFFLÉS. Not easy: eggs have a way of coating your palate. Omelettes: follow the other ingredients; mushrooms suggest red; Côtes du Rhone is a safe bet. With a truffle omelette, Vintage Champagne, or perhaps Volnay. Florentine, with spinach, is not a winey dish.

gulls' eggs Push the luxury: mature white burgundy or Vintage Champagne.

oeufs en meurette Burgundian genius: eggs in red wine with a glass of the same.

quails' eggs Blanc de Blancs Champagne; VIOGNIER.

Mozzarella with tomatoes, basil Fresh Italian white, eg. Soave, Alto Adige. VERMENTINO from Liguria or Rolle from the Midi. See also VEGETABLE/AVOCADO.

Oysters, raw NV Champagne, Chablis, MUSCADET, white Graves, Sancerre, or Guinness. Experiment with Sauternes. Manzanilla is gd.

stewed, grilled or otherwise cooked Puligny-Montrachet or gd NZ CHARD. Champagne is gd with either.

Pasta Red or white according to the sauce:

creamy sauce (eg. carbonara) Orvieto, GRECO di Tufo. Young SANGIOVESE.

meat sauce MONTEPULCIANO d'Abruzzo, Salice Salentino, MALBEC.

pesto (basil) sauce BARBERA, VERMENTINO, NZ SAUV BL, Hungarian FURMINT.

seafood sauce (eg. vongole) VERDICCHIO, Lugana, Soave, GRILLO, unoaked CHARD.

tomato sauce Chianti, Barbera, Sicilian red, ZIN, S Australian GRENACHE.

Pâté Chicken liver calls for pungent white (Alsace PINOT GR, or MARSANNE), smooth red, eg. light GARNACHA or PINOT N. More strongly flavoured (duck, venison) needs Chianti Classico, Gigondas, or gd white Graves. Amontillado can be marvellous match, as can young Port.

foie gras Sweet white: Sauternes, Tokaji Aszú 5 Puttonyos, late-harvest RIES or PINOT GR, Vouvray, Jurançon *moelleux*, GEWURZ. Old dry Amontillado. Note hot fresh foie gras (not pâté) needs mature Vintage Champagne.

Risotto Follow the flavour:

funghi porcini Finest mature Barolo or Barbaresco.

nero A rich dry white: VIOGNIER or even Corton-Charlemagne.

seafood A favourite dry white.

vegetables (eg. Primavera) PINOT GR from Friuli, Gavi, youngish SÉM, DOLCETTO or BARBERA d'Alba.

Soufflés As show dishes, these deserve ★★★ wines:

cheese Mature top PINOT N or Bx, CAB SAUV, etc. Or fine mature white burgundy, Hunter SEM or Rioja.

fish (esp smoked haddock with chive cream sauce) Dry white, ★★★ burgundy, Bx, Alsace, CHARD, etc.

spinach (tough on wine) Light non-tannic red or white. Champagne (esp Vintage) can also spark things with the texture of a soufflé.

Fish

Abalone Dry or medium white: SAUV BL, unoaked CHARD. A touch of oak works with soy sauce, oyster sauce, etc. In Hong Kong: Dom Pérignon (at least).

Anchovies Fino, obviously. Or try orange wine.

bocquerones VERDEJO, unoaked SÉM.

salade niçoise Provence rosé.

Bacalão Salt cod needs acidity: young Portuguese or Italian (r/w). Orange can be gd.

Bass, sea Fine white, eg. Clare RIES, Chablis, white Châteauneuf, ALBARIÑO, VERMENTINO, WEISSBURGUNDER. Rev up the wine for more seasoning, eg. ginger, spring onions; more powerful Ries, not necessarily dry.

Beurre blanc, fish with Deserves gd unoaked white with maturity: Hunter SEM, Premier Cru Chablis, CHENIN BL, RIES, Swartland white blend, gd Austrian, Etna CARRICANTE. Applies to most veg with beurre blanc too.

Caviar Iced vodka (and) full-bodied Champagne (eg. Bollinger, Krug). Don't (ever) add raw onion.

Ceviche Can be applied to anything now, but here, it's fish. RIES, GRÜNER V, TORRONTÉS, VERDELHO, orange. Manzanilla.

Crab (esp Dungeness) and RIES together are part of the Creator's plan. But He also created Champagne.

Chinese, with ginger & onion German Ries Kabinett or Spätlese Halbtrocken. Rhône white, GEWURZ.

cioppino SAUV BL; but West Coast friends say ZIN. Also trad-method sparkling.

cold, dressed Top Ries (Alsace, Australia, Austria, Mosel); ASSYRTIKO, CHENIN BL. **crab cakes** Any of the above.

softshell Unoaked CHARD, ALBARIÑO or top-quality German Ries Spätlese.

Cured fish Salmon can have a whisky cure, a beetroot cure; all have sweetness and pungency. With gravadlax, sweet mustard sauce is a complication. SERCIAL Madeira (eg. 10-yr-old Henriques), Amontillado, Tokaji Szamarodni, orange wine. Or NV Champagne.

Curry A vague term for a vast range of flavours. S African CHENIN BL, Alsace PINOT BL, Franciacorta, fruity rosé, not too pale and anodyne; look at other flavours. Prawn and mango need more sweetness, tomato needs acidity. Fino can handle heat. So can IPA or Pilsner.

Fish pie (with creamy sauce) Can be homely or fancier. ALBARIÑO, Soave Classico, RIES Erstes Gewächs, CHARD, Spanish GODELLO.

Grilled, roast or fried fish Also applies to **fish & chips**, **tempura**, **fritto misto**, **baked…**
   cod, haddock CHARD, PINOT BL, MALVAZIJA.
   Dover sole Perfect with fine wines: white burgundy or equivalent.
   halibut, turbot, brill Best rich, dry white; top Chard, mature RIES Spätlese.
   monkfish Meaty but neutral; full-flavoured white or red, according to sauce.
   mullet, grey VERDICCHIO, unoaked Chard, rosé.
   oily fish like herrings, mackerel, sardines More acidity, weight: ASSYRTIKO, VERDELHO, FURMINT, orange, rosé.
   perch, zander Top white burgundy, Mosel, Grand Cru Alsace, mature top fizz.
   plaice, flounder Light, fresh whites.
   red fish like salmon, red mullet PINOT N. For salmon, also best Chard, Grand Cru Chablis, top Ries.
   skate, ray Delicate, but brown butter, capers need oomph: Alsace, ROUSSANNE, CHENIN BL
   swordfish Full-bodied dry white (or why not red?) of the country. Nothing grand.
   trout Gd Chard, Furmint, Ries, Malvazija, Pinot N.
   tuna Best served rare (or raw) with light red: young Loire CAB FR or Pinot N. Young Rioja is a possibility.
   whitebait Crisp dry whites, eg. Furmint, Greek, Touraine SAUV BL, Verdicchio, white Dão, Fino, rosé, orange. Or beer.

Kedgeree Full white, still or sparkling: CHARD, SÉM, GRÜNER V, German Grosses Gewächs or (at breakfast) Champagne.

Lobster with a rich sauce Eg. Thermidor: Vintage Champagne, Cru Classé Graves, ROUSSANNE, mature CARRICANTE, top CHARD. Alternatively, for its inherent sweetness, Sauternes, Pfalz Spätlese, even Auslese.
   plain grilled, or cold with mayonnaise NV Champagne, Alsace RIES, Premier Cru Chablis, Condrieu, Mosel Spätlese, GRÜNER V, Hunter SEM, white Rioja or local fizz.

Mussels marinière MUSCADET sur lie, unoaked CHARD, ASSYRTIKO. Or try light, brisk English red.
   curried Alsace RIES or PINOT BL.

Paella, shellfish Full-bodied white or rosé, unoaked CHARD, ALBARIÑO, or GODELLO. Or local Spanish red.

Prawns, crayfish with garlic Keep the wine light, white, orange, or rosé, and dry.
   with mayonnaise CHARD or rosé.
   with spices Up to and incl chilli, go for a bit more body, but not oak: dry RIES or Italian, eg. FIANO, GRILLO. *See also* CURRY.

Sardines in saor Local neutral, fresh white with acidity.

Sashimi KOSHU comes into its own here, either as orange or white, and can deal with wasabi and soy, within reason. Otherwise, try white with body (Chablis Premier Cru, Alsace RIES) with white fish, PINOT N with red. Both need acidity. Simple Chablis can be too thin. If soy is involved, then low-tannin red (again, Pinot). Remember sake (or Fino).

Scallops An inherently slightly sweet dish, best with medium-dry whites.

in cream sauces German Spätlese, Montrachet, or top CHARD.

grilled or seared Hermitage Bl, GRÜNER V, Pessac-Léognan Bl, Vintage Champagne, or PINOT N.

with Asian seasoning CHENIN BL, GEWURZ, GODELLO, Grüner V.

Scandi fish dishes Scandinavian dishes often have flavours of dill, caraway and cardamom and combine sweet and sharp notes. Go for acidity and some weight: FALANGHINA, GODELLO, VERDELHO, Australian, Alsace, or Austrian RIES.

Shellfish Dry white with plain boiled shellfish, richer wines with richer sauces. RIES is the grape.

plateaux de fruits de mer Etna white, MUSCADET de Sèvre et Maine, PICPOUL de Pinet, Alto Adige PINOT BL.

Smoked fish All need freshness and some pungency; Fino Sherry works with all.

eel Often with beetroot, crème fraîche: Fino again, or Mosel RIES.

haddock Quality Chablis, MARSANNE, CHENIN BL, GRÜNER V. *See also* SOUFFLÉS.

kippers Try Oloroso Sherry or Speyside malt.

mackerel Not wine-friendly. Try Fino.

salmon Condrieu, Alsace PINOT GR, Grand Cru Chablis, German Ries Spätlese, Vintage Champagne, vodka, schnapps, or akvavit.

trout More delicate: Mosel Ries.

Squid / octopus Fresh white: ALBARIÑO, MUSCADET, Greek, sparkling, esp with salt-and-pepper squid. Squid ink (risotto, pasta) needs Soave.

Sushi Hot wasabi is usually hidden in every piece. KOSHU is 1st choice. Failing that, German Trocken, Greek white, ALVARINHO, GRÜNER V or NV Brut Champagne. Obvious fruit doesn't work. Or, of course, sake or beer.

Tagine N African flavours need substantial whites to balance – Austrian, Rhône – or crisp, neutral whites that won't compete. Go easy on the oak. VIOGNIER or ALBARIÑO can work well. So can Amontillado Sherry.

Taramasalata A Med white with personality, Greek if possible. Fino Sherry works well. Try Rhône MARSANNE.

Teriyaki A way of cooking, and a sauce, used for meat, as well as fish. Germans favour off-dry RIES with weight: Kabinett can be too light.

Meat / poultry / game

Barbecues The local wine: Australian, Argentine, Chilean, S African are right in spirit. Reds need tannin, vigour, freshness; don't have to be grand.

Beef (*see also* Steak), boiled Red: light Douro, BLAUFRÄNKISCH, PINOT N or SYRAH. Medium-ranking CHARD is gd. In Austria you may be offered skin-fermented TRAMINER. Mustard softens tannic reds, horseradish kills your taste; can be worth the sacrifice.

roast An ideal partner for fine red, esp Pinot N. *See* above for mustard. The silkier the texture of the beef (wagyu, Galician, eg.), the silkier the wine. Wagyu, remember, is about texture; has v. delicate flavour.

stew, daube Sturdy red: Pomerol or St-Émilion, Cornas, Hermitage, Napa CAB SAUV, Ribera del Duero, BARBERA, SHIRAZ, or Douro red.

stroganoff Dramatic red: Amarone, Barolo, Hermitage, Priorat, late-harvest ZIN. Georgian SAPERAVI or Moldovan Negru de Purkar.

Boudin blanc CHENIN BL, esp when served with apples: dry Vouvray, Saumur, Savennières, S African; mature red PINOT N if without.

Boudin noir / morcilla Local SAUV BL or CHENIN BL (esp in Loire). Or Beaujolais cru, esp Morgon. Or light TEMPRANILLO. Or Fino.

Brazilian dishes Pungent flavours that blend several culinary traditions. Rhônish grapes work for red, or white with weight: VERDICCHIO, CHARD. Or orange. Or a Caipirinha (better not have two).

Cajun food Gutsy reds, preferably New World: ZIN, CARMENÈRE, SHIRAZ. Fish or white meat: off-dry RIES, MARSANNE, ROUSSANNE. Or, of course, cold beer.

Cassoulet Fresh red from SW France (Corbières, Fitou, Gaillac, Minervois, or St-Chinian) or BAGA, SHIRAZ, TEMPRANILLO.

Chicken / turkey / guinea fowl, roast Virtually any wine, incl v. best bottles of dry to medium white and finest old reds (esp burgundy). Sauces can make it match almost any fine wine (eg. coq au vin: r or w burgundy, or *vin jaune* for that matter).

    chicken Kyiv Alsace RIES, Collio, CHARD, Bergerac rouge.

    fried Sparkling works well.

Chilli con carne Young red: Beaujolais, TEMPRANILLO, ZIN, Argentine MALBEC, Chilean CARMENÈRE. Or beer.

Chinese dishes Food in China is regional – like Italian, only more confusing. It's easiest to have both white and red; no one wine goes with all. Peking duck is pretty forgiving. Champagne becomes a thirst-quencher. Beer too.

    Cantonese Big, slightly sweet flavours work with slightly oaky CHARD, PINOT N, off-dry RIES. GEWURZ is often suggested but rarely works; GRÜNER V is a better bet. You need wine with acidity. Dry sparkling (esp Cava) works with textures.

    Shanghai Richer and oilier than Cantonese, not one of wine's natural partners. Shanghai tends to be low on chilli but high on vinegar of various sorts. German and Alsace whites can be a bit sweeter than for Cantonese. For reds, try MERLOT – goes with the salt. Or mature Pinot N, but a bit of a waste.

    Szechuan VERDICCHIO, Alsace PINOT BL, or v. cold beer. Mature Pinot N can also work; but *see* above. The Creator intended tea.

    Taiwanese LAMBRUSCO works with trad Taiwan dishes if you're tired of beer.

Choucroute garni Alsace PINOT BL, PINOT GR, RIES, or lager.

Cold roast meat Generally better with full-flavoured white than red. German or Austrian RIES, lightish CHARD are v.gd, as is light GARNACHA. Leftover Champagne too.

Confit d'oie / de canard Young, brisk CAB FR, California CAB SAUV or MERLOT, Priorat cuts richness. Alsace PINOT GR or GEWURZ match it.

Coq au vin Red burgundy. Ideal: one bottle of Chambertin in the dish, two on the table. *See also* CHICKEN.

Dirty (Creole) rice Rich, supple red: NZ PINOT N, Bairrada, GARNACHA, MALBEC.

Duck / goose PINOT N is tops. Also other red in the Pinot idiom, like GARNACHA; also BLAUFRÄNKISCH. Or rich white, esp for goose: Pfalz Spätlese or off-dry Grand Cru Alsace. With oranges or peaches, the Sauternais propose drinking Sauternes, others Monbazillac or RIES Auslese. Mature and weighty Vintage Champagne handles accompanying red cabbage surprisingly well. So does decent Chianti.

    Peking *See* CHINESE DISHES.

    roast breast & confit leg with Puy lentils Madiran (best), St-Émilion, Fronsac, Maremma.

    wild duck Worth opening gd Pinot N. Austrian or Tuscan red (but easy on oak) also gd.

    with olives Top-notch Chianti or other Tuscans.

Filipino dishes Spanish-influenced flavours, lots of garlic, bell peppers, adobo, not always super-spicy. Straightforward unoaked white with acidity (adobo can have a burst of vinegar) or fizz, Côtes de Gascogne, Rueda, RIES, rosé, even light red.

Game birds, young, roast The best red wine you can afford, but not too heavy. Partridge is more delicate than pheasant, which is more delicate than grouse. Up the weight of wine accordingly, starting with youngish PINOT N, BLAUFRÄNKISCH, SYRAH, GARNACHA, and moving up.

    cold game Best German RIES or mature Vintage Champagne.

older birds in casseroles Gevrey-Chambertin, Pommard, Châteauneuf, Dão, or Grand Cru Classé St-Émilion, Rhône.

well-hung game Vega Sicilia, great red Rhône or NZ Syrah, Ch Musar.

Game pie, hot Red: Oregon PINOT N, St-Émilion Grand Cru Classé.

cold Quality white burgundy or German Erstes Gewächs, Etna red, Champagne.

Goat (hopefully kid) As for lamb.

Jamaican curry goat *See* INDIAN DISHES. And don't forget Malbec.

Goulash Flavoursome young red: Hungarian Kékoportó, ZIN, Uruguayan TANNAT, Douro, MENCÍA, young Australian SHIRAZ, SAPERAVI; or dry Tokaji Szamarodni.

Haggis Fruity red, eg. young claret, young Portuguese or Spanish red, CAB SAUV, MALBEC or Rhône blend. Or, of course, malt whisky.

Ham, cooked A gift to wine. Softish PINOT N (Côte de Beaune, Martinborough); Loire red or BLAUFRÄNKISCH; sweetish German white (RIES Spätlese); lightish CAB SAUV (eg. Chilean), or New World Pinot N. And don't forget the heaven-made match of ham and Amontillado.

Hare Jugged hare calls for flavourful red: not-too-old burgundy or Bx, Rhône (eg. Gigondas), Bandol, Barbaresco, Ribera del Duero, Rioja Res. The same for saddle or for hare sauce with pappardelle.

Indian dishes Various options: dry Sherry is brilliant. Choose a fairly weighty Fino with fish, and Palo Cortado, Amontillado or Oloroso with meat, according to weight of dish; heat's not a problem. The texture works too. Otherwise, medium-sweet white, v. cold, no oak: Orvieto *abboccato*, S African CHENIN BL, Alsace PINOT BL, TORRONTÉS, Indian sparkling, Cava or NV Champagne. Rosé is gd all-rounder. For tannic impact Barolo or Barbaresco, or deep-flavoured reds, eg. Châteauneuf, Cornas, Australian GRENACHE or MOURVÈDRE, or Valpolicella Amarone – will emphasize the heat. Hot-and-sour flavours need acidity.

Sri Lankan More extreme flavours, coconut. Sherry, rich red, rosé, mild white.

Japanese dishes A different set of senses come into play. Texture and balance are key; flavours are subtle. A gd mature fizz works well, as does mature dry RIES; you need acidity, a bit of body, and complexity. Dry FURMINT can work well. Umami-filled meat dishes favour light, supple, bright reds: Beaujolais perhaps, or mature PINOT N. Full-flavoured yakitori needs lively, fruity, younger versions of the same reds. KOSHU with raw fish – but why not sake? Orange Koshu with wagyu beef. *See also* FISH/SASHIMI, SUSHI, TERIYAKI.

Korean dishes Fruit-forward wines seem to work best with strong, pungent Korean flavours. PINOT N, Beaujolais, Valpolicella can all work: acidity is needed. Non-aromatic whites: GRÜNER V, SILVANER, VERNACCIA. Beer too.

Lamb, roast One of trad and best partners for v.gd red Bx, or equivalents from elsewhere. In Spain, finest old Rioja and Ribera del Duero Res, or Priorat, in Italy ditto SANGIOVESE. Fresh mint is gd, but mint sauce should be banned.

milk-fed Is delicate and deserves top, delicate GARNACHA, even white Rueda or Rhône.

slow-cooked roast Flatters top reds but needs less tannin than pink lamb. *See also* TAGINES.

Liver, incl venison Young red: Bairrada, BLAUFRÄNKISCH, Breganze CAB SAUV, Italian MERLOT, Médoc, Priorat, St-Joseph, ZIN.

calf's Red Rioja Crianza, Fleurie. Or a big Pfalz RIES Spätlese.

Mexican food Californians favour RIES, esp German. Or beer.

Moussaka Red or rosé: Ajaccio, Corbières, Côtes de Provence, Greek red, SANGIOVESE, TEMPRANILLO, young ZIN.

Mutton A stronger flavour than lamb, and not usually served pink. Needs a strong sauce. Robust red; top-notch, mature CAB SAUV, SYRAH. Sweetness of fruit (eg. Barossa) suits it.

'Nduja Calabria's spicy, fiery spreadable salumi needs a big, juicy red: young Rioja, Valpolicella, CAB FR, AGLIANICO, CARIGNAN, NERELLO MASCALESE.

Osso bucco Low-tannin, supple red such as DOLCETTO d'Alba or PINOT N. Or dry Italian white such as Soave.

Ox cheek, braised Superbly tender and flavoursome, this flatters the best reds: Vega Sicilia, St-Émilion. Best with substantial wines.

Oxtail Rather rich red: St-Émilion, Pomerol, Pommard, Nuits-St-Georges, Barolo, or Rioja Res, Priorat or Ribera del Duero, California or Coonawarra CAB SAUV, Châteauneuf, mid-weight SHIRAZ, Barolo, Amarone.

Paella Young Spanish wines: red, dry white, or rosé: Penedès, Somontano, Navarra, or Rioja.

Pastrami Alsace RIES, young SANGIOVESE, or St-Émilion.

Pigeon or squab PINOT N is perfect; or young Rhône, Argentine MALBEC, young SANGIOVESE. Try Franken SILVANER Spätlese. With luxurious squab, top quite tannic red.

pastilla Depends on sweetness of dish. As above, or if authentically sweet, try RIES Spätlese, Alsace PINOT GR with some sweetness.

Pork A perfect rich background to a fairly light red or rich white.

belly Slow-cooked and meltingly tender, needs red with some tannin or acidity. Italian would be gd: Barolo, DOLCETTO or BARBERA. Or Loire red, or lightish Argentine MALBEC. With Chinese spices, VIOGNIER, CHENIN BL.

Mangalica pork Fashionable, fatty. KÉKFRANKOS or other brisk red.

pulled Often with spicy sauce: juicy New World reds.

roast Deserves ★★★ treatment: Médoc is fine. Portugal's suckling pig is eaten with Bairrada; S America's with CARIGNAN; Chinese is gd with PINOT N.

with prunes or apricots Something sweeter: eg. Vouvray.

Pot au feu, bollito misto, cocido Rustic reds from region of origin; SANGIOVESE di Romagna, Chusclan, Lirac, Rasteau, Portugal's Alentejo, Spain's Yecla, Jumilla.

Quail Succulent, delicate: try red or white. Rioja Res, mature claret, PINOT N. Or mellow white: Vouvray, Hunter SEM.

Quiche Egg and bacon are not great wine matches, but one must drink something. Alsace RIES or PINOT GR, even GEWURZ, is classical. Beaujolais could be gd too.

Rabbit Lively, medium-bodied young Italian red, eg. AGLIANICO del Vulture, REFOSCO; MALBEC, Chiroubles, Chinon or dark rosé.

as ragu Medium-bodied red with acidity: Aglianico, NEBBIOLO.

with mustard Cahors, Malbec.

with prunes Bigger, richer, fruitier red.

Satay SHIRAZ, Alsace or NZ GEWURZ. Peanut sauce: problem for wine. Orange?

Sauerkraut (German) German RIES, lager or Pils. (But *see also* CHOUCROUTE GARNI.)

Singaporean dishes Part Indian, part Malay and part Chinese, Singaporean food has big, bold flavours that don't match easily with wine – not that that bothers the country's many wine-lovers. Off-dry RIES is as gd as anything. With meat dishes, ripe, supple reds: Valpolicella, PINOT N, DORNFELDER, unoaked MERLOT, or CARMENÈRE.

Steak Rare steak needs brisker, more tannic reds; well done needs juicy, fruity reds, eg. young Argentine MALBEC. Fattier cuts need acidity, tannin.

au poivre A fairly young Rhône red or CAB SAUV. Nothing too sweetly fruity.

fillet Silky red: Pomerol or PINOT N.

fiorentina (bistecca) Chianti Classico Riserva or BRUNELLO.

from older cattle Has deep, rich savouriness. Top Italian, Spanish red.

Korean yuk whe (world's best steak tartare) Sake.

ribeye, tomahawk, tournedos Big, pungent red: Barolo, Malbec, SHIRAZ, Rioja.

sirloin Suits most gd reds. Bx blends, Tuscans.

tartare Vodka or light young red: Loire, Pinot N, BLAUFRÄNKISCH. Aussies drink GAMAY with kangaroo tartare, charred plums, Szechuan pepper.

T-bone Reds of similar bone structure: Barolo, gd Cab Sauv, SYRAH, Ribera del Duero, Douro.

wagyu Delicate, silky red, or orange.

Steak-&-kidney pie or pudding Red Rioja Res or mature Bx. Pudding (with suet) wants vigorous young wine. Madiran with its tannin is gd. Or Greek.

Stews & casseroles Village burgundy or equivalent if fairly simple; otherwise lusty and full-flavoured red, eg. young MENCÍA, Corbières, BARBERA, BLAUFRÄNKISCH, SHIRAZ, ZIN, etc.

Sweetbreads A rich dish, so needs grand white wine: top RIES or Franken SILVANER Spätlese, Grand Cru Alsace PINOT GR, MARSANNE, or Condrieu, depending on the sauce.

Tagines Depends on what's under the lid, but fruity young reds are a gd bet: GARNACHA, MERLOT, SANGIOVESE, SHIRAZ, TEMPRANILLO. Amontillado is great, as is aged Tawny Port. Amarone is fashionable.

chicken with preserved lemon, olives VIOGNIER.

Tandoori chicken RIES or SAUV BL, young red Bx or light N Italian red served cool. Also trad-method fizz or, of course, Palo Cortado or Amontillado Sherry.

Thai dishes Ginger and lemongrass call for pungent SAUV BL (Loire, Australia, NZ, S Africa) or RIES (Spätlese or Australian). Most curries suit aromatic whites with a touch of sweetness: GEWURZ also gd.

Tongue Any red or white of abundant character. Alsace GEWURZ or PINOT GR, gd GRÜNER V. Also Loire reds, BLAUFRÄNKISCH, TEMPRANILLO, full, dry rosé/orange.

Veal A friend of fine wine. Rioja Res, CAB blends, PINOT N, NEBBIOLO, German or Austrian RIES, Vouvray, Alsace PINOT GR, Italian GRECO di Tufo.

Venison Big-scale reds, incl MOURVÈDRE solo or blended. SYRAH, ZIN, Languedoc, Barolo, Bx, top mature CAB SAUV; or rather rich white (Pfalz Spätlese or Alsace PINOT GR).

with sweet & sharp berry sauce Try a German Grosses Gewächs RIES, or Chilean CARMENÈRE, or Syrah.

Vietnamese food RIES, dry or up to Spätlese, German, Austrian, NZ, also GRÜNER V, SÉM. For reds, BLAUFRÄNKISCH, CAB FR, PINOT N.

Vitello tonnato Full-bodied whites: CHARD. Light reds (Langhe Nebbiolo, TEMPRANILLO) served cool. Or a southern rosé.

Wild boar Serious red: top Tuscan or Priorat. NZ SYRAH. I've even drunk Port; Amarone would be a compromise.

Vegetable dishes

With few tannins to help or hinder, matching wine to veg is about sweetness, acidity, weight and texture. *See also* FIRST COURSES.

Agrodolce Italian sweet-and-sour, with pine kernels, sultanas, capers, vinegar and perhaps anchovies. Go to fresh white: VERDICCHIO, unoaked CHARD. Etna rosato. Or orange.

Artichokes Not great for wine. Incisive dry white: NZ SAUV BL; Greek (precisely, 4-yr-old MALAGOUSIA, but easy on the vinaigrette); VERMENTINO. Orange wine, yes; red, no. Better no wine than red.

Asparagus Is lightly bitter and needs acidity, if it needs wine at all. Asparagus solo: skip the wine. With other ingredients: go by those.

Aubergine Comes in a multitude of guises, usually strongly flavoured. Sturdy reds with acidity are a gd bet: SHIRAZ, Greek, Lebanese, Bulgarian, Hungarian, Turkish. Structured white, eg. VERDICCHIO, or go further and have orange wine.

Avocado Not a wine natural. Dry to slightly sweet RIES Kabinett will suit the dressing. Otherwise, light and fresh: ALIGOTÉ, TREBBIANO, PINOT GRIGIO.

Beetroot Mimics a flavour found in PINOT N. You could return the compliment. New-wave (ie. light) GARNACHA/Grenache is also gd, as is GAMAY.

Bitter leaves: radicchio etc. Bone-dry, aged Palo Cortado. But easy on the dressing. Fab combo. Or NEBBIOLO, LAGREIN, white VERMENTINO, orange.

  roast radicchio, chicory etc. SANGIOVESE, BLAUFRÄNKISCH, Etna red.

Cauliflower roast, etc. Go by the other (usually bold) flavours. Austrian GRÜNER V, GARNACHA, NZ PINOT N.

  cauliflower cheese Crisp, aromatic white: Sancerre, RIES Spätlese, MUSCAT, ALBARIÑO, GODELLO. CHARD too, and Beaujolais-Villages.

  with caviar – yes, really. Vintage Champagne.

Celeriac, slow-roast or purée Won't interfere with rest of dish. Acidity works well, so classic CAB blends, SANGIOVESE, PINOT N, according to dish.

  remoulade with smoked ham Needs bright red: DOLCETTO, simple GAMAY, Etna. Or white GRÜNER V.

Chestnuts Earthy, rich red: Tuscan or S Rhône.

Chickpeas Look at other flavours in the dish. Casserole works with TEMPRANILLO, S French reds.

  hummus Any simple red, pink or white, or, of course, Fino.

Chilli Some like it hot, but not with your best bottles. Tannic wines become more tannic; if you like that, go for it. Light, fruity reds and whites are refreshing: TEMPRANILLO, MERLOT, MALBEC, NZ SAUV BL. Same for **harissa**. *See also* MEAT/CHILLI CON CARNE, CHINESE DISHES, INDIAN DISHES.

Couscous with vegetables Young red with a bite: SHIRAZ, Corbières, Minervois; rosé, esp Etna; orange wine; Italian REFOSCO or SCHIOPPETTINO.

Dhal Comes with many variations, but all share aromatic earthiness. Simple, warm-climate reds work best: CARMENÈRE, Dão, S Italian.

Fennel-based dishes SYLVANER, SAUV BL, English white, or young TEMPRANILLO.

  Deep-flavoured braised fennel Light BLAUFRÄNKISCH, PINOT N.

Fermented foods *See also* CHOUCROUTE GARNI, KOREAN DISHES, SAUERKRAUT. Kimchi and miso are being worked into many dishes. Fruit and acidity are generally needed. If in sweetish veg dishes, try Alsace.

Grilled Mediterranean vegetables Italian whites, or for reds Brouilly, BARBERA, TEMPRANILLO or SHIRAZ.

Lentil dishes Sturdy reds such as Corbières, ZIN or SHIRAZ. *See also* DHAL.

Mac 'n' cheese As for CAULIFLOWER CHEESE.

Mushrooms (in most contexts) A boon to most reds and some whites. Context matters as much as species. Pomerol, California MERLOT, Rioja Res, top PINOT N, or Vega Sicilia.

  button or Paris with cream Fine whites, even Vintage Champagne.

  ceps / porcini Ribera del Duero, Barolo, Chianti Rùfina, CAB SAUV/Bx.

  on toast Best claret, even Port.

Onion / leek tart / flamiche Fruity, off-dry or dry white: Alsace PINOT GR or GEWURZ is classic; Canadian, Australian or NZ RIES; Jurançon. Or Loire CAB FR.

Peppers, cooked Mid-weight Rhône grapes, CARMENÈRE, Rioja; or ripe SAUV BL (esp with green Hungarian wax peppers).

  stuffed Full red, white, orange, or pink: Languedoc, Greek, Spanish, Etna.

Pickled foods & vinegar Vinegar and wine don't go, it's true, but pickled foods are everywhere. Try Alsace, German RIES with CHOUCROUTE/SAUERKRAUT (*see* MEAT). With pickled veg as part of a dish, just downgrade the wine a bit (no point in opening best bottles) and make sure it has some acidity. (Or have beer.) In dressings, experiment with vinegars: Sherry vinegar can work with

Amontillado, etc., big reds; Austrian apricot vinegar is delicate; balsamic can work with rich Italian reds. Wine just has to work harder than it used to.

Pumpkin / squash ravioli or risotto Full-bodied, fruity dry or off-dry white: VIOGNIER or MARSANNE, demi-sec Vouvray, Gavi or S African CHENIN. If you want red, MERLOT, ZIN.

Ratatouille (or piperade) Vigorous young red: Chianti, Languedoc, NZ CAB SAUV, MALBEC, MERLOT, TEMPRANILLO. A gd rosé can be best of all.

Roasted veg Can be root veg or more Mediterranean, but all have plenty of sweetness. Rosé, esp with some weight, or orange wine. Lightish reds with acidity to match the dressing. Pesto will tilt it towards white with weight.

Saffron Found in sweet and savoury dishes, and wine-friendly. Rich white: ROUSSANNE, VIOGNIER, PINOT GR. Orange wines can be gd too. With desserts, Sauternes or Tokaji. *See also* MEAT/TAGINES.

Salsa verde Whatever it's with, it points to more acidity, less lushness in the wine.

Seaweed (nori) Depends on the context. *See also* FISH/SUSHI. Iodine notes go well with Austrian GRÜNER V, RIES.

Sweetcorn fritters Often a hot, spicy sauce. Rosé, orange, or neutral white all safe.

Tahini Doesn't really affect wine choice. Go by rest of dish.

Tapenade Manzanilla or Fino Sherry, or any sharpish dry white or rosé. Definitely not Champagne.

Tomatoes Generally call for acidity in wine – think of Italian reds like BARBERA, NEBBIOLO, Etna, etc., for deep-flavoured cooked tomatoes. Whites with acidity for raw tomatoes.

Truffles Black truffles are a match for finest Right Bank Bx or Volnay, but even better with mature white Hermitage or Châteauneuf. White truffles call for best Barolo or Barbaresco of their native Piedmont. With buttery pasta, Lugana. Or at breakfast, on fried eggs, BARBERA.

Watercress, raw Makes every wine on earth taste revolting.

Wild garlic leaves, wilted Tricky: a fairly neutral white with acidity will cope best.

Desserts

Apples: Cox's Orange Pippins with Cheddar cheese Vintage Port.

    Russets with Caerphilly Old Tawny, or Amontillado.

    Pie, etc. Sweet Vouvray, or similar.

Bread-&-butter pudding Fine 10-yr-old Barsac, Tokaji Aszú, or Australian botrytized SEM.

Cakes *See also* CHOCOLATE, COFFEE, RUM. Bual or Malmsey Madeira, Oloroso or Cream Sherry. Asti, sweet Prosecco.

Cheesecake Sweet white: Vouvray, Anjou, or Vin Santo – nothing too special.

Chocolate Don't try to be too clever. Texture matters. BUAL, California Orange MUSCAT, Tokaji Aszú, Australian Liqueur Muscat, 10-yr-old Tawny or even young Vintage Port; Asti for light, fluffy mousses. Or *vins doux naturels* (VDN) Banyuls, Maury, or Rivesaltes. Some like Médoc with bitter black chocolate, though it's a bit of a waste of both. A trial of SYRAH with bitter chocolate showed that you shouldn't, ever. Armagnac, or a tot of gd rum.

Christmas pudding, mince pies Tawny Port, Cream Sherry or that liquid Christmas pudding itself, PEDRO XIMÉNEZ Sherry. Tokaji Aszú. Asti, or Banyuls.

Coffee desserts Sweet MUSCAT, Australia Liqueur Muscats, or Tokaji Aszú.

Creams, custards, fools, syllabubs *See also* CHOCOLATE, COFFEE, RUM. Sauternes, Loupiac, Ste-Croix-du-Mont or Monbazillac.

Crème brûlée Sauternes or Rhine Beerenauslese, best Madeira, or Tokaji Aszú.

Ice cream & sorbets PEDRO XIMÉNEZ with vanilla, or Australian Liqueur MUSCAT, or none. Sorbets: definitely none.

Lemon flavours For dishes like tarte au citron, try sweet RIES from Germany or Austria or Tokaji Aszú; v. sweet if lemon is v. tart.

Meringues (eg. Eton mess) Recioto di Soave, Asti, mature Vintage Champagne.

Nuts (incl praline) Finest Oloroso Sherry, Madeira, Vintage or Tawny Port (nature's match for walnuts), Tokaji Aszú, Vin Santo, or Setúbal MOSCATEL. Cashews and Champagne. Pistachios with Fino. **Salted nut parfait** Tokaji Aszú, Vin Santo.

Orange flavours Experiment with old Sauternes, Tokaji Aszú, or Orange MUSCAT from California .

Panettone Vin Santo. Jurançon *moelleux*, late-harvest RIES, Barsac, Tokaji Aszú.

Pears in red wine Rivesaltes, Banyuls, or RIES Beerenauslese.

Pecan pie Orange MUSCAT or Liqueur Muscat.

Raspberries (no cream, little sugar) Great with cream and something in the Sauternes spectrum.

Rum flavours (baba, mousses) MUSCAT – from Asti to Australian Liqueur, according to weight of dish.

Strawberries, wild, no cream With red Bx (most exquisitely Margaux) poured over. **with cream** Sauternes or similar sweet Bx, Vouvray *moelleux*, or Jurançon VT.

Summer pudding Fairly young Sauternes of a gd vintage.

Sweet soufflés Sauternes or Vouvray *moelleux*. Sweet (or rich) Champagne.

Tiramisù Vin Santo, young Tawny Port, MUSCAT de Beaumes-de-Venise, Sauternes, or Australian Liqueur Muscat. Better idea: skip the wine. Best idea of all: skip the tiramisù.

Trifle Should be sufficiently vibrant with its internal Sherry (Oloroso for choice).

Zabaglione Light-gold Marsala or Australian botrytized SEM, or Asti.

Wine & cheese

Counterintuitively, white is a safer option than red. Fine reds are slaughtered by strong cheeses. But aged Tawny Port is wonderful with most cheese, and orange wine is a gd standby too. Remember (despite exceptions): the harder the cheese, the more tannin the wine can have; the creamier the cheese, the more acidity is needed in the wine. Cheese is classified by its texture and the nature of its rind, so its appearance is a guide to the type of wine to match it.

Bloomy-rind soft cheeses: Brie, Camembert, Chaource CHARD, white Rhône, Swartland white blend. Not tannic red.

Blue cheeses The extreme saltiness of Roquefort or most blue cheeses needs sweetness: Sauternes, Tokaji, youngish Vintage or Tawny Port, esp with Stilton. Intensely flavoured old Oloroso, Amontillado, Madeira, Marsala and other fortifieds go with most blues. Dry red does not. Trust me.

Cooked cheese dishes: fondue Trendy again. Light, fresh white as below.

    frico Cheese baked or fried with potatoes or onions, trad in Friuli; high-acid local REFOSCO (r), or RIBOLLA GIALLA (w).

    macaroni or cauliflower cheese See VEGETABLE DISHES/CAULIFLOWER.

    Mont d'Or Delicious baked, and served with potatoes. Fairly neutral white with freshness: GRÜNER V, Jura Savagnin.

Fresh cream cheese, fromage frais, mozzarella Light crisp white: Portuguese, Jura, Loire; juicy rosé can work too.

Hard cheeses: Gruyère, Manchego, Parmesan, Cantal, Comté, old Gouda, Cheddar Hard to generalize, relatively easy to match. Gouda, Gruyère, some Spanish, and a few English cheeses complement fine claret or CAB SAUV and great SHIRAZ/SYRAH. But strong cheeses need less refined wines, preferably local ones. Granular old Dutch red Mimolette, Comté, or Beaufort gd for finest mature Bx. Also for Tokaji Aszú. But try tasty whites too: Jura, Vin Jaune. And orange.

- **Natural rind (mostly goats' cheese):** St-Marcellin Sancerre, CARICCANTE, Jurançon, Savoie, Soave, CHARD; or young Vintage Port.
- **Semi-soft cheeses:** Livarot, Pont l'Evêque, Reblochon, St-Nectaire, Tomme de Savoie Powerful white Bx, even Sauternes, CHARD, Alsace PINOT GR, dryish RIES, mature Hunter SEM, S Italian and Sicilian whites, aged white Rioja, dry Oloroso Sherry. The strongest of these cheeses kill almost any wines. Try marc or Calvados.
- **Washed-rind soft cheeses:** Carré de l'Est, mature Époisses, Langres, Maroilles, Milleens, Münster Local reds, esp for Burgundian cheeses; vigorous S French, Corsican, S Italian, Sicilian, Bairrada, S African, Australian. Also powerful whites, esp Alsace GEWURZ, MUSCAT. Gewurz with Münster, always.

Food & your finest wines

With v. special bottles, the wine guides the choice of food rather than vice versa. The following is based largely on gastronomic conventions, some bold experiments and much diligent and on-going research.

Red wines

Amarone Classically, in Verona, risotto all'Amarone or pastissada. But if your butcher doesn't run to horse, then shin of beef, slow-cooked in more Amarone.

Barolo, Barbaresco Risotto with white truffles; pasta with game (eg. pappardelle alla lepre); porcini mushrooms; Parmesan.

Great Syrahs: Hermitage, Côte-Rôtie, Grange, Vega Sicilia Beef, venison, or well-hung game; bone marrow on toast; English cheese (Lincolnshire Poacher) but also hard goats'-milk and ewes'-milk cheeses such as England's Lord of the Hundreds. I treat Côte-Rôtie like top red burgundy.

Great Vintage Port or Madeira Walnuts or pecans. A Cox's Orange Pippin and a digestive biscuit is a classic English accompaniment.

Red Bordeaux, v. old, light, delicate wines (eg. pre-82) Leg or rack of young lamb, roast with a hint of herbs (not garlic); entrecôte; simply roasted partridge; roast chicken never fails.

fully mature great vintages (eg. 82 85 89 90 00) Shoulder or saddle of lamb, roast with a touch of garlic; roast ribs or grilled rump of beef.

mature but still vigorous (eg. 05 09 10) Shoulder or saddle of lamb (incl kidneys) with rich sauce. Fillet of beef marchand de vin (with wine and bone marrow). Grouse. Avoid beef Wellington: pastry dulls the palate.

Merlot-based Beef (fillet is richest) or well-hung venison. In St-Émilion, lampreys.

Red burgundy Consider the weight and texture, which grow lighter/more velvety

---

Fail-safe face-savers

Some wines are more useful than others – more versatile, more forgiving. If you're choosing restaurant wine to please several people, or just stocking the cellar with basics, these are the wines: **Red wines** BARBERA d'Asti/d'Alba, BLAUFRÄNKISCH, Beaujolais, Chianti, GARNACHA/Grenache, young MALBEC (easy on the oak), PINOT N, SYRAH (more versatile than Shiraz). **White wines** Alsace PINOT BL, ASSYRTIKO, cool-climate CHARD, CHENIN BL, Fino Sherry, GRÜNER V, dry RIES, Sancerre, gd Soave, VERDICCHIO. And the greatest of these is Ries. Make sure to think of **orange wines**. Always go for the best producer you can afford, and don't get too hung up on appellations or even vintages, within reason. If you can't afford gd Chablis, buy Assyrtiko, not cheap Chablis.

with age. Also the character of the wine: Nuits is earthy, Musigny flowery, great Romanées can be exotic, Pommard relatively sturdy. Roast chicken or (better) capon is a safe standard with red burgundy; guinea fowl for slightly stronger wines, then partridge, grouse, or woodcock for those progressively richer and more pungent. Hare and venison are alternatives.

great old burgundy The Burgundian formula is cheese: Époisses (unfermented); a fine cheese but a terrible waste of fine old wines. *See* p.33.

vigorous younger burgundy Duck or goose roasted to minimize fat. Or faisinjan (pheasant cooked in pomegranate juice). Coq au vin, or lightly smoked gammon.

Rioja Gran Reserva, top Duero reds Richly flavoured roasts: wild boar, mutton, venison, saddle of hare, whole suckling pig.

White wines

Beerenauslese (BA) / Trockenbeerenauslese (TBA) Biscuits, peaches, greengages. But TBAs don't need or want food.

Condrieu, Ch-Grillet, Hermitage Bl Pasta, v. light, scented with herbs and tiny peas or broad beans. Or v. mild tender ham. Old white Hermitage loves truffles.

Grand Cru Alsace Gewurz Cheese soufflé (Münster cheese).

Pinot Gr Roast or grilled veal. Or truffle sandwich. (Slice a whole truffle, make a sandwich with salted butter and gd country bread – not sourdough or rye – wrap and refrigerate overnight. Then toast it in the oven. Thank you to Dom Weinbach (*see* France).

Ries Truite au bleu, smoked salmon, or choucroute garni.

Vendange Tardive Foie gras or tarte tatin.

Old Vintage Champagne (not Blanc de Blancs) As an apéritif, or with cold partridge, grouse, or woodcock. The evolved flavours of old Champagne make it far easier to match with food than the tightness of young wine. Hot foie gras can be sensational. Don't be afraid of garlic or even Indian spices, but omit the chilli.

late-disgorged old wines These have extra freshness plus tertiary flavours. Try with truffles, lobster, scallops, crab, sweetbreads, pork belly, roast veal, chicken. Saffron is flattering to old Champagne.

old Vintage Rosé Pigeon, veal.

Sauternes Simple crisp buttery biscuits (eg. langues de chat), white peaches, nectarines, strawberries (without cream). Not tropical fruit. Pan-seared foie gras. Lobster or chicken with Sauternes sauce; Ch d'Yquem recommends oysters (and indeed lobster). Experiment with blue cheeses. Rocquefort is classic but needs one of the big Sauternes. Savoury food, apart from cheese, seldom works. Cantonese dishes can be gd. A chilled glass as an apéritif can be even better.

Sherry VOS or VORS Just some almonds or walnuts, or gd cheese. And time to appreciate them.

Tokaji Aszú (5–6 Puttonyos) Foie gras recommended. Fruit desserts, cream desserts, even chocolate can be wonderful. Roquefort. It even works with some Chinese, though not with chilli – the spice has to be adjusted to meet the sweetness. Szechuan pepper is gd. Havana cigars are splendid. So is the naked sip.

Top Chablis White fish simply grilled or *meunière*. Dover sole, turbot, halibut are best; brill, drenched in butter, can be excellent. (Sea bass is too delicate; salmon passes but does little for the finest wine.)

Top white burgundy, top Graves, top aged Ries Roast veal, farm chicken stuffed with truffles or herbs under the skin, or sweetbreads; richly sauced white fish (turbot for choice) or scallops, white fish as above. Lobster, wild salmon.

Vouvray moelleux, etc. Buttery biscuits, apples, apple tart.

France

More heavily shaded areas are
the wine-growing regions.

Abbreviations used in the text:

Al	Alsace
Beauj	Beaujolais
Burg	Burgundy
Bx	Bordeaux
Cas	Castillon- Côtes de Bordeaux
Chab	Chablis
Champ	Champagne
Cors	Corsica
C d'O	Côte d'Or
Ldoc	Languedoc
Lo	Loire
Mass C	Massif Central
Prov	Provence
N/S Rh	Northern/Southern Rhône
Rouss	Roussillon
Sav	Savoie
SW	Southwest
AC	appellation contrôlée
ch, chx	château(x)
dom, doms	domaine(s)

Le Havre

Caen

Brest

LOIRE

Loire

Nantes
Muscadet Anjou-
Saumur

La Rochelle

BORDEAU

Médoc
Pomerol
Bordeaux St-Émili
Entre
Graves Deux
Sauternes
Côtes du
Marmand
Buzet
Côtes
Tursan St-Mo
Biarritz Madira
Juraçon

This edition of the book is particularly concerned with value – in a
world where, until recently, it seemed that there was no limit on what
(a few) people would pay for rare wines. Now it looks as if a limit has
been reached, and while growers' costs continue to rise, they are more
and more aware that prices at the top end must moderate. Below that top
end, however, France has a lot to offer. The Loire has never looked better;
Alsace continues to be unfashionable abroad, and as ever, unfashionable
wines are the ones to look at. Bordeaux, for example, manages to be both
in demand (still) at the top end and almost unsellable at the very bottom.
Look in the middle and there are gems. In Burgundy, look for lesser
appellations from top growers. There is relative value to be found in
every region, and on these pages you'll see lots of boxes pointing out
where to look. But always look at the name of the producer. Great
winemakers often have entry-level wines of great deliciousness;
underperforming winemakers seldom get it quite right.

France entries also cross-refer to Châteaux of Bordeaux

Calais
Lille
Reims
CHAMPAGNE
Paris
Strasbourg
Marne
ALSACE
Orléans
Loire
Chablis
Saône
Pouilly-
Fumé
Sancerre
Dijon
aine
Côte d'Or
Cher
BURGUNDY **JURA**
Côte Chalonnaise
Mâconnais
Geneva
Bugey
Beaujolais
Dordogne
Lyon **SAVOIE**
N RHÔNE
Côte-Rôtie
St-Joseph
Condrieu
Cornas
Grenoble
ac
Hermitage
Crozes-Hermitage
Rhône
ahors
S RHÔNE
Côtes du
Rhône-Villages
Gigondas
Beaumes-de-Venise
THWEST
Tarn
Châteauneuf-du-Pape
Gaillac
ôtes du Frontonnais **LANGUEDOC**
Nice
Minervois St-Chinian
louse
Montpellier **PROVENCE**
Corbières
Marseille Bandol
SSILLON Fitou
Rivesaltes
Perpignan
Banyuls

Bastia
CORSICA
Ajaccio

Recent vintages of the French classics

Red Bordeaux

Médoc / Red Graves For many wines, bottle-age is optional; for these it is indispensable. Minor chx from light vintages may need only 1 or 2 yrs these days, but even modest wines of gd yrs can improve for 10 or so, and the great chx of these yrs can profit from double that time.

2024 Difficulties ripening Cab Sauv. Variable. Earlier drinking.

2023 Mildew. Powerful but balanced Cab Sauv. Potential to age.

2022 Hot, dry. Cab Sauv dense but supple tannins; gd ageing potential.

2021 Complicated: frost, rain, mildew. Cab Sauv variable but classic. Be choosy.

2020 Cab Sauv rich, dark, expressive. High alc but elegant. Low yields.

2019 Great balance; concentrated, fresh. Much Cab Sauv in blends. Will age.

2018 Pure, aromatic Cab Sauv. Rich, powerful (alc high), balanced. Long term.
2017 Attractive wines: gd balance, fairly early drinking. Volumes often small.
2016 Cab Sauv with colour, depth, structure. Vintage to look forward to.
2015 Excellent Cab Sauv yr, but not structure of 05 10. Some variation. Keep.
Earlier fine vintages: 10 09 08 06 05 00 98 96 95 90 89 88 86 85 82 75 70 66
        62 61 59 55 53 49 48 47 45 29 28.

St-Émilion / Pomerol

2024 Mildew, coulure, rot. Low yields. Modest yr.
2023 Merlot hit hardest by mildew. Yields variable. Gd in top terroirs.
2022 As Méd. Young vines suffered. Merlot excellent on limestone, clay soils.
2021 Merlot hit by frost, mildew. Low yields, variable quality. Cab Fr did better.
2020 Merlot rich and gourmand. Cabs Fr/Sauv also v.gd. Great potential.
2019 Drought. Merlot excellent on limestone, clay soils. Sandier areas suffered.
2018 Powerful but pure. Best from limestone, clay soils. Mildew affected yields.
2017 Balanced, classic fruit-cake flavours. Will be quite early drinking.
2016 As Méd. Some young vines suffered in drought but overall v.gd.
2015 Great yr for Merlot. Perfect conditions. Colour, concentration, balance.
Earlier fine vintages: 10 09 05 01 00 98 95 90 89 88 85 82 71 70 67 66 64 61
        59 53 52 49 47 45.

Red Burgundy

Côte d'Or Côte de Beaune reds generally mature sooner than grander wines
of Côte de Nuits. Earliest drinking dates are for lighter commune wines,
eg. Volnay, Beaune; latest for GCs, eg. Chambertin, Richebourg. Red burgundy,
with less tannin, is generally more appealing young than equivalent red
Bx. But great red burgundy is more age-worthy, and rewarding, than is
generally supposed.
2024 Wet, wet summer. Dreadful mildew. Yields much reduced, esp in
        Côte de Nuits.
2023 Sunny harvest after variable summer. Careful sorting = quality, quantity.
2022 Shaping up beautifully. Lovely balance, delicious length. Nascent classic.
2021 Wicked weather. Much reduced crop, but many lovely wines for
        early drinking.
2020 Concentrated: some superb, some too robust. Avoid later-picked wines.
2019 June/July heat gave lavish wines, many great, a few too high-octane. Keep.
2018 Sumptuous reds, gd young or old. Some rather too hearty.
2017 Attractive, mostly ripe enough, stylish, enjoyable already. Don't overlook.
2016 Some spectacular reds with great energy, fresh acidity. Will keep.
2015 Dense, concentrated, as 05 but juiciness of 10. Patience needed.
        Greatness beckons.
2014 Overshadowed by 15. Attractive fresh reds, some lovely surprises.
        Drinking now.
Earlier fine vintages: (drink or keep) 12 10 09 08 05 02 99 96 93 (mature) 90
        89 85 78 76 71 69 66 64.

White Burgundy

Côte d'Or Whites are now rarely (sadly) made for long ageing, but top wines
should still improve for 10 yrs or more. Most Mâconnais and Chalonnais
(St-Véran, Mâcon-Villages, Montagny) usually best drunk young (2–5 yrs).
Scourge of premox still hangs over wines post-1995 and 5 yrs+ old. Beware.
2024 Particularly challenging; mildew, but Côte de Beaune less affected than
        Côte de Nuits.

2023 Generous harvest. Variable, some excellent, others less refined.
2022 Summer heat after early rain. Abundant flavours. Some marvellous.
2021 Trounced by frost, but survivors are promising. Will be rare jewels.
2020 Crop gd, unlike reds. Powerful, surprising freshness; v. promising.
2019 Rich after summer heat. Best retained delicious acidity. Some stellar.
2018 Hot. Many powerful, opulent. Best balanced, others less elegant.
2017 Magnificent. Poised, elegant, lingering. All excellent. Rivals 14.
2016 Small, frosted crop, inconsistent results. Most ready now. Some wonders.
2015 Lush. Early pickers gd, some heavy. 09 but more successes. Keep best.
Earlier fine vintages (ready): 14 12 10 09 08 07 05 02 99 96.

Chablis has endured more than its fair share of weather disruption in recent
yrs. Hail and frost the main offenders, allied to biblical rainfall in 2024. GCs
of top vintages need at least 5 yrs, can age superbly for 15+; PCs proportionately
less, but give them 3 yrs at least. Then serve at cellar temp, cool not iced, and
decant. Yes, really.
2024 Pummelled by rain, hit by frost, thrashed by hail. Extremely challenging,
       yet quality is promising.
2023 Summer oscillated between heat/rain. Challenging; results generally gd.
2022 Well-balanced wines in gd volumes, despite drought and heat.
2021 Frost calamity. Some remarkably gd survivors.
2020 Hot and dry, but wines have turned out well, esp at higher end.
2019 Small crop of concentrated wine: typical marine Chab, exotic notes.
Earlier fine vintages: 18 17 12 10 08 02 00.

Beaujolais

2024 Weather-beaten, esp rain. Small crop. 23 Variable summer, but
promising. 22 Early harvest, gd quality. Charming, gd future. 21 Dismal
yr, some successes. 20 V. early harvest, drinking well. 19 Hot dry summer,
gorgeously juicy, satisfying wines.

Languedoc-Roussillon

2024 Tiny in Rouss, drought; small in Ldoc. Cool autumn, extended ripening,
       pristine fruit, elegance.
2023 Dry, esp Rouss. Low yields. Intense, fresh reds, esp Carignan, Mourvèdre.
2022 Drought lowered some yields, overall gd quality. Carignan, Grenache top.
2021 Frost, drought, pre-harvest rain in Ldoc, variable. Rouss fared better, v.gd.
2020 Lovely balance, gd acidity, freshness. Rouss gd.

SW France

2024 Challenging. Spring frost, esp CAHORS; storms, hail. Best producers
       looking promising.
2023 Mixed, but generally low yields. Mildew, hail, heat. Pick carefully.
2022 Crop size reduced by frost, then drought and heat. Quality likely to be gd.
2021 Relentless frost, rain, mildew, more rain. Keep to older vintages for reds.
2020 Summer heat, drought. A little uneven but gd, occasionally exceptional.
2019 Spring storms, heatwave summer. Small crop, fine quality.

Northern Rhône

Small hillside plots, often granite, some schist; top reds (Cornas, Côte-Rôtie,
Hermitage) can live 30 yrs+. White Hermitage can age as red.
2024 Rainy, poor fruit-set, small crop, v. interesting quality. Reds have flow,
       flair, will please. Whites gd, expressive, fruity.

2023 Variable, not memorable, tannins mild, can cellar. Côte-Rôtie gd, also n of St-Joseph, Cornas. V.gd Condrieu, whites pretty gd.

2022 Prominent fruit, brio at Côte-Rôtie, Cornas, reds gd, some v.gd. Appealing, rounded, table-friendly whites.

2021 Aromatic reds. Hermitage, Cornas (depth, gd) fuller than aromatic Côte-Rôtie. Not to keep. Beautiful whites, top Condrieu.

2020 Stylish reds. Côte-Rôtie perfumed, outstanding Hermitage (r/w). Top whites, esp if Marsanne-based, v.gd.

2019 Tremendous reds, flair at Côte-Rôtie; like 16 with more stuffing. No hurry. Whites concentrated. Note Hermitage, St-Joseph.

2018 Scaled-up reds, v.gd; Hermitage (r), similar Côte-Rôtie. Crozes variable. Whites: depth, surprising freshness; Condrieu, Hermitage, St-Péray.

2017 V.gd, esp Côte-Rôtie. Full reds, more robust than 16, show sunshine, firm tannins, benefit from time. Whites for hearty food, Condrieu variable.

2016 Reds lucid, harmonious, classic at Côte-Rôtie, gd to v.gd. Stylish Cornas. Marvellous Hermitage whites, other whites gd, precise.

2015 Excellent, concentrated full-tannin reds; long-lived Côte-Rôtie, Hermitage. Time still required. Full whites, can be heady.

Southern Rhône

2024 Mildew, Grenache flower damage, crop loss. But low alc, fresh, attractive filling, stylish potential on reds. V. promising whites.

2023 Grenache handled heat, drought. Gigondas did well, Châteauneuf mixed; purity in top wines. Variable Côtes-du-Rh (r). Whites gd, balanced.

2022 Concentration, heat; dense reds, forward aromas, some tannin issues, best balanced. Châteauneuf gd. Firm, full whites, geared to *la table*.

2021 Select with care: v. drinkable, aromatic reds from best names, bright fruit, elegance. Whites can be exceptional, best-ever Châteauneuf (w).

2020 Can be variable at modest price. Top: rich, splendid, gd acidity. Whites tricky from less gd zones, stick to best.

2019 Flamboyant, deep reds, character. Intense Grenache. Châteauneuf back on form, Gigondas excellent. Top names demand patience. Whites v.gd.

2018 Mixed, can be gd. Early signs of advance in reds already. Note Valréas, Visan, Vinsobres: higher, later vyds. Also Lirac, Rasteau. Whites v. full.

2017 Drought, can be variable. Full, bold reds, tannins just easing, coming together. Top doms best, stylish. Rasteau, Visan gd. Full whites.

2016 Excellent for all. Sensuous reds, much life. Sun-filled whites; keep some.

2015 Rich, dark, body, firm tannins, often enticing flair; v.gd. Full whites v.gd.

Champagne

2024 Frost, hail, mildew, but some promising Chard.

2023 Large yield, enormous berries. Overall promising, esp Chard.

2022 Relief at big, gd yr; hot in vein of 18, but long growing season.

2021 Cold spring, April frost, mildew = v. low yields. Sad in Marne V.

2020 Miraculous trio: 18 19 20. Beautiful ripe wines.

2019 Excellent quality. Pure fruit, tension, better acidity than much-lauded 18.

2018 Best in Pinot GCs of N Montagne. Chard more mixed: heat stress.

2017 Athletic wines of grace, energy.

2016 Underrated. Gently expressive Pinot Ns give much pleasure.

Earlier fine vintages: 12 10 09 08 07 06 04 02 00 98 96 95 92 90.

The Loire

2024 Wet summer, harvest. Muscadet hit hard. Whites light; delicate reds.

2023 Warm summer, pre-harvest rain. Yields gd, quality potentially gd.
2022 Despite heat/drought, v.gd to exceptional: early, perfect fruit; gd yields.
2021 Frost, mildew, hail. Fine autumn. Fresher style than recently.
2020 Incredible 7th successive v.gd yr; gd quality, quantity. Some high alc.

Alsace

2024 No frost but v. wet (not quite 21); bio/organic difficult. Rain means wines from flatland vyds better than usual.
2023 Sunny, dry but cool; v.gd Pinot N, Ries. Outstanding Muscat (best since 10). No noble rot, so little if any memorable late-harvest.
2022 Gd, lowish acid, clay-limestone soils best; great Sylvaner.
2021 Tumultuous rain, disease. Pinots suffered, but sunny Sept gave fine Ries.
2020 Refined, elegant, scented across board, as growers master climate change.
2019 Hot; top Ries, Pinot Gr, Gewurz can be v.gd. Wines from plains could be a problem.
2018 Warm, but fresh wines. Gewurz, Pinot Gr, Ries tops in high-altitude GCs.
Earlier fine vintages: 17 16 12 10 08 07 04 02 96 95 92 90.

Abymes Sav On limestone rubble of Mont Granier by APREMONT. DYA. Vin de SAV AOP cru. Jacquère grape. Try ★ 13 Lunes, ★★ A&M QUENARD, Crocs Blancs, ★ Giachino, Labbé, P&S Ravier.

Agapé Al ★★→★★★★ Riquewihr winery, est 2007 by Vincent Sipp after split from SIPP-MACK. Pungently mineral, v. saline, bone-dry, sustainably organic; quite the following. Best: RIES GC Rosacker (20), SCHOENENBOURG (19). Nice CRÉMANT.

Agisson, Jean-Philippe Lo ★★★ Name to watch in SANCERRE, POUILLY-FUMÉ; was head winemaker at ALPHONSE MELLOT, currently ditto at DAGUENEAU. Hunt down *Equilibre* Sancerre 19 20' 21 22' (23); La Belle Endormie (Pouilly-Fumé) a challenger.

Agrapart Champ ★★★ 13' 16' 17' 18 Pascal A makes precise CHAMP from scrupulously tended vyds in AVIZE. Impressive quartet: Experience, L'Avizoise, Mineral, *Venus*. Also Terroirs Extra Brut BLANC DE BLANCS GC, Les 7 Crus.

Ajaccio Cors ★★→★★★ AOP W CORS. Lots of granite. SCIACCARELLU shines here, classy VERMENTINO too.

Alary, Dom S Rh ★★★ Top CAIRANNE estate, stylish red influenced by son Jean-Etienne's Burg education. Top sites, mature vines. Compelling, long-lived Cairanne Jean de Verde (r, gd w), full Brunote (r), gd VDF L'Exclus.

Albert de Conti, Dom SW Fr Branch of C family (CH TOUR DES GENDRES). Chez Paul CAB SAUV; unusually, pure dry MUSCADELLE Conti-ne Périgourdine. Pét-nat too.

Allemand, Thierry N Rh ★★★★ 01' 05' 06' 07' 08' 09' 10' 12' 13' 15' 16' 17' 18' 19' 20' 21' 22' 23' 24' High profile; now son Théo. Distinguished CORNAS, organic DOM, low sulphur. Deep, lingering wines, stiff prices. Top: Reynard (mineral, intricate, 20 yrs+); Chaillot (racy, floral) drinks sooner.

Alliet, Philippe Lo ★★★★ CHINON superstar, now with son Pierre. *Coteau de Noiré*, *L'Huisserie* 09 10' 15' 16 17 18' 19 20 22 23 (23). Top: VIEILLES VIGNES. Also gd white.

Aloxe-Corton C d'O ★★→★★★ 09' 10' 12' 15' 17 18' 19' 20' 21 22' 23 The n end of CÔTE DE BEAUNE, famous for GC CORTON, CORTON-CHARLEMAGNE. Others don't set pulse racing. Tasty reds improved by recent warm yrs. Reasonable value. Best: Capitain-Gagnerot, Follin-Arbelet, RAPET, Senard, TOLLOT-BEAUT.

Alsace ★★→★★★★ Vosges rain-shadow effect means driest French wine region: aromatic, fruity, full white, increasingly gd PINOT N; some gd SYRAH (strictly VDF). Varietal labelling, so wines easy to grasp. Sec (dr), demi-sec (medium-dr), *moelleux* (medium-sw), *doux* (sw) indicated on back label, or numerical scale, so you know what you're getting (more or less).

Alsace Grand Cru Al ★★★→★★★★ 08' 10' 12 13 14 (esp RIES) 15 17' 18 19 20' 23'. Only 51 GC, incl some of the world's greatest vyds (Brand, HENGST, RANGEN, Sporen). Since 22 vintage, Hengst and Kirchberg de Barr PINOT N can also be GC-labelled; Vorbourg added to list in 24. Huge geological diversity means terroir-lovers' bonanza; but some GCs are too large; PC in gd sites coming soon, but bureaucratic roadblocks delaying process. Some of world's most age-worthy wines (40 yrs+), esp 61 67 71 83 90 08 10 19.

Alzipratu Cors ★★★→★★★★ Pierre Acquaviva is leading light: gd-value Fiumeseccu; Iniziu (r), pale herbal NIELLUCCIU; Pumonte (r), velvety, powerful.

Amadieu, Pierre S Rh ★★→★★★ Consistent, value, gd vyds at GIGONDAS, note Grand Romane, Romane Machotte (50s GRENACHE). Also CAIRANNE DOM Hautes Cances (stylish). Gigondas (CLAIRETTE) gd. Merchant range: VACQUEYRAS.

Amirault, Yannick Lo ★★★★ With son Benoît, arguably top in BOURGUEIL, ST NICOLAS DE BOURGUEIL. Top: (r) Les Malgagnes, Grand Clos, Petite Cave, Quartiers 09 10' 15' 16 17 18' 19 20 22 23. Try CHENIN BL Bâtard-Princesse.

Ampeau C d'O ★★★ Step back in time at MEURSAULT DOM: long-aged releases (c.25 yrs old). Properly mature, lush, succulent white: reminder of what was lost through premature oxidation. Reds impressive, less sumptuous.

Angerville, Marquis d' C d'O ★★★→★★★★ VOLNAY bio superstar. Great range of PCs topped by CLOS des Ducs (MONOPOLE). Elegant, balanced, harmonious; *vrai* Volnay. Daughter Margot now involved. *See also* DOM DU PÉLICAN for Jura.

Anjou Lo ★→★★★★ Hotch-potch, but great CHENIN BL in (dr) ANJOU BL, SAVENNIÈRES, (sw) COTEAUX DU LAYON, QUARTS DE CHAUME. Reds varied; simple GAMAY, CABS FR/SAUV in Anjou Rouge, ANJOU-VILLAGES. Rosé incl CABERNET D'ANJOU, Rosé d'Anjou. Also fizz (esp CRÉMANT DE LO). Home to some leading VDF.

Anjou Blanc Lo ★→★★★★ 14' 15 16' 17' 18 19 20 21 22 23 Most exciting Lo AOP: laser-sharp dry CHENIN BL. Try Bablut, BAUDOUIN, *Belargus*, Bergerie, CADY, Juchepie, Le Clos Galerne, OGEREAU, PIERRE-BISE, PIERRE MÉNARD, PLAISANCE, *Richard Leroy* (VDF), SANSONNIÈRE (VdF), Terra Vita Vinum. Don't drink too young.

Anjou-Villages Lo ★→★★★ 09' 10' 11' 15' 16 17 18' 19 20 22 AOP for tannic, age-worthy CABS FR/SAUV blends; 100% CAB SAUV from warm schist soils can surprise: Bergerie, PIERRE-BISE, *Ogereau*. Enclave Anjou Brissac (previously Anjou-Villages-Brissac) covers same area as COTEAUX DE L'AUBANCE: Bablut, Montgilet, *Rochelles*.

Antech, Maison Ldoc ★★★→★★★★ Françoise A-Gazeau is queen of all styles of LIMOUX fizz: M Le Mauzac simply best BLANQUETTE; CRÉMANT Eugénie shines. Méthode Ancestrale sweetly fruity.

AOP / AC or AOC (appellation contrôlée) Government control of origin and production (but not quality) of most top French wines; around 45% of total. AOP (appellation d'origine protégée) is new term.

Aphillanthes, Dom Les S Rh ★★→★★★ 20' 22' 23 24' Organic, bio DOM on hot, stony PLAN DE DIEU. Profound, terroir wines, value. Two CUVÉES: des Galets, VIEILLES VIGNES (50s GRENACHE). CÔTES DU RH (r); GIGONDAS Promesse; RASTEAU 1921.

Apremont Sav Largest cru of SAV, thus quality varies. Steely, light Jacquère on limestone rubble. Keep up to 4 yrs. Try ★ 13 Lunes, Apffel, ★ Blard, ★ Dupraz, ★★ Giachino, ★★ Masson, Perrier, Richel.

Arbin Sav ★★ A SAV cru. Dark, spicy MONDEUSE on steep slopes. Drink to 8 yrs+. ★ A&M QUENARD, ★ Genoux, ★ Jacquet, ★ F Trosset, ★★ Magnin (last yr 22).

Arbois Jura AOP of N Jura, and Jura wine tourism capital; (w) CHARD and/or SAVAGNIN; (r) PINOT N, Poulsard/Ploussard, TROUSSEAU; VIN JAUNE. Try pristine ★★ PÉLICAN, ★★ Rijckaert and ★★★ *Stéphane Tissot*; natural ★ Bottes Rouges, ★ Gahier, ★★ MAISON OVERNOY, ★ St-Pierre, ★ Tournelle; organic ★ Borde, D Petit, ★ La Pinte, ★ Ratte, ★ Renardière, ★ Touraize, Villet. Also ever-improving ★★

Aviet, ★ Cellier Saint-Benoît, Fruitière Vinicole d'Arbois (co-op)/Ch Béthanie, Jérôme Arnoux, ★★ *Fumey-Chatelain*, ★ Rolet.

Ardèche S Rh ★→★★ 23 24' IGP Granite terraces, often less-restrictive VDF, eg. DOM des Accoles. Also HQ for Rhône Vin Nature, all VdF (A Calek, Les Deux Terres, Mazel). Quality up, often gd value. Direct reds; MARSANNE, VIOGNIER (eg. CHAPOUTIER). Best: SYRAH, also GAMAY (often old vines). Restrained, burg-style Ardèche CHARD by LOUIS LATOUR (Grand Ardèche much oak). Also CH de la Selve; DOMS de Vigier, du Grangeon, JF Jacouton; Mas d'Intras (organic).

Ardoisières, Dom des Sav IGP Vin des Allobroges organic estate, with vyds outside AOP. Superb and eclectic ★★★ range, incl Améthyste (r blend), Quartz Altesse, Schist (w blend), plus ★ Argile blends (r/w). Maison des A is gd SAV-only négociant label.

Arlaud C d'O ★★★→★★★★ Leading MOREY-ST-DENIS estate energized by Cyprien A. Hearty in past, now poised, from exceptional BOURGOGNE Roncevie up to GCS. Fine Morey PCS. Magnificent vaulted tasting room.

AR Lenoble Champ ★★★ Siblings in Damery, with Chouilly CHARD elegance underwriting subtle style with no fear of wood intervention. Archetypal BLANC DE BLANCS GC Chouilly 12 13 15' 19; BLANC DE NOIRS PC PINOT N Bisseuil perfect antidote 12 13.

Arlot, Dom de l' C d'O ★★→★★★ AXA-owned estate; stylish, fragrant across range from HAUTES-CÔTES to GC ROMANÉE-ST-VIVANT. Star: NUITS CLOS des Forêts St-Georges. Reds fully destemmed since 2021. Interesting whites too.

Burgundy 2021? Mozart delicacy, not Mahler heft. Don't ignore.

Armand, Comte C d'O ★★★→★★★★ MONOPOLE CLOS des Epeneaux may be POMMARD'S most graceful, effortless, ageless, GC quality; gd value from AUXEY, VOLNAY too.

Arnoux-Lachaux C d'O ★★★★ VOSNE superstar. All change under Charles Lachaux: no-till, high-trellised, unhedged vines, v. light-hand vinification with whole bunches, much reduced oak. Sublime. Breathtaking prices. PCS Grand Suchots, Reignots and GC ROMANÉE-ST-VIVANT.

Arretxea, Dom SW Fr ★★★→★★★★ Pioneering bio estate in remote Basque AOP IROULÉGUY. All styles, but whites (Hegoxuri, Schistes) stand out.

Aube Champ (aka Côte des Bar) CHAMP'S southerly vyds; v.gd PINOT N by great Reims houses, eg. KRUG, VEUVE CLICQUOT. Aube 11' excels, less lauded elsewhere. Torrential rain, heat spikes in 21; v. warm but promising 22. Capacious 23.

Aubuisières, Dom des Lo ★★→★★★ VOUVRAY DOM of Charles Lesaffre. Great things afoot, incl new 2nd dom, L'Arcadie. To follow. Historically fine *moelleux* 89 90 96 97 02 03 08 09 10 14 18 20 22, but focus today on SEC. Single-vyds Le Bouchet, Le Marigny, Le Petit Clos tiptop. Frolicking fizz.

Audoin, Cyril C d'O ★★→★★★★ Cyril A crafts MARSANNAY (r) of real style, smooth-textured with vibrant, lasting flavours: Au Champ Salomon. Varying use of whole bunches, seeks stem ripeness. Also rosé: "white version of PINOT N".

Aupilhac, Dom d' Ldoc ★★★ Sylvain Fadat, pioneer of MONTPEYROUX, cultivates bio s-facing old vines. Fabulous 100% CARIGNAN VDF. Les Cocalières (r/w) from high-altitude vyds on Mt Baudile have delicate touch.

Auxey-Duresses C d'O ★★→★★★★ (r) 15' 16 17 18' 19' 20' 21 22' 23 (w) 14' 15 17' 18 19' 20' 21 22' 23 MEURSAULT neighbour enjoying climate change. Whites are "junior Meursault", can be v.gd: Les Hautés vyd. Reds now ripen. Best: (r) COCHE-DURY, COMTE ARMAND, d'Auvenay (Boutonniers), Gras, Jessiaume, Paquet, Prunier; (w) Diconne, Lafouge, LEROUX, Paquet, VINCENT JM, VINCENT P.

Avize Champ ★★★★ Côte des Blancs GC CHARD; top growers AGRAPART, Bonville, SELOSSE, Thienot. Huge co-op provides base wines to biggest houses.

Aÿ Champ ★★★→★★★★ Revered PINOT N village, home of BOLLINGER, DEUTZ. Mix of merchants and growers, more oak than elsewhere (eg. Giraud). Aÿ Rouge (AOP COTEAUX CHAMPENOIS) now excellent in riper yrs: 15' 18' 19' 20 22.

Ayala Champ ★★★ 13 14 19' 20' Revitalized aÿ house, owned by BOLLINGER. Excellent BLANC DE BLANCS A 18, BRUT NATURE and No. 7 13, *La Perle 14, Collection No 16*.

Ayze Sav ★★ Cru closest to Mont Blanc, sometimes spelled Ayse. Rare Gringet grape: fruity fizz, mineral (dr) whites. Belluard winery now re-baptized ★★ Gringet (dr only) with new owners. Also seek out Montessuit and ★ Vallier (dr only).

Bachelet Burg ★★★→★★★★ Well-regarded CÔTE DE BEAUNE family. *B-Monnot* for superb village wines and BÂTARD-M, Bernard B (MARANGES), Jean-Claude B for similar quality in CHASSAGNE (PC Boudriotte), ST-AUBIN. No relation to Denis B (great GEVREY-CHAMBERTIN).

Balthazar, Franck N Rh ★★★ 18 19 20' 21 22' 23' 24' Organic, classic small dom at Cornas, led by Chaillot (incl 1914 SYRAH) also delightful zero-added-sulphur version. Fruit purity foremost. Bonny 100% ROUSSANNE ST-PÉRAY (w).

Bandol Prov ★★★→★★★★ AOP on slopes by Med, nr Toulon, renowned for noble reds that age well, majority MOURVÈDRE, plus GRENACHE, CINSAULT. Lots of rosé; some v. pale, PROV-style, many darker, gastronomic from Mourvèdre, often excellent, can age. White (5%): CLAIRETTE, UGNI BL, occasionally SAUV BL. Top: DOMS de la Bégude, de la Ribotte, des Trois Filles, du Gros'Noré, Dupuy de Lôme, Guilhem Tournier, La Bastide Blanche, Lafran Veyrolles, La Suffrène, le Galantin, Mas de la Rouvière, Pibarnon, Pradeaux, RAY-JANE, Roche Redonne, TEMPIER, Terrebrune, Val d'Arenc, Vannières.

Banyuls Rouss ★★★→★★★★ Undervalued, often brilliant VDN from steep, terraced vyds, overlooking Med, nr Spanish border. COLLIOURE same area. From GRENACHE of all colours. Young, fresh style is *rimage*, but stars are RANCIOS, long-aged, pungent, intense. Wood-aged GC, 30 mths min. Divine with dark chocolate. Best: DOMS de la Rectorie, du Mas Blanc, la Tour Vieille, MADELOC, Piétri Géraud, Vial Magnères; Bila-Haut, Clos Saint Sebastien, Coume del Mas, Les Clos de Paulilles. Co-op gd too. *See also* MAURY.

Bardi d'Alquier, Dom Ldoc ★★★→★★★★ New owners Sophie and Thibaut Bardi; FAUGÈRES DOM goes from strength to strength: Premières (r) scented, pristine; Les Grandes Bastides, brooding, truffley SYRAH, needs time.

Barmes-Buècher, Dom Al ★★→★★★ Wettolsheim estate making gd CRÉMANT, SGNS; bevy of GCS. Best: lieu-dit CLOS Sand RIES, GC Steingrubler GEWURZ.

Barrique 225-litre oak barrel. Now more subtle use, or none. Cost: €850+/barrel.

Barsac Saut ★★→★★★★ 11' 13 14 15' 16' 18 19 20 22 23 Neighbour of SAUT, similar botrytized wines from lower-lying limestone; fresher, less powerful, esp with bit of age. Top: *Climens*, COUTET, DOISY-DAËNE, *Doisy-Védrines*. Value: Cantegril, Closiot, La Clotte Cazalis, Liot.

Barthod, Ghislaine C d'O ★★★→★★★★ A reason to fall in love with CHAMBOLLE-MUSIGNY. Son Clément in charge (since 2019), further refining style. Grace and harmony abound, delicacy yet depth. Wonderful range of 11 different PCS, incl Baudes, Beaux Bruns, Cras, Fuées. BOURGOGNE Rouge can age 10 yrs.

Bâtard-Montrachet C d'O ★★★★ 08' 09' 10 12 14' 15 17' 18 19' 20' 21 22' 23 Most opulent of MONTRACHET GCS, downslope from Le Montrachet. More power than neighbours Bienvenues-B-M (more elegant) and CRIOTS B-M. Seek out: BACHELET-Monnot, BOILLOT (both H and J-M), FAIVELEY, GAGNARD, LATOUR, LEFLAIVE, LEROUX, MOREY, O LEFLAIVE, PERNOT, RAMONET, SAUZET, VOUGERAIE. Also J-C BACHELET, J CARILLON for Bienvenues version.

Baudouin, Patrick Lo ★★→★★★ Influential ANJOU DOM, organic for 20 yrs+. CHENIN BL (dr/sw) speciality. Single-vyds Bruandières, Le Cornillard, Les Gâts, Zersiles 16 18 19 20. Also top COTEAUX DU LAYON 1896, QUARTS DE CHAUME Zersilles.

Baudry, Dom Bernard Lo ★★★→★★★★ Famed organic CHINON DOM; son Matthieu upholds Bernard's legacy. Superb La Croix Boissée, Le CLOS Guillot (both limestone) 05' 09 10' 15' 16 17 18' 19 20 21 22' (23). Les Grézeaux (gravel) can be gorgeous. New Les Mollières (limestone) looking better in 23. Drink Les Granges (sand), white, rosé young.

Baumard, Dom des Lo ★★ Old ANJOU DOM now run by son Florent. Renowned for bone-dry SAVENNIÈRES CLOS du Papillon 02' 05 08 10' 14 18 19 20. Sweet COTEAUX DU LAYON CLOS de Sainte Catherine, QUARTS DE CHAUME 03 05 07' 09 10 16 18, fresh, pure-fruited gateway wines to these appellations.

Baux-de-Provence, Les Prov ★★★ Stunning, touristy village, AOP. Almost all organic, Mostly red: CAB SAUV, GRENACHE and SYRAH. White: CLAIRETTE, GRENACHE BL, Rolle and ROUSSANNE. TRÉVALLON best, prefers IGP Alpilles. Also gd: CH ROMANIN, Dalmeran, d'Estoublon, DOM HAUVETTE, Lauzieres, Mas de Carita, Mas de Gourgonnier, Mas de la Dame, Mas Ste Berthe, Terres Blanches, Valdition; atypical Milan.

Béarn SW Fr ★→★★ AOP DYA Reds from ★ JURANÇON CO-OP, DOMS Guilhémas, Lapeyre. Same grapes as MADIRAN and Jurançon.

Beaucastel, Ch de S Rh ★★★★ 05' 06' 07' 09' 10' 12' 13' 15' 16' 17' 18' 19' 20 21 22' 23 24' Organic CHÂTEAUNEUF estate, galet-stone soils: old MOURVÈDRE, 100-yr-old ROUSSANNE, base of Hommage à Jacques Perrin (r, lives 30 yrs+), Roussanne VIEILLES VIGNES (w, drink 5–25 yrs). Only 30% GRENACHE in dark-fruited, suave red (drink 2 yrs or from 7–8). Classy CÔTES DU RH Coudoulet de Beaucastel (r, age 10 yrs+). Famille Perrin GIGONDAS, RASTEAU, VINSOBRES (best) all gd, genuine. Note organic Perrin Nature Côtes du Rh (r/w). La Vieille Ferme gd value. Elegant Maison Les Alexandrins, N Rh merchant-vyds venture. New cellars, also gin, grape-scented oils, Miraval PROV rosé, shops, restaurant. (*See* Tablas Creek, US.)

Sign of crisis in Côtes du Rhône: growers seeking to rip out 6000 ha.

Beaujolais ★→★★★ Now resurgent name. Fall in love again with simple fresh fruit, and more from growers in hills. Avoid industrial examples. Also sold as COTEAUX BOURGUIGNONS. Serve cool, with a ham sandwich.

Beaujolais Primeur / Nouveau Beauj Raised the image, destroyed the reputation: BEAUJ of the new vintage, released at midnight on 3rd Wednesday in Nov. A dead-end, not a slip-road to greater delight. Enjoy juicy fruit, then move on.

Beaujolais-Villages Beauj ★★→★★★ 18' 19' 20' 21 22' 23 Challenger vyds to crus, eg. MOULIN-À-VENT. May specify best village, eg. Lantigné. Try CH de Basty, Ch des Vergers, F Berne, F Forest, JM BURGAUD, N Chemarin. Quality, value.

Beaumes-de-Venise S Rh ★★ (r) 16' 18 19' 20' 22' 23 24' Village NR GIGONDAS, punchy, grainy red: CH Redortier; DOMS de Fenouillet, Durban, LA BOUÏSSIÈRE (character), la Ferme St-Martin (organic), Les Baies Gouts, Martinelle, Mathiflo, Piéblanc (organic), St-Amant (gd w). Leave for 2–3 yrs. VDN MUSCAT apéritif/dessert, serve cold, musky-grapey, ages well: DOMS Beaumalric, Bernardins (complex), Coyeux, DURBAN (rich, lives 20 yrs), Fenouillet (brisk), Fontavin (stylish), JABOULET, Perséphone (stylish), Pigeade (racy, v.gd), VIDAL-FLEURY, CO-OP Rhonéa. Attractive CÔTES DU RH whites (incl dr Muscat, VIOGNIER).

Beaune C d'O ★★→★★★ 09' 10' 12 15' 16 17 18' 19' 20 21 22' 23 Wine capital of Burg, wines more reliable than exciting. Classic merchants: BOUCHARD, CHANSON, DROUHIN, JADOT, LATOUR; and more recent contenders Bernstein, Lemoine, LEROUX, Pacalet. Top DOMS: Bellène, Besancenot, Croix, DE MONTILLE, Dominique LAFON, Morot, plus iconic HOSPICES DE BEAUNE. Overpopulated with red PCs, but check Bressandes, Cras, VIGNES Franches for grace; more power from Grèves. White: *Clos des Mouches (Drouhin)*, CLOS St-Landry.

Beauregard, Ch de Burg ★★→★★★ Unmissable POUILLY-FUISSÉ: Frédéric Burrier: Les Reisses, Ménétrières, Vers Cras. Fine BEAUJ: FLEURIE, MOULIN-À-VENT.

Beaurenard, Dom de S Rh ★★★ 19' 20 21' 22' 23' 24' Organic, bio CHÂTEAUNEUF estate, motivated young generation, must-try. Stylish red, handsome white. Boisrenard older-vine, deeper, some oak (r/w). Two gd RASTEAU reds (complex, old-vine Argiles Bleus).

Belargus, Dom Lo ★★★★ New ANJOU superstar is born (with huge investment). Style of ANJOU BL (Bonnes Blanches, Quarts, Rouères, *Treilles* and more) is new-wave, dry, electric, mineral; similar SAVENNIÈRES (Gaudrets, Ruchères) 18 **19** 20 21 22 (23). QUARTS DE CHAUME (increasingly rare beast) also worth a try.

Bellivière, Dom de Lo ★★★→ ★★★★ Eric Nicolas and son Clément run leading DOM in COTEAUX DU LOIR, JASNIÈRES. Supremely crystalline, mineral CHENIN BL incl Calligramme, VIEILLES VIGNES Éparses (from dr to sw) 14' 15' **16' 18'** 19 20' 22 (23). Drink others younger. Reds (Rouge-Gorge), v.gd Pineau d'Aunis.

Bergerac SW Fr ★→★★★ (w) 20 22 23 (24) AOP, been in shadow of BX for too long but now breaking free, showing own identity. Varied landscape, rolling hills, more continental climate. Multitude of appellations, Côtes de Bergerac for sweet white or fuller red from lower yields. Montravel more limestone soils. Huge variations in styles, quality. Best: ALBERT DE CONTI, ★★ CH de la Jaubertie, DOM de l'Ancienne Cure, Malfourat, MOULIN CARESSE (also Montravel AOP), Thénac, Tirecul La Gravière, ★★★ *Tour des Gendres*, VIGNOBLE des Verdots, reliable co-op Cave de Sigoules. *See* sub-AOPs: MONBAZILLAC, PÉCHARMANT, SAUSSIGNAC.

Bertagna, Dom C d'O ★★★ CLOS DE VOUGEOT-based DOM, impressive roster of GCS, PCS, incl MONOPOLE CLOS de La Perrière, plus 1 ha VOSNE Beaux Monts. Abundant fruit, gd depth is hallmark. Also CHAMBOLLE Les Amoureuses, tiny quantity.

Beyer, Léon Al ★★★★ Comtes d'Eguisheim GEWURZ (GC Pfersigberg) one of best; just-as-gd RIES R de Beyer showcases underrated GC Eichberg. Dry, food-friendly, virtually ageless (40 yrs+); SGNS grand.

Bichot, Maison Albert Burg ★★→★★★★ Major BEAUNE merchant/grower with bio DOMS in BEAUJ (Rochegrès), CHAB (LONG-DEPAQUIT), MERCUREY (Adélie), NUITS (CLOS Frantin), POMMARD (Pavillon). Impressive recent improvement: humdrum days over. Major buyer at HOSPICES auction.

Billaud Chab ★★★→★★★★ Difficult CHAB choice between DOM Billaud-Simon back on form under FAIVELEY ownership and Samuel B's sensational wine under own label. Both brilliant: characterful, age-worthy. Proper Chablis.

Billecart-Salmon Champ ★★★★ Revered family house, 7th generation. Supremely reliable Rosé; Louis BLANC DE BLANCS 07' 08 12; single-plot CLOS St-Hilaire 02 04' 05' 06; NF Billecart 02 08; excellent *Elisabeth Salmon Rosé* 02 06' 09 12. Innovative Les Rendez-vous: No. 3 MEUNIER, No. 4 CHARD, No. 5 PINOT N. New focus on multi-vintage; jnr NV, *Inspiration 1818*.

Bize, Simon C d'O ★★★ Chisa B makes delicious bio whole-bunch-style reds, from BOURGOGNE to GC LATRICIÈRES-CHAMBERTIN. Also SAVIGNY Grands Liards, PCS Guettes, Vergelesses and tasty whites too. Once dependable, now exemplary.

Blagny C d'O ★★→★★★ 09' 10' 12 15' 16' 17 18' 19' 20' 21 22' 23 Remote hamlet on hillside above MEURSAULT and PULIGNY. Value. Own AOP for reds, now shedding austere cloak. Whites sold as Meursault-Blagny PC. Home to evocative vyd names: La Jeunelotte, Pièce Sous le Bois, Sous le Dos d'Ane. Best growers: (r) Lamy-Pillot, LEROUX, MATROT; (w) de Cherisey, JOBARD, LATOUR, LEFLAIVE.

Blanc de Blancs White from white grapes only, esp CHAMP. Note: describes style, not quality.

Blanc de Noirs White (or slightly pink or "blush", or "gris") wine from red grapes, esp CHAMP: much more elegant now.

Blanck, Paul & Fils Al ★★★→★★★★ GEWURZ, PINOT GR, RIES v.gd: GC SCHLOSSBERG Ries best 17' 18' 19'. SYLVANER 22 v.gd.

Blanquette de Limoux Ldoc ★★ Lively, appley fizz; 90% MAUZAC, plus CHARD/

CHENIN BL AOP CRÉMANT DE LO, more classic with Chard, Chenin Bl, PINOT N, less Mauzac. Sieur d'Arques co-op is biggest. Try Delmas, Jo Riu, La Coume-Lumet, LAURENS, Les Hautes Terres, MAISON ANTECH, Monsieur S, Robert.

Blaye Bx ★→★★ 16 17 19 20 22 23 Designation for better reds (yields, site, ageing) from AOP BLAYE-CÔTES DE BX. Name change to Blavia in 2025.

Blaye-Côtes de Bordeaux Bx ★→★★ 19 20 22 23 Mainly (90%) MERLOT-led red AOP on right bank of Gironde. A little dry white (mainly SAUV BL). Best CHX: Bel-Air la Royère, Bonnange, Bourdieu, Cantinot, des Tourtes, Gigault (CUVÉE Viva), Haut-Bertinerie, Haut-Grelot, Jonqueyres, Monconseil-Gazin, Mondésir-Gazin, Montfollet, Peybonnehomme Les Tours, Roland la Garde. Also go-ahead VIGNERONS de Tutiac co-op (r/w).

Boeckel, Dom Al ★★★ Mittelbergheim organic winery; rich but refined, outstanding SYLVANER GC ZOTZENBERG (20 esp gd); fine RIES Wibbelsberg 17' 19'; rich CLOS Eugénie 18 19'.

Boillot C d'O Leading Burg family. ★★★ Jean-Marc (POMMARD), esp fine, long-lived (w); ★★★→★★★★ Henri (MEURSAULT), stylish, thrilling (r/w); ★★★ Louis (CHAMBOLLE), great reds, both Côtes; brother Pierre (DOM LUCIEN B) ★★→★★★ (GEVREY). Marthe Henry B (Meursault), no close relation, interesting post-modern wines. Seek out all, esp Henri B.

Boisset, J-C Burg Ultra-successful merchant/grower group created over last 60 yrs. Boisset label, once humdrum, now exciting, from magnificent new winery in NUITS. Check ***Dom de la Vougeraie***. Recent additions: (Burg) Alex Gambal, VINCENT GIRARDIN. Also high-end JCB CRÉMANTS labelled as "Brut Burgundy". Projects in BEAUJ, Jura, California (Gallo connection), Canada, Chile, Uruguay.

Boizel Champ ★★★ Family-run; value. BLANC DE BLANCS NV, esp on base of 13' 17' 18' 19'. CUVÉE Sous Bois, wood well handled. Prestige Cuvée Joyau de France 08 12 (released on PLACE DE BX) also Rosé 12. ***Collection Trésor*** 90 96.

Bollinger Champ ★★★★ Great classic house, power and glory. BRUT Special NV singing since 2012, RD 02 04' 05' 07 08, Grande Année 08 12 14 15, Vintage Rosé 12 14 15. New CUVÉE showing new faces of eponymous PINOT N villages, thus far Verzenay (VZ 15 16 19), Tauxières 17, AŸ 18. Sublime ***Vieilles Vignes Françaises*** 12 15; La Côte aux Enfants (still) 14 16 and new sparkling 13 14'.

Bonnaire Champ ★★★ Cramant stalwart; supremely reliable GC BLANC DE BLANCS, some interesting lieux-dits; Le Bateau 13 16. Also JV with Paul Clouet in Bouzy, 50/50 CHARD/PINOT N, well-named as Love Story 08 12 15.

Bonnaud, Ch Henri Prov ★★★→★★★★ Top DOM in tiny AOP PALETTE, nr Aix. Silky red, elegant rosé. Quintessence (CLAIRETTE) v. fine.

Bonneau du Martray, Dom C d'O (r) ★★★ (w) ★★★→★★★★ CORTON-CHARLEMAGNE (now labelled Charlemagne), owned by Stanley Kroenke (Screaming Eagle, Napa, US); 3 ha leased to DRC. Intense, long-ageing, glorious fruit, underlying minerality. Older yrs variable. Some red CORTON. Cellar renovation 2025.

Bonnes-Mares C d'O ★★★★ 93 96' 99' 02' 05' 09' 10' 12' 15' 16' 18 19 20 21 22' 23 GC between CHAMBOLLE-MUSIGNY and MOREY-ST-DENIS with some of latter's robust, *sauvage* character. Structured, firm. Magnificence comes with age. Best: ARLAUD, d'Auvenay, Bart, BRUNO CLAIR, DE VOGÜÉ, Drouhin-Laroze, DUJAC, GROFFIER, H BOILLOT, JADOT, MORTET, ROUMIER, VOUGERAIE.

Bonnet, Alexandre Champ ★★★ Fascinating producer in Les Riceys, nearer to CHAB than Épernay. Beguiling range: CÔTEAUX CHAMPENOIS (w) 18 20, La Fôret Rosé de Saignée 16 18 19, Les Contrées (incl all) Sept Cépages 18 19. Ambassador for long-undervalued vyds of AUBE.

Bonnezeaux Lo ★★★ 07' 09' 10' 11' 13 14 15 16 17 18' 19 20 22 (23) Lesser spotted of two cru AOPS for sweet CHENIN BL in COTEAUX DU LAYON, on three slopes of schist. Best: Deux Arcs, *Fesles*, Fontaines, Mihoudy, Petit Val, Petite Croix.

Bordeaux ★→★★ 20 22 23 Catch-all AOP for generic Bx (c. half production). Most brands (*Dourthe*, MOUTON CADET, *Sichel*) in this category. Up to 10% new grapes (MARSELAN, TOURIGA N, etc.) now permitted. Try CHX Bauduc, BONNET, Lamothe-Vincent, Reignac, Turcaud.

Bordeaux Supérieur Bx ★→★★ 19 20 **22** 23 Higher min alc, lower yield, aged longer than BX. Mainly bottled at property. Consistent CHX: Argadens, Bolaire, Camarsac, de Seguin, Francs Magnus, Grand Village, Landereau, Le Grand Verdus, MÉAUME, *Parenchère* (CUVÉE Raphaël), Penin, *Pey la Tour* (Rés), Pierrail, Reignac, *Thieuley*.

Borgeot C D'O ★★★ No need to move beyond excellent BOURGOGNE CD'O CHARD from Remigny-based DOM, but if you wish to, aim for PULIGNY-MONTRACHET Le Meix.

Borie-Manoux Bx Admirable BX shipper. Part of Group BCAP: BATAILLEY, PEYRABON, TROTTEVIEILLE and NÉGOCIANT Mähler-Besse.

Bouchard Père & Fils Burg ★★→★★★ Owned by Artemis Domaines (CLOS DE TART, EUGÉNIE). Rebranded as CÔTE DE BEAUNE DOM: CÔTE DE NUITS vyds transferred to EUGÉNIE. Fingers crossed for more verve on palate. Whites best in MEURSAULT and GC, esp CHEVALIER-MONTRACHET. Flagship reds: BEAUNE VIGNE de L'Enfant Jésus, CORTON. (No longer connected with HENRIOT, WILLIAM FÈVRE.)

Boudignon, Thibaud Lo ★★★★ Young, great SAVENNIÈRES DOM; eye-popping, electric; replanted historic vyds. *Clos de la Hutte*, de Fremine, La VIGNE Cendrée, uber-rare Franc de Pied 14' 15 16 18' 19 20 21 22 23. ANJOU BL v.gd.

Bouïssière, Dom La S Rh ★★★ Quality GIGONDAS, interesting reds, robust, age well, flair. Font de Tonin 50s GRENACHE, fine white; gd VACQUEYRAS (r), Vin de Table (r).

Boulay, Gérard Lo ★★★★ Such purity, grace. Top SANCERRE in Chavignol, incl CLOS de Beaujeu, La Côte, *Monts Damnés*, all from famed vyds: 14' 16 17 **19 20** 21 22' (23). Drink DOM CUVÉE young-ish. Red Oriane also gd.

Rabelais first mentioned Chenin Blanc, in 1534 – but as a wound dressing.

Bouley C D'O ★★★ Developing stars in VOLNAY, at van of cutting-edge higher-trained viticulture. Delicious reds, esp Volnay PCS, from cousins Thomas and Pierrick at their respective DOMS. Insistent but never overbearing flavours.

Bourgeois, Henri Lo ★→★★★ Large, gd SANCERRE DOM, NÉGOCIANT; reworking range. Try ES-56 (was La Bourgeoise), *d'Antan*, Jadis, La Côte des Monts Damnées: 14' 15' 16 17 18 19 20 22' (23). Terroir-driven single-vyd Le Cotelin, Le Graveron (r), Les Côtes aux Valets, Les Ruchons all worth a pop.

Bourgogne Burg ★→★★★ (r) 15' 17 18' 19' 20' 21 22' 23 (w) 14' 17' 18 19' 20' 21 22' 23 Basic Burg AOP. Seek brilliant egs from top DOMS. Can state subregion, eg. CÔTE CHALONNAISE, HAUTES-CÔTES, or C D'O. White from CHARD unless B ALIGOTÉ. Red from PINOT N unless declassified BEAUJ crus (sold as B GAMAY) or B Passetoutgrains (Pinot/Gamay, with 30%+ of former); v.gd value.

Bourgueil Lo ★★→★★★ 05' 09' 10' 15' 16 17 18' 19 20 21 22 (23) With CHINON, top CAB FR AOP; early-drinking from alluvial soils, age-worthy from limestone and clay. Star: *Yannick Amirault*. Also Bel Air, Chevalerie, Cotelleraie, La Butte, Lamé Delisle Boucard, L'Oubliée, Minière, Ouches, Seb David.

Bouscassé, Dom SW Fr ★★★ 18 19 20 21 22 (23) MADIRAN palace. BRUMONT's Napa V-style home. Reds a shade quicker to mature than tighter flagship Montus. Star: VIEILLES VIGNES (100% TANNAT).

Bouvet-Ladubay Lo ★★→★★★ One of top houses for sparkling SAUMUR, CRÉMANT DE LO. Huge range, from cheap 'n' cheerful to serious. Trésor v. reliable; also Brut Zéro, Instinct. Or rare *Ogmius*, if you can find it.

Bouzereau C D'O ★★→★★★ Extended family, MEURSAULT to core. DOM Michel B is leader (marvellous BOURGOGNE C D'O), but try also Jean-Marie B, Philippe B (CH de Cîteaux), Vincent B or B-Gruère & Filles for gd-value whites.

Bouzeron Burg ★★→★★★ 17′ 18 19 20′ 21 22′ 23 Tiny CÔTE CHALONNAISE village with unique AOP for ALIGOTÉ. Stricter rules and greater potential than straight BOURGOGNE Aligoté. Can be wonderful. Chanzy and esp *de Villaine* outstanding. Also gd CHARD, PINOT N as Bourgogne CÔTE CHALONNAISE.

Bouzy Rouge Champ ★★★ 09 12 15′ 18′ 19′ Still red of famous PINOT N village. Formerly like v. light burg, now with more intensity (climate change, better viticulture), also refinement. Best: COLIN, Paul Bara, VEUVE CLICQUOT.

Boxler, Albert Al ★★★★ Complex, dry. Jean B one of greats. Not just GC but GC subzones (Sommerberg's Vanne, Eckberg, Dudenstein; Brand's Kirchberg, Wibtal). Rare PINOT BL Res 22′ with no AUXERROIS (regular Pinot Bl, 66% Auxerrois, v.gd). Great buy, hard-to-find SYLVANER 22′.

Brana, Dom SW Fr Illustrious Basque family helped regenerate ★★★ IROULÉGUY. Red/white; CAB FR shares star role with TANNAT. Micro-cuvées worth tracking down incl rare pre-phylloxera red.

Briday Burg ★★→★★★ Michel B, now succeeded by son Stéphane. Lovely composure and value. All wines punch above weight, esp creamy-fruited RULLY MONOPOLE CLOS de Remenot (w), from 45-yr-old vines. Seek out.

Brin, Dom de SW Fr ★★→★★★ Organic, 14-ha estate in GAILLAC championing all-local varieties. Braucol aka FER SERVADOU, Duras, Prunelart, and some tangy whites from MAUZAC, Loin de l'Oeil. Smart *méthode-ancestrale* fizz too.

Brocard, J-M Chab ★★→★★★ Quality and commercial acumen under one roof: CHAB Ste Claire and fine range of PC, GC. Son Julien B has impressive bio range under 7 Lieux label. Always reliable and slightly below radar.

Brochet, Emmanuel Champ ★★★ Bijou producer from steep Mont Bernard. Extra BRUT pure, exhilarating, organic, in barrel 9 mths. Excelled in sumptuous 18′ 19′. *Haut Chardonnay Extra Brut* 09 12 14′ 15 16. Le Mont Benoît PC excellent too.

Brouilly Beauj ★★ 18′ 19′ 20′ 21 22′ 23 Largest and most s of ten BEAUJ crus: solid, structured with some depth of flavour, approachable early but can age 3–5 yrs. Top growers: CHX de la Chaize, des Tours; DOMS Chermette, *J-C Lapalu*, L&R Dufaitre, Piron. Adjacent CÔTE DE BROUILLY is better, esp CH THIVIN.

Brumont, Alain SW Fr ★★★★ MADIRAN's pioneer, living icon, creator of BOUSCASSÉ, MONTUS and single-vyd LA TYRE ("the best terroir in Madiran"). PACHERENCS outstanding: dry 100% PETIT COURBU, sweet 100% PETIT MANSENG.

Brut Champ Term for dry classic wines of CHAMP. Dosage usually less than of yore. Under 6g residual sugar = Extra Brut, increasingly modish.

Brut Ultra / Zéro Bone-dry (no dosage) in CHAMP (aka Brut NATURE); modish; quality better with warmer summers. *Pol Roger Pure*, ROEDERER Brut Nature Philippe Starck 09′ 12′ 14′ 15 VEUVE FOURNY Nature.

Bugey ★★ Small AOP w of SAV. Light, fresh fizz; all colours of still. Crus incl Cerdon (pink GAMAY/Poulsard *méthode ancestrale*), Manicle (CHARD, PINOT N), Montagnieu (Altesse, MONDEUSE, sp). White mainly Altesse (Roussette du B AOP), Chard. Red/rosé: GAMAY, Mondeuse, Pinot N. Try Cerdon from ★ Balivet P, ★★ Dentelle, Lingot-Martin or ★★ Renardat-Fache. Try all from Bartschi, ★ Bonnard, Cortis, Duport, ★ D'Ici Là, ★ Grangeons de l'Albarine, ★★ Peillot or Tissot.

Buisson, H&G C d'O ★★→★★★ Brothers Franck and Frédérick on upward curve at bio ST-ROMAIN DOM. Vibrant. Peach- and citrus-infused Sous le Château.

Burgaud Beauj ★★★ Jean-Marc B from MORGON, top bottlings of Charmes, Côte du Py, Grands Cras, etc, best with age, when precocious flavours of youth have settled. BEAUJ standard-bearer. Nephew Alexandre promising too.

Burn, Ernest / Clos Saint-Imer Al ★★→★★★★ Picks late: dry but balanced, often off-dry. Incredibly rich MUSCAT, SYLVANER (Al's best?) from MONOPOLE CLOS Saint-Imer in GC GOLDERT 10 13 15 16 17 18 19 21 22′. PINOT GR v.gd: 10 12 15′ 18 20′. Owner Francis B believes 18′ 20′ two of Al's best recent yrs.

Bursin, Agathe Al ★★★→★★★★ 17' 18' 19' 20' Classy, often slightly off-dry, from Bollenberg and GC Zinnkoepflé; (GEWURZ 23' with creamy chicken; VT 22' magical). Outstanding SYLVANER (Eminence 23', Lutzental) from v. old vines, PINOT BL Paradox 23'. Also v.gd Gewurz.

Buxy, Caves de Burg ★→★★ Leading CÔTE CHALONNAISE CO-OP for decent CHARD, PINOT N, source of many merchants' own labels. Easily largest supplier of AOP MONTAGNY. Reliable, gd value, not to be sniffed at.

Buzet SW Fr ★★ 20 22 23 AOP along the Garonne nr Agen, BX style. Dominated by exemplary co-op: 95% of production incl CHX de Guèyze, Padère. Look also for Vigouroux-managed Dom de Tournelles.

Cabardès Ldoc ★★★ AOP on s-facing slopes of Black Mtns, overlooking Carcassonne. Where Med varieties GRENACHE, SYRAH meet Atlantic CAB SAUV, MERLOT; style is sleek black fruit with Med herbs. Rosé too. Try CHX DE SALITIS, de Pennautier (LORGERIL), La Bastide Rougepeyre; DOMS Bancalis, DE CABROL; Maison Ventenac.

Cabernet d'Anjou Lo ★→★★ Slightly sw rosé AOP from CABS FR/SAUV. Historically made to age, track down 70s/80s vintages from *Bablut*. These days, drink young; try Bergerie, Montgilet, OGEREAU.

Cabidos SW Fr ★★★ 18 19 20 22 Proper CH in BÉARN, outside JURANÇON yet similar wines: ★★ Gaston Phoebus PETIT MANSENG (dr); ★★★ St Clément, gorgeous, golden, sweet, worth seeking. Heavenly L'Or de Cabidos in best yrs.

Cabrières Ldoc ★★★ Terroir on schist in LDOC AOP nr PÉZENAS, reputed for fine rosé. Characterful reds too. Top co-op CAVES D'ESTABEL, Mas de Valbrune.

Cabrol, Dom de Ldoc ★★★→★★★★ Star AOP CABARDÈS. SYRAH-based Vent d'Est, fragrant, fiercely Med style. Vent d'Ouest, more CAB SAUV, quieter, herbal. Pique de Nore (w), floral, saline GRENACHE BL/PETIT MANSENG/CHENIN BL.

Cadillac-Côtes de Bordeaux Bx ★→★★ 19 20 22 23 Long, narrow, hilly zone on right bank of Garonne. Mainly MERLOT with CABS SAUV/FR. Medium-bodied, fresh reds. Cellar 2–8 yrs. Best: Alios de Ste-Marie, Bel-Air, Biac, *Carsin*, CH Carignan, CLOS Chaumont, Clos Ste-Anne, de Fontenille, Grand-Mouëys, Lamothe de Haux, Le Doyenné, Mont-Pérat, Plaisance, Réaut (Carat), *Reynon*, Suau.

Cady, Dom Lo ★★→★★★ ANJOU stalwart. New cellars 2023. Fine COTEAUX DU LAYON; gd dry Clos du Moulin Ste Catherine 19' 20' 21 22 (23).

Cahors SW Fr ★★★ 15' 18' 19 20 22 23 Historical AOP on River Lot. Red only, nearly all MALBEC, lots of styles. Gentler extraction today, more concrete, amphorae, large vats for ageing. Easy-drinking: ★★ CH de Hauterive, CLOS Coutale. More substance: ★★★ CHX DE CHAMBERT, DU CÈDRE, ★★ Gaudou, Hautes-Serres, La Coustarelle, Lamartine, Les Croisille, Mas La Périé, Mercuès, Ponzac; Clos d'Un Jour, *Clos Triguedina*, Clos Troteligotte, DOM Cosse-Maisonneuve, de la Bérengeraie, Haut-Monplaisir.

Cailbourdin, Alain and Loïc Lo ★★→★★★ POUILLY-FUMÉ DOM est by Alain, son Loïc increasingly in charge. Style tightening up, range refashioned. Top: *Nanogyra* (was Les Cornets) 19 20 21 22 (23). Barrel-aged Triptyque (with Silex suffix from 2019) 14 15 16 18 19, new Triptyque Calcaire both cellar-worthy.

Cailhol Gautran, Dom Ldoc ★★★ Thoughtful bio MINERVOIS, 5th generation. No added sulphur. Reds: expressive La Table du Loup, opulent Villa Lucia (rewards ageing). MUSCAT de St Jean gd.

Cailloux, Les S Rh ★★★ 09' 10' 16' 18 19' 20' 21 22' 23 24' Benchmark CHÂTEAUNEUF DOM, consistent, fab value. Profound, handmade reds; accomplished, *garrigue* white. Special Centenaire, oldest GRENACHE 1889, classy 16' 19'.

Cairanne S Rh ★★→★★★ 19' 20' 22' 23 24' Character, dark fruits, spice, herbs, esp CLOS des Mourres (organic), Clos Romane (body); DOMS ALARY (organic, style), Boisson, Brusset (depth), Chemins de Sève, Cros de Romet, des Amadieu (bio), ESCARAVAILLES, Grands Bois (organic), Grosset, Hautes Cances (polished),

Jubain, *Oratoire St Martin* (bio), Rabasse-Charavin (profound), RICHAUD (flair), Roche. Table-friendly, stylish white.

Calmel & Joseph Ldoc ★★★ Trailblazing duo seeking out fruit from top terroirs from TERRASSES DE LARZAC to COLLIOURE, plus innovative IGPS. Best PINOT N in LDOC, DOM La Magdelaine, from high vyds in CORBIÈRES.

Camin Larredya SW Fr ★★★★ Top JURANÇON estate. Excellent (dr/sw). Flagship Au Capcéu (sw): low-yield, late-harvest, delicious, from hilltop.

Canard-Duchêne Champ ★★→★★★ House owned by ALAIN THIÉNOT. Modernizing. Léonie increasingly gd. Charles VII BLANC DE BLANCS and NOIRS NV. BRUT Vintage 09' 12 13 14'; AVIZE Gamin 12 13 17' 19'. Renaissance slow but sure.

Canon-Fronsac Bx ★★→★★★ 16 18 19' 20' 22 23 Tiny enclave within FRON, otherwise same wines. Environmental action. Best: rich, full, cellar-worthy. Try Barrabaque, Canon Pécresse, Cassagne Haut-Canon la Truffière, du Gazin, GABY, Grand-Renouil, Lamarche Canon, MOULIN PEY-LABRIE.

Caraguilhes, Ch Ldoc ★★★ Big, bio CORBIÈRES DOM, never disappoints. Solus (w), delicately oaked GRENACHE/ROUSSANNE. Le Trou de l'Hermite (r) shouts out dark fruit, warm-stone Boutenac TERROIR.

Carême, Vincent Lo ★★ →★★★★ Top VOUVRAY. Excellent single-vyd dry *Le Clos* 14 15 16 17 18 19 20 21 22 23 leads pack, Clos de la Roche, Le Peu Morier close behind. Fine *moelleux* too. Brut Nature, Plaisir Ancestral (sp) v. reliable.

Carillon C d'O ★★★ Contrasting PULIGNY bros: Jacques, crafts to age (PC Referts). François, lively modern approach, pure, polished (Combettes, Folatières, Cap au Sud VDF CHARD). Village Puligny great from both.

Carré Frères Champ ★★★ Brothers from Trépail; 21 ha in Montagne. Impressive adventures in oak (300-litre casks): Le Champ Jeanvrai CHARD 16 18 20' and, by way of contrast, 100% PINOT N from Verzy, excellent Les Maladries 16 18.

Cassis Prov ★★→★★★★ Small AOP nr Marseille, known for CLAIRETTE, MARSANNE: DOMS de Ferme Blanche, DU PATERNEL, Quatre Vents. Try with bouillabasse.

Castelnau, De Champ ★★★ Co-op now merged with larger Nicolas Feuillate. Excellent BLANC DE BLANCS and Vintage 02 08. Innovative Prestige Collection Hors d'Age, different each yr: current release CCF2067 led by fine MEUNIER. Impressive Hors Categorie NV CT 2015 and BRUT Oenothèque in magnum 95 98 02. Inspiring chef de CAVE Carine Bailleul.

Castillon-Côtes de Bordeaux Bx ★★→★★★ 18 19 20 22 23 Appealing neighbour of ST-ÉM; similar, usually gd value. Growers want independent AOP Cas; also a dry white. Top: Alcée, Ampélia, Cap de FAUGÈRES, CLOS Les Lunelles, Clos Louie, *Clos Puy Arnaud*, *d'Aiguilhe*, *de l'A*, de Pitray, Joanin Bécot, La Brande, *La Clarière*, l'Aurage, *Le Rey*, *l'Hêtre*, Montlandrie, Picoron, Poupille, Veyry.

Cathiard, Dom Sylvain C d'O ★★★★ Sébastien C makes wines of astonishing

---

Chablis

There is still no CHARD to rival the tense, "stone and savour" wines of CHAB, although its style is threatened by warmer summers. The best are delicate but intense, never blowsy. Added richness comes with age. **Top:** BILLAUD, DAUVISSAT (V), DROIN, FÈVRE (W), LAROCHE, Michel (L), MOREAU (C), Pinson, RAVENEAU. **Challengers:** Bessin, BROCARD (J-M), CHABLISIENNE, Collet, Dampt (D), Davenne, *Defaix* (B), DROUHIN-Vaudon, Duplessis, Fèvre (N&G), *Garnier*, Grossot, LAROCHE, LONG-DEPAQUIT, Malandes, MOREAU-Naudet, Picq, Piuze, Pommier, Oudin, Tribut. **Up-and-coming:** Dauvissat (J & Fils), d'Henri, Gautheron, Lavantureux, Vocoret (E&E), *Vrignaud*. **Organic/natural:** Brocard (J), CH de Béru, de Moor, Goulley, *Pattes Loup*.

quality from VOSNE, esp Malconsorts, Orveaux, Reignots, plus NUITS Aux Thorey, Murgers. New range of generic BOURGOGNES. Style is pick late and destem.

Cauhapé, Dom SW Fr ★★★ Trail-blazing JURANÇON estate, exceptional whites (dr/sw). La Canopée PETIT MANSENG super-complex, barrel-fermented (dr). Folie de Janvier (sw), exceptional yrs only, picked in Jan.

Cave Cellar, or any wine establishment.

Cave coopérative Growers' co-op winery; over half of all French production. Wines often well priced, probably not most exciting. CAVE DE TAIN (N Rh), CHABLISIENNE gd eggs. Many co-ops closing down.

Cave d'Irouléguy SW Fr ★★★ Well-run co-op covering half of IROULÉGUY. All styles quality-focused, some organic; excellent tastings. Try Omenaldi (r), Xuri (w).

Cazeneuve, Ch Ldoc ★★★ Consistenly gd PIC ST-LOUP. Top: Le Causse (SYRAH), rewards ageing. ★★★ Cynarah (r) delightfully fruity, herbal; Les Calcaires (r) v.gd.

Cazes, Dom Rouss ★★★ Largest bio vyd in France. Try VDN: RIVESALTES Ambré, Tuilé, Grenat and sensational aged Aimé Cazes. MAURY SEC. Ambre (SW GRENACHE BL), Le Canon du Maréchal (GRENACHE/SYRAH). Top red: Le Crédo CÔTES DU ROUSS-VILLAGES; also Alter, Ego. Les CLOS de Paulilles (BANYULS, COLLIOURE).

Cébène, Dom de Ldoc ★★★★ Thrilling FAUGÈRES from high-altitude, n-facing, organic vyds. Flagship Felgaria, mostly MOURVÈDRE, is elegance, power. Ages well. Les Bancels SYRAH et al., earlier drinking, no less fine. Belle Lurette shows what CARIGNAN can do. Vivaciously fruity À la Venvole.

Cédre, Ch du SW Fr ★★→★★★ 15' 18 19 20 22 23 Organic, min-intervention, excellent, v. approachable CAHORS. Tamed tannins, lower alc, gentle ageing in *foudres*. Delicious everyday ★★ MALBEC IGP. Consultant to CHX Haut Monplaisir, Ponzac (both Cahors).

Cellier aux Moines Burg ★★★ Now top DOM in GIVRY based in vyd of same name; reached new heights after investment in new winery and winemaker Guillaume Marko. Interesting options in CÔTE DE BEAUNE, but star is home vyd.

Cépage Grape variety. *See* pp.12–22.

Cérons Bx ★★ 19 22 23 Tiny AOP. Sweet wines next to BARSAC (limestone soils), but less intense. Best: CHX de Cérons, DE CHANTEGRIVE, du Seuil, Grand Enclos.

Chablis Bx ★★→★★★ 15 17' 18' 19' 20 21 22 23 Wine world's most traduced name? Pure-fruited yet shot through with stony savour, gd Chab is a beguiling iteration of CHARD. Climate change adds succulence, but some challenging recent yrs. Also PETIT CHAB, DYA, lighter. (For top names, *see* box, p.51.)

Chablis Grand Cru Chab ★★★→★★★★ 10' 12' 14' 15 17' 18' 19' 20 21 22 23 Contiguous s-facing block overlooking River Serein, grandest CHAB, needs 5–15 yrs to reveal complexity. Seven vyds: Blanchots (floral), Bougros (incl Côte Bouguerots), CLOS (most patrician), Grenouilles (spicy), Preuses (finesse), Valmur (structure), Vaudésir (plus brand La Moutonne). Many gd growers. Value versus C D'O GCS.

Value Champagne

An oxymoron? Perhaps not, given the economics and logistics in play. But what to look out for? CHAMPAGNE can be divided into big brands (used to be called Grandes Marques) and smaller growers. The latter can be fantastic value: LARMANDIER-BERNIER or PIERRE PÉTERS. The former are often discounted over holiday periods, but in any event PIPER-HEIDSIECK and Nicolas Feuillatte offer genuine value. Most Champ is NV, but vintage can be relatively well priced (BOLLINGER, LOUIS ROEDERER excel) – and don't forget prestige cuvées, all reassuringly expensive, but a touch less so with such gems as RARE or POL ROGER's Sir Winston Churchill for occasions when that boat most definitely has to be pushed out.

Chablisienne, La Chab ★★→★★★ Exemplary co-op responsible for huge slice of CHAB production, esp supermarket own-labels; v.gd value. Trade up to bio CUVÉES of Chab, PETIT CHAB. Top: GC CH Grenouilles, a winner.

Chablis Premier Cru Chab ★★★ 15 17' 18' 19' 20 21 22 23 Well worth premium over straight CHAB: better hillsides sites can deliver great satisfaction, variety. Racy, pure: Montmains, Vaillons, Vaucoupin. More charming: Côte de Léchet, Fourchaume. Greater opulence: Mont de Milieu, *Montée de Tonnerre*, Vaulorent.

Chambert, Ch de SW Fr ★★★★ Gorgeous bio property in W CAHORS; v. reliable estate wine; superb yet pricey *parcellaires*. Pound for pound, best value is Grand Vin, from oldest vines. Try restaurant, stunning views over vyds.

Chambertin C d'O ★★★★ 90' 93 96' 99' 02' 05' 09' 10' 12' 14 15' 16 17 18' 19' 20' 21 22' 23' Commanding in youth, compelling with age, masculine burg. Meat and muscle abound, lavish fruit in best. Imperious; more charm recently. Producers who match potential: Bernstein, BOUCHARD PÈRE & FILS, CHARLOPIN, Damoy, DOM LEROY, DUGAT-Py, DROUHIN, MORTET, ROSSIGNOL-TRAPET, ROUSSEAU, TRAPET. Clos de Bèze next door: velvet texture, deeply graceful: Bart, B CLAIR, Damoy, Drouhin, Drouhin-Laroze, DUROCHÉ, FAIVELEY, GROFFIER, JADOT, Prieuré-Roch, Rousseau.

Chambolle-Musigny C d'O ★★★→★★★★ 99' 02' 05' 09' 10' 12' 15' 16 17 19' 20 21 22' 23 Even the name seduces. Silky, velvety, more structure recently: Charmes, Combe d'Orveau for substance, more chiselled from Cras, Fuées, bewitching Amoureuses, plus GCs BONNES-MARES, MUSIGNY. Stars: BARTHOD, GROFFIER, MUGNIER, ROUMIER, VOGÜÉ. Also gd: Amiot-Servelle, DROUHIN, Felettig, HUDELOT-Baillet, POUSSE D'OR, RION, Sigaut.

Champagne Sparkling wines of PINOT N, MEUNIER and CHARD: 33,805 ha, heartland c.145 km e of Paris. Sales 300m+ bottles/yr. Some PINOT BL further s in AUBE adds freshness. Other sparkling, however gd, cannot be called Champ. Thrives on chalky tension and biscuity development (autolysis). (*See* box, opposite.)

Champagne le Mesnil Champ ★★★ Top co-op in centre of Le Mesnil-sur-Oger; exceptional GC CHARD village. *Cuvée Sublime* 08' 09' 13' 15 17' 19 from finest site. Majestic CUVÉE Prestige 07' 05. Access to some of best GC Chard sites in region.

Champagne Marguet Champ ★★★ Unfazed by having KRUG as neighbour in Ambonnay, 5th-generation Benoît transformed estate, bio since 2009. Names reveal philosophy: Sapience Rosé 18 19 20; Shamen BRUT 12 14' 15 16 18; Shamen Rosé 20. Excellent single-vyds La Grande Ruelle, Le Parc, Les Crayères.

Champalou Lo ★★→★★★ Classically styled VOUVRAY, white flowers, minerals. Daughter Céline now in charge. Fine sweet La Moelleuse, Les Tries 89 95 96 97 02 03 09 15 18. Also gd: SEC, DEMI-SEC Les Fondraux; fizz.

Chandon de Briailles, Dom C d'O ★★★ Decade-long, incremental improvement; bio, min sulphur, whole bunches, no new oak. Brilliantly pure, perfumed (r) CORTON-Bressandes, PERNAND-VERGELESSES PC Île de Vergelesses.

Chanson Père & Fils Burg ★★→★★★★ Long-est name, 275 yrs old in 2025. Continuing improvement. Quality whites (CHASSAGNE PC Chenevottes, CLOS DES MOUCHES, CORTON-Vergennes), reduced use of whole bunches in reds. Purchase of 50 ha in CÔTE CHALONNAISE cements transition from merchant to DOM.

Chapelle-Chambertin C d'O ★★★ 99' 02' 05' 09' 10' 12' 15' 16 18' 19' 20' 21 22' 23 Lighter neighbour of CHAMBERTIN; thin soil does better in cooler, damper yrs. More elegant, less structured. Slightly overlooked. Top: Damoy, DROUHIN-Laroze, JADOT, PONSOT, ROSSIGNOL-TRAPET, TRAPET, TREMBLAY.

Chapoutier N Rh ★★→★★★★ Grower-merchant. Emphatic SYRAH: low-yield CÔTE-RÔTIE La Mordorée. HERMITAGE: L'Ermite (compelling r/w), Le Pavillon (granite, bold r), Cuvée de l'Orée (w), Le Méal (r/w). ST-JOSEPH Les Granits (r/w). Top: *Hermitage w*, complexity, all old-vine MARSANNE, *Chante-Alouette*. Cracking

CONDRIEU Chéry, also ST-PÉRAY Hongrie. Duché d'Uzès (r/w) gd value. Profound GRENACHE CHÂTEAUNEUF: Barbe Rac, Croix de Bois (r). Also CÔTES DU ROUSS-VILLAGES (gd DOM Bila-Haut), COTEAUX D'AIX-EN-PROV, RIVESALTES; FERRATON at Hermitage, BEAUJ house Trenel, CH des Ferrages (PROV); plus in AL and Australia. Hotel, wine bars in Tain.

Charbonnière, Dom de la S Rh ★★★ 10' 16' 17 18 19' 20' 22' 23 24' Maret sisters create full, resounding CHÂTEAUNEUF: (r) Estate (profound), VIEILLES VIGNES (vigour, best), Mourre des Perdrix (genuine), Hautes Brusquières; (w) stylish, crystalline. Peppery VACQUEYRAS (r).

Charlopin C d'O ★★★ Large DOM, 25 ha. Philippe C makes impressive, wide range of reds. Substance now matched by style. BOURGOGNE C D'O, MARSANNAY for value; gd range GCS for top of line. Son Yann C, DOM C-Tissier also worth following.

Charmes-Chambertin C d'O ★★★★ 99' 02' 03 05' 09' 10' 12' 15' 16 17 18' 19' 20' 21 22' 23 GEVREY GC, 31 ha, incl neighbour MAZOYÈRES-CHAMBERTIN. Abundant, smooth rich fruit, berries, cherries, sumptuous texture, fragrant finish. Best: ARLAUD, BACHELET, Castagnier, Coquard-Loison-Fleurot, DUGAT, DUJAC, DUROCHÉ, LEROY, MORTET, Perrot-Minot, Roty, ROUSSEAU, Taupenot-Merme, VOUGERAIE.

Chartogne-Taillet Champ ★★★★ Disciple of SELOSSE, now celebrated in own right; bio inclinations. BRUT Ste Anne NV, single-vyds *Couarres Château*, Le Chemin de Reims, Les Barres 15' 17' 18. Superb Hors Serie BLANC DE BLANCS 16' 18 19.

Charvin, Dom S Rh ★★★ 09' 10' 12' 15' 16' 17' 18' 19' 20' 21' 22' 23' 24' Underrated CHÂTEAUNEUF estate, one of best, true terroir expression; 85% (average) 50-yr-old GRENACHE, vat-raised; just one red, spiced, mineral, high-energy, needs time. Recent gd white. Fab, long-lived CÔTES DU RH (r).

Chassagne-Montrachet C d'O ★★→★★★★ (w) 08' 09' 12' 14' 15 17' 18' 19' 20' 21 22' 23 The C D'O's most exciting commune? Great white vyds Blanchot, Cailleret, LA ROMANÉE, Ruchottes and GCS. Thrilling flavours. Try COLIN, GAGNARD, MOREY, PILLOT families, plus DOMS HEITZ, MOREAU, Niellon, RAMONET. Overlooked reds can age superbly, from eg. Boudriotte, CLOS St-Jean, Morgeot.

Château (Ch) Estate, big or small, gd or indifferent, esp BX (see pp.105–25). Literally, castle or great house. In Burg, DOM is usual term.

Château-Chalon Jura ★★★→★★★★ 10' 14 15 16 17 Not a CH but AOP and village, summit of VIN JAUNE elegance from SAVAGNIN grape; min 6 yrs barrel-age under veil of yeast, worth investing. Drink with Comté cheese (or with/in a chicken dish). Ages for decades. Search out Baud, ★ Berthet-Bondet, Bourdy, Carlines, Chevassu-Fassenet, ★★ *Macle*, ★ Rousset-Martin, ★ Stéphane TISSOT.

Château-Grillet N Rh ★★★★ 09' 10' 12' 14' 15' 16' 17' 19 20' 21' 22' 23' 24' France's smallest AOP, 3.7-ha pretty, sand-granite-terraced amphitheatre s of CONDRIEU, minutely cared vyd. Owned by F Pinault of CH LATOUR, prices v. v. high, wine polished, fine, restrained; do not drink young. Can be great at 20 yrs. Scented, oily, pinpoint VIOGNIER: drink mildly chilled, decanted, with refined dishes. Condrieu La Carthery since 2017, vyd nearby; also sound CÔTES DU RH (w).

Châteaumeillant Lo ★→★★ 21 22 23 Tiny AOP, island of vines s of REUILLY. Simple red, rosé from GAMAY, PINOTS N/GR. Try Lecomte, Roux, Rouzé.

Châteauneuf-du-Pape S Rh ★★★→★★★★ 07' 09' 10' 12 15 16' 17 19' 20' 21 22' 23 24' Global name, 3200 ha+. Labyrinth of soils, up to 13 grapes (r/w), mostly GRENACHE, plus SYRAH, MOURVÈDRE (increasing, important), Counoise = many different styles; c.60 gd DOMS (other 80 fair to poor). Spiced, scented, herbal, best to wait 8 yrs+; should be pure, caressing. From 90s to mid-2010s too many plodding, hard to drink. Young generation more finesse-freshness aware. Small, trad DOMS often value. To avoid: new oak, 16% abv, zany prices. Lovely whites, sell fast: upfront, fruity, or rich, best can age 15 yrs+; fantastic 21. (For top names, *see* box, opposite.)

Chave, Dom Jean-Louis N Rh ★★★★ 05′ 07′ **09′** 10′ 11′ **12′ 13′** 15′ **16′** 17′ 18′ 19′ 20′ 21′ 22′ 23′ 24′ Marvellous 14-ha family DOM at HERMITAGE. Sensuous, whispering SYRAH, incl occasional, pricey Cathelin. Complexity, intrigue in long-lived whites (mainly MARSANNE). ST-JOSEPH (r), smoky, linear: single-vyd CLOS Florentin (since 2015), whizzingly fruited Offerus. Festive CÔTES DU RH Mon Coeur, sound-value merchant Hermitage Farconnet (r), Blanche (w).

Chénas Beauj ★★★ **16** 18′ **19′** 20′ 21 22 23 Smallest BEAUJ cru, between MOULIN-À-VENT and JULIÉNAS, gd value, firm, age-worthy, merits more attention. *Thillardon* is reference DOM, but try also Janodet, LAPIERRE, Pacalet, Piron, Trichard, co-op.

Chevalier-Montrachet C d'O ★★★★ 08 09′ 10 12 14′ 15 17′ 18 19′ 20′ 21 22′ 23 Just above MONTRACHET on hill, barely below in quality; brilliant, crystalline, precise. Long-lived but accessible early. LEFLAIVE; special-CUVÉES Les Demoiselles from JADOT, LOUIS LATOUR; La Cabotte from BOUCHARD. Also: Chartron, COLIN (P), Dancer, DE MONTILLE, Niellon, VOUGERAIE.

Cheverny Lo ★→★★ 21 22 23 Frost-prone AOP; mostly simple white (SAUV BL/CHARD/ Menu Pineau), red (GAMAY/PINOT N/CAB FR/CÔT). Drink young. Cazin, Huards, Montcy, Tessier. Blends with Menu Pineau from Veilloux can be ★★★.

Chevillon, R C d'O ★★★ With GOUGES, reference DOM for NUITS, dark-fruited, muscular but not overtannic PCS: Bousselots, Chaignots, Pruliers more accessible; Cailles, Les St-Georges, Vaucrains for long term.

Chevrot C d'O ★★→★★★ Appealing, juicy MARANGES, esp Sur les Chênes, PC Croix Moines. Decent whites, esp ALIGOTÉ Tilleul, Maranges Fussière. CRÉMANT too. Lively wines, fair prices.

Chidaine, François Lo ★★★→★★★★ MONTLOUIS-SUR-LOIRE star DOM, large range single vyds. Dry CLOS du Breuil, Les Bournais 15 16 17 18 19 20 22, can show oxidation with age though; Clos Habert, Les Tuffeaux (both s/sw), Moelleux (sw) v.gd. Vines in *Clos Baudoin* in VOUVRAY (VDF on label).

Chignin Sav ★→★★ AOP: Jacquère, MONDEUSE. Chignin-Bergeron is ROUSSANNE. Try ★★ A Berlioz, ★★ A&M QUENARD, ★★ Berthollier, ★★ *J-F Quenard*, ★★ Partagé.

Chinon Lo ★★→★★★ 05′ 09′ 10′ 15′ **16′** 17 18′ 19 20 22′ (23) Top CAB FR AOP, on limestone slopes, from juicy early-drinking to serious, age-worthy. Best: *Alliet*, Baudry, Charles Joguet, CLOS des Capucins, Gasnier, Grosbois, J-M Raffault,

---

Châteauneuf: kings, queens and pretenders to the castle

Leading producers at this widespread, multi-faceted (soils, blends, styles) appellation: CHX DE BEAUCASTEL, Gardine, Mont-Redon, Mourre du Tendre (depth), Nalys, Nerthe, RAYAS, Sixtine, Vaudieu; DOMS André Mathieu, Barroche (flair), BEAURENARD (bio, classy), Bois Pointu, Bosquet des Papes (full), Chante Cigale (genuine), Chante Perdrix, CHARBONNIÈRE, CHARVIN, CLOS DES PAPES, CLOS du Caillou (organic), CLOS DU MONT-OLIVET (authentic), Clos St-Jean (scale), Cristia (also max purity Chapelle St Théodoric), de la Biscarelle (fruit), de la Janasse (strength), DE LA MORDORÉE, de la Vieille Julienne (bio), du Banneret (trad), Durieu, Fontavin, Font-de-Michelle, Galet des Papes, Grand Tinel, Grand Veneur (organic), Henri Bonneau (depth), Famille Ferrando (style), LES CAILLOUX (value), MARCOUX (bio, esp VIEILLES VIGNES), Mas du Boislauzon (punch), Pegaü, Pères de l'Église, Pierre André (bio, terroir), Porte Rouge, Famille P Usseglio, R Usseglio (bio, style), Roger Sabon, Sénéchaux, Vieux Donjon (classic), VIEUX TÉLÉGRAPHE. Whites: Chx de Beaucastel (ace ROUSSANNE), Gardine, RAYAS, Vaudieu; Doms Beaurenard, Clos des Papes (long life), Les Cailloux (genuine), Marcoux (stylish), R Usseglio (v.gd Roussanne), Vieux Donjon (authentic, depth), Vieux Télégraphe (deep, terroir).

Noblaie, Olga Raffault, Pallus, Pascal Lambert, Saut au Loup, Wilfrid Rousse. Watch for DOM de Beauséjour. Tiny volumes dry CHENIN BL, rosé, can be gd.

Chiroubles Beauj ★★ 15' 18' 19' 20' 21 22' 23 A BEAUJ cru in hills above FLEURIE: fresh, fruity, savoury. Try Berne, CH de Javernand, Cheysson, LAFARGE-Vial, Métrat, Passot, Raousset, or merchants DUBOEUF, *Trenel*. Worth a look.

Chorey-lès-Beaune C d'O ★★→★★★ 15' 17 18 19' 20 21 22' 23 Village just n of BEAUNE. TOLLOT-BEAUT is standard-bearer for reliable rather than exciting, fruit-forward AOP. Also Arnoux, DROUHIN, Gay, Guyon, JADOT, RAPET, ROUGET.

Clair, Bruno C d'O ★★★ Below-radar DOM; understated, never flashy. Marked by a lighter weave than some. Promising new generation: Edouard, Margaux, Arthur. CHAMBERTIN-Clos de Bèze (standout), GEVREY-CHAMBERTIN (CLOS ST-JACQUES, Cazetiers), MARSANNAY (gd value), SAVIGNY La Dominode (old vines). Best whites from CORTON-CHARLEMAGNE, MOREY-ST-DENIS. Watch.

Clairet Bx Light red. AOP BX Clairet: CHX de Fontenille, La Freynelle, THIEULEY.

Clairette de Die N Rh ★★ Must-try low-Alps fizz – flinty or (better) MUSCAT (s/sw), great apéritif, value, low alc. Or dry CLAIRETTE, can age 3 yrs. Note Achard-Vincent (organic, bio, bright), Carod, David Bautin (organic), Jaillance (value), J-C Raspail (organic, IGP SYRAH), Poulet & Fils (terroir, Chatillon-en-Diois r).

Clape, Dom N Rh ★★★→★★★★ 05' 06' 07' 09' 10' 12' 14' 15' 16' 17' 18' 19' 20' 21' 22' 23' 24' Legendary CORNAS, old granite-hillside SYRAH. Deep fruit, complex, initially tannic red; be patient. Ideal present for a godchild. Needs 7 yrs+, live 25+. Crisp younger-vines Renaissance. Superior CÔTES DU RH, ST-PÉRAY (MARSANNE), VDF (r).

Clape, La Ldoc ★★★→★★★★ Driest, sunniest AOP in LDOC. MOURVÈDRE hotspot with SYRAH, GRENACHE for characterful herb-scented red with freshness from sea breezes. Salty, herbal white from BOURBOULENC with dash of ROUSSANNE: underrated, worth seeking out. CHX Anglès, Bouisset, Camplazens, Capitoul, LA NÉGLY, Laquirou, Le Bouïs, l'Hospitalet, Mire l'Etang, Pech-Céleyran, PECH REDON, Ricardelle, ROUQUETTE SUR MER; DOM Sarrat de Goundy; La Combe Saint-Paul.

Climat Burg Individual named vyd (almost interchangeable with lieu-dit) esp in C D'O. UNESCO World Heritage status. Say "klee-mah".

Clos Distinct (walled) vyd, often in one ownership (esp AL, Burg, CHAMP). Often prestigious. In Burg, walls on three sides, of four, suffice for "clos".

Clos Alivu Cors ★★→★★★ AOP PATRIMONIO. Stylish, fresh wines from talented Eric Poli, also owner of DOM Poli, gd-value AOP CORS (r/w/rosé), IGP Île de Beauté.

Clos Canarelli Cors ★★★ Revered bio estate in S. AOP CORS Figari. Reviving indigenous grapes plus more mainstream NIELLUCCIO, SCIACARELLO. Core range aged in and named after amphorae, worth seeking out. Excellent Tarra di Sognu (r/w), rare Tarra d'Orasi (r/w) from ungrafted vines.

Clos Cibonne Prov ★★★ Small estate nr Toulon, making red/rosé from rare local Tibouren as AOP CÔTES DU PROV. Wonderful trad labels, gastronomic, ethereal wines. Tentations range: fruitier, early drinking.

Clos Culombu Cors ★★★ Innovative DOM in Corse-Calvi, blending indigenous varieties with NIELLUCCIO, VERMENTINO. Impressive Storia di range (r/w).

Clos d'Alzeto Cors ★★★ Highest vyd in CORS, 500m (1640ft). AJACCIO (r) from SCIACARELLO, prestige VERMENTINO, floral, fine.

Clos de L'Écotard Lo ★★→★★★★ Newish; SAUMUR Bl can be v.gd; La Haie Nardin, Les Pentes 20 21 22 (23), fine Les Quarts St-Vincent (sp). Red yet to impress.

Clos de Tart C d'O ★★★★ 05' 08' 10' 13' 14 15' 16' 17 18' 19' 20' 21 22' 23 Expensive MOREY-ST-DENIS GC. MONOPOLE of Pinault/Artemis empire (CHX GRILLET, Latour, etc.). Becoming more refined with plot-by-plot vinification while retaining natural intensity. Rebuilt winery. La Forge de T gd value.

Clos de Vougeot C d'O ★★★→★★★★ 02′ 03′ 05′ 09′ 10′ 12′ 13′ 15′ 16 17 18′ 19′ 20′ 21 22′ 23 CÔTE DE NUITS GC, many owners; 50 ha, needs trimming. Finally shedding ho-hum reputation. Best wines need 10 yrs+. Gaining composure in recent warm yrs. Keys: philosophy, technique, position in vyd. Top: ARNOUX-LACHAUX, CH de la Tour, EUGÉNIE, *Faiveley*, GRIVOT, *Gros (Anne)*, Hudelot-Noëllat, LEROY, *Liger-Belair* (both), MÉO-CAMUZET, MORTET, *Vougeraie*. Also v.gd: BOUCHARD, Castagnier, Clerget (Y), Coquard-Loison-Fleurot, DROUHIN, Forey, MONTILLE, *Mugneret-Gibourg*.

Clos des Fées Rouss ★★★→★★★★ Playful names, but serious stuff. La Petite Siberie (r), sublime CÔTES DU ROUSS pure GRENACHE; Sorcières (r/w) gd value; Le Chat de Marquis, scented TEMPRANILLO, IGP CÔTES CATALANES.

Clos des Lambrays C d'O ★★★→★★★★ 09′ 10′ 15′ 16′ 18′ 19′ 20′ 21 22′ 23 All-but-MONOPOLE GC vyd at MOREY-ST-DENIS, now belongs to LVMH. Big investment, new winemaker from 2019, leap in quality. Singing fruit, sweet spice. Splendid new vat room. Also Puligny PCS CLOS du Cailleret, Les Folatières.

Clos des Mouches C d'O ★★★ (w) 02 05′ 09′ 10′ 14′ 15 17′ 18 19′ 20′ 21 22′ A PC vyd in several Burg AOPS. Mostly reds, but most famous for glorious BEAUNE white. *Mouches* = honeybees; see label of DROUHIN's iconic Beaune bottling (ages magnificently). Also BICHOT, CHANSON (Beaune); plus CLAIR, MOREAU, Muzard (SANTENAY); Germain (MEURSAULT).

"Infusion, not extraction", is Côte d'Or's mantra du jour. All sent same memo?

Clos des Papes S Rh ★★★★ 05′ 07′ 09′ 10′ 12′ 13′ 14′ 15′ 16′ 17′ 18′ 19′ 20′ 21′ 22′ 23′ 24′ Marvellous CHÂTEAUNEUF DOM, small crops, burg refinement, Swiss-watch consistency; striking red (GRENACHE/MOURVÈDRE, drink at 2–3 yrs or from 8+); complex white (demands top cuisine; 2–3 yrs, then 10–20).

Clos du Mesnil Champ ★★★★ KRUG's walled vyd in GC Le Mesnil. Dates from 1698. Richly indulgent CHARD. On-going battle between mature **95** and **96**, Cavalier vs Roundhead. Wait a little longer for similar duel between **02** and **08**. Also aristocratic **03′ 04**. Look forward to 12 13′ and, many yrs hence, 15 19′ *et seq*.

Clos de la Roche C d'O ★★★★ 90′ 93′ 96′ 99′ 02′ 05′ 08 09′ 10′ 15′ 16′ 17 18′ 19′ 20′ 21 22′ 23 Overlooked though not underpriced: finest GC of MOREY-ST-DENIS, grace and gravitas counterpoised, more savoury than sumptuous. Glorious with time. ARLAUD, *Dujac*, H LIGNIER, PONSOT references, try Amiot, Bernstein, Castagnier, Coquard, LEROY, LIGNIER-Michelot, POUSSE D'OR, Remy, ROUSSEAU.

Clos du Roi C d'O ★★→★★★ Frequent Burg vyd name, sometimes as CLOS du Roy. Best vyd in GC CORTON (DE MONTILLE, POUSSE D'OR, VOUGERAIE); top PC vyd in MERCUREY, future PC (still waiting) in MARSANNAY. Less classy in BEAUNE.

Clos del Rey Rouss ★★★ Small family DOM punching above weight, vyds on 300m (984ft) plateau. La Noia old GRENACHE, deep, spicy. Outstanding Grenache Gr.

Clos Naudin, Dom du Lo ★★★★ Thank Bacchus for the Foreau (Philippe, Vincent) family. Reference for VOUVRAY, stunning sweets incl *Moelleux Rés* 89 90 95 97 02 03 05 09 10 15 16 18 19 20 22. Also Vouvray's best fizz. Whole range tiptop.

Clos Rougeard Lo ★★★★ 05′ 09 10′ 14 15′ 16 17 18′ 19 20 21 22 (23) Cult status SAUMUR-CHAMPIGNY. Same owners as CH MONTROSE (DX), similar prices. Huge recent investments. SAUMUR Bl Brézé (w) also tiptop.

Clos St-Denis C d'O ★★★ 90′ 93′ 96′ 99′ 02′ 05′ 09′ 10′ 12′ 15′ 16′ 17 18′ 19′ 20′ 21 22′ 23 MOREY-ST-DENIS GC. Sumptuous young, silky with age. Great: DUJAC, PONSOT (Laurent P from 2016). Also gd: Amiot-Servelle, ARLAUD, BERTAGNA, Castagnier, Coquard-Loison-Fleurot, Heresztyn-Mazzini, JADOT, Jouan, LEROUX.

Clos Ste-Hune Al ★★★★ Legendary TRIMBACH single site from GC Rosacker. World's greatest dry RIES. Super 71′ 67′ 71′ 75′ 13′ 15′ 16′ 17′ 18 19′ 20′ need 10 yrs; 22′ nr perfection; 100th anniversary 2024.

Clos St-Jacques C d'O ★★★★ 90' 93 96' 99' 02' 05' 09' 10' 12' 15' 16 17 18 19' 20' 21 22' 23 Hillside PC in GEVREY, perfect se exposure. Shared by CLAIR, ESMONIN, FOURRIER, JADOT, ROUSSEAU. (Holdings run top to bottom.) Power, poise; GC in all but name, outstrips many in quality. Sublime with age.

Clos Teddi Cors ★★★ AOP PATRIMONIO; beautiful, remote DOM on granite soil of Agriates desert. Intense, powerful Grande Cuvée (r), NIELLUCCIU; rich, polished VERMENTINO, perfect with sea bass.

Clusel-Roch, Dom N Rh ★★★ 05' 09' 10' 11 12' 13' 14 15' 16' 17' 18' 19' 20' 21' 22' 23' 24' Organic (higher hillside costs, rare) CÔTE-RÔTIE, mostly Serine (pre-clone SYRAH). Tight, ferrous, spinal red; be patient. Les Schistes gd start point, La Viallière (finesse, floral), Les Grandes Places (linear, compelling, long-lived). Son Guillaume C makes v.gd Coteaux du Lyonnais (GAMAY, incl 1896 vines; w).

Coche, Fabien C d'O ★★★ Fabien C in shadow of cousin, below, but insiders' pick. Signature citrus style, ages well. Lovely MEURSAULT Rouge.

Coche-Dury C d'O ★★★★ Top MEURSAULT DOM led by Raphaël C, in succession to legend Jean-François. Exceptional, palate-dazzling whites from ALIGOTÉ to CORTON-CHARLEMAGNE; pretty reds too. Bank-breaking prices, hard to justify.

Colin C d'O ★★★→★★★★ Extended family of CHASSAGNE, ST-AUBIN vinous nobility, all noted for superlative whites: pure, poised, persistent. Current generation turning heads, esp Pierre-Yves C-MOREY, DOM MARC C, Joseph C and cousins BRUNO C, Philippe C, Simon C.

Colin-Morey Burg ★★★→★★★★ Pierre-Yves C-M continues to burnish his reputation with vibrant tingling whites, esp from *St-Aubin* and CHASSAGNE PC, with their characteristic gunflint aromas. Bland labels give no hint of complex glories within. Exemplary wines at all levels, incl NÉGOCIANT CUVÉES.

Collin, Ulysse Champ ★★★→★★★★ Cerebral grower on Côteaux du Petit Morin, sw of Vertus. Single-vyds only, all subtly oaked, low dosage. Les Pierrières and Les Enfers, both BLANC DE BLANCS, Les Maillons Rosé de Saignée, Le Jardin d'Ulysse. Value (relative) BLANC DE NOIRS. A CHAMP odyssey, not lacking drama, tension.

Collines Rhodaniennes N Rh ★★ IGP ("Rhodanienne" = "of the Rhône"); lively, value, character, incl v.gd, long-life Seyssuel (schist), granite hills, plateau reds, often top names. Mostly SYRAH (best), also GAMAY, mini-CONDRIEU VIOGNIER (best). Reds: A Chatagnier, A Paret, A PERRET, Avallet (Seyssuel), Bonnefond, Bott, CLOS de la Bonnette (organic), E Barou (organic), Eymin Tichoux (Seyssuel), Hameau Touche Boeuf, *Jamet*, JASMIN, J-M GÉRIN, L Chèze, Monier-Pérreol (bio), N Champagneux, S Pichat, Rosiers, ROSTAING, Vins de Vienne (Seyssuel), Y CUILLERON. Whites: Alexandrins, Amphores, A Perret (v.gd), Barou, F Merlin, *G Vernay*, P-J Villa, P Marthouret, X Gérard, Y Cuilleron.

Collioure Rouss ★★★ Same vyds as BANYULS, dry wines (r/w/rosé), best poised, elegant, among greatest in ROUSS. Mainly GRENACHE of all colours. Top: DOMS Augustin, Bila-Haut, de la Rectorie, du Mas Blanc, du Traginer, La Tour Vieille, MADELOC, Vial-Magnères; Coume del Mas, Clos Saint Sebastien, Les CLOS de Paulilles. Co-ops Cellier des Templiers, l'Étoile.

Comte Abbatucci Cors ★★★ Prominent bio DOM in S CORS, saviour of indigenous grapes. Humble but top-quality VDF. CUVÉE Fustine, Valle de Nero (both r/rosé). Collection range recalls military connections of ancestor, pal of Napoleon.

Condrieu N Rh ★★★→★★★★ 22' 23' 24' Physical and spiritual home of VIOGNIER, modest town, hillside sand-granite vyds, only c.225 ha. Perfumed, acacia, dried flowers, pear, apricot. Best: mystical, mineral; avoid heavy oak, sweetness, alc. Growers, and vines, adapting to hot yrs, so alc less, fruit clear recently. Top wines live 10 yrs; 80 producers, not all gd. Rare white companion for asparagus. Best: A Paret, *A Perret*, Boissonnet, CHAPOUTIER, CLOS de la Bonnette (organic), C Pichon, DELAS, L Faury (esp La Berne), F Merlin, F Villard (lighter recently),

GANGLOFF (rich), GUIGAL, *G Vernay* (fab Coteau de Vernon), M Clerc, MONTEZ, Mouton (robust), Niéro, ROSTAING, ST COSME, Semaska, X Gérard (value), Y CUILLERON (stylish).

Corbières Ldoc ★★→★★★ Huge AOP, varied, but some excellent, characterful reds, styles reflect contrast of coastal lagoons to windswept foothills of Pyrénées and inland to cooler Carcassonne. Plenty of CARIGNAN, can be fab in Cru Boutenac. Some v.gd whites. Try CHX Aiguilloux, Aussières, Borde-Rouge, CARAGUILHES, de Sérame, Grand Moulin, La Baronne, Lastours, La Voulte-Gasparets, Les Palais, OLLIEUX ROMANIS, Pech-Latt, Vaugelas; DOMS de Fontsainte, de la Cendrillon, de Villemajou, DES DEUX CLÉS, du Grand Crès, du Vieux Parc, PY, Trillol; CLOS de l'Anhel, Clos du Cers, Famille Fabre, Grand Arc, Les Clos Perdus, MAXIME MAGNON, Sainte-Croix, Serres Mazard. Castelmaure co-op.

Cornas N Rh ★★★ 01′ 05′ 09′ 10′ 12′ 15′ 16′ 17′ 18′ 19′ 20′ 21′ 22′ 23′ 24′ Often overlooked, now acclaimed granite-slope SYRAH, only 150 ha, top names now expensive. Smouldering, deep, always mineral-clad. Some made for early fruit, really need 5 yrs+. Top: A&E Verset (organic), *Allemand* (top two), BALTHAZAR (trad, incl zero sulphur), *Clape* (benchmark), Colombo (modern), Courbis (modern), DELAS, DOM DU TUNNEL (rich), Dumien Serrette (profound, value), G GILLES (stylish), J&E Durand (racy fruit), Lemenicier, Lionnet (character, organic), M Barret (bio), M Bourg (character), P&V Jaboulet, Tardieu-Laurent (stylish, oak), Voge (swish, oak), V Paris (esp v. fine La Geynale).

Clos des Marechaudes, Corton, only Burgundy vineyard that can be either GC or PC.

Corsica / Corse ★★→★★★ "Île de Beauté" aptly named IGP for whole island. Plenty of variety; altitude, sea winds give freshness. Over half is rosé. Reds elegant, spicy from SCIACARELLO, structured from NIELLUCCIO aka SANGIOVESE; tangy VERMENTINO whites. VDN sweet MUSCATS Local varieties championed by top producers CLOS CANARELLI, COMTE ABBATUCCI et al. Nine AOPS incl crus PATRIMONIO in n, AJACCIO to w. AOP Corse plus villages Calvi, Coteaux du Cap Corse, Figari, Porto-Vecchio, Sartène. Top: Antoine Arena, ALZIPRATU, CLOS ALIVU, Clos Canereccia, Clos Calviani, Clos Capitoro, CLOS CULOMBU, CLOS D'ALZETO, Clos Nicrosi, Clos Poggiale, CLOS TEDDI, Clos Venturi; DOMS de Grenajolo, Fiumicicoli, Giacometti, Maestracci, Orsucci, Peraldi, PIERETTI, PINELLI, Poli, Saperale, Torraccia, YVES LECCIA, U STILICCIONU, Vaccelli.

Corton C d'O ★★→★★★★ 03′ 05′ 09′ 10′ 12′ 15′ 17 18 19′ 20′ 21 22′ 23 Too much is GC, can be stellar, often dull. Needs trimming. Choose carefully. Best vyds: CLOS DU ROI, Bressandes, Renardes, Rognet. Top: BOUCHARD, CHANDON DE BRIAILLES, DRC, Dubreuil-Fontaine, FAIVELEY (CLOS des Cortons), Follin-Arbelet, MÉO-CAMUZET, RAPET, TOLLOT-BEAUT. Under radar, can be value: Bichot, Camille Giroud, Capitain-Gagnerot, Clavelier, DOM des Croix, H&G BUISSON, MALLARD, POUSSE D'OR, Terregelesses. Best white from Vergennes vyd: CHANSON, CH DE MEURSAULT, HOSPICES DE BEAUNE.

Corton-Charlemagne C d'O ★★★→★★★★★ 05′ 09′ 10′ 14′ 15′ 17′ 18 19′ 20′ 21 22′ 23 Potentially scintillating GC, as gd as any when on song, should age well; sw- and w-facing limestone slopes, plus band around top of hill. Top: BIZE, BONNEAU DU MARTRAY, BOUCHARD, CLAIR, *Coche-Dury*, FAIVELEY, HOSPICES DE BEAUNE, JADOT, Javillier, LATOUR, Mallard, MONTILLE, RAMONET, RAPET, Rollin. Magnificent DRC from 2019. *Dom Vougeraie* uses rare sister AOP, Charlemagne.

Costières de Nîmes S Rh ★→★★ 23 24 Sprawling 2700 ha sw of CHÂTEAUNEUF; similar stony soils, Mistral, warmth freshness; gd with bold dishes. Red (GRENACHE, SYRAH) robust, spiced, up to 15 yrs. Best: CHX de Grande Cassagne, de Montfrin (organic), de Nages (gd w), d'Or et de Gueules (full), La Tour de Beraud (fruit), L'Ermitage, Mourgues-du-Grès (organic), Roubaud, Vessière (w);

DOMS de la Patience (organic), du Vieux Relais, du Petit Romain, Galus, Gassier, M KREYDENWEISS (bio); CHAPOUTIER, CLOS des Boutes (organic, bio), Mas Carlot (organic, zappy), Mas des Bressades (organic), Mas Neuf, Terre des Chardons (bio). Up-tempo, table-friendly rosés; best white elegant (esp ROUSSANNE).

Cotat, François Lo ★★→★★★★ Cult SANCERRE vigneron, wines v. age-worthy. Give Les Culs de Beaujeu, *Les Monts Damnés* 10 yrs/+ to shine.

Coteaux Bourguignons Burg ★ DYA Mostly reds, GAMAY, PINOT N. AOP est in 2011 to replace BOURGOGNE Grand Ordinaire and to sex up basic BEAUJ. Market accepting the change. Rare whites ALIGOTÉ, CHARD, MELON, PINOTS BL/GR.

Coteaux Champenois Champ ★★★ AOP for still wines of CHAMP, eg. BOUZY. Vintages as for Champ. Better reds with climate change (12'). Impressive range of Coteaux Champenois Grands Blancs based on 17' by CHARLES HEIDSIECK, burgundian by inclination. Also gd: Drappier, Etienne Calsac, TARLANT. Not to forget BOLLINGER's La Côte aux Enfants.

Coteaux d'Aix-en-Provence Prov ★★ Mostly pale, fruity rosé from AOP centred on Aix: CINSAULT, GRENACHE. Some reds: CAB SAUV in cooler n (Pigoudet, Revelette, VIGNELAURE). In warmer spots, Med grapes often more interesting: CHX Calissanne, de Beaupré, La Realtière, Les Bastides, Les Béates, Paradis; DOM d'Eole (on Alpilles). *See also* LES BAUX-DE-PROV.

Coteaux d'Ancenis Lo ★→★★ 21 22 23 AOP e of Nantes, unfussy easy-drinking (r/w/ rosé). Malvoisie (PINOT GR) can be gd (Galloires, Landron-Chartier).

Coteaux de l'Aubance Lo ★★→★★★ 15 18' 19 20 22 (23) Underrated AOP for sweet; more nervy, mineral style than COTEAUX DU LAYON. Try *Bablut*, Bois Brinçon, Montgilet, Rochelles, Terra Vita Vinum.

Coteaux du Giennois Lo ★→★★ 22 23 AOP n of POUILLY-FUMÉ; gd-value fruity SAUV BL, red (GAMAY/PINOT N) can also be gd (drink young). Try Berthier, Langlois, Quintin, *Villargeau*.

Coteaux du Layon Lo ★★→★★★★ 07' 09 10 11' 13 14 15 **16 17** 18' 19 20 22 (23) Star Lo AOP for botrytized CHENIN BL, incl six villages and PC Chaume. Top: BAUDOUIN, BAUMARD, BELARGUS, Bergerie, Breuil, CADY, Forges, Juchepie, *Pierre-Bise*, PIERRE MÉNARD, OGEREAU.

Coteaux du Loir Lo ★→★★★ Modest AOP on the Loir (tributary of Loire); taut CHENIN BL 14' 15' 16' 18' 19 20' 22 (23); reds incl fine Pineau d'Aunis. Best: *Bellivière*, Gigou, Maisons Rouges, Roche Bleue.

Coteaux du Quercy SW Fr ★ DYA AOP between CAHORS and GAILLAC. Hearty country wines based on CAB FR, plus TANNAT or MALBEC. Active co-op challenged by independents: ★★ DOMS du Guillau, Lacoste, Revel.

Coteaux du Vendômois Lo ★→★★ Small AOP on upper Loir (tributary of Loire). Whites mostly CHENIN BL 21 22 (23), while cult variety Pineau d'Aunis dominates red, rosé. Try CAVE du Vendômois, Montrieux.

Coteaux Varois-en-Provence Prov ★★ High, cooler AOP, chalk; light, appealing rosé. GRENACHE, CINSAULT, SYRAH, VIOGNIER in cooler n. Tiny-volume red, gd, fruity with lift. Try CHX des Annibals, la Calisse, Carpe Diem, DE L'ESCARELLE, Lafoux, Miraval (Brad Pitt), St Julien, Trians; DOMS des Aspras, du Deffends, du Loou, La Grand'vigne, La Rose des Vents, Les Terres Promises, Routas, St Mitre.

Côte Chalonnaise Burg ★★→★★★ Lunatic prices for top C D'O wines should deliver recognition. Lighter, ever-improving BOUZERON for ALIGOTÉ; *Rully* for accessible, juicy wines in both colours; *Mercurey* and GIVRY, more structure, can age; MONTAGNY for leaner, often impressive CHARD.

Côte d'Or Burg Golden or e-facing slope. Département name applied to central and principal Burg vyds: CÔTE DE BEAUNE, CÔTE DE NUITS.

Côte de Beaune C d'O ★★→★★★★ The s half of C D'O. Also a little-seen AOP applying to top of hill above BEAUNE itself. DROUHIN's versions (r/w) also incl declassified

Beaune PC. Try DOM VOUGERAIE too. Confusingly, C de B-Villages is different – often a blend from lesser villages of s half of C d'O. Read label carefully.

Côte de Brouilly Beauj ★★ 18' 19' 20' 21 22' 23 Range of styles: soils vary around Mont Brouilly. Merits a premium over straight BROUILLY. Reference: CH THIVIN. Also gd: Brun, Dufaitre, LAFARGE-Vial, Le Grappin, Martray, Pacalet.

Côte de Nuits C d'O ★★→★★★★ The n half of C D'O. Nearly all red, n to s: MARSANNAY, FIXIN, GEVREY-CHAMBERTIN, MOREY-ST-DENIS, CHAMBOLLE-MUSIGNY, CLOS DE VOUGEOT, VOSNE, NUITS. Wine doesn't get more patrician, or expensive, than best Côte de Nuits.

Côte de Nuits-Villages C d'O ★★ 15' 16 17 18' 19' 20' 21 22' 23 AOP for extreme n/s of CÔTE DE NUITS; can be bargains. Specialists: Chopin, Gachot-Monot, Jourdan. Top vyds: CLOS du Chapeau (ARLOT), Croix Violette (FOURNIER, Pernot), Faulques (Millot), Leurey (J-J Confuron), Meix Fringuet (TRAPET), Montagne (many), Robignotte (Jourdan), Vaucrains (JADOT). Best (w): Monts de Boncourt.

Côte Roannaise Lo, Mass C ★★→★★★ 18' 19 20' 21 22' 23 Best GAMAY in France? High-altitude AOP, granite, basalt. Tiptop wines from *Sérol* go head to head with any BEAUJ, and they can age. Also gd: Giraudon, Pothiers.

Côte-Rôtie N Rh ★★★→★★★★ 05' 09' 10' 12' 15' 16' 17' 18' 19' 20' 21 22' 23' 24' Finest, violet-perfumed red, mainly SYRAH, dabble of VIOGNIER, granite, schist soils, style connects with burg. Allow 5–10 yrs+. Long-lived 10 15 19, silken 20, pure 21, jolly-fruited 22, expressive 23, flowing 24. Top: *Barge*, B Chambeyron, Billon (energy), Bonnefond (crisp, oak), Bonserine (La Garde), Bott (modern), Burgaud, CHAPOUTIER, *Clusel-Roch* (organic), DELAS, DOM de Rosiers, Duclaux, Gaillard (oak), Garon, GUIGAL (long oak), *Jamet*, Jean-Luc Jamet, JASMIN (pure), J-M GÉRIN, J-M Stéphan (organic), Lafoy, Levet (trad), MONTEZ, Parpette (Le Plomb), *Rostaing* (fine), Semaska, S OGIER (racy), S Pichat (Grandes Places), VIDAL-FLEURY (La Chatillonne), X Gérard, Y CUILLERON.

Côtes Catalanes Rouss ★★★ Arguably France's most thrilling IGP (r/w/rosé). From fruity gd value from big Vignerons Catalans co-op to serious age-worthy wines from some of ROUSS's finest growers. CLOS DES FÉES, DANJOU-BANESSY, Gauby, CH de l'Ou, Lafage, Le Soula, ODYSÉE, Paetzold, among others for top wines. Covers most of ROUSS except BANYULS, COLLIOURE, which are IGP Côte Vermeille.

Côtes d'Auvergne Lo, Mass C ★→★★ 21' 22' 23 AOP in Puy-de-Dôme (Central France) on the Allier (tributary of Loire); CHARD, GAMAY, PINOT N give rather light, Burgundian wines. SYRAH in IGP Puy de Dôme. Try Desprat Saint-Verny, Les Chemins de l'Arkose, Miolanne, Sauvat.

Côtes de Bordeaux Bx ★ AOP for reds. For cross-blending CAS, FRANCS, BLAYE, CADILLAC and Ste-Foy. If Cas, Cadillac, etc. comes before Côtes de Bx, expect single terroir, stiffer controls. BLAYE-CÔTES DE BX, FRANCS-CÔTES DE BX, Ste-Foy Côtes de Bx: some dry white too. Try CHX Dudon, Malagar, Vieille Tour.

Côtes de Bourg Bx ★→★★ 19 20 22 23 Solid, savoury reds, a little white from e bank of Gironde; MALBEC, key element. Top CHX: Brûlecécaille, Bujan, de la Grave, *Falfas*, Fougas-Maldoror, Grand-Maison, Haut-Guiraud, Haut-Macô, Haut-Mondésir, La Grolet (Tête de Cuvée), Le Clos du Notaire, Macay, Mercier, Nodoz, *Roc de Cambes*, Sociondo.

Côtes de Duras SW Fr ★→★★ 19 20 22 23 (24) Quirky, underrated BERGERAC AOP; BX styles with sweet twist: Mauzac, Ondenc grapes. Best known for crisp dry whites: ★★ DOMS de Laulan, Grand Mayne, Mouthes le Bihan; gd co-op, Berticot.

Côtes de Gascogne / Comté Tolosan SW Fr Usually DYA. Two catch-all IGPS covering most of sw. Kaleidoscope of styles, mostly entry level. ★★ Joy, Menard Pellehaut, Plaimont, Tariquet for Gascony. DOM de Ribonnet stands out for Tolosan. Unbeatable value, infinite possibilities, wide selection of grapes.

Côtes de Millau SW Fr ★ Small, Med-influenced AOP in beautiful Gorges du Tarn close to Millau viaduct. Home to a gd co-op. Best independents: DOMS du Vieux Noyer, La Tour-St-Martin, Montrozier.

Côtes de Provence Prov ★→★★★ DYA Huge volumes of fashionably pale rosé; AOP from swathe of vyds, Marseilles to Cannes and inland. Together with COTEAUX D'AIX, COTEAUX VAROIS accounts for 90% of PROV rosé. White (increasingly 100% Rolle) and red (GRENACHE, SYRAH; MOURVÈDRE nearer coast) can be more interesting. Five subzones: La Londe, STE-VICTOIRE best, plus Fréjus, Notre Dame des Anges, Pierrefeu. Top: CHX D'ESCLANS, de l'Île, Gasqui (bio), La Gordonne, La Mascaronne, Léoube, Malherbe; CLOS CIBONNE (primarily Tibouren), DOMS *Gavoty*, Ott (Ch de Selle, Clos Mireille); Estandon, MIRABEAU, Rimauresq.

Côtes du Brulhois SW Fr ★ 19 20 22 23 Small AOP nr Agen, most oceanic of Garonne, Tarn appellations. Softer version of TANNAT (obligatory) and CAB SAUV, MALBEC, MERLOT in support. Local co-op unusually supportive of a few independents. Best for quaffing reds, pinks.

Côtes du Forez Lo, Mass C ★→★★ 21 22 23 High-altitude AOP upstream of CÔTE ROANNAISE for fun, frivolous, rather BEAUJ-esque GAMAY. For drinking young. Try Bonnefoy, Guillot, Poyet, Verdier-Logel.

Côtes du Jura Jura AOP covering all Jura, but esp around Poligny and s. Organic, esp natural, can be pricey. White dominates: mineral CHARD, Savagnin of all styles, incl VIN JAUNE. Light, earthy PINOT N, Poulsard, TROUSSEAU. Great food wines. Try classic ★ Baud, Chevassu, Lambert; organic ★ CH d'Arlay, ★ Badoz, ★★ Berthet-Bondet, ★ *Champ Divin*, Courbet, Grand, ★ Marnes Blanches, ★★ *Pignier*, natural ★★ Dolomies, ★★ *Labet*, ★★★ GANEVAT, ★★ Miroirs, Pieds sur Terre. *See also* ARBOIS, CH-CHALON, L'ÉTOILE.

Côtes du Marmandais SW Fr ★→★★ (r) 18 19 20 22 23 AOP, 300m (984ft) as crow flies from BX, increasingly eccentric thanks to local Abouriou grape and SYRAH. ★★★ Cult winemaker ELIAN DA ROS flagship DOM. ★★ Doms Beyssac, Bonnet, Cavenac, CH Lassolle (blend with usual Bx grapes). Co-ops dominate (95%).

Côtes du Rhône S Rh ★→★★ 23 24 Crisis-hit (low sales, low prices), incl v.gd SYRAH of Brézème, St-Julien-St-Alban (N Rh). Reds interesting, gd (esp CHÂTEAUNEUF estates, top value) vs dull, mass-volume. Pressure to rip out vyds. Spice, bustling fruit to fore. Mainly GRENACHE, also Syrah, often old CARIGNAN. Most best drunk young. Vaucluse best, then Gard (Syrah). Whites improving fast, stirring value in recent yrs.

Côtes du Rhône-Villages S Rh ★→★★★ 22' 23 24 Spiced reds from 7700 ha, incl 21 named S Rh villages, some ghost-like. LAUDUN cru status 2024. Best: full, long, like white gd value. Red core: GRENACHE, plus SYRAH, MOURVÈDRE. Improving

---

Village tales: best of Côtes du Rhône-Villages

Heartlands GRENACHE: try Gadagne (hearty, spiced), MASSIF D'UCHAUX, St-Maurice (rare, gd r/w), Ste-Cécile (medium weight), Signargues (punchy), VISAN; CHX Bois de la Garde, Fontségune, Signac; DOMS Aure, Bastide, Bastide St Dominique (organic), Bois de St Jean (full), Buissonnade (organic), Cabotte (bio, stylish), Coste Chaude (organic), Crève Coeur (bio, character), Echevin (gd w), Espigouette, Florane (bio), Grand Veneur, Grands Bois (organic), Gravennes (smooth), Janasse (top class), Jérôme, *Les Aphillanthes* (bio), Martin, Montbayon, Montmartel (organic), Mourchon, Pascal Chalon (bio), Pasquiers (organic), Pique-Basse (organic, gd w), *Rabasse-Charavin*, Réméjeanne (v.gd r/w), Renjarde, Romarins, Saladin (organic), STE-ANNE, Valériane; CAVE de RASTEAU Ortas, Les VIGNERONS d'Estézargues (Grenache range best, incl Doms Génestas, Pierredon).

white, often incl ROUSSANNE, VIOGNIER added to CLAIRETTE, GRENACHE BL, best *à table*. Top three: PLAN DE DIEU, SÉGURET (quality, choice), VISAN (improving, many organic). *See* MASSIF D'UCHAUX (fresh), SABLET (notable w), VALRÉAS; St-Gervais (DOM Sainte-Anne). (*See* box, opposite, for best growers.)

Côtes du Roussillon (Villages) Rouss ★→★★★ AOP for ROUSS (r/w/rosé), often v.gd: lots of CARIGNAN, also old-vine GRENACHES BL/Gr, MACCABEO for whites. AOP Côtes du Rouss-Villages smaller area, just red, some v.gd; 32 villages: Caramany, Latour de France, Les Aspres, Lesquerde, Tautavel named on label. Fine: Boucabeille, CAZES, Charles Perez, CLOS DES FÉES, Clot de l'Oum, des Chênes, Gauby, Les VIGNES de Bila-Haut (CHAPOUTIER), Mas Becha, Mas Crémat, Mas de la Devèze, Modat, Piquemal, Rancy, ROC DES ANGES, Thunevin-Calvet, Venus. Co-ops Brial, Carmany gd. *See also* CÔTES CATALANES.

Coudoulet, Dom Ldoc ★★★ Ournac family-owned, 8th generation. Innovative. Fine La Livinière, CH de Cesseras, alongside IGP from non-LDOC varieties: ASSYRTIKO, PINOT GR, PETIT VERDOT, PINOT N.

Coulée de Serrant Lo ★ 16 18 19 20 21 Historic CHENIN BL AOP; wonderful 7-ha ANJOU vyd, but sub-par wines with high alc, botrytis, premox. Proprietor Nicolas Joly makes other SAVENNIÈRES that also seem problem-prone.

Courcel, Dom de C d'O ★★★ Idiosyncratic POMMARD estate. Late-picking, whole bunches. Pommard structure without undue heft, a dextrous combination. Top: age-worthy PCS Épenots, Rugiens. Interesting Croix Noires.

Cour-Cheverny Lo ★★→★★★ 14 16 18 19 20 22 (23) Insider's AOP, rare Romorantin, CHENIN BL-like wines, eye-popping acidity. Top: *Cazin*. Also gd: Huards, Montcy.

Crémant AOP for quality classic-method fizz in AL, BX, BOURGOGNE, Die, Jura, LIMOUX, Lo, Luxembourg, SAV. Many gd egs.

Crémant de Loire Lo ★★→★★★ Large AOP for fizz. Varied styles: elegant pure CHARD, mineral CHENIN BL (perhaps with toasty lees-aged notes). And rosé. Big-name SAUMUR houses for value, esp BOUVET-LADUBAY, Langlois-Château; small DOMS for more intrigue, esp Arnaud Lambert, Aulée, *Plaisance*.

Criots-Bâtard-Montrachet C d'O ★★★ 09 10 12 14' 15 17' 18 19' 21 22 23 Tiny MONTRACHET satellite, 1.57 ha, downslope of BÂTARD-M. D'Auvenay for lottery winners. More accessible from Blain- or Fontaine-GAGNARD, LAMY and Caroline MOREY. Hangs on Montrachet's coat-tails. Doesn't burnish the term GC.

Cros, Dom du SW Fr Philippe Teulier was pioneer of MARCILLAC. He started with 1 ha, today is largest independent producer, with 30 ha. Le Sang del Païs is flagship red, from FER SERVADOU, locally known as Mansois.

Cros Parantoux Burg ★★★→★★★★ Cult PC in VOSNE, made famous by Henri Jayer. Now made by DOMS ROUGET, MÉO-CAMUZET. If fairy godmother is paying, don't refuse (though the haunting, Jayer magic is hard to replicate).

Crozes-Hermitage N Rh ★★→★★★ 22' 23 24' Quoted as France's most profitable AOP. Two zones. SYRAH from mostly flat vyds: quality variable. Dark fruits, oiliness, licorice, black-olive flavours. Most drink 2–5 yrs. Close-knit, cooler (more intrigue) Syrah from granite, loess hills n of HERMITAGE: red-fruited, iron, take time. Simple CUVÉES ideal for festivities. Oaked, older-vine wines cost more, gradually unfurl. Top: *A Graillot* (fab La Guiraude), Aléofane (r/w), Belle (organic), Betton, CHAPOUTIER, *Dard & Ribo* (low sulphur, high character), DELAS (Le CLOS, DOM des Grands Chemins), G Robin, Les Vins de Vienne; Doms Combier (organic), de Thalabert (JABOULET), de la Ville Rouge (bio), des Entrefaux, des Hauts-Châssis (bright), des Lises (fine), *du Colombier* (*Gaby* great), Dumaine (organic), Habrard (organic), *Laurent Fayolle* (stylish, top Clos Cornirets), Les Bruyères (bio), Machon, Martinelles (trad), Melody, Michelas St Jemms, Mucyn (fine), Remizières (oak), Rousset (Picaudières), Vendome (organic), Y Chave. Drink *white* (mostly MARSANNE) early, v.gd yrs recently. Value.

Cuilleron, Yves N Rh ★★★ Leading CONDRIEU, always stylish, flowing white. Top: Les Chaillets. Note old-vine ST-JOSEPH (r) Les Serines. CÔTE-RÔTIE okay, oaked (La Viallière). COLLINES RHODANIENNES Ripa Sinistra (SYRAH, Seyssuel), MARSANNE, VIOGNIER gd. Much recent vyd-merchant expansion, now organic.

Cuve close Quicker method of making fizz in tank. Bubbles die away in glass much faster than with *méthode traditionnelle*.

Cuvée Usually indicates a blend. In CHAMP, means 1st and best juice off the press.

Dagueneau, Louis-Benjamin Lo ★★★→★★★★ Didier's son emulates father's success. Exemplary range, although all now VDF rather than POUILLY-FUMÉ/SANCERRE: Buisson Renard, Le Mont Damné, Pur Sang, *Silex* 14' 16' 17 18' 19 20 21 22' (23).

Danjou-Banessy, Dom Rouss ★★★★ Extraordinarily complex, fresh, bio. In Agly V. IGP CÔTES CATALANES; v.gd La Truffière (r/w), Roboul, mostly MOURVÈDRE. Ethereal Estaca 130-yr-old GRENACHE.

Dard & Ribo N Rh ★★★ Offbeat, talented duo, deservedly loved by natural-wine enthusiasts, but consistent too. Old-vine CROZES-HERMITAGE, ST-JOSEPH, calm winemaking, used-oak; character, charm, wines age. Note whites (ROUSSANNE); Crozes Les Bâties, St-Joseph Pitrou (both r/w).

Dauvissat, Vincent Chab ★★★★ Supreme bio CHAB, uses old barrels and local 132-litre *feuillettes*. Grand, age-worthy, similar to RAVENEAU cousins. Best: La Forest, Les CLOS, Preuses, Séchet. Try also DOM Jean D & Fils (no relation).

Deiss, Dom Marcel Al ★★★ Famous Bergheim estate favouring field blends. Altenberg de Bergheim 16, Engelgarten 18, Grasberg 19, Rotenberg 19', Schoenenbourg 13' 17' outstanding; 20 delicious. Young Mathieu D takes reins from father Jean-Michel: wines showing even more precision, purity at all levels (marvellous Burg 22, Langenberg 22).

Delamotte Champ ★★★ Fine, small, CHARD-dominated house. Managed with SALON by LAURENT-PERRIER. BRUT, fascinating Rosé, BLANC DE BLANCS 07 08 13' 14; 18 19' 20 trilogy promises much; 19 *primus inter pares*.

Delas Frères N Rh ★★★ Owner-merchant, CONDRIEU, CROZES-HERMITAGE, CÔTE-RÔTIE, notably HERMITAGE vyds. Polished reds, consistent standard, high prices. Best: Côte-Rôtie Landonne; Hermitage DOM des Tourettes (r/w), *Les Bessards* (r, granite smoke, major finesse 15 yrs+), Ligne de Crête (subtle); ST-JOSEPH Ste-Épine (r, intricate, time); S Rh Grignan-les-Adhémar (r, value); VACQUEYRAS DOM des Genêts. Whites, bit mainstream, lighter recently. Owned by ROEDERER.

Delaunay, Edouard C d'O ★★★ Old Burg name revived in NUITS and l'Étang-Vergy by Laurent D; wide range NÉGOCIANT CUVÉES all price points. Gaining widespread plaudits. On a roll. Check v.gd-value Septembre BOURGOGNE CHARD, PINOT N.

Demi-sec Half-dry – in practice more like half-sweet (CHAMP c.45g/l dosage).

Department 66 Rouss ★★★ Napa winemaker Dave Phinney's DOM in MAURY; old vines, smart winery. Smart wines too. Opulent Painted Scars CÔTES CATALANES GRENACHE, SYRAH; Others (r), mineral, approachable.

Derenoncourt, Stéphane Bx International winemaker, favours elegance. Own property, *Dom de l'A* in CAS. Project in Greece (T-Oinos).

Deutz Champ ★★★★ One of best medium-sized houses, owned by ROEDERER family. Winemaker Caroline Latrive was at AYALA. Supreme CHARD *Cuvée Amour de Deutz* 08 10 13 15' 16; AdD Rosé 12 13 15 16; superb CUVÉE William Deutz 08 12 13 14' 15; BLANC DE BLANCS 13 14 16' 17'. Supremely elegant in every way.

Deux Clés, Dom des Ldoc ★★★ Burgundians Gaëlle, Florian Richter bring light touch to terroir-driven wines (r/w) from old vines in deepest CORBIÈRES. IGP Vallée du Paradis terrific CARIGNAN.

Devaux Champ ★★★ Côte des Bars. Reliable CUVÉE D; Coeur des Bar pair BLANC DE BLANCS/NOIRS underlines provenance, style. Also high-profile project with far-from-predictable Michel CHAPOUTIER Sténopé 08 09 10 11' 12. So far so v.gd.

Dirler-Cadé, Dom Al ★★★→★★★★ Over 40 plots: top old-vines MUSCAT GC Saering 23' and Spiegel; SYLVANER VIEILLES VIGNES 16 17' 18' 19 20 22 23; v.gd Saering and Kitterlé RIES 10 14' 16 17' 18 19 20 22. Luscious Bux PINOT GR VT 23. Amazing GEWURZ Spiegel VT 19 23 (but Gewurz Saering VT almost as gd).

Dom (Domaine) Property, except next entry. *See* under name, eg. TEMPIER, DOM.

Dom Pérignon Champ ★★★★ Vincent Chaperon, chef de CAVE, firmly into his stride at luxury CUVÉE of MOËT & CHANDON. Reductive style but gains seductive creamy allure after 10–15 yrs. Plénitude releases: long bottle-age, recent disgorgement, huge price, at 7, 16, 30 yrs+ (P1, P2, P3); superb P2 98 99 00 02 04' 06', still-vibrant P3 70 82 85 90 93'. More PINOT N focus since 2000: 06 07 08 10 12 13' 15. Superb, ultra-expensive rosé too. Quantity, quality both shrouded in mythology; both v. high.

Dopff au Moulin Al ★★★→★★★★ Pioneer of AL CRÉMANT in pretty Riquewihr; some wines dilute but GEWURZ GCS Brand, Sporen 12 16 18' 20', RIES SCHOENENBOURG 13 17', SYLVANER de Riquewihr 19' v.gd. Some gd buys, hidden gems.

Dourbie, Dom de la Ldoc ★★★ Impressive bio DOM, IGP Hérault, joyful CINSAULT Intemporal. Grenache Gr, taut, complex, floral, mineral. Thirst-quenching pét-nat from old LDOC grape Terret.

Dourthe Bx Sizeable merchant-grower, eight properties (incl CHX BELGRAVE, Grand Barrail Lamarzelle Figeac, LA GARDE, PEY LA TOUR). *Dourthe No. 1* (esp w) well-made generic BX. Also Promesse (CÔTES DE BOURG) returnable bottle.

Drappier, Michel Champ ★★★→★★★★ Family-run AUBE house, children of Michel D now in charge. Fine PINOT N, 60 ha+, bio; Pinot-led NV, BRUT ZÉRO, Brut *sans souffre*, Millésime d'Exception 12 14' 16 18 19, Prestige CUVÉE Grande Sendrée 08' 09 12, plus GS Rosé 08 09 10' 12 Cuvée Quatuor (four cépages). Superb 95' 82 (magnums). Constant research into early C17 vines resistant to climate change. More use of large oak *foudres*. Thoughtful, likeable house.

DRC (Dom de la Romanée-Conti) C d'O ★★★★ Grandest estate in Burg (or world). MONOPOLES ROMANÉE-CONTI and LA TÂCHE, major parts of ÉCHÉZEAUX, GRANDS-ÉCHÉZEAUX, RICHEBOURG, ROMANÉE-ST-VIVANT (glorious 23), plus 0.68 ha of MONTRACHET. Also CORTON from 09, superb CORTON-CHARLEMAGNE since 19. Crown-jewel prices. Scintillating 22, esp LA TÂCHE.

Drouhin, Joseph & Cie Burg ★★★→★★★★ Grower-NÉGOCIANT in BEAUNE; vyds (bio) incl (w) Beaune *Clos des Mouches*, MONTRACHET (Marquis de LAGUICHE) and large CHAB holdings. Wide range of stylish reds: CHOREY-LÈS-BEAUNE, Beaune, CHAMBOLLE, VOSNE (Petits Monts) and GEVREY. Purchase of Rapet (ST-ROMAIN) and CH de Chasselas (ST-VÉRAN), added 20 ha. Avoids négociant trap of all wines tasting much the same. Also Dom Drouhin Oregon (US).

Duboeuf, Georges Beauj ★★→★★★ From hero (saviour of BEAUJ) to less so (too much BEAUJ NOUVEAU), always major player. Sound source for Beauj crus that age well, Mâcon bottlings. Don't let ubiquity obscure many other producers.

Dugat C d'O ★★★→★★★★ Cousins Claude and Bernard (Dugat-Py) made excellent, deep-coloured GEVREY-CHAMBERTIN, respective labels. Almost ageless. Both flourishing with new generation. Tiny volumes, esp GCS, huge prices deliver quality not value. Try D-P's excellent BOURGOGNE Rouge to gain hint of GC quality.

Dujac, Dom C d'O ★★★→★★★★ MOREY-ST-DENIS grower originally noted for sensual reds that aged into delicate intensity, from village Morey to outstanding GCS, esp CLOS DE LA ROCHE, CLOS ST-DENIS, ÉCHÉZEAUX. Slightly more mainstream these days; gd *whites* from Morey and PULIGNY. New eco-friendly winery 2023. Lighter merchant wines as D Fils & Père and DOM Triennes in COTEAUX VAROIS.

Durban, Dom S Rh ★★→★★★ Top MUSCAT de BEAUMES-DE-VENISE from high vyds, veteran family; rich, inviting, long-lived (20+ yrs). Sound BEAUMES red, neat IGP dry Muscat, VIOGNIER.

Dureuil-Janthial Burg ★★ Vincent D-J runs outstanding DOM in RULLY, with *fresh, punchy whites* and cheerful, juicy reds. All recommended, esp Maizières (r/w), PC Meix Cadot (w). Seek if C D'O now beyond budget.

Duroché, **Dom** C d'O ★★★→★★★★ Pierre D's deft approach yields richness, depth on one hand, elegance, finesse on other; all seamlessly blended with age. Also small NÉGOCE operation. Flag carrier for GEVREY-CHAMBERTIN.

Duval-Leroy Champ ★★★ Family-owned, over 200 ha mainly fine CHARD crus. Excellent sites. Improved Prestige Blanc de Blancs and Femme de Champagne. Fleur de CHAMP GC 96 00' 02 04. CLOS des Bouveries 05 06' 08.

Échézeaux C d'O ★★★ 02' 05' 09' 10' 12' 15' 16 17 18 19' 20' 21 22' 23 GC next to CLOS DE VOUGEOT, but different style: lacy, ethereal, scintillating. Pixellated ownership, 38 ha, 59 owners. Outstanding quality/price: ARNOUX-LACHAUX, Bizot, Coquard-Loison-Fleurot, DRC, DUJAC, EUGÉNIE, G NOËLLAT, GRIVOT, GROS, LIGER-BELAIR, MÉO-CAMUZET, *Mugneret-Gibourg*, ROUGET, TREMBLAY. Also Berthaut-Gerbet, *Guyon*, Lamarche, Millot, MUGNERET, Naudin-Ferrand, Tardy.

Edelzwicker Al ★ DYA Blended, entry-level fresh white: HUGEL Gentil, Meyer-Fonné.

Egly-Ouriet Champ ★★★→★★★★ Family affair in GC Ambonnay, Francis E heading 4th generation. Outstanding VIEILLES VIGNES: Les Crayères BLANC DE NOIRS. Also NV PC Les Prémices. Fashionable (and brilliant) COTEAUX CHAMPENOIS; CUVÉE des Grands Côtés 16 18 19 20. Also late-release VP (Vieillissement Prolongé), variant on RD theme. Fantastically subtle take on PINOT N.

Elian da Ros, Dom SW Fr ★★★→★★★★ Almost single-handedly created reputation of CÔTES DU MARMANDAIS, rare AOP of SAUTERNES. Trained with ZIND H; est 1997. Excellent bio wines: BX varieties, local speciality Abouriou.

Entraygues-le-Fel and Estaing SW Fr ★→★★ DYA Two tiny, obscure AOP neighbours, nr-vertical terraces above Lot V. Cool climate, hard to find, but worth it (esp w). Bone-dry CHENIN BL v.gd: ★★ DOMS Laurent Mousset (r, esp La Pauca, v.gd rosé), Méjanassère, ★★ Nicolas Carmarans.

Entre-Deux-Mers Bx ★→★★ DYA Often gd-value dry white BX from between rivers Garonne and Dordogne. New red AOP from 23 (stricter rules than BX SUPÉRIEUR), available 25. Best: CHX Beauregard Ducourt, BONNET, de Fontenille, Haut-Rian, La Freynelle, Landereau, Lauduc, Les Arromans, Marjosse, Nardique-la-Gravière, Sainte-Marie, *Tour de Mirambeau*, Thieuley, Turcaud, Vignol.

Escaravailles, Dom des S Rh ★★→★★★ Leading CAIRANNE, RASTEAU name, high vyds. Daughter Madeline conjuring bright fruit. Stylish Cairanne Scarabée Libérée (no sulphur); top Roaix Village (SYRAH); Rasteaus Ad Argillam (part amphorae), Héritage 1924 (fluid, rich); VDN.

Escarelle, Ch l' Prov ★★★ CÔTEAUX VAROIS-EN-PROV; nature res; elegant, aromatic rosés. Croix d'Engardin (oaked, can age); Les Deux Anges gd.

Esclans, Ch d' Prov ★★→★★★ Self-styled architect of "rosé renaissance", Sacha Lichine has built high-profile rosé brands, most for export. Whispering Angel big everywhere. Top: Garrus GRENACHE/ROLLE, oaked, expensive, will age. Les Clans, partially oaked, v. stylish. Part-owned by LVMH.

Esmonin, Dom Sylvie C d'O ★★★ Rich, dark, from fully ripe grapes, whole-bunch vinification, new oak. Best: CLOS ST-JACQUES (DOM's back garden), GEVREY-CHAMBERTIN VIEILLES VIGNES. Slightly below radar, hence reasonable value.

Estabel, La Cave de l' Ldoc ★★★ Top CABRIÈRES CO-OP: v.gd rosé; Fulcrand Cabanon CLAIRETTE even better. Super value. Fragrant, fine Cantate de Garrigue (r).

Etoile, L' Jura AOP for stony CHARD, SAVAGNIN on limestone and marl, often oxidative. VIN JAUNE, VIN DE PAILLE also allowed but not reds (sold as AOP CÔTES DU JURA). Try Cartaux-Bougaud, ★★ *Montbourgeau*, ★ Mouillard, Rolet.

Eugénie, Dom C d'O ★★★→★★★★ Artemis Estates' 1st foray into burg, also CLOS DE TART, BOUCHARD (latter's CÔTE DE NUITS vyds now transferred here). Intense, dark wines now enlivened by more whole-bunch vinification. Outstanding CLOS DE VOUGEOT, GRANDS-ÉCHÉZEAUX.

Faiveley, Dom Burg ★★→★★★ Was NÉGOCIANT, now DOM; 200 yrs in 2025. Revitalized by Erwan F since 2005. Once serviceable, now exciting. Glossy, polished style, sweet fruit. Leading light in CÔTE CHALONNAISE, but save up for top CHAMBERTIN-CLOS de Bèze, CHAMBOLLE-MUSIGNY, CORTON *Clos des Cortons*, NUITS. Also owns classy DOM Billaud-Simon (CHAB).

Faugères Ldoc ★★★ AOP in Cevennes foothills, unique schist terroir attracts innovative small growers. *Garrigue*-scented, poised reds. Will age. Elegant whites from GRENACHE BL, MARSANNE, ROUSSANNE, VERMENTINO. Drink CH de Ciffre, DE LA LIQUIÈRE. DOMS Ancienne Mercerie, BARDI-ALQUIER, CÉBÈNE, Chenaie, des Trinités, Estanilles, Grézan, LA SARABANDE, Léon Barral, Mas d'Alezon, Mas Gabinèle, Méteore, Ollier-Taillefer, St Antonin.

Ferraton Père & Fils N Rh ★★★ HERMITAGE-based grower-merchant, CHAPOUTIER-owned, bio. Several wines/appellation. Quality gd–v.gd, esp CORNAS Patou, CROZES-HERMITAGE Grand Courtil (r/w 50/50% MARSANNE/ROUSSANNE), Hermitage Le Méal (r, 60s SYRAH), Le Reverdy (w, firm, long, oak), Les Dionnières (r, finesse), ST-JOSEPH Bonneveau (r, true terroir).

Fèvre, William Chab ★★★→★★★★ Biggest owner of CHAB GCS: outstanding Bougros Côte Bougerots and Les CLOS. Small yields, no expense spared, priced accordingly. GCs can be splendid, age-worthy; humbler wines a little safe in style. Visitor-friendly. Look also for cousins N&G Fèvre, esp PC Vaulorent and GC Preuses. Now owned by DBR Lafite.

Fiefs Vendéens Lo ★→★★★ 20' 21 22 (23) Historic Atlantic AOP; whites from CHENIN BL, Grolleau Gr give Ligérian flavours, but oceanic salinity – like a VOUVRAY-MUSCADET hybrid. Bright, breezy reds: CAB FR, GAMAY, NÉGRETTE and more. Try Mourat, *Saint Nicolas* (VDF).

Fitou Ldoc ★★→★★★ AOP Lots of CARIGNAN gives rugged richness, taste of the sun. Two parts: schist on inland hills s of Narbonne; and chalk, limestone nr coast. Try CHX de Nouvelles, Grand Guilhem, Champs des Soeurs; DOMS Bertrand-Bergé, de la Rochelierre, DU VENT, JONES, Lérys, Mas des Caprices.

Fixin C d'O ★★→★★★ 09' 10' 12' 14 15' 16 17 18 19' 20' 21 22' 23 When GEVREY goes beyond budget, switch to Fixin. Continuing improvement. Structured reds, previously hearty but benefiting from climate change. Best vyds: Arvelets, CLOS de la Perrière, Clos du Chapitre, Clos Napoléon. Top locals: Berthaut-Gerbet, Gelin, Joliet, Naddef. Also gd: Bart, CLAIR, FAIVELEY, MORTET. Watch.

Fleurie Beauj ★★→★★★★ 15' 18' 19' 20' 21 22' 23 Top cru: scented, strawberry fruit, immediate appeal. Charm in a glass. PCs applied for, will be yrs. Classic: CHX BEAUREGARD, Chatelard, de Poncié; DOMS Brun, Chignard; CLOS de la Roilette, Depardon, DUBOEUF, Métrat, co-op. Naturalists: Balagny, Dutraive, Métras, Pacalet, Sunier. New: Chapel, Clos de Mez, Dom de Fa, *Hoppenot*, LAFARGE-Vial.

Fontanel, Dom Rouss ★★★ Go-ahead DOM: Arrels (r), classy MAURY Sec; VDNS Maury Grenat, moreish; RIVESALTES Ambré, nutty, orange-peel delight.

Fourrier, Dom C d'O ★★★★ GEVREY DOM producing sensual vibrant reds with magical fruit flavours, from ancient vines. Age beautifully. Best: CLOS ST-JACQUES, Combe aux Moines (complete with monk sculpture in vyd), GRIOTTE-CHAMBERTIN. Magnificent wines, cult prices. Also Bass Phillip (*see* Australia).

Francs-Côtes de Bordeaux Bx ★★ 18 19 20 22 23 Tiny CÔTES AOP next to CAS; also wants independent status. Fief of Thienpont (PAVIE MACQUIN) family. Mainly red; MERLOT-led (60%). Some gd white (Charmes-Godard, Puyanché). Try Ad Francos, Cru Godard, La Prade, Laulan, Marsau, *Puygueraud*.

Fronsac Bx ★★→★★★ 18 19' 20' 22 23 Great-value, hilly AOP w of POM. MERLOT-led on clay-limestone; mid-term ageing potential. Top CHX: Arnauton, DALEM, Fontenil,

George 7, Haut-Carles, *La Dauphine*, La Grave, Lamolière, La Rivière, LA VIEILLE CURE, LES TROIS CROIX, Mayne-Vieil (CUVÉE Alienor), *Moulin Haut-Laroque*, Villars. *See also* CANON-FRON.

Fronton SW Fr ★★ 20 22 23 AOP n of Toulouse. Home to NÉGRETTE (violets, cherries, licorice); often blended with SYRAH. Best known, vibrant, fruity, purple-hued: ★★★ CHX Baudare, Bouissel, Caze; ★★ CH BELLEVUE-LA-FORÊT, *du Roc*; La Colombière, Laurou, Plaisance. Also gd: ★ Boujac, Clamens, Viguerie de Belaygues. No AOP for whites yet.

Fuchs, Henri Al ★★→★★★ Organic Ribeauvillé winery, est 1922, 4th generation. Outstanding, deep SYLVANER VIEILLES VIGNES 19 20 21, from late-ripening, top Weinbaum site; v.gd RIES GC Kirchberg de Ribeauvillé.

Fuissé, Ch Burg ★★→★★★ Smart operation in POUILLY-FUISSÉ with long track record. Concentrated, oaky (too oaky?) whites, can be lavish. Top terroirs: Combettes, Le CLOS. Also BEAUJ crus, eg. JULIÉNAS.

Gagnard C d'O ★★★ Respected clan in CHASSAGNE. Long-lasting wines, esp BÂTARD, Caillerets from Jean-Noël G; while Blain-G, Fontaine-G have full range, incl rare CRIOTS-BÂTARD, MONTRACHET itself – gd value all round. Tasty Chassagne reds too. Hard to go wrong with any Gagnard; seek out.

Gaillac SW Fr ★→★★★ On Tarn River, stylistically most diverse AOP of SW. Cornucopia of grapes: (r) Braucol (Fer), Duras, SYRAH; (w) LEN DE L'EL, MAUZAC (w). Prunelard gaining ground for red, while Ondenc (w) has legendary status at *Plageoles*. Quality variable but also look for ★★★ CHX Lastours, *L'Enclos des Roses*; DOMS Causse-Marines, DE BRIN, d'Escausses, La Ramaye, La Vignereuse, Le Champ d'Orphée, Peyres-Roses, Rotier. Perlé is refreshing, summery white with slight prickle; can be delicious. Co-ops do it well, cheaply.

Ganevat Jura ★★★→★★★★ CÔTES DU JURA bio superstar with single-vyd CHARD (eg. Chalasses, Grands Teppes), SAVAGNIN VIGNES de Mon Père (topped up 10 yrs). Expressive reds. Cult pricing. Anne & Jean-François G NÉGOCE business too.

Gangloff, Yves N Rh ★★★ Rock-star (literally) CONDRIEU grower, fans clamour for wines; aromatic, rich. Also two CÔTE-RÔTIES: Barbarine (younger vines, dark fruit), Sereine Noire (profound, complex). Correct ST-JOSEPH (r/w).

Garrabou, Dom Ldoc ★★★ Smart AOP LIMOUX CHARD; racy L'Estrade CHENIN BL IGP. Intense MALBEC Le Gouffre de Diable, needs time.

Gayda, Dom Ldoc ★★★→★★★★ Burgundian Vincent Chansaut winemaker at this swish, innovative DOM in Malpère, nr LIMOUX, for 20 yrs. Chemin des Mouscou IGP d'Oc top (r) blends ROUSS with La Livinière grapes. Figure Libre monocépages CHENIN BL (w), CAB FR (r) classy, complex.

GC (Grand Cru) Official term meaning different things in different areas. One of top Burg vyds with its own AOP. In AL, one of 51 top vyds, each now with own rules. In ST-ÉM, 60% of production is St-Ém GC, often run of the mill. In MÉD, five tiers of GC CLASSÉS. In CHAMP, top 17 villages are GCs. Since 2011 in Lo for QUARTS DE CHAUME; emerging system in LDOC. Take with pinch of salt in PROV.

Gérard Bertrand Ldoc ★★★★ LDOC pioneer. Ex-rugby-international Gérard took on family's Ch de Villemajou in CORBIÈRES, now has 17 estates and counting. CH l'Hospitalet (LA CLAPE), Clos d'Ora (La Livinière), iconic rosé at Clos du Temple (CABRIÈRES). Lots bio. NÉGOCIANT arm covers 32 AOC, IGP.

Gérin, Jean-Michel N Rh ★★★ 19' 20' 21' 22' 23' 24' On-the-march 15-ha CÔTE-RÔTIE DOM, well-sited schist-granite vyds, busy wines, headed by Les Grandes Places (coiled-depth), Côte Brune (7% VIOGNIER, complex); also La Landonne (rich), La Viallière (stylish). Some oak. Two sound CONDRIEU.

Gevrey-Chambertin C d'O ★★→★★★★ 05' 09' 10' 12' 15' 16 17 18 19' 20' 21 22' 23 Major AOP for reds of substance, structure, from serviceable to supreme, up to great CHAMBERTIN and GC cousins. Style less forbidding today. Some trade on name, but best brilliant. Top PCS: Cazetiers, Combe aux Moines, Combottes, CLOS ST-JACQUES. Value: single-vyd village (En Champs, La Justice), VIEILLES VIGNES bottlings. Top: BACHELET, BOILLOT, *Burguet*, Damoy, Drouhin-Laroze, DUGAT, Dugat-Py, DUROCHÉ, ESMONIN, FAIVELEY, FOURRIER, Guillon, Harmand-Geoffroy, Heresztyn-Mazzini, LEROY, Magnien (H), Marchand-Grillot, MORTET, REBOURSEAU, ROSSIGNOL-TRAPET, Roty, ROUSSEAU, Roy, SÉRAFIN, TRAPET; gd merchants.

Gigondas S Rh ★★→★★★ 09' 10' 12' 13' 15' 16' 17' 18 19' 20 21 22' 23 24' Fresh, serious red; from 23 white (mainly CLAIRETTE) too. Picturesque vyds on stony, clay-sand plain and Alpine, limestone-spiked hills; GRENACHE, plus SYRAH, MOURVÈDRE. Spiced, menthol-fresh; best give fine dark-red fruit, terroir. Top: 10 15 16 19. Try Boissan, Bosquets (modern, oak), Brusset, Cayron (character), CH de Montmirail, CH DE ST COSME (tempo, oak), *Clos des Cazaux* (value), CLOS du Joncuas (organic), DOM *Famille Perrin*, Goubert, Gour de Chaulé (crystalline), Grapillon d'Or, LA BOUÏSSIÈRE (punchy), Les Pallières (cool), Longue Toque, Moulin de la Gardette (organic), Notre Dame des Pallières, P AMADIEU (consistent), PESQUIER (authentic), Piéblanc (organic), Pourra (robust), *Raspail-Ay* (ages), Roubine (punchy), *St Gayan* (long life), Santa Duc (stylish), Semelles de Vent (handmade), Teyssonières (elegant). Powerful rosés.

Gilbert, Philippe Lo ★★→★★★ Name to beat in MENETOU-SALON; bio. Superior to many an ordinary SANCERRE: *Clos des Treilles* (r/w), 35/44 Rangs 19 **20 21 22** 23.

Gilles, Guillaume N Rh ★★★ 19' 20' 21' 22' 23' 24' Classic, smoky CORNAS; only 3 ha; detailed, repay patience, esp Chaillot. Aso gd: CÔTES DU RH, GAMAY, ST-PÉRAY.

Rhône whites progress: Gigondas AOP white (mainly Clairette) from 2023.

Gimonnet, Pierre Champ ★★★★ Didier G makes beautifully consistent CHARD on N Côte des Blancs, 28 GCS, PCS. Great-value Le Perlé de Gimonnet 12 13 16 18' 19. Special Club is complex expression of great Chard 13 15 17' 19 20 for long ageing. Oger GC a (glorious) departure from philosophy of assemblage 15' 16. Ditto Chouilly 12 16, Cramant GC 12 16'.

Girardin, Vincent C d'O ★★★ MEURSAULT-based NÉGOCIANT, part of BOISSET. Top white, esp CORTON-CHARLEMAGNE. Reds much improved. Son Pierre-Vincent operates from impressive new winery in Meursault; real promise.

Givry Burg ★★→★★★ 15' 17 18' 19' 20' 21 22' 23 Top tip in CÔTE CHALONNAISE for tasty, age-worthy reds, substantial but not overweight. Rare, nutty whites if you can find. Best (r): CELLIER AUX MOINES, CLOS Salomon, *Faiveley*, F Lumpp, Joblot, Masse, Thénard.

Goisot Burg ★★★ Guilhem and J-H G, outstanding bio producers: single-vyd ST-BRIS (SAUV BL); Côtes d'Auxerre (CHARD, PINOT N). Racy, mineral, perky. Dependable quality, gd value. Deserve to be better known.

Goldert Al Exceptional AL marl-limestone GC; v. aromatic. Some of Al's best GEWURZ, MUSCAT, SYLVANER. Try ERNEST BURN, ZIND HUMBRECHT.

Gonon, Dom N Rh ★★★ 10' 13' 14 15' 16' 17 18' 19' 20' 21' 22' 23' 24' Leading ST-JOSEPH estate, works organically, hand-graft cuttings for 10-ha terraced granite vyds. Wines loved by hipsters, prices hot. Mostly whole-bunch, old 600 litre casks, floral-spiced, iron-toned red, SYRAH from heaven; rich flow 50–80-yr-old vines *Les Oliviers* (w, 80% MARSANNE, fab *à table*), both live 20 yrs.

Gosset Champ ★★★★ Oldest house, based in AŸ, owned by Cointreau. Chef de CAVE Odilon de Varine passionate about terroir. Grand Blanc de MEUNIER mainly 07, elegant, aged on CHARD lees. Outstanding *Celebris Extra Brut* 04 07' 08. Rosé 08 12 just as gd. Sublime Les Célébrissimes 95'; long-aged 12 and 15 Ans de Cave a Minima (incl rosé). Excellent double act: BLANC DE BLANCS and Millésime 12'. Plus Grand Millésime 15' 16.

Gouges, Henri C d'O ★★★ Days of forbidding concentration, structure at Gouges are over. Cousins Grégory and Antoine G now making wine in a lighter iteration, though no less compelling. Great PCs: CLOS des Porrets, Vaucrains and esp Les St-Georges. Also excellent *white Nuits*, from PINOT BL, aka "Pinot Gouges".

Graillot, Dom Alain N Rh ★★★ 18' 19' 20' 21' 22 23 24' CROZES-HERMITAGE, organic stony vyds, whole-bunch ferments. Up-tempo, smoky, dark-fruited red: La Guiraude special selection, mini HERMITAGE, long life. Crozes (w, graceful), ST-JOSEPH (r). Alain's son Maxime makes Crozes-H DOM des Lises (forward fruit, drinks early, gd old-vines merchant wines), Equis (CORNAS, St-Joseph).

Gramenon, Dom S Rh ★★–★★★ 22' 23' 24' Organic pioneer since 70s, *garrigue* vyds, bio since 2007. Fruit purity, GRENACHE *en finesse*, character wines, v. low sulphur. CÔTES DU RH: La Papesse (30s Grenache), La Sagesse (Grenache), Poignée des Raisins (toot, toot), Sierra du Sud (SYRAH).

Grande Rue, La C d'O ★★★ 05' 06 09' 10' 12' 15' 16 17 18 19' 20' 21 22' 23 MONOPOLE of DOM Lamarche, GC between LA ROMANÉE-CONTI and LA TÂCHE. Quality, consistency improved under Nicole Lamarche. Light and long rather than broad and deep. Also special bottling dubbed 1959 – not better, just different.

Grands-Échézeaux C d'O ★★★★ 93 96' 99' 02' 05' 09' 10' 12' 15' 17 18 19' 20' 21 22' 23 Superlative GC next to CLOS DE VOUGEOT, but with a MUSIGNY silkiness, 9 ha. More conviction than most ÉCHÉZEAUX. Top: BICHOT (CLOS Frantin), Coquard-Loison-Fleurot, DRC, DROUHIN, EUGÉNIE, Millot, NOËLLAT G.

Deepest cellars in Champagne are 38m (125ft). That's 80 million years of chalk.

Gratien & Meyer / Alfred Gratien Champ ★★★→★★★★ (BRUT) 12 13 15' 18' 19 Small but wonderfully idiosyncratic house, owned by Henkell Freixenet. Passionate chef de CAVE Nicolas Jaegar knows all there is to know about oak influence. Brut NV; CHARD-led Prestige *Cuvée Paradis Brut* 02 04 12 13' 15 16. Fine, v. dry, lasting, oak-fermented wines. Also Gratien & Meyer in SAUMUR.

Graves Bx ★→★★ 19 20 22 23 Appetizing fresh SAUV/SÉM (dr w), grainy CAB SAUV, MERLOT, Grav Supérieures denotes *moelleux*. "Ambassador de Graves" selected CHX. Some of best value in BX today. Top Chx: ARCHAMBEAU, Brondelle, CHANTEGRIVE, CLOS Bourgelat, *Clos Floridène*, CRABITEY, de Cérons, Grand Enclos du Ch de Cérons, Haura, Lagrange, Liber Pater, Moutin, Pont de Brion, Portets, RAHOUL, *Respide Medeville*, Roquetaillade La Grange, Seuil, Torteau Chollet, *Vieux Ch Gaubert*, Villa Bel-Air.

Graves de Vayres Bx ★ DYA Tiny AOP within E-2-M zone. Red, white, *moelleux*.

Grés de Montpellier Ldoc ★★★ Terroir in LDOC AOC nr Montpellier. Dry, stony, intense red with lift from sea breezes. Nearby St-Georges d'Orques similar. DOMS Bas d'Aumelas, de Blanville, de L'Engarran, de Roquemale, de Saumarez, Henry, La Magdelaine, La Marfée; CLOS des Nines, MAS DU NOVI, Mas de Lunés.

Grignan-les-Adhémar S Rh ★→★★ AOP, stony, wooded *garrigue*, 1200 ha, best red with incense, herbs, latent punch, drink within 4–5 yrs. Best: DELAS (value); CHX Bizard, La Décelle (incl CÔTES DU RH w); DOMS de Bonetto-Fabrol, de Montine (enjoyable r, gd w/rosé, also Côtes du Rh r), Grangeneuve best (VIEILLES VIGNES), St-Luc.

Griotte-Chambertin C d'O ★★★★ 96' 99' 02' 05' 09' 10' 12' 15' 16 17 18' 19' 20' 21 22' 23 Small, 2.7 ha, GC next to CHAMBERTIN; nobody has much volume. Perky red fruit, depth, ageing potential: DROUHIN, DUGAT, DUROCHÉ, FOURRIER, Ponsot (L).

Gripa, Dom Bernard N Rh ★★★ 17' 18' 19' 20' 21' 22' 23' 24' Top ST-JOSEPH, ST-PÉRAY, uber-elegant whites: St-Joseph Le Berceau (100% 60-yr+ MARSANNE), *St-Péray Les Figuiers* (classy). Both St-Joseph reds gd; Le Berceau (60-yr+ SYRAH), dense 17, bold 18, rich 19, stylish 20, clear 21, bright 22, smoky 23, flowing 24.

Grivot, Jean C d'O ★★★→★★★★ VOSNE DOM that may improve even further as Mathilde G takes over. Superb range of PCs (esp Beaux Monts, NUITS Boudots) topped by GCS CLOS DE VOUGEOT, ÉCHÉZEAUX, RICHEBOURG. Beautiful wines. Recent refinement in style, days of heft over beauty are gone.

Groffier C d'O ★★★→★★★★ Sizzling 22, incl two glorious versions of PC LES AMOUREUSES. Bewitching style dazzles the taste buds. Flavour-packed yet delicate. Raid the piggybank.

Gros, Doms C d'O ★★★→★★★★ Family of vignerons in VOSNE: stylish wines from Anne (compelling RICHEBOURG), succulent reds from Michel (CLOS de Réas), Anne-Françoise (now in BEAUNE), Gros Frère & Soeur (CLOS DE VOUGEOT En Musigni). Marvellous view across Vosne GCS from new tasting room at Gros F&S. Not just GC; try value HAUTES-CÔTES DE NUITS. Also Anne's DOM Gros-Tollot in MINERVOIS. Some vyds changed hands within family, 2022.

Gros Plant du Pays Nantais Lo ★→★★ 22 23 AOP for Gros Plant (FOLLE BLANCHE), bracing, occasionally anodyne alternative to MUSCADET. Decent LUNEAU-PAPIN.

Guigal, Ets E N Rh ★★→★★★★ World-famous, constantly expanding, still family affair. Grower-merchant at CÔTE-RÔTIE (expensive La Landonne, La Mouline, megarich La Turque; owns DOM de Bonserine), plus CONDRIEU, CROZES-HERMITAGE, HERMITAGE (fab Ex Voto), ST-JOSEPH (VIGNES de l'Hospice), CHÂTEAUNEUF CH de Nalys (improving), top TAVEL Ch d'Aquéria (stylish, note new Héritage). Owns VIDAL-FLEURY. *Astounding-value Côtes du Rh* (r/w/rosé). Best whites: Condrieu, Condrieu La Doriane (oak), Hermitage, St-Joseph Lieu-dit St-Joseph.

Hautes-Côtes de Beaune / Nuits C d'O ★★→★★★ (r) 18′ 19′ 20′ 21 22′ 23 (w) 17′ 18 19′ 20′ 21 22′ 23 BOURGOGNE AOP for villages in hills behind main C D'o vyds. Climate change means wines gaining style, elegance, losing rusticity. Sweet spots: villages of Arcenant, Meloisey, Nantoux, plateau above CÔTES DE NUITS. Try Carré, Champy (Boris), CHEVROT, Devevey, DOM de la Douaix, Faure, Hoffmann-Jayer, Jacob, LEPRINCE, Naudin (Claire), Parigot, Vantey. Watch.

Haut-Médoc Bx ★★→★★★ 16′ 18 19′ 20 22 23 Prime source of dry, digestible CAB/MERLOT reds. Usually gd value. Plenty of CRUS BOURGEOIS. Wines usually sturdier in n; finer in s. Five Classed Growths (BELGRAVE, CAMENSAC, *Cantemerle*, *La Lagune*, LA TOUR-CARNET). Five Crus Bourgeois Exceptionnels (de Malleret, du Taillan, *Malescasse*, Paloumey, REYSSON). Try also BEAUMONT, CISSAC, CITRAN, COUFRAN, *de Lamarque*, Doyac, LANESSAN, Madame de Beaucaillou, SÉNÉJAC, *Sociando-Mallet*.

Haut-Poitou Lo ★→★★ 21 22 23 Historically huge AOP for white (SAUVS BL/Gr), red/rosé (mostly CAB FR), n of Poitiers; now only a nubbin remains. The best offer fresh, vibrant fruit; drink young: La Tour Beaumont, Villemont.

Hauvette, Dom Prov ★★★★ Dominique H makes enchanting wines at bio DOM nr Saint-Rémy-de-prov. IGP Alpilles; Jaspe ROUSSANNE, Amethyste CINSAULT.

Heidsieck, Charles Champ ★★★★ Iconic house, small but beautiful, wines perennially exquisite. *NV Brut* all purity, subtle yet ripe complexity, a beguiling paradox. Peerless *Blanc des Millénaires* 04 06′ 07 14′ (new release after gap). Great Vintage 12′ 14. Older La Collection Crayères 83 81. Returning CHAMP Charlie multivintage prestige CUVÉE, icon if ever there was one. BLANC DE BLANCS NV nicely priced, delicious. Ditto Vintage Rosé 04 06′ 07 08.

Heitz C d'O ★★★ Armand H is in Chaudenay, off main drag of C D'o. Gentle purity marks reds, distinctive, classy. Pure, poised whites too.

Hengst Al Marl-limestone-sandstone GC, powerful wines: GEWURZ (ZIND H); AUXERROIS, PINOT GR (JOSMEYER). Now one of two al PINOT N GC sites (A MANN).

Henriot Champ ★★★→★★★★ Two changes in ownership in past 2 yrs; 1st Artemis and now co-op Terroirs et Vignes de Champagne (TEVC). Newish winemaker Alice Tétienne continues to impress. BLANC DE BLANCS de CHARD NV; BRUT 98′

02' 08; Brut Rosé 09. Exceptional prestige CUVÉE *Hemera* 05 06 08 13'. New from AVIZE: L'Inattendu 16 18 (18 did, illogically, keep the same name). Also imperious Chard Perpetual Res Cuvée 38, now on its 6th Edition (E6).

Herbert & Co Champ ★★★ PINOT N specialist from Montagne de Reims. PN DH2 EB NV tastes a lot better than it sounds. Try 1000% PINOT N or 1000% PINOT M if in need of varietal integrity.

Hermitage N Rh ★★★→★★★★ 05' 06' 07' 09' 10' 11' 12' 13' 15' 16' 17' 18' 19' 20' 21' 22' 23' 24' (10 15 20 brilliant.) Majestic hill; mighty, mystical wine (r/w). Complex terroir, grandest, most complex SYRAH and nutty, sometimes cussed, white (MARSANNE, some ROUSSANNE), best left for 7 yrs+, decanted. Best: Alexandrins, Belle (organic), *Chapoutier (bio, magic w)*, Colombier (value), Darnaud, DELAS, Faurie (pure, last vintage 20), GUIGAL, Habrard (w), *J-L Chave* (class), PAUL JABOULET AÎNÉ (sleek), Philippe & Vincent Jaboulet (r/w), SORREL (splendid Le Gréal r, deep Les Rocoules w), Tardieu-Laurent (r/w). TAIN co-op gd (esp Gambert de Loche r, stylish VIN DE PAILLE W).

Hertz, Albert Al ★★→★★★★ 15' 17' 18' 19' Father/son team; bio. GEWURZ (Eichberg GC 18, VT 15), PINOT GR (Zinnkopflé GC 18), RIES (Eichberg), SYLVANER (Eguisheim 18), v.gd, but can be uneven. Unforgettable SGNS.

Horizon, Dom de l' Rouss ★★★ Pure expression of rugged ROUSS terroir under IGP CÔTES CATALANES from old vines nr Calce. Mar y Muntanya gd-value SYRAH; mineral, gastronomic rosé.

Hospices de Beaune C d'O Massive hype and razzmatazz surround annual charity auction of CUVÉES from Hospices' 61 ha for Beaune's hospital. Once a triumph of spectacle over substance. Now much improved. Individuals can buy as well as trade. Winemaker Ludivine Griveau doing a great job. Now organic. Quality high, prices too; it's charity. Try BEAUNE cuvées, VOLNAYS or expensive GCS, (r) CORTON, ÉCHÉZEAUX, MAZIS-CHAMBERTIN, (w) BÂTARD-MONTRACHET.

Hudelot C d'O ★★★ VIGNERON family in CÔTE DE NUITS. H-NOËLLAT (VOUGEOT) is top class, esp pure and refined, harmonious and elegant GCS ROMANÉE-ST-VIVANT, RICHEBOURG, while H-Baillet (CHAMBOLLE) is challenging with punchy reds.

Huet, Dom Lo ★★★★ Reference DOM for VOUVRAY; bio. CLOS du Bourg can be breathtaking, Le Mont tiptop, Le Haut Lieu reliable. SEC to *moelleux*, all age magnificently 02' 03 10 14' 16' 17 18' 19 20' 21 22' 23 (24). Pétillant v.gd.

Hugel & Fils Al ★★★→★★★★ Wines better than ever; famed late-harvest, esp GEWURZ RIES VT, SGN. Superb Ries Schoelhammer 10 13 17 from GC SCHOENENBOURG. Don't miss 15' Grossi Laue ("great growth") wines. Brand-new, promising 1st-time release: Ries Granit (from outstanding Engelkritt lieu-dit): 23' special. Also unforgettable, 1st VT Schoelhammer (15).

IGP (indication géographique protégée) Potentially most dynamic category in France (150+ regions), scope for experimentation. Replacing VdP, but new terminology still not accepted by every area. Zonal names most individual, eg. CÔTES DE GASCOGNE, Côtes de Thongue, Pays des Cévennes, Haute Vallée de l'Orb, among others. Enormous variety in taste, quality; never ceases to surprise.

Irancy Burg ★★ 17 18' 19 21 22' 23 Structured red nr CHAB made from PINOT N and more rustic local César. Beware hot, dry vintages. Best vyds: Mazelots, Palotte. Best: Cantin, Ferrari, GOISOT, Maison Chapelle, Renaud, Richoux.

Irouléguy SW Fr ★→★★★ 18' 19 20 22 23 Frontier AOP in Pyrénées, most remote in France. More likely to hear Basque than French. Excellent whites based on PETIT COURBU, both MANSENGS; gd reds based on Axéria (CAB FR), TANNAT. Rediscovered vines like Arrouya (Manseng N), Erremaxaoua. Best: Bordaxuria, *Brana*, ★★★ *Dom Arretxea*, Ilarria. Also v.gd co-op (Xuri w).

Jaboulet Aîné, Paul N Rh International in style and price. Grower-merchant, organic vyds at CONDRIEU, CORNAS, CÔTE-RÔTIE, CROZES-HERMITAGE, HERMITAGE,

> **Jura's topsy-turvy vintages**
> While selection and a warming climate enable gd quality each yr, Jura has
> had a roller-coaster ride in terms of volumes over the past decade. Severe
> spring frosts in 17 19 21 24 reduced quantities by 30–80%, with mildew
> adding to woes in 21 24; CHARD and Poulsard suffered most. Heatwaves
> and droughts in 18 20 22 affected fragile Poulsard, but 18 23 cheered up
> producers with gd quantity and quality.

ST-JOSEPH. Red: sleek, little local ID. Best: Hermitage ★★★★ La Chapelle
(legendary 61 78 90), some revival since 2010 on reds. Also CORNAS St-Pierre,
Crozes Thalabert (can be stylish, interesting), Roure (decent). Merchant: robust
VACQUEYRAS, VENTOUX (r, quality/value). White: neat, clear, bit low on true Rh
depth, drink most young. Costly Hermitage La Chapelle.

Jacquart Champ ★★★ Simplified range from co-op-turned-brand, focus on what it
does best: PC Côte des Blancs CHARD. Fine BLANC DE BLANCS 13' 17 19'. Rosé 12
13 14' impresses. As does CUVÉE Mosaïque 08. Villers-Marméry Blanc de Blancs
16' for essence of underrated village.

Jacquart, André Champ ★★★→★★★★ Marie Doyard's flagship is MESNIL Experience
12 13. Magic Vintage trio 18 19 20. BLANC DE BLANCS specialist, with additional
CUVÉES from AVIZE and local vyd, magnificent Chétillons. Admirable Solera too.
Fantastic location, exploited with elegance. Not far from ★★★★ now.

Jacquesson Champ ★★★★ Superlative Dizy house; precise, v. dry wines. Part of
Artemis Group. Outstanding single-vyd Avize CHAMP Caïn 09 12' 13. Corne
Bautray, all CHARD. Dizy 09 10' 12 13'. Terres Rouges 09 12 13. Innovative
numbered NV cuvées 730' *et seq* 744 745' 746 747. Focus on character of each
harvest rather than consistency yr on yr. Pioneers thus, and oft imitated. 747,
eg., based on 19. Look out for Dégorgement Tardif 7 Series too; somewhat rare.

Jadot, Louis Burg ★★→★★★ Large est BEAUNE merchant (1859): 130 ha = 200+
wines. Powerful white, wide range red. Big holdings in BEAUJ, C D'O, MÂCON incl
POUILLY-FUISSÉ (DOM Ferret), MOULIN-À-VENT (CH des Jacques); GCS gaining more
conviction, excitement. Now led by Thomas Seiter, ex-BOUCHARD PÈRE & FILS.

Jamet, Dom N Rh ★★★★ 05' 09' 10' 12 13' 14 15' 16' 17' 18' 19' 20' 21 22' 23' 24'
Jean-Paul and Corinne J craft stirring, iron-filled, fresh CÔTE-RÔTIE, v. long-lived,
packed with detail. Côte Brune (r) is imperious, smoky, mysterious, 30 yrs+.
High-quality CÔTES DU RH (r/w), COLLINES RHODANIENNES (r), also age well.

Jasmin, Dom N Rh ★★★ Small CÔTE-RÔTIE DOM; fine, consistent quality, links
to Burg, iron inflection, evolve well. Try Giroflaire. Also: Oléa (oak), gd-value
COLLINES RHODANIENNES (r/w)

Jasnières Lo ★→★★★ Wonderful insider's white AOP. Pure CHENIN BL 14' 15' 16' 18'
19 20' 22 23. Best: cool, crystalline, mineral; wines of tear-jerking beauty from
Bellivière; also Gigou, Janvier, Maisons Rouges, Roche Bleue.

Jobard C D'O ★★★ Vigneron family in MEURSAULT. Antoine J for proper Meursaults
esp long-lived CHARMES, Genevrières, Poruzots; compelling whites, incl superb
BOURGOGNE Bl, plus reds from former DOM Mussy (POMMARD). Rémi J for
immediately classy Meursaults, esp Poruzots. Valentin J impressing too.

Joguet, Charles Lo ★★→★★★★ A-list CHINON DOM, currently enjoying long
renaissance. Intense, vibrant. Top CUVÉES: CLOS du Chêne Vert, *Clos de la Dioterie*
89 03 05 09 10 15 16 18 19 20 22 (23), Varennes du Grand Clos.

Jones, Dom Rouss ★★★ Englishwoman Katie J; characterful CÔTES CATALANES,
CÔTES DU ROUSS, fragrant, gd-value FITOU. Deliciously tangy orange wine. Adopt-
an-old-vine scheme.

Josmeyer Al ★★★→★★★★ Siblings Isabelle and Celine Meyer run Wintzenheim bio
AL pioneer. Top-ten Al RIES, PINOT GR GCS Brand, Hengst 13 14 16 17' 18' 19.

Hengst Pinot Gr now macerated. Al's best AUXERROIS: "H" 21' 22'. Ries Kottabe 23 (20% declassified juice from Brand and Hengst) best ever, v. smart buy.

Juliénas Beauj ★★★ 18' 19' 20' 21 22' 23 Source of firm, dark-fruited wines, to convince those who believe BEAUJ cannot age, esp CLIMATS Beauvernay, Capitans, etc. Try Audras (CLOS de Haute Combe), Aufranc, Besson, Burrier, CH BEAUREGARD, CH FUISSÉ, DOM Granit Doré, Perrachon.

Jurançon SW Fr ★→★★★ (sw) 18 19 20 22 23 (dr) 18' 19 20 22 (23) AOP nr Pau; terraced, contoured vyds. Excellent dry based on GROS MANSENG, late-harvest sweet PETIT MANSENG. ★★★ *Camin Larredya*, *Clos Lapeyre*, Clos Larrouyat; DOMS *Cauhapé*, Guirardel. ★★ CH Jolys, CLOS Benguères; Doms Bellegarde, Bordenave, Castéra, Nigri, Uroulat. ★ Gan co-op, gd value. *See also* CABIDOS.

Kientzler, Andre Al ★★→★★★★ High-acid, pure, mineral RIES, SYLVANER; sensual GEWURZ GC Kirchberg 16 17' 18' 19 20. Also v.gd: VT and entry-level MUSCAT.

Kirrenbourg Al ★★★ Successor to much-loved Martin Schaetzel. Some great crus, given deep pockets of restaurateur owner Marc Rinaldi. Talented Samuel Tottoli (also of Hurst) makes wines. Superb GC SCHLOSSBERG 20; v.gd PINOT BL 22.

Kreydenweiss, Marc Al ★★→★★★★ Age-worthy limestone GC Moenchberg PINOT GR and black-schist Kastelberg RIES 10 17' ★★★★ 18' 19; bio for decades. Also in COSTIÈRES DE NÎMES.

Krug Champ ★★★★ Supremely prestigious deluxe house. Grande CUVÉE, *Edition 168*, based on superb 12; E169 on 13 etc.; latest E172 on 16. Grande Cuvée Rosé E25 E26 E27 E28 Vintage 98 02 04 06' 08 11; Rosé; CLOS D'AMBONNAY 95' 96 98' 00 02 06'; *Clos du Mesnil* 98 02 04 06' 08; Krug Collection 69 76' 81 85 88 89 90 95 00 08. Rich, nutty, oak-fermented; highest quality, ditto price.

Kuentz-Bas Al ★★→★★★ Organic, bio. Outstanding SYLVANER 13 15 17' 20 22'. CUVÉE Caroline GEWURZ VT, winery's most balanced, 09 12 17, though CUVÉE Jeremy SGN richer, more famous.

Labet, Dom Jura ★★→★★★ Sought-after CÔTES DU JURA organic family estate in Rotalier. Best known for vibrant single-vyd CHARDS: En Chalasse, La Bardette, Les Varrons. Natural PINOT N, Poulsard, classic VIN JAUNE.

Labranche-Laffont, Dom SW Fr ★★★→★★★★ Organic estate in same family hands since French Revolution. Now run by Christine Dupuy, 1st female winemaker in MADIRAN. Gentler, long-maceration to tame TANNAT's notorious fierce tannins. Some parcels 140 yrs+, ungrafted, pre-phylloxera.

Ladoix C d'O ★★ (r) 15' 17 18' 19' 20' 21 22' 23 (w) 14' 15 17' 18 19' 20' 21 22' 23 Lively whites (PC Grechons): Chevalier, FAIVELEY, Loichet. Juicy red (PC Joyeuses): Capitain-Gagnerot, CH DE MEURSAULT, Mallard, Naudin-Ferrand, Ravaut.

Lafage, Dom Rouss ★★→★★★ Jean-Marc L, 7th-generation VIGNERON, gd winemaker, marketeer. Impressive, consistent range from ROUSS. AOP/IGP. Centenaire (w), Fundació (r), Miraflors (rosé) standout.

Lafarge, Michel Burg ★★★ VOLNAY bio estate run by Frédéric L, now joined by daughters Clothilde, Eléonore. PCS CLOS du CH des Ducs, Clos des Chênes. Also fine: BEAUNE (w Clos des Aigrots, r Grèves). FLEURIE project, Lafarge-Vial. Wines delightful in youth, but close down, time needed.

Lafon, Dom des Comtes Burg ★★★→★★★★ Celebrated bio MEURSAULT DOM now run by cousins Léa L and Pierre L. PCS Genevrières, Perrières; GC MONTRACHET. VOLNAY *Santenots* one of CÔTE DE BEAUNE's best reds. Try Dominique L's own label for BEAUNE, Volnay, Meursault. Also Héritiers du Comte L from Mâconnais.

Lafond Roc-Epine, Dom S Rh ★★★ Prominent LIRAC, TAVEL name; organic, bio, gd drive, fruit in expressive wines. Tavel La Relève rosé (low sulphur) high interest, gd Lirac (r/w), CHÂTEAUNEUF (r) *vin de terroir*.

Laguiche, Marquis de C d'O ★★★→★★★★ Largest owner of LE MONTRACHET (2 ha/one-quarter) and a fine PC CHASSAGNE, both made for yrs by DROUHIN.

Lahaye, Benoît Champ ★★★ Cerebral bio producer; GC Bouzy. *Cuvée Violaine* 12 13 15 18 19; Le Jardin de La Grosse Père 13 15 17 18'. Quintessence of PINOT N CHAMP. Flagship BLANC DE NOIRS Extra BRUT NV. Fascinating Rosé de Maceration and, counterintuitively, wonderfully rich BLANC DE BLANCS.

Lalande de Pomerol Bx ★★→★★★ 16 18 19 20 22 23 Satellite neighbour of POM; similar but less depth, class; value. Largely MERLOT planted in communes of L de P and Néac. Top CHX: Ame de Musset, Annereaux, Chambrun, Enclos de Viaud, Garraud, Grand Ormeau, Haut-Chaigneau, Jean de Gué, La Chenade, LA FLEUR DE BOÜARD, La Sergue, Les Cruzelles, *Les Hauts Conseillants*, Pavillon Beauregard, Sabines, Samion, Siaurac, *Tournefeuille*.

Lallier Champ ★★★→★★★★ Artisan CHAMP from GC AŸ. Black Label R 14' 15 16 19. Lovely Oger CHARD too. Interesting parcels, Les Sous and Loridon, BLANC DE BLANCS/NOIRS. Collection Memoire 08 10' 12 14. Owned by Campari group. Dynamic chef de CAVE Dominique Demarville. On way up.

Lamy C d'O ★★★ DOM Hubert L, now run by Olivier L, for matchless ST-AUBIN. Breathtakingly fresh, concentrated whites, tense and reserved, often from higher-density plantings. Worth decanting. Fastidious viticulture. Also L-Caillat (intense w) and don't ignore L-Pillot in CHASSAGNE.

Landron, Jo Lo ★★→★★★ Ever-popular MUSCADET vigneron, has organic DOM and best moustache in Lo V. Top: *Fief du Breil* 14' 15 16 17 18 20 23, prototype for La Haye-Fouassière cru. Classy, classic; worth trying.

Langlade Ldoc ★★★★ Retired doctor Elizabeth van der Bent makes extraordinary, age-worthy AOP LDOC: depth yet delicacy from 3.5-ha DOM w of Nîmes.

Languedoc Largest wine region in France, from Nîmes towards Perpignan, inland to Carcassonne and LIMOUX. AOP covers much of region; specific terroirs allowed to append name: CABRIÈRES, GRÈS DE MONTPELLIET, PÉZENAS, Quatourze, St-Georges d'Orques, St-Saturnin. Other AOPs incl FAUGÈRES, FITOU, MINERVOIS, ST-CHINIAN. CLAIRETTE du LDOC tiny AOP for white, Malpère. Top of hierarchy: crus incl CORBIÈRES-Boutenac, Minervois la Livinière, PIC ST-LOUP, LA CLAPE, TERRASSES DU LARZAC. Usual Ldoc grapes: (r) CARIGNAN, CINSAULT, GRENACHE, MOURVÈDRE, SYRAH; (w) GRENACHE BL, ROUSSANNE, VERMENTINO, but many others. IGP d'Oc covers whole region, regional IGPs too, source of quaffers and gd-quality, quirky wine from producers who don't follow AOP rules. (*See also* box, below.)

Lanson Champ ★★★ Major house, owned by BCC. Black Label NV, Le Vintage BRUT on a roll 02 08 12 13 14', Rosé NV. Prestige NV Noble CUVÉE BLANC DE BLANCS, Rosé, Vintage 98 02 04. Single-vyd Brut Vintage CLOS Lanson 06' 07 08 09 12. Now some malo: rounder style. Extra Age series esp gd.

Lapierre, Marcel Beauj ★★★ Mathieu and Camille L in vanguard of sulphur-free movement. Magnificent when on song, age-worthy. CUVÉES of BEAUJ, MORGON.

Languedoc value

This region does gd-value, everyday wines v. well. Expect labelling by variety, don't expect a sense of place. Mid-top ranges offer low yields, often old vines; intensity, complexity, conjure up warm sun, hot stones, wild herbs, rugged landscape. Large AOPs offer lots of choice. MINERVOIS: DOMS Pierre Cros, PIERRE FIL; in La Livinière, CHX Eulalie, Cesseras (COUDOULET), Maris. CORBIÈRES: Boutenac, top terroir for old-vine CARIGNAN, Chx CARAGUILHES, OLLIEUX ROMANIS, Voulte-Garparets, also co-op Castelmaure. ST-CHINIAN: cru Berlou on schist, eg. Doms Navarre, Rimbert, co-op Roquebrun. For white: LA CLAPE, salty/mineral BOURBOULENC, eg. Chx PECH REDON, ROUQUETTE-SUR-MER. Don't forget fizz: LIMOUX, eg. MAISON ANTECH vintage BLANQUETTE is class.

Laplace family SW Fr Oldest and at one time only producer of MADIRAN. Still at top. Best wine ★★★ *Ch d'Aydie*, needs time. Odie d'Aydie less so. Beautifully polished, less extracted than before; ★ Les Deux Vaches easy intro to TANNAT, lighter, rounder. Excellent ★★★ PACHERENCS (dr/sw). Sweet fortified Maydie (think BANYULS) gd with chocolate. Also gd-value IGP.

Larmandier, Guy Champ ★★★ Epitome of BLANC DE BLANCS elegance. Based in Vertus, but best wine GC Cramant. Also excellent CUVÉES Perlée, Signe François **07** 10 11' 12. Vertus PC well worth a look; trad, reliable.

Larmandier-Bernier Champ ★★★★ Exemplary CHARD-dominated range from Côtes des Blancs. Longitude and Latitude magnificent BLANCS DE BLANCS. Zero-dosed Terre de Vertus **12** 13 14' 15 16 18, great value; renamed *Vieille Vigne du Levant* (was du Cramant) **08** 10 12 13 14' 15 16, merely great. Pierre and Sophie a formidable team; Arthur, Geirges primed and ready.

Laroche Chab ★★→★★★ Major player in CHAB with quality St Martin blend, Vieille Voye special CUVÉE, Rés de l'Obédience made from exacting selection of GC Blanchots, named after historic HQ. Winemaker Grégory Viennois involved in NÉGOCIANT IRANCY project. Also Mas La Chevalière in LDOC.

Lascaux, Ch de Ldoc ★★→★★★ PIC ST-LOUP bio dom, 15th generation: (w) Les Pierres d'Argent, taut, fragrant; (r) La Carra, powerful, brimming with terroir.

Latour, Louis Burg ★★→★★★ Eléonore L now vice president of trad BEAUNE merchant. Rich, age-worthy CORTON-CHARLEMAGNE, far superior to other whites. Also Mâconnais, ARDÈCHE (all CHARD). Reds improved: GCS (CORTON, ROMANÉE-ST-VIVANT) deliver occasional splendour. Also Henry Fessy in BEAUJ.

Soil contains 2–3 times more carbon than atmosphere – huge carbon dioxide storage potential.

Latricières-Chambertin C d'O ★★★★ 99' 05' 09' 10' 12' 15' 16 17 18' 19' 20' 21 22' 23 A GC next to CHAMBERTIN. Deep soil, cooler site give structured, meaty wines in warm dry yrs. Best: ARNOUX-LACHAUX, BIZE, Drouhin-Laroze, Duband, DUROCHÉ, FAIVELEY, LEROY, Remy, ROSSIGNOL-TRAPET, TRAPET.

Laudun S Rh ★→★★ 22' 23 24' Now aop, ex-CÔTES DU RH-VILLAGE, in 2024, hmm, not sure, low choice of DOMS. 30% white, v. high for region, and gd, interesting, drink-young wines, led by GRENACHE BL, CLAIRETTE. Red-fruit, spiced reds, much SYRAH, bright rosés. Immediate flavours from Maison Sinnae co-op (was Laudun-CHUSCLAN). DOM Pelaquié best, esp engaging white. Also CHX Courac, de Bord; Doms Carmélisa (ex-footballer), Duseigneur (bio), Maravilhas (bio, character), Olibrius (tiny).

Laureau, Damien Lo ★★→★★★★ New-wave SAVENNIÈRES. Top: *Roche-aux-Moines* **09** 10 14' 15' 16' 18 20, one of best. Classic Bel Ouvrage, Les Genêts. New Chambourcier worth a pop if you're feeling flash.

Laurens, Dom SW Fr ★★★→★★★★ Leading light of MARCILLAC AOP. Single parcels based on Mansois (FER SERVADOU): Claus d'Ifer, La Bruyère Le Dernier Lion.

Laurent-Perrier Champ ★★★→★★★★ Important house. BRUT NV (CHARD-led) perfect apéritif; v.gd skin-contact Rosé. Fine **08** 12' 14 15. Grand Siècle multi-vintage on form, now released as a numbered "Iteration"; latest I 26 and I 24 in magnum. Peerless *Alexandra Rosé* 98 04 12. Interesting new Héritage, res from 4 yrs, youngest 19. Also owns DELAMOTTE, SALON.

Lavantureux Chab ★★→★★★ Specialist source for PETIT CHAB, CHAB, esp single-vyd Vauprin. Also PC Vau de Vey. BOURGOGNE Epineuil reds from 19 look brilliant.

Leccia, Yves Cors ★★★→★★★★ Small bio DOM. Thrilling; intense, precise fruit rather than oak. AOP PATRIMONIO El Croce, YL range IGP Île de Beauté.

Leclapart, David Champ ★★★★ High priest of bio, based in Trépail, CHARD stronghold in Montagne. Barrel-fermented, oak sourced at LEFLAIVE; min sulphur, mainly zero dosage. *L'Artiste Blanc de Blancs* 12 13 18 19. Other inspired names (and wines): L'Amateur, L'Aphrodisiaque, L'Apôtre, L'Astre.

Leclerc Briant Champ ★★★→★★★★ Impressive Épernay house, bio, guided by guru Hervé Jestin. Excels at every level. Note: NV BRUT Rés, deep-sea-matured Abyss 15 16 17 18 19', Le CLOS des Trois Clochers 15 16, intriguing oak-aged Blanc de MEUNIERS 13 16 18 (last three zero dosage). CH D'AVIZE, also BRUT ZERO.

Leflaive, Dom Burg ★★★→★★★★ Legendary PULIGNY-MONTRACHET DOM, back on form since 17. Poise, precision. High prices. Outstanding GCS incl CHEVALIER, MONTRACHET; *fabulous PCs* Combettes, Folatières, Pucelles, etc. When on song, none better. Try S Burg range. Beware premoxed older yrs, esp in auction.

Leflaive, Olivier C d'O ★★★ White specialist NÉGOCIANT at PULIGNY-M. Outstanding BOURGOGNE Les Sétilles and all levels up to own GC vyds. Reds improving. Also La Maison d'Olivier, classy hotel, restaurant, tasting room, vyd tours. Real style.

Lendemain, Dom du Rouss ★★★ Mireille Ribière herbalist, vigneronne since 2018, works astonishingly old vines. CÔTES CATALANES (w) Jeunes Pousses, intense, delicate Grenache Gr. Genese, top CARIGNAN. Lovely dry MUSCAT.

Leprince Burg ★★→★★★★ Marvellous, entry-level ALIGOTÉ is Frédéric L's calling card, perky-fruity masterclass in what can be achieved with this grape. Numerous other delights in range too. Try VOSNE, GEVREY-CHAMBERTIN.

Leroux, Benjamin C d'O ★★★ BEAUNE-based NÉGOCIANT equally at home in red or white; C D'O only, strengths (w) in MEURSAULT with increasing DOM and (r) BLAGNY, GEVREY, VOLNAY. Rock-solid consistency. Subtle labels signify subtle wines. Experimenting with glass globes in cellar. A sure buy.

Leroy, Dom C d'O ★★★★ Lalou Bize L, bio pioneer, delivers extraordinary reds, more impressive than charming, from tiny yields in VOSNE and from DOM d'Auvenay (more w). Ludicrously expensive even ex-dom, as is amazing trove of mature wines from family NÉGOCIANT Maison L. Collector territory.

Leroy, Richard Lo ★★★★ Long live Le Roi. Inspirational ANJOU vigneron, in VDF since 2008. *Les Noëls de Montbenault*, *Les Rouliers* both outstanding, hugely desirable. Prices reflect this, but you won't be disappointed.

Liger-Belair, Comte C d'O ★★★★ Comte Louis-Michel L-B makes brilliantly ethereal wines in VOSNE; ever-increasing stable headed by fabulous MONOPOLE LA ROMANÉE. Recent additions: GCS CLOS DE VOUGEOT, ÉCHÉZEAUX, GRANDS-ÉCHÉZEAUX. New La Cuverie wine bar (eclectic selection), guest rooms.

Liger-Belair, Thibault C d'O ★★★→★★★★ Succulent bio burg from generics up to Les St-Georges (could someday be upgraded to GC), GC RICHEBOURG. Outstanding ALIGOTÉ. Also stellar old-vine, single-vyd MOULIN-À-VENT. Thibault talks the talk, his wines walk the walk. Splendid eco-friendly winery.

Lignier C d'O ★★★ Family in MOREY-ST-DENIS. Understated and stylish, from Laurent L (DOM Hubert L), esp CLOS DE LA ROCHE; v.gd PCS from Virgile L-Michelot, esp Faconnières. Fresh, bordering on austere, from Dom Georges L.

Limoux Ldoc ★★★ Coolest part of LDOC, nr Carcassonne, AOPS for (r/w/sp). Cradle of fizz since 1544: gd-value, appley BLANQUETTE (aka MAUZAC) de Limoux, also CRÉMANT, more CHARD, CHENIN. Méthode Ancestrale is original pét-nat. Don't miss stylish still white AOP Limoux (CHARD, CHENIN BL, Mauzac), must be barrel-aged. Red AOP: MERLOT, plus SYRAH, GRENACHE, Cabs. PINOT N in Crémant and for IGP Haute Vallée de l'Aude. Try CHX de Gaure, Rives-Blanques; DOMS de Baronarques, Begude, de Fourn, de l'Aigle, de Mouscaillo, GARRABOU; J Laurens, J-L Denois, MAISON ANTECH, Plô Roucarels, VIGNOBLE Nicolas Therez.

Liquière, Ch de la Ldoc ★★★ AOP FAUGÈRES, family estate, never disappoints. Les Amandières (r/w/rosé) terrific value. Cistus old vines (r/w). Malpas top SYRAH. Les Racines (w) racy blend of five LDOC grapes.

Lirac S Rh ★★→★★★ 19' 20 22' 23 24' Four villages opposite CHÂTEAUNEUF, gd stony terroir. Upbeat, savoury, spiced red (6 yrs+), boost from Châteauneuf owners: clear fruit, brio. Reds best. Try CHX Boucarut (organic, revived), de Bouchassy (gd w), de Manissy (organic, bio), DE MONTFAUCON (brilliant CLAIRETTE w, incl CÔTES DU RH), Mont-Redon, St-Roch; DOMS Anglore (low sulphur), Carabiniers (bio), *de la Mordorée* (organic, best w, storming Reine des Bois r), Giraud, Joncier/Mont-Redon (bio), LAFOND ROC-EPINE (organic, bio), La Lôyane, La Rocalière (bio, gd fruit), Maby (Fermade, gd w), Maravilhas (bio), MARCOUX (stylish), Plateau des Chênes (swell); CLOS DU MONT-OLIVET, Famille P Usseglio, Mas Isabelle (handmade), Rocca Maura (esp w), R Sabon. Whites freshness, depth, go 6 yrs. Table rosés gd: Romain le Bars (character).

Listrac-Médoc H-Méd ★★→★★★ 16′ 18 19 20 22 23 Much-improved AOP for savoury red BX; now more fruit, depth and MERLOT due to clay soils. Also gd whites under AOP Bx (Le Cygne de Ch Fonréaud). Best CHX: Cap Léon Veyrin, CLARKE, FONRÉAUD, FOURCAS-DUPRÉ, FOURCAS-HOSTEN, Lafon, l'Ermitage, LESTAGE, MAYNE-LALANDE, Reverdi, SARANSOT-DUPRÉ.

Long-Depaquit Chab ★★★ BICHOT-owned CHAB DOM with famous flagship brand, GC La Moutonne. Much recent improvement, well worth trying. Value.

Lorentz, Gustave Al ★★→★★★ Bergheim grower-merchant; approachable, easy-going wines: v.gd RIES GC Altenberg de Bergheim 12 13 14 16 18 19. Best: VT, SGN (esp *Gewurz*).

Lorenzon Burg ★★→★★★ Bruno L (not dissimilar to George Orwell in looks) is maestro of MERCUREY. Practises meticulous viticulture based on high-trained vines, high-density planting, self-described as *un travail de haute couture*. Intensely flavoured wines, rare delicacy for CÔTE CHALONNAISE.

Lorgeril, Vignobles Ldoc ★★★ Family estates based at 400-yr-old CH Pennautier nr Carcassonne. Poised, gd-value CABARDÈS; classy Ch de Ciffre FAUGÈRES; gd Borie Blanche MINERVOIS LA LIVINIÈRE (r).

Loupiac Bx ★★ 17 18 19 22 23 Minor SÉM-dominant *liquoreux*. Lighter, fresher than SAUT. Some can age. Top CHX: CLOS Jean, *Dauphiné-Rondillon*, *de Ricaud*, du Cros, Les Roques, *Loupiac-Gaudiet*, Noble.

Luberon S Rh ★→★★ 23 24 Hilly, arid tourist region; terroir can be *ordinaire*. Technical oaked wines a pity, but young incomers making gd VDF (Alexandre Dalet, DOM des Passages, Laura Aillaud). SYRAH lead role, brisk fruit. Whites improving. Bright star: CH de la Canorgue (organic). Also gd: Chx Clapier, Edem, Fontvert (bio, gd w), La Verrerie, Puy des Arts (w), Ravoire, St-Estève de Neri (improving); Doms de la Citadelle (organic), Fontenille (organic), La Cavale, Le Novi (terroir), Marrenon, Maslauris (organic), Val-Joanis; top-quality/value La Vieille Ferme (w/rosé) from Famille Perrin.

Luneau-Papin, Dom Lo ★★★★ Much-loved MUSCADET DOM, only improved in recent yrs under Pierre-Marie and Marie L. Tighter range, small-volume site-specific CUVÉES. All will delight, but *L d'Or* 02′ 05 07′ 10 12′ 14 16 19 20 23 is a classic.

Lussac-St-Émilion Bx ★★ 19 20 22 23 Most n of ST-ÉM satellites; lightest in style. Top CHX: Barbe Blanche, Bellevue, Courlat, Croix de Rambeau, DE LUSSAC, des Landes, La Rose-Perrière, Le Rival, LYONNAT, Mayne-Blanc.

Macle, Dom Jura ★★★ Legendary producer of CH-CHALON VIN JAUNE for long ageing. Also expanding range of CÔTES DU JURA CHARD-dominated whites, plus supreme MACVIN.

Mâcon-Villages Burg ★★→★★★ 17′ 18 19′ 20′ 21 22′ 23 Chief appellation for Mâconnais whites. Individual villages may also use own names, eg. Mâcon-Lugny. Co-ops at Lugny, Terres Secrètes, Viré for value, plus *brilliant grower wines* from Guffens-Heynen, Guillot, Guillot-Broux, Maillet, Merlin, Paquet and C D'o-based DOMS BOILLOT (J-M), LAFON, LEFLAIVE. Also major NÉGOCIANTS DROUHIN, LATOUR, etc. Image spruced up in recent years. Worth exploring.

Macvin Jura AOP, not Scottish. Grape juice fortified by oak-matured local marc to make apéritif (s/sw) or dessert wine of 16–18% abv. Usually white, can be red or rosé. Best by far are organic.

Madeloc, Dom Rouss ★★★★ Grower in N Rh; Pierre Gaillard's deft touch evident in top COLLIOURE DOM, works with daughter Elise. Sarral (r) masterclass in GRENACHE. Penya (w, Grenache Gr/Rolle), no less fine.

Madiran SW Fr ★★→★★★★ 15' 16 18 19 20 22 (23) Gascon AOP, France's home of TANNAT grape. Worthy reds in range of styles with many keepers. Look for ★★★ CHX BOUSCASSÉ, **Montus** (owner BRUMONT has 15% entire AOP), Laffitte-Teston, **Laplace**. Wide ranges from ★★★ Chx Arricaud-Bordès, de Gayon; DOMS Berthoumieu, Capmartin, Damiens, Dou Bernés, **Labranche-Laffont**, Laffont, **Pichard**; CLOS Basté. Doms ★★ Barréjat, ★★ Crampilh, Maouries not far behind. Laougue is new kid and looking gd.

Magnon, Maxime Ldoc ★★→★★★ Farms steep, high vyds in rugged CORBIÈRES; Burg native; bio. Rozeta (r), fruit-bomb with elegance, spice. Unfashionably dark, delicious Métisse rosé.

Mailly Grand Cru Champ ★★★→★★★★ Top co-op, all GC grapes. Prestige **Cuvée des Echansons** 08 09 12 13' for long ageing. Sumptuous Echansons Rosé 12 13 14 16 18; refined, classy L'Intemporelle 15 16 18; v. reliable EXTRA BRUT Millésimé 18' 19. Sébastien Moncuit, cellarmaster since 14, a real talent. New Poétique de la Terre BLANC DE NOIRS Variation VIII. Incredibly well run by Xavier Millard.

Mann, Albert Al ★★→★★★★ Barthélmé family-owned Wettolsheim bio estate; son Antoine back after work at Rippon, DOM LEFLAIVE, Georges NOELLAT. Pure GCS HENGST, SCHLOSSBERG (esp 17' 20'), RIES Epicentre (unforgettable 22'). One of AL's two best PINOT N producers (Les Stes Claires 15 18' 19; Grand H 22). Amazing MUSCAT VT 19, refined GC Steingrubler GEWURZ 22.

Visiting Burgundy? Check Cité des Vins: Chablis, Beaune and Mâcon.

Maranges C d'O ★★→★★★ 17 18' 19' 20' 21 22' 23 Ever-improving name to watch. Robust well-priced reds from s end of CÔTE DE BEAUNE, age well. Try PCS Boutière, CLOS Roussots, Croix Moines, Fussière. Best: BACHELET-Monnot, Cassiopée, **Charleux**, CHEVROT, Giroud, MATROT, Rouges Queues.

Marchand-Tawse C d'O ★★★ Grower-NÉGOCE in NUITS. Pascal M shows deft touch across wide range. Style previously hearty, robust. More refined, elegant now. Minute production of sublime MUSIGNY. (Incorporates DOM Maume.)

Marcillac SW Fr ★★ 19 20 22 (23) Aveyron AOP based on Mansois (aka FER SERVADOU). Stunning valley, terraced vyds, alt 500m+ (1640ft+). Medium-bodied, modest alc, spicy reds, great freshness. Brilliant with food, esp charcuterie, cheese and of course **aligot** (mashed potato, garlic, an unhealthy amount of cheese). Obscure but worth seeking out. ★★ **Dom du Cros** largest independent grower (gd w IGPS too), also DOMS des Boissières, des Costes Rouges, **Laurens**, Le Mioula. Excellent co-op. Recent heatwave vintages outstanding.

Marcoux, Dom de S Rh ★★★ The 1st bio CHÂTEAUNEUF, quality with style: broadly fruited classic red; sustained, impressive VIEILLES VIGNES (1900 GRENACHE, sand-clay). Elegant, textured white; gd, forthright LIRAC La Lorentine (r).

Margaux H-Méd ★★★→★★★★ 14 15 16' 18 19' 20' 22' 23 Most s MÉD communal AOP. Famous for elegance, fragrance; reality more diverse. Top: BRANE-CANTENAC, DURFORT-VIVENS, FERRIÈRE, GISCOURS, ISSAN, KIRWAN, LASCOMBES, MALESCOT ST EXUPÉRY, MARGAUX, PALMER, PRIEURÉ-LICHINE, RAUZAN-SÉGLA. Value: ANGLUDET, Arsac, Deyrem Valentin, LABÉGORCE, LA TOUR DE MONS, Paveil de Luze, SIRAN.

Marionnet, Henry Lo ★★→★★★ 20' 21 22' 23 TOURAINE DOM, eclectic range. **Provignage** from pre-phylloxera Romorantin gd but pricy. GAMAY CUVÉES Les CÉPAGES Oubliées, Première Vendange wonderfully dark, juicy.

Maris, Ch Ldoc ★★★ Opulent polished wines, cool eco winery in MINERVOIS La Livinière; bio. SYRAH-dominant Les Amandiers, Les Anciens CARIGNAN.

Marsannay C d'O ★★→★★★ (r) 15' 17 18' 19' 20 21 22' 23 Most n AOP of CÔTE DE NUITS. PCs in (long) pipeline (eg. CHAMP Salomon, CLOS du Roy, Longeroies). Further village-level vyds added in 2019, eg. Le Chapitre. Satisfying, mildly rustic, fruit-laden reds, from energetic producers: AUDOIN, Bart, Bouvier, CHARLOPIN, CH de M, CLAIR, Derey, Fournier, *Pataille*; gd unfashionable rosé needs 1–2 yrs; whites getting better. Reputation still lags behind burgeoning quality.

Mas, Doms Paul Ldoc ★★→★★★ Jean-Claude M owns/manages 2400 ha in LDOC-ROUSS. Working on bio, low sulphur. IGP GD value, canny marketing with different labels for export: Arrogant Frog, Astelia, Côté Mas, La Forge, Les Tannes, Les VIGNES de Nicole. Owns Crès Ricards in TERRASSES DU LARZAC, Martinolles in LIMOUX; CHX Lauriga in ROUSS, Capendu in CORBIÈRES, Villegly in MINERVOIS.

Mas Amiel Rouss ★★★→★★★★ Leading MAURY, Côtes du ROUSS, IGP. Look for Altaïr (w), Origine, Vers le Nord, Vol de Nuit from v. old CARIGNAN/GRENACHE, others. Plus excellent VDN from young, fruity *grenat*, to venerable RANCIO 20–40-yr-old Maury aged in 60-litre glass demijohns, intensely sweet and savoury. Sublime.

Mas de Daumas Gassac Ldoc ★★★→★★★★ Pioneer in LDOC in 1978, now 2nd-generation Samuel Guibert. Famed for CAB SAUV-based age-worthy reds. Perfumed white from CHENIN BL blend arguably better; super-CUVÉE Émile Peynaud (r); rosé Frizant; v.gd Vin de Laurence (sw MUSCAT/SERCIAL).

Mas de Libian S Rh ★★★ Exemplary bio CÔTES du RH, VDF S ARDÈCHE. Mainly GRENACHE (r) with energy, flair. Try Khayyâm, La Calade (MOURVÈDRE). gd white.

Mas du Novi Ldoc ★★★ Once part of Cistercian abbey, now leading light in GRÉS DE MONTPELLIER; bio. Powerful Ô de Novi, Prestigi (r). Masterful SYRAH/ VIOGNIER N de Novi. Stylish IGP CHARD.

The Médoc had more Malbec planted than Cabernet Sauvignon in 1855.

Mas Jullien Ldoc ★★★★ Olivier J leader in TERRASSES DU LARZAC: outstanding Lous Rougeos (LDOC varieties at 400m/1312ft). Autour de Jonquières (MOURVÈDRE/ CARIGNAN); Carlan, États d'Âme. Sublime, mineral CARIGNAN BL (w).

Mas Llossanes Rouss ★★★ Highest vyds in ROUSS (700m/2297ft): fresh, elegant. Pure SYRAH, Pur CARIGNAN, super varietal expression; Au Dolmen, Dotrera gd red blends; Pur Chasan (w) perhaps most thrilling of all. IGP CÔTES CATALANES,

Mas Rouge, Dom du Ldoc ★★★ Next to Med, nr Montpellier. Seductive, fragrant MUSCAT VDN from both Frontignan and Miraval, latter elegant, fresh.

Mas Sibert Ldoc ★★★★ Tiny bio DOM, Swiss winemaker. Unfiltered/unfined VDF from un-LDOC grapes ALBARIÑO, PETITE ARVINE, MERLOT, PETIT VERDOT. Saramon dark rosé, SANGIOVESE-based, v.gd. Playful, pink, pét-nat 20 Ans dans la Bulle.

Massif d'Uchaux S Rh ★★ 22' 23 Superior CÔTES DU RH-VILLAGE, intimate pine-tree vyds, crisply fruited, spiced reds, not easy to sell, but best truthful, stylish. Note CH St-Estève (incl gd old-vine VIOGNIER), DOMS *Cros de la Mûre* (character, gd value), de la Guicharde, La Cabotte (bio, on great form), Renjarde (swell fruit).

Matrot Burg ★★★ Since sisters Elsa and Adèle took over, quality, consistency soared at MEURSAULT DOM. Vigorous but civil flavours. Equally gd in red (BLAGNY, VOLNAY Santenots) and white (Meursault Blagny, Charmes, Les Perrières; PULIGNY PCs). Name to watch, on gd trajectory. Prices not wild, in context of C D'O.

Maury Rouss ★★→★★★ Village beneath Cathar Castle Quéribus, gives name to two distinct AOPs. Sweet VDN from GRENACHES N/BL/Gr (on island of schist, ambré, tuilé) and RANCIO. Maury SEC is dry red. MAS AMIEL leader for both styles; CH de l'Ou; DOMS FONTANEL, de Lavail, des Soulanes, LAFAGE, of the Bee, Pouderoux; Maury co-op.

Mazis- (or Mazy-) Chambertin C d'O ★★★★ 93 96' 99' 05' 09' 10' 12' 15' 16' 17 18

19' 20' 21 22' 23 GEVREY-CHAMBERTIN GC, top class in upper part; intense, heavenly wines, reward keeping. Best: Bernstein, DUGAT-PY, FAIVELEY, HOSPICES DE BEAUNE, LEROY, MARCHAND-TAWSE, MORTET, REBOURSEAU, ROUSSEAU.

Mazoyères-Chambertin C d'O ★★★★ Usually sold as CHARMES-CHAMBERTIN, hence below radar, but style is different: less succulence, more stony structure. Try DUGAT-PY, MARCHAND-TAWSE, MORTET, Perrot-Minot, Taupenot-Merme.

Médoc Bx ★★ 18 19 20 22 23 AOP for reds in n part of Méd peninsula (whites in pipeline). Sturdy, savoury. Lots of CRUS BOURGEOIS. Can be gd value; be selective. Top CHX: Castera, CLOS Manou, d'Escurac, Fleur La Mothe, GREYSAC, La Cardonne, *La Tour-de-By*, LES ORMES-SORBET, LOUDENNE (Le Ch) Lousteauneuf, *Patache d'Aux*, POITEVIN, *Potensac*, PREUILLAC, Ramafort, *Rollan-de-By* (HAUT-CONDISSAS), TOUR HAUT-CAUSSAN, Tour Séran, Vieux Robin.

Meffre, Gabriel S Rh ★★→★★★ A gd merchant; owns GIGONDAS DOM Longue Toque (top Hommage GM, gd VACQUEYRAS r). Clearer fruit, less oak. CHÂTEAUNEUF (incl small doms), VACQUEYRAS St-Barthélemy. Reliable-to-gd oaked Laurus range, esp HERMITAGE (w), ST-JOSEPH (r).

Mellot, Alphonse Lo ★★→★★★★ Big SANCERRE name; bio. Top white *Edmond* 14' 15 16' 17 18 19 20 21 22 (23) proves SAUV BL can age. Large portfolio, incl La Moussière. Reds (En Grands Champs), some of Sancerre's best.

Menard, Pierre Lo ★★→★★★ ANJOU star; new-wave ANJOU BL, electric definition, purity. *Le Clos des Mailles* 16 17 18 19 20 (21) (22) (23), plus La Varenne de Chanzé, Le Quarts des Noëls, Pluton. COTEAUX DU LAYONS Chaos, Cosmos.

Menetou-Salon Lo ★★→★★★ 16 20' 21 22 23 AOP for SAUV BL and PINOT N from limestone; SANCERRE lookalikes, often better value (and better quality too). Try Gilbert, Henry Pellé, La Tour St-Martin, Teiller.

Méo-Camuzet C d'O ★★★★ Noted VOSNE DOM: icons Brûlées, CROS PARANTOUX, RICHEBOURG. Value from M-C Frère & Soeur (NÉGOCIANT). Full, dense, magnificent with age. Interesting HAUTES-COTES (w) CLOS St-Philibert.

Mercurey Burg ★★→★★★ 15' 17 18' 19' 20' 21 22' 23 Major CÔTE CHALONNAISE village. Reds hearty to harmonious; aromatic white. Try BICHOT, Champs de l'Abbaye, *Ch de Chamirey (esp Clos du Roi)*, CH Philippe Le Hardi, DOM de Suremain, FAIVELEY, Génot-Boulanger, *Juillot-Theulot*, LORENZON, M Juillot, Raquillet.

Merlin Burg ★★→★★★ Olivier M, wizard of the Mâconnais, plus sons. Top: MÂCON La Roche Vineuse Les Cras, expanding POUILLY-FUISSÉ range, MOULIN-À-VENT La Rochelle. Lovely 21s. Co-owner CH des Quarts with Dominique LAFON.

Mesclances, Ch les Prov ★★★ Farmed by same family since C16, delicious rosé from La Londe, terroir of CÔTES DE PROV. Try GRENACHE DOM St Honorat; Faustine more ambitious, needs food. Silky reds too.

Mesnil-sur-Oger, Le Champ Top Côte des Blancs village, v. long-lived CHARD: ANDRÉ JACQUART, JL Vergnon, PIERRE PÉTERS, not forgetting eponymous co-op with grape contracts to die for. Needs 10 yrs+ ageing. Top named vyd Les Chétillons.

Méthode champenoise Champ The trad method of putting bubbles into CHAMP by re-fermenting in the bottle. Outside Champ region, makers must use terms "classic method" or *méthode traditionnelle*.

Meunier-Centernach, Dom Paul Rouss ★★★→★★★★ Organic, horse instead of tractor, low-intervention wines vinified in old co-op. Chorèmes CÔTES DU ROUSS: (w) haunting Grenache Gr, MACCABEO; (r) CARIGNAN, perfumed, silky. Falguayra MAURY Grenat VDN.

Meursault C d'O ★★★→★★★★ 09' 10' 12 14' 15 17' 18 19' 20' 21' 22' 23 Potentially great full-bodied whites from PCS: Charmes, Genevrières, Perrières, more perky from hillside vyds Narvaux, Tesson, Tillets. Try Ballot-Millot, BOILLOT, Boisson-Vadot, BOUZEREAU, *Ch de Meursault*, COCHE-DURY, *de Montille*, Ente, F COCHE, Fichet, *Girardin*, Javillier, JOBARD, *Lafon*, *Latour-Giraud*, LEROUX,

Matrot, Michelot, *Mikulski*, P Morey, PRIEUR, Rougeot, *Roulot*. Also de Cherisey for Meursault-BLAGNY.

Meursault, Ch de C d'O ★★★ A 67-ha bio estate, CH restored; once-sleepy name now buzzing with vitality. Tasty reds: BEAUNE, POMMARD, VOLNAY. Some stunning whites: MEURSAULT. BOURGOGNE Bl, PULIGNY PC v.gd. Try long-aged Marc. Major biodiversity plantings. Visitor-friendly. Also CH de MARSANNAY.

Milhau-Lacugue, Ch Ldoc ★★★ Jean L makes joyously fruity, herb-scented ST-CHINIAN from 60 ha nr Beziers. CUVÉE Magali, gd value; Les Truffières, savoury, autumnal. IGP VERMENTINO, bargain.

Minervois Ldoc ★★→★★★ Undulating AOP; gently fruity, herbal red from SYRAH, GRENACHE, MOURVÈDRE, CARIGNAN. Some stylish white, rosé: CHX Coupe-Roses, d'Agel, Donjon, de Homs, Gourgazaud, Guery, La Grave, La Tour Boisée, Oupia, Paumarhel, St-Jacques d'Albas, Senat, Villermain-Julien; DOM A Gros & J-P Tollot; Abbaye de Tholomiès, Borie-de-Maurel, CAILHOL-GAUTRAN, CLOS Centeille; Laville-Bertrou, Pierre Cros, PIERRE FIL. La Livinière cru, fine, long-lived red: Clos d'Ora (GÉRARD BERTRAND), Combe Blanche, COUDOULET, de l'Ostal, GAYDA, MARIS, Piccinini, Ste Eulalie excel. St Jean de Minervois, delicious fresh MUSCAT VDN: Barroubio, Clos du Gravillas, Montahuc.

Mirabeau, Maison Prov ★★→★★★ Stylish, well-packaged CÔTES DE PROV rosé, bought-in fruit, by Stephen and Jeany Cronk. Brands Etoile, Pure gd. DOM Res from own vyds a further step up. Focus on regenerative viticulture.

Mis en bouteille au château / domaine Bottled at CH, property, or estate. Note *dans nos caves* (in our cellars) or *dans la région de production* (in the area of production) often used but mean little.

Moët & Chandon Champ ★★★★ By far largest CHAMP house, impressive quality for such a giant. Fresher, drier BRUT Imperial NV, dosage conspicuously and successfully lowered of late. Rare prestige CUVÉE MCIII "solera" concept now superseded by *Collection Impériale Creation No. 1* (NV or MV of seven vintages) – philosophy of "haut oenologie". Outstanding Grand Vintages Collection, showcase for urbane chef de CAVE Benoît Gouez: 02 08 09 12 13' 15 16. Outposts across New World. *See also* DOM PÉRIGNON.

Monbazillac SW Fr ★★→★★★★ 18 19 20 21 22 BERGERAC sub-AOP: Sauternes-style sweet, with more MUSCADELLE. ★★★★ *Tirecul-la-Gravière*; ★★★ CLOS des Verdots, L'Ancienne Cure, Les Hauts de Caillaval, co-op *Ch de Monbazillac*; ★★ CHX de Belingard-Chayne, Grande Maison, Kalian, Le Faget, Monestier la Tour, Pech La Calevie, Pécoula. Neighbour SAUSSIGNAC makes similar wines.

Monopole A vyd in single ownership. Usually prestigious, not common, in Burg, eg. LA ROMANÉE. Only 5 GC monopoles in C D'O.

Montagne-St-Émilion Bx ★★ 18 19 20 22 23 Largest ST-ÉM satellite. Solid reputation. Beauséjour, CLOS de Boüard, Croix Beauséjour, Faizeau, La Couronne, Maison Blanche, Malengin (Eve), Montaiguillon, Roudier, Simon Blanchard, Teyssier, Tour Bayard, Vieux Bonneau, Vieux Ch Palon, *Vieux Ch St-André*.

Montagny Burg ★★ 14' 17 18 19' 20' 21 22' 23 CÔTE CHALONNAISE village with crisp whites, best of which punch well above reputation, mostly in hands of CAVES DE BUXY. Also LOUIS LATOUR, O LEFLAIVE. Top: Aladame, Berthenet, Cognard, Feuillat-Juillot, *Lorenzon*. Well worth checking.

Montez, Stéphane N Rh ★★★ Monteillet DOM, v.gd source for racy granite SYRAHS. COLLINES RHODANIENNES (r/w), CONDRIEU Chanson (tight, time), CÔTE-RÔTIE (Bons-Arrêts, style; Grandes Places, oak, time), ST-JOSEPH (Papy).

Montfaucon, Ch de S Rh ★★★ Talented Rodolphe de Pins crafts top LIRAC: (w) notable, complex, ancient-vine CLAIRETTE (ages); (r) 50S-GRENACHE based. Two v. sound CHÂTEAUNEUF reds.

Monthélie C d'O ★★→★★★ 15' 16 17 18' 19' 20' 21 22' 23 Crisp, juicy reds, grown uphill from VOLNAY, less fine but improving. Les Duresses best PC. Also *Ch de Monthélie* (de Suremain), Changarnier, Dubuet, Dujardin, Garaudet. Whites interesting (hillside sites). Value can still be found here.

Montille, de C d'O ★★★ Supple intensity in reds: BEAUNE, CÔTE DE NUITS (Malconsorts), POMMARD (Rugiens, Pézerolles), VOLNAY (Taillepieds). Impressive whites: CORTON-CHARLEMAGNE, MEURSAULT, PULIGNY-MONTRACHET Caillerets. Glorious BOURGOGNE CHARD. Since 2017, incl CH de Puligny wines. Deux Montille label dropped. Also Sta Rita Hills (California), Hokkaido (Japan).

Montlouis sur Loire Lo ★★→★★★★ 14′ 15 16 17 18 19′ 20′ 21 22′ 23 AOP; CHENIN BL (dr/sw/sp) from opposite bank of the Loire to VOUVRAY. More clay, flint than limestone, giving slightly more tender wines: Chanson, CHIDAINE, Delecheneau, Jousset, *Taille aux Loups*, Weisskopf.

Mont-Olivet, Clos du S Rh ★★★ Authentic CHÂTEAUNEUF reds, 26-ha family DOM. Age well, v. consistent. Regular CUVÉE (80% GRENACHE), *garrigue* tones; Papet (1904 Grenache), silky, intricate; charming white. Also gd CÔTES-DU-RH, LIRAC (r).

Montpeyroux Ldoc ★★★→★★★★ Cru 40 km n of Montpellier dominated by Mt Baudile. Innovative growers: DOM D'AUPILHAC; also Chabanon, Divem, Jasse-Castel, Joncas, Mas d'Amile, Villa Dondona. Serious co-op.

Montrachet (or Le Montrachet) C d'O ★★★★ 02′ 04 05 08 09′ 10 12 14′ 15 17 18 19′ 20′ 21 22′ 23 A GC vyd straddling PULIGNY-CHASSAGNE boundary, hence both claimed it. *Should* be greatest white burg for intensity, richness of fruit and reverberating length. Top: BOUCHARD, COLIN, DRC, LAFON, LAGUICHE (DROUHIN), LEFLAIVE, RAMONET, SAUZET. Temper expectations to avoid disappointment.

Provence rosé has 139 possible colours, officially. France overall has 143.

Montus, Ch SW Fr ★★★★ 15′ 16 17 18 19 20 22 (23) Alain BRUMONT's flagship property, famous for long-extracted oak-aged wines. Long-lived all-TANNAT reds, much prized by lovers of old-fashioned MADIRAN. Classy (sw/dr w) barrel-raised PACHERENC-DU-VIC-BILH. La Tyre (tiny plot), Prestige equal to Classed Growths.

Mordorée, Dom de la S Rh ★★★ 16′ 18′ 19′ 20 22′ 23′ 24′ Leading family DOM at TAVEL, bio/organic, rosés with real flair, local ID, impetus. Also LIRAC, La Reine des Bois (cracking r, gd w). CHÂTEAUNEUFS La Dame Voyageuse (r), La Reine des Bois (incl 1929 GRENACHE). Neat, nifty VDF La Remise (r/w/rosé).

Moreau Chab ★★→★★★ Widespread family, esp *Dom Christian M*, noted for PC Vaillons CUVÉE Guy M and superlative GC Les CLOS des Hospices. Louis M, more commercial range; DOM M-Naudet, concentrated wines for longer keeping. Improving *J Moreau*. BOISSET-owned.

Moreau C d'O ★★★→★★★★ Outstanding CHASSAGNE PCS from DOM Bernard M, now divided between sons Alex and Benoît; fine La Cardeuse (r). Appealing range of SANTENAY, MARANGES from David M. Neither related to CHAB dynasty.

Morey, Doms C d'O ★★★→★★★★ VIGNERON family in CHASSAGNE. Exemplary from: Caroline M and husband Pierre-Yves COLIN-M, MARC (En Virondot), Sylvain, Thibault M-Coffinet (LA ROMANÉE), Thomas (v. fine pure w), Vincent (plumper style). Also Pierre M in MEURSAULT for Perrières and BÂTARD. All v. reliable.

Morey, Marc C d'O ★★★ Ultra-reliable source of beautifully crafted wines, made by Marc M's grand-daughter, Sabine Mollard. (Corks branded "by Sabine".) Elegant, refined, gentle persistence, not shouty.

Morey-St-Denis C d'O ★★★→★★★★ 99′ 02′ 05′ 09′ 10′ 12′ 15′ 16′ 17 18 19′ 20′ 21 22′ 23 The Janus appellation, caught between GEVREY's grandeur and CHAMBOLLE's grace. Deserves better recognition for wines of vigour with spicy note that age well; GCS CLOS DE LA ROCHE, CLOS DE LAMBRAYS, CLOS DE TART, CLOS ST-DENIS. Top: ARLAUD, CLOS DE TART, CLOS des Lambrays, *Dujac*, GROFFIER, *H Lignier*, Perrot-Minot, PONSOT, ROUMIER, TREMBLAY. Also gd: Amiot, Castagnier,

Coquard-Loison-Fleurot, LIGNIER-Michelot, Magnien, Remy, Taupenot-Merme. Interesting whites, esp PC Monts Luisants.

Morgat, Eric Lo ★★★→★★★★ Meticulous, precise vigneron who settled in SAVENNIÈRES. Wines reflect his character. Magnificent CLOS Sertaux, *Fidès* 14′ 15′ 18 20 21 (22) (23). ANJOU BL Litus also tiptop.

Morgon Beauj ★★★ 15′ 17 18′ 19′ 20′ 21 22′ 23 Commanding BEAUJ cru; the volcanic slate of Côte du Py makes meaty and age-worthy wine, the clay of Les Charmes for earlier, smoother drinking. Try *Burgaud*, CH de Pizay, Ch des Lumières (JADOT), *Desvignes*, *Foillard*, Gaget, Godard, *Lapierre*, Piron, Sunier. It's Morgon 1ST, Beauj 2nd.

Mortet C d'O ★★★→★★★★ Arnaud M on song with impressive, refined reds from BOURGOGNE Rouge to CHAMBERTIN. Key wines GEVREY-CHAMBERTIN Mes Cinq Terroirs; PCS Champeaux, Lavaut St-Jacques. Also separate Arnaud M label, equally brilliant, incl CHARMES- and MAZOYÈRES-CHAMBERTIN. Thierry M: lighter, finessed style; overshadowed, worth following.

Moueix, J-P & Cie Bx Respected Libourne-based NÉGOCIANT and proprietor, family-owned. CHX BELAIR-MONANGE, HOSANNA, LA FLEUR-PÉTRUS, LAGRANGE, *La Grave à Pomerol*, LATOUR-À-POMEROL, *Trotanoy*. *See also* Dominus Estate (California).

Moulin-à-Vent Beauj ★★★ 09′ 11′ 15′ 18′ 19′ 20′ 21 22′ 23 Grandest BEAUJ cru, transcending GAMAY grape. Weight, spiciness of Rh but matures towards gamey PINOT flavours, easily mistaken for C d'o red at 10 yrs old+. Increasing interest in single-vyd bottlings from eg. *Ch des Jacques*, Ch de Moulin-à-Vent, DOMS Janin, Janodet, Labruyère, *Merlin* (La Rochelle), Rottiers. *See also* C d'O producers eg. BICHOT (Rochegrès), L BOILLOT (Brussellions), T LIGER-BELAIR (Rouchaux).

There are 750,000 ha (1,853,290 acres) of vineyard land in France.

Moulin Caresse, Ch SW Fr ★★ Family-owned property, nine generations, organic; BERGERAC, MONTRAVEL. Excellent value (r/w/rosé/sw).

Moulin de la Gardette S Rh ★★★ 16′ 17′ 19′ 20 21′ 23′ 24′ Organic, pine tree-fringed, 10-ha GIGONDAS, made with care, true *garrigue* herbal expression, be patient. Petite Gardette strong value; main red Tradition is heart-on-sleeve GRENACHE, 20 yrs+ life. Oaked Ventabren substantial.

Moulis H-Méd ★★→★★★ 16 18 19 20 22 23 Tiny inland AOP w of MARGAUX. Honest, gd-value wines; best can age. Top CHX: Anthonic, Biston-Brillette, BRANAS GRAND POUJEAUX, Caroline, *Chasse-Spleen*, Dutruch Grand Poujeaux, *Gressier Grand Poujeaux*, Lalaudey, MAUCAILLOU, *Mauvesin Barton*, Poujeaux.

Mourgues du Grès, Ch S Rh ★★→★★★ 22′ 23′ 24′ Sure-bet, top COSTIÈRES DE NÎMES, organic, early-drinking, busy-fruited. Racy rosé (Dorés, Galets Rouges, Rosés). Firmer Capitelles: Terre d'Argence (SYRAH), Terre de Feu (GRENACHE).

Mugneret C d'O ★★★→★★★★ VIGNERON family in VOSNE. Sublime wines of grace, restrained vigour from Georges M-Gibourg (from BOURGOGNE to RUCHOTTES-CHAMBERTIN), new generation on board. Cousins at DOM Gérard M doing equally well. Also Dom Mongeard-M.

Mugnier, J-F C d'O ★★★★ Outstanding grower of CHAMBOLLE-MUSIGNY *Les Amoureuses*, *Musigny*. Do not miss PC Fuées. Finesse, never shouty; thinkers' wines. Also MONOPOLE NUITS CLOS de la Maréchale (note reversed "a" in "la" on labels, replicates error on wrought-iron vyd sign). No longer sells young vintages of magnificent MUSIGNY, to avoid infanticide.

Mumm, GH & Cie Champ ★★★ Revitalized house owned by Pernod Ricard. Yann Munier, chef de CAVE. Increasingly gd RSRV series; Mumm de Verzenay BLANC DE NOIRS 08 09 12 13, BLANC DE BLANCS (formerly Mumm de Cramant) 12′ 13 15, CUVÉE Lalou 06 08 13. RSRV 4.5. Cordon Rouge NV much improved: PINOT-led weight with tension. Also impressive in California.

Muré / Clos Saint Landelin Al ★★★→★★★★ A trad Rouffach winery, more innovative than most (NB: Dom Muré is estate; Maison Muré négociant arm); AL's best PINOT N (CUVÉE V 15' 18') and CRÉMANTS. Outstanding SYLVANER Steinstuck, Cuvée Oscar 17 18 19 22', PINOT GR 17' 18, GEWURZ 19 from iron-rich CLOS St Landelin (12-ha MONOPOLE in GC Vorbourg), up-and-coming SYRAH.

Muscadet Lo ★→★★ 21 22' 23 (24) Revitalized source of super yet affordable wines. MUSCADET is generic AOP; trade up to zonal AOPs for true joy: Coteaux de la Loire (Champ Chapron) is decent, Côtes de Grandlieu (Haut-Bourg, Herbauges) better, but best are MUSCADET SÈVRE ET MAINE.

Muscadet Crus Communaux Lo ★★→★★★ 07' 08' 09 10 12' 14 16 18 19 20 (22) (23) MUSCADET's cru system; low yields and long lees-ageing gives complex wines. Seven ratified: Ch-Thébaud, Clisson, Gorges, Goulaine, Le Pallet, Monnières-St Fiacre, Mouzillon-Tillières. Try JO LANDRON, Lieubeau, LUNEAU-PAPIN, PÉPIÈRE. Three more crus planned: Champtoceaux, La Haye Fouassière, Vallet.

Muscadet Sèvre et Maine Lo ★→★★★ 14 16 19' 20' 21 22' 23 (24) Largest MUSCADET zone; high quality. Try Bonnet-Huteau, Brégeon, Chereau-Carré, Cormerais, Gadais, Grand Mouton, Gunther-Chereau, Haute-Fevrie, Huchet, LANDRON, Lieubeau, *Luneau-Papin*, *Pépière*, Vincent Caillé.

Musigny C d'O ★★★★ 93 96' 99' 02' 05' 09' 10' 12' 15' 17 18 19' 20' 21 22' 23 Most beautiful red burg; the queen to CHAMBERTIN's king. Fragrance made flesh. Deceptive delicacy cloaks sinuous power. Never refuse – if someone else is paying. Best: DE VOGÜÉ, DROUHIN, FAIVELEY, JADOT, LEROY, MARCHAND-TAWSE, *Mugnier*, PRIEUR, ROUMIER, VOUGERAIE.

Nature Unsweetened, esp for CHAMP: no dosage. Fine if v. ripe grapes, raw otherwise. Vin Nature = natural wine; *see* A Little Learning.

Négly, Ch La Ldoc ★★★ Leading LA CLAPE estate, impressive range from salty Brise Marine (w), La Côte, La Falaise (r) for everyday to icon La Porte du Ciel (SYRAH), MOURVÈDRE-based L'Ancely.

Négociant-éleveur Merchant who "brings up" (ie. matures) the wine.

Noblaie, Dom de la Lo ★★→★★★ Excellent value CHINON from Jérôme Billard. Chiens Chiens, Les Blancs Manteaux, *Pierre de Tuf* 05' 09 10' 15' 18' 19 20 21 22' (23), latter vinified in ancient limestone vat. CHENIN BL also v.gd.

Noëllat C d'O ★★★ Noted VOSNE family. Maxime Cheurlin at DOM Georges N on top form: try NUITS Boudots, Vosne Petits-Monts and GC ÉCHÉZEAUX, also some gd-value lesser appellations. Cousins at *Michel N* starting to cause a stir (Vosne Les Suchots). *See also* v. stylish HUDELOT-N in VOUGEOT.

Nuits-St-Georges C d'O ★★→★★★★ 99' 02' 05' 09' 10' 12' 15' 16 17 18 19 20 21 22' 23 Three parts to this major AOP: Premeaux vyds for elegance (various CLOS: de la Maréchale, des Corvées, des Forêts, St-Marc), centre for dense dark plummy wines (Cailles, Les St-Georges, Vaucrains) and n side for finesse (Boudots, Cras, Murgers, Richemone). Hearty reputation of yore increasingly outdated, Nuits treads lighter today. Worth a close look. Top: ARLOT, ARNOUX-LACHAUX, CATHIARD, CHEVILLON, *Faiveley*, GOUGES, GRIVOT, LEROY, *Liger-Belair*, *Mugnier*, but try also Ambroise, Chauvenet, Chicotot, Confuron, Gavignet, Lechéneaut, Ledy, Machard de Gramont, MARCHAND-TAWSE, Michelot, Millot, Perdrix, RION.

Odyssée, Dom Rouss ★★★ Vincent Carreras's tiny DOM, superb, terroir-driven La Belle Echappé (w, MACCABEO), Chimichurri SYRAH.

Ogereau, Dom Lo ★★→★★★ Top ANJOU under Vincent, even better under Emmanuel. Dry CHENIN BL range (Bonnes Blanches, La Martinère, Vent de Spilite). ANJOU-VILLAGES (100% CAB SAUV) *Côte de la Houssaye* 05 09 10 15 18 19 20 22 (23). Excellent COTEAUX DU LAYON, QUARTS DE CHAUME.

Ogier, Stéphane N Rh ★★★ 20' 21 22' 23' 24' Increasingly high-profile CÔTE-RÔTIE DOM; driving fruit, oaking, busy tannins, several v. small, plot-specific

(Bertholon, Leyat). Top: Belle Hélène (50s SYRAH, complex), Côte Blonde (floral), La Viallière (iron). IGP Seyssuel (r, terroir), VDF Syrah, VIOGNIER.

Ollieux Romanis, Ch Ldoc ★★★★ Impeccable CORBIÈRES bio DOM. Tradition (r/w/rosé) gd value. Prestige (r/w, oaked, stylish) a step up. Terrific Atal Sia pure expression of Boutenac terroir. CUVÉE Or, opulent, sun-drenched.

Oratoire St Martin, Dom de l' S Rh ★★★ 19' 20' 21' 22' 23 24' CAIRANNE luminary, prime vyds, owned by CH Mont-Redon (CHÂTEAUNEUF). Reds v.gd, bio, deep purity: Haut Coustias (vines c.70 yrs), Les Douyes (1905 GRENACHE/MOURVÈDRE). Table-friendly whites (from two S Rh, two N Rh varieties): Haut-Coustias, Rés Seigneurs.

Ostertag, Dom Al ★★★ Top bio estate now run by Arthur O. Terroir-driven RIES Muenchberg 10 14 18', trend-setting barrique-fermented, rich Muenchberg PINOT GR 15. Excellent SYLVANER VIEILLES VIGNES 15 18' 19'.

Overnoy, Maison Jura AOP ARBOIS-Pupillin. Founded by Pierre O, run by Emmanuel Houillon. Otherworldly CHARD, ★ SAVAGNIN, ★★ Ploussard (Poulsard); new TROUSSEAU/Ploussard. Other Jura Overnoy estates are cousins.

Pabiot, Jonathan Lo ★★★→★★★★ Rockstar POUILLY-FUMÉ DOM; bio. Top: *Luminance* 14' 16 17' 19' 20' 21 22 23 (Kimmeridgian). Aubaine (Portlandian) often tiptop. Value in Léon & Elisa CUVÉES.

Pacherenc du Vic-Bilh SW Fr ★★→★★★ White AOP contiguous with MADIRAN. GROS/PETIT MANSENG (dr/sw). Made by most Madiran growers, but note ★★ CHX Arricau-Bordes (PRODUCTEURS PLAIMONT), d'Aydie, de Mascaaras. Best: PETIT COURBU (dr w) from ALAIN BRUMONT.

Hotels are sparse in Pauillac: try Hôtel des Vignes et des Anges.

Paillard, Bruno Champ ★★★→★★★★★ Top quality; est 1981. BRUT and Rosé Première CUVÉE NV; refined style, esp slow-ageing Prestige *NPU* 95 02' 08 09. BP assemblage 08 09 12' 15. BLANC DE BLANCS 04 06 09 13' 14, on the up. Bruno P heads LANSON-BCC group of mainly family houses; cerebral daughter Alice has taken over at Paillard, with impressive results.

Palette Prov ★★★ Tiny AOP nr Aix. GRENACHE, MOURVÈDRE; floral, age-worthy reds, fragrant rosés; intriguing forest-scented whites, also oddities like FURMINT. Try trad, serious CH SIMONE, Crémade, HENRI BONNAUD.

Palmer & Co Champ ★★★→★★★★ Exemplary co-op, enviable patchwork of vyds. PINOT N-dominated. Inspired leadership by Rémi Vervier; v. reliable BRUT Rés. Unsurprisingly powerful NV Amazone; Grands Terroirs 03 12 15'. Don't overlook excellent BLANC DE BLANCS from ostensibly Pinot N house.

Paradis, Les Vignes de Sav ★→★★ Above Lac Léman (Lake Geneva), IGP Vin des Allobroges (shunning AOP), organic estate uses eggs, amphorae to bring v. best from CHASSELAS, plus CHENIN BL, Savagnin.

Partagé, Dom Sav ★★→★★★ Tiny bio DOM of Gilles Berlioz in CHIGNIN. Energetic ★ Altesse, ★★ Jacquère, ★★ MONDEUSE and range of various ★★★ Chignin-Bergeron (ROUSSANNE).

Pascal, J C d'O ★★★ Look hard enough, and value can still be found in C D'O. Pascal's BOURGOGNE C d'O CHARD offers unrivalled quality at fair price. Move up to PULIGNY village for even greater delight. Uber-reliable.

Pas de l'Escalette, Dom du Ldoc ★★→★★★ Exciting TERRASSES DE LARZAC. Ze CINSAULT, exuberantly fruity. Las Clapas (r/w) consistently gd, intense.

Pataille Burg ★★★ Wild-haired guru Sylvain P is MARSANNAY's standard-bearer. Cult following for single-vyd red (whole bunches), white (esp site-specific ALIGOTÉ), rosé (Fleur de PINOT), low sulphur, long-ageing. Cutting-edge, consistent.

Paternal, Dom du Prov ★★→★★★ Santini bros make consistently elegant (w) CASSIS. Also gd BANDOL, CÔTES DE PROV.

Patrimonio Cors AOP in N CORS with cru status, along with AJACCIO. Sumptuous reds, fresh rosé from NIELLUCCIO, VERMENTINO for white. Lots of organic.

Pauillac H-Méd ★★★→★★★★ 09' 10' 15 16' 18' 19' 20' 22' 23 Communal AOP in N MÉD with 18 Classed Growths, incl LAFITE, LATOUR, MOUTON. Famous for long-lived wines, the acme of CAB SAUV. Other top CHX: CLERC MILON, DUHART-MILON, GRAND-PUY-LACOSTE, LYNCH-BAGES, PICHON BARON, PICHON LALANDE, PONTET-CANET. BATAILLEY, HAUT-BAGES-LIBÉRAL, HAUT-BATAILLEY also on song.

Pays d'Oc, IGP Ldoc ★→★★★ Largest French IGP, covering whole of LDOC-ROUSS. Extremes of quality from simple, quaffing varietals to innovative, exciting. At last count, 58 different grapes allowed. Big players: Fortant de France, GÉRARD BERTRAND, Jeanjean, PAUL MAS and co-ops Cèbezan, Foncalieu.

PC (Premier Cru) First Growth in BX; 2nd rank of vyds (after GC) in Burg; 2nd rank in Lo: one so far, COTEAUX DU LAYON Chaume.

Pécharmant SW Fr ★★→★★★ 18 19 20 22 (23) BERGERAC inner AOP on edge of town. Iron, manganese in soil generate biggest, longest-living wines of area. Veteran ★★★ CH DE TIREGAND, DOM du Haut-Pécharmant, l'Ancienne Cure; ★★ CHX Beauportail, Corbiac, du Rooy, Terre Vieille; Dom des Bertranoux.

Pech Redon, Ch Ldoc ★★★ Christophe Bousquet's bio DOM in rugged heart of LA CLAPE. L'Epervier (r) brims with wild herbs, dark fruit. White even better.

Pélican, Dom du Jura ★★★ VOLNAY'S MARQUIS D'ANGERVILLE venture nr ARBOIS; bio vyds incl those from retired legend Jacques Puffeney – giving pristine range.

Pellé, Dom Lo ★★→★★★ One of handful of superstar MENETOU-SALON DOMS. Top single vyds: (w) Le Carroir, *Les Blanchais* 19 20 21 22 (23), VIGNES de Ratier; (r) Le Carroir, Les Cris 15 18 19 20 22 (23), rarely seen Coeur de Cris.

Pena, Ch de Rouss ★★ Tiny co-op of 20 families making cracking, approachable wines. Try Ninet de Pena ("little stone" in Catalan), IGP CÔTES CATALANES.

Pépière, Dom de la Lo ★★→★★★★ 14 18 19' 20 23 MUSCADET name to know. Wines frequently best there are. Top: Briords (old vines, ages well). Look for crus, eg. *Clisson*, CH-Thébaud, Gorges, Monnières-St-Fiacre.

Pernand-Vergelesses C d'O ★★★ (r) 10' 12 15' 17 18' 19' 20' 21 22 23 (w) 14' 15' 17' 18' 19' 20' 21 22' 23 Village hosting w-facing part of CORTON-CHARLEMAGNE. Some other vyds w-facing. Lacks recognition due to clumsy name. Different vyds thrive in each colour: (r) Île des Vergelesses; (w) Combottes, Sous Frétille. Local DOMS CHANDON DE BRIAILLES, Dubreuil-Fontaine, RAPET, Rollin lead way.

Perret, André N Rh ★★★ 19' 20' 21 22' 23' 24' Top CONDRIEU DOM. Three whites: Classic, lucid fruit; stylish, mineral-lined CLOS Chanson; full, intriguing Chéry. ST-JOSEPH (r/w); bustling-fruit, classic red (smoky, old-vine Les Grisières). Also gd COLLINES RHODANIENNES (r/w).

Perrier, Joseph Champ ★★★ Fine family-run CHAMP house with v.gd PINOTS N/M vyds, esp in own Cumières DOM. Prestige CUVÉE Joséphine 12'; BRUT Royale NV more focused with lower dosage. Distinctive, tangy BLANC DE BLANCS 08 13' 17' 19 20. Cuvée Royale 08 12 15' 16; older BLANC DE BLANCS vintages age well, esp 95. Owner Jean-Claude Fourmon easing reins to son.

Perrier-Jouët Champ ★★★ The 1st (in C19) to make dry CHAMP for UK; strong in GC CHARD, best for vintage, deluxe Belle Époque in painted bottle 08 12' 13 15; BRUT NV; Blason de France NV Brut and Rosé; Belle Époque Rosé 12 13 14' 15; Belle Époque BLANC DE BLANCS 07' 12 13 14' 15.

Pesquié, Ch S Rh ★★ Central name at VENTOUX. Fresh, organic, bio vyds; gd range clear-drinking, polished reds and attractive whites. Try Terrasses, IGP Mediterranée Paradou.

Pesquier, Dom du S Rh ★★★ Admirable GIGONDAS DOM; terroir, real grass-roots-truth red, value. Also genuine CÔTES DU RH, VACQUEYRAS (r).

Pessac-Léognan Bx ★★★→★★★★ 10' 15 16 18 19' 20' 22 23 AOP for best part of N GRAV, incl all Crus Classés: DOM DE CHEVALIER, HAUT-BAILLY, HAUT-BRION, LA MISSION HAUT-BRION, PAPE CLÉMENT, SMITH HAUT LAFITTE, etc. Aspiring unclassified: LES CARMES HAUT-BRION. Firm, full-bodied, earthy reds; BX's finest dry whites. Try also LA LOUVIÈRE, LARRIVET HAUT-BRION, OLIVIER.

Péters, Pierre Champ ★★★★ Superb Côte des Blancs estate. *Les Chétillons* probably longest-lived CHARD in CHAMP 08 09 12 13 14' 15 16. Fascinating project with CH DE BEAUCASTEL: Fleur de Miraval (ER I, II, III: Exclusivement Rosé, not late Queen). CUVÉE Montjolys 15 16. Also L'Espit, Rés, unforgettable Rés Oubliée. Rodolphe P one of Champ's finest winemakers.

Petit Chablis Chab ★ DYA Refreshing mini-CHAB from outlying vyds mostly not on Kimmeridgian clay. Move up when refreshed. Best: BILLAUD, BROCARD, DAUVISSAT, Defaix, LAVANTUREUX, Pommier, RAVENEAU and co-op LA CHABLISIENNE.

Pézenas Ldoc Charming medieval town. AOP LDOC, diverse soils, fun to explore. Big gun PAUL MAS and smaller Mas Gabriel. Also DOMS Allegria, des Aurelles, de Nizas, Les Trois Puechs, Magellan, Prieuré St Jean de Bebian, Villa Tempora.

Philipponnat Champ ★★★→★★★★ Small house based in Mareuil-sur-AŸ, distinct PINOT N style. Now owned by LANSON-BCC group, but Charles P has hand firmly on the tiller. NV BRUT, NV Rosé, CUVÉE 1522 12 13 15 16. Famous for majestic single-vyd *Clos des Goisses* 08 09 12 13 14' 15. Goisses Juste Rosé 12 13 14' 15. And from within Goisses itself, minute production of Les Cintres 08 09 12. Also exceptional late-disgorged vintage CLOS des Goisses LV (Long Vieillissement) 94' 95 96 99. Rare Léon 06 08 14, Rémissionne 09 12 15.

Picpoul de Pinet Ldoc ★→★★★ DYA AOP for PICPOUL, popular, versatile white, vyds overlooking oyster farms by Med, cooled by sea breezes. Salty tang, lemony freshness. Perfect with seafood. Best not oaked. Co-ops l'Ormarine, Pomerols do gd job, also DOMS de Belle Mare, des Lauriers, Félines-Jourdan, Font-Mars, La Croix Gratiot, Petit Roubié, Reine Juliette, St Martin de la Garrigue.

Pic St-Loup Ldoc ★★★★ AOP n of Montpellier with dramatic scenery dominated by eponymous peak. Higher, cooler, wetter; more elegance to wines; 50% min SYRAH plus GRENACHE, MOURVÈDRE. Reds for ageing, rosé gd; white potential considerable but still AOP LDOC or IGP Val de Montferrand. Growers: Chx CAZENEUVE, de Lancyre, de LASCAUX, de Valflaunès, La Roque, Puech-Haut; CLOS de la Matane, Clos Marie; Doms de l'Hortus, Pegaline; Bergerie du Capucin, Le Chemin des Rêves, Mas Bruguière, Mas Gourdou, Mas Peyrolle. Tiny co-op, eight growers, Hommes & Terres du Sud v.gd.

Pieretti, Dom Cors ★★★ Small estate in windswept Cap CORSE, n of Bastia. Lina Pieretti-Venturi makes top rosé, also delicious red and sweet MUSCAT. Star: Marine (w), predictably perfect with seafood.

Pierre-Bise, Ch Lo ★★→★★★★ Supeb ANJOU DOM run by René Papin. Fine range of dry CHENIN BL ANJOU BL, incl SAVENNIÈRES, ROCHE-AUX-MOINES (ages well). Contracted range of COTEAUX DU LAYON now, still top dog in QUARTS DE CHAUME 07' 09 10 11' 13 14' 15 16 17 18' (22) (23). Also gd reds, fizz.

Pierre Fil, Dom Ldoc ★★★ MINERVOIS; USP MOURVÈDRE with carbonic maceration. Top Dolium and CUVÉE M superb, reward ageing. Drink *garrigue*-scented Orebus while waiting.

Pillot C d'O ★★★ Ultra-reliable family in CHASSAGNE, all branches on form: F&L P (sound all round), Jean-Marc P (esp CLOS St-Marc) and Paul P (Grandes Ruchottes, LA ROMANÉE, etc.). Also red Chassagne PCS from all three. Explore.

Pinard, Vincent Lo ★★→★★★ Top SANCERRE, single-vyds: Le Château **20 21 22** (23), *Le Grand Chemarin*, Le Petit Chemarin. Reds: Charlouise, Vendanges Entières.

Pinelli, Dom Cors ★★→★★★ Marie-Charlotte P, young talent at family DOM, PATRIMONIO; Campo Vecchio (r), Impassitu MUSCAT, VIN DE FRANCE (sw).

Pinon, François et Julien Lo ★★★★ Leading VOUVRAY DOM now expertly run by Julien.

FRANCE

Super DEMI-SEC (speciality) Les Trois Argiles, Silex Noir; recently introduced dry *Deronnières* also excellent. Great fizz. Long history of tiptop *moelleux* under late François: CUVÉE Botrytis 89' 90' 96' 02 03 05' 09 10 14 18' 19' 20 22.

Piper-Heidsieck Champ ★★★→★★★★ On surging wave of quality, inspiring newish chef de CAVE, Emilien Boutillat. Dynamic BRUT Essentiel with more age, less sugar, floral yet vigorous. Vintage back on form 08 12 14 16' 18. Hors Serie late-disgorged, only 71 82 released so far.

Place de Bordeaux, La Bx Internal BX NÉGOCIANT marketplace. Négociants buy through brokers, sell to other merchants, or to you and me.

Plageoles, Dom SW Fr ★★★ Defenders and rebels guarding true GAILLAC style. Rare local grapes rediscovered incl Ondenc (base of ace sw ★★★ Vin d'Autan), ★★ Prunelard (r, deep, fruity), Verdanel (dr w, oak-aged) and countless sub-varieties of MAUZAC. More reds from Braucol (FER SERVADOU), Duras.

Plaisance, Ch de Lo ★★→★★★ Exemplifying new ANJOU BL style, electric, dry, mineral: La Grande Pièce, Ronceray, Zerzilles 19 20 21 22 (23).

Plan de Dieu S Rh ★★ 20 22' 23 24' Top village, stony, wind-hammered plain, can need irrigation. Robust, spice-tannin, mainly GRENACHE. Selection broad. Best: CH la Courançonne, CLOS St Antonin (50s Grenache), Le Plaisir; DOMS APHILLANTHES (bio), Arnesque, Durieu (stylish), Espigouette (genuine), Favards (organic), Grand Retour, La Bastide St Vincent, Longue Toque, Martin (full, trad), Pasquiers (organic), St-Pierre (60s Grenache, trad).

Pol Roger Champ ★★★★ Family-owned Épernay house, *sine qua non* of elegance. BRUT Rés NV excels, dosage lowered since 2012; Brut Vintage 08 09 12' 13 15' 16 18; Rosé 09 15 16 18; BLANC DE BLANCS 08 09' 12 13 15' also fine *Pure* (no dosage). Sumptuous *Cuvée Sir Winston Churchill* 02 09 12 13 14' 15, a serious keeper. More focus on Vinothéque promised.

Grenache delivers what Pinot Noir promises: true or false?

Pomerol Bx ★★★→★★★★ 10' 15 16' 18' 19' 20' 22 23 Tiny, pricey AOP; MERLOT-led, plummy to voluptuous, but long life. Top CHX on clay, gravel plateau: CLINET, HOSANNA, L'ÉGLISE-CLINET, L'ÉVANGILE, LA CONSEILLANTE, LAFLEUR, LA FLEUR-PÉTRUS, LE GAY, LE PIN, PETRUS, TROTANOY, *Vieux Ch Certan*. Relative value from BOURGNEUF, CLOS du Clocher, FEYTIT-CLINET.

Pommard C d'O ★★★→★★★★ 96' 99' 05' 09' 10' 12 15' 16' 17 18 19' 20' 21 22' 23 As with NUITS, reputation for heft over grace is increasingly outdated. Best PC: Epenots (grace), Rugiens (power). Try Noizons at village level. Top: BICHOT (DOM du Pavillon), Ch de Pommard, Clerget, Commaraine, COMTE ARMAND, DE COURCEL, DE MONTILLE, HOSPICES DE BEAUNE, J-M BOILLOT, Launay-Horiot, Lejeune, Parent, Rebourgeon-Mure, Violot-Guillemard. Relative value.

Pommery Champ ★★→★★★ Historical house with spectacular cellars but now few vines; brand owned by Vranken. BRUT NV steady bet, no fireworks; Rosé NV; Brut 04 08 09 12'. Apanage 1874 range more promising: BLANC DE BLANCS/NOIR, Brut. Once-outstanding CUVÉE Louise slowly regaining ground 02 04 05 06'. Celebrated Le CLOS de Pompadour 02 04, a fading beauty.

Ponsot, Dom C d'O ★★→★★★★ Famed MOREY-ST-DENIS DOM. Rose-Marie P in charge. Largest landholder in *Clos de la Roche*, 3.35 ha, marvellous wine. Exceptional, age-worthy PC Monts Luisants, standard-bearer for all ALIGOTÉ.

Ponsot, Laurent C d'O ★★→★★★★ Man who made DOM PONSOT wines for 30 yrs left family business to create own haute-couture label nearby (2016). Kept sharecropping contracts, incl amazing CLOS ST-DENIS, GRIOTTE-CHAMBERTIN. Buying vines and developing whites, in new purpose-built winery (Gilly).

Pouilly-Fuissé Burg ★★→★★★ 14' 15 17 18 19' 20' 21 22' 23 Top AOP of Mâcon; potent, rounded but intense whites from around Fuissé, more mineral in Vergisson.

Offers value compared to C D'O; PC classification finally in place from 2020. Top: Barraud, Bret, Carette, **Ch de Beauregard**, CH DE FUISSÉ, CH des Quarts, Ch des Rontets, Cornin, *Ferret*, Forest, Lassarat, **Merlin**, Paquet, Renaud, Robert-Denogent, Rollet, Saumaize, Saumaize-Michelin, VERGET.

Pouilly-Fumé Lo ★★→★★★★ 14 19′ 20′ 21 22′ (23) Famed AOP for SAUV BL close to SANCERRE. Best stunning, nervy as Sancerre, but quality variable. Mostly DYA; best can age. Super CAILBOURDIN, LOUIS-BENJAMIN DAGUENEAU, *Jonathan Pabiot*, Masson-Blondelet, Michel Redde, Tracy.

Pouilly-Vinzelles Burg ★★ 14′ 15 17 18 19′ 20′ 21 22′ 23 Close to POUILLY-FUISSÉ geographically and in quality. New PCs from 2024: Les Longeays, Les Pétaux, Les Quarts. Best: CH de V, DROUHIN, Soufrandière (Bret), Valette. Volume from CAVE des GCS Blancs.

Pousse d'Or, Dom de la C D'O ★★★ Substantial VOLNAY DOM; choice holdings in CÔTE DE NUITS also, esp CHAMBOLLE. Lovely, pure Volnay PCs. Amphorae used for portion of some wines, giving lighter "weave" in texture.

Premières Côtes de Bordeaux Bx ★→★★ 20 22 23 Same zone as CADILLAC-CÔTES DE BX but sweet whites only; SÉM-dominated *moelleux*. Generally early drinking. Best: CHX Crabitan-Bellevue, Faugas, Fayau, Marsan.

Prieur, Dom Jacques C D'O ★★★ Major MEURSAULT estate, wide range of GCS from MONTRACHET to MUSIGNY. Style: weight from late-picking, oak. More verve, excitement would be welcome. New project Labruyère-Prieur in Burg. Owners Famille Labruyère also CHAMP, CH ROUGET (BX), MOULIN-À-VENT projects.

Producteurs Plaimont SW Fr ★→★★ France's most dynamic co-op: CÔTES DE GASCOGNE, MADIRAN, SAINT MONT (best). Champions of SW vines eg. MANSENGS, Petit Courbu, TANNAT, pre-phylloxera finds. All colours, styles, mostly ★★, all tastes, budgets. Top: Le Faîte. Colombelle, entry level (w/rosé).

Propriétaire-récoltant Champ Owner-operator, literally owner-harvester.

Provence Think pink, 89% production rosé. Most from three AOPS: COTEAUX D'AIX-EN-PROV, CÔTES DE PROV, VAROIS-EN-PROV (and subzones). Pale, dry, crisp, some v.gd. Look beyond to serious reds: AOPs BANDOL, BAUX-DE-PROVENCE standout. Intriguing white, incl CASSIS. IGP Alpilles et al.

Puech-Haut, Ch Ldoc ★★→★★★★ AOP LDOC St Drézéry. Powerful Prestige (r/w), Tête de Belier (r/w/rosé) swish wine, packaging. IGP Argali rosé gd value. Owns ★★★ PIC ST-LOUP CH Lavabre.

Puisseguin St-Émilion Bx ★★ 19 20 22 23 Most e of four ST-ÉM satellites; MERLOT-led; meaty but firm. Top: CHX BEAUSÉJOUR, Branda, Clarisse, de l'Anglais, DES LAURETS, de Roques, Durand-Laplagne, Fongaban, Guibeau (Noé), Haut-Bernat, La Mauriane, Soleil.

Puligny-Montrachet C D'O ★★★→★★★★ 09 10′ 12 14′ 15 17′ 18 19′ 20′ 21 22′ 23 Floral, fine-boned, tingling white burg. At its best, finest of all. Deceptive delicacy cloaks memorable intensity. Curiosity red too. Outstanding PCs, esp Caillerets, Champ Canet, Combettes, Folatières, Pucelles, plus fabled MONTRACHET GCS. Producers: *Carillon (F&J)*, *Chartron*, Chavy, *Dom Leflaive*, *Drouhin*, Ente, *J-M Boillot*, *O Leflaive*, *Pascal*, *Sauzet*, Thomas-Collardot.

Py, Dom Ldoc ★★★ On n flank of Mt Alaric, nr Carcassonne; bio. Antoine (r/w) expressive, approachable CORBIÈRES. Succulent PINOT N IGP.

Quarts de Chaume GC Lo ★★★→★★★★ 07′ 09 10 11′ 13 14′ 15 16 17 18′ 22 Greatest sweet CHENIN BL AOP in Lo, but much of its 40 ha now making dry: sweet doesn't sell. Try BAUDOUIN, BAUMARD, BELARGUS, Bergerie, Forges, OGEREAU, *Pierre-Bise*, PLAISANCE.

Quenard Sav Six separate Q estates in CHIGNIN, incl (all ★★) super-reliable A&M Q, excellent J-F Q, small-but-lovely organic P&A Q. All offer top ROUSSANNE (Chignin-Bergeron), Jacquère, MONDEUSE. Try J-F Q Persan.

Quincy Lo ★★ 20' 21 22' (23) AOP, SAUV BL. More texture, generosity than SANCERRE, POUILLY-FUMÉ. Largely (not always) earlier drinking. Try Ballandors, Tatin, Tremblay (all Domaines Tatin), plus Adèle Rouzé, Lecomte, Mardon, Jacques Rouzé, Villalin.

Ramonet, J-C C d'O ★★★→★★★★ Distinctive, verging on idiosyncratic, often ethereal white. Excellent, age-worthy reds remain largely under radar, *value*. J-C now joined by daughters. Watch for new label from Noël R's sons.

Rancio Rouss Describes complex, evolved aromas from extended, oxidative ageing. Reminiscent of Tawny Port, or old Oloroso Sherry. Associated specifically with BANYULS, MAURY, RASTEAU, RIVESALTES. Can be a grand experience; don't miss.

Rangen Al Uniquely steep, volcanic, hot, most S GC of AL at Thann. Top: ZIND HUMBRECHT PINOT GR CLOS St Urbain 08' 10' 17' 21' (world's greatest dr Pinot Gr), SCHOFFIT RIES St-Théobald 15' 17'.

Rapet, Père et Fils C d'O ★★→★★★ On hill of CORTON, 4 ha+ form substantial base for significant family DOM of 25 ha. Style ranges from lush, plump CORTON-CHARLEMAGNE to lean, mineral ALIGOTÉ.

Rare Champ Was PIPER-HEIDSIECK, now separate; 02 06 07' 08 12 13. Little made.

Rasteau S Rh ★★ 19' 20 22' 23 24' Mostly GRENACHE (r) of character, depth, terroir, often peppery, some suave, early drinking, gd in hot yrs, consistent, now more finesse. BEAURENARD (bio, major, ages), CAVE Ortas/Rhonéa, CH La Gardine (old Grenache), Ch du Trignon, Famille Perrin; DOMS Beau Mistral, Collière (handmade, style), Combe Julière (punchy), Coteaux des Travers (bio), Elodie Balme (soft), ESCARAVAILLES (style), Girasols, Gourt de Mautens (supreme character, IGP from 2010), Gramiller (organic), Grand Nicolet (deep, character), Grange Blanche, M Boutin (handmade, organic), Rabasse-Charavin (punchy), Soumade (polished), *St Gayan*, Trapadis (bio). Grenache dessert VDN, long life, quality on the up: Doms Banquettes, Bressy Masson, Combe Julière, Coteaux des Travers, Escaravailles, Trapadis. Also gd CÔTES DU RH (r).

Red Puligny-Montrachet? Yes, there is such a thing – for adventurous palates only.

Raveneau Chab ★★★★ One of Burg's great names, using classic methods for ***extraordinary long-lived wines***. A little more modern while still growing in stature of late. Excellent value (except in secondary market). Look for PC Butteaux, Chapelot, Vaillons and GC Blanchots, Les CLOS.

Rayas, Ch S Rh ★★★★ 05' 06' 07' 09' 10' 11' 12' 15' 16' 17' 19' 20' 21' 22' 23' 24' Mystical, shrouded, wonderful, one-off CHÂTEAUNEUF estate, tiny yields, sandy soils, tree-sheltered, nr-garden plots, late harvesting. Pale, sensuous, spiced, aromatic reds (100% GRENACHE) age superbly, 30 yrs+. Pricey. White Rayas (CLAIRETTE, GRENACHE BL) rich, mysterious, v.gd over 20 yrs+. Also *en finesse* second wine, Pignan. Supreme CH Fonsalette CÔTES DU RH, incl marvellous, long-lived, complex SYRAH. Decant all; each an occasion for joy. No 18 (mildew). In VACQUEYRAS, Ch des Tours, gd VDP.

Ray-Jane, Dom Prov ★★★→★★★★ AOP BANDOL. Third of vyds 100 yrs+; de Sanary (90% CLAIRETTE), floral, elegant; Le Falun (r), intensity, silky power.

Rebourseau, Dom Henri C d'O ★★★ Resurgent GEVREY name: major investment from Bouygues family (CH MONTROSE, CLOS ROUGEARD). Splendid new winery; 13 ha incl significant GCS. Sumptuous, sweet-fruit style. Watch.

Regnié Beauj ★★ 19 20' 21 22' 23 Most recent BEAUJ cru, lighter wines on sandy soil, meatier nr MORGON. Starting to get some gd growers now. Try Burgaud, Chemarin, de la Plaigne, Dupré, Rochette, Sunier (A), Sunier (J). Watch.

Reuilly Lo ★★→★★★★ 20' 21 22' (23) Small AOP for SAUV BL, stylistically similar to SANCERRE, esp from Kimmeridgian soils. Also pale rosés from PINOTS GR and/ or N, and Pinot N reds. Try Claude Lafond, Denis Jamain, Jacques Rouzé.

Riceys, Les Champ Key AOP in AUBE for notable PINOT N rosé. Producers: A Bonnet, Brice, Jacques Defrance, Morize. Excels, almost counterintuitively, in warm yrs, *viz.* **09 15' 18 19 (20)**.

Richaud, Dom S Rh ★★★ Rightly popular organic CAIRANNE, true *garrigue* reds, multi-variety blends, high-octane style: classy Ebrescade (high MOURVÈDRE). Sound white, gd CÔTES-DU-RH (r).

Richebourg C d'O ★★★★ **02' 05' 09' 10' 12'** 15' 16 17 18' 19' 20' 21 22' VOSNE GC, cheek-by-jowl with ROMANÉE-CONTI. Magisterial; extraordinary depth and endless waves of flavour. Sonorous name, sonorous wine. Growers: *DRC*, GRIVOT, GROS, HUDELOT-NOËLLAT, LEROY, LIGER-BELAIR (T), MÉO-CAMUZET.

Rion C d'O ★★→★★★ Related DOMS in NUITS, VOSNE. Patrice R for excellent Nuits CLOS St-Marc, Clos des Argillières and CHAMBOLLE-MUSIGNY. Daniel R for Nuits and Vosne PCS, now being split between family members; A&B R Vosne-based, visitor-friendly. All dependable, fairly priced.

Rivesaltes Rouss ★★→★★★ Underappreciated VDN with various styles: Ambré, RANCIO/Hors d'Age, Rosé, Tuilé. Mostly GRENACHE, except MUSCAT de Rivesaltes AOP fragrant, youthful. Try Boucabeille, des Chênes, des Schistes, DOM CAZES, Puig-Parahy, Rancy, Roc des Anges, Sarda-Malet, Valmy, Vaquer. *See also* ROUSS VDNs BANYULS, MAURY.

R&L Legras Champ ★★★ Essence of Chouilly CHARD from flamboyant Julien Barbier (punts of bottles bright red like certain shoes); longevity, filigree finesse, esp St-Vincent BLANC DE BLANCS GC **02 08 12 13**, Présidence VV GC **07 12 13 14'**.

Roc, Dom Le SW Fr ★★ Organic FRONTON estate, run by multi-talented Ribes family. Pleasing crunchy red based on NÉGRETTE; lovely white from rare Bouysselet.

La Romanée in words? Would take Yeats to capture its poetic beauty.

Roc des Anges, Le Rouss ★★★→★★★★ Standout DOM, with quartz, schist terroir; freshness and minerality in Llum Grenache Gr. IGP CÔTES CATALANES. Reliefs CARIGNAN (120-yr-old vines).

Roches Neuves, Dom des Lo ★★★→★★★★ Exemplary SAUMUR-CHAMPIGNY DOM. Remarkable reds CLOS de L'Échelier, Les Mémoires **14 16** 18 19 20 22 (23). Stunning limestone-derived whites, *Clos Romans* **14 16** 18 19 20 22 (23).

Rodez, Eric Champ ★★★ Flamboyant former mayor of Ambonnay; wines equally flamboyant. Supremely complex Grands Vintages. Also CUVÉE des Crayères, fascinating Les Beurys maceration PINOT N Rosé **13 14 16'**.

Roederer, Louis Champ ★★★★ Family ownership par excellence. Enviable vyds, largest bio holdings. Brilliant chef de CAVE Jean-Baptiste Lecaillon. BRUT Premier NV phased out in favour of MV Collection; **242 243 244 245**. BLANC DE BLANCS **13 14'** 15 16. Vintage LR **12 13 14 15 16'** Far-from-disagreeable Cristal **08 09 12 13 14 15 16**, Cristal Rosé **08 09 12 13 14**. Superb *Cristal Vinothèque Bl* and *Rosé* 95; Brut NATURE Philippe Starck (all Cumières **09 12 15'**). *Late Release Vintage* 90 95 96 97 99 00. Also CH PICHON LALANDE, DEUTZ and *see* California.

Rolland, Michel Bx Veteran international consultant, MERLOT specialist. Own wines: The Rolland Collection.

Rolly Gassmann Al ★★★ Outstanding now bio DOM, mostly off-dry, rich, luscious wines (and v. many of them); maybe too sweet for some. Outstanding SGNS. Mineral RIES, rich SYLVANER **13 16 17' 18 19'**.

Romanée, La C d'O ★★★★ 09' **10' 12'** 15' 16' **17 19** 19' 20 21 22' 23' Tiniest GC in VOSNE, 0.85 ha, MONOPOLE of COMTE LIGER-BELAIR. Contiguous with, and upslope of, ROMANÉE-CONTI. Exceptionally fine, perfumed, intense. Vines planted n–s, unusual for C D'O. Superlative burg, superlative price.

Romanée-Conti, La C d'O ★★★★ **90' 93' 96' 99'** 00 **02'** 05' **09' 10' 12' 14'** 15' 16' 17 18' 19' 20' 21 22' 23' A GC in VOSNE, MONOPOLE of DRC. Grandest name in all

Burg (and the world); needs long ageing before it unfolds into splendour. When on song, no superlative captures its haunting delight. Magnificence made wine.

Romanée-St-Vivant C d'O ★★★★ 90' 99' 02' 05' 09' 10' 12' 15' 16' 17 18' 19' 20' 21 22' 23' A GC in VOSNE, downslope from LA ROMANÉE-CONTI. Seductive perfume, delicate but intense. Less magisterial, perhaps more beautiful, than famous neighbours. Growers: if you can't afford ARNOUX-LACHAUX, DRC, LEROY, CATHIARD, or HUDELOT-NOËLLAT, try ARLOT, Follin-Arbelet, J-J Confuron, LATOUR, Poisot. Hard to fault, and delivers boundless delight, in right hands.

Romanin, Ch Prov ★★★ Leading bio DOM in BAUX-EN-PROV, worth visiting for magnificent cathedral cellar. Grand vin (r/w), equally majestic.

Rosé de Loire Lo ★→★★ Decent, dry, multi-regional AOP for rosé, usually Grolleau-based blend. Bablut, CADY, Passavant.

Rossignol-Trapet C d'O ★★★→★★★★ Brothers Nicolas and David R-T doing great job. Removed from hearty GEVREY stereotype, yet not lacking in penetrating, memorable flavours. Healthy holdings of GCs, esp CHAMBERTIN; gd value across range from GEVREY VIEILLES VIGNES up. BEAUNE vyds from Rossignol side.

Rostaing, Dom N Rh ★★★→★★★★ 09' 10' 12' 13' 15' 16' 17' 18' 19' 20' 21 22' 23' 24' Top quality CÔTE-RÔTIE: five iron-cool, understated wines from prime plots, all v. fine, low-level oak, wait 6 yrs+, decant. Genuine Ampodium (value), complex, top-class, terroir Côte Blonde (5% VIOGNIER), Côte Brune (mineral), also La Landonne (intensity, 20–25 yrs), occasional Viallière (crisp, rocky). Mineral CONDRIEU, also IGP COLLINES RHODANIENNES (r/w), LDOC Puech Noble (r/w).

Rouget, Dom C d'O ★★★ Renamed as DOM R rather than Emmanuel R, with new generation refreshing dom famed for Henri Jayer connection and CROS PARANTOUX vyd. Style more robust than in Jayer era. Not as stellar.

Roulot, Dom C d'O ★★★→★★★★ Outstanding MEURSAULT DOM. Poised, precise, never flashy. Now holding back some wines for later release, when mature. Great PCs: CLOS des Bouchères, Perrières. Value from top village sites Luchets, Meix Chavaux, esp Clos du Haut Tesson. Excellent BOURGOGNE Bl.

Roumier, Georges C d'O ★★★★ Reference DOM for BONNES-MARES and other **brilliant Chambolle** (incl Amoureuses, Cras) from Christophe R, now joined by nephews Alexis, Clément. Long-lived but attractive early. Silly prices for tiny amount of MUSIGNY, secondary market. Best value: MOREY CLOS de la Bussière.

Rouquette sur Mer, Ch Ldoc ★★★→★★★★ Impressive LA CLAPE estate, vyds, *garrigue* by beach. *Arpège* (w), crisp, herbal, terrific value. L'Esprit terroir-benchmark red. Le CLOS de la Tour, top MOURVÈDRE.

Rousseau, Dom Armand C d'O ★★★★ Legendary GEVREY-CHAMBERTIN DOM: balanced, fragrant, majestic, age-worthy GCs. Chambertin doesn't get any better than here. Celebrated PC CLOS ST-JACQUES. Village wines less commanding.

Roussette de Savoie Sav AOP, same area as AOP SAV; 100% ALTESSE. Age to 5 yrs+. Carrel-Senger, CH de Lucey, Chevalier Bernard, ★★ Chevillard ★ Côtes Rousses ★★ Dupasquier, ★ Lupin, ★ Orchis, ★★ St-Germain, ★★★ Prieuré St-Christophe.

Roussillon Often linked with LDOC, and incl in AOP Ldoc, but has distinct Catalan ID. From Pyrénéan foothills to Med. Different soils, topography attract innovative producers; some brilliant wines. Lots of old vines, tiny yields, intense. GRENACHE is key. Largest AOP CÔTES DU ROUSS, gd-value spicy reds. Original, sometimes stunning, trad VDN (BANYULS, MAURY, RIVESALTES). Also serious age-worthy table wines (r/w). *See also* COLLIOURE, CÔTES DU ROUSS (VILLAGES), Maury (SEC). IGP excellent CÔTES CATALANES, Côte Vermeille.

Ruchottes-Chambertin C d'O ★★★★ 02' 05' 09' 10' 12' 15' 16 17' 18' 19' 20' 21 22' 23 Small GC, upslope of MAZIS-C. Ethereal, great finesse when mature. Worth the wait: MUGNERET-Gibourg, ROUMIER, ROUSSEAU. Also gd: CH de MARSANNAY, F Esmonin, H Magnien, Marchand-Grillot, Pacalet. LAMBRAYS from 2021.

Ruinart Champ ★★★★ Oldest sparkling CHAMP house (1729). High standards getting higher still. Rich, elegant R de Ruinart BRUT NV; Ruinart Rosé NV; R de Ruinart Brut 10' 15 16. BLANC DE BLANCS now MV Blanc Singulier Editions 17 18 19. Prestige DOM Ruinart Blanc de Blancs 02 04' 06 07 09 10 13. No 08 made; shame. Magnificent gastronomic *DR Rosé* 90 96 98' 02 04 07 09. Winemaker Fred Panaïotis at top of game; ages best under cork rather than crown cap.

Rully Burg ★★→★★★ (r) 15' 17 18 19' 20' 21 22' 23 (w) 17' 18 19' 20' 21 22 23 CÔTE CHALONNAISE village. Slowly gaining more recognition for tasty whites and fruity reds. Best vyds: Grésigny, Pucelle, Rabourcé. Try BRIDAY, Champs l'Abbaye, Devevey, *de Villaine*, DOM de la Folie, DROUHIN, *Dureuil-Janthial*, FAIVELEY, *Jacqueson*, Jaeger-Defaix, Jobard (C), Leflaive (O). *Picamelot* for top CRÉMANT.

Sablet S Rh ★★ 23 24' Eminent CÔTES DU RH-VILLAGE on mainly sand soils (hence name), some higher terraces nr GIGONDAS. Neat red-berry fruit, mainly GRENACHE, some deeper. Try CAVE co-op Gravillas; CHX Cohola (organic), du Trignon (stylish); DOMS de Boissan (organic, full), Les Goubert (r/w), Pasquiers (organic, full, best). Sturdy whites gd, for apéritifs/food: Boissan (ages well), Notre Dame des Pallières, ST GAYAN.

St-Amour Beauj ★★ 18' 19' 20' 21 22' Most 1 cru, mixed soils, character; signs of revival. Try Cheveau, DOM de Fa, Patissier, *Pirolette*, Revillon. Watch.

St-Aubin C d'O ★★★ (w) 14' 15 17' 18 19' 20' 21 22' 23 *Increasingly complex white*; St-A PC now merits comparison with big three: CHASSAGNE, PULIGNY, MEURSAULT. Also juicy, easy-drinking red. Best vyds: *Chatenière*, *En Remilly*, *Murgers Dents de Chien*. Best growers: BACHELET (JC), COLIN (Joseph, Marc), COLIN-MOREY, *Lamy*, Larue. Value Prudhon. Worth exploring.

St-Bris Burg ★ DYA Unique AOP for SAUV BL in N Burg. Fresh, lively, but can age (de Moor, GOISOT). Also gd: Bersan, Davenne, Felix, Simonnet-Febvre, Verret.

St-Chinian Ldoc ★★→★★★ Hilly AOP between MINERVOIS, FAUGÈRES. Two zones. Schist in ne, fragrant, nervy red, crus Berlou (mostly CARIGNAN), Roquebrun (mostly SYRAH). Limestone clay in s, broader, spicy. Usual suspects Syrah, GRENACHE, Carignan, MOURVÈDRE. White from GRENACHE BL, MARSANNE, ROUSSANNE, VERMENTINO. Roquebrun co-op excels; CHX Cazal Viel, Castigno; DOMS Borie la Vitarèle, Canet-Valette, Comps, des Jougla, La Dournie, La Lauzeta, LA LINQUIÈRE, La Madura, Les Eminades, MILHAU-LACUGE, Navarre, Rimbert; CLOS Bagatelle, Mas Champart, Mas de Cynanques, Quartironi de Sars, Viranel.

St Cosme, Ch de S Rh ★★★ 09' 10' 11' 12' 13' 14' 15' 16' 17' 18' 19' 20' 21' 22' 23 24' Top-rank, bio GIGONDAS estate; reds with brio, energy, oak, live well. Plot-specific CÔTES DU RH Les Deux Albion (r), Gigondas Classique (genuine, value), Hominis Fides (1902 GRENACHE, complex), Le Poste (class). Owns CH de Rouanne (VINSOBRES). Superior N Rh merchant range (CONDRIEU, CÔTE-RÔTIE).

Ste-Anne, Dom S Rh ★★ Outstanding CÔTES DU RH-VILLAGE DOM on limestone above St-Gervais; pioneer in 60s/70s (so old vines). Full reds, need time, have character: Mourillons (mostly SYRAH), Rouvières (60s MOURVÈDRE), live 15 yrs+. Subtle, superior VDF from 1977 VIOGNIER worth tracking down.

Ste-Croix-du-Mont Bx ★★ 18 19 20 22 23 Tiny AOP for sweet white. Soils consist of fossilized oysters. Best: rich, creamy, can age. Top CHX: Bel Air, Crabitan-Bellevue, des Arroucats, du Mont, La Caussade, La Rame, *Loubens*.

St-Émilion Bx ★★→★★★★ 10' 15' 16 18 19' 20' 22' 23 Big MERLOT-led AOP on BX's Right Bank; CAB FR also strong. Many GCS, mixed quality. Environmental certificate obligatory. Top designation St-Ém PREMIER GRAND CRU CLASSÉ (14 in 2022 classification). Warm, full, rounded style but much diversity due to terroir, winemaking and blend. Best firm, v. long-lived. Top CHX: ANGÉLUS, AUSONE, CANON, CHEVAL BLANC, FIGEAC, PAVIE.

> **Value: Sauvignon beyond Sancerre**
> There is better value here – flavour, quality, price – than in any other
> French region. And some appellations really overperform. Look beyond
> SANCERRE for SAUV BL. MENETOU-SALON: DOM PELLÉ Le Carroir (citrus
> rubbed on chalk), PHILIPPE GILBERT CLOS des Treilles (w fruit, salty
> minerality). QUINCY: Doms Tatin Victoires (blood orange, rose).
> REUILLY: Denis Jamain Les Chênes de Reuilly (sw citrus, smoky oak).

St-Estèphe H-Méd ★★→★★★★ 09' 10' 15 16' 18 19' 20' 22' 23 Most n communal AOP
in MÉD. Gravel, but more limestone, clay. Solid, structured wines for ageing. Five
Classed Growths: CALON SÉGUR, COS D'ESTOURNEL, COS LABORY, LAFON-ROCHET,
MONTROSE. Top unclassified estates: CAPBERN, DE PEZ, LE BOSCQ, LE CROCK, LILIAN
LADOUYS, MEYNEY, ORMES-DE-PEZ, PHÉLAN SÉGUR, TRONQUOY.

Ste-Victoire Prov ★★→★★★ Subzone of CÔTES DE PROV, majority rosé. Limestone
slopes of Montagne Ste-Victoire: much-needed freshness in hotter yrs. DOMS de
St Ser, des Diables, Gassier, Mas de Cadenas, St Pancrace. IGP Dom Richeaume.

St Gayan, Dom S Rh ★★★ 05' 07' 10' 15' 16' 17' 18' 19' 20' 21 22' 23 24' Top,
consistent GIGONDAS, *garrigue*, long-lived red, value: Origine (80% GRENACHE),
RASTEAU Ilex. Also CHÂTEAUNEUF (w), SABLET L'Oratory (w, pure).

St-Georges-St-Émilion Bx ★★ 18 19 20 22 23 Smallest ST-ÉM satellite. Sturdy,
structured. Best CHX: Calon, Cap St-Georges, CLOS Albertus, Haut St-Georges,
Macquin, St-André Corbin, St-Georges, Tour du Pas-St-Georges.

St-Joseph N Rh ★★→★★★ 15' 16' 17' 18' 19' 20' 21 22' 23 24' A v.gd substitute for
big-name CÔTE-RÔTIE etc. SYRAH red. Oldest vyds nr Tournon: stylish, red-
fruited, need time; further n nr Chavanay darker, peppered, younger oak.
More character, terroir than CROZES-HERMITAGE: CHAPOUTIER (Les Granits),
Gonon (brilliant), *Gripa*, GUIGAL (VIGNES de l'Hospice), *J-L Chave* (max interest).
Also gd: Alexandrins, Amphores (bio), A PERRET (Grisières), B Jolivet (rising
force), Boissonnet, Chèze, Courbis (modern), Coursodon (racy, modern),
E Darnaud (bespoke), DELAS, Farge, Faury, FERRATON, F Villard, Gaillard
(CLOS de Cuminaille), Gouye (trad), Iserand (handmade), J Cécillon (energy),
J-B Souillard, J&E Durand (fruit), Marsanne (trad), Monier-Perréol (bio),
MONTEZ, P-J Villa (style), P Marthouret, S Blachon (trad), Sept Lunes (bio), Vallet,
Vins de Vienne, Y CUILLERON. Interesting *white (mainly Marsanne)*: A PERRET,
Barge, *Chapoutier* (Les Granits), Curtat, DOM Faury, *Gonon*, Gouye (trad), *Gripa*,
Guigal, J P Marthouret, Pilon (style), Vallet, Y Cuilleron.

St-Julien H-Méd ★★★→★★★★ 09' 10' 15 16' 18 19' 20' 22' 23 Epitome of harmonious,
fragrant, savoury red; v. consistent mid-MÉD communal AOP; 11 classified (1855)
estates own most of vyd area; incl BEYCHEVELLE, DUCRU-BEAUCAILLOU, GRUAUD-
LAROSE, LÉOVILLES (x3). Also gd: GLORIA, Moulin Riche.

Saint Mont SW Fr ★★ (r) 18 19 20 22 (23) AOP on way to the Pyrénées, but with some
Atlantic influence. Red similar to MADIRAN, but often softer, less intense. White
is intriguing blend often incl pithy Arrufiac. PRODUCTEURS PLAIMONT dominates
and makes almost all. Try ★★★ *Ch de Sabazan*. Fantastic value.

St Nicolas de Bourgueil Lo ★→★★★ 10' 15' 16 17 18' 19' 20 22' (23) Underrated
CAB FR AOP, w of BOURGUEIL; stylistically indistinguishable. Ranges from easy-
drinking bistro wines to cellar-worthy. Try Cotelleraie, Frédéric Mabileau,
Sébastien David, Xavier Amirault, *Yannick Amirault*.

St-Péray N Rh ★★→★★★ 23' 24' Wines of interest, style (MARSANNE/ROUSSANNE) from
hilly granite, with limestone opposite Valence, much new planting, core quality
gd. Was *famous for fresh fizz*: A Voge (vintaged), Pic & CHAPOUTIER (vintaged),
R Nodin, TAIN co-op. Best still white: Chapoutier (Hongrie), Clape (pure),
Colombo (calm richness), *du Tunnel* (stylish), Gripa (best; mainly Roussanne

Figuiers), J&E Durand, J Michel, L Fayolle, R Nodin (old-vine Suchat), TAIN co-op, Vins de Vienne, Voge (Fleur de Crussol, oak), Y CUILLERON (Biousse).

St-Pourçain Lo, Mass C ★→★★★ 21 22' 23 Little-known AOP nr Vichy. Whites from CHARD, SAUV BL, but intriguing citrus, acid-bright white blends with Tressalier are ones to look for. Also some red/rosé from GAMAY/PINOT N. Try *Bérioles*, Terres d'Ocre, Vignerons de St-Pourçain.

Mondeuse Blanche – sounds like a medieval queen. Mother of Syrah, grown for Savoie white.

St-Romain C d'O ★★→★★★ (w) 17' 18 19' 20' 21 22' 23 *Crisp whites* from picturesque side valley of CÔTE DE BEAUNE. Gaining in stature, gd value by Burg standards. Best vyds: Combe Bazin, Sous la Roche, Sous le CH. Specialists: *Alain Gras*, de Chassorney, *H&G Buisson* (outstanding). Most négociants reliable. Fresh reds.

St-Véran Burg ★★ 18' 19 20' 21 22' 23 AOP either side of POUILLY-FUISSÉ. Best sites in Davayé. CH de Beauregard, Chagnoleau, Corsin, Deux Roches, Litaud, Merlin; gd-value DUBOEUF, Poncetys, Terres Secrètes co-op. Watch for DROUHIN.

Salitis, Ch de Ldoc ★★ Historic DOM, once part of Lagrasse Abbey before Frédéric Maurel's ancestor won it in a bet. Cabardès trad (r), delight of warm Med fruit with CAB SAUV lift; gd-value rosé.

Salon Champ ★★★★ Original BLANC DE BLANCS, from LE MESNIL in Côte des Blancs. Tiny quantities. Long-lived luxury-priced wines. On song recently, quality once again catching up with reputation, *viz.* 90 96 97' 02 04' 08 10 12 13 14'. *See also* DELAMOTTE. Both owned by LAURENT-PERRIER.

Sancerre Lo ★→★★★★ 19' 20 21 22 23 AOP famed for SAUV BL, but (r/rosé) PINOT N increasingly gd. Top whites go beyond simple varietal flavours to incorporate mineral and ripe citrus. Great acidity. Best can age. Try A Mellot, Anne Vatan, *Boulay*, Bourgeois, C Riffault, Delaporte, F or P Cotat, François Crochet, J-M Roger, L Crochet, P&N Reverdy, Paul Prieur, Pierre Martin, *Pinard*, Raimbault, Roblin, Thomas Labaille, VACHERON.

Sang des Cailloux, Dom Le S Rh ★★★ 16' 17' 18' 19' 20' 21 22' 23 24' Top VACQUEYRAS, bio, character, peppery, *garrigue* thrust, mostly GRENACHE (r). Classic red rotates name: Floureto (22), Azalaïs (24), Doucinello (23). Majestic, deep, rich Lopy (r) deserves patience. Sturdy, table-suited Un Sang Bl (w).

Sansonnière, La Ferme de Lo ★★→★★★ Cult ANJOU DOM, home to inspirational Mark Angeli, son Martial and pal Bruno Ciofi. Intriguing dry CHENIN BL, all VDF since 2006. Track down blended CUVÉE *La Lune* 08 09 10 12 14' 16 21', but snap up single-vyd du Houet, Les Fouchardes, Les Vieilles des Blanderies if you see them. Rosés, reds more hit and miss.

Santenay C d'O ★★★ 12 15' 16 17 18 19' 20' 21 22' 23 At s end of COTE DE BEAUNE, fine red, lovely white. Best vyds: CLOS de Tavannes, Clos Rousseau, Gravières (r/*w*). Local producers: *Bachey-Legros*, *Capuano-Ferreri*, *Ch Philippe le Hardi*, CHEVROT, Girardin (Justin), Jessiaume, MOREAU, *Muzard*, *Olivier*, VINCENT. Also gd: Giroud, JADOT (incl DOM Prieur-Brunet), LAMY. Evenstad for CÔTE DE NUITS (r).

Sarabande, Dom La Ldoc ★★→★★★ Australian/Irish couple, impressive FAUGÈRES. Les Espinasses powerful SYRAH-based. ROUSSANE/MARSANNE stylish, schist.

Saumur Lo ★→★★★★ 19' 20' 21 22' 23 AOP and region, latter home to AOPs SAUMUR-CHAMPIGNY, Saumur Le Puy-Notre-Dame (both r); range from simple fare to stunning cellar-worthy wines, also rare Coteaux de Saumur (sw). White (CHENIN BL) can be v. fine. Try Antoine Sanzay, Arnaud Lambert, BOUVET-LADUBAY (sp), CLOS DE L'ÉCOTARD, *Clos Rougeard*, Guiberteau, Le Porte Saint Jean, Nerleux, ROCHES NEUVES, Rocheville, Targé, Villeneuve, Yvonne.

Saumur-Champigny Lo ★★→★★★★ 05' 10' 15' 16 17 18' 19 20 21 22' 23 AOP for top CAB FR. Usually more structured/complex than SAUMUR. Try Antoine Sanzay,

Arnaud Lambert, Bruno Dubois, *Clos Rougeard*, Guiberteau, Hureau, Le Porte Saint Jean, Nerleux, ROCHES NEUVES, Rocheville, Targé, Villeneuve, Yvonne.

Saussignac SW Fr ★★→★★★ 18' 19 20 22 (23) BERGERAC sub-AOP, adjoining MONBAZILLAC, similar sweet wines, but best challenge SAUTERNES: ★★★ DOMS de Richard, La Maurigne, *Les Miaudoux*, Lestevenie; ★★ CHX Le Chabrier, Le Payral, Le Tap.

Sauternes Bx ★★→★★★★ 11' 13 14 15' 16' 18 19 20 22 23 AOP making France's best *liquoreux* from "noble rotted" grapes. Luscious, golden, age-worthy. Plenty of dry white BX too. Top classified (1855) CHX: GUIRAUD, *Lafaurie-Peyraguey*, LA TOUR BLANCHE, RAYNE VIGNEAU, SUDUIRAUT, YQUEM. Exceptional unclassified: *Fargues*, *Gilette*, *Raymond-Lafon*.

Sauzet, Etienne C d'O ★★★→★★★★ Leading DOM in PULIGNY with superb range of PCS (Combettes, Champ Canet best) and GC BÂTARD-M. Concentrated, lively, bio, age-worthy. Magnificent BOURGOGNE Bl. (Also sublime MONTRACHET from bought grapes.)

Savennières Lo ★★→★★★★ 10' 14' 15 16 18 19 20 22' (23) ANJOU's most prestigious dry AOP. Best from schist, complex, cellar-worthy. From sand, drink young. Try BAUDOUIN, BAUMARD, BELARGUS, Bergerie, *Boudignon*, Closel, DOM FL, Epiré, Laureau, Mahé, MORGAT, OGEREAU, PIERRE-BISE, Soucherie.

Savennières Roche-aux-Moines Lo ★★★→★★★★★ 10' 14' 15 16 18 19 20 22' Peak of SAVENNIÈRES, must-try CHENIN BL from 35-ha AOP. Breathtaking, mineral, electric from best: *Dom aux Moines*, FL, Forges, Laureau, PIERRE-BISE.

Savigny-lès-Beaune C d'O ★★→★★★ 10' 15' 18' 19' 20' 21' 22' 23 Important village next to BEAUNE; similar mid-weight wines, more excitement recently. Top vyds: Dominode, Guettes, Lavières, Vergelesses. Local growers: A Guyon, *Bize*, Camus-Bruchon, *Chandon de Briailles*, Chenu, Girard, Guillemot (w), Pavelot, RAPET, *Tollot-Beaut*. Exceptional CUVÉES: CLAIR, DROUHIN, JP Guyon, LEROY.

Savoie AOP Alpine wines, two-thirds white. 20 crus incl APREMONT, ARBIN, AYZE, Chautagne, CHIGNIN, Jongieux, St Jean de la Porte; regional AOPs incl CRÉMANT de Sav, ROUSSETTE DE SAV, SEYSSEL 25 grapes (r) mainly GAMAY, MONDEUSE, Persan, PINOT N; (w) Altesse, CHARD, CHASSELAS, Gringet, Jacquère, ROUSSANNE. Organic stars: ★★ A Berlioz, ★ Baraterie, ★ Berthollier, ★★ Chevillard, ★ Côtes Rousses, ★ *Giachino*, ★★ Prieuré St-Christophe, ★ St-Germain. Safe bets: Carrel-Senger, L'Idylle, Perrier, ★ P Grisard, Vendange. Promising natural newbies: Albatros, Archer, C Houillon, Sonjon. *See also* QUENARD.

Schaal, Julien Al ★★★ Marvellous set of organic RIES GC 19' 21; clean, precise; identified on labels by dominant mineral (SCHOENENBOURG: Gypse. RANGEN: Volcanique). Also in S Africa.

Schlossberg Al Famed GC at Kientzheim, since C15. Glorious compelling RIES from WEINBACH 10 and new TRIMBACH 15 20 21 22.

Schlumberger, Doms Al ★★★→★★★★ Huge (owns c.1% all AL vyds); GCS Kessler, Kitterlé, Saering. Superb Saering RIES 08 17' 18 19, but GEWURZ tops, esp VT CUVÉE Christine (unforgettable 76'; 20' excellent) and SGN Cuvée Anne (masterpiece 89'). New, v.gd Ries CLOS St Leger 17 19 vies with TRIMBACH CLOS STE-HUNE as most expensive Al.

Sancerre has six colours of silex (flint): black, white, grey, pink, salmon, blue-green.

Schoenenbourg Al Historic Riquewihr GC famous for RIES. (Voltaire owned vines here.) Top: HUGEL Ries Schoelhammer. Fine VT, SGN Ries DOPFF AU MOULIN.

Schoffit, Dom Al ★★★★ Rare winery situated in Colmar. Contrast RIES RANGEN CLOS St-Théobald 10' 17' 18' 20' (volcanic soil) and Ries GC Sommerberg 13 15 16 17' (granite). Harth CHASSELAS VIEILLES VIGNES, AL best. Superb VT, SGN, hard-to-find pure SYLVANER.

Sec Literally means dry, though CHAMP so called is medium-sweet.

Séguret S Rh ★★ 22' 23 **24**' Pretty hillside village in Rh-Villages top three; hot plain, fresh heights. Primarily GRENACHE, peppery, crisp, berried red; peachy white. Try CH la Courançonne (gd w); DOMS Bosquets (w), Crève Coeur (handmade, organic, bio), de Cabasse (hotel), de l'Amauve (organic, gd w), Fontaine des Fées (organic), Garancière (organic, bio), Maison Plantevin (organic), Malmont (rosé), Mourchon (profound), Pourra (intense, character).

Melon à Queue Rouge in Jura is just local Chardonnay. Sounds far more exotic.

Selosse, Anselme Champ ★★★★ Leading grower, prophet no longer in wilderness. Vinous, oxidative style, oak-fermented. Son Guillaume adding finesse: Version Originale still vibrant after 7 yrs on lees. NV BRUT Initial and fantastically rare Substance. Well-named Contraste BLANC DE NOIRS. Côte des Blancs parcels wonderfully different: lieux-dits Les Carelles, Le Bout du Clos, *La Côte Faron* Blanc de Noirs. Much of range NV; but Millésime **02** 04 06 08 09 10' 12 13.

Selz, Albert Al ★★★→★★★★ King of SYLVANER, with vyds in Mittelbergheim's clay-calcareous GC Zoztenberg. Outstanding 19 20 22; also v.gd RIES 19', marvellous late-harvest. Son Jeremy now joined.

Sérafin, Dom C d'O ★★★ Niece Frédérique in charge, continuing Christian S recipe: deep colour, intense flavours, new wood. Wines need age. Full-throttle, structured, firm, trad GEVREY. Robust, vibrant Cazetiers (DOM's back garden), CHARMES-CHAMBERTIN, Gevrey-Chambertin VIEILLES VIGNES.

Sérol, Dom Lo ★★★ 18' 19 20' 21 22' 23 Overlook this DOM in CÔTE ROANNAISE AOP at your peril. Combination of granite/basalt with local clone of GAMAY gives beautifully fresh, shapely wines. Top (Millerands, Perdrizière, Oudan): rich, dark, cellar-worthy. Most (eg. Eclat de Granite) drink young.

Seyssel Sav Small regional AOP with long history. Light white, fizz (Altesse, Molette). Try ★ Caves de Seyssel (esp Royal Seyssel).

SGN (Sélection des Grains Nobles) Al Term coined by HUGEL for AL equivalent of German Beerenauslese. Today, *grains nobles* mostly made with noble rot-affected grapes, not just v. sweet grapes that meet legal SGN requirement.

Sichel & Co Bx Notable BX merchant: Sirius a top brand. Family-run. Interests in CHX ANGLUDET, Daviaud, PALMER; DOM Peter Sichel (CORBIÈRES).

Sigoulès, Les Vignerons de SW Fr Much-improved source for BERGERAC, incl top CLOS d'Yvigne.

Simone, Ch Prov ★★★ Historic estate outside Aix, where Churchill painted Mont Ste-Victoire. Rougier family-owned for c.200 yrs. AOP PALETTE; n-facing slopes on limestone with clay and gravel give freshness. Seek age-worthy whites; iconic rosé, elegant reds from GRENACHE, MOURVÈDRE, with rare grape varieties Castet and Manosquin (r).

Sipp, Louis Al ★★→★★★ Trades in big volumes of young wines, but also two GC: fine RIES Kirchberg 13 16; luscious GEWURZ Osterberg VT 09 15 16 18 19.

Sipp-Mack Al ★★→★★★ Large range of lively, easy-drinking, dry, mineral wines, but not last word in concentration. Caroline S at helm now: lovely RIES GC Rosacker, expansive PINOT GR best.

Sorg, Bruno Al ★★★ Small grower at Eguisheim, GCS Florimont (RIES 13 14 16' great 17'), PFERSIGBERG (MUSCAT) 18'. Immaculate eco-friendly vyds.

Sorrel, Dom N Rh ★★★→★★★★ 18' 19' 20' 21 22' 23' 24' Small 3rd-generation HERMITAGE grower; the real thing. Top: Le Gréal (r, complex, long life), Les Rocoules (w, rich, a marvel at 10 yrs+). Also old-vine CROZES-HERMITAGE (r/w).

Sousa, De Champ ★★★ Erick and daughters enter 2nd decade as bio heroes in AVIZE. CUVÉE Les Caudalies BLANC DE BLANCS 08 10 12 13' 14 15. Well-named Cuvée Umami 13 15 16'; GC Blanc de Blancs Rés consistently excellent.

Sur lie "On the lees", as in MUSCADET. Bottled straight from vat: zest, body, character.

Tâche, La C d'O ★★★★ 90' 93' 96' 99' 02' 03 05' 09' 10' 12' 15' 16' 17 18' 19' 20' 21 22' 23 VOSNE GC, DRC MONOPOLE. Firm but always appealing in youth, glorious with age, a merry-go-round of flavour. More tannic than stablemates, develops extraordinary complexity and allure with time, floral and perfumed. Can age for decades – then, fairest of all DRCs?

Taille-aux-Loups, Dom de la Lo ★★★→★★★★ 14' 15 16 17' 18 19' 20' 21 22' (23) Leading DOM in MONTLOUIS SUR LO run by Jean-Philippe Blot. Brilliant MONTLOUIS, VOUVRAY (labelled VDF), all barrel-fermented, dry, touch burgundian, top quality and only get better with age. Try CLOS Michet, Clos Mosny, Les Hauts de Husseau, Remus. Triple Zéro, one of Lo's top fizzes.

Tain, Cave de N Rh ★★→★★★ Consistent CO-OP, mature vyds, incl 25% of all HERMITAGE. Sound-to-v.gd red Hermitage, esp Gambert de Loche (best, genuine, value), rich MARSANNE Hermitage Au Coeur des Siècles (w, value). ST-JOSEPH (r/w), ST-PÉRAY, interesting Bio (organic) range (St-Joseph r, CROZES w); others modern, run-of-mill, can be dull. Stylish Marsanne VIN DE PAILLE.

Taittinger Champ ★★★→★★★★ Family-run Reims house, unfailing elegance. BRUT NV, Rosé NV, Brut Vintage Collection Brut 89 95'. Epitome of apéritif style, inimitable weightlessness. Luxury **Comtes de Champagne** 95' 02 04' 08 09 12 13 14'. Opinions differ on tricky 11, but for some, wine of the vintage. Comtes Rosé also shines in 12' 13 14. Children Clovis and Vitalie now key to business. *See also* DOMS Evremond (England), Carneros (US).

Tarlant Champ ★★★→★★★★ Marne family in Oeuilly, 12th-generation, specializing in bone-dryness, *viz.* influential **Zero Brut Nature**; BAM!, CUVÉE Louis, Entracte.

Tasque, Dom La Ldoc Contributor Juliet Bruce Jones MW's small bio DOM. In MINERVOIS, but most IGP. Easy-drinking SYRAH-led Appia; old-vine CARIGNAN; intriguing ASSYRTIKO.

Tavel S Rh ★★ 24' Historical, red-tinted, full-bodied rosé from *garrigue* soils, across River Rhône from CHÂTEAUNEUF, based on GRENACHE, CINSAULT, aided by white grapes for lovely texture. Should be deep, herbal; for colourful Med garlicky, spiced dishes and sunny terraces. Best show well 3–4 yrs. Now some lighter, PROV-apéritif style. Top: CHX Aquéria (stylish), de Manissy (organic, bio), La Genestière (organic), Ségriès, **Trinquevedel** (fine, organic); DOMS A Hote (organic, character), Corne-Loup, *de la Mordorée* (top, bio), des Carabiniers (bio), LAFOND ROC-EPINE (organic, bio, interest), Maby (Prima Donna), Moulin-la-Viguerie (interest), Rocalière (bio); Alain Jaume, GUIGAL, L'Anglore (character, no sulphur), Tardieu-Laurent (organic, full), VIDAL-FLEURY, Vignerons de Tavel (Lauzeraies, value).

Tempier, Dom Prov ★★★→★★★★ Iconic BANDOL: Lucien and Lulu Peyraud revived AOP in 30s. Tops for elegance, concentration, longevity. Single-vyds Cabassaou, La Tourtine, pure expressions of MOURVÈDRE; v.gd rosé.

Terrasses du Larzac Ldoc ★★★→★★★★ One of LDOC's four cru terroirs, situated

---

SW France value

A hotbed of gd value. If what you want is real stylishness, this is where to look. CAHORS: CH les Croisille (modern, crunchy), CUVÉE Maurin (powerful), DOM La Berangeraie. CÔTES DU MARMANDAIS: DOM ELIAN DA ROS Abouriou (spicy). FRONTON: Dom Plaisance-Penavayre Alabets (quintessential NÉGRETTE). GAILLAC: DOM DE BRIN Pierres Blanches (saline). IROULÉGUY: DOM ARRETXEA Hegoxuri (stunning white). MARCILLAC: DOM DU CROS VIEILLES VIGNES (concentrated). SAINT MONT: Ch de Sabazan (outrageous value).

nw of Montpellier. High AOP on limestone with cold nights makes poised and complex reds. Attracts innovative growers, with small plots of vines; 50%+ organic, bio. Try CH de Jonquières; DOMS de La Rés d'O, de Malavielle, de Montcalmès, du PAS DE L'ESCALETTE; La Peira, Le Clos du Serres, L'Écriture, Mas Cal Demoura, Mas Combarèla, Mas Conscience, Mas d'Agamas, Mas des Brousses, MAS JULLIEN. Neighbouring AOP Ldoc St-Saturnin: Doms Archimbaud, Virgile Joly.

Thénard, Dom Burg ★★→★★★★ Historical; large holding of MONTRACHET, mostly sold on to NÉGOCIANTS. Look out for v.gd reds from home base in GIVRY.

Thévenet, Jean Burg ★★★ Top Mâconnais purveyor of rich, some semi-botrytized CHARD, eg. CUVÉE Levroutée at *Dom de la Bongran*. Also DOMS de Roally, Emilian Gillet. Opulent flavours, distinctive style divides opinion.

Thiénot, Alain Champ ★★★ Young house, new generation in charge. Ever-improving quality: watch. BRUT NV; Brut Rosé NV; Vintage Stanislas BLANC DE BLANCS 02 04 06 08'. Voluminous VIGNE aux Gamins (single-vyd AVIZE 06' 08 09 10). CUVÉE Garance CHARD 07 08. Interesting Garance Blanc des Rouges 08 10 12 13. Owns CANARD-DUCHÊNE, JOSEPH PERRIER; CH Ricaud (LOUPIAC).

Thivin, Ch Beauj ★★★ Long-est Geoffray family make great CÔTE DE BROUILLY. Single-vyd bottlings cover soil types. Sept VIGNES blend also a winner.

Tiregand, Ch de SW Fr ★★★ Leading estate in PÉCHARMANT. Age-worthy BX-style reds, greater freshness, distinctive SW twist; v. small but excellent SAUV BL. New owners 2023 after nearly 200 yrs in St-Exupéry family.

Greek grapes Agiorgitiko, Moschofilero, Xinomavro now allowed for some Provence red/rosé.

Tissot Jura Dominant family around ARBOIS. Jacques T (volume); ★ Jean-Louis T (value). ★★★ *Stéphane T* (also as A&M Tissot), bio with top single-vyd CHARD, VIN JAUNE, brooding reds and classy CRÉMANT du Jura selections. T-Maire, unrelated BOISSET brand.

Tollot-Beaut C d'O ★★★ Utterly dependable CÔTE DE BEAUNE grower with 20 ha in BEAUNE (Grèves, CLOS du Roi), CORTON (Bressandes), SAVIGNY (MONOPOLE PC Champ Chevrey) and CHOREY-LÈS-BEAUNE base (Pièce du Chapitre). Immediately appealing gd-value wines that can age. Also gd CORTON-CHARLEMAGNE.

Touraine Lo ★→★★★ Region and AOP. Latter a source of easy-going white/red. Some more serious, even age-worthy, esp from sub-AOPs: Amboise, Azay-le-Rideaux, Chenonceaux, Mesland, Oisly. Best: Biet, Clos du Porteau, Echardières, Garrelière, Gosseaume, Grosbois, J-F Mérieau, Joël Delaunay, La Grange Tiphaine, Marionnet, Morantin, *Ricard*, Roussely, Tue-Boeuf, T/X Frissant. Also look for Touraine-Noble-Joué, a triple-Pinot rosé AOP.

Tour des Gendres, Ch SW Fr Flagship estate in BERGERAC; bio. ALBERT DE CONTI other part of same family. Mostly BX varieties, but interesting additions ie. CHENIN BL, SAVAGNIN. Try Antholgia, single-parcel, old-vine SAUV BL. One to make Sancerrois quake.

Tour Saint-Martin, La Lo ★★→★★★ Bertrand Minchin, top name in MENETOU-SALON: (w) Fumet, Honorine 19 20 21 22 23; (r) age surprisingly well. VALENÇAY CUVÉES for value (Le Claux Delorme).

Trapet C d'O ★★★ →★★★★ Long-est GEVREY DOM. Sensual bio wines: eye-catching COTEAUX BOURGUIGNONS to majestic GC CHAMBERTIN, plus AL by marriage. Sons Pierre, Louis trying glass globes, steel barrels, eggs.

Tremblay, Dom Cecile C d'O ★★★ Wines of harmony, persistence. Style firmer recently. Doubled in size 2022, adding 4 ha, incl VOSNE PC, Les Beaux Monts.

Trévallon, Dom de Prov ★★★★ Famous DOM at LES BAUX; daughter Ostiane now in charge. No GRENACHE, so must be IGP Alpilles. Huge reputation fully justified:

meticulous viticulture, age-worthy wines. Intense CAB SAUV/SYRAH. Barrique-aged MARSANNE/ROUSSANNE, drop of CHARD and now GRENACHE BL. Terrific.

Trimbach, FE Al ★★★★ Top, refined, ageless: RIES CLOS STE-HUNE, peerless 67' 71' 75' 89'; VT and VT Hors Choix 90' (still great) 13 17' 18 19' 21' 22' 23' (classic); almost-as-gd (much cheaper) *Frédéric Emile* 10 12 13 14 16 17' 20' 21 22' 23'. Improved Ries SCHLOSSBERG, exceptional 20 21' 22' 23' (one of best ever: Mandelberg, Brand 23' both excellent). Underrated, fresh PINOT GR: superb Osterberg 15'. Knockout Ries-like SYLVANER Weinbaum from Trottacker lieu-dit, ages spectacularly well.

Tunnel, Dom du N Rh ★★★ Four top, stylish ST-PÉRAY, notably Prestige, Pur Blanc (30s MARSANNE, serious, evolves). Richly styled, scaled CORNAS, incl Pur Noir (1900s SYRAH), ST-JOSEPH (r).

Tursan SW Fr Mostly DYA AOP in LANDES. Super-chef Michel Guérard makes ★★★ lovely wines in chapel-like cellar at CH de Bachen, but not trad Tursan. Real thing from ★★ DOM de Perchade. Lovely dry white from ★★ Dom de Cazalet (two MANSENGS plus rare local Baroque). Worthy co-op rather outclassed.

U Stiliccionu, Dom Cors ★★★ In AJACCIO; 7 ha; bio (min sulphur). Granite, finesse; Antica (r) GRENACHE, SCIACCERELLO. Emy-Lidia VERMENTINO.

Vacheron, Dom Lo ★★→★★★ Leading DOM in SANCERRE. Single-vyd Chambrates, Guigne-Chèvres, Le Paradis, *Les Romains* 14' 15 16 17 19 21 22, 23. Iconic cellar-worthy PINOT N, Belle Dame.

Vacqueyras S Rh ★★→★★★ 16' 17' 18 19' 20 22' 23 24' Spiced, deep, tannic GRENACHE-led red from hot, flat, stony vyds nr GIGONDAS; hearty dishes suited. Lives 10 yrs+. CHX de Montmirail, *des Tours* (finesse, RAYAS stable); CLOS de Caveau (organic), *Clos des Cazaux* (value); DOMS Amouriers (organic), Archimbaud-Vache, CHARBONNIÈRE, Couroulu (v.gd, last yr 22), Famille Perrin, Font de Papier (organic), Fourmone (fine), Garrigue (genuine), Grapillon d'Or, Monardière (organic, v.gd), Montirius (bio), Montvac (organic), Ouréa (organic, pure), Roucas Toumba (organic, character), SANG DES CAILLOUX (organic, bio, esp Lopy), Semelles de Vent (handmade), Verde; JABOULET, P AMADIEU. Solid whites: Ch des Roques, Clos des Cazaux, Fourmone, Mas des Restanques, Sang des Cailloux.

Val de Loire Lo ★→★★★ Main regional IGP in Lo. Mostly minor wines (DYA, no fuss). Occasional gem: YANNICK AMIRAULT Bâtard-Princesse CHENIN BL (BOURGUEIL).

Valençay Lo ★→★★★ 21 22' 23 AOP; gd-value, easy-drinking, mostly SAUV BL/CHARD or CÔT/GAMAY/PINOT N: Domaines Minchin, Lafond, Preys, Sinson.

Valréas S Rh ★★ 23 24' CÔTES DU RH-VILLAGE in N Vaucluse, truffle, wine, lavender, olive area; high vyds, cool breezes, quality on the up; large co-op. Spiced, crisp, red-fruited mainly GRENACHE (r); stylish white. Try CH la Décelle, CLOS Bellane incl Val des Rois (organic, gd w), Mas de Ste-Croix; DOMS des Grands Devers, du Séminaire (organic, pure r), Prévosse (organic).

VdF (Vin de France) Replaces Vin de Table, but with mention of grape variety, vintage. Often blends of regions with brand name. Can be source of unexpected delights if talented winemaker uses this category to avoid bureaucractic hassle, eg. Mark Angeli, Y CUILLERON VIOGNIER. ANJOU, S ARDÈCHE hotbeds of VdF.

VDN (*vin doux naturel*) ROUSS Sweet wine fortified with wine alc, so sweetness natural, not strength. Speciality of ROUSS based on GRENACHES BL/Gr/N. Top, esp aged RANCIOS, can finish a meal on a sublime note. MUSCAT from BEAUMES DE VENISE, FRONTIGNAN, Lunel, RIVESALTES, ROUSS, St Jean de MINERVOIS gd.

VdP (Vin de Pays) *See* IGP.

Vendange Harvest. VT (Vendange Tardive) Late-harvest; AL equivalent to German Auslese but usually higher alc.

Venoge, de Champ ★★★ Venerable house, precise, more elegant under LANSON-BCC ownership; articulate boss in Gilles de la Bassetière. Cordon Bleu Extra-

BRUT, Vintage BLANC DE BLANCS 12 13' 16 17. Prestige CUVÉE Louis XV 10-yr-old BLANC DE NOIRS 08 10' 12 14'. Less Anglophone following than it deserves.

Vent, Dom du Ldoc ★★ Natalie and Benjamin Boyer have worked all over France, been in LDOC since 2022. Made cracking start. Perfumed, delicate Comme un Souffle FITOU, floral, zippy VERMENTINO IGP Aude. Also fine MUSCAT de Rivesaltes. To watch.

Ventoux S Rh ★★ 23 24 Sprawling 5400-ha AOP on fringes of Mont Ventoux: mixed soils, hot plain, cool heights. Some top DOMS: value red, gd choice. Frisky red (GRENACHE/SYRAH, café-style to fuller, peppery, quality rising), lucid rosé, stylish white (more oak). Best: CH Unang (organic, gd w), Ch Valcombe, Chêne Bleu (oak, rosé), CLOS de Trias (long raising), Clos des Patris (organic), Gonnet, La Ferme St Pierre (w/rosé, organic), La Vieille Ferme (r, also VDF), St-Marc, Terra Ventoux, Vignerons Mont Ventoux; Doms Allois (organic), Anges, Berane, Brusset, Cascavel, Champ-Long, Croix de Pins (gd w), du Tix, Fondrèche (organic, fun), Grand Jacquet, Martinelle (organic, stylish), Murmurium, Olivier B (organic), PAUL JABOULET, PESQUIÉ (polished), Piéblanc (organic, fresh depth), Pigeade, St-Jean du Barroux (organic, character, incl w), Terres de Solence, Tix, Verrière, VIDAL-FLEURY, Vieux Lazaret, VIGNOBLES Brunier, co-op Bédoin.

Vernay, Dom Georges N Rh ★★★★ 22' 23' 24' Save up to try CONDRIEU: balance, restraint, finesse. Terrasses de l'Empire *apéritif de luxe*; Chaillées d'Enfer, fine richness; Coteau de Vernon, subtle, mystery, lives 20 yrs+. CÔTE-RÔTIE, ST-JOSEPH (r), lucid, tight; upmarket IGP COLLINES RHODANIENNES (r/w).

Veuve Clicquot Champ ★★★★ Historical house, both trad and creative. Improving Yellow Label NV; 5% oak. Impressive DEMI-SEC NV. Vintage Rés 12 a wonder of perfect maturity. Luxe La Grande Dame (GD) 12' 15; PINOT N takes control with aplomb. Older vintages of GD stay course, *viz.* 04' (no 02, deemed too muscular for GD), glorious in 89. GD Rosé 06 08 12 13 15', ready.

Veuve Fourny Champ ★★★→★★★★ Superb archetypal Côte des Blancs specialist, delightful bros. Sustainable (HVE) in Vertus. Also PINOT N. BLANC DE BLANCS PC 13 14' 15 17' 18 19 and NV exceptional value.

Vézelay Burg ★→★★ Age 1–2 yrs. Lovely location (with abbey) in NW Burg. Promoted to full AOP for tasty whites from CHARD. Also try revived MELON (COTEAUX BOURGUIGNON), light PINOT (generic BOURGOGNE): Best: DOM de la Cadette, des Faverelles, Elise Villiers, La Croix Montjoie.

Vidal-Fleury N Rh ★→★★★ Since 1781 merchant-grower based at Côte-Rôtie, GUIGAL-owned. Top, distinguished, deep *La Chatillonne* (from Blonde, 12% VIOGNIER, much oak, leave min 7 yrs) miles ahead of rest of range: decent CAIRANNE (r), gd CHÂTEAUNEUF (w), sound CÔTES DU RH (w/rosé), GIGONDAS, MUSCAT de BEAUMES-DE-VENISE, VENTOUX.

Vieilles vignes Old vines. Can give extra depth, complexity. But no rules about age and can be a tourist trap. Can a vine be old if it's younger than you are?

Vieux Télégraphe, Dom du S Rh ★★★ 05' 07' 09' 10' 12' 14' 15' 16' 17' 18' 19' 20' 21 23' 24' Much-celebrated, high-level estate, in gd form; massed big-stone plateau soils, tight, slow-burn, deep-set terroir-herbal red CHÂTEAUNEUF. Top two wines: La Crau (long life, no 22), Piedlong et Pignan (pure, silky). Splendid, compelling, true-*garrigue* Med table-white *La Crau* (complex if patient), CLOS La Roquète (slinky). Owns cool, slow-to-evolve, spiced, intricate GIGONDAS DOM Les Pallières with US importer Kermit Lynch.

Vignelaure, Ch de Prov ★★★→★★★★ Top estate for reds, AOP COTEAUX D'AIX EN PROVENCE. CAB SAUV, SYRAH at 300m (984ft) give depth, freshness. Will age 10 yrs. Rosé up to 5 yrs; intriguing ROUSSANNE, Rolle, SÉM.

Vigne or vignoble Vineyard (vyd), vineyards (vyds). **Vigneron** Vine-grower.

Vignoble du Rêveur Al ★★★ Project by Mathieu DEISS and Emanuelle Milan using

Mathieu's maternal family vines; bio field blends in Bennwihr, crafted by this uncommonly talented duo, make dry, food-friendly, pure styles that won't make a horse faint like many "natural" wines. Superb Singulier and Pierre Sauvages 17' 18 20 21.

Vigouroux, Georges SW Fr Top name in CAHORS, instrumental in reviving AOP. Estates incl Haute Serre and Mercues. Generations have changed; wines seem to be getting better after slightly dull period.

Villeneuve, Ch de Lo ★★→★★★ 18' 19' 20' 21 22' 23 Underrated DOM, delicious SAUMUR (w) and tiptop SAUMUR-CHAMPIGNY. Burgundian Les Cormiers (w) and finely structured Le Grand Clos (r) age beautifully.

Vilmart & Cie Champ ★★★→★★★★ Exemplary grower farming 11 ha of PC in relatively unfashionable Montagne village Rilly. Oak fermentation, attention to detail from long-serving chef de CAVE Laurent Champs. Superb Coeur de CUVÉE 08 09 12 13 15' 16, Grand Cellier d'Or 14 16 18 19. Try Rubis Rosé.

Vincent, Jean-Marc C d'O ★★★ Few people devote as much thought/effort to viticulture. Excellent, age-worthy whites; v.gd reds (Gravité). Check daring, multi-vintage ALIGOTÉ blend Soler-Al. Now joined by daughter Anaïs.

Vincent, Pierre C d'O ★★★ Now est own name in AUXEY-DURESSES (ex-DOM LEFLAIVE, VOUGERAIE). Small CUVÉES of some 20 appellations. Many old vines yielding pure, delicate wines. Best to come.

Vin de paille From grapes dried before pressing, so concentrated sweetness, acidity; esp in Jura, also HERMITAGE.

Vin gris Pale pink. "Oeil de perdrix" means much the same; so does "blush".

80% of France's *vins doux naturels* come from Roussillon.

Vin jaune Jura ★★→★★★★ Speciality of Jura; inimitable not-so-"yellow" wine. SAVAGNIN, 6 yrs+ in barrel without topping up, develops flor like Sherry but no added alc. Ages for decades. Sold in unique 62cl clavelin bottles. Top spot, CH-CHALON has own AOP; S TISSOT specializes in single-vyd bottlings, Bourdy in old vintages. *See also* ARBOIS, CÔTES DU JURA, L'ETOILE.

Vinsobres S Rh ★★ 19' 20 21 22' 23 24' Out-of-limelight AOP starting to move, led by quality, fresh SYRAH, gd hillside, high-plateau vyds, deserves a try. Best reds peppery, lustre in fruit; age 10 yrs. New DOMS emerging. Leaders: CAVE la Vinsobraise (Diamant N), CH Rouanne (plot-specific), CLOS Volabis (organic), Doms Autrand (stylish), Chaume-Arnaud (bio, v.gd, incl w), Constant-Duquesnoy, du Tave, Famille Perrin (**Hauts de Julien** top, Cornuds value), Jaume (fruit), Moulin (trad, gd r/w), Péquélette (bio, VDF taking over from Vinsobres), Serre Besson (gd VdF), Vallot (bio, fruit).

Viré-Clessé Burg ★★ 17' 18 19' 20' 21 22' 23 AOP, two of best white villages of MÂCON. Exuberant rich style, esp from Quintaine area, sometimes late-harvest. Try **Bonhomme**, Chaland, DOM de la Verpaille, Gandines, Gondard-Perrin, Guillemot-Michel, J-P Michel, THÉVENET and all gd Mâconnais NÉGOCIANTS.

Visan S Rh ★★ 23 24' Upwardly mobile CÔTES DU RH-VILLAGE, top three: peppery, mainly GRENACHE red; some softer, plenty organic. White fair. DOMS Au 7ème Clos (organic), Bastide (fruit), Coste Chaude (organic), Dieulefit (bio, low sulphur), Florane (bio, v.gd), Fourmente (bio, esp Nature), Guintrandy (organic, full), Montmartel (organic), Philippe Plantevin (organic), Roche-Audran (organic, style), VIGNOBLE Art Mas (organic).

Vogüé, Comte Georges de C d'O ★★★★ Patrician CHAMBOLLE estate with lion's share of MUSIGNY. Winemaker Jean Lupatelli using more whole bunches, making style more accessible in youth. Also plot-by-plot vinification. Unique and splendid **Musigny Bl**, a one-off.

Volnay C d'O ★★★→★★★★ 05' 09' 10' 15' 16 17' 18 19 20 21 22' 23 Top CÔTE DE

BEAUNE reds, except when it hails or gets too hot. The southern echo of CHAMBOLLE, similar grace and slightly more structure. Wonderful evolution with age. (Ban on weedkillers in PC vyds.) Best vyds: Caillerets, Champans, CLOS des Chênes, Santenots (more clay), Taillepieds and MONOPOLES Clos de la Bousse d'Or, Clos de la Chapelle, Clos des Ducs, Clos du CH des Ducs. Growers: BOULEY, D'ANGERVILLE, *de Montille*, Lafarge, *Pousse d'Or*. Also v.gd: *Bitouzet-Prieur*, Buffet, Clerget, Glantenay, H BOILLOT, HOSPICES DE BEAUNE, LAFON, Rossignol.

Vosne-Romanée C d'O ★★★→★★★★ 90' 93' 96' 99' 02' 05' 09' 10' 12 15' 16' 17 18 19' 20' 21 22' 23 Most patrician village in Burg, with celebrated GCS and outstanding PCS Beaumonts, Brûlées, Malconsorts, Suchots and more. Should always be special and regularly sublime. No excuses for anything less. Just a question of price... Top: ARNOUX-LACHAUX, Bizot, CATHIARD, Coquard-Loison-Fleurot, DRC, EUGÉNIE, GRIVOT, GROS, Lamarche, LEROY, LIGER-BELAIR, MÉO-CAMUZET, MUGNERET, Noëllat, ROUGET. Also v.gd: Clavelier, *Confuron-Gindre*, Forey, Guyon Tard.

Vougeot C d'O ★★★ 02' 05' 09' 10' 12' 15' 16 17 18 19' 20 21 22' 23 Mostly GC as CLOS DE VOUGEOT (variable, but improving). Also village and PCS Les Cras, Les Petits Vougeots, plus MONOPOLES *Clos Blanc de V* (outstanding w), *Clos de la Perrière*. Try *Bertagna*, Clerget, *Fourrier*, GROS (A), HUDELOT-NOËLLAT, LEROUX and *Vougeraie*.

Pink Chardonnay is now a thing: brown-skinned mutation discovered in Jura.

Vougeraie, Dom de la C d'O ★★★→★★★★ BOISSET's vyd holdings; bio. Fine-boned, perfumed, whole-bunch vinified, sensual GCS, esp *Bonnes-Mares*, CHARMES-CHAMBERTIN, MUSIGNY. Fine white: superb, age-worthy *Clos Blanc de Vougeot*, four GCs incl unique Charlemagne. Gaining stature each yr.

Vouvray Lo ★→★★★★ (dr) 18' 19' 20' 21 22 23 (sw) 02' 03 05 08' 09 10 11' 15' 16 17 18' 20' 22 Famed AOP for CHENIN BL. All styles; much fizz (great from top DOMS, but others often disappointing). Dry (bright, minerally), demi-sec (super with acid/sugar in harmony), top sweet (can be astonishing). Try Aubuisières, Autran, Brunet, CHAMPALOU, *Clos Naudin*, FRANÇOIS CHIDAINE (VDF), FRANÇOIS ET JULIEN PINON, Gaudrelle, HUET, Meslerie, Perrault-Jadaud, TAILLE-AUX-LOUPS (VDF), Vigneau-Chevreau, *Vincent Carême*.

Weinbach, Dom Al ★★★★ World's best GEWURZ (from Altenbourg, Furstentum, Mambourg) and PINOT GR SGN, but all exceptionally elegant, pure gastronomic wines: MUSCAT 22', SYLVANER 19' 20, RIES GC SCHLOSSBERG (Cuve Ste Catherine 22 is exceptional), Pinot Gr Altenbourg 10' 13' 17' 18' 19' 21'. Théo Faller is making superlative wines, all styles (even superb orange if you like). Slowly changing (and adding) many wine names to French, eg. Les Caracoles and Les Treilles du Loup.

Zind Humbrecht, Dom Al ★★★★ Four new wines from AL quality leader (AUXERROIS Rotenberg, RIES Hengst, Ries Sommerberg, also CHARD fizz). But estate's stars still stellar Ries, GEWURZ, PINOT GR from GCS Brand, HENGST, GOLDERT, RANGEN, plus MUSCAT GC Goldert (Al's best along with Ernest BURN's). CLOS Windsbuhl (not GC) Ries, Pinot Gr great too. Splendid 21 and 22, classic 19, sumptuous 18. Heimbourg a high-quality lieu-dit: marvellous Pinot Gr 22.

Zotzenberg Al Only GC for SYLVANER (should be many more). Different geological-era limestone marls give full, fresh, age-worthy wines. Best: Albert Seltz, BOECKEL, Hirtz, Rieffel.

Zusslin, Valentin Al ★★★ Much-admired, 13th-generation bio estate. Excellent lieu-dit Bollenberg, marly-sandstone CLOS Libenberg MONOPOLE (4 ha, top of Pfingstberg hill; v.gd 17 18), Pfingstberg GC RIES (spectacular 18).

Châteaux of Bordeaux

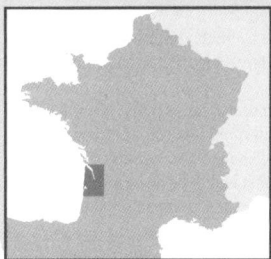

Abbreviations used in the text:

Bx	Bordeaux
Bar	Barsac
Cas	Castillon-Côtes de Bordeaux
E-2-M	Entre-Deux-Mers
Fron	Fronsac
Grav	Graves
H-Méd	Haut-Médoc
L de P	Lalande de Pomerol
List	Listrac
Marg	Margaux
Méd	Médoc
Mou	Moulis
Pau	Pauillac
Pe-Lé	Pessac-Léognan
Pom	Pomerol
Saut	Sauternes
St-Ém	St-Émilion
St-Est	St-Estèphe
St-Jul	St-Julien

B ordeaux's en primeur system appears to be broken. The 2022 campaign flopped due to overpricing (nothing to do with the quality of the wines, which are good); and despite a reduction in prices for the 23s (again generally well received in terms of quality) that campaign went the same way, the cuts not deemed to have gone far enough. And whereas in the past, the négociants funded and carried the stock, this time the négoce refused certain allocations because their cellars were already full with back vintages. The financial situation for some négociants is precarious. Pricing a new vintage attractively without undermining the prices of back vintages is one of the problems. The

Châteaux of Bordeaux entries also cross-refer to France

other is to continue to convince consumers to part with hard-earned cash for unfinished wines when there is so much else on offer and the general trend is for wines to drink now. Would a one year break, say, and a serious price reset make the difference? It's hard to say, because châteaux are already hedging their bets by holding more stock and releasing older vintages later. And for some négociants, en primeur is gradually becoming less important.

Vintage 2024 was something of an ordeal for growers. A rainy winter then spring, intense pressure from mildew, coulure (particularly in the old Merlot) and hail that affected about 6000 hectares to varying degrees, were some of the adversities that had to be dealt with. Then, when there was a gleam of sunshine and hope, heavy rain fell in September. Expect lower alcohol, higher acidity and variable quality. Luckily there are plenty of vintages for drinking now. The luscious 09s are tempting at whatever level; 08s have come into their own; 10s are opening, as are the "classic" 14s, although the Grands Crus need longer. For early drinking, try the often-charming 12s or underrated 11s, which have improved with bottle-age.

Of recent years, the softer 17s will be the first to broach. Mature vintages to look for are 96 (best Médoc), 98 (particularly Right Bank, Graves), 00 01 (Right Bank, but don't dismiss Médoc), 02 04 06. The splendid 05s are also opening, although patience is still a virtue here. Dry white Bordeaux remains consistent in quality and value, the whites in 24 seemingly balanced and fresh. Fine white Graves can age as well as white burgundy, providing there's acidity and freshness. And Sauternes continues to offer an array of remarkable years: 24 looks to have excellent potential. Even moderate years like 08 14 16 offer approachability and a fresher touch, while great years, 09 11 15 17, have the concentration and hedonistic charm that make them indestructible.

A, Dom de l' Cas ★★ 17 18 19 20 22 23 CAS property owned by STÉPHANE DERENONCOURT. Consistent quality. Also VDF CHARD.

Agassac, D' H-Méd ★★ 18 19 20' 22 23 In S H-MÉD. Modern, accessible. Blend of CAB SAUV/MERLOT.

Aiguilhe, D' Cas ★★ 16 18 19 20 22 23 Large von Neipperg-owned estate. MERLOT-led *power and finesse*. Some ageing potential. Also a BX white. CANON-LA-GAFFELIÈRE same stable.

Andron-Blanquet St-Est ★★ 16' 18 19 20 Last vintage 21. Integrated into COS LABORY.

Angélus St-Ém ★★★★ 10' 11 12 14 15' 16' 17 18' 19' 20 21 22' 23 24 Declined classification in 2022. Dark, rich, sumptuous. More finesse from 19. Second label: Carillon d'Angélus. Also No. 3 d'Angélus and BX red Tempo d'Angélus; all made in state-of-the-art winery. Blanc du Milie (w) too.

Angludet Marg ★★ 15' 16' 18' 19 20 21 23 Owned by NÉGOCIANT SICHEL; bio from 23. Lots of PETIT VERDOT in blend. Fragrant, stylish. Often gd value.

Archambeau Grav ★★ (r) 19 20 22 (w) 22 23 Family-owned property. 20 ha in a single block. Organic methods. *Fruity dry white*; fragrant reds (50/50% MERLOT/ CAB); all gd value.

Arche, D' Saut ★★ 15 16 17 18 20 22 23 Second Growth steadily being overhauled. Also Arche Perlée CRÉMANT.

Armailhac, D' Pau ★★★ 14 15' 16' 17 18 19 20 21 22' 23 (MOUTON) ROTHSCHILD-owned Fifth Growth; 83% CAB SAUV/CAB FR in 23. Fair value.

Aurelius St-Ém ★★ 18 19 20 21 Top CUVÉE from go-ahead ST-ÉM CO-OP; MERLOT/ CAB FR (80/20%), new oak, concentrated.

Ausone St-Ém ★★★★ 05' 06' 08 09' 10' 12 14 15' 16' 17 18' 19' 20' 21 22 23 24 Tiny, illustrious CH owned by Vauthier family. Declined classification in 2022, so now just basic ST-ÉM. Only 1500 cases; vyds s- and se-facing, sheltered; lots of CAB FR (60% in 23). Long-lived wines with volume, texture, finesse. At a price. Second label: Chapelle d'Ausone (500 cases). *La Clotte*, FONBEL, MOULIN ST-GEORGES, Simard same stable.

Balestard la Tonnelle St-Ém ★★ 15 16 18 19 20 22' 23 Capdemourlin-owned property on limestone plateau. More CAB FR these days (35% in 23).

Barde-Haut St-Ém ★★→★★★ 15' 16 18 19' 20 22 23 MERLOT-led GRAND CRU CLASSÉ; s-facing vyd in one block. Limestone terroir. Modern touch.

Bastor-Lamontagne Saut ★★ 15 17 19 21 22 23 24 Large Preignac estate; SÉM/SAUV BL; organic. Second label: Les Remparts de Bastor. Visitor-friendly. On gd form since 2021.

Batailley Pau ★★★ 10' 11 12 15 16 17 18 19' 20 21 22 23 24 Relatively gd value, CAB SAUV-led Fifth Growth.

Beaumont H-Méd ★★ 18 19 20 22 23 Large CRU BOURGEOIS Supérieur. Approachable early. Usually gd value. Same stable as BEYCHEVELLE.

Beauregard Pom ★★★ 14 15 16 18 19' 20' 21 22 23 Much improved; organic; modern winery. MERLOT-led with CABS FR/SAUV. Second label: Benjamin de Beauregard.

Beauséjour St-Ém ★★★ 14 15 16 17 18' 19' 20' 22 23 24 Tiny PREMIER GRAND CRU CLASSÉ (B). Owned by Joséphine Duffau-Lagarrosse and Courtin family (Clarins cosmetics). New *cuvier* in 2024. Rich, cellar-worthy.

Beau-Séjour Bécot St-Ém ★★★ 12 14 15 16 17 18 19 20' 21 22 23 24 Distinguished PREMIER GRAND CRU CLASSÉ (B) on limestone plateau. Family-owned. More finesse these days, but still gd ageing potential.

Beau-Site St-Est ★★ 16 18 19 20 22 23 Owned by BORIE-MANOUX. CAB SAUV-led (70%). Supple, fresh, accessible.

Bélair-Monange St-Ém ★★★ 10' 11 12 14 15 16' 17 18 19 20 21 22 23 24 PREMIER GRAND CRU CLASSÉ (B) on limestone plateau and côtes. MOUEIX-owned. Huge investment in vyd and Herzog & de Meuron-designed winery. Refined style; more intensity, precision these days. Second label: Annonce.

Belgrave H-Méd ★★ 14 15 16 18 19 20 21 22 23 DOURTHE-owned Fifth Growth (since 1979). Steady investment. Understated but consistent. Value.

Bellefont-Belcier St-Ém ★★ 15' 16 17 18 19' 20 21 22 23 24 Much-improved GRAND CRU CLASSÉ on s côtes. More interest and precision.

St-Émilion classification – 2022 edition

The 2022 classification incl a total of 85 CHX: 14 PREMIERS GRANDS CRUS CLASSÉS and 71 GRANDS CRUS CLASSÉS. FIGEAC received promotion, joining PAVIE as the only Premiers Grands Cru Classés (A), ANGÉLUS, AUSONE and CHEVAL BLANC having officially withdrawn from the classification. There were no other changes at Premier Grand Cru Classé (B) level barring the absence of LA GAFFELIÈRE, which had also withdrawn. New to status of Grand Cru Classé were Badette, Boutisse, Clos Badon Thunevin, Clos Dubreuil, Clos St-Julien, La Confession, Corbin Michotte (declassified in 2012), Croix de Labrie, La Croizille, Lassègue, MANGOT, Montlabert, Montlisse, ROL VALENTIN, Tour Baladoz and TOUR SAINT CHRISTOPHE. Among the absentees from the 2012 classification, Grand Pontet, L'Arrosée and Tertre Daugay are now all part of newly created QUINTUS. Others withdrew (LA CLOTTE, QUINAULT L'ENCLOS), and some were absorbed by a sister property (PAVIE DECESSE by PAVIE). Classification reviewed every 10 yrs, so the next, theoretically, in 2032.

Belle-Vue H-Méd ★★ 15′ 16′ 17 18 19 20 22 In S H-MÉD. Dark, dense but firm. Owned by TWE (*see* Australia).

Berliquet St-Ém ★★ 14 15′ 16′ 17 18 19′ 20 21 22 23 Tiny GRAND CRU CLASSÉ on plateau and côtes. Same stable as CANON. To watch.

Bernadotte H-Méd ★★ 16′ 17 18′ 19 20 23 Hong Kong-based ownership. CAB SAUV/MERLOT (50/50%). Savoury; gd value.

Beychevelle St-Jul ★★★ 11 12 14 15′ 16′ 17 18 19′ 20 21 22 23 24 Sizeable Fourth Growth owned by Castel and Suntory. Wines of consistent *elegance* rather than power. Manager Philippe Blanc's 30th vintage in 2024.

First pecan tree in Europe was given to Carbonnieux by Thomas Jefferson, 1787.

Biston-Brillette Mou ★★ 16′ 18 19 20 22 Family-owned CRU BOURGEOIS Supérieur. Attractive, early drinking, gd value. MERLOT/CAB SAUV (50/50%). Second label: Biston. Environmental certification.

Bonalgue Pom ★★ 15 16 18 19 20 22 23 Much-improved MERLOT/CAB FR (90/10%) POM from sand, gravel, clay soils; gd value for AOP. Owned by Domaines Bourotte-Audy. CLOS du Clocher same stable.

Bonnet Bx ★★ (r) 19 20 22 (w) DYA Forged by André Lurton; now run by son Jacques. Large producer of some of best E-2-M white and red (oak-aged Rés) BX. E-2-M red in 23 (available 25). Also Oh Oui! 0% alcohol.

Bon Pasteur, Le Pom ★★★ 14 15′ 16 17 18 19 20 22 23 Tiny cru on ST-ÉM border. MERLOT/CAB FR (80/20%). MICHEL ROLLAND makes the wine. Ripe, opulent, seductive, but ages well.

Boscq, Le St-Est ★★ 15′ 16′ 18′ 19′ 20 22 23 Owned by DOURTHE, consistently great value wines.

Bourgneuf Pom ★★ 14 15′ 16′ 17 18 19′ 20 21 22 23 MERLOT-led (85%). Frédérique Vayron at helm. Subtle, savoury wine; gd value for POM.

Bouscaut Pe-Lé ★★★ (r) 15 16′ 17 18 19 20 21 22 (w) 20 21 22 23 24 Classed Growth. Structured, MERLOT/CAB SAUV/MALBEC reds. Sappy, age-worthy SAUV BL/SÉM *whites*. Organic.

Boyd-Cantenac Marg ★★★ 14 15 16 18 19 20 22 Tiny (17 ha) Cantenac-based Third Growth. Owned by Guillemet family since 1932. CAB SAUV-based plus MERLOT/PETIT VERDOT/CAB FR. Needs time. Also POUGET.

Branaire-Ducru St-Jul ★★★ 14 15 16′ 17 18′ 19 20 21 22 23 24 Consistent Fourth Growth; regularly gd value; ageing potential. Modern, gravity-fed *cuvier* with 65 suspended tanks.

Branas Grand Poujeaux Mou ★★ 15′ 16′ 17 18 19′ 20′ 22 23 Neighbour of CHASSE-SPLEEN, POUJEAUX. Now 25 ha of vyd. Rich, modern style. Second label: Les Eclats de Branas.

Brane-Cantenac Marg ★★★→★★★★ 12 14 15′ 16′ 17 18 19′ 20 22 23 24 Second Growth owned by Henri Lurton; CAB SAUV-led (77% in 23) with 1% CARMENÈRE. Classic, fragrant MARG to age. Second label: *Baron de Brane*; value.

Brillette Mou ★★ 16′ 18 19 20 Reputable DOM on gravelly soils. Acquired and integrated into CHASSE-SPLEEN in 2023.

Cabanne, La Pom ★★ 15 16′ 18 19 20 22 23 MERLOT-dominant (94%) DOM on w slope. Firm when young; needs bottle-age.

Caillou Saut ★★ 15′ 16 19 20 23 Second Growth BAR for pure *liquoreux;* 100% SÉM. Second label: Les Erables. Also young-vine Les Tourelles.

Calon Ségur St-Est ★★★★ 12 13 14 15′ 16′ 17 18′ 19′ 20 21 22 23 24 Third Growth on top form; more CAB SAUV these days (72% in 23). Powerful but fine, complex. Second label: Le Marquis de Calon.

Cambon la Pelouse H-Méd ★★ 16′ 18 19 20 22 Large and reliable. Owned by TWE (*see* Australia).

Camensac, De H-Méd ★★ 15 16 18' 19 20 22 Sizeable Fifth Growth in N H-MÉD. Owned by Merlaut family (CHASSE-SPLEEN, GRUAUD-LAROSE). Steady improvement; CAB SAUV/MERLOT; ageing potential.

Canon St-Ém ★★★★ 09' 10' 12 14 15' 16' 17 18' 19' 20 21 22' 23 24 Esteemed PREMIER GRAND CRU CLASSÉ (B) with vyd on limestone plateau. Wertheimer-owned, like BERLIQUET, RAUZAN-SÉGLA, so plenty of investment. MERLOT/CAB FR (70/30%). Elegant, complex, for long ageing. Second label: Croix Canon (separate winery formerly a C12 chapel).

Canon-la-Gaffelière St-Ém ★★★ 10' 14 15' 16 17 18 19' 20 22 23 PREMIER GRAND CRU CLASSÉ (B) on s foot slope. MERLOT/CAB FR/CAB SAUV blend. Stylish, impressive. Organic. Also D'AIGUILHE, LA MONDOTTE.

Cantemerle H-Méd ★★★ 10' 14 15 16 18 19' 20 22 23 Large Fifth Growth in S H-MÉD. Replanted over past 40 yrs. New gravity-fed *cuvier* with 120 tanks from 2025. On gd form and gd value too; 22 best yet.

Cantenac-Brown Marg ★★★ 14 15 16' 17 18 19' 20 21 22 23 24 Third Growth being revamped. New gravity-fed winery from 2023 with 70 tanks (33 before). More voluptuous, refined these days. CAB SAUV-led (71.5% in 23). Second label: BriO de Cantenac-Brown. Also SAUV BL-led (90%) dry white AltO.

Capbern St-Est ★★ 15' 16' 17 18 19 20 21 22 23 Same ownership/team as CALON SÉGUR; CAB SAUV-led (69% in 23); gd form and value.

Cap de Mourlin St-Ém ★★ 15 16 18 19 20 22 GRAND CRU CLASSÉ on n slopes. Same family ownership since C16. MERLOT-led (75% in 22). Firm, tannic wines. Also BALESTARD LA TONNELLE.

Carbonnieux Pe-Lé ★★★ 15' 16' 18 19' 20 21 22 23 Classed Growth GRAV, owned by Perrin family. Sterling red/white; large volumes of both. Fresh *whites*, 65% SAUV BL, eg. 21 22 23. Red can age. Old-vine white (100% SÉM) CUVÉE 1741 from 20. Second label: La Croix de Carbonnieux.

Carles, De Fron ★★ 16 18 19 20 22 23 Haut-Carles is prestige CUVÉE; MERLOT/CAB FR (90/10%) blend.

Carmes Haut-Brion, Les Pe-Lé ★★★ 14 15 16' 17 18' 19' 20' 21 22' 23 24 Tiny, high-flying property in heart of Bordeaux city; CABS FR (50% in 23)/SAUV-led wines, structured but suave. Philippe Starck-designed winery. Second label: Le C des Carmes Haut-Brion.

Caronne Ste Gemme H-Méd ★★ 16 18 19 20 Now integrated into LA TOUR CARNET; CAB SAUV-led wines; fresh, structured; 21 last vintage.

Carruades de Lafite Pau ★★★ Second-label of CH LAFITE; 20,000 cases/yr. Second Growth prices. Accessible but has ageing potential.

Carteau Côtes-Daugay St-Ém ★★ 16' 18 19 20 22 Small s-facing GRAND CRU ST-ÉM. MERLOT-led, supple, gd value.

Certan de May Pom ★★★ 14 15' 16' 17 18 19' 20 21 22 23 24 Much-improved neighbour of VIEUX CH CERTAN; POM of an elegant nature.

Chantegrive, De Grav ★★→★★★ 16 18 19 20' 21 22 23 Leading large estate at Podensac; v.gd quality, value. MERLOT/CAB SAUV (r). *Fragrant Cuvée Caroline* (w) 21 22 23 24.

Celebratory years

2022 and 23 were celebratory vintages for a number of CHX in BX. Olivier Bernard marked his 40th vintage at DOM DE CHEVALIER, Denis Lurton his 30th at DESMIRAIL and Gérard Perse his 25th at PAVIE, all in 22. There will be special labels at the 1st two and specially engraved bottles at the latter. Meanwhile, in 23, it was the 40th vintage for Suntory at LAGRANGE and the 25th for the Wilmers family at HAUT-BAILLY. How time flies when you're having fun.

Chasse-Spleen Mou ★★★ 15 16' 17 18 19' 20 21 22 23 Well-known CH owned by Céline Villars. Often impressive, long-maturing; classical structure, fragrance. Now 125 ha with acquisition of CH BRILLETTE in 2023.

Chauvin St-Ém ★★ 16' 18' 19' 20' 21 22' 23 24 GRAND CRU CLASSÉ on constant progression since 2014. Owner Sylvie Cazes, president of Association de GRANDS CRUS CLASSÉS de ST-ÉM.

Médoc has 89 growers making white, from 208 ha. Time for an AOP Médoc white?

Cheval Blanc St-Ém ★★★★ 09' 10' 12 13 14 15' 16' 17 18' 19' 20' 21 22 23 24 Declined classification in 2022. Superstar, easier to love than buy. Sustainable viticulture. MERLOT/CAB FR (46% in 23)/CAB SAUV. Firm, fragrant, verging on POM. Delicious young; lasts a generation. Second label (r/w): Le Petit Cheval.

Chevalier, Dom de Pe-Lé ★★★★ 08 09' 10' 12 14 15' 16' 17 18' 19' 20 21 22 23 24 Reliable Classed Growth owned by the Bernard family. Elegant, finely textured red. Impressive, complex, long-ageing white (drink early on the fruit or later for more complexity) 18 19' 20 21 22 23. Second label (r/w): L'Esprit de Chevalier.

Cissac H-Méd ★★ 16' 17 18 19 20 22 23 Large CRU BOURGEOIS Supérieur in N H-MÉD, owned by Vialard family. Classic CAB SAUV-led wines; structured but more fruit than in past; 23 v.gd.

Citran H-Méd ★★ 15 16 18 19 20 22 Sizeable S H-MÉD estate owned by Merlaut family (GRUAUD-LAROSE). Accessible but structured.

Clarence de Haut-Brion, Le Pe-Lé ★★★ 10' 11 12 14 15 16' 17 18 19' 20 21 22 23 Second label of CH HAUT-BRION, known as Bahans Haut-Brion until 2007. Usually MERLOT-led (55.5% in 23), stylistically similar to the *grand vin*. More approachable but can age.

Clarke List ★★→★★★ 15 16' 17 18 19 20 21 22 23 Greater length and precision since 2016. Investment in *cuvier* with 50 new tanks in 2022. Also gd dry white: Le Merle Blanc du CH Clarke.

Clerc Milon Pau ★★★ 09 10' 12 14 15 16' 17 18' 19' 20 21 22 23 Fifth Growth owned by (MOUTON) ROTHSCHILD since 1970; CAB SAUV-based. Powerful but harmonious; consistent quality but prices up.

Climens Bar ★★★★ 07 09' 10' 11' 12' 13' 14 15 16' 19 22 23 Classed Growth owned by Moitry family. Concentrated, vibrant acidity; ageing potential guaranteed; bio. No 17 18 20 21 (frost). Second label: Les Cyprès. Also dry whites (100% Sém) Lilium, Asphodèle, Petite Lily.

Clinet Pom ★★★ 11 12 14 15' 16' 17 18 19 20 21 22 23 24 Plateau-based property owned by Ronan Laborde. MERLOT-led, CAB SAUV (20%). Sumptuous, modern, to age. Also generic BX Ronan by Clinet.

Clos des Jacobins St-Ém ★★→★★★ 12 14 15' 16' 17 18 19 20 22 23 Côtes GRAND CRU CLASSÉ owned by Decoster family. MERLOT-led (80%), great consistency; powerful, modern style. Also restaurant L'Atelier de Candale.

Clos du Marquis St-Jul ★★→★★★ 11 14 15' 16' 17 18' 19' 20 21 22 23 24 Owned by Domaines Delon (LÉOVILLE LAS CASES, NÉNIN); gd ST-JUL character. Second label: La Petite Marquise (young vines).

Clos de l'Oratoire St-Ém ★★ 15 16' 17 18 19 20 22 23 Supple GRAND CRU CLASSÉ in ne of ST-ÉM; 80% MERLOT. Organic.

Clos Floridène Grav ★★ (r) 16 18' 19 20 22 23 (w) 21 22 23 Dubourdieu family-owned/run. SAUV BL/SÉM from limestone, *fine modern white*; vibrant, CAB SAUV-led red (75% in 23). CHX DOISY-DAËNE, REYNON same stable.

Clos Fourtet St-Ém ★★★ 10' 14 15' 16' 17 18 19 20 21 22 23 PREMIER GRAND CRU CLASSÉ (B) on limestone plateau owned by Cuvelier family; CH Les Grands Murailles integrated in 2022. Classic, stylish ST-ÉM. Consistently gd form. Second label: La Closerie de Fourtet.

Clos Haut-Peyraguey Saut ★★★ 13 14 15 16 17 18 19 20 21 22 23 24 First Growth in Bommes. Owned by magnate Bernard Magrez (PAPE CLÉMENT, LA TOUR CARNET). Harmonious wines; mostly SÉM with SAUV BL; can age. Second label: Symphonie.

Clos l'Église Pom ★★★ 10 14 15' 16 18 19 20 22 23 Tiny (4.4 ha) estate on edge of plateau. MERLOT/CAB FR (80/20%) on clay-gravel. Winemaker Patrice Lévêque. Seductive, will age.

Clos Puy Arnaud Cas ★★ 15 16' 17 18 19' 20' 22 23 Leading CAS estate run with passion by Thierry Valette. Vibrant wines with plenty of energy, bio. MERLOT-led with CABS FR/SAUV.

Clos René Pom ★★ 14 15' 16 18' 19 20 22 Owned by Garde family. MERLOT-led with spicy MALBEC (10%). Classical rather than modern; reasonable value for POM.

Clotte, La St-Ém ★★→★★★ 15' 16' 17 18 19' 20 21 22' 23 24 Top flight ST-ÉM. Owned by Vauthier family (AUSONE). Classification declined.

Conseillante, La Pom ★★★★ 09' 10' 12 14 15' 16' 17 18 19' 20 22 23 Nicolas family-owned for over 150 yrs. Some of noblest, most fragrant POM. Organic practices. Flying at present but expensive.

Corbin St-Ém ★★ 16' 18 19 20 22 23 GRAND CRU CLASSÉ owned by Anabelle Crus; gd value. Relatively accessible; mid-term ageing.

Cos d'Estournel St-Est ★★★★ 09' 10' 11 12 13 14 15' 16' 17 18 19' 20' 21 22 23 24 Big Second Growth owned by Michel Reybier (COS LABORY). Refined, suave, long-ageing. Pricey SAUV BL-dominated white; now more zest. Second label (r/w): Les Pagodes de Cos. Also G d'Estournel in MÉD.

Cos Labory St-Est ★★→★★★ 10' 12 14 15 16' 18 19 20 21 22 23 24 Small Fifth Growth; acquired by Michel Reybier (COS D'ESTOURNEL). Savoury and firm, usually gd value. More precision in 22 23.

Coufran H-Méd ★★ 15' 16' 18 19 20 22 Atypical: 85% MERLOT (since 20s). Supple wine, some ageing potential. Miailhe family-owned (1924).

Couhins-Lurton Pe-Lé ★★→★★★ (r) 15 16 18 19 20 22 23 (w) 19 20 22 23 *Fine white*, tense, long-lived SAUV BL (100%). MERLOT-led red. Act II (r/w) for earlier drinking.

Couspaude, La St-Ém ★★★ 10' 14 15 16 18 19 20 22 23 GRAND CRU CLASSÉ on limestone plateau. MERLOT-led; more refined these days.

Coutet Saut ★★★ 11' 12 13 14' 16 17' 18 19' 20 21 22 23 24 First Growth; majority SÉM. Consistently v. fine. CUVÉE Madame: v. rich, old-vine selection 97 01 03 09. Second label: La Chartreuse. Dry white Opalie (Sauv Bl/Sém) v.gd.

Couvent des Jacobins St-Ém ★★ 12 14 15 16' 18 19' 20 22 23 GRAND CRU CLASSÉ in town of St-Émilion; trad rather than modern ST-ÉM.

Crabitey Grav ★★ (r) 18 19 20 22 (w) 20 22 On gravelly soils of Portets. Harmonious CAB SAUV-led reds; small volume of lively SAUV BL dominant white.

Cru Bourgeois – 2025 edition

The Alliance des CRUS BOURGEOIS implemented a number of changes for the 2025 edition of the three-tier classification (CB, CB Supérieur, CB Exceptionnel). All candidates have to have environmental certification – HVE level 2 for CB and 3 for higher (Haute Valeur Environnementale). The five vintages tasted are 17–21, and all candidates present wines for the blind tasting, whatever level desired. Also, as of 2022 all those wishing to use the CB certificate needed to present their wines in bottles that weigh no more than 390g (a reduction of 22% on the previous max weight). The results showed 170 CHX classified in 2025 (down from 250 in the 2020 edition) of which 120 CB, 36 CB Supérieur, 14 CB Exceptionnel. The classification is now organized every 5 yrs.

Crock, Le St-Est ★★ 14 15 16' 18 19' 20 21 22 23 CRU BOURGEOIS Exceptionnel. Same stable as LÉOVILLE POYFERRÉ. Firm but polished, can age. Usually gd value.

Croix, La Pom ★★ 14 15 16 18 19 20 22 Owned by NÉGOCIANT Joseph Janoueix. Rich, MERLOT-led (90%) wine. Also HAUT-SARPE.

Croix de Gay, La Pom ★★★ 15 16 17 18 19 20 22 Tiny MERLOT-dominant (95%) vyd on gravelly soils. Rich, round wines.

Croix du Casse, La Pom ★★ 15' 16 18 19 20 Supple, early drinking. MERLOT-based (90%+), sandy/gravel soils. Castéja-owned (BORIE-MANOUX).

Croizet-Bages Pau ★★ 14 15 16' 18 19 20 20 23 Striving, CAB SAUV-led (70% in 23) Fifth Growth. Steady improvement in recent yrs. Quié family-owned (1942).

Cru Bourgeois Méd Three-tier classification in 2025 (CB, CB Supérieur, CB Exceptionnel). 170 CHX all told. *See box, p.111.*

Cruzelles, Les L de P ★★ 14 15' 16' 17 18 19' 20 21 22 23 Consistent, expressive, gd-value, MERLOT-led wine. Same stable as L'ÉGLISE-CLINET.

Dalem Fron ★★ 16 17 18' 19 20 21 22 23 MERLOT-dominated (90% in 23) property. Smooth, ripe, fresh. Eric Boissenot consults.

Dassault St-Ém ★★ 14 15 16 18' 19 20 22 23 Rich, modern GRAND CRU CLASSÉ on sandy soils. Dassault-owned since 1955. New gravity-fed *cuvier* in 2022. Second label: D de Dassault. Also CH La Fleur.

Dauphine, De La Fron ★★→★★★ 15 16 17 18' 19 20 21 22 23 A reference in FRON. Expansion, renovation over past 20 yrs. Organic. Second label: Delphis. Also BX white, rosé.

Dauzac Marg ★★→★★★ 14 15 16' 17 18' 19 20 22 Busy Fifth Growth at Labarde. Dense, rich, dark wines. Second label: La Bastide Dauzac. Also ungrafted Franc de Pied (100% CAB SAUV).

Desmirail Marg ★★→★★★ 10' 14 15 16' 18 19 20 21 22 23 Discreet Third Growth; fine, delicate style. Also La Perle white (BLANC DE NOIRS).

Destieux St-Ém ★★ 14 15 16 18 19 20 22 23 GRAND CRU CLASSÉ. MERLOT-based; firm, powerful, modern. Christian Dauriac owner.

Doisy-Daëne Bar ★★★ 11' 13' 14 15' 17' 18' 19 20 21 22 23 24 *Fine, sweet* but tangy BAR. Pure SÉM. L'Extravagant 17' 18' 19' 22 23 intensely rich, expensive, 100% SAUV BL CUVÉE. Also dry white Doisy-Daëne SEC.

Doisy-Védrines Bar ★★★ 11' 12 13 14 15' 16' 17 18' 19 20 22 23 24 *Long-term fave*; delicious, gd value; SÉM/SAUV BL (90/10% in 23).

Dôme, Le St-Ém ★★★ 15 17 18 19 20 22 Micro-wine; rich, modern, powerful. Majority old-vine CAB FR (80%), lots of new oak. Circular, Norman Foster-designed cellar. Also CH Teyssier (value).

Dominique, La St-Ém ★★★ 10' 14 15 16' 17 18' 19 20 21 22 23 24 GRAND CRU CLASSÉ.

Value in Bordeaux

BORDEAUX is often accused of being overpriced, an assertion that may ring true at Classed Growth level. But these wines represent only 5% of total production. Beyond them, among the CRUS BOURGEOIS and other *petits* CHX, there's great value to be found, the character of Bx assured, the drinking window shorter (5–10 yrs). Among the CBs in the MÉD, try D'AGASSAC, BEAUMONT, La Cardonne or PATACHE D'AUX. Further s in the GRAVES, there's Cérons, CHANTEGRIVE and CLOS FLORIDÈNE. Heading e across the Dordogne river, there's value to be found in MERLOT-centric FRONSAC (LA DAUPHINE, Villars) or CASTILLON-CÔTES DE BX (La Brande, La Clarière). Another tip for drinking at a higher level is to take a look at the less-hyped vintages like 11 12 14 or 17. There's value to be found and wines ready to drink now.

MERLOT-led (88% in 23); complex and refined. Visitor-friendly (restaurant). Also CH Fayat in POM.

Ducru-Beaucaillou St-Jul ★★★★ 09' 10' 12 14 15' 16 17 18' 19' 20' 21 22 23 Outstanding Second Growth. Majors in CAB SAUV (85% in 23). Excellent form; classic cedar-scented claret for long ageing. New gravity-fed *cuvier* in 2024.

Duhart-Milon Rothschild Pau ★★★ 09' 10' 14 15 16' 17 18' 19' 20 21 22 23 Fourth Growth owned by LAFITE ROTHSCHILD; CAB SAUV-dominated (80% in 23); v. fine quality. On up and up. Winery in PAUILLAC town.

Château Dauzac uses dehydrated potatoes for fining so can be labelled vegan.

Durfort-Vivens Marg ★★★ 09' 10' 14 15' 16' 17 18' 19' 20' 21 22 23 24 High-flying Second Growth; recent yrs tiptop; 90% CAB SAUV. Organic, bio. Three CUVÉES *parcellaires* (Les Plantes, Le Plateau, Le Hameau). Gonzague Lurton owner.

Eglise, Dom de l' Pom ★★ 10' 14 15 16 18 19 20 22 Owned by BORIE-MANOUX. MERLOT-led (98% in 22). Clay/gravel soils of plateau. Consistent, fleshy of late. BATAILLEY, CROIX DU CASSE same stable.

Église-Clinet, L' Pom ★★★★ 08 09' 10' 11' 12 13 14 15' 16' 17 18 19' 20' 21 22 23 24 Tiny, top-flight. Great consistency; full, concentrated, fleshy but expensive. Needs time; long ageing. Also LES CRUZELLES in L DE P.

Evangile, L' Pom ★★★★ 10' 11 14 15' 16' 17 18' 19' 20' 21 22 23 24 Rothschild (LAFITE)-owned since 1990. MERLOT-led but more CAB FR these days (21% in 23) and more finesse. Second label: Blason de L'Evangile.

Fargues, De Saut ★★★ 09' 10' 11' 13 14 15' 16' 17' 18 19 20 21 22 23 First vintage 1943. Philippe de Lur Saluces now at helm. Unclassified but top quality; rich, refined, age-worthy.

Faugères St-Ém ★★→★★★ 14 15 16' 18 19' 20 22 23 Sizeable GRAND CRU CLASSÉ owned by Silvio Denz. Rich, bold, modern wines. Sister CH Péby Faugères, and LAFAURIE-PEYRAGUEY (SAUT).

Ferrand, De St-Ém ★★→★★★ 10' 14 15 16 18 19 20 22 23 Big GRAND CRU CLASSÉ. Organic. More CAB FR and more refined these days.

Ferrande Grav ★★ 16' 18 19 20 22 Sizeable (100 ha) property owned by Castel. Easy-going MERLOT-driven red; creamy SÉM/SAUV BL/Gr white.

Ferrière Marg ★★★ 09 10' 14 15 16' 17 18 19 20 22 23 Small (24 ha) Third Growth. Organic, bio. Dark, firm, perfumed.

Feytit-Clinet Pom ★★→★★★ 10' 14 15 16' 17 18 19' 20 22 23 Tiny 6-ha property owned by Chasseuil family since 2000. 90% MERLOT. Top, consistent form; rich, seductive. Relatively gd value.

Fieuzal Pe-Lé ★★★ (r) 10' 14 15 16' 18' 19' 20 21 22 23 (w) 21 22 23 Classified estate. Full-bodied SAUV BL-led white; rich and firm red. Second label (r/w): L'Abeille de Fieuzal.

Figeac St-Ém ★★★★ 05' 06 08 09' 10' 11 12 14 15 16' 17 18' 19' 20' 21 22 23 24 PREMIER GRAND CRU CLASSÉ (A) on a roll. Owned by Manoncourt family. Gravelly vyd with unusual 70% CABS FR/SAUV. Now richer, but always elegant; needs long ageing. Visitor-friendly. Second label: Petit-Figeac.

Filhot Saut ★★ 10' 11' 12 13 14 15 16 18 20 22 23 Second Growth; SÉM/SAUV BL/MUSCADELLE blend (60/36/4%). Richer, purer in recent yrs.

Fleur Cardinale St-Ém ★★ 14 15 16' 18 19' 20' 21 22 23 GRAND CRU CLASSÉ on flying form. Ripe, unctuous, modern. MERLOT and CABS FR/SAUV. Second label: Intuition. Organic.

Fleur de Boüard, La L de P ★★→★★★ 15 16' 17 18 19 20 23 Dark, dense, modern. Special CUVÉE Le Plus: 100% MERLOT; more extreme. State-of-the-art winery. Visitor-friendly. Second label: Le Lion.

Fleur-Pétrus, La Pom ★★★★ 09' 10' 14 15 16 17' 18 19' 20' 21 22 23 24 J-P MOUEIX property on plateau. Sizeable (18.7 ha) for POM. MERLOT-led with unusual PETIT VERDOT (0.5% in 23). Refined, long-ageing.

Fombrauge St-Ém ★★→★★★ 10 14 15 16' 18 19 20 22 23 Substantial GRAND CRU CLASSÉ in St-Christophe-des-Bardes. Bernard Magrez-owned since 1999. Rich, dark, creamy, opulent. Magrez Fombrauge is special CUVÉE.

Fonbadet Pau ★★ 10' 15 16' 18 19' 20' 22 23 Small non-classified estate; gd value, less long-lived but reliable. Pascale Peyronie owner.

Fonbel, De St-Ém ★★ 15 16 18 19 20 22 23 Consistent, juicy, fresh, gd-value ST-ÉM. Owned by Vauthier family (AUSONE) since 1971.

Fonplégade St-Ém ★★ 14 15 16' 18' 19 20' 21 22 23 RIP owner Stephen Adams. GRAND CRU CLASSÉ; bio. Fruit and balance these days.

Fonréaud List ★★ 10' 14 15 16' 17 18 19 20 21 22 23 Consistent, satisfying, savoury wines that are CAB SAUV-led (53%). Next generation Chanfreau (Guillaume and Loïc) at helm.

Fonroque St-Ém ★★★ 15 16 18 19 20' 21 22 23 Côtes GRAND CRU CLASSÉ; bio. Medium-bodied, mineral, fresh. Guillard family-owned.

Fontenil Fron ★★ 14 15' 16 18' 19 20 22 23 Owned by Dany and MICHEL ROLLAND. Ripe, chocolatey, opulent.

Forts de Latour, Les Pau ★★★★ 09 10 11 12 14 15 16' 17 18 19' 20 21 (22) Second label of CH LATOUR; authentic PAU flavour in slightly lighter format; high price. Primeur sales finished; only released when deemed ready to drink (18 in 2024), but another 10 yrs often pays.

Fourcas Dupré List ★★ 15' 16' 17 18 19 20 22 Well-run property, fairly consistent; medium-bodied, dry, fresh. Dry white as well.

Fourcas-Hosten List ★★→★★★ 15 16 17 18 19 20 22 23 Large estate owned by Hermès connections. Organic. Finesse, precision these days. Second label: Les Cèdres.

France, De Pe-Lé ★★ (r) 15 16' 18 19 20 22 23 (w) 21 22 23 Owned by Thomassin family since 1971. Ripe, modern reds. Fresh, balanced SAUV BL/SÉM (80/20%). Value wines.

Franc Mayne St-Ém ★★ 15 16 17 18 19' 20 22 23 24 Improving GRAND CRU CLASSÉ on côtes. 100% MERLOT. Fresh, structured. Organic.

Gaby Fron ★★ 15 16 18 19' 20 22 Well-sited CANON-FRON estate. MERLOT-dominated. Visitor-friendly. Organic.

Gaffelière, La St-Ém ★★★ 14 15 16' 17 18 19' 20 21 22 23 24 Top, unclassified ST-ÉM owned by Malet Roquefort family. Investment, improvement; part of vyd replanted. Lots of CAB FR (40%); on fine, elegant form. Long-ageing.

Garde, La Pe-Lé ★★ (r) 15 16' 18 19 20 22 23 (w) 21 22 23 Unclassified, owned by DOURTHE; supple, CAB SAUV/MERLOT reds. Tiny production SAUV BL/SÉM (90/10%) white. Second label: La Terrasse (r/w).

Gay, Le Pom ★★★ 12 14 15 16 17 18 19' 20 22 23 24 Owned by Henri Parent. MERLOT dominant (90%+). Rich, suave with ageing potential. Also CH La Violette.

Gazin Pom ★★★ 14 15' **16' 18' 19'** 20 22 23 Large DOM on plateau. On v.gd form; generous (90% MERLOT), long-ageing. Second label: l'Hospitalet.

Gilette Saut ★★★ 86 88 89 90 96 **97 99** 01 Extraordinary small Preignac CH. Stores its sumptuous wines untouched in concrete vats for 18–20 yrs; c.400–500 cases/yr. Vintages back to 53.

Giscours Marg ★★★ 11 12 14 15 **16' 17** 18' 19' 20' 21 22 23 24 Substantial Third Growth. Albada Jelgersma family-owned. CAB SAUV-led (60%). Full-bodied, long-ageing MARG; recent vintages on song. Second label: La Sirène de Giscours.

Glana, Du St-Jul ★★ 15 16' 17 18 19' 20 22 Unclassified; CAB SAUV/MERLOT (65/35%). Undemanding, robust, value. Owned by Jean-Paul Meffre and his sons. Second label: Pavillon du Glana.

Gloria St-Jul ★★·→★★★ 10' 11 14 15 16' 17 18 19' 20 21 22 23 24 Domaines Henri Martin owner; CAB SAUV-dominant (65%) with MERLOT, CAB FR, PETIT VERDOT. Unclassified but sells at Fourth Growth prices. On superb form.

Grand Corbin-Despagne St-Ém ★★·→★★★ 14 15 16' **18' 19' 20'** 21 22 23 GRAND CRU CLASSÉ discerningly run by François Despagne, gd value. Aromatic now, with riper, fuller edge. Organic, bio practices. Ampélia (CAS) sister estate. Second label: Petit Corbin-Despagne.

Grand Cru Classé St-Ém 2022: 71 classified; reviewed every 10 yrs (next in 2032).

Grand Mayne St-Ém ★★★ 14 15 16' 17 18 19' 20 21 22 23 24 Consistent GRAND CRU CLASSÉ on the côtes and pied de côtes. MERLOT/CAB FR (80/20%); full-bodied, structured. Owned by the Nony family.

Grand-Puy Ducasse Pau ★★★ 15' 16' 18 19' 20 21 22 23 24 Fifth Growth, steady rise in quality; CAB SAUV/MERLOT (60/40%). New state-of-the-art winery with suspended vats. Visitor-friendly. Sister to MEYNEY.

Grand-Puy-Lacoste Pau ★★★ 09' 10' 12 14 15' 16' 17' 18' 19' 20 22 23 24 Fifth Growth famous for CAB SAUV-driven (75%+) PAU to lay down; vyd in one block around CH. Borie family-owned.

Grave à Pomerol, La Pom ★★★ 14 15 16' 17 18 19' 20 21 22 23 Small J-P MOUEIX property on gravel soils with fine clay; value for POM. MERLOT-led (100% in 23). Refined; can age.

Greysac Méd ★★ 16' 18 19 20 22 Fine, fresh and consistent wines, MERLOT-led. Sister to Rollan de By.

Gruaud-Larose St-Jul ★★★★ 09' 10' 14 15' 16' 17 18' 19' 20' 22' 23 24 One of biggest, best-loved Second Growths. Vigorous claret to age. Organic, bio practices. Recent vintages on song. Second label: *Sarget de Gruaud-Larose.*

Guadet St-Ém ★★ 14 15 16' 18 19 20 22 Tiny GRAND CRU CLASSÉ on the limestone plateau. Better form recently. Bio since 2015.

Guiraud Saut ★★★ 08 09 10' 11' 13 14 15' 16' 17 19 20 22 23 24 Classed Growth SAUT; organic. More SAUV BL than usual. Two dry whites: G de Guiraud, Grand Vin Blanc Sec. Restaurant Le Cercle Guiraud in Sauternes.

Gurgue, La Marg ★★ 15 16' 18 19 20 21 22 23 Organic, bio; CAB SAUV-led. Light but fine. Also FERRIÈRE.

Hanteillan, D H-Méd ★★ 15 16 18 19 20 22 Sizeable family-owned estate at Cissac-Médoc. Reliable; early drinking. Second label: CH Laborde.

Mouton Cadet launched 1930; now 10 million bottles/year, 120 countries.

Haut-Bages-Libéral Pau ★★★ 10' 14 15' 16 18 19' 20' 21 22 23 Improving Fifth Growth; CAB SAUV-led (86% in 23); organic, bio. Reasonable value. Also Ceres: 100% Merlot, no sulphur.

Haut-Bailly Pe-Lé ★★★★ 09' 10' 11 12 14 15' 16' 17 18' 19' 20' 21 22 23 24 Top-quality Classed Growth. Refined, elegant, CAB SAUV-led. Astutely managed by Véronique Sanders. Visitor-friendly. Second label: Haut-Bailly II (was La Parde de H-B).

Haut-Batailley Pau ★★★ 12 14 15 16' 17 18' 19' 20' 22 23 24 Fifth Growth owned by Cazes family (LYNCH-BAGES). On top form. Planted 910 trees/shrubs in 2022. Second label: Verso.

Haut-Bergeron Saut ★★ 13 14 15' 18 19 20 22 Family-owned, 9th generation. Consistent, unclassified. Vines in SAUT, BAR. Mainly SÉM (90%). Rich, opulent, gd value.

Haut-Bergey Pe-Lé ★★→★★★ (r) 15 16' 18' 19 20' 21 22 23 (w) 23 Garcin family-owned. Organic, bio. Rich, bold red. Fresh, SAUV BL-led dry white.

Haut-Brion Pe-Lé ★★★★ 05 06 07 08 09' 10' 11' 12 13 14 15' 16' 17' 18' 19' 20' 21 22 23 24 Only non-MÉD First Growth in list of 1855, owned by American Dillon family since 1935; 1st written reference 1521. Prince Robert de Luxembourg titular head. Jean-Philippe Delmas manages. Deeply harmonious, wonderful texture; for many, top choice of all. Wine shop. A little ***sumptuous dry white*** (SAUV BL/SÉM) for tycoons: 19 20 21 22 23 24. Also La Clarté (w) from both H-B and LA MISSION HAUT-BRION. Second label: LE CLARENCE DE HAUT-BRION (previously Bahans H-B).

Haut Condissas Méd ★★★ 16 18 19' 20 22 23 Top wine from Jean Guyon stable (GREYSAC, Rollan de By). Rich, exuberant, modern. MERLOT-led (60%) plus 20% PETIT VERDOT.

Haut-Marbuzet St-Est ★★→★★★ 10' 15 16 17 18 19' 20' 21 22 23 Situated between MONTROSE and COS D'ESTOURNEL; owned by Duboscq family. Easy to love, but unclassified; 60%+ sold directly by CH. Unctuous, matured in 100% new oak. Approx 30,000 cases. MERLOT-led. Second label: Mac Carthy.

Haut-Sarpe St-Ém ★★ 14 15' 16' 18 19 20 22 GRAND CRU CLASSÉ owned by Joseph Janoueix; MERLOT/CAB FR; ripe, modern style.

Hosanna Pom ★★★★ 10' 12 14 15 16' 17 18 19' 20' 21 22 23 Tiny vyd in heart of plateau. Clay/gravel soils, iron-rich subsoil. MERLOT (70%), old-vine CAB FR (30%). Created by J-P MOUEIX (1999). Power, complexity, balance; needs time.

Issan, D' Marg ★★★ 09' 10' 12 14 15' 16' 17 18' 19' 20 21 22 23 Third Growth. Fragrant, CAB SAUV-led (60%) wines that age. Unusual dry white (VIOGNIER, ROUSSANNE, MARSANNE, Rolle) from 24. Second label: Blason.

Jean Faure St-Ém ★★ 14 15 16 18' 19' 20' 22 23 GRAND CRU CLASSÉ on clay, sand, gravel soils. Organic, bio; CAB FR-led (plus 5% MALBEC), fresh, elegant style. Second label: La Réserve.

Kirwan Marg ★★★ 09 10' 14 15' 16' 18 19' 20' 21 22 23 Third Growth owned by Schÿler family. Freshness, finesse, charm. Visitor-friendly. Dry white Vin de Franc (100% CHARD) from 23. Second label: Charmes.

Labégorce Marg ★★→★★★ 10' 14 15 16' 17 18' 19 20 21 22 23 Substantial unclassified property; CAB SAUV-led (50%). Perrodo family-owned since 1989. Ripe, modern but fresh. Second label: Zédé de Labégorce.

Lafaurie-Peyraguey Saut ★★★ 10' 11 14 15' 16' 17 18 19 20 21 22 23 24 Leading First

---

The vineyard of the future

LARRIVET HAUT-BRION in PE-LÉ has started planting what it terms "the vineyard of the future". A 12-ha parcel (17% of the total vyd) has been set aside for replanting, taking into consideration sustainability, biodiversity, climate change and the eventual quality of the wine. Over the coming yrs, low-density CABS SAUV/FR and MALBEC will be planted, along with hedges, flowers and a variety of trees. Among the latter, 300 Paulownia trees will be planted between rows to create a protective mesoclimate thanks to the rapidity of their growth, the form of the leaves and their higher-than-average capacity to absorb carbon dioxide. An existing park with lakes will assist with the biodiversity. Sounds perfect if it works.

Growth (1855). Rich, harmonious, sweet. SÉM (93%), MUSCADELLE (1%). Second label: La Chapelle. Also Grand Vin Sec (dr w).

Lafite Rothschild Pau ★★★★ 06 07 08 09' 10' 11' 12 13 14 15' 16' 17 18' 19' 20' 21 22 23 24 Big (112 ha) First Growth of famously elusive perfume, style; never great weight, although more dense, sleek these days. Lots of CAB SAUV (93% in 23). Great vintages need keeping for decades. More affordable, approachable (MERLOT-led) Anseillan. Second label: CARRUADES DE LAFITE. Acquired WILLIAM FÈVRE (CHAB) in 2023. Also CHX DUHART-MILON, L'EVANGILE, RIEUSSEC.

Cab Fr is very old: probably Basque. Parent of Cab Sauv, Merlot, Sauv Bl.

Lafleur Pom ★★★★ 09' 10' 11 12 13 14 15' 16' 17' 18' 19' 20 21 22 23 24 Superb but tiny; Guinaudeau family-owned. Elegant, intense, to age. Expensive. Second label: *Les Pensées*. Also gd-value CH Grand Village (BX r/w).

Lafleur-Gazin Pom ★★ 14 15 16' 18' 19 20' 21 22 23 24 Small (8.5 ha), gd-value J-P MOUEIX estate. 100% MERLOT. Elegant, fresh.

Lafon-Rochet St-Est ★★★ 09' 10' 14 15' 16' 17 18' 19 20' 21 22 23 24 Fourth Growth owned by Jacky Lorenzetti (LILIAN LADOUYS, PÉDESCLAUX). Christophe Congé (ex-LAFITE) in charge. On gd form; firm but zesty. Second label: Les Pélerins de Lafon-Rochet.

Lagrange St-Jul ★★★ 09' 10' 12 14 15' 16' 17 18 19' 20 21 22 23 Large (118 ha) Third Growth owned by Suntory. Serious investment. Consistent, fresh; CAB SAUV-driven. Special bottling of various vintages (2009–15) aged in ancient oaks. Dry white Les Arums de Lagrange. Second label: Les Fiefs de Lagrange (gd value).

Lagrange Pom ★★ 15' 16' 17 18 19 20 21 22 23 J-P MOUEIX-owned since 1953, on n edge of plateau. 100% MERLOT. Supple, round, accessible; gd value.

Lagune, La H-Méd ★★★ 09' 10' 11 14 15' 16' 17 19 20 21 22 23 24 Substantial Third Growth in v. s of MÉD. On gd form; fine-edged with structure, depth. Organic, bio. Caroline Frey at helm.

Lamarque, De H-Méd ★★ 14 15 16 18 19' 20 22' 23 Medium-sized estate owned by Gromond family. Competent, savoury, mid-term wines; value. Lots of PETIT VERDOT (18% in 23). Second label: D de Lamarque.

Lanessan H-Méd ★★ 14 15' 16' 17 18 19' 20 22 23 Reliable, gd-value claret from just s of ST-JUL. Part of Aussie group TWE.

Langoa Barton St-Jul ★★★ 10' 11 12 14 15' 16' 17 18' 19' 20 21 22 23 24 Small Third Growth sister CH to LÉOVILLE BARTON; CAB SAUV-led, with MERLOT, CAB FR; charm, elegance. New gravity-fed cellar.

Larcis Ducasse St-Ém ★★★ 09' 10 14 15' 16' 17 18 19' 20 21 22 23 24 PREMIER GRAND CRU CLASSÉ on top form. Wine to mature; MERLOT (80%). On-going renovation. David Suire now in charge (ditto LAROQUE).

Larmande St-Ém ★★ 14 15 16 18' 19' 20 22 23 GRAND CRU CLASSÉ owned by La Mondiale insurance. Sound but lighter weight; accessible. Visitor-friendly.

Laroque St-Ém ★★→★★★ 14 15 16 18' 19' 20' 21 22 23 Large GRAND CRU CLASSÉ. MERLOT (98%); more finesse these days.

Larose-Trintaudon H-Méd ★★ 16 18 19' 20 22 Largest vyd in MÉD at 202 ha. Generally for early drinking. Larose Perganson same stable. Second label: Les Hauts de Trintaudon.

Laroze St-Ém ★★ 14 15 16' 18' 19' 20 21 22 23 GRAND CRU CLASSÉ on sandy-gravel soils. MERLOT/CAB FR (60/40% in 23). Lighter framed wines but fruit, balance. Second label: La Fleur Laroze.

Larrivet Haut-Brion Pe-Lé ★★★ (r) 12 14 16' 18' 19 20 21 22 23 24 Unclassified; 70-ha vyd. More CAB SAUV these days (75% in 23). Refined, refreshing red. Rich, creamy, SAUV BL-led *white* 21 22 23 24. Environmental programme. Second label (r/w): Les Demoiselles.

Lascombes Marg ★★ 09 10′ 14 15′ 16′ 17 18 19′ 20 21 22 23 24 Large Second Growth; chequered history. Opulent; change of style from 23; more MARG elegance. Ex-Ornellaia (*see* Italy) winemaker. Second label: Chevalier de Lascombes.

Latour Pau ★★★★ 05′ 06 07 08 09′ 10′ 11 12 13 14 15′ 16′ 17 18′ 19′ 20′ 21 22 23 First Growth considered grandest statement of BX. Profound, intense, almost immortal in great yrs; even weaker vintages have unique taste and run for many yrs. Sustainable and organic. Ceased en primeur sales 2012; wines now only released when considered ready to drink (17 in 2024 and another 1000 cases of 09). Owned by Pinault family; technical director Hélène Génin. Second label: LES FORTS DE LATOUR. *Third label: Pauillac;* even this can age 20 yrs.

Crémant de Bx is on up and up – now 3% of production. Popular because it sells.

Latour à Pomerol Pom ★★★ 09′ 10′ 14 15′ 16′ 17 18 19′ 20 21 22 23 24 J-P MOUEIX property. 100% MERLOT. Consistent, structured but balanced wines that age.

Latour-Martillac Pe-Lé ★★→★★★ (r) 10′ 14 15′ 16 18′ 19 20 21 22 23 Cru Classé owned by Kressmann family. Fresh, fragrant red. Appetizing *white* 21 22 23 24. Usually gd value. Also old-vine white Grapecap 1884 (from 21).

Laurets, Des St-Ém ★★ 16 18 19 20 22 Edmond de Rothschild Heritage wine. Large estate in PUISSEGUIN ST-ÉM. 90% MERLOT. Supple, early drinking.

Laville Saut ★★ 16 18 19 22 (23) Non-classified Preignac estate; SÉM-dominated (85%); lush, gd-value, botrytized. Jean-Christophe Barbe at helm.

Léoville Barton St-Jul ★★★★ 08 09′ 10′ 11 12 14 15′ 16′ 17 18′ 19′ 20′ 21 22 23 24 Second Growth owned by Anglo-Irish Bartons since 1826; Lilian B with daughter Mélanie and son Damien in charge. Harmonious, classic, long-ageing claret; CAB SAUV-dominant (87% in 23). New gravity-fed *cuverie* shared with LANGOA-BARTON. Second label: La Rés de Léoville Barton.

Léoville Las Cases St-Jul ★★★★ 05′ 08 09′ 10′ 11′ 12 13 14 15′ 16′ 17 18′ 19′ 20′ 21 22 23 24 Largest Léoville and original "Super Second" owned by Jean-Hubert Delon (CLOS DU MARQUIS, POTENSAC). Elegant, complex wines built for long ageing. CAB SAUV-led (86% in 23). Second label: Le Petit Lion.

Léoville Poyferré St-Jul ★★★★ 09′ 10′ 11′ 12 13 14 15′ 16′ 17 18′ 19′ 20′ 21 22 23 24 In Cuvelier family hands since 1920. "Super Second" level; dark, rich, spicy, long-ageing; CAB SAUV-led with MERLOT/CAB FR/PETIT VERDOT. Second label: Pavillon de Léoville Poyferré.

Lestage List ★★ 15 16′ 18 19′ 20 22 Exceptionnel wines; firm, ripe, toasty. Also dry white La Mouette.

Lilian Ladouys St-Est ★★ 15 16′ 17 18′ 19′ 20 22 23 Sizeable (75 ha). Lorenzetti family-owned (*see* LAFON-ROCHET, PÉDESCLAUX). investment, expansion. Organic. Full but fine. Second label: La Devise de Lilian.

Liversan H-Méd ★★ 16′ 18 19 20 22 In N H-MÉD; owned by Advini group. MERLOT/CAB SAUV; round, savoury, early drinking.

Loudenne Méd ★★ 16 18 19′ 20 22 23 Large estate owned by Christophe Gouache. Landmark C17 pink-washed *chartreuse* by river. Supple reds, MERLOT/CAB SAUV (50/50%); SAUV BL-led white. Also Clos Albus (w) from 23.

Louvière, La Pe-Lé ★★★ (r) 14 15 16′ 17 18 19 20 21 22 23 (w) 21 22 23 24 VIGNOBLES André Lurton property (run by son Jacques). Excellent white (100% SAUV BL), savoury red that can age (60% MERLOT in 23).

Lussac, De St-Ém ★★ 18 19 20 22 Top estate in LUSSAC-ST-ÉM. MERLOT-led (75%). Supple, accessible red.

Lynch-Bages Pau ★★★★ 08 09′ 10′ 11 12 13 14 15 16′ 17 18 19′ 20′ 21 22 23 24 Large (110 ha) estate; always popular, far higher than its Fifth Growth rank; pricier. Rich, dense CAB SAUV-led (71%), for ageing. Owned by Cazes family. Second label: Echo de Lynch-Bages. *Blanc de Lynch-Bages* (gd w). Also HAUT-BATAILLEY.

Lynch-Moussas Pau ★★ 10' 14 15 16 18 19' 20 22 23 Fifth Growth owned by Castéja family (BORIE-MANOUX). Less gravitas than top PAU, but improving.

Lyonnat St-Ém ★★ 18 19 20 22 Sizeable LUSSAC-ST-ÉM owned by Milhade family. MERLOT-led (90%); consistent. Also special CUVÉE Emotion.

Malartic Lagravière Pe-Lé ★★★ (r) 10 14 15' 16' 17 18 19' 20' 21 22 23 24 (w) 20 21 22 23 Classed Growth. Bonnie family-owned. Rich, appetizing red; fresh, creamy **white** (majority SAUV BL). Visitor-friendly. Second labels (r/w): Le Comte, La Réserve.

Malescasse H-Méd ★★ 16' 18 19 20 22 CRU BOURGEOIS Exceptionnel. Ripe, fleshy, polished. Second label: Les Moulin Rose.

Malescot St Exupéry Marg ★★★ 14 15' 16' 17 18' 19 20 21 22 23 24 Third Growth. Ripe, fragrant, finely structured. New-generation Léa Zuger now runing estate.

Malle, De Saut ★★★ 11' 12 13 14 16' 17' 18 19 Second Growth. Medium-bodied SAUT. Ex-GUIRAUD winemaker now at helm. Expect change.

Mangot St-Ém ★★ 15 16 18 19 20 22 23 GRAND CRU CLASSÉ; vyd e of ST-ÉM; clay-limestone. MERLOT-led (85%). Organic, bio.

Margaux, Ch Marg ★★★★ 08 09' 10' 11 12 13 14 15 16' 17 18' 19' 20' 21 22 23 24 First Growth; most seductive, fabulously perfumed, consistent, long ageing; CAB SAUV-dominated (89% in 23). Mentzelopoulos family-owned (1977). Second label: Pavillon Rouge 14 16' 17 19 20 21 22 23 24. Third label: Margaux du CH Margaux. **Pavillon Blanc** (100% SAUV BL) best white of MÉD 20 21' 22 23 24. Second label (from 22): Pavillon Blanc Second Vin.

Marojallia Marg ★★★ 16 17 18' 19' 20 22 Micro-CH; big, rich, un-MARG-like wines. Absorbed into MARQUIS DE TERME in 2023.

Marquis d'Alesme Marg ★★→★★★ 15 16 17 18 19 20 22 23 Third Growth revived by Perrodo family. Investment: upward curve. Visitor-friendly (restaurant May–Oct). MARG on lush side.

Marquis de Terme Marg ★★→★★★ 10' 14 15 16' 17 18' 19' 20 21 22 23 Fourth Growth. Investment, progression in recent yrs, but solid side of MARG. Paloma Sénéclauze heads up (from 2024).

Maucaillou Mou ★★ 14 15' 16' 17 18 19' 20 21 22 23 Dourthe family-owned. Consistent, medium-term. 30,000 cases/yr. Second label: No. 2 de Maucaillou.

Mayne Lalande List ★★ 15 16 18 19 20 23 Full and finely textured. Alice-Jeanne Lartigue in charge.

Mazeyres Pom ★★ 15 16' 18 19' 20 21 22 23 Lightish but consistent. Earlier-drinking, MERLOT-led (73%). Organic, bio.

Méaume Bx ★★ 19 20 22 (23) Consistent BX SUPÉRIUR in Libournais; Rés du CH (MERLOT-led) from oldest vines.

Meyney St-Est ★★→★★★ 05 08 09' 10' 12 15' 16' 17 18' 19' 20' 21 22 23 Big river-slope vyd, superb site next to MONTROSE. Structured, age-worthy; CAB SAUV-led, but lots of PETIT VERDOT; gd value. Anne Le Naour leads the estate. Second label: Prieur de Meyney.

First Bordeaux wine classification (price/provenance): 1647, 200 yrs before the 1855.

Mission Haut-Brion, La Pe-Lé ★★★★ 05' 06 08 09' 10' 11 12 13 14 15' 16' 17' 18' 19' 20' 21 22 23 24 Owned by DOM Clarence Dillon (like HAUT-BRION, QUINTUS). Considerable investment over past 40 yrs. Consistently grand-scale, full-blooded, long-maturing. Second label: La Chapelle de la Mission. Magnificent SÉM-led white: previously Laville Haut-Brion; renamed La Mission Haut-Brion Blanc 20' 21' 22 23 24. Second label: La Clarté.

Monbousquet St-Ém ★★★ 14 15 16' 18 19 20 22 23 GRAND CRU CLASSÉ on sand and gravel plain; 30 yrs' devotion from owner Gérard Perse (see PAVIE). Voluptuous. Dry white BX discontinued. Second label: Angélique de Monbousquet.

> **En primeur angst**
> What makes an en primeur campaign a success? According to the trade, the 2022 campaign was a disaster: price rises from the CHX that misjudged the market, consumers who sat on their hands. Yet the chx will say they sold everything. They did: to the NÉGOCES, who will have to fund it until they can sell it. And the amount the top chx release en primeur every yr is maybe half their total. The 22 vintage was v.gd but by no means the best ever. Just the most expensive ever. Until the next time.

Monbrison Marg ★★→★★★ 14 15' 16 17 18 19 20 21 22 Tiny property owned by Laurent Vonderheyden. Delicate, fragrant. H-MÉD and rosé too.

Mondotte, La St-Ém ★★★→★★★★ 11 12 14 15' 16 17 18 19' 20' 22 23 24 Tiny (4.5 ha) PREMIER GRAND CRU CLASSÉ on limestone-clay plateau; MERLOT/CAB FR (75/25%); intense, powerful. Organic. Owned by VIGNOBLES Comtes von Neipperg.

Montrose St-Est ★★★★ 08 09' 10' 12 13 14 15' 16' 17 18' 19' 20' 21 22 23 24 Second Growth with riverside vyd. Famed for forceful, long-ageing claret. Vintages 1979–85 were lighter. Bouyges bros-owned. Massive environmental programme. From 23, *grand vin* from Terrace 4 vyd only. Second label: *La Dame de Montrose*. Third label: Tertio.

Moulin du Cadet St-Ém ★★ 15' 16 18' 19' 20' 22 23 24 Tiny GRAND CRU CLASSÉ; 100% MERLOT. Lefévère family-owned. Structured, lithe, fresh.

Moulinet Pom ★★ 15 18 19 20 22 Large CH for POM: 18 ha on clay and gravel soils. MERLOT-led (90%). Lighter style.

Moulin Haut-Laroque Fron ★★ 15' 16 18' 19' 20' 21 22 23 Leading FRON. MERLOT-led (65%). Consistent, can age.

Moulin Pey-Labrie Fron ★★ 16 18 19 20' 22 MERLOT-led CANON-FRON; organic, natural. Hubau family-owned. Can age.

Moulin St-Georges St-Ém ★★★ 14 15' 16' 17 18' 19' 20 22 23 24 Unclassified: lively, fresh, harmonious; gd value. Same stable as AUSONE.

Mouton Rothschild Pau ★★★★ 05' 06 08' 09' 10' 11 12 13 14 15' 16' 17' 18' 19' 20' 21 22 23 24 Rothschild-owned (1853). Most exotic, voluptuous of PAU First Growths; at top of game. 2022 label created by French artist Gérard Garouste. White Aile d'Argent (SAUV BL/SÉM) now more graceful. Second label: *Le Petit Mouton*. Also D'ARMAILHAC, CLERC MILON.

Nairac Bar ★★ 11 12 13 15 16 17 18 22 23 24 Second Growth run by Les Grands Chais de France since 2022. Rich but fresh, SÉM-led (92% in 22). Second label: Esquisse de Nairac.

Nénin Pom ★★★ 09' 10' 12 14 15' 16' 17 18' 19' 20' 21 22 23 24 Owned by Domaines Delon (LÉOVILLE LAS CASES); investment. Restrained but generous, ageable; MERLOT-led with CABS FR/SAUV. Second label: Fugue de Nénin.

Olivier Pe-Lé ★★★ (r) 14 15 16' 18 19' 20 21' 22 23 24 (w) 21 22 23 24 Vast DOM; C16 CH. Structured red (CAB SAUV-led), juicy white (majority SAUV BL). Second label (r): Le Dauphin.

Ormes de Pez St-Est ★★ 09' 10' 11 14 15' 16' 17 18' 19 20' 22 23 24 Cazes family (LYNCH-BAGES) owned. CAB SAUV-led. Cool, classic, age-worthy.

Ormes Sorbet, Les Méd ★★ 16' 18 19 20 22 23 Reliably consistent MÉD cru owned by Boivert family. CAB SAUV-led (65%); 12,500 cases/yr. Elegant, gently oaked wines.

Palmer Marg ★★★★ 08 09' 10' 11 12 13 14 15' 16' 17 18' 19' 20' 21 22' 23 24 Third Growth on par with "Super Seconds" (occasionally Firsts). Voluptuous wine of power, complexity and much MERLOT. Mähler-Besse/Sichel-owned. Organic, bio, environmental. Sells 50% en primeur, releases rest at 10 yrs (14 in 2024). Second label: *Alter Ego de Palmer*.

Pape Clément Pe-Lé ★★★★ (r) 09' 10' 14 15' 16' 17 18' 19' 20 22 23 24 (w) 21 22 23 24

Historic estate in Bordeaux suburbs, owned by Bernard Magrez. Dense, long-ageing reds. Tiny production of rich, oaky white. Visits/tastings/B&B. Second label (r/w): Clémentin.

Patache d'Aux Méd ★★ 16' 18 19 20 22 Sizeable CRU BOURGEOIS Supérieur owned by Advini; CAB SAUV-led, classic, savoury, gd value.

Pavie St-Ém ★★★★ 06 08 09' 10' 12 14 15' 16' 17 18 19' 20' 21 22 23 24 PREMIER GRAND CRU CLASSÉ (A) owned by Gérard Perse (*see* MONBOUSQUET). Splendidly sited on plateau and s côtes. Intense, powerful, for long ageing; recent vintages less extreme (more CABS FR/SAUV). Second label: Arômes de Pavie.

Pavie Decesse St-Ém ★★★ 09' 10' 12 14 15' 16 17 18 19' 20' 21 Former GRAND CRU CLASSÉ now integrated into PAVIE. Tight, tannic, needs time.

Pavie Macquin St-Ém ★★★ 09' 10 14 15 16' 17 18' 19' 20' 21 22 23 24 PREMIER GRAND CRU CLASSÉ (B); vyd in one block on limestone-clay; 80% MERLOT, rest CAB FR and 2% old CAB SAUV. Sturdy, needs time. Second label: Les Chênes de Macquin.

Pédesclaux Pau ★★ 10' 14' 15 16' 17 18 19' 20 22 23 24 Underachieving Fifth Growth expanded and transformed by owner Jacky Lorenzetti. Organic. Lighter than top PAU, but well defined.

Petit Village Pom ★★★ 09' 10 15' 16' 17 18' 19 20' 22 23 24 Much improved; atypical 40% CABS FR/SAUV. Now greater precision. Second label: Le Petit de Petit Village.

Petrus Pom ★★★★ 05' 06 08 09' 10' 11' 12 13 14 15' 16' 17 18' 19' 20' 21 22 23 24 (Unofficial) First Growth of POM: MERLOT solo *in excelsis*. 11.5-ha vyd on blue clay gives massively rich, concentrated wine for long ageing; at a price. Owned by Jean-François MOUEIX and son Jean.

Pey La Tour Bx ★★ 19 20 22 23 Large DOURTHE property (135 ha). Quality-driven generic BX. Two red CUVÉES: Rés du CH (MERLOT-led) top.

Peyrabon H-Méd ★★ 16 17 18 19 20 22 Savoury CRU BOURGEOIS Supérieur in N H-MÉD; owned by Castéja family (*see* BATAILLEY).

Pez, De St-Est ★★★ 10' 14 15' 16' 17 18' 19' 20 21 22 23 24 Dense, reliable, for ageing; vyd in one block. Owned by Louis ROEDERER.

Phélan Ségur St-Est ★★★ 09 10' 14 15' 16' 17 18' 19' 20 21 22 23 24 Reliable, top-notch, unclassified CH with Irish origins; long, supple style. Visitor-friendly (lunch possible at Table du Chef). Second label: Frank Phélan.

Pibran Pau ★★ 10' 14 15 16' 17 18' 19' 20 21 22 23 Tiny (17 ha) AXA property. Earlier-drinking. Almost 50/50% MERLOT/CAB SAUV.

Pichon Baron Pau ★★★★ 05' 06 08 09' 10' 11 12 14 15' 16' 17 18' 19' 20 21 22 23 24 AXA-owned. Second Growth on flying form. Powerful, long-ageing PAU at a price. Second labels: Les Tourelles de Longueville (more approachable); Les Griffons de Pichon Baron. Les Griffons Grand Vin Blanc Sec from 23 (100% SÉM).

Pichon Longueville Comtesse de Lalande (Pichon Lalande) Pau ★★★★ 08 09' 10' 11 12 14 15' 16' 17 18' 19' 20' 21 22 23 24 ROEDERER-owned Second Growth. Always among top performers; long-lived wine of famous breed. More elegance, less power than PICHON BARON. Nicolas Glumineau manager. More CAB SAUV in recent yrs (80% in 23). Second label: *Rés de la Comtesse.*

Ch Palmer's Historical XIXth Century Wine: "hermitaged" by Rhône Syrah in blend.

Pin, Le Pom ★★★★ 08' 09' 10' 11 12 14 15 16' 17 18' 19' 20' 21 22 23 24 Original BX cult wine owned by Jacques Thienpont. Only 2.8 ha. Neighbour of TROTANOY. MERLOT (100%) on deep gravel and sand. Almost as rich as its drinkers; prices out of sight. Aged in new oak barrels. Potential to age. Also L'If (ST-ÉM), L'Hêtre (CAS).

Plince Pom ★★ 14 15 16' 18 19 20 22 23 Lighter POM on sandy soils. MERLOT-led. Oaky when young. Neighbour of NÉNIN.

Pointe, La Pom ★★ 14 15' 16' 18 19 20 21 22 23 Large, well-run estate; less intense than top POM. Second label: Ballade de La Pointe.

Poitevin Méd ★★ 17 18 19 20 22 CRU BOURGEOIS Supérieur. Consistent quality, value; organic. Also a dry white.

Pontet-Canet Pau ★★★★ 08 09′ 10′ 14 15 16′ 17 18′ 19′ 20 21 22 23 24 Large, bio, Tesseron family-owned Fifth Growth. Radical improvement has seen prices soar; CAB SAUV-led (52% in 23); ageing in amphora (for 35%). Classic PAU but generous, refined.

Forget horses: automatic GPS tractors are latest. Light, very eco-friendly.

Potensac Méd ★★ →★★★ 14 15 16′ 17 18′ 19′ 20′ 21 22 23 Firm, long-ageing wines; gd value. Usually MERLOT-led, but lots of old-vine CAB FR too. Owned by Domaines Delon (see LÉOVILLE LAS CASES).

Pouget Marg ★★ 14 15′ 16 18 19 20 22 23 Tiny Fourth Growth sister of BOYD-CANTENAC. CAB SAUV-led and lots of PETIT VERDOT (12% in 23). Sturdy; needs time.

Poujeaux Mou ★★ 10 14 15′ 16′ 17 18′ 19 20 21 22 23 24 Large MOU estate; CAB SAUV-led on gravelly soils. Full, robust, ageing potential.

Premier Grand Cru Classé St-Ém 2022: 14 classified, two ranked (A) and 12 (B). See box, p.107.

Pressac, De St-Ém ★★ 14 15′ 16′ 17 18′ 19′ 20′ 21 22 23 GRAND CRU CLASSÉ e of St-Émilion town. Ripe, full, engaging. Includes MALBEC, CARMENÈRE.

Preuillac Méd ★★ 16 18 19′ 20 23 Savoury, structured CRU BOURGEOIS Supérieur. MERLOT-led (54%). Solid, value.

Prieuré-Lichine Marg ★★★ 12 14 15′ 16′ 17 18′ 19′ 20′ 22 23 24 Fourth Growth owned by Ballande group. Parcels in all five MARG communes. Fragrant; on gd form. Visitor-friendly. Second label: Confidences. Also gd Le Blanc (w) and H-MÉD (Le Clocher).

Puygueraud Bx ★★ 16′ 17 18′ 19 20 22 23 Leading CH of tiny FRANCS-CÔTES DE BX AOP. Thienpont family-owned. MERLOT-led (90% in 23); top yrs can age a bit. Also MALBEC/CAB FR-based George (540 cases); dry white (SAUVS BL/Gr).

Quinault L'Enclos St-Ém ★★→★★★ 16′ 17 18′ 19′ 20 21 22 23 Same team/owners as CHEVAL BLANC. MERLOT-led, but more CABS SAUV/FR these days (33% in 23); more freshness, finesse. No longer sold en primeur.

Quintus St-Ém ★★★ 15 16′ 17 18′ 19′ 20′ 22 23 24 Owned by Dillons of HAUT-BRION. Composed of ex-Tertre Daugay, L'Arrosée and Grand Pontet vyds. Grand vin 25% of production in 23. Gaining in stature; expensive. Second label: Le Dragon de Quintus. Third label: St-Émilion de Quintus.

Rabaud-Promis Saut ★★→★★★ 11 13 14 15′ 16′ 17′ 18 19 20 23 First Growth (1855). Majority SÉM. Quality, gd value.

Rahoul Grav ★★ (r) 16′ 18 19 20 21 22 23 24 DOURTHE property; reliable, MERLOT-led red. White: gd-value, SÉM-dominated 22 23 24.

Ramage la Batisse H-Méd ★★ 18 19 20 23 CRU BOURGEOIS Supérieur owned by insurance company; CAB SAUV, MERLOT, lots of PETIT VERDOT.

Rauzan-Gassies Marg ★★★ 14 15 16′ 18 19 20′ 22 23 Second Growth. Quié family-owned. Some improvement but still lacks a little finesse. Second label: Gassies.

Rauzan-Ségla Marg ★★★★ 09′ 10′ 11 12 13 14 15′ 16′ 17 18′ 19′ 20′ 21 22 23 24 Leading Second Growth; fragrant, structured; owned by Wertheimers of Chanel. Limestone-clay and gravel soils; CAB SAUV-led (85% in 23). Second label: Ségla.

Raymond-Lafon Saut ★★★ 11′ 13 14 15′ 16′ 17′ 18 19 20 22 23 Unclassified SAUT, but First Growth quality. Meslier family-owned (1972). Rich, complex, gd value.

Rayne Vigneau, De Saut ★★★ 11′ 12 14 15′ 16′ 17′ 18′ 19′ 20 21 22 23 24 Substantial First Growth. Trésor du Patrimoine group-owned. Suave, age-worthy. Visitor-friendly. Second label: Madame de Rayne.

Respide Médeville Grav ★★ (r) 18 19 20 22 (w) 22 23 Tiny property. Part of VIGNOBLES Gonet-Médeville. Elegant red, complex white.

Reynon Bx ★★ Leading CADILLAC-CÔTES DE BX estate. Same stable as CLOS FLORIDÈNE. MERLOT-led red 19' 20' 22 23; BX white SAUV BL (DYA).

Reysson H-Méd ★★ 19 20 22 23 CRU BOURGEOIS Exceptionnel owned by DOURTHE. Mainly MERLOT with PETIT VERDOT. Consistent; rich but fragrant.

Rieussec Saut ★★★★ 11' 13 14 15' 16' 17 18' 19 20 22 First Growth; substantial vyd in Fargues (85 ha), owned by (LAFITE) Rothschild. Powerful, opulent; SÉM-led (91% in 22). Special bottle from recycled glass. Second label: Carmes de Rieussec.

Rivière, De la Fron ★★ 16' 18 19 20 21 22 Largest (65 ha), most impressive FRON property. MERLOT-led, CABS SAUV/FR, MALBEC. Fresh and more refined these days. Visitor-friendly.

Roc de Cambes Bx ★★★ 11 14 15' 16' 17 18 19 20 21 22 23 Undisputed leader in CÔTES DE BOURG; MERLOT/CAB SAUV (80/20%); savoury, opulent, pricey. Can age. Same approach as TERTRE ROTEBOEUF. Also DOM de Cambes.

Rochemorin, De Pe-Lé ★★ (r) 16 18' 19 20 22 (w) 22 23 Sizeable (68 ha) property owned by VIGNOBLES André Lurton. Fleshy, earlier-drinking, dark-fruit red; aromatic white (100% SAUV BL). Fairly consistent quality.

Rol Valentin St-Ém ★★ 14 15' 16' 18 19 20' 21 22 GRAND CRU CLASSÉ; MERLOT-led, CAB FR, MALBEC. Ripe, modern, structured.

Rouget Pom ★★ 14 15 16' 18 19 20 22 23 Sizeable (for POM) estate on n edge of plateau. Labruyère family-owned. MERLOT-led (85% in 23), CAB FR. Powerful, unctuous. Second label: Le Carillon de Rouget.

St-Georges St-Ém ★★ 16 18 20 22 This vyd represents 25% of ST-GEORGES AOP. MERLOT-led (80%), with 10% each CABS FR/SAUV; gd wine sold direct to the public – c.23,000 cases/yr.

St-Pierre St-Jul ★★★ 10' 12 14 15' 16' 18' 19' 20 21 22 23 24 Tiny Fourth Growth; CAB SAUV-led, stylish, consistent, classic. Worth following. Same stable as GLORIA. Second label: Esprit de St-Pierre.

Sales, De Pom ★★ 15 16 18 19' 20' 22' 23 Biggest vyd of POM (47.6 ha). Investment and improvement. Honest, drinkable; can age; value. Jean-Claude Berrouet consults. Second label: CH Chantalouette.

Sansonnet St-Ém ★★→★★★ 14 15 16' 17 18 19' 20 21 22 23 Plateau-based GRAND CRU CLASSÉ. MERLOT-led (85%). Modern but refreshing. Visitor-friendly.

Saransot-Dupré List ★★ 15 16 18 19 20 23 CRU BOURGEOIS Supérieur. Yves Raymond owner. Firm, generous. Also gd dry white BX.

Sénéjac H-Méd ★★ 15 16' 18 19' 20' 22 23 Cru in S H-MÉD (Pian). Consistent, well balanced. Drink young or age. Visitor-friendly.

Serre, La St-Ém ★★ 15 16' 18' 19' 20' 21 22 23 Small GRAND CRU CLASSÉ on plateau. MERLOT/CAB FR (80/20%). Fresh, consistent, stylish wines.

Sigalas Rabaud Saut ★★★ 11' 12 13 16 17' 18 19' 21 22 23 24 Tiny First Growth. 100% SÉM; *v. fragrant and lovely*. Second label: Le Lieutenant de Sigalas. Also La Sémillante de Sigalas (dr w).

AI vs counterfeiting

Could AI be used to help stamp out wine counterfeiting? A machine fed an algorithm can apparently identify the precise origin of BX wines by analyzing their chemical makeup. The experiment was carried out by a team from the University of Geneva (Switzerland), which used AI to appraise the chemical composition of 80 red wines from seven different CHX. Twelve different vintages between 90 and 07 were used, and the results were found to be totally accurate, each estate revealing its own, unique chemical signature. If the algorithm can be used to reveal an individual terroir, then it could also be used to expose bogus wines.

Siran Marg ★★→★★★ 09' 10' 14 15' 16' 17 18' 19' 20 21 22 23 Unclassified MARG. Substance, fragrance, can age. Miailhe family-owned. MERLOT/CAB SAUV/PETIT VERDOT (49/41/10% in 23). Second label: S de Siran.

Smith Haut Lafitte Pe-Lé ★★★★ (r) 09' 10' 11 12 14 15' 16' 17 18 19' 20 21 22 23 24 (w) 21 22 23 24 Celebrated Classed Growth with spa hotel (Caudalie). White is full, ripe, sappy; red precise, generous. Own cooperage. Organic, bio practices. Second labels: Le Petit Haut Lafitte (r/w); Les Hauts de Smith (r/w).

Sociando-Mallet H-Méd ★★★ 10' 12 14 15' 16' 17 18 19' 20 22 23 Large (83 ha), unclassified but esteemed estate. MERLOT/CABS SAUV/FR (54/42/4%). Wines for ageing. Second label: La Demoiselle de Sociando-Mallet.

Sours, De Bx ★★ Large property owned by Jack Ma of Alibaba fame. State-of-the-art winery. New range: Quarry.

Soutard St-Ém ★★★ 10 14 15 16' 17 18' 19' 20' 21 22 23 24 *Potentially excellent* GRAND CRU CLASSÉ on limestone plateau. La Mondiale insurance-owned (*see* LARMANDE); massive investment, making strides in recent yrs. Visitor-friendly.

Suduiraut Saut ★★★★ 10' 11' 13 14 15' 16' 17' 19' 20' 21 22 23 24 AXA property. One of v. best SAUT; 100% SÉM, luscious quality, pure, long. Second labels: Castelnau de Suduiraut; Lions de Suduiraut (fruitier). Dry wines: VIEILLES VIGNES, Pur Sém and entry-level Lions de Suduiraut.

Taillefer Pom ★★ 15 16 18' 19 20' 22 23 MOUEIX-owned, 100 yrs in 2023. Lighter weight but refined. Usually gd value.

Talbot St-Jul ★★★ 10' 11 14 15 16 17 18 19 20 21 22 23 24 Substantial ST-JUL Fourth Growth (110 ha). Bignon Cordier family-owned. Wine rich, age-worthy, *consummately charming, reliable.* Approachable SAUV BL-based Caillou Blanc. Second label: Connétable de Talbot (more approachable).

Tertre, Du Marg ★★★ 10' 14 15' 16' 17 18' 19' 20 21 22 23 Fifth Growth isolated s of MARG. CAB SAUV-led (70% in 23). Fragrant, fresh and fruity but structured wines. Eric Boissenot consults. Second label: Les Hauts du Tertre. Also Tertre Blanc VDF (dr w).

Tertre Roteboeuf St-Ém ★★★★ 09' 10' 12 14' 15' 16' 17 18' 19 20 21 22 23 24 Tiny, unclassified côtes star; lush, concentrated, toasty. François Mitjavile's creation; frightening prices. Also v.gd ROC DE CAMBES.

Thieuley Bx ★★ An E-2-M supplier of consistent-quality AOP BX (r/w); run by Sylvie and Marie Courselle. Clos Ste-Anne CÔTES DE BX gd.

Tour Blanche, La Saut ★★★ 10' 11' 13 14 15 16' 17 18' 19' 20 21 22 23 24 Excellent First Growth. Rich, bold, powerful, on sweeter end of scale; SÉM-dominant, SAUV BL, MUSCADELLE. Second label: Les Charmilles. Also lighter, less sweet Brumes.

Tour Carnet, La H-Méd ★★★ 09' 10' 14 15 16' 18' 19' 20 21 22 23 Large Fourth Growth owned by Bernard Magrez (*see* FOMBRAUGE, PAPE CLÉMENT). MERLOT-led (75% in 23); ripe, sweet, savoury. Also dry white BX (SÉM/SAUV BL). Second label: La Mémoire de La Tour Carnet.

Tour de By, La Méd ★★ 15' 16' 18 19' 20' 21 22 23 Substantial estate in N MÉD. Owned by Pagès family. Popular, sturdy, reliable, CAB SAUV-led (60%) wines; can age.

Tour de Mons, La Marg ★★ 15' 16' 18' 19 20 22 23 Owned by Perrodo family (MARQUIS D'ALESME). Upward curve; gd value.

Tour du Haut Moulin H-Méd ★★ 15' 16' 18 19 20 22 23 In N H-MÉD. Owned by Tzora Vyds (2024). Classic wines; structured, to age.

Tour du Pas St-Georges St-Ém ★★ 16 18 19 20 22 ST-GEORGES-ST-ÉM estate; Delbeck family-owned; wines made by FLEUR DE BOÜARD. MERLOT-led (66%). Classic style.

Tour Figeac, La St-Ém ★★ 15' 16' 18' 19' 20 22 23 GRAND CRU CLASSÉ neighbour of FIGEAC; fine, floral. Organic, bio practices.

Tour Haut-Caussan Méd ★★ 16' 18 19 20 22 Small cru owned by Véronique and Fabien Courrian; CAB SAUV/MERLOT on clay-limestone. Consistent, value.

Tournefeuille L de P ★★ 16 18 19 20 21 22 Reliable; MERLOT-led (62%); round, firm, fleshy. Also C315 Ouest without sulphur.

Tour Saint Christophe St-Ém ★★ 16 18 19 20 21 22 23 GRAND CRU CLASSÉ. MERLOT-led; ripe, structured. Same VIGNOBLES K stable as BELLEFONT-BELCIER. Also Enclos Tourmaline (POM).

Trois Croix, Les Fron ★★ 16' 18' 19' 20 22 23 Fine, balanced, gd-value wines from consistent producer; MERLOT-led (83% in 23).

Tronquoy St-Est ★★★ 11 12 14 15' 16' 17 18' 19' 20 21 22 23 Was Tronquoy-Lalande until 2019. MERLOT/CAB SAUV/PETIT VERDOT (11% in 23); consistent, satisfying.

Troplong Mondot St-Ém ★★★ 10 12 14 15' 16 17 18' 19' 20 21 22 23 24 PREMIER GRAND CRU CLASSÉ (B) on limestone plateau. Lots of investment; new winery, restaurant. *Wines of power, depth*; major style change from 17; more elegance, freshness. MERLOT-led with CABS SAUV/FR. Second label: Mondot.

Trotanoy Pom ★★★★ 12 14 15' 16' 17 18' 19' 20 21 22 23 One of jewels in J-P MOUEIX crown; MERLOT on clay/gravel soils; dense, powerful, long-ageing.

Trottevieille St-Ém ★★★ 12 14 15 16' 17 18' 19' 20 22 23 PREMIER GRAND CRU CLASSÉ (B) owned by BORIE-MANOUX. Greater consistency; wines long, fresh, structured; lots of CAB FR (53% in 23). New cellar from 2021. Second label: La Vieille Dame de Trottevieille.

Valandraud St-Ém ★★★★ 10 12 14 15' 16' 17 18 19' 20 21 22 23 24 PREMIER GRAND CRU CLASSÉ (B). Garage wonder turned First Growth. Creation of Jean-Luc Thunevin. Formerly super-rich; now dense, balanced. Also Virginie de V and V Bl.

Vieille Cure, La Fron ★★ 17 18' 19' 20 22 23 Leading FRON estate; appetizing, fruit-evident, MERLOT/CABS FR/SAUV. Value.

Vieux Château Certan Pom ★★★★ 08 09' 10' 11' 12 13 14 15' 16' 17 18' 19' 20' 21 22 23 24 One of the great POMS. In Thienpont hands, 100 yrs in 2024. Different in style from neighbour PETRUS; *elegance, harmony, fragrance*. Plenty of old-vine CABS FR/SAUV one of reasons. Great consistency; long-ageing.

Vieux Château St-André St-Ém ★★ 16' 18 19 20 22 23 Small MERLOT-based vyd in MONTAGNE-ST-ÉM; *gd value*. Berrouet-owned. Also Samion (L DE P).

Villegeorge, De H-Méd ★★ 16 18 19 20 22 Tiny S H-MÉD owned by Marie-Laure Lurton; Eric Boissenot consults; light but elegant wines.

Vray Croix de Gay Pom ★★★ 14 15 16' 17 18' 19' 20' 22 23 24 Tiny vyd in best part of POM. More finesse of late. MERLOT-led (98% in 23). Organic, bio practices. Same stable as CALON SÉGUR.

Yquem Saut ★★★★ 03' 04 05' 06' 07 08 09' 10' 11' 13' 14 15' 16' 17' 18' 19 20 21' King of sweet, *liquoreux* wines. Owned by LVMH. Strong, intense, luscious; kept 2 yrs in barrel. Most vintages improve for 15 yrs+, some live 100 yrs+ in transcendent splendour; 100 ha in production (75/25% SÉM/SAUV BL). No Yquem made 51 52 64 72 74 92 2012. Older vintages available in Time Capsule series. Makes small amount (c.830 cases) off-dry (5g/l sugar) Sauv Bl/Sém (75/25%) "Y" (pronounced "ee-grec"). Organic from 2022.

Alternative ways

The economic difficulties experienced at generic level have incited one BX CO-OP group, Bordeaux Families, to explore alternative avenues. From only 25,000 bottles 15 yrs ago, the co-op is now the leading producer of CRÉMANT de Bx, with 2.5m bottles and rising. In 2024, it invested €2.5m in a vacuum distillation plant to make no- and low-alc wines; and among certain members, disease-resistant grape varieties such as Floréal and others like MARSELAN and SYRAH are replacing trad Bx varieties, even if it means adopting the VDF label. When needs must...

Italy

VALLE
D'AOSTA
L Maggiore
Turin
PIEDMONT
LOMBAR
Genoa
Po
LIGURIA
Ligurian Sea

More heavily shaded areas are
the wine-growing regions.

Abbreviations used in
the text:

Ab	Abruzzo	Mol	Molise
Bas	Basilicata	Pie	Piedmont
Cal	Calabria	Pu	Puglia
Cam	Campania	Sar	Sardinia
E-R	Emilia-Romagna	Si	Sicily
FVG	Friuli Venezia Giulia	T-AA	Trentino-Alto Adige
Lat	Latium	Tus	Tuscany
Lig	Liguria	Umb	Umbria
Lom	Lombardy	VdA	Valle d'Aosta
Mar	Marches	Ven	Veneto

For a country so completely (some might say tragically) dominated
by bureaucracy, wine could hardly escape. And so, in order to enjoy
the greatness of Italian wine to its fullest, it helps to know and remember
a few facts. There are 407 different denominations (330 DOCs and
77 DOCGs) in Italy, each with its own official production regulations.
(Imagine how much fun it is to sit down, read and analyze them all.)
Of those denominations, there are more than 100 that have a certified
production of less than 400 hectolitres per year (that's just over 50,000
bottles, folks). Now that's perfectly fine, provided the wines truly speak
of a specific parcel of land, or of specific grape varieties that express
wines like nobody else's. Alas, it is not always so.

Small Italian wine denominations, such as Loazzolo (in Piedmont)
and Faro (in Sicily), are just what they should be: small enclaves of
often wonderful wines quite unlike those made anywhere else. In
the former, it's a common grape, Moscato Bianco, but a very specific
geology and microclimates that combine to give Muscat wines different
from any others you might have tried. With the latter, you are tasting
wines that are (or should be) dominated by the Nocera grape, a rare
local native that grows basically nowhere else in the world (rest of Italy
included). These are wines, although limited in their annual output
and availability, for which it actually makes sense to speak of specific
terroirs and, hence, denominations. The same is also true of a few
(not many) larger-volume production zones: the wines of the Verdicchio
dei Castelli di Jesi and those of Verdicchio di Matelica denominations
could not be more different, even though they are both made with
exactly the same grape, Verdicchio. And why should it not be so?
The former's territory is made of gently rolling hillsides close to the sea
and temperate climates; the latter's is inland, high-altitude and windy.
If the two wines were in fact similar, then that would be a real problem.
Another example is that of Prosecco DOC and Prosecco DOCG: same
grape, resoundingly different wines.

RENTINO-
LTO ADIGE

Bolzano

FRIULI
VENEZIA
GIULIA

Trento

VENETO

L Garda

Trieste

Verona

Venice

Po

MILIA-
OMAGNA

Bologna

orence

TUSCANY

ena

L Trasimeno

MARCHES

UMBRIA

L Bolsena

LATIUM

ABRUZZO

L Bracciano

Rome

MOLISE

Adriatic Sea

CAMPANIA

Bari

Naples

PUGLIA

BASILICATA

Taranto

SARDINIA

Tyrrhenian Sea

CALABRIA

Cagliari

Palermo

Reggio Calabria

SICILY

However, far too many Italian wine denominations are marred
by production regulations that do little to bring terroir to the fore.
For example: wines made from any variety, indigenous or international;
white, red, rosé, orange, sparkling; Classico, Riserva, Superiore;
ridiculous production volumes; it goes on... Such denominations can
hardly represent a territory, terroir, or a specific place and its history
(because they have nothing specific or recognizable about them). By
reading on here, you will learn about those denominations and their
wines for which it makes sense to speak of terroir, and that help make
Italy the uniquely great wine-producing country that it is (or could be).

Recent vintages

Amarone, Veneto & Friuli

2024 Ven: complicated, gd whites. FVG: high quality (r/w), low quantity.

2023 Ven: better than expected in difficult yr. FVG: uneven; okay where no hail or downy mildew; better whites.

2022 Ven: dry, gd quality. FVG: v.gd quality. Better than expected.

2021 Ven: dry, v.gd quality, less quantity. FVG: vgd quality, uneven volume.

2020 Ven: balanced, gd quality, quantity. FVG: wet June, uneven, better whites.

2019 Low quantity. Ven: gd for Amarone, Soave. FVG: fair quality.

2018 Optimal weather conditions; gd for quantity, quality, esp fresh whites.

2017 V. difficult (non-stop rain); weedy Amarones a risk, green reds in general.

Campania & Basilicata

2024 Warm, gd quality, quantity (r/w).

2023 V. difficult: downy mildew, hail. Small crop. What escaped is gd.

2022 Cam: classic, v.gd quality (r/w). Bas: warm, classic, v.gd.

2021 Cam: balance, quality, less quantity (best r). Bas: late harvest, classic, v.gd.

2020 Similar to 19. Classic, balanced but lower quantity; gd (r/w).

2019 Classic, balanced. Best for Aglianico, gd for whites.

2018 Rainy, but whites fresh, lively; sleek reds (Aglianico best).

2017 Low-volume yr of reds plagued by gritty tannins. Whites flat; Greco best.

Marches & Abruzzo

2024 Mar: complicated, low quantity. Ab: v. difficult due to drought.

2023 V. difficult: downy mildew; small crop; better for whites.

2022 Mar: similar to 21, uneven. Ab: dry, better than 21. Both best for red.

2021 Hot, dry late vintage, gd quality but low yields; gd for late-ripening grapes.

2020 Uneven; quality peaks; wet June, fresh weather; late-ripening grapes gd.

2019 Difficult yr. Rainy, cold spring. Low quantity, medium quality.

2018 Patchy spring. More balanced than 17; v. high volume, gd quality (r/w).

2017 Best to forget: hot, droughty. Reds gritty, whites overripe. Low volume.

Piedmont

2024 Complicated, uneven, lower alc, gd quality. Alto Piemonte: less quantity.

2023 Better than expected, though still difficult. Alto Piemonte v.gd.

2022 Better than expected, uneven quantity, gd quality.

2021 Gd, despite warm dry summer; gd quality, less quantity.

2020 Classic, 19 better balance, but elegant; better Barbera than Nebbiolo.

2019 Classic, more balanced than 18. Lower quantity but higher quality.

2018 Despite difficult spring, potentially classic Barolo, Barbaresco.

2017 Among earliest harvests in living memory. Can lack depth.

Earlier fine vintages: (drink or keep) 16 13 10 06 04 99 96 (mature) 12 11 09 08 07 03 01 98 97.

Tuscany

2024 Challenging. Style as in 90s. Elegance more than power.

2023 Complicated but promising, crop reduction, but gd quality.

2022 Better than expected, high quality; gd structure, acidity for Sangiovese.

2021 V.gd (even if warm, dry) mainly for Sangiovese (better: fresher sites).

2020 V.gd, but complicated. Less power, alc than 19, elegant.

2019 Maybe one of best since 2000. Classic, balanced; gd quality, quantity.

2018 Reds gd: of steely personality, age-worthiness.

2017 Hot, v. difficult vintage. Better in Chianti Classico than coastal Maremma. Earlier fine vintages: (drink or keep) 16 15 11 10 08 01 99 (mature) 09 07 06 04 03 00 97 95 90.

Abate Nero T-AA ★★★ Roberta Lunelli runs artisanal winery, devoted to sparkling Trento. Top: Domini, Domini Nero, RISERVA Cuvée dell'Abate. Look for Brut Riserva Collezione Luciano Lunelli 03 07 and Rosé 09 (disgorged 2022).

Abbona, Anna Maria Pie ★★★ Anna Maria is 5th generation in Dolcetto (since 1850). Top: ALTA LANGA, BAROLO San Pietro (also RISERVA), DOGLIANI SUPERIORE (Maioli, San Bernardo).

Abrigo, Orlando Pie ★★★ Some of most mineral, steely, refined BARBARESCOS. Top: Meruzzano (and RISERVA), Montersino, CN III (100% NEBBIOLO rosé). Trés Plus (w blend CHARD/Nascetta) v.gd.

Adanti Umb ★★★ One of three best estates in Montefalco, benchmark of DOC. Top MONTEFALCO SAGRANTINO (Il Domenico, Passito); v.gd Montefalco Rosso RISERVA and GRECHETTO.

Aglianico del Taburno Cam ★→★★★ DOCG Around Benevento. Generally cooler microclimate than TAURASI. Spicier notes (leather, tobacco), herbs, higher acidity than other AGLIANICOS. Best: Cantina del Taburno (Apis, Delius), Fontanavecchia (RISERVAS: Grave Mora, VIGNA Cataratte) and La Rivolta (Taburno Aglianico, Terra di Rivolta)

Aglianico del Vulture Bas ★→★★★ DOC(G) 15 17′ 19 20 21′ DOC after 1 yr, SUPERIORE after 3 yrs, RISERVA after 5. From slopes of extinct volcano Monte Vulture; soils with high content of clay-rich tuff. More floral (violet), dark fruits (plum), smoke, spice than other AGLIANICOS. Try: Elena Fucci. Then try Basilisco, Cantina di Venosa, Cantine del Notaio, Donato d'Angelo, Grifalco, Mastrodomenico (Likos), Paternoster. Also gd: Mustocarmelitano, Terre degli Svevi.

Alba Pie Truffles, hazelnuts and PIE's, if not Italy's, most prestigious wines: Alba, BARBARESCO, BARBERA D'ALBA, BAROLO, DOLCETTO d'Alba, NEBBIOLO D'ALBA.

Alessandri, Massimo Lig ★★★ One of best with Pigato grape. Top: Pigato Vigne Veggie (35-yr-old vines), Viorus (VIOGNIER/ROUSSANNE). Also v.gd: Pigato, Puro (Roussanne), VERMENTINO, Granaccia.

Alessandria, Fratelli Pie ★★★ Since 1870 top BAROLO producer in VERDUNO. Best crus: Monvigliero, Gramolere, San Lorenzo. Also v.gd: Barolo di Verduno and Verduno Pelaverga Speziale.

Almondo, Giovanni Pie ★★★→★★★★ Top ROERO estate. Best: Roero ARNEIS Bricco delle Ciliegie, Rive del Bricco. Outstanding FREISA; v.gd Roero Bric Valdiana (r).

Alta Langa Pie ★★★ DOCG The 1st METODO CLASSICO made in Italy, since mid-C19 in "underground cathedrals". Vintage only, and simply CHARD, PINOT N. Best: COCCHI-BAVA, Contratto (For England Blanc de Noirs, Millesimato), ETTORE GERMANO. Then try BANFI, Bera, Brandini (Blanc de Blancs), Colombo (Blanc de Blancs, Rosé), Del Tetto (PN+CH, RISERVAS), Enrico Serafino (Zero Pas Dosé, M+M 18 Perpetuelle Sbagliato, Zero 140), Fontanafredda (VIGNA Gatinera 108 Mesi and 84 Mesi, Rosé), GANCIA (120 Mesi, 60 Mesi), Mirafiore (Blanc de Noirs), Monsignore, Paolo Berruti, PODERI COLLA, RIZZI, ROBERTO GARBARINO. Also gd: CASCINA CERRUTI, Cascina Bretta Rossa, Giribaldi, Isolabella della Croce, Ivaldi Dario, Marcalberto, Massimo Rivetti, Pecchenino, San Silvestro, San Biagio.

Alto Adige (Sudtirol) T-AA DOC Mountainous region with Bolzano its chief city (Austrian until 1919); arguably best Italian whites today but also underrated reds. Germanic vines dominate. GEWURZ, KERNER, SYLVANER, but PINOT GR too. Probably world's best PINOT BIANCO. PINOT N often overoaked; *Lagrein* in gd yrs.

Alto Piemonte Pie Cradle of PIE quality in C19 (40,000 ha). Acidic soil, exposure, climate and altitude diversity, ideal for many different NEBBIOLO expressions (here called Spanna). Main DOC(G): BOCA, BRAMATERRA, Colline Novaresi, Coste della Sesia, Fara, GATTINARA, GHEMME, LESSONA, Sizzano, Valli Ossolane. Many outstanding wines. Actually, rarely 100% Nebbiolo: small additions of Croatina, Uva Rara, Vespolina common.

Ama, Castello di Tus ★★★★ Among 1st to produce single-vyd CHIANTI CLASSICO. Gran Selezione VIGNETO Bellavista best; La Casuccia close 2nd; v.gd San Lorenzo and RISERVA Montebuoni. MERLOT L'Apparita one of Italy's three best.

Amarone della Valpolicella Ven ★★→★★★★ DOCG 11′ 13 15 16 18 (19) (20) (21) CLASSICO area (from historic zone), Val d'Illasi and Valpantena (from extended zone) can make unique world-class reds from raisined grapes. Alas, many less than what they should be, despite hype. Choose carefully. (*See* VALPOLICELLA, and box p.156.)

Ambra, D' Cam ★★★ On ISCHIA; fosters rare local native grapes. Best: single-vyd Frassitelli (w, 100% Biancolella). Also v.gd: (w) Biancolella, Forastera, Ischia Bianco; (r) La VIGNA dei Mille Anni (blend), Per' 'e Palummo.

Antinori, Marchesi L&P Tus ★★→★★★★ Top CHIANTI CLASSICO (TENUTE and *Badia a Passignano*), two excellent SUPER TUSCANS (TIGNANELLO, SOLAIA) and Prunotto (PIE BAROLOS). Also gd FVG (JERMANN), La Braccesca, MONTALCINO (Pian delle Vigne).

Argiano, Tenuta di Tus ★★★→★★★★ Since 1580. High-quality BRUNELLOS (esp RISERVA, VIGNA del Sudlo); trad-style Brunello and single-vyd, modern Riserva.

Argiolas Sar ★★★ Top producer, native island grapes. Outstanding CRUS: Iselis (Monica, Nasco), *Turriga* ★★★★, *Vermentino* di SARDEGNA (Cerdeña), Antonio 100 (CANNONAU PASSITO). Bovale Korem, Cannonau RISERVA Senes, CARIGNANO del Sulcis (Cardanera, Is Solinas) and new (sp) Argiolas METODO CLASSICO (from Nuragus grapes) v.gd.

Arnaldo Rivera Pie ★★★ Starting from vintage 13, top-quality line of Terre del BAROLO CO-op. Small parcels (less than 0.5 ha) in most prestigious Barolo crus. Best: Barolo Bussia, Monvigliero, Rocche dell'Annunziata, Vignarionda and new Cannubi.

Asti Pie ★→★★ NV sparkler from MOSCATO Bianco grapes, inferior to MOSCATO D'ASTI. Try Bera, Cascina Fonda, Caudrina, Vignaioli di Santo Stefano.

Top Barbaresco by MGA

BARBARESCO has four main communes, four distinct styles: **Barbaresco** most complete, balanced. Growers incl Asili (BRUNO GIACOSA, CA' DEL BAIO, CERETTO, PRODUTTORI DEL BARBARESCO), Martinenga (MARCHESI DI GRÉSY), Montefico (Produttori del B, ROAGNA), Montestefano (Giordano Luigi, Produttori del B, Rivella Serafino), Ovello (CANTINA del Pino, ROCCA ALBINO), Pajè (Roagna), Pora (Ca' del Baio, MUSSO, Produttori del B), Rabaja (Bruno Giacosa, BRUNO ROCCA, CASTELLO DI VERDUNO, GIUSEPPE CORTESE, Produttori del B), Rio Sordo (Cascina Bruciata, Cascina delle Rose, MUSSO, Produttori del B), Roccalini (Cascina Roccalini), Roncaglie (PODERI COLLA). **Neive** most powerful, fleshiest. Albesani (Cantina del Pino, CASTELLO DI NEIVE, MASSOLINO), Basarin (MARCO E VITTORIO ADRIANO, Giacosa Fratelli, Negro Angelo, PAITIN, SOTTIMANO), Bordini (La Spinetta), Currà (Bruno Rocca, Sottimano), Gallina (Castello di Neive, Ceretto, La Spinetta, Lequio Ugo, ODDERO), Serraboella (Cigliuti, PAITIN). **San Rocco Seno d'Elvio** readiest to drink, soft. Rocche Massalupo (Lano, TENUTA Barac), Sanadaive (Marco e Vittorio Adriano). **Treiso** freshest, most refined. Bernardot (Ceretto), Bricco di Treiso (PIO CESARE), Marcarini (Ca' del Baio), Montersino (ORLANDO ABRIGO, Rocca Albino), Nervo (RIZZI), Pajoré (Rizzi, Sottimano), Rombone (Fiorenzo Nada, Luigi Oddero).

Attimis Maniago, Conte d' FVG ★★★ One of best trad estates; standout FRIULANO, MALVASIA, RIBOLLA, Pignolo, SCHIOPPETTINO; Tazzelenghe knockout.

Avignonesi Tus ★★★ Large bio estate. *Italy's best Vin Santo*. Top: VINO NOBILE single-vyd Grandi Annate, Poggetto di Sopra. Also gd MERLOT Desiderio.

Azelia Pie ★★★ Distinctive, elegant BAROLOS from Luigi Scavino and son Lorenzo. Some of best crus. Top: Bricco Fiasco, Cerretta, Margheria, San Rocco, RISERVA Bricco Voghera. Also v.gd BARBERA D'ALBA, LANGHE NEBBIOLO.

Azienda agricola / agraria Estate (large or small) making wine from its own grapes.

Badia a Coltibuono Tus ★★★ One of top CHIANTI CLASSICO producers; buy every wine, great terroirs spell non-stop success. Montebello (blend of nine historic CHIANTI grapes), SANGIOVETO v.gd. Organic.

Banfi (Castello or Villa) Tus ★★→★★★ Giant of MONTALCINO, but top, limited-production POGGIO all'Oro is great BRUNELLO; v.gd ALTA LANGA (Aurora 100 Mesi, Cuvée Aurora), Moscadello.

Barbaresco Pie ★★→★★★★ DOCG 13 14 15 16 18 19 20 21 Often better than BAROLO, Barbaresco's lesser reputation is undeserved. When spot-on, the gracefulness, age-worthiness and perfumed intensity are like those of no other wine in Italy – the world, really. Min 26 mths' ageing, 9 mths in wood; at 4 yrs becomes RISERVA. Two main types of soil: Serravalian (alternation of sandy levels and grey silty marls), on average, elegant and v. perfumed wines, not too fleshy Tortonian (blue-grey marls with more or less sand), v. structured wines (mainly in Barbaresco, Neive). (For top crus/producers, *see* box, opposite.)

Barbera d'Alba Pie DOC Unique, luscious, sultry Barbera, quite different from d'Asti's more nervy, higher-acid version. AZELIA (Punta), BREZZA, BROVIA, GB BURLOTTO, CAVALLOTTO (Cuculo), CLERICO DOMENICO, CORREGGIA, CONTERNO FANTINO (Vignota), Cortese, Fratelli Revello, ETTORE GERMANO (della Madre), GD VAJRA, MASSOLINO, Paolo Conterno, PODERI ALDO CONTERNO (Conca Tre Pile), PODERI COLLA, Renato Corino, ROAGNA, SOTTIMANO, TREDIBERRI, VIETTI (Scarrone VIGNA Vecchia) make benchmarks. COGNO's Pre-Phylloxera is *hors classe*.

Barbera d'Asti Pie Huge DOCG, encompassing v. different soils (from sandy to marly) and climatic characteristics. Wines vary, but usually high acidity and fruity notes. Superiore: higher quality (but often overoaked). (*See also* NIZZA.) Best: BRAIDA, BAVA, Colle Manora, MARCHESI DI GRÉSY, Marchesi Incisa della Rocchetta, SCARPA (La Bogliona), TENUTA Olim Bauda (Le Rocchette). Also v.gd: BERSANO, Cascina Castlet, Gianni Doglia, Marchesi Alfieri (Alfiera), ODDERO, Spertino, Tenuta Garetto, *Vietti* (La Crena), Vinchio Vaglio (Vigne Vecchie).

Barbera del Monferrato Superiore Pie DOCG From soils rich in limestone, full-bodied BARBERA with sharpish tannins, gd acidity. Top: Accornero, Castello di Uviglie, Iuli (Barabba, Rossore).

Barolo Pie DOCG 10' 11 12 13' 15 16' 17 19' 20 21' "King of wines and wine of kings", 100% NEBBIOLO. 2000-ha zone. Must age 38 mths before release (5 yrs for RISERVA), of which 18 mths in wood. Best are age-worthy, able to join power and elegance, with alluring floral scent and sour red-cherry flavour. Now most is single vyd, but trad a blend of vyds from different communes. The concept of "cru" is replaced (in Barolo and BARBARESCO at least) by subzones known officially as MGA (menzioni geografiche aggiuntive). Currently Barolo has 11 village mentions and 170(!) additional geographical mentions. Often underrated: Village MGA ("Barolo del Comune di...") best way to understand different Barolo terroirs. Best: "di Barolo" (ROAGNA, SCARZELLO, Virna), "di Castiglione" (Monchiero Fratelli), "di Grinzane" (Canonica), "di La Morra" (Brandini, CIABOT BERTON, GIANNI GAGLIARDO, TREDIBERRI), "di Novello" (Le Strette), "di Serralunga" (ETTORE GERMANO, GIOVANNI ROSSO, PALLADINO, RIVETTO), "di VERDUNO" (FRATELLI ALESSANDRIA). Three main types of soil: Messinian (chalk-sulphur formation),

---

Top Barolos by MGA

Here are a few top crus and their best producers: **Bricco Boschis** (Castiglione Falletto) CAVALLOTTO (RISERVA VIGNA San Giuseppe). **Bricco delle Viole** (BAROLO) GD VAJRA, MARENGO, VIBERTI. **Bricco Rocche** (Castiglione Falletto) CERETTO. **Briccolina** (Serralunga) RIVETTO. **Brunate** (La Morra, Barolo) Ceretto, FRANCESCO RINALDI, GIUSEPPE RINALDI, Marengo, ODDERO, VIETTI. **Bussia** (Monforte) ALDO CONTERNO (Gran Bussia e Romirasco), ARNALDO RIVERA, Ceretto, EINAUDI, GIACOMO FENOCCHIO (also Riserva 90 Dì), Oddero (Vigna Mondoca), PODERI COLLA (Dardi Le Rose). **Cannubi** (Barolo) BREZZA, Giacomo Fenocchio, LUCIANO SANDRONE, PIRA E FIGLI – CHIARA BOSCHIS, Einaudi, Virna. **Cerequio** (La Morra, Barolo) BOROLI, GAJA. **Falletto** (Serralunga) BRUNO GIACOSA (Riserva Vigna Le Rocche). **Francia** (Serralunga) GIACOMO CONTERNO (Cascina Francia and Monfortino). **Ginestra** (Monforte) CONTERNO FANTINO (Sorì Ginestra and Vigna del Gr), DOMENICO CLERICO (Ciabot Mentin). **Lazzarito** (Serralunga) ETTORE Germano (Riserva), GIANNI GAGLIARDO, VIETTI. **Monprivato** (Castiglione Falletto) GIUSEPPE MASCARELLO (Mauro). **Monvigliero** (VERDUNO) Arnaldo Rivera, CASTELLO DI VERDUNO, Einaudi, FRATELLI ALESSANDRIA, GB BURLOTTO, PAOLO SCAVINO, Viberti. **Mosconi** (Monforte) Conterno Fantino, Domenico Clerico, Pira e Figli – Chiara Boschis, PIO CESARE. **Ornato** (Serralunga) Pio Cesare, PALLADINO. **Ravera** (Novello) ELVIO COGNO (Bricco Pernice), GD Vajra, Vietti. **Rocche dell'Annunziata** (La Morra) Arnaldo Rivera, Paolo Scavino (Riserva), Ratti, Rocche Costamagna, TREDIBERRI. **Rocche di Castiglione** (Castiglione Falletto) BROVIA, Oddero, ROAGNA, Vietti. **Sarmassa** (Barolo) Bergadano, Brezza, Scarzello. **Vigna Rionda** (Serralunga) Ettore Germano, GIOVANNI ROSSO, Figli Luigi Oddero, MASSOLINO VR, Oddero. **Villero** (Castiglione Falletto) Boroli, Brovia, Giacomo Fenocchio, Giuseppe Mascarello. And the Barolo of Bartolo Mascarello blends together Cannubi San Lorenzo, Ruè and Rocche dell'Annunziata. A sommelier's delight.

---

readier to drink more open Barolo, w slope of La Morra; Serravalian (greyish yellow/red looser calcareous marl soil and sands), Castiglione Falletto (bold), Monforte (structure), Serralunga (power); Tortonian (blue-grey compact marl soil and calcareous sands, younger), Barolo (grace), La Morra (fragrance). Newcomers to follow: La Contrada di Sorano. (For top crus and producers, *see* box, above.)

Barone Pizzini Lom ★★★ One of top FRANCIACORTA estates; bio. Top: Animante (also LA, Long Ageing), Naturae (Brut), RISERVA Bagnadore (Dosage Zero).

Bartoli, Marco De Si ★★★★ One of best estates in all Italy. Marco spent life promoting "real" MARSALA, and his must be tried. Top: VECCHIO SAMPERI, 20-yr-old Ventennale. Also v.gd: GRILLO (Grappoli del Grillo, Terzavia sp), ZIBIBBO (Pietranera). Outstanding sweet Zibibbo di PANTELLERIA *Bukkuram*.

Benanti Si ★★★★ This family turned world on to ETNA BIANCO SUPERIORE *Pietramarina* (one of Italy's best whites), Contrada Rinazzo. Top: (r) Etna RISERVA (Rovittello, Serra della Contessa), Selezione Contrade (Calderara Sottana, Cavaliere, Dafara Galluzzo, Monte Serra, Rinazzo), Etna's best whites. Also v.gd: Lamorèmio (sp, NERELLO MASCALESE), Noblesse 48 Mesi (sp, CARRICANTE).

Berlucchi, Guido Lom ★★★ Created FRANCIACORTA wine with Franco Ziliani in 1961, hence names of wines. Top: 61 Nature, 61 Nature Blanc de Blancs, 61 NV Extra Brut, and RISERVAS Cuvée Franco Ziliani, Palazzo Lana Extreme.

Bersano Pie ★★→★★★ Large volume but gd quality. BARBERA D'ASTI, BAROLO, GRIGNOLINO, NIZZA (Generala), Ruchè, all inexpensive, delightful.

Bertinga Tus ★★★ Estate in Gaiole, CHIANTI. Best: Bertinga (SANGIOVESE/MERLOT), Punta di Adine (Sangiovese), Volta (Merlot). Original.

Biondi-Santi Tus ★★★★ Invented BRUNELLO. High quality, high in acid, tannin requiring decades to develop fully.

Bio Vio Lig ★★★ Top Ponente estate, Aimone and daughter Caterina, super-star winery. Outstanding Pigato Bon in da Bon; v.gd Marené, Pigato EsSenza (no sulphites), Pigato Grand-Père, 4C ROSATO.

Bisol Ven ★★★ Owned by FERRARI's Lunelli family; quality leader in PROSECCO. Top: CARTIZZE, Relio Rive di Guia. Also v.gd: Crede, Molera, Rive di Campea.

Boca Pie DOC *See* ALTO PIEMONTE. Potentially among greatest reds resurfaced thanks to Christoph Kunzli (Le Piane). Blend of NEBBIOLO (70–90%), incl up to 30% Uva Rara and/or Vespolina. Volcanic quartz porphyry soils. Needs long ageing. Best: *Le Piane*. Carlone Davide, Castello Conti gd.

Bolgheri Tus DOC Mid-Maremma, on w coast, cradle of many expensive SUPER TUSCANS, mainly based on French varieties. Big name and excellent quality. Top: Masseto (100% MERLOT), SAN GUIDO (SASSICAIA, original Super Tuscan). Also v.gd: Campo alla Sughera, GAJA (Ca' Marcanda), GRATTAMACCO, LE MACCHIOLE, Michele Satta (Marianova, Piastraia), ORNELLAIA (FRESCOBALDI).

Borgo del Tiglio FVG ★★★→★★★★ Nicola Manferrari (one of Italy's top white wine makers) and his son Mattia run one of best COLLIO estates. Top is Black Label collection: Collio FRIULANO RONCO della Chiesa, MALVASIA Selezione, Rosso della Centa, Studio di Bianco esp impressive.

Borgogno, Virna Pie ★★★ Family estate run by Virna B and sister Ivana. Great-value BAROLO from famous crus: Cannubi and Sarmassa. Barolo del Comune di Barolo, Barolo Noi, RISERVA, BARBERA D'ALBA v.gd.

Boroli Pie ★★★ Achille now runs this winery, devoted to BAROLOS. Best: Brunella (monopole), Cerequio, Villero. New v.gd Langhe NEBBIOLO 1661.

Bosco, Tenute Si ★★★ Small ETNA estate owned by Sofia B, high quality. Best: Etna Rosso VIGNA Vico Prephylloxera. Piano dei Daini (r/w/rosé) v.gd.

Botte Big barrel, anything from 6–250 hl, usually 20–50, trad Slavonian but increasingly of French oak. To traditionalists, ideal vessel for ageing wines without adding too much oak smell/taste.

Braida Pie ★★★ If BARBERA D'ASTI is known today, it's thanks to the Bologna family, world ambassadors for this wine. Top: Ai Suma, Bricco dell'Uccellone, Bricco della Bigotta. Also v.gd: Montebruna. Their GRIGNOLINO d'Asti Limonte is one of Italy's best; new Limonte GB is bigger, esp age-worthy.

Bramaterra Pie DOC Volcanic porphyry and marine deposits. Most variegated in terms of soils. Wines tend to be lighter and less massive than the other ALTO PIEMONTE denominations. Top: Antoniotti Odilio, PROPRIETÀ SPERINO.

Brezza Pie ★★★→★★★★ Organic. Certainty for lovers of trad BAROLOS. Great value, from famous crus Cannubi, Castellero, Sarmassa (esp RISERVA VIGNA Bricco); v.gd BARBERA and DOLCETTO D'ALBA, LANGHE NEBBIOLO; outstanding FREISA.

Brolio, Castello di Tus ★★→★★★ Since 1141 run by Ricasoli family. (Bettino R devised the classic CHIANTI blend.) Historic estate of CHIANTI CLASSICO. Outstanding Gran Selezione offerings.

Brovia Pie ★★★→★★★★ Since 1863, classic BAROLOS in Castiglione Falletto. Organic. Top: Ca' Mia, Garblèt Sue, Rocche, Villero. After 10 yrs again iconic DOLCETTO d'ALBA Solatio. BARBERA and Dolcetto d'Alba v.gd.

Bruna Lig ★★★ Historical producer of Pigato. Best: Russeghine, U Baccan. Also v.gd: Majè.

Brunelli, Gianni Tus ★★★ Lovely refined user-friendly BRUNELLOS (top RISERVA) and Rossos from two sites: Le Chiuse di Sotto n of MONTALCINO, Podernovone to s.

Brunello di Montalcino Tus 09 10' **12 13** 15' 16' **18** 19' (20') (21) DOCG World-famous,

but quality all over the shop. When gd, memorable and ageless, archetypal
SANGIOVESE. Problems derive mostly from greedily enlarged production area (a
ridiculous 2000 ha+), much less than ideal for fickle Sangiovese and world-class
wines. Recent push to turn wine into a blend has been successfully stopped (thus
far, at least). Generally speaking, MONTALCINO's soils vary from the limestone-rich
Galestro of the n sector (wines are sleeker, more floral and mineral, generally
higher acidity), to the loamier, siltier sandy clays of the s (wines broader, more
powerful). (For top producers, *see* box, above.)

Bucci Mar ★★★★ Villa Bucci RISERVA one of Italy's ten best whites. All wines quasi-
Burgundian, v. elegant, esp complex VERDICCHIOS. All age splendidly; v.gd red
Pongelli. Outstanding Vintage Collection.

Burlotto, Commendatore GB Pie ★★★★ Fabio Alessandria maintains his ancestor
Commander GB Burlotto's (among 1st to make/bottle BAROLO, 1880) high
quality and focus. Barolo Monvigliero and superlative FREISA best. Barolos
(Acclivi, Cannubi, Castelletto), VERDUNO Pelaverga also outstanding.

Bussola, Tommaso Ven ★★★★ Self-taught maker of some of the great AMARONES,
RECIOTOS, RIPASSOS of our time. The great Bepi QUINTARELLI steered him; he
steers his two sons. Top TB selection.

Ca' del Baio Pie ★★★ Family estate; best-value producer in BARBARESCO. Outstanding
Asili (RISERVA too) and Pora; v.gd Autinbej, LANGHE RIES, Vallegrande.

Ca' del Bosco Lom ★★★★ Arguably Italy's best METODO CLASSICO fizz, famous
FRANCIACORTA estate owned by Zanella family and Santa Margherita Group.
One of Italy's most innovative and avant-garde wineries, with new immersive
sensory room. Outstanding, unforgettable Dosage Zéro Annamaria Clementi
RISERVA (rosé too) and new Annamaria Clementi RS 1980 (aged for over
40 yrs). Great Cuvée Prestige (esp Edizione RS). Vintage Collection (Dosage
Zéro, Dosage Zéro Noir) practically as gd. Excellent Bx-style Maurizio Zanella
(r), PINOT N, CHARD.

Cadinu, Francesco Sar ★★★ Micro size, mega quality. Top CANNONAU di SARDEGNA
(Ghirada Elisi, Ghirada Fittiloghe). Mattìo (w, rare Granatza) v.gd.

Caiarossa Tus ★★★ Dutch-owned (Ch Giscours; *see* Bordeaux) estate, n of BOLGHERI.
Excellent Caiarossa Rosso plus reds Aria, Pergolaia.

Ca' La Bionda Ven ★★★ Some of finest VALPOLICELLA. Top: AMARONE, CORVINA.

Calcagno Si ★★★→★★★★ Lilliputian size and Brobdingnagian quality from ETNA
family estate. Outstanding mineral NERELLO MASCALESE. Arcurìa, Feudo di
Mezzo top reds; plus v.gd Ginestra (w), Nireddu (r), Romice delle Sciare (rosé).

Calì, Paolo Si ★★★ Passionate Paolo C makes numerous wines highly typical of
Vittoria's sandy terroir. Top: CERASUOLO DI VITTORIA new single-vyd Forfice, Niscia,
Pruvuletta; Frappato. Blues (w Grillo), Nero d'Avola (r), Mood (rosé/sp) all v.gd.

Caluso / Erbaluce di Caluso Pie ★★→★★★ DOCG Morainic soils give v. interesting and mineral wines. Can be still, sparkling or sweet (Caluso Passito). Top: FERRANDO (Cariola), Giacometto, TAPPERO MERLO (Kin, sp). Also v.gd: Cieck (Misobolo), Favaro (Le Chiusure), Gnavi (Vigna Crava, sp Turbante), Orsolani, San Martin (Memento), Scelte di Vite (also sp 36 mths), SORPASSO. Outside DOCG: MONTE MALETTO, Sopravvento.

Campania Some of Italy's greatest and most age-worthy whites, terroir-driven, full of character. Reds unfortunately less consistent due to combination of overripe grapes and too much oak, with some remarkable exceptions. Few international varieties cloud native grapes panorama. FIANO DI AVELLINO may well be Italy's best white zone, TAURASI makes better and better reds. Try BENITO FERRARA, Caggiano, CANTINE Lonardo, CANTINE MAZZELLA, *Colli di Lapio*, D'AMBRA, De Angelis, Di Prisco, FATTORIA LA RIVOLTA, FEUDI DI SAN GREGORIO, Galardi, Guastaferro, I FAVATI, Il Cancelliere, La Sibilla, Luigi Maffini, *Marisa Cuomo*, MASTROBERARDINO, Molettieri, Perillo, Pierlingeri, Pietracupa, QUINTODECIMO, Reale, Rocca del Principe, Sarno 1860, SORRENTINO, Terredora, TRAERTE. MONTEVETRANO: world-class, international, mostly CAB SAUV wine.

Canalicchio di Sopra Tus ★★★★ Top-ten BRUNELLO estate. Owner Francesco Ripaccioli keen observer of terroir, MONTALCINO typicity. Top: Brunello RISERVA, single-vyd (La Casaccia, Montosoli). Also v.gd: Brunello, ROSSO DI MONTALCINO.

Cantina A cellar, winery or even a wine bar.

Capezzana, Tenuta di Tus ★★★ Organic production from noble Bonacossi family that made Carmignano's reputation. Excellent Carmignano (Trefiano, Villa di Capezzana), UCB (SANGIOVESE), Ghiaie della Furba (Bx blend). Exceptional VIN SANTO, one of Italy's five best.

Caprai Umb ★★★→★★★★ MONTEFALCO leader thanks to Marco C. Top: Montefalco (25 Anni, Spinning Beauty). Also v.gd: Collepiano (less oak), GRECHETTO Grecante, Montefalco Rosso RISERVA (elegant).

Caprili Tus ★★★ Family-run; based on Alfo Bartolommei's experience, making top BRUNELLO: classic, RISERVA Adalberto.

Carema Pie ★★★ DOC 13 15 16' 18' 20' 22' Only 22 ha, n of Turin. Steep terraces, morainic agglomerate soils for light, mineral, intense, outstanding NEBBIOLO. Top: FERRANDO, MONTE MALETTO, Murajè, SORPASSO. Also v.gd: Chiussuma, Milanesio, Produttori Nebbiolo di Carema (esp RISERVA), Sopravvento.

Carpineti, Marco Lat ★★★ Phenomenal bio whites from little-known Bellone, GRECO Moro, Greco Giallo varieties. Benchmark Moro, and Ludum (one of Italy's best stickies).

Cartizze Ven ★★★→★★★★ DOCG At 107 ha, this PROSECCO super-cru is 2nd-most expensive vyd land in Italy, after BAROLO; v. steep hills in heart of Valdobbiadene showcase just how great Prosecco DOCG can be. Usually on sweet side due to fully ripe grapes. Best: Adami, Andreola, BISOL, Bortolomiol, COL VETORAZ, Le Colture, NINO FRANCO, Ruggeri, Silvano Follador.

Cascina Cerruti Pie ★★★ Small estate in gd area for MOSCATO: best sweet Sol, naturally dried Moscato. Also v.gd Fol (dr).

Case Basse Tus ★★★★ Gianfranco Soldera's children keep up similar lofty level of iconic BRUNELLO. Long-oak-aged. Rare, precious.

Castel de Paolis Lat ★★→★★★★ One of quality-leading estates in Lat. Best: Frascati SUPERIORE, Donna Adriana (VIOGNIER/MALVASIA del Lazio).

Castel Juval, Unterortl T-AA ★★★ Distinctive, crystalline wines. Best: WEISSBURGUNDER (old-vine Himmelsleiter). Also v.gd: RIES (Windbichel), MÜLLER-T, PINOT N RISERVA.

Castell' in Villa Tus ★★★ CHIANTI CLASSICO estate in extreme sw of zone. Wines of class, trad, excellence; v. age-worthy. Top RISERVA.

Castello Romitorio Tus ★★★→★★★★ Filippo Chia produces some of BRUNELLO's sleekest, most perfumed. Top: single-vyd Filo di Seta (also RISERVA), classic Brunello. Also v.gd: Metafisica (w blend), Romitoro (r), ROSSO DI MONTALCINO.

Castiglion del Bosco Tus ★★★ One of best organic BRUNELLO producers. Top: Campo del Drago. Cecilia Leoneschi made possibly 1st single-vyd Rosso di Montalcino.

Caudrina Pie ★★★→★★★★ Romano Dogliotti, one of best for MOSCATO D'ASTI. Top: ASTI La Selvatica, La Galeisa. Also gd: La Caudrina, NIZZA Montevenere.

Cavallotto Pie ★★★★ Organic. Solid reference for trad BAROLO, in Castiglione Falletto. Outstanding RISERVA VIGNA San Giuseppe and RISERVA Vignolo, v.gd BARBERA D'ALBA SUPERIORE Vigna Cuculo, LANGHE NEBBIOLO, FREISA.

Cave Mont Blanc VdA ★★★ Quality co-op at foot of Mont Blanc, with ungrafted indigenous 60–100-yr-old Prié Bl vines. Organic. Outstanding sparkling. Top: Blanc de Morgex et de la Salle Rayon and cru La Piagne (oaked), sparkling (Blanc du Blanc, Cuvée des Guides, Cuvée du Prince, XT).

Cerasuolo d'Abruzzo Ab ★ DOC DYA ROSATO version of MONTEPULCIANO D'ABRUZZO. Can be brilliant. Best (by far): TIBERIO, VALENTINI. Also v.gd: Masciarelli – Villa Gemma, Terraviva, Torre dei Beati, Valle Reale. Plus gd: Barone Cornacchia, Cataldi Madonna, De Fermo, I Fauri, Illuminati, La Valentina, Praesidiumo.

Cerasuolo di Vittoria Si ★★ 14 16 17 18 19 20 (21) Blend of Frappato/NERO D'AVOLA. Only SI DOCG, in se, around city of Vittoria, best terroir for Frappato. Top: GULFI, PAOLO CALÌ. Also v.gd: COS, OCCHIPINTI ARIANNA, PLANETA, Valle dell'Acate.

Ceretto Pie ★★★★ Leading organic/bio producer of BARBARESCO (Asili, Bernadot, Gallina), BAROLO (Bricco Rocche, Brunate, Bussia, Cannubi San Lorenzo, Prapò and new Rocche di Castiglione), plus LANGHE Bianco Blange (ARNEIS). Wines now more classic, elegant.

Cesanese (Comune and di Affile) Lat ★→★★★ Two grapes: Comune (more common in Olevano Romano area, s of Lat), d'Affile (in Affile and Piglio). Three wines: C del Piglio, try Casale della Ioria (Torre del Piano); C di Affile, try Colline di Affile (Le Cese); Olevano Romano C, try DAMIANO CIOLLI. Outstanding Colacicchi (Cesanese Tufano IGT).

Chianti Tus ★→★★★ DOCG When gd, delightfully delicious, easy-going and food-friendly fresh red. Modern-day production zone covers most of TUS; v. big differences in topography, climate and soils among various Chianti denominations. RÙFINA is only terroir of quality comparable to historic Chianti production zone (now called CHIANTI CLASSICO).

Chianti Classico Tus ★★→★★★ DOCG 15 16' 18 19' 20' 21 No wine in Italy has improved more over past 20 yrs+, now often 100% SANGIOVESE. More than 500 producers means inconsistent quality, but best are among Italy's greatest. Made in historic (high, rocky) CHIANTI production zone between Florence and Siena in nine townships. Climate varies greatly from n to s sectors, three main soil types – Alberese (whitish marls), Galestro (clay schist) and macigno (mix of sands and compacted sands) – so potentially wines are v. different from each other. From 2019, new UGA (unità geografiche aggiuntive) only for Gran Selezione (new top level, above RISERVA). (For top producers, *see* box, opposite.)

Chiuse, Le Tus ★★★ Simonetta BIONDI-SANTI (great-granddaughter of Ferruccio) runs small but great family estate. Top: classic, BRUNELLO RISERVA, ROSSO DI MONTALCINO.

Ciabot Berton Pie ★★★ Marco Oberto and wife Federica; best-value producer of BAROLO in La Morra. Top: Barolo 1961, crus Roggeri, Rocchettevino have distinctive single-vyd characters, LANGHE NEBBIOLO, BARBERA D'ALBA.

Cinque Terre, CS Lig ★★→★★★ Quality co-op in beautiful area. Top: Cian Auti, Costa da Posa, Sciacchetrà (sw, one of Italy's best stickies).

Ciolli, Damiano Lat ★★★ One of most interesting wineries in central Italy. Best:

ITALY

> **Who makes really good Chianti Classico?**
>
> CHIANTI CLASSICO is a large zone with hundreds of producers, so picking the best is tricky. Top get a ★: ★ AMA, ★ BADIA A COLTIBUONO, BROLIO, Castellare di Castellina, CASTELL' IN VILLA, ★ CASTELLO DI MONSANTO, ★ CASTELLO DI VOLPAIA, ★ FELSINA, ★ FONTODI, ★ I Fabbri, ★ ISOLE E OLENA, ★ Le Cinciole, ★ Monteraponi, NITTARDI, Nozzole, Palazzino, Poggerino, Poggiopiano, ★ QUERCIABELLA, Rampolla, RIECINE, Rocca di Castagnoli, ★ Rocca di Montegrossi, Ruffino, San Fabiano Calcinaia, SAN FELICE, ★ SAN GIUSTO A RENTENNANO, Tenuta Perano – FRESCOBALDI, ★ Vecchie Terre di Montefili, ★ Villa Calcinaia, ★ Villa La Rosa, Viticcio.

Cirsium, 100% CESANESE d'Affile, 80-yr-old vines. Also v.gd: Botte 22, Silene, Trebbiano Verde (aka VERDICCHIO)/Ottonese.

Cirò Cal ★→★★★ DOC Brisk strong red from Cal's main grape, Gaglioppo, or light, fruity white from GRECO (DYA). Best: *Librandi*, IPPOLITO 1845. Also v.gd: 'A Vita, Caparra & Siciliani, Cataldo Calabretta.

Classico Term for wines from a restricted, usually historic and superior-quality area within limits of a commercially expanded DOC. *See* CHIANTI CLASSICO, SOAVE, VALPOLICELLA, VERDICCHIO DEI CASTELLI DI JESI, numerous others.

Clerico, Domenico Pie ★★★→★★★★ Influential BAROLO innovator, modernist producer of Monforte d'ALBA, esp crus Ginestra (Ciabot Mentin, Pajana), Mosconi (Percristina only in best vintages). BARBERA D'ALBA (Trevigne), Barolo Aeroplanservaj (from Baudana cru), LANGHE NEBBIOLO (Capisme-e) v.gd.

Clivi, I FVG ★★★ Wealth of old vines in FRIULI COLLI ORIENTALI and COLLIO), even up to 90 yrs of age. Some of FVG's purest, most age-worthy, mineral wines, ranking with Italy's best whites. Top: FRIULANO, MALVASIA cru, also outstanding dry Verduzzo.

Cocchi-Bava Pie ★★★ Since 1891 producer of vermouth. Top Cocchi: ALTA LANGA (Pas Dosé, Toto Corde, new Espressione Bianc and Noir), Vermouth Storico di Torino and Extra Dry. Top: BARBERA D'ASTI Stradivario, BAROLO Scarrone, NIZZA Piano Alto, Ruchè, Serre di San Pietro (NEBBIOLO).

Cogno, Elvio Pie ★★★★ Top estate; super-classy, austere, elegant BAROLOS from Ravera cru. Best: Bricco Pernice, Ravera, RISERVA VIGNA Elena (NEBBIOLO Rosé clone). Also v.gd: Anas-Cëtta (100% Nascetta), BARBERA D'ALBA Bricco Merli, Barolo Cascina Nuova.

Col d'Orcia Tus ★★★ Top MONTALCINO estate (3rd-largest), owned by Francesco Marone Cinzano. Best: BRUNELLO Nastagio, Brunello RISERVA POGGIO al Vento. Also v.gd: Brunello, Ghiaie Bianche (CHARD), Moscadello di Montalcino.

Colla, Poderi Pie ★★★★ Family-run, with experience of Beppe C. Classic, trad, age-worthy. Top: BARBARESCO Roncaglie, BAROLO Bussia, LANGHE Bricco del Drago, new RISERVA Beppe Colla and Bonmè (vermouth). Also v.gd: ALTA LANGA Pietro Colla, NEBBIOLO D'ALBA, PINOT NERO, RIES.

Colli = hills; singular: colle. **Colline** (singular collina) = smaller hills. *See also* COLLIO and POGGIO.

Colli di Lapio Cam ★★★ Clelia Romano's estate makes Italy's *best Fiano*. Outstanding FIANO Clelia, v.gd GRECO DI TUFO, TAURASI Andrea.

Colli di Luni Lig, Tus ★★→★★★ DOC nr Spezia. Albarola, VERMENTINO whites; SANGIOVESE-based reds easy-drinking charm. Top: Giacomelli, LUNAE, OTTAVIANO LAMBRUSCHI, TERENZUOLA. Also v.gd: Il Monticello, La Baia del Sole, La Pietra del Focolare, Zangani.

Collio FVG ★★→★★★★ DOC Famous white denomination, unfortunately moved steadily to nonsensical Collio Bianco blend rather than highlight terroir differences of its communes, incl coolish San Floriano and Dolegna, warmer

Capriva. Happily, Collio boasts glut of talented producers. Best: BORGO DEL TIGLIO, Doro Princic, Gravner, I CLIVI, LIVIO FELLUGA, *Schiopetto*. Also v.gd: Alessandro Pascolo, Attems, Ca' Ronesca, Castello di Spessa, Drius, Gradis'Ciutta, Isidoro Polencic, Primosic, Radikon, Ronc dai Luchis, RONCO dei Tassi, RUSSIZ SUPERIORE, Toros, Venica & Venica, VILLA RUSSIZ.

Colombera, La Pie ★★★ Elisa Semino is "queen" of the Timorasso grape. Top: DERTHONA (Il Montino, Santacroce), Monleale (100% BARBERA).

They say on Etna that it's not the last eruption that matters; it's the next one.

Colombo, Gianluca Pie ★★★ One of Italy's most promising young winemakers. Top: BAROLO, VERDUNO. Also v.gd: Langhe NEBBIOLO.

Colterenzio, CS / Schreckbichl T-AA ★★★ Cornaiano-based main player among ALTO ADIGE CO-ops. Top whites: Lafóa CHARD, SAUV BL; PINOT BIANCOS Berg, LR. Lafóa reds: CAB SAUV, PINOT N. New outstanding SAUV BL RISERVA Gran Lafóa 2021. Cru range v.gd.

Col Vetoraz ★★★ Top VALDOBBIADENE PROSECCO producer: CARTIZZE, Coste di Ponente (Extra Dry), Millesimato Dry Coste di Mezzodì.

Conegliano Valdobbiadene Ven ★→★★ DOCG DYA Name for top PROSECCO: may be used separately or together. Extremely steep hills; quality should be better.

Conterno, Aldo Pie ★★★★ Top estate of Monforte d'ALBA, 25 ha for only 80,000 bottles of highest quality. Granbussia, iconic expression of greatness of BAROLO and one of best. Top: BAROLOS Cicala, Colonello, esp Romirasco; Bussiador CHARD. Also v.gd: BARBERA D'ALBA, LANGHE NEBBIOLO, Quartetto (r blend).

Conterno, Giacomo Pie ★★★★ Monfortino, one of best wines of Italy. Outstanding BARBERAS, BAROLOS. Owns Nervi in GATTINARA.

Conterno Fantino Pie ★★★→★★★★ Organic. One of top producers of excellent modern-style BAROLO crus at Monforte, aims to valorize each single different vyd of MGAs: Castelletto (VIGNA Pressenda), Ginestra (Vigna Sorì Ginestra, Vigna del Gris), Mosconi (Vigna Ped). Ginestrino, iconic Monprà (NEBBIOLO/BARBERA); Bastia CHARD (one of PIE's best).

Contini Sar ★★★ Benchmark VERNACCIA DI ORISTANO, oxidative-styled whites (like dry Sherry). Antico Gregori one of Italy's best whites. Amazing Flor 22 and RISERVA; gd I Giganti (r).

Cornelissen, Frank Si ★★★★ One of ETNA's top producers, esp for red. Practically all crus outstanding. Don't miss Magma (from vyd at 910m/2986ft, planted in 1910), usually SI's most expensive wine, and Munjebel crus CS, SC, Cuvée VA (r/w) and Perpetuum (using perpetual solera).

Coroncino, Fattoria Mar ★★★ Organic, trad estate now run by Valerio Canestrari (Lucio's son), specialist in VERDICCHIO DEI CASTELLI DI JESI. Top: Cenobita, Gaiospino (also Fumè), Stracacio, Stragaio (also Fumè). Also v.gd: Coroncino, Il Bacco.

Correggia, Matteo Pie ★★★ Organic. Leading producer of ROERO (RISERVA Rochè d'Ampsej, Val dei Preti), Roero ARNEIS, plus BARBERA D'ALBA (Marun) and Roero Arneis Val dei Preti (aged 6 yrs). ALTA LANGA Severina, new Apapà (100% NEBBIOLO) v.gd.

Cretes, Les VdA ★★★ Costantino Charrère is father of modern VALLE D'AOSTA viticulture, saved many forgotten varieties. Outstanding *Petite Arvine*, incl Rebàn Pas Dosé; Cuvée Bois CHARD (one of Italy's best), Fumin, Neige d'Or (w blend), Torrette.

Cristo di Campobello, Baglio del Si ★★→★★★ Bonetta family estate just e of Agrigento. Top: GRILLO La Luci, NERO D'AVOLA Lu Patri. New METODO CLASSICO (100% Grillo). Solid wines.

Crotta di Vegneron, La VdA ★★→★★★ Quality co-op in Chambave. Top: La Griffe des Lions line (Fumin, Nus MALVOISIE). Also v.gd: Chambave MUSCAT Attente, Chambave Superieur, sparkling range Quatremillemètres Vins d'Altitude.

CS (cantina sociale) Cooperative winery.

Cuomo, Marisa Cam ★★★★ Fiorduva is *one of Italy's greatest whites*; Top: (r) RISERVAS (Furore, Ravello), (w) Furore, Ravello.

Cupertinum Pug ★★→★★★ Quality CS since 1935. Best: Copertino Rosso (RISERVAS, Settantacinque), NEGROAMARO (also SW).

Custodi delle Vigne dell'Etna, I Si ★★★→★★★★ Run by Mario Paoluzi. Member of consortium I VIGNERI. Outstanding ETNA (r) Aetneus, RISERVA Saeculare; (w) Contrada Caselle. Etna whites (Ante, Contrada Muganazzi) and rosé v.gd.

Dal Forno Romano Ven ★★★★ VALPOLICELLA, AMARONE, RECIOTO (latter not identified as such any more) v. high quality; vyds outside CLASSICO zone but wines great.

Derthona Pie ★→★★★ Wine from Timorasso grapes grown only in COLLI Tortonesi. One of Italy's most *interesting whites*, like v. dry RIES from Rheinhessen (*see* Germany). Best: Boveri Giacomo (Piazzera, Lacrime del Bricco), LA COLOMBERA (Il Montino), Mariotto (Pitasso), Ricci, ROAGNA (Montemarzino), VIGNETI MASSA, VIETTI.

Di Barrò VdA ★★★ Small family estate, top quality from typical VDA grapes. Best: (r) Mayolet, Torrette Sup (Ostro), (w) Petite ARVINE.

DOC / DOCG Quality wine designation: *see* box, p.159.

Dogliani Pie ★→★★★ DOCG Varietal DOLCETTO. Some to drink young, some for moderate ageing. Best: Chionetti, PODERI LUIGI EINAUDI. Also v.gd: ANNA MARIA ABBONA, Francesco Boschis, FRANCESCO VERSIO, Marziano Abbona, Osvaldo Barberis, Pecchenino, San Fereolo, TREDIBERRI.

Donnafugata Si ★★→★★★ Classy range: (r) ETNA Rosso (Contrada Fragore, Marchesa, Sul Vulcano), Mille e Una Notte, Tancredi; (w) Chiaranda, Lighea. MOSCATO PASSITO di PANTELLERIA Ben Ryé v. fine.

Due Terre, Le FVG ★★★ Small family-run FRIULI COLLI ORIENTALI estate. Top: Sacrisassi Rosso (SCHIOPPETTINO/REFOSCO). MERLOT, Sacrisassi Bianco (w) v.gd.

Einaudi, Luigi Pie ★★★ Founded late C19 by ex-president of Italy, 52-ha estate in DOGLIANI. Solid BAROLOS from Bussia, Cannubi, Monvigliero, Terlo, new Villero. Barolo Ludo, Dogliani from VIGNA Tecc v.gd.

Enoteca Wine library; also shop or restaurant with ambitious wine list. There is a national enoteca at the *fortezza* in Siena.

Etna Si ★★→★★★★ DOC (r) 14' **15** 16' 17 19' 20 21 (22) Remarkable development; 900 ha on n slopes, high-altitude, volcanic soils. Etna Rosso typically NERELLOS MASCALESE/Cappuccio (90/10%), Bianco can be pure CARRICANTE or incl CATARATTOS Comune or Lucido and other varieties. (*See also* box, below.)

Summit of Etna

Some of Italy's most exciting wines come from this famous volcano. Vines grow up to 1000m (3281ft) on SI's e coast. *Contrada* is Si's way to express cru: differences in soil, altitude and age of lava flows. Of Etna's 133 *contrade*, the greatest number are in Castiglione di Sicilia (46), Randazzo (25) and Linguaglossa (10). Following producers make gd to great wine (top get a ★): Alberelli di Giodo, ★ BENANTI, Calabretta, ★ CALCAGNO, Cottanera, Cusumano Alta Mora, DONNAFUGATA, ★ FRANK CORNELISSEN, ★ GIROLAMO RUSSO, Graci (Arcuria, Feudo di Mezzo), ★ GULFI, ★ I CUSTODI DELL'ETNA, ★ I VIGNERI, PALMENTO COSTANZO, ★ PIETRADOLCE, Statella (Pignatùni Vecchie Vigne), TASCA D'ALMERITA, TENUTE BOSCO (VIGNA Vico), ★ TENUTA DELLE TERRE NERE, ★ TENUTA DI FESSINA, Tornatore (Pietrarizzo, Trimarchisa), ★ VINI FRANCHETTI.

Favati, I Cam ★★★ Rosanna Petrozziello runs high-quality family winery. Top: Etichetta Bianca (white label) range (FIANO, GRECO, TAURASI).

Fay Lom ★★★ Run by Fay family in VALTELLINA since 1971. Alpine wines. Top: SFORZATO (RONCO del Picchio), Valgella (Carterìa RISERVA, Il Glicine).

Felline Pug ★★★→★★★★ Gregory Perucci was pioneer in rediscovery of PRIMITIVO and Susumaniello vines. Top: PRIMITIVO DI MANDURIA (Cuvée Anniversario, Dunico, Giravolta, ZIN). Also v.gd: Verdeca (w), Edmond Dantès 24 Mesi (sp VERMENTINO), Pietraluna (NEGROAMARO), Sum (Susumaniello).

With sesame tuna cutlet, drink Etna Bianco.

Felluga, Livio FVG ★★★→★★★★ Consistently fine, age-worthy FRIULI COLLI ORIENTALI, esp blends Abbazia di Rosazzo, Terre Alte. Also Bianco Illivio, FRIULANO (Sigar), *Pinot Gr* (Curubella), SAUV BL Potentilla; MERLOT/REFOSCO blend Sossó; PICOLIT (Italy's best?).

Felsina Tus ★★★ CHIANTI CLASSICO estate of distinction in se of zone. Best (100% SANGIOVESE): Gran Selezione Colonia, classic RISERVA Rancia and IGT Fontalloro.

Fenocchio, Giacomo Pie ★★★→★★★★ Small but outstanding Monforte d'ALBA-based BAROLO cellar; trad style. Crus: Bussia (also RISERVA 90 Dì), Cannubi, Catsellero, Villero. Outstanding FREISA, one of Italy's 2–3 best.

Ferrando Pie ★★★→★★★★ Historic, iconic producer of outstanding Caluso Cariola (one of best), CAREMA Black Label. Also v.gd C White Label.

Ferrara, Benito Cam ★★★ One of Italy's best GRECO DI TUFO producers (Terra d'Uva, VIGNA Cicogna). Talent shows in excellent TAURASI (Vigna Quattro Confini).

Ferrari – Tenute Lunelli T-AA ★★★★ TRENTO maker of one of two best Italian METODO CLASSICOS. Outstanding Giulio Ferrari (RISERVA del Fondatore, Rosé, new Selezione 04), Riserva Bruno Lunelli 06 (2nd vintage since 1995). Also v.gd: CHARD-based Brut Riserva Lunelli, Perlè Bianco (gd value), Perlè Zero, PINOT N-based Perlè Nero. TENUTE Lunelli: Castelbuono, Umb (MONTEFALCO: Carapace Lunga Attesa, Lampante Riserva); Margon, T-AA (Chard, Pinot N), Podernovo, Tus.

Fessina, Tenuta di Si ★★★→★★★★ Jacopo Maniaci continues Silvia Maestrelli's path, in one of youngest and best ETNA estates. Elegant wines. Best: EB A' Puddara (w), Il Musmeci (r/w), new red Il Musmeci RISERVA Speciale (dedicated to Roberto and Silvia). Also v.gd: Erse Moscamento 1911 (r).

Feudi di San Gregorio Cam ★★★ Much-hyped CAM producer, with DOCGS FIANO DI AVELLINO (Pietracalda, RISERVA *Campanaro*), GRECO DI TUFO Cutizzi, TAURASI Riserva Piano di Montevergine. Ranges: *FeudiStudi* (most expressive vyds, selected every yr among 700 sites), Storie Feudi.

Feudo di San Maurizio VdA ★★★★ Outstanding wines from rare native grapes CORNALIN, Mayolet, Vuillermin; last two among Italy's greatest reds. Try (r) Torrette (and SUPERIORE), Ch de Sarre (NEBBIOLO); (w) GEWURZ, PETITE ARVINE.

Feudo Montoni Si ★★★★ Exceptional estate in upland E SI. Best: NERO D'AVOLA Lagnusa, Vrucara. Try (w) CATARRATTO del Masso, GRILLO della Timpa; (r) Perricone del Core; (sw) PASSITO Bianco. Authentic wines.

Fiano di Avellino Cam ★★→★★★★ DOCG 16 18 19' 20 21 Can be either steely (most typical) or lush. Best: CANTINA del Barone, Ciro Picariello, COLLI DI LAPIO, Di Prisco, FEUDI SAN GREGORIO, I FAVATI, MASTROBERARDINO, Marsella, Pietracupa, Rocca del Principe, QUINTODECIMO, TENUTA Sarno, TRAERTE (Vadiaperti).

Fino, Gianfranco Pug ★★★★ Greatest PRIMITIVO, old, low-yielding bush vines: outstanding Es among Italy's top 20 reds, Es Selezione Red Label. Jo (NEGROAMARO), Se (Primitivo) v.gd.

Florio Si ★★→★★★★ Historic quality maker of MARSALA. Specialist in Marsala Vergine Secco. Best: RISERVA Donna Franca, Targa. Also v.gd: Baglio Florio.

Fongaro Ven ★★★★ METODO CLASSICO Lessini Durello (100% Durella). High quality, even higher acidity, age-worthy. Top: RISERVAS (Brut, Pas Dosé), new Degorgement Tardif. Also v.gd: Pas Dosé.

Fonterutoli Tus ★★★ Historic CHIANTI CLASSICO estate of Mazzei family at Castellina. Characterful wines, Chianti Classico Gran Selezione: Badiola, Castello Fonterutoli, Vicoregio 36, outstanding Ipsus (Caggio vyd). IGT Siepi (SANGIOVESE/MERLOT). Also owns Tenuta di Belguardo (Maremma), Zisola (SI).

Fontodi Tus ★★★★ One of v. best CHIANTI CLASSICOS: Filetta di Lamole, Flaccianello (100% SANGIOVESE); Gran Selezione San Leolino, VIGNA del Sorbo. New white. IGT SYRAH Case Via among best TUS Syrah.

Foradori T-AA ★★★ Much-loved Elisabetta F is "lady of Trentino wine"; outstanding **Teroldego**, lovely macerated, amphora-aged Incrocio Manzoni and Nosiola. TEROLDEGOS Morei, Sgarzon (also amphora-aged Cilindrica), white Nosiola Fontanasanta. Top remains TEROLDEGO-based Granato.

Franchetti, Vini Si ★★★→★★★★ Contributor to fame of ETNA (was Passopisciaro), run by Franchetti (*see* TENUTA DI TRINORO). Outstanding Rosso Franchetti (PETIT VERDOT/Cesanese d'Affile), NERELLO MASCALESE single *contrada*. Best: Contradas C, G, S (R also v.gd). New Contrada PC (CHARD).

Franciacorta Lom ★★→★★★★ DOCG Italy's zone for top-quality METODO CLASSICO fizz. Soils extremely complex (50+ types). Two large sectors: e generally most elegant, freshest; w generally broadest, richest. Top: BARONE PIZZINI, CA' DEL BOSCO, Cavalleri, MOSNEL, TERRA MORETTI (Bellavista, Contadi Castaldi), UBERTI, VILLA, VILLA CRESPIA. Also v.gd: Ca' del Vent, Cola-Battista (Extra Brut, Millesimato Dosaggio Zero), Majolini, Monte Rossa, Ricci Curbastro.

Franco, Nino Ven ★★★→★★★★ Owner Primo F makes large volumes of top PROSECCO that age surprisingly well. Among finest: Grave di Stecca Brut, Primo Franco Dry, Riva di San Floriano Brut, Rustico. Excellent CARTIZZE.

Frascole Tus ★★→★★★★ Most n winery of most N CHIANTI RÙFINA zone, small estate run organically by Enrico Lippi. Top: Chianti Rùfina, VIN SANTO

Frescobaldi Tus ★★★→★★★★ Ancient noble family, leading CHIANTI RÙFINA pioneer at NIPOZZANO estate (look for ★★★ **Montesodi**), also BRUNELLO from Castelgiocondo estate, MONTALCINO. Sole owner of LUCE estate (Montalcino), ORNELLAIA (BOLGHERI), TENUTA Perano (top: CHIANTI CLASSICO Gran Selezione Rialzi). Also vyds in COLLIO (Attems), Maremma (Ammiraglia), Montespertoli (Castiglioni), Gorgona Island (state prison).

Friuli Colli Orientali FVG ★★→★★★★ DOC 15 16 20 21 (was COLLI Orientali del Friuli) Hilly area of FVG next to COLLIO. Unlike latter, not just whites, but outstanding reds, v.gd stickies from likes of red Pignolo, REFOSCO dal Peduncolo Rosso, SCHIOPPETTINO, Tazzelenghe and white MALVASIA Istriana, RIBOLLA GIALLA, PICOLIT, Verduzzo, FRIULANO. Top: Grillo Iole, I CLIVI, LA VIARTE, LIVIO FELLUGA, MEROI, MIANI, RONCHI DI CIALLA, VIGNA PETRUSSA. Also v.gd: Abbazia di Rosazzo, Aquila del Torre, D'ATTIMIS, Ermacora, Gianpaolo Colutta, Gigante, Jacuss, La Sclusa, LE DUE TERRE, Polencic, Specogna, Volpe Pasini (Zuc di Volpe range). Ramandolo DOCG, best sweet Verduzzo (Anna Berra, Giovanni Dri). Picolit can be Italy's best sweet: Aquila del Torre, Livio Felluga, Marco Sara, RONCHI DI CIALLA, Vigna Petrussa.

Visiting Como? Buy a can of fresh Como air. €9.90. One born every minute.

Friuli Isonzo FVG ★★★ DOC (previously just Isonzo). One of world's best flatland wine denominations. High-alc, powerful, rich, unfailingly complex whites, from gravel-rich, clay-loam soils and hot mesoclimate. Best: LIS NERIS, RONCO DEL GELSO, VIE DI ROMANS. Also gd: Brandolini, Drius, Pierpaolo Pecorari.

Friuli Venezia Giulia FVG A ne region hugging Slovenian border, home to Italy's best whites (along with ALTO ADIGE). Hills to ne give best, but alluvial seaside regions (DOC from Annia, Aquilea, Latisana) improving markedly. DOCs Carso, COLLIO, F COLLI ORIENTALI, F ISONZO best.

Frizzante Semi-sparkling, up to 2.5 atmospheres, eg. MOSCATO D'ASTI, much PROSECCO, LAMBRUSCO and the like.

Fucci, Elena Bas ★★★★ AGLIANICO DEL VULTURE Titolo from 55–70-yr-old vines in Mt Vulture's Grand Cru; one of Italy's 20 best; also RISERVA, SUPERIORE. Organic. Also v.gd: By Amphora, Pink Edition.

In Piedmont, hazelnuts suffer more from drought than vines do.

Fuligni Tus ★★★★ Outstanding, trad: BRUNELLO (top RISERVA), ROSSO DI MONTALCINO.

Gagliardo, Gianni ★★★ High-quality BAROLOS from six different crus. Best: Castelletto, Lazzarito VIGNA Preve, Castelletto, Monvigliero, Mosconi. Iconic v.gd Fallegro (Favorita).

Gaja Pie ★★★★ Old family firm at BARBARESCO led by eloquent Angelo G; daughter Gaia G following. One of Italy's top wineries. Best: Barbaresco (Costa Russi, Sorì San Lorenzo, Sorì Tildìn, classic Barbaresco), BAROLO (Conteisa, Sperss). Splendid CHARD (Gaia e Rey). Also owns Ca' Marcanda in BOLGHERI (Camarcanda, Magari, Promis), Pieve di Santa Restituta in MONTALCINO, TENUTA Garetto in Monferrato.

Gancia Pie Famous old brand of ASTI. Best ALTA LANGA ★★★ Cuvée (120, 60).

Garbarino, Roberto Pie ★★★ One of most talented young producers of ALTA LANGA DOCG. Top: Le Rapide (PINOT N/CHARD). Also v.gd: Il Viaggio (Chard), La Sorgente (Pinot N).

Gattinara Pie 13 15 16' 17 18 19' 21 Best known of a cluster of ALTO PIE DOC(G)s based on NEBBIOLO. Steep hills; wines suitable for long ageing. Best: Antoniolo, CANTINA del Signore, Iarretti Paride, Nervi, Torraccia del Piantavigna, TRAVAGLINI. *See also* Alto Piemonte.

Gavi / Cortese di Gavi Pie ★→★★★ DOCG At best, subtle dry white of CORTESE grapes. Best: ***Bruno Broglia***/La Meirana, Castellari Bergaglio (Rovereto, Rolona), Castello di Tassarolo, Chiarlo, La Giustiniana, Enrico Serafino (Maneo, Poggio della Rupe), LA SCOLCA, Nicola Bergaglio (Minaia), Villa Sparina.

Germano, Ettore Pie ★★★→★★★★ Family Serralunga estate run by Sergio G and wife Elena. Top BAROLOS: Cerretta, RISERVA Lazzarito, outstanding VIGNA Rionda. Also v.gd: ALTA LANGA (also Riservas Blanc de Noirs, Blanc de Blancs, both 65 mths), BARBERA D'ALBA SUPERIORE della Madre, Barolo Prapò, Del Comune di Serralunga, LANGHE RIES Hérzu.

Ghemme Pie ★★→★★★ DOCG NEBBIOLO (at least 85%), incl up to 15% Uva Rara and/or Vespolina. Mainly morainic agglomerate soils of friable pebbles and rich in minerals, poor and not v. fertile (actually, youngest among those of ALTO PIEMONTE). Top: ***Antichi Vigneti di Cantalupo*** (Collis Braclemae, Collis Carellae), Ioppa (Balsina), Rovellotti (RISERVA). Also v.gd: Torraccia del Piantavigna (VIGNA Pelizzane).

Ghizzano, Tenuta di Tus ★★★ Historic bio estate on Pisa's hills; non-interventionist. Best: (r) Nambrot (Bx blend), Il Ghizzano. New Mimesi Project (r/w).

Giacosa, Bruno Pie ★★★★ Now run by daughter Bruna; wines still top. Splendid iconic trad-style BARBARESCOS (Asili, Rabajà), BAROLOS (Falletto, Falletto VIGNA Rocche). Top wines (ie. RISERVAS) get famous red label. Amazing METODO CLASSICO Brut (one of best in PIE), ROERO ARNEIS (w), Valmaggiore (r).

Ginestre, Le Pie ★★★ Barbara Audasso runs historical family estate; gd value. Top: BAROLO Sottocastello di Novello (also RISERVA), LANGHE NEBBIOLO.

Gini Ven ★★★ Gini family since 1500s; bio. Best: SOAVE CLASSICO Contrada Salvarenza Vecchie Vigne, La Froscà. Also v.gd: AMARONE RISERVA Scajari, RECIOTO DI SOAVE.

Girlan, Cantina T-AA ★★→★★★ Quality co-op. Top: Solisti (PINOT NS Trattmann, VIGNA Ganger; CHARD Curlan, VERNATSCH), Flora (esp PINOT BL) ranges.

Giuseppe Cortese Pie ★★★ A trad producer of outstanding BARBARESCO Rabajà (also RISERVA). Also gd Barbaresco, LANGHE NEBBIOLO, Scapulin (CHARD).

Grappa Pungent spirit made from grape pomace (skins, etc., after pressing), can be anything from disgusting to inspirational. What the French call "marc".

Grattamacco Tus ★★★ Owned by Colle Massari Group; historic estate (BOLGHERI's 2nd). Long line of outstanding wines (salinity, power): Bolgheri Grattamacco (r, c.15% Sangiovese; w, Vermentino), L'Alberello, Montecucco ROSSO RISERVA.

Greco di Tufo Cam ★★→★★★ DOCG Better versions among Italy's best whites (tannic, oily) made with local Greco (different from Cal's also outstanding Greco Bianco). Best: Bambinuto, BENITO FERRARA, Di Prisco, Pietracupa, QUINTODECIMO, TRAERTE (Vadiaperti). Also v.gd: CANTINA dei Monaci, Colle di San Domenico, COLLI DI LAPIO, FEUDI DI SAN GREGORIO, I FAVATI, MASTROBERARDINO, SALVATORE MOLETTIERI, Terredora.

Grifalco Bas ★★★→★★★★ Small estate in high-quality Ginestra and Maschito subzone; purity, trad. Best: AGLIANICO DEL VULTURE SUPERIORE Daginestra, Damaschito. Also v.gd: Gricos, Grifalco.

Grignolino Pie DYA Two DOCS: Grignolino d'ASTI, Grignolino del Monferrato Casalese. At best, light, perfumed, crisp, high in acidity, tannin. D'Asti: BERSANO, BRAIDA, Cascina Tavijin, Crivelli, Incisa della Rocchetta, Spertino, TENUTA Garetto, Tenuta Santa Caterina (also Monferace). M Casalese: Accornero (Bricco del Bosco, Vigne Vecchie), Bricco Mondalino, Castello di Uviglie, PIO CESARE.

Grosjean VdA ★★★ Top quality, native grapes; best CORNALIN, Premetta. Vigne Rovettaz one of VDA's oldest, largest.

Guerrieri Rizzardi Ven ★★→★★★ Noble family making top AMARONE (Calcarole, Villa Rizzardi), Bardolino; v.gd SOAVE CLASSICO Costeggiola.

Gulfi Si ★★★★ Best producer of NERO D'AVOLA in SI; 1st to bottle single-*contrada* (cru) wines. Organic. Outstanding: Nerobufaleffj, Nerosanlorè; iconic Nerojbleo; new RISERVAS. Also v.gd (r) CERASUOLO DI VITTORIA CLASSICO, Nerobaronj, NeroMàccarj; (w) Carjcanti. Interesting Pinò (PINOT N), ETNA red Reseca.

IGT (indicazione geografica tipica) Increasingly known as IGP (indicazione geografica protetta). (*See* box, p.159.)

Inama Ven ★★★ Important producer in COLLI Berici, Soave. Some of denomination's best: Soave CLASSICO (Carbonare, Du Lot, Foscarino, new I Palchi Grande Cuvée), CARMENÈRE RISERVA Oratorio di San Lorenzo, Bradisismo (r blend).

Ippolito 1845 Cal ★★→★★★ Since 1845 in heart of CIRÒ. Best: Cirò Bianco Mare Chiaro (GRECO Bianco); Cirò Rosato Mabilia, red Cirò (Liber Pater, RISERVA COLLI del Mancuso).

Ischia Cam ★★→★★★ DOC DYA Island off Naples, green volcanic tuff soils, own grape varieties (w: Biancolella, Forastera; r: Piedirosso, also found in CAM). Best for Biancolella: Frassitelli, VIGNA del Lume vyds. Top: CANTINE MAZZELLA, Cenatiempo (Kalimera), D'AMBRA. Also v.gd: Crateca, Giardini Arimei (Arcipelago Muratori), Tommasone, Perrazzo.

Ischia has vineyards so steep that grapes must be taken to winery by boat.

Isole e Olena Tus ★★★★ Top CHIANTI CLASSICO estate, owned by EPI group. Superb red IGT Cepparello. Outstanding Chianti Classico, CHARD, VIN SANTO. Also v.gd: CAB SAUV, SYRAH.

Kaltern, Cantina T-AA ★★★ Quality co-op close to Caldaro lake. Best: Quintessenz range (PINOT BL, Kalterersee). Also v.gd: Selezioni range. Look for limited-edition Kunst Stück (celebrating the grape that best interprets the vintage), new Brut Nature (sp).

Köfererhof T-AA ★★★→★★★★ Great whites: KERNER, SYLVANER; PINOT GR (new "K"); excellent MÜLLER-T ("R").

Lageder, Alois T-AA ★★★ Famous ALTO ADIGE producer. Exciting single vyds: CAB SAUV Cor Römigberg; CHARDS Gaun, Löwengang; GEWURZ Am Sand; PINOT N Krafuss; MCM (MERLOT Vecchie Viti).

Lagrein Alto Adige T-AA ★★→★★★ DOC 16′ 18′ 20 21′ Alpine red with deep colour, rich palate (plus a bitter hit at back); refreshing pink *Kretzer rosé* (LAGREIN). Top: ALTO ADIGE: CANTINA Bolzano (Taber), CS TERLANO, CS COLTERENZIO (Lafóa), IGNAZ NIEDRIST, LAGEDER, MURI GRIES, TIEFENBRUNNER.

Lessona was the wine that toasted the first government of united Italy, 1870.

Lambruschi, Ottaviano Lig ★★★ One of best COLLI DI LUNI VERMENTINO producers: Costa Marina, SUPERIORE. Also v.gd: Il Casale

Lambrusco E-R ★→★★★ DYA The 17 different Lambrusco grapes (five mostly planted) make for highly distinct wines. When gd, delightful fizzy fresh, lively red that pairs divinely with rich, fatty fare. DOCS: Best **Grasparossa** Cleto Chiarli (Enrico Cialdini), Moretto (Monovitigno and VIGNA Canova), Pederzana (Canto Libero Semi Secco), *Vittorio Graziano* (Fontana dei Boschi); **Maestri** Ceci, Dall'Asta, **Marani** Medici Ermete; **Salamino** Cavicchioli, Luciano Saetti, Medici Ermete; **Sorbara** Cavicchioli (Cristo Secco, Cristo Rose), Cleto Chiarli (Antica Modena Premium), Medici Ermete, PALTRINIERI.

Langhe Pie The hills of central PIE, home of BAROLO, BARBARESCO, etc. DOC name for several Pie varietals plus Bianco and Rosso blends. Those wishing to blend other grapes with NEBBIOLO can at up to 15% as LANGHE NEBBIOLO – a label to follow.

Langhe Nebbiolo Pie ★★→★★★ Like NEBBIOLO D'ALBA (Nebbiolo 85%+) but from a wider area: LANGHE hills. Unlike N d'Alba, may be used as a downgrade from BAROLO or BARBARESCO. Try ALDO CONTERNO, AZELIA, Bergadano, BOROLI, BREZZA, BURLOTTO, Cascina Roccalini, CIABOT BERTON, CLERICO, ETTORE GERMANO, FRANCESCO RINALDI, GIACOMO FENOCCHIO, GIOVANNI ROSSO (Ester Canale), GIUSEPPE RINALDI, MASSOLINO, PALLADINO, PIO CESARE, SCARZELLO, TREDIBERRI, VAJRA, VERSIO.

Lessona Pie DOCG *See also* ALTO PIEMONTE. NEBBIOLO (at least 85%). Mostly clay-free marine sandy soils, rich in minerals. Elegant, age-worthy, fine bouquet, long savoury taste. Best: PROPRIETÀ SPERINO. Also v.gd: Colombera & Garella, La Prevostura, Massimo Clerico, Noah, TENUTE Sella.

Librandi Cal ★★★ Top producer pioneering research into Cal varieties. Best: CIRÒ (*Riserva Duca San Felice* ★★★), IGT Asylia (GRECO Bianco), Efeso (w Mantonico), Gravello (CAB SAUV/Gaglioppo), Megonio (r Magliocco).

Liguria ★→★★★ Narrow ribbon of extreme mtn viticulture produces memorable (w) PIGATO, VERMENTINO, (r) ROSSESE DI DOLCEACQUA. Riviera di Levante (in e): CS CINQUE TERRE, De Battè, Giacomelli, La Baia del Sole, LUNAE, OTTAVIANO LAMBRUSCHI, TERENZUOLA. Riviera di Ponente (in w): BIO VIO, BRUNA, Ka' Manciné, Maccario, MASSIMO ALESSANDRI, Rocche del Gatto, TENUTA di Selvadolce (Pigato), Terre Bianche, Terre Rosse. For Ormeasco di Pornassio (r Ligurian DOLCETTO biotype): Cascina Nirasca, Fontanacota, Maffone. *See also* ROSSESE DI D.

Lis Neris FVG ★★★ Top ISONZO estate for whites. Best: Confini (w blend), FRIULANO (Fiore di Campo), PINOT GR (Gris), SAUV BL (Picol).

Lo Triolet VdA ★★★ Top PINOT GR. Also GEWURZ, MUSCAT, Fumin, Torrette.

Luce Tus ★★★ FRESCOBALDI's estate. Lovely BRUNELLO DI MONTALCINO; SANGIOVESE/ MERLOT for oligarchs.

Lugana ★★→★★★ DOC DYA Much-improved white of S Lake Garda, rivals gd SOAVE next door. Main grape, Turbiana (was TREBBIANO di Lugana). Best: Ca' dei Frati (esp *Brolettino*), Cavalchina, Corte Sermana (Due Rive, RISERVA), Le Morette, MONTE DEL FRÀ, Ottella, Roveglia, TOMMASI.

Lunae, Cantine Lig ★★★ Owned by Bosoni family, in COLLI DI LUNI. Terroir-expressive wines: VERMENTINO (Cavagino, Etichetta Nera, Numero Chiuso). Rare Vermentino Nero v.gd.

Lungarotti Umb ★★→★★★ Leading producer of TORGIANO. Stars: DOC Rubesco, DOCG RISERVA *Monticchio*. Also Giubilante, MONTEFALCO SAGRANTINO, Sangiorgio (SANGIOVESE/CAB SAUV), VIGNA Il Pino (VERMENTINO/GRECHETTO/TREBBIANO).

Macchiole, Le Tus ★★★★ Organic. One of few native-owned wineries of BOLGHERI; one of 1st to emerge after SASSICAIA, makes *Italy's best Cab Fr* (Paleo Rosso), one of best MERLOT (Messorio), SYRAH (Scrio).

Maculan Ven ★★★ Quality pioneer of Ven. Excellent CAB SAUV (Fratta, Palazzotto). Best known for sweet Torcolato (esp RISERVA Acininobili).

Malvasia delle Lipari Si ★★★ DOC Luscious sweet, from one of many MALVASIA varieties. Best: Caravaglio, Fenech, Marchetta, TASCA D'ALMERITA – TENUTA Capofaro (Dydime, VIGNA di Paola), Tenuta di Castellaro. Also gd: Hauner.

Malvirà Pie ★★★→★★★★ Top ROERO producer. Organic. Best single vyd: (r/w) Renesio, Trinità; (w) Saglietto. New ARNEIS RISERVA Saglietto.

Manduria (Primitivo di) Pug ★★→★★★ DOC Cradle of PRIMITIVO, alias ZIN; gutsy, alc, can be Porty. Best: FELLINE, GIANFRANCO FINO, MORELLA. Also v.gd: Attanasio, Commenda Magistrale (Supremo), Conti Zecca, Feudi di San Marzano, Leone de Castris, Pirro Varone, Zicari. For Gioia del Colle: PIETRAVENTOSA, Polvanera, Tenute Chiaromonte.

Marchesi di Grésy Pie ★★★ Historic BARBARESCO (1797), Martinenga cru (monopole). Best: Gajun, Martinenga, RISERVA Camp Gros. Also v.gd: BARBERA D'ASTI Monte Colombo.

Marenco, Luca Pie ★★★ Young talent between Barolo and Novello. Terroir-driven wines. Top: BAROLO La Volta, Nascetta del Comune di Novello (w). Also v.gd: DOLCETTO, NEBBIOLO.

Marengo Pie ★★★ Marco is one of most talented Barolo producers. Top: Bricco delle Viole, Brunate, Classico, NEBBIOLO D'ALBA Valmaggiore.

Marrone, Agricola Pie ★★★ Small estate producing gd-value BAROLOS. Top: Bussia, Pichemej, new Castellero. Also gd: ARNEIS, BARBERA D'ALBA SUPERIORE, Favorita, San Carlo (r).

Marsala Si ★→★★★★ DOC Once-famous fortified of SI. Can be dry to v. sweet; best is bone-dry Marsala Vergine. *See also* MARCO DE BARTOLI.

Mascarello Pie ★★★★ Two iconic producers of BAROLO: Bartolo M, of Barolo (daughter Maria Teresa continues father's highly trad path), outstanding FREISA, BARBERA D'ALBA, LANGHE NEBBIOLO; Giuseppe M, of Monchiero (son Mauro now makes), v. fine, trad-style Barolo from great *Monprivato* vyd in Castiglione Falletto.

Masi Ven ★★→★★★ Archetypal yet innovative producer of Verona, led by inspirational Sandro Boscaini; v.gd Rosso Veronese *Campo Fiorin* and Osar (Oseleta). Top AMARONES: Campolongo di Torbe, Costasera. Also Masi Wine Estates: Canevel (CARTIZZE, Valdobbiadene Campofalco), Conti Bossi Fedrigotti (Fojaneghe Bx blend, Trento Conte Federico) and Serego Alighieri (Amarone Vaio Armaron).

Clay soil is c.2°C (3.6°F) cooler than sand or rock at the same altitude.

Maso Martis T-AA ★★★ Stelzer family-owned. Organic TRENTO reference. Top: Madame Martis Dosaggio Zero Limited Edition, Monsieur Martis Rosé (PINOT M), Dosaggio Zero RISERVA. Also v.gd: AL-MA 800 MÜLLER-T.

Massa, Vigneti Pie ★★★ Walter M brought Timorasso (w) grape back from nr extinction. Top: Coste del Vento, Montecitorio, Sterpi. Also v.gd: Anarchia Costituzionale (MOSCATO Bianco), BARBERAS Bigolla, Monleale.

Massolino Vigna Rionda Pie ★★★ One of finest BAROLO estates, in Serralunga. Top:

long-ageing VIGNA Rionda RISERVA (Black Label). Excellent Margheria, Parafada, Parussi, new BARBARESCO Albesani. Also v.gd: LANGHE NEBBIOLO.

Mastroberardino Cam ★★★ Historic top-quality producer of mtn Avellino province. Top: More Maiorum (GRECO/FIANO), Stilema range, *Taurasi* (Radici RISERVA).

Mastrojanni Tus ★★★ Classic BRUNELLOS from Castelnuovo dell'Abate. Top: VIGNA Schiena d'Asino, Vigna Loreto. Also v.gd: ROSSO DI MONTALCINO.

Mattoni, Lorenzo Umb ★★★ Young talent in Umb. Best: MONTEFALCO, Trebbiano Spoletino (w, unrelated to TREBBIANO Toscana).

Mazzella, Cantine Cam ★★★ Siblings Nicola and Vera M's high-quality winery on ISCHIA. Top: single-vyd Biancolella VIGNA del Lume. Also v.gd: Ischia Biancolella, Forastera, Villa Campagnano (w blend).

Meroi FVG ★★★ Dynamic estate. Top: CHARD Dominin, FRIULANO, MALVASIA Zittelle Durì, RIBOLLA GIALLA, SAUV BL Zittelle Barchetta; REFOSCO Dominin.

Metodo classico (MC) or tradizionale Italian for "Champagne method".

Miani FVG ★★★★ Enzo Pontoni is Italy's best white-wine maker. Top: FRIULANO (Buri, Filip), RIBOLLA GIALLA Pettarin, SAUV BL Zitelle. Also v.gd: CHARD Zitelle, Sauv Bl Saurint, MERLOT, REFOSCO Buri.

Mirizzi and Montecappone Mar ★★★ Two estates owned by Gianluca Mirizzi, with focus on VERDICCHIO DEI CASTELLI DI JESI. Mirizzi on marly sandstone, deep slopes; organic, trad winemaking: Ergo, Ergo Sum RISERVA, Millesimè Pas Dosè. Montecappone on calcareous clay; reductive winemaking: Federico II, Riserva Utopia.

Molettieri, Salvatore Cam ★★★ Outstanding RISERVA VIGNA Cinque Querce, TAURASI; gd FIANO DI AVELLINO Apianum, GRECO DI TUFO.

Molino, Mauro Pie ★★★ High-quality BAROLO producer in La Morra. Top: Conca. Excellent: Bricco Luciani, Gallinotto, La Serra.

Monacesca, Fattoria La Mar ★★★ Family-run, Aldo Cifola in charge; top VERDICCHIO DI MATELICA. Best: RISERVA Mirum, Terra di Mezzo (longer ageing). Outstanding: Mirum 30 Year (multi-vintage blend). Also v.gd: Criptico (VERDICCHIO/CHARD), Ecclesia Brut (sp Verdicchio).

Monsanto, Castello di Tus ★★★ Historic, top-quality CHIANTI CLASSICO. Top: Il Poggio Gran Selezione (1st single-vyd Chianti Classico), iconic RISERVA, IGT Fabrizio Bianchi (r SANGIOVETO Grosso, w CHARD).

Montalcino Tus Hilltop town, Siena province; fashionable, famous for concentrated, expensive BRUNELLO and more approachable, better-value ROSSO DI MONTALCINO, both still 100% SANGIOVESE.

Monte del Frà Ven ★★→★★★ Bonomo family-owned; v.gd value. Top: AMARONE (Lena di Mezzo, RISERVA), Custoza (Bonomo Sexaginta, Ca' del Magro). Also v.gd: Bardolino (Bonomo), LUGANA.

Montefalco Sagrantino Umb ★★★→★★★★ DOCG Once sweet PASSITO only (still best wine of area); drier version is Italy's most powerfully tannic red, requiring optimal growing seasons to show best. Top: ADANTI, Antano Milziade, Antonelli San Marco, CAPRAI (25 Anni, Collepiano, Spinning Beauty), Colpetrone, TENUTE LUNELLI – Castelbuono (Lampante, Carapace, Carapace Lunga-Attesa), Ruggeri. Also v.gd: Bellafonte, LORENZO MATTONI, Lungarotti, Pardi, Romanelli, Tenuta Alzatura, Terre dei Capitani.

Monte Maletto Pie ★★★ Gian Marco Viano one of Italy's most talented young producers. Best: CAREMA Sole e Roccia, single vyds La Costa, Le Rue.

Montepulciano d'Abruzzo Ab ★★→★★★ DOC (r) 16 18 19 20' 22 Thanks to new generation of winemakers, Ab's wines (MONTEPULCIANO, TREBBIANO D'ABRUZZO too) never been better. Reds: light, easy-going or structured, rich. Best: Cataldi Madonna (Piè delle Vigne, Tonì), Praesidium, TIBERIO, Torre dei Beati, *Valentini* (age-worthy), Valle Reale. Also v.gd: Cingilia, Filomusi Guelfi.

Montevertine Tus ★★★★ Organic estate in Radda. Outstanding IGT Le Pergole Torte, world-class, pure, long-ageing SANGIOVESE; v.gd Montevertine.

Montevetrano Cam ★★★ Iconic CAM AZIENDA. Superb IGT Montevetrano (AGLIANICO/ CAB SAUV/MERLOT); v.gd Core Bianco (FIANO/GRECO), Rosso (Aglianico).

Morella Pug ★★★→★★★★ Gaetano M and wife Lisa Gilbee make outstanding PRIMITIVO (La Signora, Mondo Nuovo, Old Vines) from c.90-yr-old vines. Also v.gd: Mezzogiorno (FIANO), Mezzarosa rosé (Primitivo/NEGROAMARO).

Morellino di Scansano Tus ★→★★★ DOCG 16' 17 18 19' 20 21' Maremma's famous SANGIOVESE-based red is better when cheerful, light than overoaked, gritty. Best: Fattoria dei Barbi, *Le Pupille* (plus RISERVA), MORIS FARMS, PODERE 414, POGGIO ARGENTIERA, Roccapesta, TENUTA Belguardo.

Moris Farms Tus ★★★ One of 1st new-age producers of TUS Maremma. Top: iconic IGT Avvoltore (rich SANGIOVESE/CAB/SYRAH), MORELLINO DI SCANSANO (regular, RISERVA). Also VERMENTINO, Rosato Rosamundi.

Moscato d'Asti Pie ★★→★★★ DYA Similar to DOCG ASTI, but usually better grapes; lower alc, lower pressure, sweeter, fruitier, often small producers. Best DOCG MOSCATO: Ca' d'Gal, *Caudrina* (La Galeisa), Forteto della Luja, Mongioia, *Saracco*, Vignaioli di Santo Stefano. Also v.gd: BRAIDA, GD VAJRA, RIZZI.

Mosnel Lom ★★★→★★★★ Barzanò family-run, in FRANCIACORTA (1836). Organic. Elegance, complexity, long-ageing: EBB, Nature, Pas Dosé RISERVA, Riedizioni Late Release Vintage.

Muri Gries T-AA ★★→★★★ Monastery in Bolzano suburb of Gries; trad and still top producer of LAGREIN ALTO ADIGE DOC. Best: Abtei Muri, Klosteranger.

Musso Pie ★★★ Musso family-run (1929). Underrated: BARBARESCOS Pora (also RISERVA), Rio Sordo.

Nals Margreid T-AA ★★★ Small quality co-op making mtn-fresh whites (esp PINOT BIANCO Sirmian), CHARD RISERVA, new cuvée (w) Nama.

Nebbiolo d'Alba Pie ★★→★★★ DOC 15 16' 18 19' 21 (100% NEBBIOLO) Sometimes a worthy replacement for BAROLO/BARBARESCO, though it comes from a distinct area between the two. Best: BREZZA, BRUNO GIACOSA, CERETTO, Hilberg-Pasquero, LUCIANO SANDRONE, ORLANDO ABRIGO, PAITIN, PODERI COLLA.

Neive, Castello di Pie ★★★ Historic estate, owns single greatest cru of all BARBARESCO, famous Santo Stefano (Albesani MGA). Top: Gallina, Santo Stefano (also RISERVA). Also v.gd: Albarossa, Barbarossa.

The value list – reds

Italy's a big place. Here's my pick of great value from top to toe, starting (more or less) at the top. DI BARRÒ (VDA), mineral, refined Mayolet; ETTORE GERMANO (PIE), fresh, velvety BARBERA D'ALBA della Madre; ELENA WALCH (T-AA), deep, balanced, silky LAGREIN; Tamburino Sardo (Ven), juicy, savoury, spicy VALPOLICELLA CLASSICO SUPERIORE; RONCHI DI CIALLA (FVG), fresh, juicy, vibrant Schioppettino; ISOLE E OLENA (TUS), deep, refined, classic CHIANTI CLASSICO; PODERE SABBIONI (Mar), gorgeous, fresh ROSSO PICENO; LORENZO MATTONI (Umb), nobly tannic, powerful, harmonious MONTEFALCO SAGRANTINO; DAMIANO CIOLLI (Lat), suave, juicy, dense CESANESE di Olevano Romano-Silene; SORRENTINO (CAM), balsamic, lively, juicy Vesuvio Lacryma Christi 5 Viti; FELLINE (PUG), rich, suave, v.long ZIN PRIMITIVO DI MANDURIA; Parco dei Monaci (Bas), mineral, fresh, balanced Monacello ROSATO; TENUTA del Travale (Cal), lovely, rare, dark-rosato Epicarma; FEUDO MONTONI (SI), clean, smooth, flinty NERO D'AVOLA Lagnusa; La Dolce VIGNA (SAR), balanced, refined, powerful Mandrolisai.

Niedrist, Ignaz T-AA ★★★ LAGREIN Berger Gei RISERVA is reference. So are RIES, WEISSBURGUNDER (Limes, Berg), BLAUBURGUNDER Riserva. Also v.gd: CHARD (vom Kalk), SAUV BL (Limes, Porphyr & Kalk), Trias (w blend).

Nipozzano, Castello di Tus ★★★→★★★★ FRESCOBALDI estate in RÙFINA, e of Florence, making excellent CHIANTI Rùfina. Top: IGT *Montesodi*, Nipozzano RISERVA (Vecchie Viti). Also v.gd: Mormoreto (Bx blend).

2024 rain: Monferrato (Piedmont) over 4000mm (157.5in), but in droughty 2023, only 400mm (15.7in).

Nittardi Tus ★★→★★★ Reliable source of quality modern CHIANTI CLASSICO (Casanuova di Nittardi, RISERVA). German-owned; oenologist Carlo Ferrini.

Nizza Pie ★★→★★★ DOCG (100% BARBERA) Only from best-exposed sites of 19 villages around town of Nizza Monferrato; also RISERVA. Needs time. Best: BAVA, BERSANO, Cacina Garitina (900, Riserva), Chiarlo (La Court), Doglia Gianni, La Barbatella, ODDERO, Olim Bauda (also Riserva), TENUTA Garetto, Villa Giada, Vinchio Vaglio.

Nössing, Manni T-AA ★★★★ Outstanding benchmark GRÜNER V, KERNER, MÜLLER-T Sass Rigais, SYLVANER.

Occhio di pernice Tus "Partridge's eye". Type of VIN SANTO made predominantly from black grapes, mainly SANGIOVESE. *Avignonesi's is definitive*.

Occhipinti, Arianna Si ★★★ Cult producer, deservedly so. Organic. Top: CERASUOLO DI VITTORIA CLASSICO Grotte Alte, Il Frappato.

Oddero Pie ★★★→★★★★ Traditionalist La Morra estate for excellent BAROLO (Brunate, Bussia RISERVA, Villero, outstanding VIGNA Rionda Riserva), BARBARESCO (Gallina) crus, plus other serious PIE wines; v.gd-value Barolo, RIES.

Oltrepò Pavese Lom ★→★★★ Multi-DOC, lots of varietals, blends from Pavia province: METODO CLASSICO best. Try Barbacarlo, Bruno Verdi, Conte Vistarino (MC 1865, PINOT N Bertone), Isimbarda, Mazzolino, Travaglino.

Ornellaia Tus ★★★★ 15 16' 18 19' 20 21 Fashionable, indeed cult, estate nr BOLGHERI now owned by FRESCOBALDI. Top (Bx grapes/method): Bolgheri DOC Ornellaia; IGT Masseto (MERLOT), now its own winery; Ornellaia Bianco (SAUV BL/VIOGNIER). Also gd: Bolgheri DOC Le Serre Nuove, POGGIO alle Gazze (w).

Orvieto Umb ★→★★★ DOC DYA One of few areas of Italy where noble rot occurs spontaneously and often. Sweet late-harvest can be memorable. Off-dry Amabile less in favour today but delicious. Top: Barberani (Luigi e Giovanna, sw Calcaia), Palazzone, Sergio Mottura (Lat). Also v.gd: Castello della Sala, Decugnano dei Barbi, Todini.

Ottin VdA ★★★ Elio O one of top interpreters of VDA terroir. Best: PETITE ARVINE Nuances, PINOT N (also L'Emerico), Torrette Superieur.

Paitin Pie ★★★ Pasquero-Elia family bottling BARBARESCO since C19. Today back on track, "real" Barbaresco from cru Serraboella in large barrels. Star: Sorì Paitin Vecchie Vigne. Also v.gd: new Barbaresco (Basarin, Faset), BARBERA D'ALBA (Campolive), NEBBIOLO D'ALBA.

Palladino Pie ★★★ Family estate, talented interpreter of Serralunga BAROLO. Top: Ornato, RISERVA San Bernardo. Also v.gd: BARBERA D'ALBA, Parafada.

Palmento Costanzo Si ★★→★★★ In several ETNA *contrade*. Top: (r/w) Contrada Santo Spirito; (r) Etna Prefillossera, Nero di Sei; (w) Bianco di Sei.

Paltrinieri E-R ★★→★★★ One of top three LAMBRUSCO; among 1st to produce 100% L di Sorbara. Best: La RISERVA, Leclisse, Secco Radice.

Pantelleria Si ★★★ Windswept, black (volcanic) earth SI island off Tunisian coast, famous for superb MOSCATO d'Alessandria stickies. Dense, intense PASSITO. Try Coste Ghirlanda, MARCO DE BARTOLI (Bukkuram), DONNAFUGATA (Ben Ryé), Ferrandes, Vinisola (A'mmare, Arbaria, Zefiro).

Parusso, Armando Pie ★★★ Excellent BAROLO. Best: Bussia (and RISERVAS Munie, Rocche), Mariondino. Also v.gd: Mosconi, Perarmando.

Passito Si, Tus, Ven One of Italy's most ancient, characteristic styles, from grapes dried briefly under harvest sun (in s) or over a period of weeks or mths in airy attics (*appassimento*). Best-known versions: AMARONE/RECIOTO, VALPOLICELLA/ SOAVE (Ven); VIN SANTO (TUS); Pantelleria (SI). Try Loazzolo, MONTEFALCO, ORVIETO, Torcolato. Never cheap.

Pavese Ermes VdA ★★★ One estate, one grape: Prié Bl, ungrafted vines up to 1219m (4000ft). Top: Blanc de Morgex et de la Salle (Classic, Le 7 Scalinate, Nathan), Ninive (sw), MC Pavese (sp XLVIII and LX, mths of ageing).

Pepe, Emidio Ab ★★★ Artisanal, 15 ha, bio/organic. Top: MONTEPULCIANO D'ABRUZZO. Old-vine PECORINO, TREBBIANO D'ABRUZZO. Nicely funky, maybe not for everyone.

Petrolo Tus ★★★ DOC Valdarno di Sopra. Luca Sanjust is an artist, painter, passionate winemaker. Top: Boggina A and C (SANGIOVESE), Galatrona (MERLOT).

Petrussa, Vigna FVG ★★★ Small, high quality. Best: PICOLIT, Richenza (indigenous w grapes, old vines), SCHIOPPETTINO di Prepotto (and RISERVA).

Pian dell'Orino Tus ★★★★ Small MONTALCINO estate, committed to bio. BRUNELLO seductive, technically perfect, Rosso nearly as gd. Many epic wines.

Piane, Le Pie ★★★★ Christoph Kunzli one of best ALTO PIEMONTE producers. Top: (r) BOCA (also new single-vyd Antonio Cerri), Plinius; (w) Bianko, Eos (Erbaluce). Also v.gd: new Maggiorina, Mimmo (NEBBIOLO/Croatina), Nebbiolo, Piane (Croatina).

Picolit FVG ★★→★★★ DOCG 13 15 16' 17 18 (20') Potentially Italy's best sweet (most from air-dried grapes; rare late-harvests even better), but plagued by poor versions that don't speak of the grape. Texture ranges from light, sweet (rare) to super-thick (PASSITO). Best: Aquila del Torre, d'Attimis, I Comelli, LIVIO FELLUGA, Marco Sara, Perusini, RONCHI DI CIALLA, Valentino Butussi, VIGNA PETRUSSA. Also v.gd: Ermacora, Girolamo Dorigo, Paolo Rodaro.

Piedmont / Piemonte In ne, bordering France to the w. Turin is capital. Main areas: ALTO PIEMONTE, Monferrato, LANGHE, ROERO. With TUS, Italy's most important region for quality (10% of all DOC[G] wines). No IGTS allowed. Grapes incl BARBERA, Brachetto, CORTESE, DOLCETTO, FREISA, GRIGNOLINO, MALVASIA di Casorzo, Malvasia di Schierano, MOSCATO, NEBBIOLO, Ruchè, Timorasso. *See also* BARBARESCO, BAROLO.

Pieropan Ven ★★★★ Andrea and Dario, Leonildo's sons, now run winery. Organic. Cru *La Rocca* still ultimate oaked SOAVE; Calvarino best of all. Outstanding new Calvarino 5 (blend of Calvarino 08–12). Also v.gd AMARONE, RECIOTO DI SOAVE (Le Colombare).

Pietradolce Si ★★★→★★★★ Faro bros in key ETNA crus, often pre-phylloxera vines. Top: (r/w) Archineri; (r) Barbagalli, Feudo di Mezzo, Rampante, Santo Spirito; (w) Sant'Andrea (100% CARRICANTE). Precise wines.

Pietraventosa Pug ★★★ Small family estate, one of top producers of PRIMITIVO di Gioia del Colle. Top: Allegoria, RISERVA, Rosé Est-Rosa.

Pievalta Mar ★★★ Founded by BARONE PIZZINI, bio. Top: VERDICCHIO DEI CASTELLI DI JESI (RISERVA San Paolo, Tre Ripe, sp Perlugo).

2024 rain: Bolgheri 200mm (7.9in); third of annual rainfall in just 2 hours in Sept.

Pio Cesare Pie ★★★ Veteran ALBA producer; BAROLO, BARBARESCO in modern (barrique) and trad (large cask-aged) versions. NEBBIOLO D'ALBA esp gd, *a little Barolo at half the price*. Best: Single-vyd (Bricco, Mosconi, Ornato), Classic (Pio, dedicated to Pio Boffa) collections. Also gd: Barolo Chinato, vermouth.

Pira e Figli – Chiara Boschis Pie ★★★★ Organic. Top: Cannubi, Mosconi, Via Nuova. Also v.gd: BARBERA D'ALBA SUPERIORE, LANGHE NEBBIOLO. Must visit.

Planeta Si ★★★ Leading SI estate, vyds all over island, incl Menfi (GRILLO Terebinto), Noto (NERO D'AVOLA Santa Cecilia, PASSITO di Noto), Vittoria (CERASUOLO Dorilli, Frappato), most recently on ETNA (NERELLO MASCALESE Eruzione 1614). Also gd: Cometa (FIANO). Reliable.

Podere Tus Small TUS farm, once part of a big estate.

Podere Sabbioni Mar ★★★ Best Ribona (grape, also called Maceratino) in Italy: della Famiglia. Also v.gd ROSSO PICENO.

Poggio Tus Means "hill" in TUS dialect. **Poggione** means "big hill".

Turin has its own DOC wine: Vigna della Regina. Freisa grapes, less than 1 ha.

Poggio Antico Tus ★★★ Paola Gloder looks after 32-ha estate, one of highest in MONTALCINO (500m/1640ft). Restrained, consistent, at times too herbal.

Poggio Argentiera Tus ★★★ In Maremma, TUA RITA-owned: fresh, drinkable. Best: Capatosta (95% SANGIOVESE), MORELLINO DI SCANSANO.

Poggio di Sotto Tus ★★★★ Small MONTALCINO estate, big, well-deserved reputation. Top: BRUNELLO, RISERVA, ROSSO, trad character with idiosyncratic twist.

Poggione, Tenuta Il Tus ★★★ MONTALCINO estate, in s. Consistently excellent BRUNELLO (RISERVA VIGNA Paganelli), Rosso; v.gd VIN SANTO.

Potazzine, Le Tus ★★★★ Gorelli family just s of MONTALCINO; organic, vyd quite high. Outstanding, serious, v. drinkable BRUNELLO (and RISERVA), ROSSO. Try at family restaurant.

Prà Ven ★★★★ Leading SOAVE CLASSICO: Colle Sant'Antonio, Monte Grande, Staforte. Excellent AMARONE (15 top), VALPOLICELLA La Morandina.

Produttori del Barbaresco Pie ★★★ One of Italy's earliest and best co-ops. Excellent trad, classic BARBARESCO plus crus Asili, Montefico, Montestefano, Ovello, Pora, Rio Sordo. Super value.

Proprietà Sperino Pie ★★★★ Top estate of LESSONA. One of best of ALTO PIEMONTE run by Luca De Marchi. Outstanding BRAMATERRA, Lessona (and RISERVA Covà). Also v.gd: 'L Franc (one of best Italian CAB FR), Rosa del Rosa (NEBBIOLO/Vespolina rosé), Uvaggio (r blend).

Prosecco Ven ★→★★ DOC(G) DYA Prosecco is the wine, GLERA the grape variety. Quality is higher in Valdobbiadene and Conegliano (DOCG zones). Best: Adami, BISOL, Bortolomiol, COL VETORAZ, Gemin, Marchiori, Masottina, NINO FRANCO, Ruggeri, Silvano Follador, Sorelle Bronca, Zucchetto. Also v.gd: Andreola, Biancavigna, Bosco del Merlo, Fratelli Bortolin, Le Colture, Najma.

Puglia The "heel" of Italy. Many gd-value reds from Bombino Nero, NEGROAMARO, PRIMITIVO, Susumaniello, Uva di Troia. Bombino Bianco, aromatic Minutolo, Verdeca most interesting whites. Castel del Monte, Gioia del Colle Primitivo, PRIMITIVO DI MANDURIA, SALICE SALENTINO best denominations.

Querciabella Tus ★★★ Top CHIANTI CLASSICO estate, bio (2000). Best: Batàr (CHARD/PINOT BL), Chianti Classico (RISERVA, Gran Selezione), IGT Camartina (CAB SAUV/SANGIOVESE). Also v.gd: Mongrana (VIOGNIER/VERMENTINO), Palafreno (MERLOT).

Quintarelli, Giuseppe Ven ★★★★ Arch-traditionalist artisan producer of sublime VALPOLICELLA, RECIOTO, AMARONE. Daughter Fiorenza and sons now in charge, altering nothing, incl the ban on spitting when tasting.

Quintodecimo Cam ★★★→★★★★ Oenology professor/winemaker Luigi Moio's beautiful estate. Outstanding: TAURASI (VIGNA Grande Cerzito, Vigna Quintodecimo, new Grand Cru Luigi Moio), Grande Cuvée Luigi Moio (w blend native grapes). Great: AGLIANICO, FALANGHINA, FIANO D'AVELLINO, GRECO DI TUFO.

Ragnaie, Le Tus ★★★ Makes trad BRUNELLOS revealing essence of SANGIOVESE. Top: Casanovina Montosoli, Passo del Lume Spento, VV

Recioto della Valpolicella Ven ★★★→★★★★ DOCG Sweet-wine marketing problems mean this trad Italian beauty is being made less and less. Shame, esp as always much better than many disappointing overly sweet/tannic AMARONE. Top: Brigaldara, Roccolo Grassi, Secondo Marco, TEDESCHI, TOMMASO BUSSOLA.

Recioto di Soave Ven ★★★→★★★★ DOCG SOAVE from half-dried grapes: sweet, fruity, slightly almondy; sweetness is cut by high acidity. *Drink with cheese*. Best: Anselmi, Coffele, GINI, PIEROPAN, SUAVIA, Tamellini. Often v.gd: Ca' Rugate, Pasqua, PRÀ, Trabuchi.

Redalmo Ven ★★★ Elisa and Mattia run family estate over two territories of great geological value: Val d'Alpone and Berici Hills. Top: GARGANEGA, Rosso Veneto (100% MARSELAN, one of the few in Italy).

Refosco (dal Peduncolo Rosso) FVG ★★ 15 16 19' 20 21 Most planted native red grape of the region. Best from FRIULI COLLI ORIENTALI DOC. Top: MIANI, Ronchi di Cialla, VIGNA PETRUSSA, Volpe Pasini. Also gd: Jacuss, La Viarte, LIVIO FELLUGA, MEROI.

Revello, Fratelli Pie ★★★ Small family estate, delicious BAROLO from some of La Morra's best crus (Conca, Gattera, Rocche dell'Annunziata), new Cerretta; v.gd L'Insieme (NEBBIOLO/BARBERA/CAB SAUV).

Riecine Tus ★★★→★★★★ SANGIOVESE specialist at Gaiole since 70s. Riecine di Riecine, La Gioia (100% Sangiovese) potentially outstanding; Tresette (MERLOT).

Rinaldi, Francesco Pie ★★★ Paola and Piera R make classic, elegant BAROLOS. Top: Brunate, Cannubi (also RISERVA), Rocche dell'Annunziata. Also v.gd: Classic Barolo, LANGHE FREISA, NEBBIOLO.

Rinaldi, Giuseppe Pie ★★★ Marta and Carlotta R produce some of most iconic LANGHE wines: FREISA, BAROLO (plus new Bussia), LANGHE NEBBIOLO.

Riserva Wine aged for a statutory period, usually in casks or barrels.

Rivetto Pie ★★★ Enrico R one of most talented young winemakers; bio. Top: BAROLOS Briccolina, Leon. Also v.gd: Langhe Nascetta (w), BARBERA D'ALBA, Barolo Serralunga, LANGHE NEBBIOLO.

Rivolta, Fattoria La Cam ★★★ Paolo Cotroneo, in an ancient farm on ne slope of Taburno, since 1998. Best: AGLIANICO del Taburno (Terra di Rivolta), Sogno di Rivolta (GRECO/FIANO/FALANGHINA). Also v.gd: Coda di Volpe, Falanghina.

Rizzi Pie ★★★→★★★★ Sub-area of Treiso, commune of BARBARESCO, where Dellapiana family looks after 35 ha. Organic. Top: Barbaresco Pajorè, Rizzi RISERVA Boito. Also v.gd: ALTA LANGA, Barbaresco (Nervo, Rizzi), MOSCATO D'ASTI, vermouth. Mineral, steely wines.

Roagna Pie ★★★★ Old vines, massal selection, organic, wild yeast, long maceration and long ageing in large oak casks. Outstanding BARBARESCO Crichet Pajet (also RISERVA), BAROLO and Barbaresco Vecchie Viti ("old vines") ranges, Riservas "Black Label". More than v.gd: Solea (CHARD/NEBBIOLO), Timorasso Montemarzino, Barbarescos (Pajè, Albesani, Gallina and Faset), Barolos (Pira, Del Comune di Barolo, Rocche di Castiglione).

Rocca, Albino Pie ★★★→★★★★ Foremost producer of elegant, sophisticated BARBARESCO: Cottà, Ovello VIGNA Loreto, Ronchi; RISERVAS (Cottà, Ronchi).

With Castelmagno cheese, drink Barolo or Barbaresco.

Rocca, Bruno Pie ★★★→★★★★ Family estate run by Francesco and Luisa R, Bruno's children. BARBARESCO with more trad style. More elegance than power. Top: Currà, Maria Adelaide, Rabajà, RISERVAS. Also v.gd: BARBERA D'ASTI, LANGHE NEBBIOLO.

Roero Pie ★★→★★★★ DOCG 14 16' **18** 19' 20 21 Wilder, cooler compared to LANGHE. Wines have typically moderate alc and tannin, gd elegance, freshness, aromatics. ARNEIS, NEBBIOLO. Best: ANGELO NEGRO, BRUNO GIACOSA, GIOVANNI ALMONDO, MALVIRÀ, MATTEO CORREGGIA. Also v.gd: Ca' Rossa, Cornarea, Deltetto, Francesco Rosso, GIOVANNI ROSSO, Monchiero Carbone, Val del Prete, Valfaccenda.

Romagna Sangiovese Mar ★★→★★★ DOC At times too herbal and oaky, but often well-made, even classy SANGIOVESE red. Top: Condè, Condello, Drei Donà, Fattoria Zerbina, Nicolucci, Papiano, Ronchi di Castelluccio, Tre Monti. Also v.gd: TENUTA Mara (Guiry, Maramia).

Ronchi di Cialla FVG ★★★→★★★★ Leading FVG estate, in Cialla subzone of FRIULI COLLI ORIENTALI, Rapuzzi family-run, devoted to local old native grapes. Best: Ciallabianco (RIBOLLA GIALLA/Verduzzo/PICOLIT), Picolit di Cialla, SCHIOPPETTINO. Also v.gd REFOSCO dal Peduncolo Rosso di Cialla, Sol (dr Picolit).

Ronco Term for a hillside vyd in NE Italy, esp FVG.

Ronco del Gelso FVG ★★★→★★★★ Tight, pure ISONZO. Regional benchmarks: FRIULANO Toc Bas, MALVASIA VIGNA della Permuta, PINOT GR Sot lis Rivis. Latimis (w blend), RIES Schulz, MERLOT, all v.gd.

Rosato General Italian name for rosé. Other rosé names incl Chiaretto from Lake Garda; CERASUOLO from Ab; Kretzer from ALTO ADIGE.

Rossese di Dolceacqua, or Dolceacqua Lig ★★→★★★ DOC Interesting reds. Intense, salty, spicy; greater depth of fruit than most. Best: Ka' Manciné, Maccario-Dringenberg (Curli, Luvaira, Posaù, Sette Cammini), Terre Bianche (Bricco Arcagna), TENUTA Anfosso. Also v.gd: Poggi dell'Elmo.

Rosset VdA ★★→★★★ Innovative young winery. Best: CHARD 770, SYRAH 870.

Rosso, Giovanni Pie ★★★ Davide R is talented interpreter of Serralunga BAROLO. Best: Cerretta, LANGHE NEBBIOLO Ester Canale Rosso, Serra, Vignarionda Ester Canale. Also v.gd Langhe Nebbiolo, ROERO ARNEIS. In ETNA too.

Rosso di Montalcino Tus ★★→★★★ 13 15 16 18 19' 20 21 DOC for earlier-maturing wines from BRUNELLO grapes, usually from younger or lesser vyd sites; watch out for bargains.

Rosso Piceno / Piceno Mar ★→★★★ DOC 18 19 (20) Blend of MONTEPULCIANO (35%+) and SANGIOVESE (15%+). SUPERIORE means it comes only from the far s of the region. Top: BUCCI, Garofoli, MONTECAPPONE (Utopia). Also v.gd: Boccadigabbia, Moncaro, Monte Schiavo, Saladini Pilastri, Santa Barbara, TENUTA DI TAVIGNANO, Velenosi.

Rùfina Tus ★★→★★★ Most n subzone of CHIANTI, e of Florence, is by far best and most interesting non-CHIANTI CLASSICO denomination. Highest of all Chiantis, so refined, age-worthy. Soils are varied and incl limestone, sand, Galestro, Alberese, marly clays and others. Top: Colognole, Fattoria il Capitano, Fattoria Lavacchio, Frascole, Grignano, I Veroni, NIPOZZANO (*see* FRESCOBALDI), Ormaevini, Podere Il Pozzo, *Selvapiana*, Travignoli.

Russiz Superiore FVG ★★→★★★ LIVIO FELLUGA's brother Marco est vyds in various parts of FVG. Now run by Marco's granddaughter Ilaria. Wide range. Best: Col Disôre (COLLIO Bianco blend), PINOT GRIGIO. Also v.gd: PINOT BIANCO RISERVA.

Russo, Girolamo Si ★★★→★★★★ Giuseppe R is one of three or four best ETNA producers. Among 1st on Etna to bottle crus separately. Top: (r) Caldera Sottana, Feudo, Feudo di Mezzo, San Lorenzo; (w) Nerina, San Lorenzo.

Salento Pug ★→★★★ Home to Italy's best rosé from NEGROAMARO (alongside Ab's CERASUOLO from MONTEPULCIANO). Plus v.gd red Negroamaro, with a bit of help from MALVASIA Nera, and now red from local Susumaniello. Best: Conti Zecca (Nero, Rodinò), CUPERTINUM, Leone de Castris (Five Roses); Rosa del Golfo (VIGNA Mazzi classic, rosé). *See also* SALICE SALENTINO.

Salice Salentino Pug ★★→★★★★ DOC 16 17 20' 22 Best known of Salento's too many NEGROAMARO-based DOCS. RISERVA after 2 yrs. Top: Agricole Vallone, Leone de Castris (Riserva). Also v.gd: Cantele, Due Palme, Mocavero, For ROSATO: Candido, FELLINE, Leone de Castris, Rosa del Golfo.

Salvioni Tus ★★★★ (aka La Cerbaiola) Iconic small, highest-quality MONTALCINO estate. BRUNELLO, ROSSO DI MONTALCINO among v. best available.

Sandrone, Luciano Pie ★★★→★★★★ Modern-style ALBA. Deep BAROLOS: Aleste (from 2013, previously Cannubi Boschis), Le Vigne, Vite Talin. Also gd NEBBIOLO D'ALBA Valmaggiore.

San Felice Tus ★★★ Historic winery, owned by Gruppo Allianz, run by Leonardo Bellaccini. Fine: CHIANTI CLASSICO and RISERVA POGGIO Rosso from Castelnuovo Berardenga. Also gd: BRUNELLO DI MONTALCINO Campogiovanni, IGT *Vigorello* (1st SUPER TUSCAN, from 1968).

San Giusto a Rentennano Tus ★★★★ Top CHIANTI CLASSICO. Organic. Outstanding: IGTS La Ricolma (MERLOT), Percarlo (SANGIOVESE); Chianti Classico (and RISERVA Le Baroncole); Vin San Giusto (PASSITO).

San Guido, Tenuta Tus *See* SASSICAIA.

San Leonardo T-AA ★★★★ Top Trentino estate of Marchesi Guerrieri Gonzaga. Main wine is Bx blend, *San Leonardo* (now released 1 yr later). Also v.gd: RIES, CARMENÈRE, Villa Gresti (MERLOT/Carmenère), TRENTO (sp Cuvée Pietra, RISERVA Privata).

San Lorenzo, Fattoria Mar ★★★ Age-worthy VERDICCHIOS from Montecarotto, bio/ organic. Top: Campo delle Oche (also Integrale), Il San Lorenzo Bianco. Also v.gd: Il San Lorenzo Rosso (SYRAH), Le Oche, VIGNA La Gattara (r).

San Michele Appiano T-AA ★★★ Historic co-op; *mtn-fresh whites* a speciality brimming with varietal typicity, drinkability. Best: Appius (selected by Hans Terzer), Sanct Valentin, The Wine Collection. Also v.gd PINOT BL Schulthauser.

Santadi Sar ★★★ Best SAR co-op (and one of Italy's), esp for Carignano del Sulcis (Rocca Rubia RISERVA, *Terre Brune*). Also v.gd: VERMENTINO DI SARDEGNA (Cala Silente), Villa di Chiesa (w blend), Latinia (PASSITO).

Saracco, Paolo Pie ★★★★ Top MOSCATO D'ASTI; v.gd CHARD, LANGHE RIES, PINOT N.

Sardinia / Sardegna Italy's 2nd-largest island is home to world-class whites and reds. Look for: VERMENTINO DI GALLURA, VERMENTINO DI SARDEGNA (fruitier, less mineral), Sherry-like VERNACCIA DI ORISTANO, NURAGUS, Nasco, Semidano. CANNONAU (GARNACHA), Carignano, most famous reds. Bovale, Monica, Pascale just as gd.

Sartarelli Mar ★★★ High-quality VERDICCHIO DEI CASTELLI DI JESI CLASSICO. Top: Balciana, Milletta RISERVA, Tralivio.

Sassicaia Tus ★★★★ 10 13 15' 16' 18 19' 20 21' Single-vyd DOC (BOLGHERI), a CAB (SAUV/FR) made on First Growth lines by Marchese Incisa della Rocchetta at TENUTA SAN GUIDO. More elegant than lush, made for age – and often bought for investment, but hugely influential in giving Italy a top-quality image; 16 extremely elegant, one of best recent yrs.

Satta, Michele Tus ★★★ Virtually only BOLGHERI grower to succeed with 100% SANGIOVESE (Cavaliere). Best: BOLGHERI Marianova, Piastraia.

The value list – whites

Whites can be less expensive than reds; either way, these are also great value. They start in n and work down. CAVE MONT BLANC (VDA), aristocratic, saline, deep La Piagne; LA COLOMBERA (PIE), absolute gem DERTHONA; BIO VIO (Lig), saline, lively Pigato Marenè, KÖFERERHOF (T-AA), enticing, layered SYLVANER R; PIEROPAN (Ven), enveloping, silky SOAVE CLASSICO Calvarino; I CLIVI (FVG), deep, charming, clean Friulano San Lorenzo; TENUTA DI TAVIGNANO (Mar), deep, balanced, refined Misco VERDICCHIO DEI CDJ Classico SUPERIORE; TIBERIO (Ab), balanced, multi-faceted, mineral TREBBIANO D'ABRUZZO; COLLI DI LAPIO (CAM), clean, saline FIANO D'AVELLINO; Vinisola (SI), bright, saline, energetic PANTELLERIA Bianco Amanolibera; SANTADI (SAR), herbal, fresh, different Nuragus di Cagliari Pedraia.

Scarpa Pie ★★★ Historic trad winery in NIZZA Monferrato. Top: BARBERA D'ASTI La Bogliona, Rouchet (Ruchè). BARBARESCO Tettineive, FREISA v.gd.

Scarzello Pie ★★★ Classic, refined BAROLO. Top: Boschetti, Sarmassa. Also v.gd: BARBERA D'ALBA, LANGHE NEBBIOLO.

Scavino, Paolo Pie ★★★ Modernist BAROLO producer of Castiglione Falletto: Bric del Fiasc, Monvigliero, Prapò, Ravera, Rocche dell'Annunziata.

The smallest MGA of Barolo? Bricco Rocche (1.46 ha).

Schiava Alto Adige T-AA ★ DOC DYA Schiava (VERNATSCH in German): blend of the three main Schiava varieties (Gentile, Grigia, Grossa). Used to make DOC wines called Lago di Caldaro, St-Magdalener (Santa Maddalena). Light- to medium-bodied, v. fresh, pleasant red. Best: CS Bolzano, Caldaro, GIRLAN, Merano.

Schiopetto, Mario FVG ★★★ Legendary late COLLIO pioneering estate now owned by Rotolo family; v.gd DOC FRIULANO, SAUV BL, *Pinot Bl*, RIBOLLA GIALLA and IGT blend Blanc des Rosis, etc.

Scolca, La Pie ★★★ Among 1st to make GAVI known in world, with legendary Black Label. Best: Gavi dei Gavi (Black Label, Limited Edition), Soldati D'Antan (and SPUMANTE Millesimato).

Sella & Mosca Sar ★★→★★★ Major SAR grower-merchant. *See* TERRA MORETTI.

Selvapiana Tus ★★★★ RÙFINA organic estate among Italian greats. Best: RISERVA Bucerchiale, IGT Fornace; but even *basic Chianti Rùfina is a treat*. Also fine red Petrognano, Pomino, Riserva VIGNETO Erchi.

Sesta di Sopra Tus ★★★ High-quality BRUNELLO (top RISERVA), ROSSO DI MONTALCINO.

Sesti – Castello di Argiano Tus ★★★ Distinctive, refined yet flavourful BRUNELLOS from Sesti family estate; trad-style. CLASSICO Brunello, RISERVA Phenomena equally gd, if different.

Sforzato / Sfursat Lom ★★★ DOCG Sforzato di VALTELLINA is made AMARONE-like, from air-dried NEBBIOLO grapes. Ages beautifully. Best: FAY (RONCO del Picchio). Also v.gd: Dirupi (Vino Sbagliato), Mamete Prevostini (Albareda, Corte di Cama), Nino Negri (Cinque Stelle), Triacca. *See* VALTELLINA.

Sicily The Med's largest island, and modern source of exciting original wines and value. Grows native grapes: (r) Frappato, NERELLO MASCALESE, NERO D'AVOLA; (w) CARRICANTE, CATARRATTO, Grecanico, GRILLO, INZOLIA. Also internationals. The vyds are on flatlands in the w, hills in the centre and volcanic altitudes on Mt Etna. (*See also* ETNA.)

Soave Ven ★★→★★★ DOC Famous, hitherto underrated Veronese white. Soils: mix of mainly volcanic or calcareous elements. Wines from volcanic soils of CLASSICO zone can be intense, saline, v. fine, quite long-lived. Best: PIEROPAN, GINI, INAMA, PRÀ, SUAVIA. Also v.gd: Agostino Vicentini (Il Casale), Ca' Rugate, Casato 1922 (Vite Torta), Coffele (Alzari), Filippi, Nardello (Monte Zoppega), Roccolo Grassi (Broia). *See also* RECIOTO.

Solaia Tus ★★★★ 15 16' 18 19' 21 CAB/SANGIOVESE by ANTINORI; needs age.

Sorpasso Pie ★★★ Vittorio Garda is one of most talented young winemakers in PIE. Top: CALUSO, CAREMA. Elegant, refined.

Sorrentino Cam ★★→★★★ Benni S makes top (r/w) Lacryma Christi (5 Viti, VIGNA Lapillo). Best: AGLIANICO Don Paolo (r), Caprettone (Benita 31), Catalò (w).

Sottimano Pie ★★★→★★★★ Family estate. One of most inspired in BARBARESCO (crus: Basarin, Cottá, Currá, Fausoni, Pajoré). Also v.gd: BARBERA D'ALBA, DOLCETTO d'ALBA, LANGHE NEBBIOLO.

Speri Ven ★★★ VALPOLICELLA family estate. Organic; trad style. Top: AMARONE Sant'Urbano, RECIOTO DELLA VALPOLICELLA (La Roggia).

Spumante Sparkling.

Strette, Le Pie ★★★ Makes gd-value BAROLO: B. del Comune di Novello, Bergera

Pezzole, Corini Pallaretta. Also LANGHE Nas-cëtta del Comune di Novello (plus single-vyd Pasinot).

Suavia Ven ★★★ Tessari sisters make v. refined SOAVE CLASSICO. Top: Le Rive (GARGANEGA), Massifitti (TREBBIANO di Soave), Soave Classico (and Monte Carbonare). I Luoghi (The Places) project (Garganega).

Südtirol T-AA German name for ALTO ADIGE.

Superiore Wine with more ageing than normal DOC and 0.5–1% more alc. May indicate a restricted production zone, eg. ROSSO PICENO Superiore.

Super Tuscan Tus Wines of high quality and price developed in 70s/80s to get around silly laws then prevailing. Now, esp with Gran Selezione on up, scarcely relevant. Wines still generally considered in Super Tuscan category, strictly unofficially: BERTINGA, Ca' Marcanda, Flaccianello, Guado al Tasso, Messorio, ORNELLAIA, Redigaffi, SASSICAIA, SOLAIA, TIGNANELLO.

Tappero Merlo Domenico Pie ★★★ Roots in the past, eyes to the future and Erbaluce grape as life partner. Top: Acini Perduti (80/20% rare MALVASIA Moscata/Erbaluce), ERBALUCE DI CALUSO (Cuvée des Paladins, Kin). Also v.gd: Bohemien (PASSITO).

Tasca d'Almerita Si ★★★ New generation runs historic TENUTE. Top: (r) Regaleali (NERO D'AVOLA-based *Riserva del Conte*); (w) CHARD VIGNA San Francesco, Nozze d'Oro. Also v.gd: Capofaro (MALVASIA delle Lipari – Didyme, Vigna di Paola), Sallier de la Tour (SYRAH La Monaca), Tascante (ETNA r – Contrada Rampante, Contrada Sciaranuova Vigna Vecchia), Whitaker (GRILLO Mozia).

Taurasi Cam ★★★ DOCG 12 13 15 16 19 20 21' The 1st DOCG in S Italy. Best is AGLIANICO of CAM. None so potentially *complex, demanding, ultimately rewarding*. With 17 communes, four subzones: nw, w, Taurasi, s. Top: Contrade di Taurasi, Guastaferro (and RISERVA VV Primum), MASTROBERARDINO, QUINTODECIMO, SALVATORE MOLETTIERI. Also v.gd: BENITO FERRARA, COLLI DI LAPIO, Contrada Vini, Di Prisco, Fratelli Urciuolo, I FAVATI, Perillo, Pietracupa, Rocca del Principe, Tecce, Terredora.

Tavignano, Tenuta di Mar ★★★ Organic. One of best VERDICCHIO DEI CASTELLI DI JESI. Top: Misco (and RISERVA), new Dosaggio Zero (sp). Also v.gd: Villa Torre.

Tedeschi Ven ★★★ Bevy of v. fine VALPOLICELLA, AMARONE. Best: Amarones Capitel Monte Olmi, La Fabriseria, Maternigo; RECIOTO Capitel Monte Fontana. Also v.gd: Valpolicella La Fabriseria, Amarone Marne 180.

Tenuta An agricultural holding (*see* under name – eg. SAN GUIDO, TENUTA).

Terenzuola Lig, Tus ★★★ Passionate, talented Ivan Giuliani makes some of best wines in Cinque Terre, COLLI DI LUNI. Top: Colli di Luni-VERMENTINO (Fosso di Corsano, I Pini di Corsano), rare Vermentino Nero (r). Also v.gd: Cinque Terre Bianco, Sciacchetrà.

Terlano, Cantina di T-AA ★★★★ High-quality co-op, benchmark PINOT BL. Outstanding LAGREIN RISERVA Porphyr, Pinot Bl Riserva Vorberg, Primo *Terlaner I* Grande Cuvée (Pinot Bl/SAUV BL/CHARD), *Rarity* (w special editions, aged min 10 yrs on lees), Sauv Bl Quarz, Terlaner Cuvée Riserva Nova Domus. Also v.gd: GEWURZ Lunare, iconic Terlaner (Pinot Bl/Sauv Bl/Chard).

Got €1m to spare? You could buy a hectare of Brunello di Montalcino. Just the one.

Teroldego Rotaliano T-AA ★★→★★★ DOC Trentino's best local grape makes seriously tasty wine on flat Campo Rotaliano. Top: *Foradori*. Also gd: Cipriano Fedrizzi (Due Vigneti), Dorigati (Diedri), Mezzacorona (Musivum, Nos).

Terra Moretti Lom, Sar, Tus ★★★→★★★★ Three regions, six estates owned by Moretti family. In FRANCIACORTA: Bellavista with new chef de cave Richard Geoffroy, ex-Dom Pérignon (top Pas Operé, Vittorio Moretti; v.gd new Alma Assemblage 1, Teatro alla Scala Brut), Contadi Castaldi (new Pinot Nero RISERVA

> **Valpolicella: the best**
> Time to take gd VALPOLICELLA more seriously. AMARONE DELLA VALPOLICELLA
> and RECIOTO DELLA VALPOLICELLA are now DOCG, while RIPASSO has new
> rules. Following producers make gd to great (★) wine: Allegrini, Begali,
> Bertani, BOLLA, Boscaini, ★ Brigaldara, BRUNELLI, ★ BUSSOLA, Ca' la
> Bianca, ★ CA' LA BIONDA, Ca' Rugate, Campagnola, CANTINA Valpolicella,
> Castellani, Corteforte, Corte Sant'Alda, CS Valpantena, ★ DAL FORNO,
> ★ GUERRIERI RIZZARDI, Le Ragose, Le Salette, ★ MASI, ★ Mazzi, MONTE DEL
> FRÀ, Nicolis, ★ PRÀ, ★ QUINTARELLI, ★ Roccolo Grassi, Secondo Marco,
> ★ Serego Alighieri, ★ SPERI, ★ Stefano Accordini, ★ TEDESCHI, ★ TOMMASI,
> Valentina Cubi, Venturini, ★ Viviani, ZENATO, Zeni.

2017, Zéro). In SAR: Sella & Mosca (top r CAB SAUV Marchese di Villamarina,
Tanca Farrà, CANNONAU Mustazzo; top w Torbato Terre Bianche Cuvée 161,
VERMENTINO DI GALLURA Monte Oro; v.gd new Tintas range, Vermentino and
Cannonau). In TUS: Acquagiusta La Baiola, Petra (Petra, Quercegobbe), Teruzzi
(VERNACCIA DI SAN GIMIGNANOS Isola Bianca, RISERVA Sant'Elena).

Terre Nere, Tenuta delle Si ★★★★ Marc de Grazia shows great wine can be made from
NERELLO and CARRICANTE, on coveted n side of Mt Etna. Top: Cuvée delle Vigne
Niche, Guardiola and pre-phylloxera La VIGNA di Don Peppino. Le Vigne di Eli
v.gd. Look for new ER Bocca d'Orzo (monopole) and EB Montalto.

Teularju Sar ★★★ Family estate, dedicated to CANNONAU and its ancient biotypes.
Top: crus (*ghiradas*) Cara'Gonare, Ocruarana.

Tiberio Ab ★★★★ Outstanding TREBBIANO D'ABRUZZO Fonte Canale (60-yr-old vines),
one of Italy's best whites; MONTEPULCIANO D'ABRUZZO single-vyds Archivio, Colle
Vota; CERASUOLO D'ABRUZZO (one of Italy's best ROSATOS); PECORINO (also new
single-vyd Quarmarì).

Tiefenbrunner T-AA ★★★→★★★★ Christof T runs one of most historical estates
in Turmhof Castle in S ALTO ADIGE. Wide range of mtn-fresh white and
well-defined red varietals, esp 1000m (3281ft)-high MÜLLER-T *Feldmarschall*,
one of Italy's best whites, now also late-harvest. Top VIGNA range: CHARD Au,
SAUV BL Rachtl, CAB SAUV Toren. Linticlarus range v.gd: Chard (esp new RISERVA),
LAGREIN, PINOT N.

Tignanello Tus ★★★ 16' 17 19 20 21 ANTINORI's dense SANGIOVESE/CAB SAUV blend.

Tommasi Ven ★★★ Now 4th generation, elegant wines. Top: AMARONE (RISERVA
Ca' Florian, iconic De Buris), LUGANA Riserva Le Fornaci, VALPOLICELLA Rafael.
Classic. Other estates in Bas (Paternoster), OLTREPÒ PAVESE (TENUTA Caseo), PUG
(Masseria Surani), Ven (Filodora).

Torgiano Umb ★★ DOC ★★→★★★ RISERVA DOCG 13 15 16 19' 20 21 Range of
gd to excellent reds, esp LUNGAROTTI *Vigna Monticchio* Rubesco RISERVA, keeps
many yrs.

Torrette VdA ★→★★★ DOC Blend based on Petit Rouge and other local varieties.
Best: Torrette Superieur. Also gd: Anselmet, D&D, DI BARRÒ, Didier Gerbelle,
FEUDO DI SAN MAURIZIO, GROSJEAN, LES CRETES, LO TRIOLET, OTTIN.

Traerte Cam ★★★ Raffaele Troise, v. talented maker of Torama, one of Italy's best
whites (100% Coda di Volpe Bianca). Top: GRECO DI TUFO Tornante, GRECO Fuori
Limite Le Vecchie Vigne, FIANO DI AVELLINO Aipierti.

Tramin, Cantina T-AA ★★★ Quality co-op with benchmark GEWURZ. Outstanding
Epokale, Nussbaumer, Terminum, (CHARD) Troy, (PINOT GR) Unterebner. Best:
Selezioni range the highest expression.

Travaglini Pie ★★★ Solid producer of GATTINARA. Best: RISERVA, Tre Vigne. Also v.gd:
Coste della Sesia, Gattinara, METODO CLASSICO Nebolé (NEBBIOLO).

Trebbiano d'Abruzzo Ab ★→★★★★ DOC DYA Generally crisp, simple, but TIBERIO'S

(Fonte Canale) and VALENTINI's are *two of Italy's greatest* whites. Also v.gd: Talamonti, Valle Reale. And gd: Ciavolich, Cingilia, Marramiero.

Trediberri Pie ★★★ Dynamic estate. Top: BAROLO Rocche dell'Annunziata (value). Also v.gd: BARBERA D'ALBA, Barolo Berri, DOGLIANI, LANGHE NEBBIOLO.

Trento T-AA ★★→★★★★ DOC High-quality METODO CLASSICO fizz. Top: ABATE NERO, FERRARI, MASO MARTIS, SAN LEONARDO. Also v.gd: Cembra (Oro Rosso), Cesarini SFORZA, Letrari.

Trinoro, Tenuta di Tus ★★★★ Individualist TUS red estate, pioneer in DOC Val d'Orcia. Heavy accent on Bx grapes in flagship TENUTA di Trinoro, also in Camagi, Magnacosta, Palazzi, Tenagli. *See also* VINI FRANCHETTI (ETNA).

Tua Rita Tus ★★★★ As new BOLGHERI in 90s, 1st producer of possibly Italy's greatest MERLOT in Redigaffi (19, 25th anniversary); outstanding Bx-blend *Giusto di Notri*, SYRAHS Keir (amphora), Per Sempre. Also owns POGGIO ARGENTIERA in Maremma (best: Capatosta, MORELLINO DI SCANSANO).

Tuscany / Toscana Home of world's top SANGIOVESE. CHIANTI CLASSICO, BRUNELLO DI MONTALCINO, RÙFINA best, but BOLGHERI just as gd and world-class for international grapes (CAB FR, MERLOT), but SASSICAIA (CAB SAUV) most famous.

Uberti Lom ★★★→★★★★ Historic estate, excellent interpreter of FRANCIACORTA's terroir. Outstanding: Comarì del Salem, Dequinque (blend of 15 yrs), Quinque (blend of 5 yrs). Also v.gd: Dosaggio Zero Sublimis RISERVA, Francesco I.

Vajra, GD Pie ★★★→★★★★★ Leading BAROLO producer in Vergne. Top: Bricco delle Viole, LANGHE FREISA Kyè, both outstanding. Also gd: Langhe RIES, Barolos (Coste di Rose, Ravera), DOLCETTO Coste & Fossati, Serralunga's Baudana Barolos (Cerretta).

Valentini, Edoardo Ab ★★★★ Collectors seek CERASUOLO D'ABRUZZO, MONTEPULCIANO D'ABRUZZO, TREBBIANO D'ABRUZZO; among Italy's v. best. Age-worthy, trad.

Valle d'Aosta ★★→★★★ DOC Italy's smallest region makes some of its best reds/ whites, but hard to find. Soil of morainic origin (heterogeneous glacial deposits of gravel sands). Famous names: Arnad-Montjovet, Blanc de Morgex (w/sp from Prié Bl), Chambave (local biotype of MUSCAT), Donnas (NEBBIOLO-based), Nus MALVOISIE (with PINOT GR), Torrette (r mostly Petit Rouge). Lovely wines from (r) Cornalin, Mayolet, Premetta; (w) CHARD, PETITE ARVINE.

Valle Isarco T-AA ★★ DYA ALTO ADIGE DOC for seven Germanic varietal whites made along Isarco (Eisack) River, ne of Bolzano. Top: Abbazia di Novacella, Eisacktaler, KÖFERERHOF, Kuenhof, MANNI NÖSSING. Also gd: GEWURZ, MÜLLER-T, RIES, SILVANER.

Vallerosa Bonci Mar ★★★ Historic estate famous for its VERDICCHIO (pioneer of sp). Top: RISERVA Pietrone, San Michele, trad-method Caterina.

Valpolicella Ven ★→★★★★ DOC(G) Light, easy-going red (Valpol), medium-bodied to powerfully alc, rich, tannic (AMARONE) and super-sweet (RECIOTO). Popular RIPASSO, between Valpol and Amarone, but few noteworthy. (*See* box, opposite.)

Valpolicella Ripasso Ven ★★→★★★ DOC 13 15 16 18 19 20 21' In huge demand, so changes from 2016. Used to be only from VALPOLICELLA SUPERIORE re-fermented (only once) on RECIOTO or AMARONE grapeskins to make a more age-worthy wine. Now can blend 10% Amarone with standard Valpol and call it Ripasso. Best: Brigaldara, BUSSOLA, CA' LA BIONDA, PRÀ, SPERI, Tamburino Sardo, TEDESCHI, TOMMASI, ZENATO.

Valtellina Lom ★→★★★ DOC/DOCG Rare e-w valley, just s of the Swiss border. Soils are sandy-loamy. Home of CHIAVENNASCA. Best labelled Valtellina SUPERIORE (five subzones: Grumello, Inferno, Maroggia, Sassella, Valgella), *see* SFORZATO. Top: ArPePe (Grumello RISERVA Sant'Antonio, Inferno Fiamme Antiche, Nuova Regina, Sassella Rocce Rosse), Dirupi, FAY, Mamete Prevostini (Sassella Sommarovina).

Vecchio Samperi Si *See* MARCO DE BARTOLI.

Venissa Ven ★★★ Owned by BISOL family. Beautiful vyd on island of Mazzorbo in Venice lagoon. Top: Venissa (100% rare w Dorona). Also v.gd: Rosso Venissa (Bx blend). Unique wines.

Verdicchio dei Castelli di Jesi Mar ★★→★★★ Versatile white from nr Ancona on Adriatic; light and quaffable or sparkling or structured, complex, long-lived (esp RISERVA DOCG, min 2 yrs old), usually lighter and more floral than those of Matelica. Montecarotto more structured. Cupramontana more vibrant. Also CLASSICO. Best: *Bucci*, La Staffa, Marotti Campi, MIRIZZI, MONTECAPPONE, SARTARELLI, TENUTA DI TAVIGNANO, VALLEROSA BONCI. Also v.gd: Casalefarneto, CORONCINO, Garofoli Podium, PIEVALTA, Serra Fiorese), Edoardo Dottori (Kochlos, Nardì), FATTORIA SAN LORENZO, TENUTA dell'Ugolino, Vignamato.

Verdicchio di Matelica Mar ★★→★★★ Higher acidity level, but also more body, alc and intense minerality than wines of Jesi; so longer-lasting though less easy-drinking young. Lower-lying vyds grow on alluvial soils, while higher hillsides have complex soils of calcarenites, marl, limestone, gravel and conglomerates. RISERVA is likewise DOCG. Top: Belisario (Cambrugiano), Bisci, Borgo Paglianetto (Jera Riserva, Petrara, Vertis), Collestefano, LA MONACESCA.

Verduno Pie ★★★ DOC DYA Berry and herbal flavours. Top: ARNALDO RIVERA, Diego Morra, CASTELLO DI VERDUNO, FRATELLI ALESSANDRIA, GB BURLOTTO, GIANLUCA COLOMBO. Also v.gd: Cadia, PODERI EINAUDI, Reverdito.

Verduno, Castello di Pie ★★★ Husband-and-wife team, making v.gd terroir-driven BARBARESCOS Rabajà, Rabajà-Bas and BAROLOS Massara, Monvigliero (also RISERVA), VERDUNO Basadone.

Vermentino di Gallura Sar ★★★ DOCG More flinty and saline than VERMENTINO DI SARDEGNA. Different soils characterized by pink granite (rarity in Italy) with high acidity and minerality. Maybe best in Italy. Top: Cantina di Gallura (Canayli), Capichera (Santigaini, VT), CS del Vermentino (Funtanaliras), Masone Mannu (top Costarenas, Petrizza, Roccaìa), Mura (Sienda), Pala (Stellato), Paolo Depperu (Ruinas), SELLA & MOSCA (Monteoro), Surrau.

Vermentino di Sardegna Sar ★★ DOC DYA From anywhere on SAR; generally fruitier (less structured) and offer earlier, uncomplicated appeal compared to VERMENTINO DI GALLURA. Best: ARGIOLAS, Deiana, Mora e Memo, Quartomoro, *Santadi*, *Sella & Mosca*.

Vernaccia di Oristano Sar ★→★★★★ DOC Flor-affected wine, similar to light Sherry, a touch bitter, full-bodied. Delicious with bottarga. Must try. Top: CONTINI (*Antico Gregori*, Flor 22, RISERVA), Silvio Carta. Also v.gd: Fratelli Serra, Josto Puddu.

Vernaccia di San Gimignano Tus ★★→★★★ Better at entry level than RISERVA. Top: Fontaleoni (VIGNA Casanuova), Giovanni Panizzi, Guicciardini Strozzi/Fattoria di Cusona (1933), La Lastra, Sono Montenidoli (Fiore), Turizzi (Sant'Elena).

Versio, Francesco Pie ★★★ Young talented winemaker in BARBARESCO. Top: refined Barbaresco, DOGLIANI, LANGHE NEBBIOLO.

Vevey Albert, Maison VdA ★★★ From vyds at 1000m+ (3281ft), Vevey bros make some of best Blanc de Morgex et La Salle (Priè Bl). Blanc Flapi (PASSITO) v.gd.

Viarte, La FVG ★★→★★★ Organic estate of FRIULI COLLI ORIENTALI; v.gd terroir-driven FRIULANO, SCHIOPPETTINO di Prepotto, Tazzelenghe.

Viberti Pie ★★★ High-quality, classic BAROLO (Bricco delle Viole, La Volta, Monvigliero, San Pietro), RISERVAS; v.gd BARBERA D'ALBA, LANGHE NEBBIOLO.

Vie di Romans FVG ★★★★ Gianfranco Gallo has built up his father's ISONZO estate to top status. Outstanding: Climat range (six different CHARDS, from six different sites, for authentic terroir expression), Flors di Uis blend, Isonzo PINOT GR Dessimis, MALVASIA, SAUV BLS Piere, Vieris.

Vietti Pie ★★★★ Organic estate at Castiglione Falletto owned by Krause Group but still run by Luca Currado and Mario Cordero. Characterful. Textbook BAROLOS: Brunate, Cerequio, Lazzarito, Monvigliero, Ravera, Rocche di Castiglione, Villero RISERVA. Also v.gd: BARBERA D'ALBA, BARBERA D'ASTI, BARBARESCO, DERTHONA.

Vigna (or vigneto) A single vyd, generally indicating superior quality.

Vigneri, I Si ★★★★ Consortium of growers, also ETNA estate within that consortium, run by Salvo Foti, greatest expert on NERELLO MASCALESE and all Etna varieties. Consortium focus on bush-trained vines, native grape varieties and respect for the land. Outstanding: Etna Bianco SUPERIORE (Palmento Caselle, VIGNA di Milo), Etna Rosso (Vinupetra, Viti Centenarie). Also v.gd Aurora (w), I Vigneri (r), Vinudilice (rosé).

Villa Lom ★★★ Owned by Bianchi family, in small medieval hamlet (C15) in FRANCIACORTA. Consistent. Best sparkling: Diamant Pas Dosè, Emozione Brut Millesimato and RISERVA, Selezione Riserva.

Villa Crespia Lom ★★★ Family estate in FRANCIACORTA, organic. Top: Brut Millè RISERVA, Dosaggio Zero Numero Zero, Riserva del Gelso. Also v.gd: Brut Millè.

Villa Russiz FVG ★★★ Historic estate for DOC COLLIO, v.gd SAUV BL and MERLOT (esp de la Tour selections), CHARD, FRIULANO, PINOTS BL/GR.

Vino Nobile di Montepulciano Tus ★★→★★★★ 15 16 17 18 19 20 21 The 1st Italian DOCG (1980). Prugnolo Gentile (SANGIOVESE)-based, from TUS town MONTEPULCIANO (distinct from grape). Recent focus on single vyds. Complex, long-lasting Sangiovese expression; often tough, drying tannins. Top: AVIGNONESI, Boscarelli (Costa Grande, Nocio, RISERVA Sotto Casa), Dei (Bossona, cru Madonna della Querce), La Braccesca, Poliziano, Salcheto. Also gd: Bindella, Fattoria del Cerro, Fattoria della Talosa, Montemercurio, Valdipiatta. Riserva after 3 yrs.

Vin Santo / Vinsanto / Vino Santo T-AA, Tus ★★→★★★★ DOC Sweet PASSITO, usually TREBBIANO, MALVASIA and/or SANGIOVESE in TUS (Vin Santo), Nosiola in Trentino (Vino Santo). Versions from TUS extremely variable, anything from off-dry and Sherry-like to sweet and v. rich. May spend 3–10 unracked yrs in small barrels called *caratelli*. *Avignonesi's is legendary*; plus CAPEZZANA, FELSINA, FRASCOLE, ISOLE E OLENA, Rocca di Montegrossi, SAN GIUSTO A RENTENNANO, SELVAPIANA, Villa Sant'Anna, Villa di Vetrice. *See also* OCCHIO DI PERNICE.

Volpaia, Castello di Tus ★★→★★★★ Top CHIANTI CLASSICO at Radda, organic. Best: Balifico (SANGIOVESE/CAB SAUV), Chianti Classico RISERVA, Gran Selezione Coltassala (Sangiovese/Mammolo).

Walch, Elena T-AA ★★★→★★★★ Sisters Karoline and Julia carry on winery founded by mother with passion and talent. Top: Kastelaz and Ringberg vyds, Grande Cuvée (Beyond the Clouds, Kermesse), PINOT N Res Aton.

Zenato Ven ★★★ Garda wines: v. reliable, inspired. Also AMARONE, LUGANA, SOAVE, VALPOLICELLA. Look for labels RISERVA Sergio Zenato.

What do the initials mean?

DOC (denominazione di origine controllata) controlled denomination of origin, cf. AOP in France.

DOCG (denominazione di origine controllata e garantita) "G" = "guaranteed". Italy's highest quality designation. Guarantee? It's still caveat emptor.

IGT (indicazione geografica tipica) geographic indication of type. Broader and more vague than DOC, cf. IGP in France.

DOP / IGP (denominazione di origine protetta / indicazione geografica protetta) "P" = "protected". The EU's DOP/IGP trump Italy's DOC/IGT.

MGA (menzione geografica aggiuntiva) or UGA (unità geografiche aggiuntiva), eg. subzones, cf. crus in France.

Germany

Abbreviations used in the text:

Bad	Baden
Frank	Franken
Hess	Hessische Bergstrasse
M-M	Mittelmosel
M Rh	Mittelrhein
Mos	Mosel
Na	Nahe
Pfz	Pfalz
Rhg	Rheingau
Rhh	Rheinhessen
Sa-Un	Saale-Unstrut
Sachs	Sachsen
Würt	Württemberg

Hamburg

Bremen

Elbe

Berlin

Hanover

Rhein

Leipzig

Weser

SAALE-UNSTRUT

SACHSEN

Erfurt

Dresden

Bonn

AHR **MITTELRHEIN**

Koblenz

MOSEL- **RHEINGAU**
SAAR-RUWER

Frankfurt

RHEINHESSEN

FRANKEN

Trier

Mannheim

Würzburg

NAHE

HESSISCHE
BERGSTRASSE

PFALZ

Nürnberg

WÜRTTEMBERG

Main

Stuttgart

Baden-Baden

Danube

BADEN

München

Freiburg

Bodensee

More heavily shaded
areas are the wine-
growing regions.

It's considered a truism that German wine is benefiting from global warming. But the downsides of climate change are also making themselves felt: in 2021, the Ahr Valley experienced a terrible flood that killed 135 people and destroyed villages and cellars throughout the valley. 2023 brought many regions the worst mildew infections in decades. In 2024, the vines were hit hard by frost after a mild winter and early bud-burst. Numerous estates lost half their crop or more. Of course, there have always been rain and frost, but the suddenness with which weather phenomena change and the extremes encountered have reached a new level. In 2024, the effects were so existential that the VDP, which sets the tone in quality wine-growing, allowed its members to leave the grape eagle – the association's insignia – on the capsule even for wines made from bought-in grapes, provided the grapes came from other VDP growers. But where there are risks, there are also opportunities: Germany has never experienced a Pinot Noir vintage like 2022. The growing season was warm and dry, but the wines have an extra kick of freshness that is almost inexplicable from a year like this. Don't miss out on these wines. They will delight you in three, five and probably even 20 years' time.

Recent vintages

Baden, Franken, Württemberg
Germany's s regions produce wines capable of ageing too: white and red Pinots from Bad, Frank Silvaner, and Ries, Pinot N, Lemberger from Würt improve for 5–10 yrs if from gd producers.

2024 No frost in S Bad, but almost everywhere else. Challenging (mildew). Dense, aromatic wines, but low quantities.
2023 Rollercoaster season with happy end, v.gd whites.
2022 Hot, dry: Pinot N of class and surprising freshness, whites more variable.
2021 Cool summer with plenty of rain. Exceptional whites, middling reds.
2020 Remarkable Frank Silvaner; v.gd Bad, Würt reds where drought hadn't hit too hard.
Earlier fine vintages: 19 16 15 12 10 (Pinot N) 07 05 97 90.

Mosel, Saar, Ruwer
Don't drink them too young. Certainly, Mosels are delicious v. soon after bottling, but to enjoy their max complexity, allow Grosses Gewächs (GG) a min of 3 yrs, Kabinett 3–5 yrs, Spätlese 5–7 yrs, Auslese 7–10 yrs.

2024 Frost cut quantity (up to 80%), esp Saar, Ruwer; overall sound quality.
2023 Conditions improved just in time and lasted: mid-weight wines of fine balance.
2022 Another dry, hot summer. Sept rain complicated harvest.
2021 Mildew, rain, harvest into Nov, lighter wines, outstanding freshness and balance.
2020 3rd yr running of drought, gd quality, quantity.
2019 Low quantity (Mos -25%, Ruwer -40%: frost), but textbook raciness.
Earlier fine vintages: 18 15 12 11 09 08 07 05 04 03 01 99 97 95 94 93 90 89 88 76 71 69 64 59 53 49 45 37 34 21.

Rheingau, Nahe, Pfalz, Ahr, Rheinhessen, Mittelrhein
Rhg tends to be longest-lived of all German regions, improving for 15 yrs or more, but best Ries from Rhh, Na and Pfz can last as long – and this applies not only to Spätlese and Auslese; GGs undoubtedly have potential to age for 10 yrs+ too. The same holds for Ahr V reds.

2024 Devastating frost in Na, Ahr, parts of M Rh, Rhg. Plus mildew: mixed bag.
2023 Spring wet, summer dry, hail too (Rhh). Sept wet, warm; Oct fine. Ries better than Pinot N, but tight selection crucial.
2022 Hot, dry; whites mixed results. Cool autumn nights. Outstanding Pinot N.
2021 Classical yr like those of 80s, gd acidity, moderate alc, intense flavours.
2019 Drought, heatwaves, rain. Excellent Ries with gd acidity.
2018 Record summer, powerful wines. Growers allowed to acidify.
2017 Roter Hang and Mittelhaardt outstanding: freshness with extract.
2016 Quality and quantity mixed.
2015 Hot, dry summer; Rhg excellent, both dry and nobly sweet.
Earlier fine vintages: 12 11 09 08 05 03 02 01 99 98 97 96 93 90 83 76 71 69 67 64 59 53 49 45 37 34 21.

Acham-Magin Pfz ★★★ Organic family estate at FORST; vines in Kirchenstück, Jesuitengarten, Pechstein; crisp, age-worthy. Restaurant too, continuously open since 1712.

Adams, Simone Rhh ★★★ A PhD oenologist putting emphasis on vibrant freshness of INGELHEIM's calcareous soils. Best: single-vyds Auf dem Haun and Pares.

Adelmann, Graf Würt ★★→★★★ Estate (est 1297) kept young by Count Felix A, wide range: lush Süssmund RIES, tight Oberer Berg LEMBERGER, finely tuned red cuvées, skin-fermented Ries Neben Frank.

Adeneuer, JJ Ahr ★★★ Prime producer, best usually Gärkammer, from enclave in famous Kräuterberg, planted with ancient Kastenholz clone of PINOT N.

Ahr Small river valley s of Bonn; PINOT N of outstanding complexity from slate. Terrible flood in July 2021 destroyed buildings and equipment, but not the steep slopes – 22 likely best vintage ever produced. Best: ADENEUER, BERTRAM-BALTES, Brogsitter, BURGGARTEN, DEUTZERHOF, KREUZBERG, KRIECHEL, MEYER-NÄKEL, NELLES, Riske, SCHUMACHER, SERMANN, STODDEN. Also gd co-ops: Dagernova, Mayschoss-Altenahr.

Aldinger, Gerhard Würt ★★★→★★★★ Outstanding family estate at Fellbach nr Stuttgart. Reliable (RIES, LEMBERGER, PINOT N), and inventive: Brut Nature SEKT, TROLLINGER ALTE REBEN Blanc de Noirs, GJA (Bx blend), magnificent Mönchberg Ries EISWEIN 21.

Alte Reben Old vines. But no min age.

Amtliche Prüfungsnummer (APNr) Official test number for quality wine. Useful for discerning different lots of AUSLESE a producer has made from the same vyd.

Assmannshausen Rhg ★★→★★★★ Steep Höllenberg (45 ha) makes delicate *Spätburgunder* (age potential 50 yrs+). Growers: Allendorf, Berg, BISCHÖFLICHES WEINGUT RÜDESHEIM, CHAT SAUVAGE, HESSISCHE STAATSWEINGÜTER, KESSELER, König, KRONE, KÜNSTLER, SOLVEIGS, SAALWÄCHTER.

Aust, Karl Friedrich Sachs ★★★ Fine family estate (brilliant TRAMINER, PINOT N) nr Dresden, brand-new winery at foot of steep, terraced Goldener Wagen vyd.

Ayl Mos ★→★★★ All vyds known since 1971 by name of historically best site: Kupp. Growers: BISCHÖFLICHE WEINGÜTER TRIER, *Lauer*, Vols, ZILLIKEN.

Bacharach M Rh ★→★★★ Small, idyllic Rhine-side town; centre of M RH RIES. Growers: BAER, JOST, KAUER, RATZENBERGER.

Baden Huge region in sw and former Grand Duchy, its 15,000 ha stretch over 300 km. Nine districts with v. different conditions, eg. BODENSEE, KAISERSTUHL, MARKGRÄFLERLAND, ORTENAU.

Baer M Rh ★★→★★★ Former Bastian estate, taken over and enlarged by Baer family (wine merchants and pharmacists), vyds farmed by hand, concentrated, taut wines to age (1st vintage 21). Watch.

Barth, Wein- und Sektgut Rhg ★★→★★★ Family estate at HATTENHEIM, 22 ha; specializes in finely chiselled RIES SEKT from single vyds (Hassel, Schützenhaus).

Bassermann-Jordan Pfz ★★★ Famous historic estate producing powerful RIES from DEIDESHEIM and FORST: trad GGS; experimental vinifications (Ries Ancestrale, amphora CAB SAUV).

Battenfeld-Spanier Rhh ★★★→★★★★ Passionate HO Spanier (*see also* KÜHLING-GILLOT) is leading grower in calcareous sites at Hohen-Sülzen, Mölsheim and ZELLERTAL (auction RIES about to get cultish), bio. Brilliant Brut Nature SEKT.

Becker, Friedrich Pfz ★★★★ Age-worthy, terroir-driven PINOT N (Heydenreich, Kammerberg, Sankt Paul) from SÜDPFALZ. Some vyds actually lie across border in Alsace.

Becker, JB Rhg ★★→★★★ Delightfully old-fashioned, cask-aged (and long-lived) dry RIES, SPÄTBURGUNDER at Walluf and Martinsthal. Mature vintages (back to 90s) great value.

Bercher Bad ★★★ KAISERSTUHL family estate, v. reliable from ORTSWEIN up to GG, long experience in barrique ageing of PINOTS BL/GR/N.

Bergdolt Pfz ★★★ Organic estate at Duttweiler, known for food-friendly WEISSBURGUNDER GG Mandelberg, mineral RIES, taut SPÄTBURGUNDER. Stunning SEKT (Brut Nature Fluxus).

Bergweiler-Prüm Mos ★★★ Erni LOOSEN's grandfather was Zacharias Bergweiler, who married two daughters of the Prüm family in succession. The old brand (and according cellar at WEHLEN) is now used for wines exclusively sold through the Place de Bx (*see* France); 1st vintage, 18, marketed in 2024 (SONNENUHR dr ALTE REBEN, KABINETT, AUSLESE). Vines 130 yr old, no machines in vyd or cellar, grass mowed by hand, basket press from 1910. Fairly priced.

Bernhart Pfz ★★★ Gerd B and son Marius at Schweigen, S PFZ: dense, straight-forward, classically structured PINOT varieties (r/w).

Bernkastel M-M ★→★★★★ Centre of M-M, misrepresented by Kurfürstlay GROSSLAGE (avoid!). Rightly famous sites: Alte Badstube am Doctorberg, Badstube, DOCTOR, Graben, Johannisbrünnchen, Lay.

Bernkasteler Ring Mos One of two MOS growers' associations organizing an auction every Sept, eg. MOLITOR, THANISCH Erben Müller-Burggraef.

Bertram-Baltes Ahr ★★★ Shooting stars in AHR, engaged in regenerative viticulture (eg. no more plastic in vyd or cellar; cover crops and sheep). Early picking, moderate use of new oak, and ageing on lees bring fresh, racy, almost slim SPÄTBURGUNDER from prime vyds.

Bischel Rhh ★★★ VDP family estate in Appenheim, outstanding RIES GGS Heerkretz, Hundertgulden 19' 21' 23, Scharlachberg.

Bischöfliches Weingut Rüdesheim Rhg ★★★ Not to be confused with BISCHÖFLICHE WEINGÜTER TRIER: 9 ha of best sites in ASSMANNSHAUSEN, RÜDESHEIM. Age-worthy, dense *Pinot N.* (Cellarmaster Peter Perabo vinified legendary vintages at KRONE before.) Brilliant 22 SPÄTBURGUNDER, esp RÜDESHEIM S.

Bischöfliche Weingüter Trier Mos ★★ 130 ha of potentially 1st-class historic donations. Not v. reliable; do not buy without prior tasting.

Bocksbeutel Frank Belly-shaped bottle dating back to C18, today only permitted in FRANK and village of Neuweier, BAD.

Bodensee Bad Idyllic district of S BAD and on (particularly dynamic) Bavarian shore of Lake Constance, at altitude: 400–580m (1312–1903ft). Dry, elegant MÜLLER-T, light, firm SPÄTBURGUNDER.

Böhme & Töchter Sa-Un ★★→★★★ Rising star in e, top vyds at Freyburg (Unstrut) and purist winemaking shape expressive PINOTS (BL/GR/N), culinary CHARD, mineral RIES.

Boppard M Rh ★→★★★ Wine town of M RH with GROSSE LAGE Hamm, an amphitheatre of vines. Growers: Heilig Grab, Lorenz, M Müller, Perll, WEINGART. Unbeatable *value*.

Brauneberg M-M ★★★→★★★★ Excellent full RIES from Juffer and Juffer-Sonnenuhr vyds. Growers: *F Haag*, KESSELSTATT, M Conrad, MF RICHTER, Paulinshof, Sankt Nikolaus Hospital, SCHLOSS LIESER, THANISCH, *W Haag*.

Rent a Doctor

Of the 3.2 ha of the famous BERNKASTELER DOCTOR vyd, two plots (totalling 0.26 ha) belong to the local Heilgen Geist Foundation. The charitable organization does not cultivate the land itself, but auctions the lease for 9 yrs. In Nov 2024, the land was auctioned off for use until 2033. One of the plots went for €16/m², the other for €19/m². That's around €50,000/yr for the charity – and two or three small casks of unique RIES for wine-lovers.

Bremer Ratskeller Town-hall cellar in N Germany's commercial town of Bremen, founded in 1405, UNESCO World Heritage Site. Oldest wine is a barrel of 1653 RÜDESHEIMER Apostelwein.

Breuer Rhg ★★★→★★★★ Exquisite RIES from RAUENTHAL, RÜDESHEIM and LORCH. Nonnenberg transforms austerity into age-worthiness, Berg Schlossberg 90' 93' 96' 97' 02' 08' 12' 13' 14 15' 16 17' 18 19 20 21' has depth at 12% alc, Pfaffenwies full of floral elegance.

Buhl, Reichsrat von Pfz ★★★ Historic PFZ estate at DEIDESHEIM. After several changes in cellar, unstable – but signs of things turning round.

Bürgerspital zum Heiligen Geist Frank ★★★→★★★★ Ancient charitable estate, founded 1316. Long-time director Robert Haller has retired, but continuity for whites trad-made from best sites in/around WÜRZBURG, eg. SILVANER GG from monopole Stein-Harfe 15' 16' 17' 18' 19' 20' 21' 22 23', RIES Randersacker Pfülben and STEIN-BERG.

Burggarten Ahr ★★★ PINOT N from best sites in lower AHR, tight, aromatic (esp Alte Lay, Burggarten, Kräuterberg). Family runs hotel at Heppingen.

Bürklin-Wolf, Dr. Pfz ★★★→★★★★ Finely chiselled RIES full of finesse from 30 ha of best MITTELHAARDT vyds, incl FORST (Jesuitengarten, Kirchenstück, Pechstein), Ruppertsberg (Gaisböhl), WACHENHEIM (Rechbächel); bio. Forerunner of VDP classifcation (1994).

Busch, Clemens Mos ★★★★ Steep Pündericher Marienburg farmed by hand, bio. Seven GGs from different parcels, eg. Felserrasse (mineral, deep), Raffes (power, balance), Rothenpfad (silky, balsamic). Also Res range (2 yrs barrel ageing). Son Johannes taken over.

Castell'sches Fürstliches Domänenamt Frank ★★★ Ferdinand Fürst zu Castell vigorously increases quality: SILVANER GG Schlossberg 12 14 15' 16 17' 18 19', now sold only 5 yrs after harvest, ERSTE LAGE Silvaners outstanding value.

Chat Sauvage Rhg ★★★→★★★★ Dense PINOT N from ASSMANNSHAUSEN, JOHANNISBERG, LORCH, RÜDESHEIM; crisp CHARD. And no RIES!

Christmann Pfz ★★★→★★★★ VDP President Steffen C, bio pioneer, now joined by daughter Sophie, PINOT N expert. Estate owns only classified vyds. Also CHRISTMANN & KAUFFMANN.

Christmann & Kauffmann Pfz ★★★ SEKT estate, est 2019 by Sophie and Steffen C and ex-Bollinger cellarmaster (*see* France) Mathieu K. Triple-digit codes on labels: 101 = RIES-based, 1st disgorgement; 203 = PINOTS N/BL/CHARD-based, 3rd disgorgement.

Clüsserath, Ansgar Mos ★★★ Tense TRITTENHEIMER Apotheke RIES from Eva Clüsserath-WITTMANN (married to Philipp W); KABINETTS delicious.

Corvers-Kauter Rhg ★★★ Organic estate at Mittelheim, 37 ha, textbook dry RIES from MARCOBRUNN, RAUENTHAL (Baiken), RÜDESHEIM, occasionally also TBA; PINOT N from ASSMANNSHAUSEN.

Crusius, Dr. Na ★★★ Family estate at TRAISEN. Young Rebecca C produced outstanding 23: Bastei, Kupfergrube RIES GGS, stylish PINOT BL/CHARD blend, magnificent Ries TBAS (Felsenberg, Kupfergrube).

Dautel Würt ★★→★★★★★ Christian D produces CHARD, PINOTS BL/N, LEMBERGER, in Burgundian spirit. Breathtaking S 22 Pinot Bl: flinty, with distinctive minerality.

Deidesheim Pfz ★★→★★★★ Centre of MITTELHAARDT (also economically). Best: Grainhübel, Hohenmorgen, Kalkofen, Langenmorgen. Top: BASSERMANN-JORDAN, Biffar, BUHL, BÜRKLIN-WOLF, CHRISTMANN, Fusser, MARGARETHENHOF, MOSBACHER, SECKINGER, Siben, Stern, VON WINNING; gd co-op.

Deutzerhof Ahr ★★★ Quality pioneer in AHR in 90s, now top again; GGS (Eck, Mönchberg), Res range (Grand Duc). Sensational 22 FRÜHBURGUNDERS (Herrenberg, Mönchberg).

Germany's quality levels

The official range of qualities and styles in ascending order is (take a deep breath):

1 **Wein** Formerly known as Tafelwein. Light wine of no specified character, mostly sweetish.

2 **ggA (geschützte geographische Angabe)** or protected geographical indication, formerly known as LANDWEIN. Dryish Wein with some regional style. Mostly a label to avoid, but some thoughtful estates use the Landwein designation to bypass official constraints.

3 **gU (geschützte Ursprungsbezeichnung)** or protected designation of origin. Replacing QUALITÄTSWEIN. Up to now, only six small-scale appellations in the narrower sense of the word approved by the EU.

4 **Qualitätswein** Dry or sweetish wine with sugar added before fermentation to increase its strength, but tested for quality and with distinct local and grape character. Don't despair.

5 **Kabinett** Lightest of German wines, dry/dryish, unsugared, subtle yet long-lived, production complicated by climate change: altitude vyds needed, and early, speedy picking.

6 **Spätlese** Late-harvest. One level riper and sweeter than KABINETT. Needs to be aged for 5 yrs at least. Dry SPÄTLESE (or what could be considered as such) is today mostly sold under Qualitätswein designation (even if not sugared).

7 **Auslese** Wines from selective picking of super-ripe bunches affected by noble rot (*Edelfäule*). Unctuous, but – trad – elegant rather than super-concentrated; 99% are sweet, but specialists (JB BECKER, Koehler-Ruprecht) show Auslese TROCKEN can be elegant too.

8 **Beerenauslese (BA)** Luscious sweet wine from exceptionally ripe, individually selected berries concentrated by noble rot.

9 **Eiswein** Made from frozen grapes with the ice (ie. water content) discarded, thus v. concentrated: of BA ripeness or more. Outstanding Eiswein vintages: 98 02 04 08. Less and less produced in past decade: climate change is Eiswein's enemy.

10 **Trockenbeerenauslese (TBA)** Sweetest, most expensive category of German wine, extremely rare, viscous and concentrated, with dried-fruit flavours. Made from selected dried-out berries affected by noble rot (botrytis). Half-bottles a gd idea.

Diel, Schlossgut Na ★★★→★★★★ Caroline D reliably produces exquisite *GG Ries*, best usually Burgberg. Magnificent SPÄTLESEN, serious *Sekt* Cuvée Mo, Goldloch RIES.

Doctor M-M Emblematic steep vyd at BERNKASTEL, place where TBA was invented 1921 by THANISCH. RIES of unique balsamic flavours from 3.2 ha, five owners: both Thanisch estates, WEGELER (1.1 ha), Lauerburg and local Heiligen Geist charity (0.26 ha, leased until 2033 to MOLITOR, SCHLOSS LIESER).

Dolde, Helmut Würt ★★→★★★ Some of Germany's highest vyds (up to 530m/1739ft), meticulously managed by retired grammar-school teacher. Stunning SILVANERS, delicate and age-worthy SPÄTBURGUNDER, serious pét-nat.

Dönnhoff Na ★★★★ Outstanding in every respect: solid basic wines, excellent GGS (balance, ageing potential), and fruity and nobly sweet wines of great distinction. In 24, many vyds affected by frost.

Dörflinger Bad ★★★ Famous for single-vyd GUTEDELS, pleasant young and age well; CHARD, PINOT N v.gd too.

Egon Müller zu Scharzhof Mos ★★★★ 59 71 83 90 01 03 15 18 19 20 21 22 23 Legendary SAAR family estate at WILTINGEN, treasury of old vines. Racy

SCHARZHOFBERGER RIES among world's greatest: sublime, vibrant, immortal. *Kabinetts* feather-light, long-lived (but meanwhile costly).

Einzellage Individual vyd site. Never to be confused with GROSSLAGE.

Emrich-Schönleber Na ★★★ Werner S and son Frank make precise RIES from Monzingen's classified Frühlingsplätzchen and Halenberg vyds.

Erden M-M ★★★→★★★★ Village on red slate soils; RIES (dr/sw) with rare spiciness, delicacy. GROSSE LAGE: Prälat, Treppchen. Growers: BREMER RATSKELLER, Erbes, JJ Christoffel, LOOSEN, MAX F RICHTER, MERKELBACH, MOLITOR, Mönchhof, Rebenhof, Schmitges.

Erste Lage Classified vyd, 2nd-from-top level in VDP classification, similar to Burgundy's Premier Cru.

Erzeugerabfüllung Analogous to GUTSABFÜLLUNG, but also allowed on co-op labels.

Escherndorf Frank ★★★ Village with steep GROSSE LAGE Lump ("scrap" – as in tiny inherited parcels). Marvellous *Silvaner*, RIES (dr/sw). Growers: Fröhlich, H SAUER, R SAUER, Schäffer, zur Schwane.

Eser, August Rhg ★★→★★★ Fine Oestrich family estate known for emphatically dry, but elegant RHG RIES; gd PINOT N too.

Falkenstein, Hofgut Mos ★★★ Weber family; emphatically fresh RIES from early harvested grapes in Krettnach and Niedermennig, located in SAAR side valley.

Feinherb Imprecisely defined trad term for wines with around 10–30g/l sugar.

Forst Pfz ★★→★★★★ Famous MITTELHAARDT village; Kirchenstück was PFZ's highest taxed vyd on 1828 tax map. Pechstein, Jesuitengarten, Ungeheuer vyds almost equally outstanding. Top: ACHAM-MAGIN, BASSERMANN-JORDAN, BÜRKLIN-WOLF, H Spindler, MARGARETHENHOF, MOSBACHER, VON BUHL, VON WINNING, WOLF.

Franken / Franconia Region of distinctive dry wines, esp SILVANER, often bottled in round-bellied flasks (BOCKSBEUTEL).

Fricke, Eva Rhg ★★★ Dense, full-bodied, even silky RIES from 17 ha at KIEDRICH, LORCH, eg. 23 Mélange, Lorch ORTSWEIN TROCKEN.

Full Rhh ★★→★★★★ Christopher F is cellarmaster at Battenfeld-Spanier; his family estate in RHH (part of ZELLERTAL) is reliable source of deeply mineral RIES (Silberberg, Zellerweg am Schwarzen Herrgott).

Fürst, Weingut Frank ★★★→★★★★★ *Spätburgunders* 97' 03' 05' 09 10' 15' 16' 17 18' 19 20 21 of great finesse from red sandstone (most dense, Hundsrück; most powerful, Schlossberg; most typical, Centgrafenberg). Also tight CHARD in burgundian style, and underrated RIES.

Gallais, Le Mos EGON MÜLLER ZU SCHARZHOF 2nd estate, with 4-ha monopoly Braune Kupp at WILTINGEN. AUSLESEN can be exceptional.

Grosse Lage / Grosslage: spot the difference

Up to now, German wine labels can say GROSSLAGE or GROSSE LAGE. They are not the same: the former is a mix of usually hundreds of ha of secondary vyds, the latter refers to the exact opposite – to a top single vyd, an EINZELLAGE, a German "Grand Cru" according to the classification set up by growers' association VDP. Until now, a *Grosslage* could disguise itself as a single vyd: who would know if Forster Mariengarten is an *Einzellage* or a *Grosslage*? (It's Gross.) But luckily, this is not the end of the story: after 2026, a *Grosslage* name will not be allowed to be mentioned together with a village name. Instead of Forster Mariengarten, it must be written: region Mariengarten. The term *Bereich* will also be replaced by region. *Bereich* means district within an *Anbaugebiet* (region). *Bereich* on a label should equally be treated as a flashing red light; the wine is a blend from arbitrary sites within that district.

Geisenheim Rhg Town primarily known for Germany's university of oenology and viticulture. GROSSE LAGE Rothenberg (WEGELER) is less famous but one of RHG's best.

GG (Grosses Gewächs) "Great/top growth". The top dry wine from a VDP-classified GROSSE LAGE.

Goldkapsel / Gold Capsule Mos, Na, Rhg, Rhh Designation (and bottle seal) mainly for AUSLESE and higher; v. strict selection of grapes, which should add finesse and complexity, not primarily weight and sweetness. Lange Goldkapsel (Long Gold Capsule) even better. Not a legal term.

Patron saint of Hermannshöhle? Hermes, the messenger of the gods.

Graach M-M ★★★→★★★★ Small village between BERNKASTEL and WEHLEN. GROSSE LAGE vyds: Domprobst, Himmelreich, Josephshöfer. Growers: *JJ Prüm*, Kees-Kieren, KESSELSTATT, LOOSEN, MAX F RICHTER, MOLITOR, SA PRÜM, SCHAEFER, *Selbach-Oster*, Studert-Prüm, WEGELER.

Grans-Fassian M-M ★★★ Catharina Grans (13th generation) has treasure of prime sites at TRITTENHEIM, PIESPORT, Leiwen. Kitsch-free RIES (dr/sw), drive, balance.

Griesel & Compagnie Hess ★★★ SEKT startup (2013) at Bensheim, known for crisp, dry style, eg. RIES Rés Perpétuelle, single-vintage Dosage Zero PINOTS BL/N from Höllberg and Fürstenlager vyds (both granite).

Gröhl Rhh ★★→★★★★ Young Johannes G advocates v. early picking for bitingly acidic RIES (Pettenthal TROCKEN); in 23, breathtaking Pettenthal TBA.

Grosse Lage Top level of VDP classification, but only for VDP members. Dry wine from a Grosse Lage site is called GG. Note: not on any account to be confused with GROSSLAGE. Stay awake, there.

Grosser Ring Mos Group of top (VDP) MOS estates, whose annual Sept auction at TRIER sets world record prices.

Grosslage Term destined, maybe even intended, to confuse: a collection of secondary vyds without identity. Not on any account to be confused with GROSSE LAGE. Newest legislation stipulates term "region" must precede *Grosslagen* name; mention of village together with *Grosslage* (eg. Piesporter Michelsberg) no longer permitted, but transition period lasts until 2026.

Gunderloch Rhh ★★★→★★★★★ Historical NACKENHEIM estate portrayed in Carl Zuckmayer's play *Der fröhliche Weinberg* (1925). Deeply mineral Rothenberg RIES both TROCKEN (GG 15 16 17' 18' 19' 20 21' 22 23') and sweet. New VERSTEIGERUNGSWEIN/GG from Rothenberg parcel Fenchelberg. *Kabinett Jean-Baptiste* is perfect match for spicy dishes.

Gut Hermannsberg Na ★★★ Historic Prussian state dom at NIEDERHAUSEN, now in private hands. RIES GGS (Kupfergrube) need time to develop; v.gd Res range (Hermannsberg and Kupfergrube 19, marketed 2024).

Gutsabfüllung Estate-bottled, and made from own grapes.

Gutswein Entry-level wine, no vyd or village designation, but only producer's name. Ideally, produced from own grapes, but not always the case.

Gutzler Rhh ★★★ Reliable, versatile: refined Morstein RIES, dense SILVANER, subtle SPÄTBURGUNDERS from Gundersheim and Westhofen. Historic grapes: Blauer Arbst, Kleiner Fränkischer Burgunder.

Haag, Fritz Mos ★★★★ BRAUNEBERG's top estate; Oliver H is more modern in style than father Wilhelm was. *See* SCHLOSS LIESER.

Haag, Willi Mos ★★→★★★★ BRAUNEBERG family estate, led by Marcus H. Old-style RIES, mainly sweet, rich but balanced, inexpensive.

Haart, Reinhold M-M ★★★→★★★★★ Best estate in PIESPORT, with important holding in famous Goldtröpfchen ("gold droplet") vyd; RIES SPÄTLESEN and higher PRÄDIKAT wines are *racy, copybook Mosels.*

Haidle Würt ★★★→★★★★ Moritz H uses cool climate of Remstal area for distinctive freshness. Outstanding LEMBERGER GGS Berge, Gehrnhalde, RIES Pulvermächer.

Halbtrocken Medium-dry with 9–18g/l unfermented sugar, inconsistently distinguished from FEINHERB.

Hallgarten Rhg ★★→★★★★ Village situated away from River Rhine in heights; vyds (eg. Jungfer, Hendelberg) more and more sought-after with climate change. Growers: FÜRST LÖWENSTEIN, KÜHN, H Nicolai, PRINZ, Querbach, SPREITZER.

Hattenheim Rhg ★★→★★★★ Town famous for *Brunnen* ("well") vyds (Nussbrunnen, Wisselbrunnen), with water-bearing layers underneath, and legendary STEINBERG high above village. Estates: BARTH, HESSISCHE STAATSWEINGÜTER, Kaufmann, Knyphausen, Ress, Schloss Reinhartshausen, SPREITZER.

Heger, Dr. Bad ★★★→★★★★ Young Rebecca H continues work of father Jochim in steep slopes of Achkaren, IHRINGEN, setting new accents by picking earlier. Best parcel selctions: Häusleboden Pinot N from old Clos de Vougeot (*see* France) cuttings, planted 1956; Winklerberg Vorderer Berg (PINOTS BL/GR/N).

Heitlinger / Burg Ravensburg Bad ★★→★★★★ Two leading estates of Kraichgau, N BAD, under same ownership. Heitlinger more elegant, Burg Ravensburg fuller.

Hessische Bergstrasse Germany's smallest wine region (460 ha), n of Heidelberg.

Hessische Staatsweingüter Hess, Rhg ★★→★★★★ State dom with vinotheque in KLOSTER EBERBACH; 210 ha in top sites all along RHG and HESSISCHE BERGSTRASSE. Rich stock of mature wines back to 1706. Quality, with an upward trend: brilliant 21 PINOT N from ASSMANNSHAUSEN; manificent 20 STEINBERG TBA; foot-trodden, phenolic 20 STEINBERG Wild Ferment RIES (entirely vinified in vyd).

Hey, Weingut ★★★ Leading estate in e, at Naumburg, SA-UN. Impressive RIES, PINOTS BL/GR GGS from Steinmeister vyd.

Heymann-Löwenstein Mos ★★★ Sarah L has taken over from father Reinhard, continues to produce terroir-minded, nonconformist RIES from steep terraces at WINNINGEN, nr Koblenz.

Hochheim Rhg ★★→★★★★ Town e of main RHG, on River Main, rich RIES from loess and limestone soils, best usually Domdechaney, Hölle, Kirchenstück.

Value in Germany

Germany follows the usual pattern for value: don't bother with the cheapest, and look in the sweet spot (*see* p.355) for the best price:quality ratio. Estates known for this incl Karl Pfaffmann (PFZ); Manz, Kissinger (RHH); Karl Erbes, MERKELBACH (MOS). SILVANER-lovers can find amazing wines all over FRANK, eg. BÜRGERSPITAL (WÜRZBURG ORTSWEIN), Neder (St. Klausen), Schmachtenberger (Quaderkalk), and many more. Decent entry-level German PINOT N is almost unbeatable internationally, esp compared with Burgundy prices, try Baumann (Waldulm), Baum-Barth (INGELHEIM), DOLDE, Shelter Winery (Kenzingen, BAD), WASSMER (both). Connoisseurs in search of affordable luxury find excellent RIES offerings at the ORTSWEIN level. A paradigm is FORST: 80% of the village is GROSSE LAGE sites – Ortswein usually contains declassified lots of Ungeheuer or Pechstein; M RH Ries is generally underrated and underpriced, esp JOST (Devon S, KABINETT FEINHERB), Lanius-Knab (Rheingold, Rheinschiefer), WEINGART (whole range). All over Germany, Feinherb Ries is out of fashion and often sold much too cheaply for what it is (outstanding: DÖNNHOFF Gutsriesling Feinherb 22'). If you love mature wines, WEGELER's vintage collection has many fairly priced Mos, RHG bargains; the same holds for JB BECKER (RHG), Nick Köwerich (Mos), VON NEIPPERG (WÜRT, esp r).

Growers: Domdechant Werner, Flick, HESSISCHE STAATSWEINGÜTER, Himmel, Im Weinegg, KÜNSTLER.

Hock A trad English term for Rhine wine, derived from HOCHHEIM.

Hövel, Weingut von Mos ★★★ Passionate Max von Kunow, now joined by ex-KESSELSTATT cellarmaster Wolfgang Mertes, takes light, crystalline SAAR style to highest level. Superb 22 SCHARZHOFBERG VERSTEIGERUNGSWEIN KABINETT. Brilliant 22 GGS too.

Huber, Bernhard Bad ★★★→★★★★ PINOT N ALTE REBEN, Sommerhalde, Wildenstein have generous fruit, and world fame. Same holds for Julian H's tight, demanding CHARD.

Ihringen Bad ★→★★★ Village in KAISERSTUHL known for fine PINOTS N/GR/BL on steep volcanic Winklerberg. Top: DR. HEGER, Konstanzer, Michel, Stigler.

Immich-Batterieberg Mos ★★→★★★ Handcrafted, balanced RIES, mostly dry, from Enkirch and surroundings. Name alludes to dynamite "batteries" used to create steep, rocky Batterieberg vyd.

Ingelheim Rhh ★★→★★★★ Town with limestone banks under vyds, and historic fame for PINOT N. Dynamic estates ADAMS, Baum-Barth, Bettenheimer, Dautermann, NEUS, Schloss Westerhaus, SAALWÄCHTER, Wasem, Werner put wines back on map.

Iphofen Frank ★★→★★★ Town in E FRANK (Steigerwald area = altitude) famous for rich, aromatic, well-ageing SILVANER from gypsum soils in Julius-Echter-Berg and neighbouring vyds. Growers: Arnold, Emmerich, JULIUSSPITAL, Popp, RUCK, Seufert, Vetter, Von der Tann, Weigand, WELTNER, *Wirsching*, Zehntkeller.

Johannisberg Rhg ★★→★★★★ Legendary SCHLOSS JOHANNISBERG has made town's name synonymous with RIES; other wineries incl CHAT SAUVAGE, JOHANNISHOF (Eser), Prinz v. Hessen, Schamari-Mühle. GROSSLAGE (avoid!): Erntebringer.

Johannishof (Eser) Rhg ★★→★★★ Family estate with vyds at JOHANNISBERG, RÜDESHEIM: RIES with perfect balance of ripeness and steely acidity.

Jost, Toni M Rh ★★★ Leading estate in BACHARACH with monopoly Hahn, now led by Cecilia J.

Jülg Pfz ★★→★★★★ Dense PINOT N, sharply mineral CHARD, SAUV BL from limestone soils at SCHWEIGEN. Top: Opus Oskar (named after Johannes J's grandfather).

Juliusspital Frank ★★★ Ancient WÜRZBURG charity with top vyds all over FRANK, known for firmly structured *dry Silvaners* that age well. New director 2023.

Kaiserstuhl Bad Extinct volcano nr Rhine in S BAD, notably warm climate, black soil. Altitudes up to 400m (1312ft). PINOTS N/GR of class, renown.

Kanzem Mos ★★★ SAAR village with steep GROSSE LAGE vyd Altenberg (green and grey slate, weathered red rock). Growers: BISCHÖFLICHE WEINGÜTER TRIER, Cantzheim (plus guesthouse), VAN VOLXEM, VON OTHEGRAVEN.

Karthäuserhof Mos ★★★ Historic RUWER estate with emblematic neck-only label. After mixed results over past decade, a new team: Mathieu Kauffmann (ex-Bollinger, *see* France), Dominik Völk (ex-VAN VOLXEM).

Kauer M Rh ★★→★★★ Randolf K was professor of organic viticulture at GEISENHEIM; daughter Anne now about to take over family estate at BACHARACH, aiming at fresher, crisper style.

Keller, Franz Bad *See* SCHWARZER ADLER.

Keller, Klaus Peter Rhh ★★★★ Star of RHH, cultish for ALTE REBEN RIES G-Max from undisclosed (calcareous) parcel, and GGS Hubacker, Morstein. Also Ries from NIERSTEIN (Hipping, Pettenthal), M-M (PIESPORT Schubertslay). Record prices at auction.

Kesseler, August Rhg ★★★★ August K's 85 ASSMANNSHAUSEN Höllenberg PINOT N was start of new German Pinot N miracle. Meanwhile, long-time employees taken over.

Kesselstatt, Reichsgraf von Mos ★★ Top vyds on Mosel and tributaries, 46 ha. In troubled waters after death of visionary Annegret Reh-Gartner (2016), but now 1st signs of improvement.

Kiedrich Rhg ★★→★★★★ Top village, almost monopoly of WEIL estate; other growers (eg. FRICKE, Knyphausen, PRINZ VON HESSEN) own only small plots. Famous church and choir.

Botrytis works by concentrating flavours, facilitating release of phenols into juice.

Kloster Eberbach Rhg Atmospheric C12 Cistercian abbey in HATTENHEIM, where *The Name of the Rose* was filmed. Domicile of HESSISCHE STAATSWEINGÜTER.

Klumpp Bad ★★★ Top family estate in Kraichgau, N BAD, led by bros Markus and Andreas K, esp fruit-driven PINOT N, refined PINOT GR from Rothenberg vyd at Bruchsal, and Unteröwisheim Kirchberg CHARD. Also inexpensive Hand in Hand series together with Markus K's wife Meike Näkel (MEYER-NÄKEL).

Knebel Mos ★★★ Family estate in top form at WINNINGEN. Refined TBA, and elegant, aromatic dry wines.

Knewitz Rhh ★★★ Practically unknown 10 yrs ago; today VDP member, and one of RHH's leaders. Best: CHARD Res (22'), RIES Hundertgulden 15' 16' 17' 18 19' 20' 21' 22' 23'. Organic.

Knipser Pfz ★★★→★★★★ Top estate in N PFZ, best for age-worthy PINOT N (15' RdP a monument), CHARD and specialities like Gelber Orleans, SYRAH, Cuvée X (Bx blend). Now PETIT MANSENG too: grape gets botrytis under climate change conditions in Pfz.

Königin Viktoriaberg Rhg ★★→★★★ Historic RIES vyd at HOCHHEIM, today run by Flick estate, Wicker. After 1845 visit, Queen Victoria granted owner right to rename vyd as "Queen-Victoria-mountain".

Kopp Bad ★★★ In ORTENAU, bio estate and fine restaurant nr Baden-Baden city. Tight CHARD; dense, mineral PINOT N.

Kranz, Weingut Pfz ★★★→★★★★ Top organic estate at Ilbesheim, S PFZ. Intense RIES, SPÄTBURGUNDER, WEISSBURGUNDER from classified Kalmit SE – and superb Blanc de Noirs Brut Nature SEKT. Kerstin and Boris K now assisted by son Xaver.

Kreuzberg, HJ Ahr ★★★ Prime producer. Best: Devonschiefer R PINOT N and Hardtberg FRÜHBURGUNDER.

Kriechel, Peter Ahr ★★→★★★ Fine family estate at Ahrweiler. Round, full SPÄTBURGUNDER (Kräuterberg GOLDKAPSEL).

Krone, Weingut Rhg ★★★ Famous SPÄTBURGUNDER estate with a treasure of old vyds in ASSMANNSHAUSEN, run by WEGELER.

Kühling-Gillot Rhh ★★★★ Top bio estate, run by Caroline Gillot and husband HO Spanier. Best in outstanding range of ROTER HANG RIES: GG Rothenberg Wurzelecht from ungrafted vines.

Kühn, Peter Jakob Rhg ★★★→★★★★ Obsessive bio vyd management and long macerations shape **nonconformist but exciting** RIES; Res RPJK Unikat aged 4 yrs in cask. St Nikolaus and Doosberg GGs reliable at highest level.

Kuhn, Philipp Pfz ★★★→★★★★ Outstanding estate at Laumersheim, N PFZ: RIES (eg. Saumagen, Schwarzer Herrgott), age-worthy SPÄTBURGUNDER, terrific specialities CHARD, SAUV BL, VIOGNIER.

Künstler Rhg ★★★ Gunter K's family estate at HOCHHEIM has vyds and GGs in every part of RHG, incl ex-Schönborn vyd in MARCOBRUNN; trad, reliable style.

Kuntz, Sybille Mos ★★★ Progressive organic 12-ha estate at Lieser, esp Niederberg-Helden vyd. Pioneer of MOS TROCKEN; intense wines, one of each ripeness category, intended for gastronomy, listed in many top restaurants.

Kurek, Jonas Würt ★★→★★★ Young grower on Bavarian shores of BODENSEE. Trained with Bernhard and Julian HUBER, makes outstanding Seehalde PINOT N.

Laible, Andreas Bad ★★★ Crystalline dry RIES, fine TRAMINER from Durbach's Plauelrain vyd (granite). Younger brother Alexander has own estate.

Landwein Technically "ggA" (*see* box, p.165), meant to label wines with only broadly defined origin. Now popular among ambitious growers to avoid narrow-minded official quality testing. Best known: Brenneisen, Enderle & Moll, Forgeurac, Greiner, Höfflin, Nieger, Vorgrimmler, WASENHAUS, ZIEREISEN (all BAD); Drei Zeilen, Vetter, Weigand (FRANK); Schmitt (RHH); Konni & Evi (SA-UN).

Lauer Mos ★★★ Fine, precise SAAR RIES: tense, poised. Parcel selections from huge Ayler Kupp vyd. Best: Kern, Schonfels, Stirn.

Leitz, Josef Rhg ★★★ Important RÜDESHEIM estate, 160 ha, producing anything from respectable discount RIES to outstanding GGS (Berg Schlossberg 21' 22). Inexpensive, reliable Eins-Zwei-Dry label, and soundly produced de-alc wines.

Loersch M-M ★★–★★★ Fine family estate (since 1640) with energetic KABINETT and aromatically complex dry wines from 1st-class vyds (PIESPORT Goldtröpfchen, TRITTENHEIM Apotheke).

Loewen, Carl Mos ★★★ RIES of complexity, best vyd Longuicher Maximin Herrenberg (planted 1896, ungrafted). Entry-level Ries Varidor too: excellent *value*.

Loosen, Weingut Dr. M-M ★★–★★★★ Ernie L is Germany's most important RIES ambassador; his wines convince from entry-level Blauschiefer, Rotschiefer and even Dr. L from bought-in grapes, over nine different GGS and four Res wines (2 yrs cask-ageing) up to cultish Prälat AUSLESE. New projects incl Tradition range for KABINETT, SPÄTLESE with less sweetness, and extended barrel-ageing (3, 5, 8 yrs) for dry wines. *See also* BERGWEILER-PRÜM; VILLA WOLF; Appassionata, J Christopher (Oregon, US); Ch Ste Michelle (Washington State, US).

Lorch Rhg ★ ·★★★ Village in extreme w of RHG, conditions more M RH-like than Rhg-like. Sharply crystalline wines, both RIES, PINOT N. Best: BREUER, CHAT SAUVAGE, FRICKE, KESSELER, SOLVEIGS, von Kanitz.

Löwenstein, Fürst Frank, Rhg ★★★ Princely estate, classic RIES from HALLGARTEN (RHG), unique SILVANER, Ries from ultra-steep Homburger Kallmuth (FRANK).

Marcobrunn Rhg Historic 7-ha vyd in Erbach, VDP-classified GROSSE LAGE. Potential for rich, long-lasting RIES. Growers: CORVERS-KAUTER, HESSISCHE STAATSWEINGÜTER, Höhn, Knyphausen, KÜNSTLER, PRINZ, Schloss Reinhartshausen, von Oetinger.

Margarethenhof Pfz ★★★ Up-and-coming family estate in FORST, organic conversion. Classy RIES from Jesuitengarten, Pechstein, Ungeheuer vyds.

Markgräflerland Bad District s of Freiburg, cool climate nr Black Forest, limestone soils. Typical GUTEDEL a pleasant companion for local cuisine. PINOT varieties increasingly successful.

Markgräfler Winzer Bad ★→★★★ Innovative MARKGRÄFLERLAND co-op (900 ha) with distinctive approach to quality, led by former LVMH (*see* Moët & Chandon, France) manager. Best: DER series (CHARD, GUTEDEL, PINOT N).

Markgraf von Baden Bad ★★→★★★ Important noble estate, at Staufenberg Castle (ORTENAU) and at Salem castle (BODENSEE), had more than 100 ha in production, but 60 ha Bodensee vyds given up in winter 2024/25.

Plant-protection with drones and robots is at an advanced experimental stage.

Mathis, Gebrüder Bad ★★★ Young couple (3rd generation) take over family estate (formerly known as Kalkbödele) on Tuniberg. Stylish PINOT N (Rosenloch 20'), CHARD, PINOT BL from vyds next to a lime plant.

Maximin Grünhaus Mos ★★★★ Maximin von Schubert now at helm at supreme RUWER estate; v. trad winemaking shapes herb-scented, *delicate, long-lived Ries*. To be taken more seriously each yr: creamy WEISSBURGUNDER, elegant PINOT N (terroir-driven GG 22', v.gd ORTSWEIN).

May, Rudolf Frank ★★★ SILVANER at its best, reliable entry-level, sophisticated, oak-influenced GGs, ultra-rare Kniebrecher from estate's oldest vines.

Merkelbach M-M ★★→★★★ Tiny estate at ÜRZIG, 1.4 ha. Brothers Alfred and Rolf (RIP 2023) M handed over day-to-day business to SELBACH-OSTER, but wine still made in bros' cellar.

Meyer-Näkel Ahr ★★★→★★★★ Refined PINOT N from steep terraces at Walporzheim Kräuterberg 13' 15' 16' 17' 18 19' 21 and Dernau Pfarrwingert 15' 16' 17 18' 19 21. Vintage 20 almost completely lost in flood. In Portugal (Quinta da Carvalhosa), S Africa (Zwalu, with Neil Ellis).

Michel Bad ★★★ Leading estate at Achkarren, KAISERSTUHL, VDP member since 2018, bitingly mineral Schlossberg CHARD, GRAUBURGUNDER, PINOT N.

Minges Pfz ★★→★★★ Father and daughter team, Theo and Regine M, shape purist, steely RIES from prime S PFZ vyds (Schäwer, Unterer Faulenberg). Delicate GEWÜRZ AUSLESE too.

Mittelhaardt Pfz North-central and best part of PFZ, incl DEIDESHEIM, FORST, RUPPERTSBERG, WACHENHEIM; largely planted with RIES.

Mittelmosel Central and best part of MOS, a RIES Eldorado, incl BERNKASTEL, BRAUNEBERG, GRAACH, PIESPORT, WEHLEN, etc.

Mittelrhein M Rh ★★→★★★ Dramatically scenic Rhine area, nr tourist magnet Loreley. *Steely, underrated Ries.* Today's vyds only quarter size (466 ha) of 1980.

Molitor, Markus M-M, Mos ★★★→★★★★ Perfectionist producer, trad winemaking from 120 ha in 24 EINZELLAGEN; almost 100 different bottlings/yr. Capsules indicate degree of sweetness (white = dry, green = off-dry, golden = sweet). *See also* DOMÄNE SERRIG.

Mosbacher Pfz ★★★ Some of best GG RIES of FORST, refined rather than massive; trad ageing in big oak casks; 23 Leinhöhle ERSTE LAGE a bargain.

Mosel Growing area for lightest of German RIES, 8575 ha, 62% Ries. Conditions on RUWER and SAAR tributaries (also subsumed under "Mosel" in wine law) significantly different.

Münzberg Pfz ★★→★★★ Tight PINOTS BL/GR, CHARD from limestone in S PFZ. Best usually Schlangenpfiff Pinot Bl GG.

Nackenheim Rhh ★→★★★★ ROTER HANG village famous for *Rhh's richest Ries*, superb TBA from Rothenberg on red shale. Top: *Gunderloch*, KÜHLING-GILLOT, Marbé-Sans, SCHÄTZEL.

Nahe Tributary of the Rhine and dynamic region (4230 ha), with couple of famous (eg. DIEL, DÖNNHOFF, SCHÄFER-FRÖHLICH) and dozens of lesser-known but trustworthy producers, excellent *value*. Great soil variety.

Neipperg, Graf von Würt ★★★→★★★★ One of most reliable estates in all Germany, strongold of elegance (LEMBERGER, SPÄTBURGUNDER), but also PINOT BL, RIES. Aus dem Reifekeller series has appropriate bottle-age. Count Philipp N's uncle Stephan makes wine at Canon-la-Gaffelière (*see* Bordeaux) and elsewhere.

Nelles Ahr ★★★ Family estate, est 1479, when ancestor paid high rent for plot in Landskrone vyd. Splendid SPÄTBURGUNDER 22 from Burggarten, Landskrone and Schieferlay.

Neus Rhh ★★★ Revived historic estate at INGELHEIM, excellent PINOT N (best: Pares).

Niederhausen Na ★★→★★★★ Village known for RIES from Hermannshöhle vyd and neighbouring steep slopes. Growers: CRUSIUS, *Dönnhoff*, GUT HERMANNSBERG, Jakob Schneider, Mathern.

Nierstein Rhh ★→★★★★ Avoid by any means GROSSLAGE Gutes Domtal designation. Genuine Nierstein RIES is rich, complex: Hipping, Oelberg, Pettenthal. Growers: Bunn, Gehring, GRÖHL, GUNDERLOCH, Guntrum, Hofmann, Huff (both), KELLER, KÜHLING-GILLOT, Manz, SCHÄTZEL, ST-ANTONY, Strub.

Ockfen Mos ★★→★★★ SAAR village known for GROSSE LAGE Bockstein. Growers:

KESSELSTATT, MOLITOR, OTHEGRAVEN, SANKT URBANS-HOF, VAN VOLXEM, WAGNER, ZILLIKEN. Historical Geisberg now re-cultivated (Van Volxem).

Odinstal, Weingut Pfz ★★→★★★ Highest vyd of PFZ, 150m (492ft) above WACHENHEIM; bio farming, low-tech vinification bring pure GEWÜRZ, RIES, SILVANER. Now PINOT N from Herxheim.

Oechsle Scale for sugar content of grape juice. Until 90s, more Oechsle meant better wine. But climate change has altered game.

Oppenheim Rhh ★→★★★ Village s of ROTER HANG with different soil (limestone) and no direct Rhine influence. Growers: GRÖHL, Guntrum, Kissinger, KÜHLING-GILLOT, Manz. Spectacular C13 church.

Ortenau Bad ★★→★★★ District around and s of city of Baden-Baden. Mainly RIES (locally called Klingelberger) and SPÄTBURGUNDER from granite soils.

Ortswein The 2nd rank up in VDP's pyramid of qualities: a village wine, many bargains. *See* next entry.

Ortswein aus Ersten Lagen Rhh New designation of VDP RHH indicating village wine grown in classified vyds. Typically, blend of different ERSTE LAGE sites. Funnily enough, no Erste Lage single-vyd wines in Rhh.

Östreicher, Richard Frank ★★★ Organic viticulture, low-intervention winemaking: concentrated CHARD Rossbach, flinty SILVANER Maria im Weingarten, smoky PINOT BL Hölzlein.

Othegraven, von Mos ★★★ Family estate owned by German TV star Günther Jauch; important holdings in superb Altenberg at KANZEM. KABINETT and SPÄTLESE VERSTEIGERUNGSWEIN among SAAR's finest.

Palatinate Pfz English for PFALZ.

Latest (?) trend: de-alcoholized wines. Carl Jung at Rüdesheim made since 1907.

Pfalz The 2nd-largest German region, 23,698 ha, balmy climate, Lucullian lifestyle. MITTELHAARDT RIES legendary; SÜDPFALZ produces outstanding PINOTS N/BL, plus CHARD. ZELLERTAL now fashionable: cool climate.

Piesport M-M ★→★★★★ Village in M-M for rich, aromatic RIES from famous Goldtröpfchen vyd. Growers: GRANS-FASSIAN, Hain, Joh Haart, Julian Haart, KESSELSTATT, LOERSCH, *Reinhold Haart*, SANKT URBANS-HOF, SCHLOSS LIESER. Avoid GROSSLAGE Michelsberg.

Prädikat Legally defined category of ripeness at harvest. *See* QMP and box, p.180.

Prinz, Weingut ★★★ Distinctly fresh, elegant RIES from HALLGARTEN's altitude vyds; organic. KABINETT GOLDKAPSEL can be magnificent. Now also MARCOBRUNN.

Prüm, JJ Mos ★★★★ 59 71 76 83 90 03 11 15 18 19 20 21 22 Legendary WEHLEN estate; also BERNKASTEL, GRAACH. Delicate but extraordinarily long-lived wines with finesse, recognizable character.

Prüm, SA Mos ★★→★★★★ Old estate at WEHLEN. Saskia Antonia P took over 2017, noticeable improvements.

QbA (Qualitätswein bestimmter Anbaugebiete) "Quality Wine", controlled as to area, grape(s), vintage. May add sugar before fermentation (chaptalization). Intended as middle category, but VDP obliges its members to label their best dry wines (GGS) as QbA. New EU name gU is scarcely found on labels (*see* box, p 165).

QmP (Qualitätswein mit Prädikat) Top category, six levels according to ripeness of grapes: KABINETT to TBA. (*See* box, p.165.) No sugaring of must or other forms of enrichment allowed.

Ratzenberger M Rh ★★★ Jochen R, 3rd generation, had 10 ha of vines and took over another 10 ha on steep slopes at BACHARACH (2017). Full range: sound, typical M RH RIES, occasionally with magnificent BA, TBA.

Rauenthal Rhg ★★→★★★★ *Spicy, austere but complex* RIES from inland slopes. Baiken, Gehrn, Rothenberg vyds contain GROSSE LAGE, ERSTE LAGE parcels, while neighbouring Nonnenberg (monopole of BREUER) is unclassified, despite its equal quality.

Raumland Rhh ★★★ SEKT house with deep cellar and full range of fine cuvées; 1st Sekt-only estate to become VDP member. Best: CHARD Brut Nature (disgorged after 10 yrs), Triumvirat cuvée (15'), sensational (and rare) MonRose 07' 09' 12'.

Rebholz, Ökonomierat Pfz ★★★ Top Südpfalz estate: bone-dry, best usually RIES GG Kastanienbusch from red schist, also outstanding CHARD, SPÄTBURGUNDER.

Try aged (7 years+) Riesling Spätlese or Auslese with game.

Ress Rhg ★★→★★★ Top sites, all at HALLGARTEN, HATTENHEIM, RÜDESHEIM; gd classic RHG RIES (dr/sw). PINOT N too.

Restsüsse Unfermented grape sugar remaining in (or added in the form of süssreserve to) wine to give it sweetness. Can range from 1g/l in TROCKEN to 300g in TBA.

Rheingau Birthplace of RIES, famous for substantial, age-worthy wines with steely backbone (dr/sw). Soils are either pyhillite, schist, quarzite (in mtn villages) or limestone, loess, river sediments nr Rhine. Only 3200 ha (8th-biggest region). Small but increasing amounts of SPÄTBURGUNDER.

Rheinhessen Germany's largest region by far (27,312 ha and rising), between Mainz and Worms. Much *Fasswein* (bulk wine), but also treasure trove of well-priced wines from gifted young growers.

Richter, Max F M-M ★★→★★★ Fine, reliable M-M estate wealthy in prime vyds at BRAUNEBERG, ERDEN, GRAACH, WEHLEN: full, aromatic RIES (dr/sw).

Riffel Rhh ★★★ Family estate, bio, known for purist style, to put Bingen's once-famous Scharlachberg (red soils) back on map.

Rings Pfz ★★★→★★★★ Dense, emphatically fresh RIES and SPÄTBURGUNDER from prime sites in N PFZ.

Roter Hang Rhh ★★→★★★★ Leading RIES area of RHH (NACKENHEIM, NIERSTEIN). Name ("red slope") refers to red shale soil.

Ruck, Johann Frank ★★★ Spicy, age-worthy RIES, SCHEUREBE, SILVANER, TRAMINER from IPHOFEN.

Rüdesheim Rhg ★★→★★★★ Tourist magnet in RHG. Unique RIES from Berg (mtn) vyds on slate (Kaisersteinfels, Roseneck, Rottland, Schlossberg). Full but never clumsy, esp gd in off-yrs. Best: Allendorf, BISCHÖFLICHES WEINGUT RÜDESHEIM, *Breuer*, CHAT SAUVAGE, CORVERS-KAUTER, HESSISCHE STAATSWEINGÜTER, JOHANNISHOF, Jörn Wein, *Kesseler*, KÜNSTLER, *Leitz*, Prinz von Hessen, Ress.

Ruwer Mos ★★→★★★★ Tributary of Mosel nr TRIER, cool and late-ripening, esp renowned for dry RIES. Best: Beulwitz, Karlsmühle, KARTHÄUSERHOF, KESSELSTATT, MAXIMIN GRÜNHAUS.

Saale-Unstrut Small but fine ne region (847 ha) around confluence of these two rivers 50 km w of Leipzig. Terraced vyds have Cistercian origins. Best: Böhme, BÖHME & TÖCHTER, Born, Gussek, HEY, Kloster Pforta, Konni & Evi (LANDWEIN), Pawis, Proppe. Severely hit by frost in 24.

Saalwächter, Carsten Rhh ★★★ Shooting star at INGELHEIM; outstanding SILVANER Grauer Stein, elegant CHARD, delicate PINOT N (ASSMANNSHAUSEN, Ingelheim).

Saar Mos Tributary of Mosel, bordered by steep slopes. Most austere, steely, *brilliant Ries* of all, consistency favoured by climate change.

Sachsen Region in Elbe V around Meissen and Dresden. Characterful dry whites, TRAMINER a speciality. Best: AUST, Drei Herren, F Fourré, Gut Hoflössnitz, Rothes Gut, SCHLOSS PROSCHWITZ, SCHLOSS WACKERBARTH, Schuh, SCHWARZ and ZIMMERLING.

St-Antony Rhh ★★→★★★ NIERSTEIN organic estate. Exceptional vyds, known for sturdy, ageable ROTER HANG RIES. Steep slopes all worked by hand.

Salm, Prinz zu Na, Rhh ★★→★★★ Owner of Schloss Wallhausen, vyds there and at BINGEN (RHH); ex-president of VDP.

Salwey Bad ★★★→★★★★ Leading KAISERSTUHL estate, forerunner of fresher PINOTS N/GR style (from 2008). Best: GGS Henkenberg Pinot Gr (21'), Steingrubenberg CHARD and Kirchberg PINOT BL, Henkenberg and Kirchberg Pinot N.

Sankt Urbans-Hof Mos ★★★ Large family estate (45 ha) led by Nik Weis, vyds along M-M and SAAR; vine nursery too. Limpid RIES, impeccably pure, racy, age well.

Sauer, Horst Frank ★★★ Man who put FRANK on sweet-wine map. Sensational BA, TBA from ESCHERNDORF's steep Lump vyd. Daughter Sandra now in charge.

Sauer, Rainer Frank ★★★ Top family estate producing seven different dry SILVANERS from ESCHERNDORF's steep slope Lump. Best: GG am Lumpen, and L.

Schaefer, Willi Mos ★★★ ★★★★ Small (4.8 ha) but outstanding family estate, MOS RIES at its best, pure, crystalline, feather-light and long-lasting. Christoph S cultivates dozens of tiny parcels, mainly in GRAACH, also Wehlener SONNENUHR.

Schäfer, Joh. Bapt. Na ★★★ Fine family estate; handcrafted, low-intervention RIES mainly from Dorsheim (GGS Goldloch, Pittermännchen). Brilliant KABINETT too.

Schäfer-Fröhlich Na ★★★→★★★★ Family estate in NA, spontaneously fermented RIES of great intensity; GGS Bockenau Felseneck, Kupfergrube, Schlossböckelheim Felsenberg. Outstanding 23 Felseneck GOLDKAPSEL SPÄTLESE.

Scharzhofberg Mos ★★→★★★★ Superlative SAAR vyd, 28 ha: a rare coincidence of microclimate, soil and human intelligence to bring about the perfection of RIES. Top: EGON MÜLLER, KESSELSTATT, VAN VOLXEM, VON HÖVEL.

Schätzel Rhh ★★★ VDP member with prime ROTER HANG vyds, advocating regenerative viticulture and low-alc, low-sulphur, tannic RIES. Mostly LANDWEIN, eg. Fuchs (Hipping), vintage-blend Reh 16-23 (Pettenthal Ries aged under flor, like Fino Sherry – *see* Spain). Steiner (= NIERSTEINER) ORTSWEIN a gd introduction into this idiosyncratic world eg. 17-23 Ries, 20-23 SILVANER. Brilliant Pettenthal KABINETT and AUSLESE 23'.

Schlipf, Weingut am Bad ★★★ Brothers Christoph and Johannes Schneider excel with GUTEDEL (El Fayoum, no added sulphur) and PINOT N.

Schlör Bad ★★★ Best grower in remote TAUBERTAL, perhaps only world-class red from SCHWARZRIESLING (aka PINOT M): Fyerst 1476 Res. Also v.gd: PINOTS BL/N.

Schloss Johannisberg Rhg ★★★→★★★★ Historic RHG estate and Metternich mansion, place where SPÄTLESE was invented (1775); 100% RIES, owned by Henkell (Oetker group). Seal colour indicates wine type. Currently on top form and in conversion to organic. Ex Bibliotheca Subterranea and Goldlack TROCKEN are pricey, but entry-level Gelblack shows nobility of site too.

Schloss Lieser M-M ★★★★ Thomas Haag, elder brother of Oliver (FRITZ HAAG) makes painstakingly elaborate RIES (dr/sw) from BRAUNEBERG, Lieser (Niederberg Helden), PIESPORT, WEHLEN. Hotel Lieser Castle has no ties to wine estate.

Resurrecting old vines

There are many ways to respond to climate change in viticulture; a particularly exciting one is to revitalize old grape varieties, abandoned in C19 because they never ripened back then. Here are some old grapes to remember: (w) Grüner Adelfränkisch, Gelber Kleinberger, Gelber Orleans, Muskatgutedel; (r) Blauer Arbst, Fränkischer Burgunder, Hartblau, Schwarzblauer Ries, Süssschwarz, Tauberschwarz. Growers making wine from one or more of these varieties incl AM SCHLIPF, B Ellwanger, BREUER, DÖRFLINGER, Genheimer-Kiltz, Goldschmidt, GUTZLER, J Hofmann, J Kiefer, Metzler, MF RICHTER, Sander, H SAUER, Schauss, Scheu, Schloss Reinhartshausen, WINZER SOMMERACH, ZIEREISEN.

Schloss Neuweier Bad ★★★ A C16 castle and some of BADEN's best RIES vyds on porphyry soils. Remarkable Late Release series: Mauerberg Ries 19, Heiligenstein PINOT N 16.

Schloss Ortenberg Bad ★★→★★★ Had been underperforming; taken over in 2021 by hotelier Thomas Althoff (Schloss Bensberg, St. James's Hotel & Club) and made remarkable progress since.

Schloss Proschwitz Sachs ★★→★★★ New team brings notable improvements in Prince zur Lippe's 70-ha estate. Top: WEISSBURGUNDER, SPÄTBURGUNDER, delicious TRAMINER Brut SEKT.

Schloss Rattey ★→★★★ Hotel and winery in ne state of Mecklenburg-Vorpommern, 30 ha, remarkable dry Solaris.

Schloss Vaux Rhg ★★→★★★ Co-owned by PRINZ ZU SALM. SEKT house, best known for single-vyd RIES Sekt.

Schloss Wackerbarth ★★→★★★ Saxon state dom on outskirts of Dresden, conceived as experience winery, with restaurant, park, events, 190,000 visitors/yr. Also wine-wise on top form. Best: ALTE REBEN, Protze RIES TROCKEN, TRAMINER SPÄTLESE, all from Radebeul's Goldener Wagen vyd.

Schnaitmann Würt ★★★→★★★★ Excellent barrel-aged reds from Fellbach nr Stuttgart. Whites (eg. RIES, SAUV BL), SEKT (Evoé!) tasty too. Burgundy-inspired TROLLINGER ALTE REBEN.

Schneider, Markus Pfz ★★→★★★ Marketing genius Markus S founded estate, having just come of age, in 1994. Full range of soundly produced, trendily labelled wines. Joint venture with Kaapzicht Estate in Stellenbosch (see S Africa).

Schneider, Reinhold & Cornelia Bad ★★★ Fine family estate at Endingen, KAISERSTUHL. Delightfully old-fashioned GRAUBURGUNDER labelled "Ruländer"; v.gd SPÄTBURGUNDER too.

Schoppenwein Café (or bar) wine, ie. wine by the glass.

Schumacher, Paul Ahr ★★★ Perfectionist grower at Marienthal, only 4 ha. Age-worthy PINOT N: Kräuterberg 12 13 15' 16 17' 18 19' 20' 21 22', Rosenthal (Magna Essentia), Trotzenberg. FRÜHBURGUNDER Alegria 22', depth, appeal. After devastating flood in 2021, new winery building on way.

Schwarz, Martin Sachs ★★★ Perfectionist grower (6 ha) at Meissen, SACHS: CHARD, RIES, PINOT N – and, believe it or not, NEBBIOLO.

Schwarzer Adler Bad ★★★→★★★★ Michelin-starred restaurant and top estate at Oberbergen, KAISERSTUHL: PINOTS N/BL/GR and CHARD to show France is nr.

Schwegler Würt ★★★→★★★★ Family estate, 11 ha, red blends full of charcter: Beryll, Granat, Saphir. Powerful CHARD.

Seckinger Pfz ★★→★★★ Three brothers from Niederkirchen/MITTELHAART making name for RIES from DEIDESHEIM in style of Vin Nature but without becoming too extreme. Organic.

Seeger Bad ★★★→★★★★ Fine family estate nr Heidelberg. 12th-generation, Thomas S, is PINOT N expert, but CHARD, SAUV BL, BLAUFRÄNKISCH equally remarkable.

Seehaldenhof Würt ★★→★★★ Gifted young grower Simon Hornstein making

> **The Trollinger revival**
> In the 70s, WÜRT's TROLLINGER was a bestseller, but then the ever-lighter, ever-sweeter litre bottles of it progessively descended into the lower shelves of supermarkets. And today? The glou-glou trend is bringing Trollinger back: stylistically exciting, still light but also dense, dry, revisited in a burgundian sytle. Try ADELMANN, ALDINGER, B Ellwanger, DAUTEL, Idler, Leon Gold, SCHNAITMANN, vom Haigst, Weinmanufaktur Stuttgart. Old vines + sand or limestone + hard work/intelligence = superb results.

name for CHARDS Seehalde (*allegro ma non troppo*), Sonnenbichl (*largo*) from Bayerischer BODENSEE. Trained at FÜRST.

Sekt ★→★★★★ German sparkling. Avoid cheap offers: bottle fermentation is not mandatory. Serious producers: ALDINGER, Bardong, BARTH, BATTENFELD-SPANIER, BERGDOLT, BREUER, BUHL, DIEL, Dr. Lippold, F John, GRIESEL, GUT HERMANNSBERG, H Bamberger, HEYMANN-LÖWENSTEIN, LAUER, Leiner, MAX F RICHTER, Melsheimer, MOLITOR, RAUMLAND, Reinecker, Schembs, SCHLOSS VAUX, SCHWARZER ADLER, Solter, S Steinmetz, Strauch, WAGECK, WEGELER, Wilhelmshof, ZILLIKEN.

Selbach-Oster M-M ★★★ Scrupulous family estate with excellent vyd portfolio, known for classical style and focus on sweet PRÄDIKAT wines.

Sermann, Lukas Ahr ★★→★★★ Young grower in Altenahr, village worst affected by 2021 floods. Resilient: made BA 21, opened small restaurant 22. Superb: Im Eck ALTE REBEN (30–80 yrs) PINOT N, RIES TROCKEN from ungrafted vines.

Serrig, Domäne Mos ★★★→★★★★ Former state dom at Serrig, 25 ha in one piece. After 2016 acquisition, MARKUS MOLITOR started the tremendous work of conversion, reconstruction. Only two wines, 1st vintage 2020: crytalline GROSSE LAGE Vogelsang (slightly off-dr); dense, bitingly fresh Vogelsang KABINETT. Wines sold on Place de Bx (*see France*).

Solveigs Rhg ★★→★★★★ PINOT N from red slate at ASSMANNSHAUSEN, LORCH; only 2 ha, organic. Best: plots Micke **13'** 15' **16'** 18' 19' 20', Present **09' 12 13'** 15' 16' 18' 19' 20'.

Sonnenuhr M-M Sundial. Name of vyds at BRAUNEBERG, Pommern, WEHLEN and Zeltingen.

Sorentberg Mos ★★→★★★ Steep slope in cool side valley nr Reil, fallow for decades until 2014, 1000 old vines on red slate, 3.5 ha cleared from bushes and newly planted by friends Tobias Treis (local) and Ivan Giovanett of Italy's Castelfeder.

Spreitzer Rhg ★★★ Deliciously *racy, harmonious* RIES from vyds in HATTENHEIM, Mittelheim, Oestrich. Mid-price range ALTE REBEN a bargain. Breathtaking TBA (Eiserberg 23'), EISWEIN.

Staatlicher Hofkeller Frank ★★→★★★ Bavarian state dom, with 115 ha of vyds; cellars in WÜRZBURG's baroque Residence. Recently significantly improved.

Staatsweingut / Staatliche Weinbaudomäne State wine estates or doms exist in BAD (IHRINGEN, Meersburg), NA (Bad Kreuznach), PFZ (Neustadt), RHG (HESSISCHE STAATSWEINGÜTER), RHH (OPPENHEIM), SACHS (Wackerbarth), SA-UN (Kloster Pforta), WÜRT (Weinsberg).

Steinberg Rhg ★★★ Walled-in vyd above HATTENHEIM, est by Cistercian monks 700 yrs ago: a German Clos de Vougeot (*see France*). Monopoly of HESSISCHE STAATSWEINGÜTER. Best parcels have unique soil: clay with fragments of decomposed schist in various colours.

Stein-Berg Frank Best parcels of famous Stein vyd at WÜRZBURG (39 ha out of 71 ha), since 2020 acknowledged by EU as gU (in sense of AOP, *see France*).

Steintal, Weingut Frank ★★★ SPÄTBURGUNDER from Klingenberg in modern style: dense, fleshy, influenced by ageing in barrels and on lees.

Steinwein Frank Wine from WÜRZBURG's best vyd, Stein. Goethe's favourite. Only six producers: BURGERSPITAL, JULIUSSPITAL, L Knoll, Meinzinger, Reiss, STAATLICHER HOFKELLER. Hugh J once tasted the 1540 vintage.

Stodden Ahr ★★★→★★★★ AHR SPÄTBURGUNDER with Burgundian touch, best usually ALTE REBEN, Herrenberg. Rech Spätburgunder ORTSWEIN 22 a bargain.

Sturm, Martin M Rh ★★→★★★ Journalist turned grower-winemaker; perfectionistic CHARD, RIES, PINOT N from most n part of M RH. Organic.

Südpfalz Pfz On the Alsace border, S PFZ, known for PINOTS (r/w). Best: BECKER, DR. WEHRHEIM, JÜLG, KRANZ, Leiner, MINGES, MÜNZBERG, REBHOLZ, Siegrist.

Taubertal Bad, Frank, Würt ★→★★★ Cool-climate river valley, divided by

Napoleon into BAD, FRANK, WÜRT sections. SILVANER (limestone soils), local red Tauberschwarz. Hofmann, SCHLÖR, gd co-op at Beckstein.

Thanisch, Weingut Dr. M-M ★★★ BERNKASTEL estate, founded 1636, famous for its share of DOCTOR vyd. After family split in 1988, two homonymous estates with similar qualities: Erben (heirs) Müller-Burggraef (more modern), Erben Thanisch (VDP, classical style).

Thörle Rhh ★★★ Brothers Christoph and Johannes T propelled fine family estate to highest ranks; dense RIES Hölle TROCKEN, racy KABINETT, rich Probstey SILVANER, delicate SPÄTBURGUNDER.

Trier Mos The n capital of ancient Rome, on the MOSEL, between RUWER and SAAR. Big charitable estates have cellars here among awesome Roman remains.

Trittenheim M-M ★★ →★★★ Racy, textbook M-M RIES if from gd plots within extended Apotheke vyd. Growers: A CLÜSSERATH, Clüsserath-Weiler, E Clüsserath, F-J Eifel, GRANS-FASSIAN, LOERSCH, Milz.

Trocken Dry. Defined as max 9g/l unfermented sugar. Generally, the closer to France, the more Trocken wines.

Ürzig M-M ★★★→★★★★ MOS village on red sandstone and red slate, famous for ungrafted old vines and *unique spicy Ries* from Würzgarten vyd. Growers: Berres, Christoffel, Erbes, *Loosen*, MERKELBACH, *Molitor*, Mönchhof, Rebenhof.

Van Volxem Mos ★★★ Historical SAAR estate, spectacular castle-like new cellar building in a Saar loop nr WILTINGEN. Low yields from top sites (SCHARZHOFBERG and Gottesfuss of Wiltingen, Bockstein and restored, formerly fallow Geisberg of OCKFEN) bring about monumental, mostly dry RIES.

VDP (Verband Deutscher Prädikatsweingüter) Influential association of 200 premium growers setting highest standards. Look for its eagle insignia on wine labels and for GG logo on bottles. VDP wine is usually a gd bet. President is Steffen CHRISTMANN.

Versteigerungswein ★★★★ Wines of extraordinary quality, auctioned off by one of the historic growers' associations (ie. BERNKASTELER RING or VDP), easily recognized by a sticker on bottle stating the auction from which the bottle was purchased.

Villa Wolf Pfz ★★→★★★ WACHENHEIM estate, leased by Ernst LOOSEN of BERNKASTEL. Quality sound; consistent rather than dazzling.

Wachenheim Pfz ★★★ Celebrated village with, according to VDP, NO GROSSE LAGE vyds. See what you think. Top growers: Biffar, BÜRKLIN-WOLF, Karl Schäfer, ODINSTAL, WOLF, Zimmermann (bargain).

Wachstetter Würt ★★→★★★ Rainer W has knack for LEMBERGER: depth, distinction; trad local cuisine in family restaurant.

German vintage notation

The vintage notes after entries in the German section are mostly given in a different form from those elsewhere in the book. If the vintages of a single wine are rated, or are for red wine regions, the vintage notation is identical to the one used elsewhere (*see* p.6). But for regions, villages or producers, two styles of vintage are indicated.

Bold type (eg. **22**) indicates classic, ripe vintages with a high proportion of SPÄTLESEN and AUSLESEN; or in the case of red wines, gd phenolic ripeness and must weights.

Normal type (eg. 23) indicates a successful but not outstanding vintage. Generally, German white wines, esp RIES, can be drunk young for their intense fruitiness or kept for a decade or even two to develop their potential aromatic subtlety and finesse.

Wageck Pfz ★★★ Family estate at Bissersheim; CHARD, PINOT N (best: Geisberg), SEKT and Portugieser ALTE REBEN (planted 1931).

Wagner, Dr. Mos ★★→★★★ Christiane W follows four generations in producing crisp dry and off-dry SAAR RIES from prime vyds in OCKFEN, Saarstein.

Wagner-Stempel Rhh ★★★ Seriously crafted RHH wines from Siefersheim nr NA border. Best: usually powerful RIES GGS Heerkretz 05 08 11' **15** 18 21 23'. Excellent Res SILVANER, v.gd SPÄTBURGUNDER.

Wasenhaus Mos ★★★ Burgundy-inspired PINOT N Bellen, Kanzel and PINOT BL Möhlin from limestone sites in MARKGRÄFLERLAND, all vines farmed by hand, all wines labelled as LANDWEIN.

Wassmer, Fritz Bad ★★★ One of finest producers of PINOT varieties in Breisgau, esp full, rich Herbolzheim Kaiserberg CHARD, PINOT N.

Wassmer, Martin Bad ★★★ Top producer of PINOT varieties in MARKGRÄFLERLAND, esp tight, vertical Dottingen Castellberg CHARD, PINOT N.

Weedenborn Rhh ★★★ Gesine Roll is SAUV BL expert; her wines (Res, Terra Rossa) have great density and freshness without superficiality.

Wegeler M-M, Rhg ★★→★★★ Important estate in Oestrich and BERNKASTEL (both in top form) plus a stake in the famous KRONE estate of ASSMANNSHAUSEN. Geheimrat J (TROCKEN RIES blend from best RHG sites 83' 85' 95' 00 **15'** 17 19 21') on par with GGS. Sensational 23' TBAS (DOCTOR, Eiserberg). Old vintages available: Vintage Collection.

Wehlen M-M ★★★→★★★★ Wine village with legendary steep SONNENUHR vyd expressing RIES from slate at v. best: rich, fine, everlasting. Top: BERGWEILER-PRÜM, JJ PRÜM, Kerpen, KESSELSTATT, LOOSEN, MAX F RICHTER, MOLITOR, Pauly-Bergweiler, SA PRÜM, Sankt Nikolaus Hospital, SCHLOSS LIESER, SELBACH-OSTER, Studert-Prüm, THANISCH, WILLI SCHAEFER, WEGELER.

Wehrheim, Dr. Pfz ★★★ SÜDPFALZ family estate known for outstanding Kastanienbusch Köppel RIES, PINOT N, Mandelberg WEISSBURGUNDER.

Weil, Robert Rhg ★★★★ Outstanding estate in KIEDRICH of great qualitative consistency, GROSSE LAGE vyd Gräfenberg gives superb sweet KABINETT to TBA, and GG. Parcel-selection Monte Vacano available only by subscription.

Weingart M Rh ★★★ Passionate grower at Spay, vyds in BACHARACH, BOPPARD (esp Hamm Feuerlay). Refined, steely but balanced RIES, low-tech in style, superb value. Also v.gd PINOT N.

Weingut Wine estate.

Weissherbst Pale-pink wine, made from a single variety, often SPÄTBURGUNDER; v. variable quality.

Weltner, Paul Frank ★★★ Family estate at Rödelsee in cool, high-altitude Steigerwald. Densely structured, age-worthy SILVANER from underrated Küchenmeister vyd.

Wiltingen Mos ★★→★★★★ Heartland of the SAAR. SCHARZHOFBERG crowns a series of GROSSE LAGE vyds (Braune Kupp, Braunfels, Gottesfuss, Kupp). ORTSWEIN usually a bargain.

Wind, Katrin Pfz ★★→★★★ Shooting star at Arzheim. Straightforward but nuanced wines, eg. Kalmit FRÜHBURGUNDER and SPÄTBURGUNDER, RIES.

Winning, von Pfz ★★★→★★★★ DEIDESHEIM estate with prime vyds there and at FORST. *Ries of great purity*, terroir expression, fermented in partly new Fuder casks. Recently increased emphasis on CHARD, PINOT BL.

Winningen Mos ★★→★★★ Lower MOS town nr Koblenz; powerful dry RIES. GROSSE LAGES: Röttgen, Uhlen. Top: HEYMANN-LÖWENSTEIN, KNEBEL, Kröber, R Richter.

Winzer Sommerach Frank ★★→★★★ Top co-op, 195 ha; outstanding parcel-selection SILVANER (Wilm, Tiefes Thal), plus expressive dry TRAMINER. Labels display names of grape suppliers – obviously a gd idea.

GERMANY

Wirsching, Hans Frank ★★★ Renowned estate in ɪᴘʜᴏFᴇɴ known for classically structured dry ʀɪᴇs, *Silvaner*. Occasionally crystal-clear ʙᴀ, ᴛʙᴀ: breathtaking Julius-Echter-Berg Ries TBA 22'.

Wittmann Rhh ★★★→★★★★ Leading bio estate; pure, zesty dry ʀɪᴇs ɢɢs Brunnenhäuschen 23', Kirchspiel, Morstein o8 ɪɪ ɪ2' ɪ5 ɪ6 ɪ7 ɪ8 ɪ9' 20 2ɪ' 23'. Top Morstein ᴀʟᴛᴇ ʀᴇʙᴇɴ selection La Borne.

Wöhrle Bad ★★★ Organic pioneer (30 yrs+) in Breisgau. Top ɢɢs (eg. Kirchgasse ɢʀᴀᴜʙᴜʀɢᴜɴᴅᴇʀ, sᴘäᴛʙᴜʀɢᴜɴᴅᴇʀ, Teufelslochgasse ᴄʜᴀʀᴅ).

Wöhrwag Würt ★★★ Family estate at Untertürkheim (district of Stuttgart), long known for some of best ʀɪᴇs in ᴡüʀᴛ. Now also successful with ʟᴇᴍʙᴇʀɢᴇʀ, ᴘɪɴᴏᴛ ɴ and Bx blend *Cuvée X*, always in a finely chiselled and fresh style that nevertheless matures v. well.

Württemberg Dynamic region in s, nr Stuttgart, with many young growers eager to experiment. Best: usually ʟᴇᴍʙᴇʀɢᴇʀ, sᴘäᴛʙᴜʀɢᴜɴᴅᴇʀ, red blends. Light, bright trad ᴛʀᴏʟʟɪɴɢᴇʀ has renaissance. Only 30% white varieties, ʀɪᴇs needs altitude vyds.

Würzburg Frank ★★→★★★★ Great Baroque city on the Main, famous for its best vyd Stein (sᴛᴇɪɴᴡᴇɪɴ, sᴛᴇɪɴ-ʙᴇʀɢ).

Zellertal Pfz ★★→★★★★ Area in N ᴘꜰᴢ, high, cool, recent gold-rush: ʙᴀᴛᴛᴇɴꜰᴇʟᴅ-sᴘᴀɴɪᴇʀ, ᴋᴘ ᴋᴇʟʟᴇʀ, ᴘʜɪʟɪᴘᴘ ᴋᴜʜɴ have bought in Zellertal's best vyd Schwarzer Herrgott or neighbouring ʀʜʜ plot Zellerweg am Schwarzen Herrgott. Local estates incl Bremer, Full, Janson Bernhard.

Ziereisen Bad ★★→★★★★ Outstanding estate in ᴍᴀʀᴋɢʀäꜰʟᴇʀʟᴀɴᴅ, advocating ʟᴀɴᴅᴡᴇɪɴ. Best: sᴘäᴛʙᴜʀɢᴜɴᴅᴇʀs from small plots – Rhini, Schulen, Talrain. Jaspis = old-vine selections. Top: ɢᴜᴛᴇᴅᴇʟ ɪᴏ⁴ (provocatively priced at €125) has great terroir expression.

Zilliken, Forstmeister Geltz Mos ★★★→★★★★ sᴀᴀʀ family estate with unique track record of mature fruity and noble sweet *Ries from Saarburg Rausch* and ᴏᴄᴋꜰᴇɴ Bockstein. Dorothee Z follows her father's path of elegance, delicacy (eg. ᴀᴜsʟᴇsᴇ ɢᴏʟᴅᴋᴀᴘsᴇʟ 2ɪ', ᴛʙᴀ ɪ8'); v.gd sᴇᴋᴛ and Ferdinand's gin.

Zimmerling, Klaus Sachs ★★★ Small, perfectionist estate, ᴠᴅᴘ, one of ɪsᴛ to be est after Berlin Wall came down. Best vyd: Königlicher Weinberg (King's vyd) at Pillnitz nr Dresden.

EU terminology

Germany's part in new EU classification involves, firstly, abolishing the term **Wein** – this is, up to now, the only visible change on labels. ʟᴀɴᴅᴡᴇɪɴ is still called Landwein, even if its bureaucratic name would be **geschützte geographische Angabe (ggA)**, or protected geographical indication. Brussels generally allows continued use of est designations. **Geschützte Ursprungsbezeichnung (gU)**, or protected designation of origin, should technically be replacing ǫᴜᴀʟɪᴛäᴛsᴡᴇɪɴ and ǫᴜᴀʟɪᴛäᴛsᴡᴇɪɴ ᴍɪᴛ ᴘʀäᴅɪᴋᴀᴛ but is, up to now, mainly in place for large geographical units such as ᴀʜʀ, ʙᴀᴅ, ꜰʀᴀɴᴋᴇɴ, etc. Since it's hard and time-consuming (4–6 yrs) to get recognition for a village- or vyd-specific gU, only six such gUs were in place by end of 2023: Bürgstadter Berg (*see* ᴡᴇɪɴɢᴜᴛ ꜰüʀsᴛ), ᴡɪɴɴɪɴɢᴇɴ Uhlen (parcel-specific Blaufuesser Lay, Laubach, Roth Lay, *see* ʜᴇʏᴍᴀɴɴ-ʟöᴡᴇɴsᴛᴇɪɴ), ᴡüʀᴢʙᴜʀɢᴇʀ sᴛᴇɪɴ-ʙᴇʀɢ, and Monzinger Niederberg (ɴᴀ). Another gU, ɪᴘʜᴏꜰᴇɴ Echter-Berg (*see* ᴡɪʀsᴄʜɪɴɢ), is in the application process. The existing predicates – sᴘäᴛʟᴇsᴇ, ᴀᴜsʟᴇsᴇ and so on (*see* box, p.165) – stay in place; the rule for these styles hasn't changed and isn't going to.

Luxembourg

Luxembourg's vineyards (1246 ha) lie on the upper Moselle, but they have more in common with Chablis than Piesport: limestone soils. 90% are white, usually with some sweetness – often too much now that high acidity is a thing of the past. Every fourth bottle is Crémant. 2022: top year for reds, 2023: complicated, 2024: frost.

Alice Hartmann ★★★→★★★★ Rich, slightly off-dry RIES from prime sites (Wormeldange Koeppchen). In Burgundy (St-Aubin), Mittelmosel (Trittenheim).

Aly Duhr ★★★ Carefully crafted Koeppchen RIES (organic). In 2022, outstanding PINOT N Barrique, amazingly gd TEMPRANILLO/MERLOT blend Legado de Léon.

Bernard-Massard ★→★★★ Big producer, esp Crémant. Top: Ch de Schengen/Thill and Clos des Rochers. Sekt in Germany too.

Charta Luxembourg 16 independent growers, high quality standards (eg. cover crops in vyd, yield max 60 hl/ha, no chaptalization).

Domaine et Tradition Leading growers' association, eight members, high quality.

Gales ★★→★★★ Reliable producer, cellar labyrinth worth seeing. Classical DOMAINE ET TRADITION whites, stylish Crémant, esp Brut Nature Héritage 17, PINOT N 22.

Kox, R&L ★★★ Avant-garde with craftsmanship: planting trees in the vyd (Orchard series), Crémant without added sulphur. Trad wines gd too: Charta AUXERROIS Remich Fels 22 (cashew aromas, silky texture), PINOT BL Charta 20 (creamy).

Pauqué, Ch ★★★→★★★★ Abi Duhr's RIES come close to those of German neighbours downstream (eg. Sous la Roche-Rue, "15 hl"), but also barrel-fermented AUXERROIS (Clos du Paradis) and CHARD (Clos de la Falaise).

Schram ★★→★★★ SYLVANER (Kurschels), Franken-like (*see* Germany) Keuper soils.

Sunnen-Hoffmann ★★★ Round, aromatic concrete-egg RIES Wintrange Felsberg, and old-school full-bodied DOMAINE ET TRADITION PINOT GR.

Other good estates: Bentz, Cep d'Or, Desom, Häremillen, Kohll-Leuk, Krier Frères, Mathes, Mathis Bastian, Ruppert, Schmit-Fohl, Schumacher-Lethal. The co-op Doms Vinsmoselle has gd young growers series.

Belgium

Since 2000, Belgium's vineyards have grown from under 100 hectares to c.1000, scattered over all provinces, led by Hainaut and Limburg. Most estates are small (c.20 producers own over ten hectares). Chardonnay and Pinot Noir prevail, followed by Johanniter, Pinot Gris, Auxerrois, Souvignier Gris, Meunier and Solaris. These make lively, food-friendly, premium-priced, cool-climate wines, mainly sparkling and white. Export is growing, but most sell locally: at cellar doors, specialist retailers, wine bars and restaurants, and increasingly at seasonal festivals and oenotourism events. Best recent vintages: 23 22.

Try Agaises, Aldeneyck, Beekborne, Bioul, Bon Baron, Bousval, Chant d'Eole, Chapitre, Chenoy, Clos d'Opleeuw, Cruysem, Cuvelier, Dappersveld-Woestijn, d'Hellekapelle, Domaine W, Entre-Deux-Monts, Genoels-Elderen, Glabais, Gloire de Duras, Haksberg, Hoenshof, Kitsberg, Kluisberg, La Falize, Leeflank, Lijsternest, Marnières, Mérula, Monteberg, Nobel, Oud Conynsbergh, Petrushoeve, Près De Gand, Ravenstein, Rhode, Ry d'Argent, Schorpion, Steinberg, Stuyvenberg, ten Gaerde, Thilesna, Valke Vleug, Vandersteene, Vandeurzen, Vin de Liège, Waes, Wijnfaktorij.

Spain

Abbreviations used in the text:

SPAIN

Alel	Alella	P Vas	País Vasco
Alic	Alicante	R Bai	Rías Baixas
Ara	Aragón	Rib Sac	Ribeira Sacra
Bier	Bierzo	Rib del D	Ribera del Duero
Bul	Bullas	Rio	Rioja
Cád	Cádiz	R Ala	Rioja Alavesa
Can	Canary Islands	R Alt	Rioja Alta
C-La M	Castilla-La Mancha	R Or	Rioja Oriental
		Rue	Rueda
C y L	Castilla y León	Som	Somontano
Cat	Catalonia	U-R	Utiel-Requena
C de Bar	Conca de Barberá	Vald	Valdeorras
Cos del S	Costers del Segre	Vcia	Valencia
Emp	Empordà		
Ext	Extremadura		
Gal	Galicia	**PORTUGAL**	
Jum	Jumilla	Alen	Alentejo
La M	La Mancha	Alg	Algarve
Mál	Málaga	Bair	Bairrada
Mall	Mallorca	Bei Int	Beira Interior
Man	Manchuela	Dou	Douro
Mén	Méntrida	Lis	Lisboa
Mont-M	Montilla-Moriles	Mad	Madeira
Mont	Montsant	Min	Minho
Mur	Murcia	Set	Setúbal
Nav	Navarra	Tej	Tejo
Pen	Penedès	Vin	Vinho Verde
Pri	Priorat		

"The rain in Spain stays mainly in the plain." Well, no, it doesn't. We are starting to discover that the songster was wrong – shockingly so. Spain is confronting the extremes of climate change. On the one hand, destructive floods sweeping all before them. On the other hand, the conversation and the Instagram posts have been about extreme drought. Priorat underwent three years of perilous lack of water; growers in Catalonia have posted pictures of vines that have shrivelled and died. Yet time is not up for Spain as a vine-grower: the country has vineyards at higher altitudes and different orientations; it is blessed with dry-farmed bush vines; it is adapting its viticulture to the conditions. Add to this the energy and creativity that a new generation brings. The people taking over now are the children of those who relaunched the industry after Franco's death and Spain's entry into the European Community. They have travelled the world and returned passionate to defend their own terroir. The country is full of bodegas making wines with local varieties, experimenting with winemaking techniques, using concrete, clay *tinajas* and different sizes and origins of oak. If there's one problem,

pain & Portugal

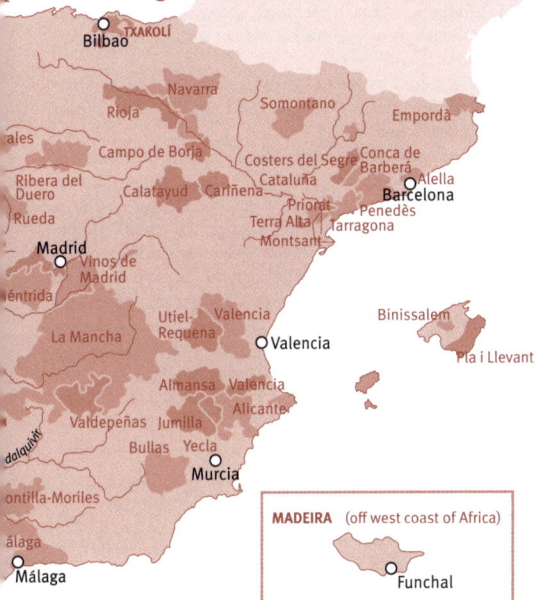

Bilbao
TXAKOLÍ
Navarra
Rioja
Somontano
Empordà
ales
Campo de Borja
Costers del Segre
Conca de
Barberá
Ribera del
Duero
Calatayud
Cariñena
Cataluña
Alella
Barcelona
Rueda
Priorat
Penedès
Terra Alta
Tarragona
Madrid
Montsant
Vinos de
Madrid
éntrida
Utiel-
Requena
Valencia
Binissalem
La Mancha
Valencia
Almansa
Valencia
Pla i Llevant
Valdepeñas
Alicante
dalquiw
Jumilla
Bullas
Yecla
Murcia
ontilla-Moriles
álaga
Málaga

SPAIN

MADEIRA (off west coast of Africa)

Funchal

their production is often small, and their distribution scant. For foreign
consumers, a holiday in Spain is often the best solution for those keen
to enjoy the New Spain. Make time to visit specialist bars in Madrid,
Barcelona, Valencia, Jerez. Don't forget northwest Spain and the islands.
If you can't make the trip this year, be assured that the quality of wines
from the larger wineries that have international distribution is also
excellent. Spain's star shines bright.

Recent Rioja vintages

2024 Cool, wet vintage; low production. Those harvested early are best.
2023 Difficult: drought in many areas. Lower yields. Depends on producer.
2022 A few v. hot summer days. Lower yields. Generally lighter wines.
2021 Deep-coloured structured, fresh reds, fine ageing potential.
2020 Difficult yr with mildew. Fresh wines, moderate alc.
2019 Low yield, overall fine quality. Some wines outstanding.
2018 Gd yr with generous yields, lower alc, fresh wines.
2017 Dramatic frost. What was left is v.gd. Enjoy now or soon.
2016 Largest harvest since 05, well-balanced wines, plenty to like.
2015 Top vintage. Wines gd as 10. Savour now, best still keepers.

Aalto Rib del D ★★★→★★★★ Stylish, polished wines: Aalto and flagship PS (from 200 plots). Winemaker MARIANO GARCÍA. Owner Masaveu also has Enate (SOM), Fillaboa (R BAI), Leda (C Y L), Murua (RIO), Pagos de Araiz (NAV); v.gd Asturias cider (Valverán).

Abadía Retuerta C y L ★★→★★★ No expense spared at Spain's newest VINO DE PAGO with spa hotel, Michelin restaurant. Just outside RIB DEL D. Serious single-vyd reds, eg. Pago Garduña SYRAH, Pago Valdebellón CAB SAUV, PV PETIT VERDOT. Fine Le Domane (w). Novartis owned.

Águila, Dominio del Rib del D ★★→★★★★ Jorge Monzón proves there is another face to RIB DEL D: crisp, delicate. Field-blend Peñas Aladas, exceptional; pale *clarete*, refreshing; Albillo, v.gd.

Álava / País Vasco / Basque Country ★→★★★★ Stretching s from the TXAKOLIS of the Atlantic to RIO, Álava is home to a people with a proud history and their own language. Young, trad R Ala wines use carbonic maceration; R Ala known for old vines, different village characters. Campaigns for regional identity encouraging some producers to break from Rio to unite under an Ala umbrella.

Algueira Rib Sac ★★→★★★ Exceptional producer in RIB SAC, expert in its extreme viticulture on vertiginous river banks. Fine selection of elegant wines from local varieties. Outstanding is Merenzao (aka Jura's TROUSSEAU), almost burgundian in style.

Alicante ★→★★★ Spiritual home of MONASTRELL: spicy reds and rare, trad, unfortified *Fondillón*. Dry white from formerly unloved MOSCATEL de Alejandría coming to fore; and local (r) Giró. Top: GUTIÉRREZ DE LA VEGA, PEPE MENDOZA CASA AGRÍCOLA. Also COLECCIÓN DE TONELES CENTENARIAS, Les Freses, Murviedro.

First wine regulatory body? Alicante (1510) says they beat Burgundians to it.

Allende, Finca R Alt ★★→★★★★ Top (in all senses) BODEGA at BRIONES in merchant's house with tower looking over town to vyds, run by irrepressible Miguel Ángel de Gregorio. Outstanding white.

Almacenista Man, Sherry Sherry stockholder; cellars wines for BODEGAS to increase or refresh stocks. Important in MANZANILLA production. Can be terrific. Few left; many have changed direction and now sell direct to consumers, eg. EL MAESTRO SIERRA, GUTIÉRREZ COLOSÍA.

Alma de Carraovejas C y L, R Bai, Rib, Rib del D, Rio ★★→★★★★ Exceptional project, started in RIB DEL D (Milsetentayseis, PAGO DE CARRAOVEJAS), now across Spain. Founded/acquired blue-chip bodegas: Aiurri (RIO), Marañones (GREDOS), Ossian (C Y L), Tricó (R BAI), VIÑA MEÍN – EMILIO ROJO (RIBEIRO).

Alonso del Yerro Rib del D, Toro ★★→★★★ Stéphane Derenoncourt (*see* France) entices elegance from RIB DEL D's extreme continental climate. Vintages from 16 on showing great delicacy. Family business, estate wines. Top: María. Paydos is TORO. Owner María del Yerro chairs Grandes Pagos (*see* PAGO).

Alta Alella Cava, Pen ★★→★★★ Family business with toes in Med, closest to Barcelona. Excellent CAVAS, fine, full-bodied Pansa Blanca (XAREL·LO), sweet red Dolç Mataró from MONASTRELL. Organic. Separate Celler de les Aus is brand for min-intervention, no-added-sulphur wines.

Alvear Ext, Mont-M ★★→★★★★ Historic; superb array of PX in MONT-M; gd FINO CB and Capataz, lovely sweet SOLERA 1927, unctuous DULCE Viejo; v. fine vintage. RAMIRO IBÁÑEZ of SANLÚCAR advises on Miradas still wines aged under FLOR. Palacio Quemado is in Ribera del Guadiana.

Añada Vintage.

Antídoto Rib del D ★★ A different face of RIB DEL D from Bertrand Sourdais, revealing delicacy, purity of Soria province. Old-vine TEMPRANILLO. Charming Le Rosita rosado.

Anza R Ala ★★ Elegance from Diego Magaña, part of impressive, well-travelled new generation in RIO.

Aragón Mighty medieval kingdom, stretching s from Pyrénées, home to Calatayud, CAMPO DE BORJA, CARIÑENA, Som DOPS. Once a land of bulk wine, co-ops, now gaining attention for new generation recuperating old vines, esp GARNACHA, also MACABEO, Moristel (r). Try ESCOCÉS VOLANTE, Familia NAVASCUÉS, FRONTONIO, SAN ALEJANDRO CO-OP.

Arfe, Bodegas Sherry ★★★ Unique project for JEREZ, Luis Arroyo makes just one wine: v. fine PALO CORTADO de la Cruz de 1767.

Arizcuren Rio ★★ Engaging Javier A trained as architect, designs wineries in RIO, incl his own urban BODEGA in downtown Logroño (worth a visit, as is trad cave in cliffs in Quel town). Specializes in GARNACHAS at altitude from R OR, Mazuelo (CARIÑENA; relatively rare as single variety in Rio) and amphora wine.

Artadi Ala, Alic, Nav, P Vas ★★→★★★★ Juan Carlos López de Lacalle makes wine within RIO DOP but prefers to label with ÁLAVA origin. Single-vyd focus: luxuriant La Poza de Ballesteros; dark, stony El Carretil; outstanding El Pisón. Also in ALIC (r El Sequé), NAV (r Artazuri, ROSADO DYA). Izar-Leku TXAKOLÍ (w) from Getaria.

Artuke Rio ★★→★★★ Family's wines transformed by bros Arturo and Kike de Miguel. One of new generation of "Rioja 'n' Rollers" now seriously gd. Exponent of villages in R Ala. Gloriously elegant, subtle use of large oak. Two top single vyds: El Escolladero, on limestone; La Condenada, on iron-rich sandstone.

Astobiza Ala ★★ In smallest of TXAKOLÍ DOPS, v. fine, advised by Ana Martín (*see* CASTILLO DE CUZCURRITA). Mineral Malkoa; also gin.

Atlantic wines Gal, P Vas, Rio Unofficial term for bright, often unoaked whites with firm acidity. Increasingly used to describe crisp, delicate reds, esp in R BAI, or TXAKOLÍS. Claimed by JEREZ. Describes cool-climate influences on specific vintages, eg. in inland GAL DOPS, and RIO. Not forgetting CAN in mid-Atlantic.

Axarquía Mál Beautiful mtn region inland from MÁL, worth a visit, renowned for sweet wines, esp BENTOMIZ, Jorge Ordoñez, Sedella.

Baltá, Pares Cava, Pen ★★→★★★ Dynamic family led by Marta Casas proving ageability of XAREL·LO. CAVAS and still wines. Electio (Xarel·lo) still lively with 12 yrs age.

Barbadillo Cád, Man ★→★★★★★ From supermarket to superb. Astonishingly fine portfolio. Sherry guru Armando Guerra works with Montse Molina seeking out specialities from cellars, incl unfortified PALOMINO. Pioneered MANZANILLA EN RAMA. Top-of-range Reliquía, esp AMONTILLADO, PALO CORTADO. Innovating in whites. Glorious As de Mirabras Sumatorio, delicate Manzanilla. Also Vega Real (RIB DEL D), BODEGAS Pirineos (SOM).

Barrio de la Estación Rio The "station quarter" of Haro, from where trains shipped wine to Bx when latter's vines were destroyed by phylloxera. Now home to seven top wineries: BODEGAS Bilbaínas (CODORNÍU), CVNE, Gómez Cruzado, LA RIOJA ALTA, LÓPEZ DE HEREDIA, MUGA, RODA. Annual open-house tastings; *see* barrioestacion.com.

Belondrade C y L, Rue ★★→★★★ Consistent leader in VERDEJO as it should be but so rarely is. Didier B was early (1994) exponent of finesse in RUE, and lees ageing. Impressive Les Parcelles shows benefits of 5 yrs' age.

Bentomiz, Bodegas Mál ★★→★★★ Dutch by birth, Spanish by adoption: Clara (winemaker) and André (chef) are welcoming hosts in Axarquía. Sweet MOSCATEL, MERLOT. Rare dry Romé (rosé). New: CAVA with PENEDÈS grapes and Bentomiz *licor de expedición*. Fine restaurant.

Bhilar, Bodegas R Ala ★→★★ David Sampedro Gil is a single-minded pioneer in El Villar. Focus on vyds, old vines, bio. Whites are textured, reds show elegance.

Phinca Revilla Sexto Año spends 6 yrs in oak, homage to trad whites of RIO. *See also* ETÉREA KRIPAN

Bideona R Ala ★→★★ Promising project (backed by two MWs), reflects specific terroirs. Founded when RIO prevented use of village name on wines not made in that village, so Bideona uses abbreviations, eg. V1BN4 (Villabuena). Part of Península Viticultores (C Y L, CEBREROS, GREDOS, TXAKOLÍ de Bizkaia).

Rioja, Priorat... How many DOPs can you remember? Spain now has 105.

Bierzo ★→★★★★ Looking for a different flavour in Spain? Find it in aromatic, mid-weight, often crunchily fresh reds from MENCÍA in nw. On slate soils they become perfumed, *Pinot-like*. The DOP shot to international fame with RAÚL PÉREZ and Ricardo Pérez Palacios (no relation). Look for CÉSAR MÁRQUEZ, DESCENDIENTES DE J PALACIOS, Raúl Pérez, plus Dominio de Tares, Losada, Luna Berberide, Mengoba, MICHELINI, Peique, Veronica Ortega. Also fine GODELLO (w).

Bilbao, Ramón R Bai, Rib del D, Rio, Rue ★→★★★ Part of huge Zamora company (producer of Licor 43). Research-driven BODEGAS. In RIO, centenary winery delivers classics but also fresh GARNACHA from R OR. Sister winery Lalomba, paradise of concrete tanks, with single-vyd reds, pale ROSADO. Also in RUE, R BAI (v.gd Mar de Frades), bio Cruz de Alba (RIB DEL D).

Bimbache Can ★★ If you are on a walking tour of El Hierro, smallest of the Canaries, check out this promising project. Local varieties, vividly fresh whites, small in quantity, big in ambition.

Bodega A cellar; a wine shop; a business making, blending and/or shipping wine.

Butt Sherry 600-litre barrel of long-matured American oak used for Sherry. Filled 5/6 full, allows space for FLOR to grow, protecting wine from oxygen and consuming nutrients. Trend for wineries – and whisky distillers – to use former butts for maturation for Sherry influence – eg. CVNE Monopole Clásico, BARBADILLO Mirabras.

Campo de Borja Ara ★→★★ Self-proclaimed "Empire of GARNACHA". Heritage of old vines, plus young vyds = 1st choice for gd-value Garnacha, now starting to show serious quality: Alto Moncayo, Aragonesas, Borsao.

Campo Viejo Rio ★→★★ Bestselling RIO, CAVA brand. Now owned by Accolade wines (*see also* YSIOS).

Canary Islands ★→★★★ Seven main islands, nine DOPS. Tenerife has five of them. Favourite of wine-hunters: unusual varieties, old vines, distinct micro-climates, volcanic soils, unique pruning and vines untouched by phylloxera, on their own rootstocks. Diverse varieties include dry white LISTÁN (aka PALOMINO) and Listán Negro, Marmajuelo, Negramoll (TINTA NEGRA), Vijariego. MOSCATELS, MALVASÍAS, incl fortified El Grifo from Lanzarote. Top: Borja Pérez, ENVINATE, SUERTES DEL MARQUÉS; try also Viñátigo. In volcano-hit La Palma: Victoria Pecís Torres (esp Malvasía Volcánica). Lanzarote: EL GRIFO. Gran Canaria: Agala, CARMELO PEÑA, Lava, TAMERÁN. Tourism rules, but fine wines to be found.

Cangas ★→★★ Isolated DOP in wild Asturias just beginning to be known. Unique varieties USP: fresh Albarín Blanco, crunchy reds from Albarín Negro, Verdejo Negro and, most promising, Carrasquín. Producers: Dominio de Urogallo, Monasterio de Corias, VidAs.

Can Sala Cava ★★★★ Exceptional CAVA winery still belonging to Ferrer family, founder of FREIXENET. Cava de Paraje, from PARELLADA.

Cariñena Ara ★→★★ The one DOP that is also the name of a grape variety. Co-op country transformed by talented winemakers. ESCOCÉS VOLANTE; Jorge NAVASCUÉS. Bold, characterful, value.

Casa Castillo Jum ★★→★★★★ One of Spain's greats, José María Vicente, proves JUM can be tiptop. Family business high up in *altiplano*. Outstanding MONASTRELLS, esp PIE FRANCO.

Castaño Mur Yecla is trad bulk-wine country, but Castaño stands apart. Castaño Dulce a modern classic sweet MONASTRELL.

Castell d'Encús Cos del S ★★→★★★ Shades of a philosopher-king, Raül Bobet (also of PRI FERRER BOBET) is constantly planning. At over 1000m (3281ft) he can make *superbly fresh, original wines*. Grapes fermented in C12 granite *lagares*. Acusp PINOT, Ekam RIES, Thalarn SYRAH all classics.

Castilla y León ★→★★★ Spain's largest wine region. Diversity means exciting discoveries. DOPS: Arlanza, Arribes, BIER, Cigales, RUE, Sierra de Salamanca (one to watch, with red Rufete grape), Tierra de León, Tierra del Vino de Zamora, TORO, Valles de Benavente, Valtiendas. Catch-all IGP Vino de la Tierra de C y L can be source of v. fine wines, eg. Barco del Corneta, Máquina y Tabla. Top: ABADÍA RETUERTA, MARQUÉS DE RISCAL (VERDEJO), Mauro, Ossian, Prieto Pariente. Recuperating unique grapes, eg. Cenicienta, Juan García, Puesta en Cruz.

Castillo de Cuzcurrita R Alt ★★ Lovely walled vyd and castle, v. fine RIO. Inky, pure, single-vyd Tilo.

Castillo Perelada Emp, Nav, Pri, Rio ★→★★ Glossy tourist destination: hotel, casino, Michelin restaurant, striking winery. Vivacious value CAVAS. Also modern red blends. Rare 12-yr-old, SOLERA-aged Garnatxa de l'EMPORDÀ. Fine Casa Gran del Siurana (PRI). Owns Chivite (NAV). Viña Salceda (RIO), now under new management, looks promising.

Catalonia Vast umbrella DOP, covers whole of Cat: seashore, mtn, in-between. Top chefs and top BODEGAS. Actual DOP too large to have identity.

Cava ★→★★★ Spain's trad-method sparkling; 90%+ made in PEN. Cava de Guarda, youngest, min 9 mths' age. Cava de Guarda Superior, incl all older wines, all certified organic 2025. Res (min 18 mths), Gran Res (min 30 mths). Single-vyd Cava de Paraje (min 36 mths), low or no dosage. Brut Nature v. common in top categories; XAREL·LO v. highly rated for ageability; MACABEO less able to tolerate climate change. Important innovation: Elaboradores Integrales, producers who grow/make/bottle their own wines. Regulatory changes partly driven by breakaway producer groups, eg. CLÀSSIC PEN, Conca del Ríu Anoia and CORPINNAT, plus RIO now has own category of trad-method sparkling not called Cava. Latest initiatives give potential for recognition of Cava's top-quality wines. *See* ALTA ALELLA, CAN SALA, CODORNÍU, MESTRES, JUVÉ Y CAMPS.

Cebreros C y L ★→★★ Youthful (2017) DOP illustrating dynamic development of GREDOS, with distinct zones identifying themselves. As elsewhere, GARNACHA (r) dominates; also Albillo Mayor (w). Look for Daniel Ramos, Rico Nuevo, Ruben Díaz, Soto Manrique, TELMO RODRÍGUEZ.

Celler del Roure Vcia ★→★★ Interested in TINAJAS? Then visit this BODEGA in S VCIA. Impressive underground cellar of vast *tinajas* buried up to necks; gd, fresh, elegant. Cullerot, Parotet, Safrà from local varieties. Many old houses in Alforins district have trad *tinajas*, none quite so remarkable as this.

Cerrón, Bodegas Jum ★★→★★★ Enthusiastic Cerdán bros working with family's v. old vines at up to 960m (3150ft); bio. New style of fresh, delicate JUM.

Take a morning to visit Vinseum, Catalonia's new wine museum in Vilafranca.

Chipiona Sherry Sandy coastal zone, source of MOSCATEL. Best: floral delicacies, far less dense than PX.

Clàssic Penedès Pen Category of DOP PEN for trad-method fizz: min 15 mths' ageing, organic grapes. Members incl Albet i Noya, Colet, Loxarel, Mas Bertrán.

Clos Mogador Pri ★★→★★★ René Jnr's father, René Barbier, is one of PRI's founding quintet and mentor to many. One of 1st wineries to gain a Vi de

Finca designation. Lovely Manyetes CARIÑENA. Gratallops Vi de Vila ROSADO (1st vintage 2021), vinous treat.

Codorníu Raventós Cos del S, Pen, Pri, Rio ★→★★★★ Historic art nouveau CAVA winery worth a visit. Single-vyd, single-variety Cavas de Paraje Calificado trio v. fine. Mass-market Cavas continue to improve. Elsewhere, Legaris in RIB DEL D has v.gd village wines; Raimat in COS DEL S is Europe's largest organic estate; BODEGAS Bilbaínas in RIO has bestseller VIÑA Pomal – back on form. Jewel is outstanding PRI SCALA DEI, which it part owns.

Colección de Toneles Centenarios Alic ★★★★ Superb aged FONDILLÓN: forgotten casks discovered, revived, commercialized under brand Luis XIV; v. limited release. Also excellent dry wines from local varieties.

Conca de Barberà Cat Small DOP once a feeder of fruit to large enterprises, now some excellent wineries, incl Abadía de Poblet, TORRES.

Consejo Regulador Organization that controls a DOP; each DOP has its own. Quality as inconsistent as wines they represent: some bureaucratic, others enterprising.

Contador, Bodega ★★→★★★★ Became an icon of modern, polished RIO. Contador is the eponymous wine, Predicador the little brother; white Que Bonito Cacareaba.

Contino R Ala ★★→★★★★ Estate incl one of RIO's great single vyds. Winemaker Jorge NAVASCUÉS developing tiptop range. CVNE-owned. Known for use of GRACIANO.

Corpinnat Cat ★★→★★★★ Independent group of producers of trad-method fizz, more stringent quality than CAVA: Bufadors, Can Descregut, Can Feixes, Cisteller, GRAMONA, Júlia Bernet, Llopart, Mas Candí, Nadal, Pardas, RECAREDO, Sabaté i Coca, Torelló.

Can a Premier League footballer make a wise wine investment? Yes, David Silva (Tamerán, Gran Canaria).

Cortijo de los Aguilares Mál ★→★★★ The bodega that proves PINOT N can be made in Andalusia. How? Because vyds nr Ronda are at 900m (2953ft). Tadeo PETIT VERDOT; GRACIANO; Tadeo TINAJA all v.gd. New GARNACHA BL/VIOGNIER/Vijiriega.

Costers del Segre ★→★★★ Geographically divided DOP combines mountainous CASTELL D'ENCÚS and lower-lying Castell del Remei, Raimat.

Cota 45 Sherry ★★ From thoughtful, ever-interesting SANLÚCAR winemaker RAMIRO IBÁÑEZ. Ube is PALOMINO from different famous PAGOS, eg. Carrascal, Miraflores. Saline, appley, unfortified, briefly matured in Sherry BUTTS. Reveals strong terroir differences. *See also* DE LA RIVA, WILLY PÉREZ.

Crianza Declaration of wine age – not quality – in RIO. Indicates use of oak. Must be min 2 yrs old; reds min 1 yr in oak barrels, whites and ROSADOS min 6 mths.

Cuentaviñas Rio ★★ Personal project of Eduardo Eguren, son of Marcos (SIERRA CANTABRIA), in Peciña (San Vicente de la Sonsierra). Old-vine (1923) El Tiznado.

Cusiné, Tomás C de Bar, Cos del S ★★→★★★ Winemaker leading innovative group: wines incl Finca collection, Tomás Cusiné blends. In MONT, C DE BAR, COS DEL S.

CVNE R Ala, R Alt ★★→★★★★ One of RIO's great names, based in Haro's BARRIO DE LA ESTACIÓN, owns 545 ha vyds. Pronounced *"coo-neh"*, Compañia Vinícola del Norte de España, founded 1879. Four Rio wineries: CONTINO, CVNE (incl Real de Asúa), Imperial, VIÑA Real. Most impressive at top end. Also wineries in CAVA (Roger Goulart), R BAI (La Val), RIB DEL D (Bela), VALD (Virgen del Galir).

De Alberto Rue ★★★ Exceptional demijohn- and SOLERA-aged oxidative VERDEJO: caramel and walnut, vanilla and raisin.

Dinastía Vivanco R Alt ★→★★★ Family business in Briones known for varietal wines and *outstanding wine museum* in Briones. Impressive trad-method sparkling RIO.

DO / DOP (denominación de origen / protegida) DOP replaced former DO category.

Dominio de Atauta Rib del D ★★→★★★★ A star among elegant wines of RIB DEL D's Soria province. Pre-phylloxera vyds; v. different from typically bold wines of DO.

Dulce Sweet. Can be late-harvest, botrytis, or fortifed. Seek out treasures: ALTA ALELLA, BENTOMIZ, GUTIÉRREZ DE LA VEGA, OCHOA, TELMO RODRÍGUEZ, TORRES. Also EMPORDÀ, MÁL, Sherry, TXAKOLÍ, Yecla.

El Escocés Volante Ara, Cal ★→★★★ Scot Norrel Robertson MW was flying winemaker in Spain, hence the brand. Focus on old-bush-vine GARNACHA grown at altitude, often field blends. Individual, characterful wines, part of movement transforming ARA; v. fine, single parcels.

El Grifo, Bodegas Can ★→★★ Historic winery on Lanzarote, celebrated 250 yrs of unbroken winemaking on the island 2025. Specializes in white MALVASIA Volcánica (dr/sw).

El Maestro Sierra Sherry ★★★ Discover how a JEREZ cellar used to be. Run by Mari-Carmen Borrego Plá, following on from her mother, the redoubtable Pilar. Fine AMONTILLADO 1830 VORS, FINO, OLOROSO 1/14 VORS.

El Puerto de Santa María Sherry Few BODEGAS remain, incl GUTIÉRREZ COLOSÍA, OSBORNE (gd wine bar). Puerto FINOS are less weighty than JEREZ, not as "salty" as SANLÚCAR. Lustau's EN RAMA trio shows differences of Sherries aged in the three different towns.

El Reventón C y L ★★→★★★ Argentine arrivals in GREDOS: Adrianna Catena and wunderkind Alejandro Vigil purchased vyd from DANI LANDI. Expect gd things.

Empordà Cat ★→★★ One of number of centres of creativity in CAT, incl CASTILLO PERELADA, Celler Martí Fabra, Pere Guardiola, Vinyes dels Aspres. Sumptuous natural sweet wine from Celler Espolla: SOLERA GRAN RES.

Envínate Alm, Can, Rib Sac ★→★★★ Sparkling quartet of winemakers unlocking lesser-known regions: Almansa (Albahra), RIB SAC (Lousas), Tenerife (Táganan).

Equipo Navazos Man, Mont-M, Sherry ★★★→★★★★ Pioneering collection by academic Jesús Barquín and Sherry-maker Eduardo Ojeda working as négociants, bottling individual BUTTS. Not just JEREZ: v. fine MONT-M selections; also vermouths and aged vinegar.

Espumoso Means "sparkling", but confusing: incl cheap, injected-bubble wine as well as quality trad-method – like CAVA.

Etérea Kripan R Ala ★→★★ Personal project of Melanie Hickman, partner of David Sampedro of BODEGAS BHILAR; bio. Phinca Hapa Blanco (v. fine), Sasikume (fascinating, delicate) from (illegal) TROUSSEAU grapes.

Extremadura For tourists, magnets are conquistador city of Trujillo and Roman city of Mérida. But linger: Extremadura has some ambitious projects, esp HABLA, Pago de los Balancines, Palacio Quemado (*see* ALVEAR). Ribera del Guadiana is DOP. Almendralejo, "city of CAVA", v. distant subzone of DOP Cava.

Faustino Rib del D, Rio ★→★★ One of the famous names of RIO's boom yrs. With some 650 ha of vyd, it makes wines in all classic categories. Celebrating 160 yrs; new winery by UK architect Norman Foster + Partners. Other wineries: Marqués de Vitoria (Rio), Portia (RIB DEL D).

Fernando de Castilla Sherry ★★→★★★★ Gloriously consistent quality. Antique range all qualify as VOS or VORS, but label doesn't say so. Complex Antique FINO is fortified to historically correct 17% abv. OLOROSO, PX Singular v.gd. Plus v. fine brandy, vermouth, vinegar. Favoured supplier to EQUIPO NAVAZOS.

Ferrer Bobet Pri ★★→★★★★ Gloriously velvety, polished CARIGNAN stars. Sergi F and Raúl B (*see* CASTELL D'ENCUS) celebrated two decades of focused brilliance in 2025. Exceptional Selección Especial. Winery worth a visit.

Flor Sherry Spanish for "flower": refers to the layer of *Saccharomyces* yeasts that typically grow and live on top of FINO/MANZANILLA Sherry in a BUTT 5/6 full. Flor consumes oxygen and other compounds ("biological ageing") and protects wine from oxidation. It grows a thicker layer nearer the sea at EL PUERTO and SANLÚCAR, hence finer character of Sherry there. VINO DE PASTO often aged for a short time with flor. Growing interest in flor winemaking elsewhere in Spain.

Florido, César Sherry ★→★★★ Master of MOSCATEL, since 1887. Working with underrated sweet-style Sherry. Explore gloriously scented, succulent: Dorado, Especial, Pasas. Based in CHIPIONA.

Fondillón Alic ★→★★★ Fabled unfortified *rancio* semi-sweet wine from overripe MONASTRELL. Matured in oak for min 10 yrs; some SOLERAS of great age. Unfairly fallen out of fashion, production shrinking too fast: Brotons (v. fine 64' 70'), MG Wines, COLECCIÓN DE TONELES CENTENARIOS.

Freixenet Cava, Pen ★→★★★ Biggest CAVA producer. Best known for black-bottled Cordón Negro. CAN SALA is Cava de Paraje. Plus: Morlanda (PRI), Solar Viejo (RIO), Valdubón (RIB DEL D), Vionta (R BAI). Also Finca Ferrer (Argentina), Gloria Ferrer (US), Katnook (Australia). Owned by sparkling giant Henkell.

Frontonio Ara ★→★★★ Fernando Mora MW and Mario López continue to make waves, seeking out old-vine GARNACHA, GARNACHA BLANCA. Also v.gd MACABEO, from old-vine El Jardin de la Iguales vyd.

Galicia Spain's nw corner. Isolation has ensured rare varieties. Outstanding whites, esp from RAFAEL PALACIOS; delicate, fresh reds, esp ALGUEIRA, DESCENDIENTES DE J PALACIOS, QUINTA DA MURADELLA, ZARATE (*see* MONTERREI, R BAI, RIB SAC, RIBEIRO and VALD).

García, Mariano & Sons C y L, Rib del D, Rio Mariano G is fixture in N and NW Spain. For many yrs winemaker at VEGA SICILIA. Co-founded AALTO and launched Mauro (C Y L). He and sons Alberto, Eduardo also run Garmón Continental (RIB DEL D), San Román (TORO). Arrived in RIO 2020 in Baños de Ebro.

Genérico Rio If there's no age category shown on the RIO bottle – such as RES – then it's a *genérico*. *Genéricos* need not follow all DOP rules on ageing (such as barrel size, min ageing). Unattractive and unhelpful name, but can be v.gd or outstanding. Case of needing to know producer.

Gil, José R Ala ★★→★★★ Rapidly rising star in R Ala, with precise single parcels El Bardallo, La Canoca. Plenty more to come.

González Byass Cava, Cád, Rib del D, Rio, Sherry ★→★★★★ Family business (1845). Cellarmaster Antonio Flores is debonair presence, born in the winery; daughter Silvia also a winemaker. From the *Tío Pepe* SOLERA, Flores extracts fine EN RAMA and *glorious Palmas series*. Consistently gd. Exceptional 1975 AMONTILLADO. Boutique hotel (1st hotel in a working BODEGA in JEREZ). Other wineries: Beronia (RIO), Pazos de Lusco (R BAI), vivacious Vilarnau (CAVA), VIÑAS DEL VERO (Som); Dominio Fournier (RIB DEL D); plus (not so gd, but popular) Croft Original Pale Cream Sherry. Finca Moncloa, close to Jerez, produces still reds.

Value wines

There are two kinds of value wine in Spain. First, those that are really cheap – gd reds are easier to find than whites, and often best served cool in summer. Look for GARNACHAS from CAMPO DE BORJA and across ARA: bright, juicy, with warming alc. BOBAL from U-R and MAN is a gd choice, with bold, deep-coloured reds and expressive rosados. For low-priced whites, choose VERDEJO, usually from RUE: crisp, SAUV BL-like. Second are those excellent wines that are v. fairly priced for the quality. Sherry and MONT-M lead with aged wines that are frankly too cheap. Also fine RIO, which is still underpriced compared to, say, Italian or French wines. Choose jnr wines from top names such as LA RIOJA ALTA's Viña Ardanza, and LÓPEZ DE HEREDIA's Bosconia RES. Pick "unpopular" categories such as CAVA. Fine Cava is underpriced: try ALTA ALELLA, JUVÉ Y CAMPS.

Gramona Cat, Pen ★★→★★★★ Specialist in long-aged trad-method sparkling, esp Enoteca, *III Lustros*, *Celler Batlle*. Co-founder of CORPINNAT. Also still wines. Next-generation cousins Leo and Roc G run business; also make v. fine, mainly XAREL·LO, L'Enclòs de Peralba (PEN); bio.

Gran Reserva In RIO, red Gran Res ages min 60 mths, of which min 2 yrs in 225-litre barrel, min 2 yrs in bottle. Whites and ROSADOS age min 4 yrs, of which 6 mths in barrel. Seek out older vintages, often great value.

Gredos, Sierra de C y L ★→★★★★ The mtn region nw of Madrid. Renowned for new-wave GARNACHA. Best: pale, ethereal. DOPS gradually appearing: CEBREROS, Madrid, MÉN. Try 4 Monos, Bernabeleva, Canopy, Comando G, DANIEL GOMEZ JIMÉNEZ-LANDI, Marañones, TELMO RODRÍGUEZ, Vitícola Mentridana.

Guita, La Man ★→★★★ Classic *Manzanilla* distinctive for sourcing fruit from vyds close to maritime SANLÚCAR. Grupo Estévez-owned (also VALDESPINO).

Gutiérrez Colosía Sherry ★→★★★ Rare remaining riverside BODEGA in EL PUERTO. Family business. Former ALMACENISTA. Excellent old PALO CORTADO.

Gutiérrez de la Vega Alic ★→★★★ Remarkable BODEGA specializing in sweet wine. In ALIC, but not DOP, after disagreement over regulations. Expert in MOSCATEL, FONDILLÓN. Daughter Violeta now leading business alongside own project Curii (with partner Alberto Redrado, focus on Giró r).

Habla, Bodegas Ext ★→★★ Impressive estate: vyds, prime cattle, Andalusian horses in conquistador country. Distinctive series of red varietals numbered from one. Plus curiosities, incl white aged underwater.

Hidalgo, Emilio Sherry ★★★→★★★★ Outstanding family BODEGA. All wines (except the PX) start by spending time under FLOR. Excellent unfiltered 15-yr-old La Panesa FINO, thrilling 50-yr-old AMONTILLADO Tresillo 1874 and rare Santa Ana PX 1861.

Hidalgo-La Gitana Man ★★→★★★★ Historic (1792) SANLÚCAR firm. MANZANILLA La Gitana, popular favourite. Top Manzanilla: classic single-vyd Pastrana Pasada, verging on AMONTILLADO. Outstanding VORS, incl Napoleon Amontillado, Triana PX.

Ibáñez, Ramiro Mont-M, Sherry Leading thinker in returning Sherry country to v. best of its old ways. Co-author with WILLY PÉREZ of book on their research. SANLÚCAR native, winemaker (eg. COTA 45), influential consultant to others, eg. ALVEAR (MONT-M), VIÑA CORRALES (PETER SISSECK). Member TERRITORIO ALBARIZA.

IGP (indicación geográfica protegida) Quality category less strict than DOP. Covers immense geographical possibilities; may incl prestigious producers, non-DOP by choice to be freer of inflexible regulation and to use other grapes.

Jerez de la Frontera Capital of Sherry region. "Sherry" is corruption of C8 "Sherish", Moorish name of city. Pronounced "hereth". In French, Xérès. Hence DOP is Jerez-Xérès-Sherry. MANZANILLA has own DOP: M-SANLÚCAR DE BARRAMEDA.

Joven Young, unoaked wine.

Jumilla Mur ★→★★★ Arid vyds in mtns n of Mur with heritage of old MONASTRELL vines. Top: CASA CASTILLO. Try CERRÓN, El Nido, Juan Gil, VIÑA Elena.

Juvé y Camps Cava, Pen ★★→★★★ Consistently gd CAVA. Family business. Stalwart is RES de la Familia (though qualifies as GRAN RES), La Capella is Cava de Paraje, released with decade of ageing.

Lalomba Rio ★→★★★ Ambitious winery of RAMÓN BILBAO. Paradise of concrete tanks, with two single-vyd reds and Provençal-style ROSADO.

La Mancha C-La M ★→★★ Don Quixote country; Spain's least impressive (except for its size) wine region, s of Madrid. Key source of grapes for distillation to brandy, particularly neutral AIRÉN. Too much bulk wine, yet excellence still possible: Martínez Bujanda's Finca Antigua and newbie VERUM.

Landi, Dani C y L, Mén ★★→★★★ DANIEL GÓMEZ JIMÉNEZ-LANDI, pioneer in new generation of GARNACHA producers, making wines at higher altitude across GREDOS (CEBREROS, Mén, etc.). *See also* EL REVENTÓN.

López de Heredia R Alt ★★→★★★★ Haro's oldest (1877), a family business in the BARRIO DE LA ESTACIÓN with wines that have become a cult. Famous "Txori-toki" tower and Zaha Hadid-designed shop. See how RIO was made (as it still is, here). Cubillo is younger range with GARNACHA; darker Bosconia; delicate, ripe *Tondonia*. Whites have seriously long barrel- and bottle-age; GRAN RES ROSADO is like no other. No shortcuts here.

1912: 44 different grape varieties grown in Rioja. 1942: 11. 2000: 7. Now: 14.

Lupier, Dom Nav ★→★★★ Put NAV and its GARNACHA back on map, rescuing old vines to create exceptional, bold El Terroir, ethereal La Dama; bio. RAÚL PÉREZ now in charge.

Lustau Sherry ★★★→★★★★ Benchmark Sherries from JEREZ, SANLÚCAR, EL PUERTO. Originators of ALMACENISTA collection; each one is worth trying. Only BODEGA to produce EN RAMA from three Sherry towns. Consistently excellent.

Málaga ★→★★★ From the Med to the mtns, in five different zones, Mál surprises; sweet wines of course. TELMO RODRÍGUEZ revived ancient glories with subtle, sweet *Molino Real*. Jorge Ordóñez, dry mtn wines from PX and MOSCATEL, plus barrel-aged No. 3 Old Vines Moscatel, gloriously succulent. BENTOMIZ, unique varieties (r/w, dr/sw). VICTORIA ORDÓÑEZ, excellent mtn wines. Try Pajarete, local sweet liqueur made with grape syrup. A historic curiosity.

Mallorca ★→★★★ Uneven quality, some v.gd, some simply prestige projects. Can be high-priced and hard to find off island: 4 Kilos, Ánima Negra, Bàrbara Mesquida, Biniagual, Binigrau, Can Ribas, Miquel Gelabert (with wide array), Soca-Rel, Son Bordils, Toni Gelabert, Tramuntana. Reds blend trad varieties (Callet, Fogoneu, Mantonegro) plus CAB, SYRAH, MERLOT. Whites improving fast. DOPS: Binissalem, Pla i Llevant.

Manchuela Man ★→★★★ Take another look: Juan Antonia PONCE, quietly superb, working with BOBAL and field blends. Also revitalized FINCA SANDOVAL.

Marqués de Cáceres R Alt, R Bai, Rue ★→★★ Famous for introducing French techniques in 70s. Fresh (w/rosé). Modern Gaudium; classic GRAN RES. In RUE and R BAI.

Marqués de Murrieta R Alt, R Bai ★★★→★★★★ Between them, the marquesses of RISCAL and Murrieta launched RIO. Two styles, classic and modern: Castillo Ygay GRAN RES is one of Rio's trad greats. Latest release of Gran Res Blanco is **86**. Dalmau is impressive contrast, glossy modern Rio, v. well made. *Capellania* is fresh, taut, complex white, one of Rio's v. best; v. pale, crisp Primer Rosé from MAZUELO. In R BAI, relaunched Pazo de Barrantes shines gloriously; La Comtesse, brilliantly intense.

Marqués de Riscal C y L, R Ala, Rue ★★→★★★★ Riscal is living history of RIO, able to put on a tasting of every vintage going back to 1st, 1862. Take your pick of styles: reliable RES, modern Finca Torrea, balanced GRAN RES. Powerful *Barón de Chirel Res*. Tapias sold on Place de Bx (*see* France). Marqués launched RUE (1972) and today makes vibrant DYA SAUV BL, VERDEJO and v.gd Barón de Chirel Verdejo, though prefers to put wines in C Y L not Rue. Eye-popping Frank Gehry hotel attached to Rio BODEGA.

Márquez, César Bier ★★→★★★★ Exciting entrant in Valtuille. Nephew of RAÚL PÉREZ. Outstanding El Val GODELLO.

Mas Doix Pri ★★→★★★★ Treasure is old vines, esp superb CARIÑENA (grape). Top – all blueberry and velvet, astonishingly pure, named after yr vyd was planted – *1902*, *Tossal d'en Bou*, one of few Gran Vinya Clasificada. Also v. fine old-vine GARNACHA *1903*, *Coma de Casas*. Murmuri and Salix (w).

Mas Martinet Pri ★★→★★★ Sara Pérez is daughter of one of original PRI quintet. Vociferous, adventurous, ready to try new approaches.

Mendoza, Abel R Ala ★★→★★★ For knowledge of RIO villages and varieties, Abel and Maite M have few equals. Discover no fewer than five varietal whites. Grano a Grano are only-the-best-berry-selected TEMPRANILLO and GRACIANO.

Merino, Miguel R Alt ★★ Son of famous father with same name, Miguel Jnr growing the winery: classics, yes, but also varietal Mazuelo, single-vyd wines.

Mestres, Cava Pen ★★→★★★ Specialist in aged CAVAS; 1st producer of Brut Nature (no dosage) Cava, in 1945. Fascinating Cavateca series with different disgorgement dates, and time in bottle.

Michelini I Muffato Bier, Rio ★★ The Michelinis (parents) from Argentina have old-vine project in BIER. Son Matías, in RIO at Dominio de Challao.

Monasterio, Hacienda Rib del D ★★★ PETER SISSECK co-owns/consults, where he 1st started in RIB DEL D. More accessible in price than his DOMINIO DE PINGUS.

Monterrei Gal ★→★★★ Small DOP on Portuguese border, with traces of Roman winemaking. Best by far: QUINTA DA MURADELLA.

Montilla-Moriles ★→★★★ Andalusian DOP nr Córdoba. Unfairly still in JEREZ'S shadow; PX makes unfortified dry FINOS but also sweet wines from sun-dried grapes. *Albariza* soils. Top wines superbly rich, some long ageing in SOLERA. Trend for dry whites aged in large amphorae. Top: ALVEAR, PÉREZ BARQUERO, TORO ALBALÁ. Important source of PX for use in Jerez DOP.

Montsant Cat ★→★★★ Tucked in around PRI; gd-value neighbour. Fine GARNACHA BLANCA (Acústic). Reds worth exploring: Can Blau, Capçanes, Domènech, Espectacle, Joan d'Anguera, Mas Perinet, Masroig, Venus la Universal.

Muga R Alt ★★ ·★★★★ Family business with siblings, cousins. Two styles: classical GRAN RES **Prado Enea**; modern, powerful **Torre Muga**. Also pale ROSADO; elegant white; lively trad-method sparkling.

Murciano, Bruno U-R, Vcia ★→★★ Former Ritz London sommelier returned to family and launched lively brand giving new profile to BOBAL. Now on to next phase: greater elegance.

Mustiguillo Rib del D ★★→★★★ Toni Sarrión led renaissance of BOBAL grape, also Merseguera (w); created VINO DE PAGO Finca El Terrerazo with top Quincha Corral. Also at Hacienda Solano (RIB DEL D).

Navarra ★→★★★ Formerly in shadow of neighbour RIO. Early focus on international varieties confused its identity. Today's GARNACHA revival relaunching region. Try Artazu, Aseginolaza & Leunda, DOM LUPIER, Gonzalo Celayeta, OCHOA, Tandem, VIÑA ZORZAL. Also sweet MOSCATELS.

Navascués Ara ★★ Jorge N, working wonders all over Spain. At family winery PAGO Aylès in ARA, winemaker at CONTINO in RIO, and CVNE properties in GAL, consults in other properties.

Numanthia Toro ★★→★★★★ One of TORO's heavyweights. Founded by Egurens of SIERRA CANTABRIA, who sold to LVMH. Exceptional, powerful wines gradually becoming more elegant. Top Termanthia comes round with 10 yrs of age.

Spain's oldest wine region? Probably Sherry: founded by Phoenicians. 2nd: Penedès.

Ochoa Nav ★→★★ Ochoa *padre* led modern growth of NAV, with focus on CAB, MERLOT. Winemaker daughter Adriana calls her range 8a, a play on her surname, developing different styles, incl Mil Gracias GRACIANO; fun, sweet, Asti-like sparkling MdO; classic MOSCATEL.

Ordóñez, Victoria Mál ★→★★★ Independent-minded former medical doctor rescuing old vyds, making v. fine wines in Montes de MÁL. Vividly fresh dry whites from MOSCATEL, PX; pure, fresh reds.

Osborne Sherry ★★→★★★★ Historic BODEGA in EL PUERTO, treasure trove, incl

AOS AMONTILLADO, PDP PALO CORTADO. Owns former Domecq VORS incl 51–1a Amontillado. FINO Quinta and mature Coquinero Fino typical of town. Wineries in RIO (Montecillo), RUE, RIB DEL D.

Pago de Carraovejas Rib del D ★★★ Refined, elegant, from a winery strikingly situated on slopes below Peñafiel's romantic castle; on-site Ambivium, Michelin-starred restaurant. Owned by ALMA DE CARRAOVEJAS.

Congratulations to Penedès: in 2025 was world's first DOP to be 100% organic.

Pago / Vino de Pago / Grandes Pagos *Pago* is a vyd, usually with est name, ie. Sherry's *pago* Miraflores and *pago* Balbaína. **Vino de Pago** is officially the top category of DOP; actually, not always. Typically Vinos de Pago are estates in less famous zones. Not to be confused with **Grandes Pagos**, the network of mainly family-owned estates. Some are Vinos de Pago, but not all.

Palacio de Fefiñanes Gal ★★→★★★★ Reliable DYA R BAI ALBARIÑO. Two superior styles: barrel-fermented 1583 (yr winery was founded, oldest of DOP); super-fragrant, lees-aged III. Visit palace/winery at Cambados.

Palacios, Álvaro Bier, Pri, Rio ★★★→★★★★ Almost single-handedly built modern reputation of Spanish wine through his obsession with quality. One of quintet that revived PRI. L'Ermita on a magical hilltop site helped place Spain on the modern fine-wine map. His other wines have captured Pri characters. He has also driven recent designations from village to Grand Cru: Gran Vi de Vinya. In RIO, at Palacios Remondo, transforming reputation of R OR and its GARNACHAS. Complex Plácet (w) originally created by brother RAFAEL P. Top: Quiñón de Valmira from slopes of Monte Yerga. In BIER with nephew Ricardo at DESCENDIENTES DE J PALACIOS. Lola, Álvaro's daughter, has now joined her father and uncle in the business.

Palacios, Descendientes de J Bier ★★★→★★★★ MENCÍA at its best. Ricardo Pérez P, Álvaro's nephew, grows old vines on steep slate. Floral Pétalos and Villa de Corullón gd value; Las Lamas and Moncerbal are different soil expressions, one clay, one rocky. Exceptional *La Faraona* (only one barrel), grows on tectonic fault; bio.

Palacios, Rafael Vald ★★★→★★★★ Impossible to find fault with Rafael's wines. In VALD, focus on GODELLO across many rocky parcels (*sortes*). Lovely Louro do Bolo; As Sortes, a step up; *Sorte O Soro*, surely Spain's best white. Sorte Antiga (old vines), v. delicate orange wine, Sorte Souto (tiny production, late harvest).

Pasto, Vino de Sherry ★→★★★ White from the Sherry zone, from Sherry grapes, but unfortified, revival of a former style. Grapes may be sun-dried for a day, then wine aged in Sherry casks. Have distinct *albariza* (chalky) soil character and may have FLOR aromas. Growing in popularity. A delicate introduction to Sherry. BODEGAS DE LA RIVA, COTA 45, LUIS PÉREZ La Escribana. Own DOP overdue.

Pazo de Señorans Gal ★★★ Consistently excellent ALBARIÑOS from glorious R BAI estate. Outstanding Selección de Añada, min 30 mths on lees, proof v. best Albariños age beautifully.

Peña, Carmelo Can ★→★★ One of new generation putting Gran Canaria on map. CV incl RAÚL PÉREZ, Puro Rofe (Lanzarote), Niepoort (*see* Portugal). Two projects: Bien de Altura (Gran Canaria, incl Ikewen), mineral, fresh; Jable de Tao (Lanzarote), saline, crunchy.

Penedès Cat ★→★★★★ Region w of Barcelona, most diverse of CAT. Mix of soils and mix of varieties, a little mixed in message. XAREL·LO should be star; 1st DOP to be 100% organic. Best: Agustí Torelló Mata, Alemany i Corrio, Can Rafols dels Caus, Enric Soler, GRAMONA, Jean León, Pardas, PARÉS BALTÀ, TORRES. Fizz has own CLÀSSIC PEN category.

Pepe Mendoza Casa Agrícola Alic ★★→★★★ Left family wine business (Enrique M) in

2016 to launch personal project with great success. Elegant Giró (r), MONASTRELL, MOSCATEL. Pequeñas Producciones experimental range. Top: Fierroca.

Pérez, Raúl Bier ★★→★★★★ A star, but avoids celebrity. Renowned for finesse, non-intervention. Provides generous house-room for new winemakers in cellar in BIER. Magnet for visiting (eg. Spanish, Argentine) winemakers. Outstanding Vizcaina Mencías; *El Rapolao* exceptionally pure. Other projects incl DOM LUPIER.

Pérez, Willy Sherry With RAMIRO IBÁÑEZ leading return to old ways in JEREZ, researching and reviving practices, trads, rare varieties, terroirs – and jointly writing the history. Interest in unfortified PALOMINO. Projects incl VINO DE PASTO DE LA RIVA. Founder member TERRITORIO ALBARIZA.

Pérez Barquero Mont-M ★→★★★ Leading producer of MONT-M; Gran Barquero FINO, AMONTILLADO, OLOROSO; La Cañada PX. Supplier to EQUIPO NAVAZOS.

Pie franco Ungrafted vine, on own roots. Typically on sandy soils where phylloxera cannot penetrate. Some 110 yrs+ – many in TORO, some in C Y L, RUE, CAN.

Pingus, Dominio de Rib del D ★★★→★★★★ One of RIB DEL D's greats. Tiny bio winery of Pingus (PETER SISSECK's childhood name), made with old-vine TINTO FINO, shows refinement of variety in extreme climate. Flor de Pingus from younger vines; Amelia is single barrel named after wife. PSI uses grapes from growers, long-term social project to encourage them to stay on land. *See also* HACIENDA MONASTERIO, SAN FRANCISCO JAVIER.

Pomares, Eulogio R Bai, Rib Sac ★★→★★★ No better way to understand R BAI and ALBARIÑO than this. Winemaker for ZARATE; launched eponymous project. Also recent project with wife Rebecca: Quinta do Estranxeiro (RIB SAC).

Ponce Man ★★→★★★ Quietly spoken Juan Antonio P has single-mindedly transformed family business into pre-eminent producer in DOP. One of leaders building reputation of BOBAL; bio. PIE FRANCO bottling: PF.

Priorat ★★→★★★★ Some of Spain's finest. Named after former monastery tucked under craggy cliffs. Key is *llicorella* (slate) soil, although there's clay too. Best show remarkable purity, finesse, sense of place; Pri has pioneered classification pyramid from village wines through Vi de Vila to Gran Vi de Vinya. After a period when CAB, SYRAH were thought best, producers have returned to trad CARIÑENA, GARNACHA and have toned down new oak.

Quinta da Muradella Monterrei ★→★★★ José Luis Mateo continues to charm and surprise. From some 15 ha in GAL's tiniest DOP he releases v. accomplished wines, from range of local grapes (r/w).

Raventós i Blanc Cat ★★→★★★ Pepe R led historic family business out of CAVA in 2012. Created Conca del Riu Anoia for high-quality sparklings with strict controls; bio. Wines: De Nit ROSADO, Mas del Serral, ringingly pure Textures de Pedra. Can Sumoi estate natural-wine project (2017), incl XAREL·LO, pét-nats.

Recaredo Pen ★★→★★★★ Outstanding trad-method sparkling, small family concern, celebrated centenary 2024. Wines aged under cork, not crown cap; still hand-disgorges. Top: precise, mineral *Turó d'en Mota*, from vines planted 1940, ages brilliantly; classic RES Particular; Enoteca library releases. Member CORPINNAT. Celler Credo: still wines, low in alc, strikingly pure. All bio.

Driving Barcelona to Priorat? Eat only when you arrive: horribly winding roads.

Remelluri, La Granja Nuestra Señora R Ala ★★→★★★ TELMO RODRÍGUEZ's family property; v. fine white blend; old-vine TEMPRANILLOS; exceptional old GARNACHA single vyds, ethereal wines. Yjar a sell-out on Place de Bx (*see* France). Lindes de Remelluri is project with local growers, different parcels.

Remírez de Ganuza R Ala ★★→★★★ Late Fernando R de G hit 100-point jackpot with 04 GRAN RES from selected vyds around Samaniego. Winery is diversifying: excellent Gran Res Blanco, also Iraila GARNACHA.

Reserva (Res) Has actual meaning in RIO. Reds: aged min 3 yrs, of which min 1 yr in oak of 225 litres and min 6 mths in bottle. Whites and ROSADOS: min 2 yrs age, of which min 6 mths barrel. Note: age does not mean quality.

Revert, Javier Vcia ★→★★★ Remarkably pure Med wines from family vyds, local grapes, eg. Tortosí, Trepadell and others. Three wines: Micalet, Sensal, Simeta, a benchmark.

Rías Baixas Gal ★→★★★★ Atlantic DOP in GAL split in five subzones, mostly DYA. Best: Forjas del Salnés, Fulcro, Gerardo Méndez, Martín Códax, PALACIO DE FEFIÑANES, Pazo de Barrantes (MARQUÉS DE MURRIETA), *Pazo de Señorans*, Terras Gauda, ZÁRATE. Land of *minifundia*, tiny landholdings. Until recently Spain's premier DOP for whites, now like RUE at risk of overproduction. ALBARIÑO is variety here; v. best can age, reaching burgundian elegance. A few reds, strikingly fresh, crisp.

Ribeira Sacra Gal ★★→★★★ Magical DOP with vyds running dizzyingly down to River Sil. Some impressive, original, fresh, light MENCÍA reds: Adegas Moure, ALGUEIRA, Castro Candaz, Dominio do Bibei, Guímaro, Rectoral de Amandi.

Ribeiro Gal ★→★★★ Historic region, famed in Middle Ages for Tostado (sw). Promising textured whites made from GODELLO, LOUREIRO, Treixadura. Some reds, fresh, crunchy. Top: Casal de Armán, Coto de Gomariz, Finca Viñoa, VIÑA MEÍN – EMILIO ROJO.

Ribera del Duero ★→★★★★ Ambitious DOP with great appeal in Spain, created 1982. Anything that incl AALTO, HACIENDA MONASTERIO, PINGUS, VEGA SICILIA has to be serious. Orihginally dominated by domestic demand for oaky concentration. At last, elegance breaking through. Wineries in Soria (to e) provide most delicate wines (DOMINIO DE ATAUTA, Dominio de Es, DOMINIO DEL AGUILA). Try ALMA DE CARRAOVEJAS, ALONSO DEL YERRO. Also: Arzuaga, Bohórquez, Cillar de Silos, Garmón, Hacienda Solano, Marta Maté, Sei Solo, Tomás Postigo, Valduero. *See also* C Y L neighbours ABADÍA RETUERTA, Mauro.

Rioja ★→★★★★ Spain's most famous wine region. Three subregions: R Ala, R Alt and R OR. Two key provinces: La Rioja and ÁLAVA, with NAV to e. Growing political differences between provinces and between producers and the CONSEJO REGULADOR reflected in proposal for some Ala producers to separate from DOP. Introduction of Viñedo Singular category was criticized, but gradually est itself; trad-method sparkling permitted since 2017, v. promising, esp Bilbaínas, Conde Valdemar, URBINA, VIVANCO. New generation of producers also taking different approaches, diversifying trad image of Rio.

Rioja Alta, La R Ala, R Alt, R Bai ★★→★★★★ For lovers of classic RIO, a favourite choice. Standard keeps going up. *Gran Res 904* and GRAN RES 890 are stars. But rest of range from ***Ardanza*** down to Arana, Alberdi each carry classic house style; all qualify as Gran Res. Also owns R Ala modern-style Torre de Oña, R BAI Lagar de Cervera, RIB DEL D Àster. Hard to fault.

Rioja Oriental Rio Name of what was Rioja Baja. Most easterly and largest subregion of RIO. Was poor relation, rapidly gaining attention for vyds at altitude and quality of GARNACHA. Led by ÁLVARO PALACIOS. Also RAMÓN BILBAO's LALOMBA. ARIZCUREN in town of Quel worth a visit.

Heroic viticulture

Aka mtn viticulture; formally defined as vines grown on slopes steeper than 30%. In Spain, some reach 85%. In GAL, RIB SAC easily qualifies; Cangas in Asturias; PRI is famed for the trad *costers* or steep slopes; and CAN with vyds up to 1800m (5906ft). Impossibly and improbably difficult to manage.

Riva, M. Ant de La Sherry ★★→★★★ Project from WILLY PÉREZ and RAMIRO IBÁÑEZ based on abandoned De La Riva BODEGA. Exceptionally fine.

Roca, AT Cat, Pen ★★→★★★ Impressive father-and-son business, both named Agustí R. Tiptop trad-method CLÀSSIC PEN AT Roca. Newer project is Anima Mundi, no sulphur, TINAJA-aged, ancestral-method; v. fine, expresses terroir.

Roda R Alt, Rib del D ★★→★★★ At far tip of BARRIO DE LA ESTACIÓN. TEMPRANILLO specialist: polished Roda, Roda I, Cirsion, approachable Sela, and more recently launched VIURA-dominant white. Also RIB DEL D BODEGAS La Horra, Corimbo (w), Corimbo I.

Rosado Rosé. The trad dark rosados of NAV were defeated by Provence pinks. Spain has fought back with pale hues, esp SCALA DEI's Pla dels Àngels (PRI), MARQUÉS DE MURRIETA's Primer Rosé (RIO), DOMINIO DEL ÁGUILA Pícaro Clarete (RIB DEL D), LALOMBA Finca Lalinde.

Rueda C y L ★→★★★ Spain's response to SAUV BL: zesty VERDEJO. Mostly DYA. Too much poor quality. Exceptional SOLERA-aged DE ALBERTO. New Gran Vino quality category for older vines, lower yields. Emina has 1st Gran Vino aged fizz. Chapirete Prefiloxérico v.gd.

Saca Sherry A withdrawal of Sherry from the SOLERA (oldest stage of ageing) for bottling. For EN RAMA wines, most common *sacas* are in *primavera* (spring) and *otoño* (autumn), when FLOR is richest, most protective.

Sánchez Romate Sherry ★★→★★★ Historic (1781) BODEGA with wide range, also sourcing and bottling rare BUTTS for négociants and retailers; 8-yr-old *Fino Perdido*, nutty AMONTILLADO NPU, PALO CORTADO Regente, excellent VORS Amontillado and OLOROSO La Sacristía de Romate, unctuous Sacristía PX.

Sandoval, Finca Man ★→★★ Consultant winemaker JAVIER REVERT making impressive changes. Top: La Rosa.

San Francisco Javier, Bodegas Sherry ★★★ PETER SISSECK's BODEGA in JEREZ. FINO is VIÑA Corrales from PAGO Balbaína, 8–9-yr-old EN RAMA. Aim is single-vyd Sherries from organic vines. Viña La Cruz is FINO-AMONTILLADO from Pago Macharnudo.

Sanlúcar de Barrameda Man, Sherry Town on River Guadalquivir. Port where Magellan, Columbus, admiral of Armada, set sail. Humidity in low-lying cellars encourages FLOR. Sea air said to encourage "saltiness". Wines aged here qualify for DOP MANZANILLA-Sanlúcar de Barrameda.

Scala Dei Pri ★★→★★★ Tiny vyds of "stairway to heaven" cling to craggy slopes. Part-owner CODORNÍU. Winemaker Ricard Rofes, leader in GARNACHA revival, expresses exceptional terroir, esp in single-vyd *Mas Deu*, Sant'Antoni. Also unusual GARNACHA BLANCA/CHENIN BL.

Sierra Cantabria R Ala, Toro ★★★ Exceptional family business run by bros Marcos (winemaker) and Miguel Ángel Eguren. Elegant, single-vyd, low-intervention. Reds all TEMPRANILLO. Also Viñedos de Paganos, Señorío de San Vicente, both RIO, Teso la Monja in TORO. Next-generation cousins have own R Ala wineries: Eduardo at CUENTAVIÑAS, Koldo at Ukan.

Sierra de Toloño R Ala ★★ Sandra Bravo's wines are all about elevation, cool climate, purity; assisted by old vines, field blends, neutral oak and time in amphora. Bravo indeed.

Sisseck, Peter Rib del D, Sherry Dane who attracted world interest to RIB DEL D with DOMINIO DE PINGUS starting to work magic on JEREZ. His purchase with a partner of SAN FRANCISCO JAVIER plus vyd in PAGO Balbaína, and his commitment to creating wines from organically-grown grapes has re-energized sector. His statement "Sherry is the best white wine in Spain" has worked wonders. Also at Ch Rocheyron (Bx).

Solera Sherry System for blending Sherry, less commonly Madeira (*see* Portugal), plus specialities such as DE ALBERTO Dorado and res wine of GRAMONA. Consists of topping up progressively more mature BUTTS with younger wines of same sort from previous stage, or *criadera*. With FINOS, MANZANILLAS it maintains vigour of FLOR. For all wines gives consistency; refreshes mature wines.

Suertes del Marqués Can ★★ Start here in discovering new-wave wineries in Tenerife. Unique local *trenzado* (plaited) vines. Edición 1 (r/w) v.gd. Worth a visit. Owner Jonatán García advises at TAMERÁN.

Tamerán Can ★★ Impressive Gran Canaria project from local boy and former UK (Man City) football star David Silva, working with Jonatán García of SUERTES DEL MARQUÉS (Tenerife). Subtle, delicate.

Telmo Rodríguez, Compañía de Vinos Mál, Rib del D, Rio, Toro, Vald ★★→★★★★ Telmo Rodríguez's family base is REMELLURI in RIO, but he and Pablo Eguzkiza work across Spain reviving old vines and traditions: in ALIC (Al-Murvedre), GREDOS (Pegaso), MÁL (*Molino Real* MOSCATEL), RIB DEL D (Matallana), RUE (Basa), TORO (Dehesa Gago), VALD (Gaba do Xil GODELLO, plus exceptional r single vyds). In Rio, BODEGA Lanzaga recuperates old vyds, with village wines, exceptionally pure single vyds. La Estrada, Las Beatas, Tabuérniga are stars. *See also* REMELLURI.

Terra Alta Cat Top GARNACHA country, with 90% of CAT's GARNACHA BLANCA vyds and 75% of Spain's. Deliciously complex, textured. Producers: Bárbara Forés, Celler Piñol, Edetària, Herencia Altés, Lafou.

Territorio Albariza Sherry Network of new-wave producers in JEREZ dedicated to *albariza* soils, and leading producers of VINO DE PASTO. Members incl Alejandro Muchada (Muchada-Leclapart), Blanco bros (CALLEJUELA), Forlong, M Ant De La Riva, Primitivo Collantes (Chiclana), RAMIRO IBÁÑEZ (COTA 45), SAN FRANCISCO JAVIER (Meridiano Perdido), WILLY PÉREZ (Luis Pérez). Not part of Sherry DOP, may form their own.

Terroir al Limit Pri ★★→★★★ Dominik Huber, based in Torroja village, was once something of an "angry young man" but now shows true understanding of his vyds. Wines of infusion not extraction; great refinement.

Tinaja Aka amphora, which come in range of sizes from small to vat. *See* A Little Learning. In Spain, widely used, and also eg. by ALVEAR, CELLER DEL ROURE, Colección de Toneles Centenarias, MAS MARTINET, SIERRA DE TOLOÑO. Prestige wineries such as NUMANTHIA also investing.

Toro ★→★★★★ Small DOP on Duero. Famed for bold reds from Tinta del Toro (phenotype of TEMPRANILLO, similar but not identical). Today best more restrained, but still firm tannic grip. Glamour from VEGA SICILIA-owned Pintia, LVMH-owned NUMANTHIA, and early investor the Egurens of SIERRA CANTABRIA, now owners of Teso la Monja. San Román, owned by MARIANO GARCÍA and family, also working with GARNACHA and v.gd zesty MALVASÍA Castellana (w). Growing trend for Garnacha, a lighter alternative to trad reds. New plan for sparkling; white, ROSADO and apparently red too. Also: Dominio del Bendito, Fariña, Las Tierras de Javier Rodríguez, Matsu.

Toro Albalá Mont-M ★★→★★★★ Why is MONT-M not better known? Unique treasure trove of wines from PX, incl AMONTILLADO Viejísimo, sumptuous Don PX Convento Selección 31, v.gd GRAN RES 90.

Torres Cat, Pri, R Bai, Rib del D, Rio ★★→★★★★ Torres family never stops. After 150 yrs they might ease off, but no more. Miguel T Snr takes lead on many eco fronts. Miguel Jnr engaged with business; sister Mireia technical director, runs Jean León. Clear pyramid of quality in wines. Top is Torres Antología, outstanding Catalan terroir collection: Bx blend *Res Real*, top PEN CAB *Mas la Plana*; C DE BAR duo (burgundy-like *Milmanda*, one of Spain's finest CHARDS, tiptop *Grans Muralles* blend of local varieties); single-vyd *Mas de la Rosa* will become Gran Vi de Vinya (top category of PRI) in due course. Also Camino de Magarín (RUE), La Carbonera (RIO), PAGO del Cielo (RIB DEL D), Pazo Torre

Pezelas (R BAI). Also famous, consistent, gd-value portfolio, eg. Viña Sol. Pioneer in Chile. Marimar T est in Sonoma (US).

Tradición, Bodegas Sherry ★★→★★★★ Fabulous collection of VOS/VORS Sherries. Must-visit for outstanding collection of Spanish art. Based on oldest-known Sherry house (1650), fascinating archives.

Txakolí P Vas ★→★★ Wines from the Basque Country DOPS: ÁLAVA, Bizkaya, Getaria. Once were DYA acidic wines poured into tumblers from a height to add to spritz. Bizkaya wines, with less exposed vyds, have depth, ageability. Fizz less essential. Top: Ameztoi, ASTOBIZA, Doniene Gorrondona, Izar-Leku (from ARTADI), Txomín Etxaníz. Bodega Gorka Izagirre has Michelin three-star restaurant Azurmendi.

Urbina Rio ★★→★★★ For lovers of gloriously mature RIO. Seemingly bottomless store of fine aged wines.

Valdeorras Gal ★→★★★★ Warmest, most inland of GAL'S DOPS, named after gold (*oro*) the Romans mined. GODELLOS more interesting than many ALBARIÑOS. RAFAEL PALACIOS's Godello miraculously gd. TELMO RODRÍGUEZ's MENCÍA v. fine. Also Godeval, Valdesil.

Valdepeñas C-La M ★→★★ Big DOP of LA MANCHA. Historic favourite for value reds.

Valdespino Sherry ★★→★★★★ Inocente FINO from top Macharnudo single vyd is rare oak-fermented Sherry. Terrific dry AMONTILLADO Tío Diego; outstanding 80-yr-old *Toneles* MOSCATEL, JEREZ's v. best. The Macallan whisky purchased 50% stake, thus ensuring supply of Sherry casks for whisky ageing.

Valencia ★→★★ On the move: higher-altitude old vines and min-intervention winemaking: Aranleon, Baldovar 923, CELLER DEL ROURE, El Angosto, Fil-loxera & Cia, JAVIER REVERT, Los Frailes, Rafael Cambra. Still a source of supermarket sweets, but now so much more.

Vinoble: biennial wine fair, Jerez. Innoble: irreverent sidekick, Sanlúcar.

Vega Sicilia Rib del D, Rio, Toro ★★★★ Carries a heavy burden of history, its reputation placing it above fashion. In Alvarez family ownership for four decades. Wines built to last, but developing a notable elegance under new regime. Valbuena has 5 yrs in oak and bottle, Único has almost 10 yrs in oak of different sizes and in bottle. Star is outstanding RES Especial, NV blend of three vintages. Neighbouring Alión (modern take on RIB DEL D). Pintia (TORO) now much fresher. Macán (RIO), joint venture with Benjamin de Rothschild, going in right direction. Oremus in Tokaj (*see* Hungary), in addition to sweet wine, has electrically fresh dry FURMINTS Mandolás, Petracs. Latest project: R BAI.

Verum C-La M ★ Elias López family business in Tomelloso, heart of brandy distilling. Old-vine wines original and new, number made in TINAJA. Watch.

Viña Literally, a vyd.

Viña Meín – Emilio Rojo Rib ★★★ Rojo's eponymous wine is a Treixadura blend with thrilling freshness. Star of RIBEIRO, v. fine (r/w). Now owned by ALMA DE CARROVEJAS group. Rojo remains to advise, with winemaker Laura Montero.

Vinegar Mont-M, Sherry ★→★★★ The trad unwanted by-product of winemaking that Sherry and Montilla producers did not wish to publicize. Gastronomes rate it highly now. Favourites incl FERNANDO DE CASTILLA, TORO ALBALÁ GRAN RES.

Vintae Nav, Rib del D, Rio, Toro ★→★★★ Entrepreneurial pair from Badarán making gd-value RIO at LÓPEZ DE HARO, but also v.gd Bodega Classica GRAN RES (esp rosado). Brands incl El Pacto (Rio); Aroa (NAV), Bardos (RIB DEL D), Matsu (TORO). Also lively Logroño wine bar: Wine Fandango.

Williams & Humbert Sherry ★→★★★★ Historic BODEGA famed for classic brands: Dry Sack, Winter's Tale AMONTILLADO, As You Like It OLOROSO (sw). Paola Medina introduced new vision: pioneering organic Sherry, Vintage Sherries.

Sherry styles

Palomino Fino Dominant grape of Sherry zone. Strong trend to unfortified PALOMINO aka VINO DE PASTO, eg. COTA 45, Muchada-Leclapart, Primitivo Collantes.

Manzanilla From SANLÚCAR, v. dry, biologically aged. Serve cool with seafood, eg. I Think (EQUIPO NAVAZOS), LA GUITA.

Manzanilla Pasada With 7 yrs+, where FLOR is dying, starting to turn into AMONTILLADO; v. dry, complex, eg. LUSTAU'S ALMACENISTA Cuevas Jurado.

Fino Dry, biologically aged in any of the 8 Sherry towns (except Sanlúcar); weightier than MANZANILLA; min age 2 yrs (as Manzanilla) but don't drink so young. Trend for mature FINOS aged 7 yrs+, eg. EMILIO HIDALGO. Trend to cellar and age Finos and Manzanillas in bottle.

Fino Viejo New category for DOP JEREZ, parallel to Manzanilla Pasada. Min 7 yrs+.

En Rama Sherry as if bottled directly from BUTT; not clarified or cold stabilized, low filtration = max flavour. Understood to refer to Manzanilla and Fino, but any Sherry bottled this way is En Rama. SACA typically when flor is most abundant, in spring.

Amontillado Started as Fino, then protective flor died. Oxidative ageing gives complexity. Naturally dry, eg. Lustau Amontillado del Castillo. If sweetened, indicated by "medium" label.

Palo Cortado Between Amontillado and v. delicate OLOROSO. Each winery has own style, eg. BARBADILLO Reliquía, Fernando de Castilla Antique.

Oloroso Typically not originally aged under flor. Naturally ultra-dry, superbly savoury, even fierce. May be sweetened and sold as CREAM, eg. Emilio Hidalgo Gobernador (dr), Old East India (sw).

Cream Blend sweetened with grape must, PX and/or MOSCATEL for a commercial medium-sweet style.

Pedro Ximénez (PX) Raisined sweet, from partly sun-dried PX grapes. Unctuous, decadent, bargain. Sip with ice cream, eg. Emilio Hidalgo Santa Ana 1861, Lustau VORS.

Moscatel Aromatic appeal, around half sugar of PX, eg. Lustau Emilín, VALDESPINO Toneles.

VOS / VORS Age-dated Sherries, some of treasures of Jerez BODEGAS. Wines assessed by carbon dating to be 20 yrs old+ are VOS (Very Old Sherry/Vinum Optimum Signatum); 30 yrs old+ are VORS (Very Old Rare Sherry/Vinum Optimum Rare Signatum). Also 12-yr-old, 15-yr-old examples. Applies only to Amontillado, Oloroso, PALO CORTADO, PX, eg. VOS Hidalgo Jerez Cortado Wellington. Some VORS wines softened with PX; sadly producers may overdo the PX.

Vintage / Añada Sherry with declared vintage. Runs counter to trad of SOLERA. Formerly private bottlings now winning public accolades, eg. WILLIAMS & HUMBERT series, Lustau Sweet Oloroso Añada 1997.

Ysios Rio ★→★★ Visitors delight in undulating roof of Calatrava-designed winery. Wines now also worth a detour.

Zárate Gal ★★→★★★ El Palomar is from centenarian vyd, one of DOP's oldest, on own rootstock, aged in *foudre*. Fontecon is unusual rosé. Fascinating set of local single-variety reds.

Zorzal, Viña Nav ★→★★★ Watch Xabi Sanz: entrepreneurial family business moving focus back to NAV: v.gd GRACIANO; fine old-vine GARNACHAS (Malayeto, Señora de la Alturas). Elegant new wine with Spain-born Swiss DJ Fredi Torres (Fitero).

Portugal

Portugal is a wine-lover's dream. The country blends tradition and innovation, coastal and high-altitude vineyards, and more than 250 indigenous varieties. From light to robust table wines, to fortifieds like Port and Madeira, there are options (and value) for everyone. Two trends are pushing the country forward. Sustainable viticulture is helping to fight climate change (and make fresher wines), and experimentation is rife. Consumers want authenticity, which usually means reinventing grapes or styles or terroirs that were unfashionable or hardly known: unfortified table wines on Madeira, for example, or new wines from sandy Colares, or using Alicante Bouschet in Port, or wines from Porto Santo island near Madeira. *See* **Portugal map p.174**

Recent Port vintages

Don't think you have to age classic Vintage Port for half your lifetime. Yes, it will age for decades, but it's delicious young (just bottled; that sort of young) and it doesn't close up in the way it used to. Silkier tannins are one reason (better viticulture, better winemaking) and better spirit is the other. The rough stuff used for fortification in ye olden days is a thing of the past; and better spirit means better Port. Single-quinta vintages too can be drunk from release – and are delicious, believe me, and better with cheese than any unfortified red. Despite a challenging growing season, marked by severe drought and heatwaves, leading producers have declared 2022 Vintage Ports. Notably, Taylor (new Sentinels), Quinta do Noval (incl Nacional), Symington, Sogrape and Sogevinus also announced multiple 2022 Vintage Ports.

2024 Exceptional harvest, v.gd concentration. Potential classic Vintage year.
2023 Increased production, gd quality if harvested before rain.
2022 Smaller quantities, but overall gd quality, some excellent.
2021 Gd quality; gd weather conditions: mild July after fairly wet winter. Best: Graham's Stone Terraces, Noval, Nacional, Ramos Pinto.
2020 Challenging yr; tiny vols of v. concentrated Graham's, Warre's Vinhas Velhas, Vargellas, Noval, Nacional, Ventozelo, Gaivosa Amphitheatrum.
2019 Balance, freshness but less structure. Best: Niepoort, Noval (incl Nacional), Pintas, Vesúvio.
2018 Gd quality, declaration for some, esp Dou Superior. Best: Ferreira, Noval, Sandeman, Taylor's, Vesúvio.
2017 Superlative yr, widely declared; v. hot, dry, compared to historic 1945.
2016 Classic yr, widely declared. Great structure, finesse.
2015 Controversial yr; v. dry, hot. Declared by many (drink: Niepoort, Noval) but not Fladgate, Sogrape or Symington.
2014 Excellent from vyds that ducked September's rain; production low.
2013 Single-quinta yr; mid-harvest rain. Stars: Fonseca Guimaraens, Vesuvio.
Earlier fine vintages: 09 07 03 00 97 94 92 91 87 83 80 77 70 66 63 45 35 31 27.

Recent table-wine vintages

2024 Low rainfall, relatively cool temp; v.gd quality all round.
2023 Portugal avoided weather crisis; v.gd whites; elegant reds.
2022 V. v. dry; light, fruity whites; elegant low-alc reds.
2021 Quality, quantity; v.gd whites and fresh, elegant reds.
2020 Gd quantity overall; v.gd whites; pick your red producer.

2019 No rain, cool summer; v.gd quality all round. Keep.

2018 Heavy rains; v. low yields. Aromatic whites, concentrated reds.

2017 3rd consecutive fine vintage; v.gd quality all round. Keep for yrs.

Creamy, room-temperature Serra da Estrela cheese is LBV/VP's best friend.

Açor, Domínio do Dão ★★★★ Deservedly acclaimed new boutique project: stunning, modern, old-vine, cement/oak-aged Bical, ENCRUZADO, Jaen, Tinta Pinheira.

Açores / Azores ★→★★★★ Portugal's historic volcanic heaven, fighting to revive rare, indigenous varieties, esp Arinto dos Açores, *Terrantez do Pico*. Mid-Atlantic nine-island archipelago with three DOCS: Pico, Biscoitos, Graciosa. Vines often protected by laborious-to-cultivate *currais* (pebble walls). Best winemakers make crisp, mineral, saline whites. Try ★★ Adega do Vulcão, ★★★ Azores Wine Company, ★★★ Cerca dos Frades, ★★★ Eruptio, ★★ Magma, ★★★ Pico Wines. Rare late-harvest *licoroso* is luscious treat. Star: ★★★★ Czar.

AdegaMãe Lis ★→★★★ Modern estate n of Lisbon, owned by codfish group Riberalves. Fresh, bright, age-worthy Atlantic-influenced whites v.gd. Dory range (esp ARINTO, *Viosinho*) gd value. Top-notch Terroir oak-aged range (r/w). *Estate restaurant* well worth 1-hr trip from Lisbon.

Aldeia de Cima Alen ★★★★ Auspicious project by Luisa Amorim (QUINTA NOVA) blends region's heritage with modernity. High-quality (r/w), fresh terroir, old vines, alternative ageing (amphora, concrete, oak vats). Superb, age-worthy range, esp GARRAFEIRA and Myndru, v.gd RES.

Alentejo ★→★★★★ Large, popular, reliable, hot, dry region known for wheat, cork, olive oil and fruit-forward reds. Leader in sustainability initiatives. Subregional diversity allows for other styles: mineral, seaside Costa Vicentina (Cebolal, VICENTINO); fresh, high-altitude PORTALEGRE (CABEÇAS DO REGUENGO), ★★ Fonte de Souto, RUI REGUINGA, Teixinha); fresh Vidigueira (★★★ CORTES DE CIMA, ROCIM); earthy, ancient clay amphora VINHO DE TALHA DOC (★★ XXVI Talhas, Rocim). Also look for ALDEIA DE CIMA, CARTUXA, ESPORÃO, Herdade dos Grous, JOÃO PORTUGAL RAMOS, JOSÉ DE SOUSA, MALHADINHA NOVA, MOUCHÃO, MOURO. Age-worthy classics often made with ALICANTE BOUSCHET.

Alorna, Quinta da Tej ★★ Historic noble estate known for majestic 300-yr-old tree. Consistent (r/w): rich, oak-aged Marquesa de Alorna; elegant RES das Pedras; single-variety and COLHEITA gd value.

Ameal, Quinta do Vin ★★★ Benchmark ESPORÃO-owned boutique estate. Organic, age-worthy LOUREIRO range incl v.gd-value Bico Amarelo, racy single-vyd Solo Único, v.gd oaked *Res.*

Andresen Port ★★→★★★★ Historic, boutique, Portuguese-owned house with superb TAWNIES: v.gd 20-yr-old; ethereal *Colheitas* 1900′ 1910′ (bottled on demand) 68′ 80′ 91′ 92′ 97′ 00′ 03′ 05′. Pioneered age-dated WHITE PORTS: 10-, 20-, v.gd 40-yr-old.

Aveleda Vin ★→★★ Most popular, largest VIN available worldwide. Now B-Corp, focused on sustainability. Makes gd-value, reliable white range, esp ALVARINHO, LOUREIRO. Owns top estate VALE D MARIA (DOU), ★★ D'Aguieira (BAI), ★ Villa Alvor (Alg). A gd visitor centre nr Porto.

Bacalhôa Vinhos Alen, Lis, Set ★★→★★★ Large group with popular brands. Top: age-worthy, v.gd QUINTA da Bacalhôa Bx blend incl CAB SAUV 1st planted 1974, also used in iconic red *Palácio da Bacalhôa*. MOSCATEL DE SETÚBAL barrels, incl rare Roxo; gd fruit-forward ALEN Quinta do Carmo reds; gd-value Catarina, Serras de Azeitão (SET). Owns several art museums.

Bágeiras, Quinta das Bair ★★★ Reputed family-owned estate, using trad low-intervention methods, techniques. Top-notch old-vines GARRAFEIRA (r/w). RES, sparkling range, entry level (r/w) gd value.

Bairrada ★★→★★★★ Atlantic-influenced DOC famous for world-class, age-worthy, structured BAGA (often v. old vines), charming whites and v.gd sparkling, esp Baga Bair. Best: ★★★ BÁGEIRAS, CAVES SÃO JOÃO, *Filipa Pato*, *Foz de Arouce*, *Giz by Luis Gomes*, *Kompassus*, LUÍS PATO, ★★ Principal, ★★ São Domingos, ★★★ *Sidónio de Sousa*, *Vadio*. Watch: ★★★ *Mira do Ó*, ★★ NIEPOORT. Unmissable local *roast suckling pig*.

Barbeito Mad ★★→★★★★ Highly regarded 75-yr-old firm. Elegance: unique, single-vyd, single-cask FRASQUEIRAS; outstanding 20-, 30-, 40-yr-old MALVASIAS, 50-yr-old BASTARDO; New 50-yr-old Familias. Historic series honours MAD's US popularity in C18, C19. Also v.gd *table wines*.

Barca Velha Dou ★★★★ Portugal's most prized and expensive red; 1st made in 1952. Blend of low/high-altitude plots. Cellar release only in exceptional yrs: 91' 95' 99 00 04 08' 11' 15. Too expensive? Try v.gd *Res Especial*, cellar release in great-but-not-BV yrs, from CASA FERREIRINHA's best barrels: 89' 94' 97' 01' 07 09 14. Both last decades. Lucky for us: 89' 94' 97' 01' 09 14 could (arguably) have been BV.

Blandy's Mad ★★→★★★★ Reputed family-run firm. Superlative, rare, library of old stocks: FRASQUEIRA (BUAL 1920' 57' 66' 72' 76', MALMSEY 88' 77' 81' 91', SERCIAL 68' 75' 80' 88' 89' 90', Terrantez 75' 77' 80' 87', VERDELHO 76 79' 82'); v.gd 20-yr-old Malmsey, *Terrantez* and COLHEITAS (Bual 96 08 09 10, Malmsey 99 04 07 10, Sercial 02 08 09 10, Verdelho 00 08 09 10). Superb *50-yr-old Malmsey*. Expensive, rare MCDXIX blends 11 yrs between 1863 and 2004. Unique 77 Listrão from Porto Santo Island. Popular, affordable RAINWATER. Atlantis table-wine range. Unmissable, historic *Funchal lodges*.

Boavista, Quinta da Dou ★★★★ Fine, rising Cima-Corgo estate, run by SOGEVINUS. Superb, age-worthy, old field blends (80-yr-old vines): single-vyd spicy Oratório, piney Ujo. Single-variety range v.gd; seductive *Res*; oak-aged Vinha do Levante.

Bual (or Boal) Mad Classic grape for medium-sweet MAD: tangy, smoky; balances acidity/sweetness. Pairs exquisitely with aged hard cheeses or alone. Thriling old vintages are a treasure.

Cabeças do Reguengo Alen ★★→★★★ Boutique estate, trad winemaking. Elegant, low-intervention range from high-altitude, v. old field blends in PORTALEGRE. Try cement-fermented Vira Cabeças (incl r/w grapes). Cosy guesthouse.

Canteiro Mad Natural, slow-warming ageing in humid lodges; trad reserved for more expensive MAD (now also TINTA NEGRA). Superior to ESTUFAGEM.

Carcavelos Lis ★★★ Tiny, true hidden-gem seaside DOC. Unique, mouthwatering, gripping, off-dry fortified. Try Villa Oeiras.

Cardo, Quinta do Bei Int ★★ Historic 90-yr-old, high-altitude (750m/2461ft), bio estate, revamped by new owners. Star winemakers (also LÉS-A-LÉS) make elegant, fresh range: top-notch Grande Res (w), single-vyd *Lomedo* (w), *Pombal* (r); gd-value Cardo, Res (r/w) labels.

Cartuxa, Adega da Alen ★★→★★★★ Historic, reputed ALEN firm run by Eugénio de Almeida Foundation. Home to flagship, full-bodied Pêra Manca (r); v.gd, age-worthy, best-buy *Cartuxa Res*; v.gd single-variety Scala Coeli changes every yr. Popular EA range.

Driving from Porto to Lisbon without stopping in Bairrada for suckling pig is a sin.

Carvalhais, Quinta dos Dão ★→★★ SOGRAPE-owned classic DÃO estate. Benchmark, age-worthy: gd oak-aged, flinty ENCRUZADO; rich RES (*esp w*); earthy *Alfrocheiro*; floral TOURIGA N; dense, top red Único; unusual, rich Branco Especial. Popular, gd-value Duque de Viseu, Grão Vasco.

Casa da Atela Tej ★★ Historic (C14) large estate; unique 75-yr-old plot of CASTELÃO (origin of top r). Native/international varieties range gd, esp CHARD, SYRAH, PETIT VERDOT, RES (r/w). Estate label gd value.

Cazas Novas Vin ★★→★★★ Dynamic firm, owns largest Avesso vyd, benchmark range: crisp COLHEITA; lees-aged Pure; v.gd oak-aged Origens.

Chocapalha, Quinta de Lis ★★★ Coastal family-run estate. Winemaker Sandra Tavares da Silva (WINE & SOUL) makes vibrant, *mineral, saline whites* (v.gd CHARD, RES, old-vine ARINTO CH, Arinto Antigo from old vyds). Vinha Mãe v.gd; also gd-value red, esp CASTELÃO, and gd wine tourism.

Porto's hearty sandwich, the Francesinha, best enjoyed with a local beer.

Chryseia Dou ★★★★ Modern classic. Prestigious, consistent, fine, elegant TOURIGA-driven red. Born from SYMINGTON FAMILY ESTATES, Bruno Prats (Bx) partnership. *Post Scriptum* v.gd value.

Churchill Dou, Port ★★★ Boutique, family-run, with v.gd *reds* (gd-value Churchill's Estates Grafite range, esp Grande RES). Top Port: Dry WHITE PORT, 20-, 30-yr-old, unfiltered LBV, VINTAGE PORT. Popular Meio Queijo. Charming C19 guesthouse.

Cockburn's Port ★★→★★★★ Refreshed, younger-focused, SYMINGTON-owned, consistently gd Port: Special RES aged longer in wood than others; vibrant LBV aged 1 yr less; v.gd single-QUINTA dos Canais; drier, fresher style of VINTAGE PORT. Tails of the Unexpected cocktail range.

Coelheiros, Tapada de Alen ★★★ Historic C15 estate, converting large vyds, orchard, forest property to bio. Top-notch GARRAFEIRA; classy CAB SAUV/ALICANTE BOUSCHET (r), ARINTO/Roupeiro (w); gd-value Coelheiros (r/w).

Colares Lis ★★★ Historic treasure-trove DOC with windswept, ungrafted vines on sand. Europe's w-most vyds. Age-worthy; tannic Ramisco reds and crisp, saline MALVASIA whites. Try ★★★ Adega Regional de Colares. Visit ★★★ VIÚVA GOMES, ★★ Casal Santa Maria.

Colheita Mad, Port Single-yr TAWNY Port. Bottling date fine-printed on label (look for recent dates); nutty, oxidative, thrilling. Cask-aged: min 7 yrs, often 50 yrs+, rare superb 100 yrs+ bottled on demand. Best (serve chilled): ANDRESEN, DALVA, GRAHAM'S, KOPKE, NIEPOORT, NOVAL, POÇAS, TAYLOR'S. Also in MAD, cask-aged min 5 yrs.

Cortes de Cima Alen ★★★→★★★★ Family-run estate undergoing bio revolution, now led by Anna Jorgensen (daughter of ALEN SYRAH pioneers). Revamped, repriced, fresher range: iconic 100% Syrah Incógnito; elegant Chaminé range, esp Atlantic-coast white. Also saline Lour-inho (ALVARINHO/LOUREIRO), Salino (r/w), Palhete with Dirk NIEPOORT.

Cossart Gordon Mad ★★★ Oldest MAD shipper (1745) known for fine, drier style; v.gd single-yr bottlings. Try: Colheitas (VERDELHO 09'; Bual 89' 06'; Malmsey 08' 95'); frasqueira (Verdelho 75'). MADEIRA WINE COMPANY owned.

Costa do Pinhão, Quinta da Dou ★★★ Historic estate, run by 6th generation. High-altitude, elegant, bio range: fine, 90-yr-old-vines Peladosa; old-vines *Gradual*, v.gd-value estate label (r/w);

Crasto, Quinta do Dou, Port ★★→★★★★ Prestigious C17 family-run estate with striking hilltop pool/lodge. Reputed for expensive single-vyd, field-blend reds Vinha da Ponte and Vinha Maria Teresa. Superb varietals, esp age-worthy TINTA RORIZ. Popular, gd value: rich old-vyd Res, Dou Superior range.

Croft Port ★★→★★★★ Historic C16 FLADGATE-owned VINTAGE PORT-focused house; v.gd-value, single-QUINTA **Quinta da Roêda**. Superlative old-vine *Sêrikos 17'*. Popular treat Pink Rosé Port, Triple Crown. Visitor centre in Pinhão.

Crusted (Port) Wallet-friendly, delicious Port treat. Luscious, rare, age-worthy NV style. Blend of two or more vintage-quality yrs, aged up to 4 yrs in casks, 3 yrs in bottle. Forms deposit ("crust"), so decant. CHURCHILL, DOW'S, FONSECA, *Niepoort*.

Dalva Port ★★★→★★★★ Quality-focused C19 house, 1st-class TAWNIES: gd-value 20-yr-old; superior **50-yr-old**. Superb COLHEITAS; 10-, 20-, 30-, 40-, 50-yr-old dry white range, stunning *golden white* 52' 63' 71' 89'. Pure bio Port v.gd. Table wines gd-value. Owned by GRANVINHOS.

Dão ★★→★★★★ Historic mtn-encircled DOC rising in reputation. Fresh, elegant ENCRUZADO-based whites, food-friendly, age-worthy reds. Often called Portugal's Burgundy but not v. similar. Classics incl ★★ Boas Quintas, ★ Cabriz, ★★ CARVALHAIS, ★★ Casa de Santar, ★ Lusovini. Try low-intervention ★★ ANTONIO MADEIRA, organic CASA DE MOURAZ, 1st-class ★★★★ Druida, characterful ★★ JOÃO TAVARES DE PINA WINES. Top designation, Dão Nobre ("noble"): ★★★ Vinha do Contador. Watch: ★★ CASA DA PASSARELA, ★★★★ DOMÍNIO DO AÇOR, ★★ Terra Chama, ★★★ TABOADELLA, ★★★ TEXTURA. Best buy: rare, age-worthy GARRAFEIRAS.

DOC (denominação de origem controlada) Quality wine designation. Increasingly ignored by wine-lovers. Newer denomination DOP rarely used.

Dona Maria Alen ★★★ Classic, reputed estate. Once a cheeky gift by the king to his mistress. Run by charismatic owner Júlio Bastos and winemaker Sandra Gonçalves. Age-worthy range with native and French varieties v.gd. Foot-trodden, old-vine ALICANTE BOUSCHET reds, esp Grande RES, Júlio Bastos; v.gd single-variety (esp PETIT VERDOT), elegant Amantis; v.gd-value *estate label*.

Douro Dou, Port ★→★★★★ Historic, dreamy UNESCO World Heritage Site made of hard-to-work steep hills. Tourists visit for river views, Port and quality table wine (Dou DOC). Powerful, structured reds; fine, high-altitude seductive whites. Three subregions (cooler Baixo Corgo, milder Cima Corgo and warmer, fast-expanding Dou Superior). Vinhas Velhas (old vines) now regulated: min 40 yrs+ old, low yields, min four varieties. Rare 100-yr+ field blends (30+ varieties) planted in terraces of unforgiving schist. Classics: *Boavista, Casa Ferreirinha* (incl top *Barca Velha*), *Chryseia*, CHURCHILL, CRASTO, ★★ MENIN, NOVAL, ★★ POÇAS, QUANTA TERRA, QUINTA NOVA, RAMOS PINTO, *Vale D Maria*, ★★★ VALE MEÃO, *Vesuvio, Wine & Soul*. Best for elegance: ALVES DE SOUSA, ★★ Carolina, ★★ COSTA DO PINHÃO, KRANEMANN, *Luis Seabra*, ★★ Manoella, *Maria Izabel, Niepoort*.

Dow's Port ★★★★ Historic, reputed SYMINGTON-owned. Age-defying, drier-style VINTAGE PORT. Legendary yrs: 27 45 63 66 70. Recent yrs: 00' 03' 07' 11' 16' 17'. In non-declared yrs, v.gd single QUINTAS do Bomfim 19 20 21, *Senhora da Ribeira* 15 18 19 22. Plus v.gd 10-, 20-, 30-, 40-yr-old Tawnies, LBV. Pinhão highlight: classy *Bomfim visitor centre*, v.gd restaurant.

Duorum Dou, Port ★★→★★★ Joint venture in DOU Superior between JOÃO PORTUGAL RAMOS (ALEN) and José Maria Soares Franco (ex-CASA FERRERIRINHA/BARCA VELHA). Top, aged several yrs pre-release *O Leucura*; v.gd-value range with fine RES, fruity Altitude (r/w); gd-value Tons, COLHEITA. Dense, v.gd VINTAGE PORT from 100-yr-old vines; LBV gd value.

Best-value fortified wines

★ for outstanding value: **Vintage Port** ★ Burmester, Cálem, CROFT, La Rosa, MENIN, ★ POÇAS, VALLADO. **Single-Quinta VP** Bomfim, Cavadinha, Croft, ★ FONSECA Guimaraens, ★ Malvedos, Roêda, ★ Vargellas. **LBV** FERREIRA, GRAHAM'S, NIEPOORT, ★ NOVAL, OFFLEY, ★ RAMOS PINTO. **Crusted** CHURCHILL, Graham's, ★ Niepoort, Quevedo. **20-yr-old Tawny** Cálem, Côrte, ★ DALVA, ★ Dona Antónia, ★ Graham's, Manoella, Royal Oporto, SANDEMAN. **10-yr-old Tawny** ★ KOPKE, ★ POÇAS, ★ Ramos Pinto. **10-yr-old White Port** ★ ANDRESEN, Manoella, ★ Poças, ★ Vieira de Sousa. **Mad** ★ BLANDY'S COLHEITA, ★ HENRIQUES & HENRIQUES MALVASIA 20 yrs, BARBEITO Single Cask. **Moscatel de Setubal** 20 yrs – BACALHÔA Superior, ★ JOSÉ MARIA DA FONSECA Alambre; 10 yrs – Bacalhôa Roxo. **Azores** PICO 10 yrs. **Carcavelos** ★ Villa Oeiras Superior.

Espera Wines Lis ★★ Low-intervention boutique winery run by winemaker Rodrigo Martins. Native-variety bio range v.gd: fresh, fruity CASTELÃO, Palheto; mineral ARINTO, Bical; skin-contact Curtimenta; low-alc Nat'Cool.

Esporão Alen ★★→★★★ Dynamic, eco-focused firm. Vast, consistent wine and olive oil range. High-end, rare Torre do Esporão; fine GARRAFEIRA-like wood-aged Private Selection (creamy SEM w and rich, dense r). High-quality, fruit-focused, modern RES. Popular Monte Velho, RES. *Visitor centre, restaurant* v.gd. Interests in DOU (Murças), VIN (AMEAL).

Espumante Sparkling. Wallet-friendly gem. Best are age-worthy with BAGA BAIR quality designation. Try Abibes, Aliança, Colinas, Marquês de Marialva, Poço do Lobo, São Domingos, São João. Távora-Varosa gd value. Undisputed best: DOU'S ★★★ VÉRTICE.

Esteban, Susana Alen ★★★ Galician (*see* Spain) trailblazer winemaker reviving v. old PORTALEGRE vyds. Fine, elegant range: top-notch Procura (two plots r, field-blend w); earthy CASTELÃO *Sem Vergonha*; fruit-forward Aventura (r/w); oak-aged *A Centenária*; exotic Vinyle; vibrant VINHO DE TALHA. Collaboration series: v.gd *Sidecar*, esp Jorge Lucki; complex DOU Crochet, ALEN Tricot with Sandra Tavares da Silva (WINE & SOUL).

Estufagem Mad Sea voyage-inspired MAD ageing method (up to 50°C/122°F, min 90 days) for unique scorched-earth tang in entry-level wines.

Falua Tej ★→★★ French-owned estate with multi-region interests: Barão do Hospital auspicious VIN project (esp ALVARINHO, LOUREIRO); QUINTA de São José (v.gd DOU range); Quinta do Mourão (v.gd PORT stocks). Falua range incl gd-value Conde de Vimioso (RES a step up), gd Res (r/w, esp Sommelier Edition). Top: stony-soil Vinha do Convento (r/w).

Ferreira Port ★★★→★★★★ Historic, prestigious, SOGRAPE-owned. Stand-out VINTAGE PORT 11' 16' 18', top Vinhas Velhas 16', v.gd-value single-QUINTA do Porto 17' 19' 20', LBV. Elegant TAWNY v.gd value: Dona Antonia RES, 10-, *20-*, 30-yr-old. GAIA visitor centre.

Ferreirinha, Casa Dou ★→★★★★ Large, highly reputed SOGRAPE-owned brand. Winemaker Luís Sottomayor makes iconic *Barca Velha*, rare *Res Especial*, age-worthy, 1st-class *Quinta da Leda*, v.gd *Castas Escondidas*, single-variety Tinta Francisca, v.gd-value Vinha Grande. Popular: Esteva, Papa Figos.

Fladgate Port Large, dynamic, independent family-owned Port firm, expanding to table wine. Owns: leading Port brands CROFT, FONSECA, Krohn, TAYLOR'S; multi-region table wines VIN (Palmeira, Pedra), DÃO Bella, BAIR Principal; growing travel empire incl hotels in GAIA, Lisbon, Pinhão, Porto; Michelin-starred The Yeatman; seven-museum WOW (World of Wine) Gaia visitor centre.

Folias de Baco Dou ★★ Natural boutique project run by PhD winemaker Tiago Sampaio. High-altitude, low-intervention Uivo range (skin contact Curtido) v.gd; fresh old-vine (r/w grapes) Renegado; low-alc Piquette.

Fonseca Port ★★★→★★★★ FLADGATE-owned house from 1815. Reputed, age-defying VINTAGE PORT 63' 70' 77' 94' 97' 11' 16' 17'. Superb *Fonseca Guimaraens* 13' 15' 18' 19' 22'. Single-QUINTA Panascal; v.gd 20-, 40-yr-old TAWNY; Bin 27 popular, gd value.

Portuguese canned fish has gourmet status. Try sardines, tuna and mackerel.

Fonseca, José Maria da Alen, Set ★→★★★★ Large, 190-yr-old, 7th-generation, family-run firm. Jewel in crown is fortified *Moscatel de Setúbal*, esp stocks of old MOSCATEL: stunning *20-yr-old Alambre* and *Moscatel Roxo*, lavish *Superior* 55' 66 71. Table-wine range: top-notch, dense Hexagon (r/w); gd-value single-variety DSF range; popular BSE, João Pires, Lancers, Periquita. Owns v.gd-value ALEN classic ★★★ *José de Sousa*.

> **Best-value reds**
> Worth more than the price tag: CARTUXA, Castelão (HUGO MENDES),
> DONA MARIA, Quinta da Bacalhôa, Dom Rafael (MOUCHÃO), Gradual
> (COSTA DO PINHÃO), Grainha (QUINTA NOVA), JOSÉ DE SOUSA, FOZ DE AROUCE,
> KOMPASSUS, Manoella (WINE & SOUL), MONTE D'OIRO, Pegos Claros RES;
> Pretexto (TEXTURA), VADIO, PORMENOR, Terra a Terra RES (QUANTA TERRA),
> VALLE PRADINHOS, Vinha Grande (FERREIRINHA).

Foz de Arouce Bei At ★★★★ Hidden gem, esp classy older vintages. JOÃO PORTUGAL RAMOS's family-run BAIR outpost making age-worthy range: vivid Cercial, TOURIGA N/BAGA blend, top-notch old-Baga-vines *Vinhas Velhas.*

Frasqueira Mad Pinnacle of MAD wines. Aged for decades (min 20 yrs) in CANTEIRO, best over 100 yrs old. Single yr (aka Vintage), single (noble) variety. Bottling date on label. Best: BARBEITO, MADEIRA WINE COMPANY.

Gaia, Vila Nova de Dou, Port Historic home of major Port shippers, also walkable tourist attraction: working cellars, tasting rooms, cable car, boat tours, hotels (The Yeatman, Michelin-starred), wine shops, museums (WOW), restaurants/bars (Enoteca 17·56, Espaço Porto Cruz, Vinum). Best: GRAHAM's. Also: Cálem, CHURCHILL, COCKBURN's, FERREIRA, NIEPOORT, POÇAS, SANDEMAN, TAYLOR's. Get to Porto: cross the double-deck bridge or take the taxi boat.

Garrafeira Designation for aged wine, esp ALEN, BAIR, DÃO. Having a comeback. Reds aged for min 30 mths (often longer), min 1 yr in bottle. Whites need 12 mths, min 6 in bottle. Also, wine shop.

Giz By Luis Gomes Bair ★★★ Reputed project; century-old-vyds revival, low-intervention range: fine VINHAS VELHAS (r/w), esp BAGA; vibrant rosé, gd fizz.

Global Wines Bair, Dão ★★→★★★ Large DÃO-based firm. Owns: gd-value, popular Cabriz range, Casa de Santar (v.gd Res, superb Nobre); fine, age-worthy Vinha do Contador range (dense r; rare, creamy, organic Grand Jury w). In other regions: Encostas do DOU (Dou), Lourosa (VIN), Monte da Cal (ALEN) and QUINTA do Encontro (BAIR), incl visitor centre with striking architecture.

Graham's Port ★★★→★★★★ Highly reputed SYMINGTON-owned 200-yr-old house. Top-notch VINTAGE PORT 27' 63' 66' 85' 91' 94' **97** 00' 03' **07'** 11' 16' 17' 20' (delightful at release, heaven with age); lavish Stone Terraces 11' 15' 16' 17' 21'; single QUINTA (Malvedos 12 15 18' 19', new old-vines Tua). CRUSTED, LBV, RES RUBY Six Grapes all gd value. Superb, seductive 20-, 30-, 40-, 50-yr-old TAWNIES; luscious Single Harvest (COLHEITAS) collection 40' 50' 52' 61' 63' 69' 72' 82 94' 97 03. Ne Oublie VERY VERY OLD TAWNY is 1882 bottled history. Best-in-class *visitor centre, restaurant in Gaia.*

Granvinhos Port ★→★★★ Ex-Gran Cruz. Owns: reputable DALVA; DOU Ventozelo; Port's largest export brand Porto Cruz (volume, cocktails); Porto Presidential. Stylish museum, bar, hotel, restaurants in GAIA/Porto; Owned by La Martiniquaise.

Grous, Herdade de Alen, Dou ★★→★★★ Prestigious eco-focused estate: RES (rich, oak-aged w; ripe, fine r); fruity Moon Harvested, best-barrels 23 Barricas labels; thrilling cement-aged *Concrete.* Reputed wine tourism. Watch: DOU outpost QUINTA de Valbom.

Henriques & Henriques Mad ★★→★★★★ Leading MAD shipper, thrilling range: *20-yr-olds (Malvasia, Terrantez),* 50-yr-old TINTA NEGRA; top-notch FRASQUEIRAS (some aged in bourbon barrels): BASTARDO 27, BUAL 00' 09, VERDELHO 32 57, SERCIAL 28 71' 01', Terrantez 54'. Entry-level range gd value; gd tasting room. Owned by La Martiniquaise.

Javali, Quinta do Dou ★★★ Boutique family-owned bio estate making trad-techniques range: v.gd VINHAS VELHAS, RES; light, fruity Clos Fonte do Santo, Crazy Javali. Also gd Port: 10-, 20-, 30-yr-old TAWNY, VINTAGE PORT, LBV.

PORTUGAL

João Tavares de Pina Wines Dão ★★→★★★ Rebel natural-wine pioneer, lost many vyds to forest fires. Native-varieties range: classic, increasingly natural Torre, Terra de Tavares. Young, fresh, low-intervention: Rufia range, Tretas.

Justino's Mad ★→★★★★ Largest MAD shipper. Winemaker Juan Teixeira blends tradition, modernity. Gems: Terrantez *50-yr-old* and *78'* (oldest in cask), MALVASIA *64' 68' 88' 97'*. Try also Verdelho *98'*, SERCIAL *97'*, TINTA NEGRA *99'*. Makes popular Broadbent label. Owned by La Martiniquaise.

Ginjinha, a cherry liqueur, is best enjoyed in edible chocolate cups.

Kopke Port ★→★★★★ Oldest Port house, now making DOU wines. Known for thrilling TAWNY (10-, 20-, 30-, 40-, *50-yr-old*, COLHEITAS *35' 40'* onwards) and exceptional WHITE PORT (esp now-rare *35' 40'* and 20-, 30-, 40-, *50-yr-old*). SOGEVINUS owned.

Kranemann Wine Estates Dou ★★→★★★★ Historic estate renovation. Quality range, esp v.gd high-altitude whites. RES; gd-value, fresh Hasso (r/w), single-variety Ponte do Fumo brand (Rabigato, Tinta Barroca); v.gd 10-, *20-*, 30-yr-old TAWNY.

LBV (Late Bottled Vintage) Port Budget-friendly, widely available alternative to VINTAGE PORT. Arguably as gd as last decade's Vintage Port. Cask-aged 4–6 yrs (twice as long as VP) for early drinking. Best are age-worthy, unfiltered versions: FERREIRA, NIEPOORT, NOVAL, RAMOS PINTO, SANDEMAN, TAYLOR'S, WARRE'S. Serve lightly chilled: chocolate's dream pair or a luscious sumptuous stand-alone treat.

Lés-a-Lés ★★ Tiny coast-to-coast project recovering trad varieties, methods; v.gd unique range, esp Távora-Varosa, Trás-os-Montes, VIN.

Lisboa ★→★★★★ Underrated N Lisbon coastal region making great-value fresh, crisp, mineral whites (ARINTO-based) and age-worthy reds (CASTELÃO, SYRAH, TINTA RORIZ). Historic, microclimate COLARES subregion (MALVASIA, Ramisco). Quality-focused, dynamic, often bio producers balance large firms. Best: CHOCAPALHA, ★★★ *Monte Bluna*, top Syrah pioneer MONTE D'OIRO. Try also ADEGAMÃE, ★★ Pancas (age-worthy range), ★★ Pinto (value blends), SANT'ANA. Young, often natural, producers to watch: ★★ *Casal Figueira*, ★★ COZs, ★★ ESPERA WINES, ★★ HUGO MENDES, ★★ Humus, ★★ Marinho, ★★ Olival da Murta, ★★ Serradinha, ★★★ *Vale da Capucha*, VIÚVA GOMES. Best to visit: AdegaMãe, Monte d'Oiro, Sant'Ana.

Lopes, Márcio Dou, Vin ★★→★★★ Rising-star winemaker. *Pequenos Rebentos* range (gd-value ALVARINHO/LOUREIRO); top Caminho; DOU (Permitido/Proibido).

Maçanita, António Alen, Dou ★★→★★★ Star winemaker/consultant, many projects, regions. Home ALEN (popular Sexy, seductive Fita Preta, v.gd Palpite, trad Chão dos Eremitas), AZORES (superb *Terrantez do Pico*, old-vine Vinha das Utras), sister-led DOU (Letra A, F range), MAD (rare, thrilling Porto Santo island range). Wine tourism in Alen, Dou, Azores.

Madeira ★→★★★★ Dramatic Island and DOC, cliff-hanging vines, mouthwatering wines, only eight firms making world-famous fortified. Treasured decades-old stocks. Best: BARBEITO, MADEIRA WINE COMPANY. Also: BORGES, HENRIQUES & HENRIQUES, JUSTINO'S, ★★ PEREIRA D'OLIVEIRA, ★ Faria & Filhos, ★ Madeira Vintners. Watch: table wines rise, ★★ Atlantis, ★★★ Barbeito, ★★ Barbusano; unique Porto Santo wines.

Madeira, Antonio Dão ★★★ Reputed French-born engineer/winemaker reviving v. old vyds (up to 120 yrs). Fine bio range: old-vine A Palheira; eponymous label Vinha da Serra; v.gd VINHAS VELHAS (r/w). Light, fruity Ainda Palhete.

Madeira, Rui Roboredo Bei Int, Dou ★★→★★★ High-altitude pioneer; DOU: v.gd mineral *Pedra Escrita (r/w)*, top, eponymous old-vines label; Bei Int: great-value *Beyra* range, esp *Jaen*, Grande RES, GARRAFEIRA. Popular: Castello d'Alba.

Madeira Wine Company Mad Reputed, largest MAD firm, led by 7th-generation Chris Blandy. Owns BLANDY'S, COSSART GORDON, Leacock, Miles.

Malhadinha Nova, Herdade da Alen ★★★→★★★★ Leading Soares-family S ᴀʟᴇɴ bio estate, high-end *country house*; v.gd, age-worthy range, incl *estate label*; rich, late-released Marias da Malhadinha; piney, dense ᴀʟɪᴄᴀɴᴛᴇ ʙᴏᴜsᴄʜᴇᴛ *Menino António* and ᴄᴀʙ sᴀᴜᴠ Pequeno João. Old-vine (1949) Vale Travessos (r/w) v.gd; single-variety, often single-vyd range gd. Watch: high-altitude ᴘᴏʀᴛᴀʟᴇɢʀᴇ outpost Teixinha growing range.

Malvasia (Malmsey) Mad Sweetest, richest of ᴍᴀᴅ's noble varieties. Sharp tang: thrilling, luscious crème brûlée, dark chocolate pair. Look for older yrs.

Maria Izabel, Quinta Dou ★★★ Brazilian-owned estate revival; v.gd, elegant range made with Dirk ɴɪᴇᴘᴏᴏʀᴛ, esp ǫᴜɪɴᴛᴀ, top-notch, oak-aged, old-vine Vinhas da Princesa (r/w), unique Sublime range (light, complex r, oak-aged w). Rare, pricey ʙᴀsᴛᴀʀᴅᴏ.

Mateus Rosé ★ Bestseller in a flask-shaped bottle. Fresh, off-dry bubbly rosé with dry edition.

Mendes, Anselmo Vin ★★★→★★★★ "Mr. Alvarinho": benchmark minerality. Try lees-aged *Contacto* (now co-owned by sʏᴍɪɴɢᴛᴏɴ); v.gd-value, crisp Muros de Melgaço, Muros Antigos range; superb, flinty Parcela Única.

Mendes, Hugo Lis ★★ Dynamic, crowdfunding pioneer, elegant multi-region range: ʟɪs (Claret, *Castelão*, *Vital*); Tejo (Fernão Pires); ᴀʟᴇɴ (ᴠɪɴʜᴏ ᴅᴇ ᴛᴀʟʜᴀ). Eponymous label (r/w) gd value; gd skin-contact Underdog.

Menin Dou ★★→★★★ Firm to watch. Large investments, new winery, consultant star winemaker Tiago ᴀʟᴠᴇs ᴅᴇ sᴏᴜsᴀ. Classy range, incl ʀᴇs (r/w), single-variety labels, top Grande Res, New Legacy and D Beatriz. Also HO Wines, gd value.

Menina d'Uva Trás M ★★ Natural-wine project by Parisian Aline Domingues, back to ancestral roots, old vyds. Elegant, native-varieties, low-intervention range, esp blend of Ciste (r/w grapes).

Mira do Ó Bair ★★★ Dynamic project led by eponymous winemaker Nuno Mira do Ó. Low-intervention old-vines range: (w) top-notch ᴇɴᴄʀᴜᴢᴀᴅᴏ *Druida Res*, Grande; (r) fresh, elegant Caminhante, Vidente. Mineral Bucelas (ʟɪs) ᴀʀɪɴᴛᴏ.

Monte Bluna Lis ★★★→★★★★ Classy Atlantic-influenced min-intervention project, high-altitude vyds n of Lisbon: superb ᴀʀᴀɢᴏɴᴇ̂ᴢ-based Blunissima; fine, elegant, rare native-variety *Tinta Miúda*; seductive *Res* and TicTac range.

Monte d'Oiro, Quinta do Lis ★★→★★★★ Family-owned, Atlantic-influenced, Hermitage-inspired bio estate. Superb range: sʏʀᴀʜ/ᴠɪᴏɢɴɪᴇʀ *Res*; v.gd Viognier *Res*; 1st-class Ex Aequo Syrah/ᴛᴏᴜʀɪɢᴀ ɴ label; thrilling limited-edition 100% ᴀʀɪɴᴛᴏ. Entry-level range gd value.

Monte da Casteleja Alg ★★ Boutique winery keeping ancestral techniques alive (foot-treading, wooden vats). Elegant bio range. Plus gd visitor centre.

Monte da Ravasqueira Alen ★★→★★★ Part of family-run ᴡɪɴᴇsᴛᴏɴᴇ group. Consultant David Baverstock (ex-ᴇsᴘᴏʀᴀ̃ᴏ) makes quality range, esp Premium, ᴀʟɪᴄᴀɴᴛᴇ ʙᴏᴜsᴄʜᴇᴛ. Single-vyd Vinhas das Romãs (r/w) gd value. Visitor centre incl carriage museum.

Morgado do Quintão Alg ★★ Historic family-run bio estate focused on native varieties. Winemaker Joana Maçanita makes sandy-soil, old-vine range:

Best-value whites
Worth more than the price tag: Abanico (ᴄᴀsᴀ ᴅᴀ ᴘᴀssᴀʀᴇʟʟᴀ), ᴄᴀʀᴠᴀʟʜᴀɪs, ᴄᴀsᴀ ᴅᴇ ᴍᴏᴜʀᴀᴢ, ᴄʜᴏᴄᴀᴘᴀʟʜᴀ, Monólogo Avesso (A&D), Morgado de Sta Catarina, Muros de Melgaço, Contacto (ᴀɴsᴇʟᴍᴏ ᴍᴇɴᴅᴇs), Frei Gigante (ᴘɪᴄᴏ ᴡɪɴᴇs), Pequenos Rebentos (ᴍᴀ́ʀᴄɪᴏ ʟᴏᴘᴇs), Pure (ᴄᴀᴢᴀs ɴᴏᴠᴀs), ʀᴇs (ʜᴇʀᴅᴀᴅᴇ ᴅᴏs ɢʀᴏᴜs), sᴏᴀʟʜᴇɪʀᴏ, Vinha do Altar (ᴡɪɴᴇ & sᴏᴜʟ), Viosinho (ᴀᴅᴇɢᴀᴍᴀ̃ᴇ).

NEGRA MOLE (elegant: rosé, *clairet*); CASTELÃO (estate r); amphora (blends both). Charming wine tourism.

Moscatel de Setúbal Set ★★→★★★★ Thrilling, exotic, sweet MOSCATEL fortified treasure, esp richer *Roxo*. Superlative *Superior* designation. Star: JOSÉ MARIA DA FONSECA (100-yr-old+ stocks). Also try v.gd BACALHÔA VINHOS, ★★ Horácio Simões. Value: ★★ Palmela Wine Company, ★★ Piloto. Pair with crème brûlée, hard, salty cheeses, or the right company.

Top 3 petiscos (arguably): amêijoas (clams), bifana (pork sandwich), octopus salad.

Mouchão, Herdade de Alen ★★★ Historic family-run estate, fine foot-trodden range: large-barrel-aged *estate red* (1st bottled 1949); prestigious ALEN fortified Tonel No. 3-4; v.gd-value perfumed *Ponte* (r) and old-vine *Dom Rafael* (r/w).

Mouraz, Casa de Dão ★★★ A bio pioneer. Vibrant range: estate label; Planet Mouraz (esp natural Bolinha, *clairet* Nina); gd-value Air. Best: v.gd 80-yr-old field blend *Elfa*; top-notch 100-yr-old-vines Boot.

Mouro, Quinta do Alen ★★★ Impressive estate of dentist Miguel Louro. Vines barely trained, look wild; v.gd age-worthy flagship red; fruit-forward, ripe Zagalos RES. Vinha do Mouro gd value. Try uconventional Erro range.

Muxagat Dou ★★★ Boutique estate, elegant range: salty, mineral, high-altitude Rabigato-based *Xistos Altos*; v.gd varietal reds, unique *Cisne* (blends, r/w grapes), 100% Tinta Francisca.

Nicolau de Almeida Dou ★★★ Boutique project; grandfather created BARCA VELHA. Superb, seductive Monte Xisto; v.gd elegant Órbita, Oriente.

Nicolau de Almeida, Mateus Dou ★★→★★★ Star winemaker, 5th-generation NICOLAU DE ALMEIDA making v.gd bio wines: Trans Douro Express mirrors DOU's subregions (cooler Baixo Corgo, balanced Cima Corgo, rich Dou Superior); Eremitas (100% Rabigato, three plots); cellar experiments Curral Teles.

Niepoort Bair, Dou, Dão ★★→★★★★ Run by larger-than-life DOU pioneer Dirk N and family. Fine, fresher-than-ever, age-worthy Dou range: 1st-class Batuta, *Charme*, *Coche* (w), v.gd Redoma (esp *Res* w), single-vyd, structured Robustus, elegant 100% TINTA AMARELA, 130-yr-old-vines *Turris*. Diálogo/Fabelhaft is gd-value globetrotter. Popular Nat'cool easy-drinking, low-intervention range. Other regions: BAIR (esp GARRAFEIRA, Poeirinho, VV), DÃO (esp top-notch Lomba, gd-value Conciso), PORTALEGRE (Ximena), VIN (ADN). Port range v.gd, often superb: VINTAGE PORT 45' 87' 00' 15' 17' 19', trad *Pisca*; organic Bioma VV; great-value *Crusted*; unique demijohn-aged *Garrafeira*; ethereal 1983 VV; TAWNY v.gd (esp bottle-aged COLHEITAS). International collaborations, esp Navazos; private GAIA Niepoort Temple requires booking.

Noval, Quinta do Dou, Port ★★★→★★★★ Historic AXA-owned (1993) estate known for Port, table wines. Enjoyable-young *Vintage* released every yr v.gd; jewel-in-crown, pricey *Nacional* 00' 01' 03' 04' 11' 16' 17' 19' 21' 22' from 2.5 ha ungrafted vines; v.gd unfiltered LBV; superior *Colheitas*, 20-, 50-yr-olds. Try DOU range: top-notch, expensive, single-plot, v. old field-blend Terroir Series; v.gd age-worthy RES (classic r, oak-aged *Viosinho-based w*); gd-value Cedro (r/w); elegant, single-variety Tinto Cão, SYRAH, TOURIGA N. Passadouro range gd value.

Offley Port ★★ Historic C18 brand. Fruit-driven VINTAGE PORT, gd-value unfiltered LBV. Cocktail-ready Clink. SOGRAPE owned.

Pacheca, Quinta da Dou, Port ★→★★ Historic estate famous for sleep-in-barrel hotel; gd-value table wines, esp RES. Owner group Terras & Terroir expanding: ★★ Caminhos Cruzados, esp Teixuga (DÃO), Ortigão (BAIR), Ribafreixo, Rocha (ALEN), Valle de Passos (Trás-os-Montes).

Passarella, Casa da Dão ★★→★★★★ Historic, boutique estate, led by star winemaker Paulo Nunes. Fine, late-release *Vindima 09' 11'* (80-yr-old field blend); classy

Villa Oliveira range (esp ENCRUZADO); bold, 80-yr-old-vine Pedras Altas; v.gd-value *Fugitivo* range (esp BASTARDO, PINOT N).

Pato, Filipa Bair ★★★★ Star bio BAGA couple. Fine, v. old-vine Baga reds, esp pre-phylloxera vines *Nossa Missão*, elegant *Nossa Calcario*. Fresh, mineral Bical whites, esp Nossa Calcario, Nossa Tola. Amphora-aged Post-Quercus v.gd.

Pato, Luis Bair ★★→★★★★ Opinionated, nonconformist, modern BAIR pioneer following rebelious family tradition. Father of FILIPA P. Fine range: *age-worthy, single-vyd Baga* (Barrio, Barrosa, Pan) and Pé Franco (ungrafted) wines (bright, sandy-soil *Ribeirinho*); age-worthy whites (rich, single-vyd Vinha Formal, sharp Parcela Cândido, fine *Ribeirinho*). BAGA Rebel, VINHAS VELHAS (r/w) v.gd value.

Perdigão, Quinta do Dão ★★→★★★ Historic family-owned bio estate, now run by daugher Mafalda. Classic native varieties-focused range, esp ALFROCHEIRO, ENCRUZADO, Jaen, TOURIGA N; v.gd RES.

Pereira d'Oliveira Mad ★★→★★★★ Run by 5th generation. Vast stocks, on-demand FRASQUEIRA, many available at time-machine touristy cellar door. Ask nicely for C19 vintages MOSCATEL 1875, SERCIAL 1875, Terrantez 1880, or rare *Bastardo 1927*. Owns Barros & Sousa.

Pico Wines ★★→★★★ Largest, oldest AZORES co-op makes consistent quality volcanic range: gd-value Frei Gigante, Terras de Lava; v.gd salty, single-variety ARINTO/Terrantez do Pico/VERDELHO range. Top: *Rola Pipa*, 100-yr-old-vine *Gruta das Torres*. 10-yr-old Licoroso a treat.

Poças Dou, Port ★★→★★★ Centenarian, family-run firm with gd Port, dynamic table-wine range. Old Tawny stocks: fine 20-, *30-, 50-yr-old*, COLHEITAS fabulous 90-yr-old+ 1918. LBV, VINTAGE PORT v.gd. Top-notch: sumptuous, oaked Branco da Ribeira (w); dense Símbolo; new field-blend Vinha do Cerro; RES gd-value; *Fora da Série* range, esp *Vinho da Roga*.

Pormenor Dou ★★★ Exciting min-intervention project. Elegant, mineral, high-altitude field-blend *Trilho*; firm, austere A de ARINTO; creamy yet vibrant, high-altitude *Pormenor Res*; gd-value entry-level (r/w).

Portalegre Alen ★→★★★ Old, now trendy n subregion; high-altitude, cooler climate, old field-blend vyds. Best: ★★★ CABEÇAS DO REGUENGO, ★★★ RUI REGUINGA, *Susana Esteban*, ★★ Tapada do Chaves. Trend followers to try: ESPORÃO, MALHADINHA (Teixinha), NIEPOORT, SOGRAPE (Série Ímpar), SYMINGTON (Fonte Souto).

Quanta Terra Dou ★★★→★★★★ Underrated estate run by star winemakers Jorge Alves (QUINTA NOVA), Celso Pereira (VÉRTICE). Fine range: unique, oak-aged *Gold Edition*; top-notch Grande Res (r/w); old-vines Inteiro; unique Phenomena PINOT N Rosé; Pouca Terra gd value. Book to visit DOU art centre.

Quinta Wine-producing estate. "Herdade" in ALEN.

Quinta Nova Dou ★★★→★★★★ Historic family-run estate, led by Luisa Amorim (cork family) and star winemakers. Predictably cork-taint-free range: fine, rich oaked Mirabilis (r/w); outstanding rich, layered Vinha Centenária range (100-yr-old vines: *Tinta Roriz* or TOURIGA N); superior 100-yr-old-vines Aeternus; v.gd-value rosé, *Grainha* (r/w). *Charming hotel*, award-winning wine tourism. DÃO outpost: TABOADELLA.

Portugal supplies over half the world's cork – no wonder screwcaps are scarce here.

Rainwater Mad Seductive chilled apéritif. Lighter, drier style of MAD Estufa aged min 5 yrs, usually TINTA NEGRA.

Ramos, João Portugal Alen ★→★★★ Large, family-run, ALEN pioneer firm. Best: Marquês de Borba RES, Estremus, single-vyd range. Popular: Loios, Pouca Roupa. Value brands: Marquês de Borba, Vila Santa, VINHAS VELHAS. Outposts: VIN, DOU (DUORUM), Beira Atlântico (FOZ DE AROUCE).

Ramos Pinto Dou, Port ★★★→★★★★ Historic Port estate, growing DOU range: top-notch silky Ervamoira; classy **Res** (r); great-value Duas Quintas (r/w); popular Bons Ares. Best Ports: 1st-class, vibrant 20-yr-old; v.gd VINTAGE PORT, incl single-quintas Bom Retiro, Ervamoira. Owned by Champagne Roederer (*see* France).

Real Companhia Velha Dou, Port ★→★★★ Oldest (1756) wine firm in Portugal, now run by young generation. Diverse range: fine Carvalhas (esp v.gd old-vines r/w); international-variety/style Cidrô, incl popular oaked CHARD and seductive, fine **Marquis** (TOURIGA N/CAB SAUV); bio, native-variety Síbio; gd-value Aciprestes, Evel; best-in-class **Grandjó** late-harvest. Value Port brands: Carvalhas, Delaforce, RCV, Royal Oporto, Silva Reis. GAIA wine bar.

For goodness' sake, serve your Port chilled – it will warm up in the glass.

Regueiro, Quinta do Vin ★★★ Family-run, boutique estate renowned for ALVARINHO. Top: blend-of-yrs Jurássico, cellar-release Maturado, old-vines **Primitivo**. Oak-aged Barricas, Foral, mineral RES v.gd. Secreto Alvarinho/Trajadura gd value.

Reguinga, Rui Alen, Tej ★★★ Consultant's own v.gd brand. ALEN, PORTALEGRE: bio, high-altitude, old-vines **Terrenus** range, incl centenarian-vine **Vinha da Serra** (w). Rhône-inspired Tejo: **Tributo**, Vinha da Talisca (w).

Reserve / Reserva (Res) Port Bottle- or oak-aged designation. Rules vary by region. Often higher quality, not always. Grande Res much better. Port bottled without age indication: often gd-value RUBY, TAWNY.

Rocim Alen ★★→★★★★ Dynamic, family-run, increasingly bio firm. Also VINHO DE TALHA-revival pioneer. Top: fine Grande Rocim (dense, piney ALICANTE BOUSCHET r; firm, oaky ARINTO w), late-release Crónica #328, 1st-class **Vinha da Micaela**. Clay-pot range v.gd: luxury-priced amphora-aged Júpiter Code 01; foot-trodden, polished **Clay Aged** (r); elegant Amphora (r/w). Also gd old-vine, single-vyd Olho de Mocho (r/w). Other regions: seductive old-field-blend DOU Bela Luz; fine DÃO **O Estrangeiro** (r/w). Visitor centre in Vidigueira, ALEN.

Romeira, Quinta da Lis ★★ Popular, historic Bucelas estate. Fresh, mineral, ARINTO-based range v.gd value: Morgado Sta Catherina, Prova Regia. SOGRAPE-owned.

Rosa, Quinta de la Dou, Port ★★★ Classic, family-run estate. Value range by Poeira's Jorge Moreira: La Rosa, RES (r/w); Passagem label. Best PORT: v.gd LBV, 30-yr-old TAWNY, VINTAGE PORT. Riverside guesthouse, restaurant.

Rozès Dou, Port ★★ Vranken-Pommery (*see* France) PORT brand (gd DOU Superior LBV); gd Terras do Grifo range (fine RES, VINHAS VELHAS, Grande Res).

Ruby Port Major PORT style/category. Bottle-aged, fruitier (vs TAWNY), yrs in wood before bottling: VINTAGE PORT (2), LBV (4–6), RES (6). Also, most simple, young, cheap, often delicious sweet Port.

Sandeman Port Port ★★→★★★ Renowned house famous for caped-image "The Don", modern labels. VINTAGE PORT back on form. Also v.gd-value range: 20-, 30-, 40-, 50-yr-old TAWNY; unfiltered LBV. DOU visitor centre, restaurant. SOGRAPE-owned.

Sant'Ana, Quinta de Lis ★★★ Idyllic, family-run bio estate known for crisp, saline whites: v.gd ALVARINHO, ARINTO, FERNÃO PIRES, esp pricey Marreco. Age-worthy reds. Rare, native **Ramisco**.

São João, Caves Bair ★★→★★★★ Historic firm famous for cellar releases incl sparkling: BAIR (Frei João, Luiz Costa, Poço do Lobo); DÃO (Porta dos Cavaleiros).

Seabra, Luis Dou, Vin ★★★→★★★★ Reputed winemaker (ex-NIEPOORT) makes elegant, low-intervention, single-vyd range; DOU (v.gd Ilimitado r/w, Indie, **Xisto Cru** r/w); VIN (fine lees-aged ALVARINHO **Granito Cru**).

Sercial Mad Racy, tart, driest style of MAD. **Supreme apéritif**, perfect with smoked fish, caviar, or fresh goat's cheese.

Setúbal, Península de ★→★★★ Seaside region s of Lisbon, home of world-class fortified MOSCATEL DE SETÚBAL. Table wines: look for crisp whites, sandy-soil reds, esp CASTELÃO. Best: BACALHOA, ★★ Brejinho da Costa, ★★ Horácio Simões, JOSÉ MARIA DA FONSECA, ★★ *Pegos Claros*, ★★ Piloto, ★★ Portocarro, ★★★ *Trois*. Popular: Adega de Pegões, Casa Ermelinda Freitas.

Soalheiro, Quinta de Vin ★★→★★★ Leading ALVARINHO firm now without winemaker Luís Cerdeira; gd-value Classico; mineral *Granit*; v.gd, subtly barrel-fermented *Primeiras Vinhas*; oaked RES.

Sogevinus Dou, Port ★→★★★ Large Spanish-owned Port group, with growing table-wine range: gd-value São Luiz range esp unique Winemaker's Collection; high-end QUINTA DA BOAVISTA. Owns gd Port houses: ★★→★★★★ Barros (v.gd-value COLHEITAS from every decade since 30s; also v.gd 20-, 30-, 40-yr-old TAWNY); ★→★★★★ Burmester (elegant, gd-value Tawny; 20-, 40-yr-old Colheitas; delectable 30-, 40-yr-old WHITE PORTS); ★→★★★★ Cálem (bestseller, entry-level Velhotes; 10-, 40-yr-old Tawny); KOPKE. Visit: GAIA (three popular cellars); DOU (São Luiz guesthouse).

Sogrape Alen, Dou, Vin ★→★★★★ Largest wine firm in Portugal, global interests. Home of MATEUS ROSÉ. Fine-wine range 1st class: 100-yr-old+ vines Legado, *Série Ímpar*; ALEN (gd-value from BARCA VELHA, v.gd CASA FERREIRINHA); DOU (CARVALHAIS); DÃO (iconic BARCA VELHA, v.gd CASA FERREIRINHA); LIS (v.gd-value QUINTA DA ROMEIRA); VIN (★ Azevedo). Port: FERREIRA, OFFLEY, SANDEMAN. Outposts: Argentina (Finca Flichman); Chile (Los Boldos); NZ (Framingham); Spain (LAN, Santiago Ruiz, Viña Mayor).

Sousa, Alves de Dou, Port ★★→★★★ Family-run table-wine pioneer, large, dynamic range: v.gd, classic *Quinta da Gaivosa*, unique late-released RES Pessoal (r/w); fine, old field blends Abandonado, Vinha de Lordelo; refined Port. Value: Caldas, Oliveirinha, Vale da Raposa.

Sousa, José de Alen ★★→★★★ Historic estate keeping ALEN trad alive with largest (100+) TALHA collection in use: v.gd *Mayor* and *J.* Spicy, ripe *José de Sousa* and RES v.gd value. JM DA FONSECA's ALEN outpost.

Symington Family Estates Dou, Port ★★→★★★★ Historic, family-run, B Corp-certified Port firm (owns top brands COCKBURN'S, DOW'S, GRAHAM'S, WARRE'S). Growing table-wine range. Top: CHRYSEIA, fruit-driven ★★★ VESUVIO, thrilling high-altitude DOU whites (esp Ilustres Desconhecidos range, *Pequeno Dilema*). Altano RES, *Contacto* (alongside ANSELMO MENDES), Pombal, Post Scriptum all gd value. Fabulous historic 1890 lodge visitor centre/restaurant in GAIA. Outposts: high-altitude ALEN/PORTALEGRE Fonte Souto (try fine Taifa); new VIN range; co-owner of VÉRTICE, Hambledon (see England). Primum Familiae Vini member.

Taboadella Dão ★★★ Amorim-family DÃO project in Serra da Estrela microclimate. QUINTA NOVA's star team makes classy range: top, oaked Grande Villae (r/w); seductive varietal RES range, esp *Alfrocheiro*. Unoaked entry-level Villae v.gd value. Charming guesthouse.

Talha, Vinho de Alen DOC. 2000-yr-old clay-amphora trad undergoing revival. Vinification: some whole-bunch, 5–6-wk maceration in decades-old amphorae, now hunted treasures. Best: ★★ XXVI Talhas, esp *Mestre Daniel*, ★★ Gerações da Talha, ★★ Herdade Grande, JOSÉ DE SOUSA, ★★ José Piteira, ROCIM. Creamy, room-temperature Serra da Estrela cheese IS LBV/VP's best friend.

Pastel de nata and 20-year-old Tawny Port are a match made in heaven.

Tawny Port ★→★★★★ Port style (alternative to RUBY). Entry-level RES (6 yrs in wood) a wallet-friendly treat. Age-dated, a big step up: 10-, 20-, 30-, 40, 50-yr-old; single-yr, cask-aged COLHEITAS up to 100 yrs, incl luscious, expensive *Very Very Old Tawny* (80-yr-old+). Top: ANDRESEN, DALVA, GRAHAM'S, KOPKE, NIEPOORT, NOVAL, Otima (WARRE'S), POÇAS, RAMOS PINTO, SANDEMAN, TAYLOR'S, VASQUES DE CARVALHO. Crowd-pleaser: wood-aged, oxidative, nutty, sweet; perfect dessert on its own or with crème brûlée. Ready to drink on release, lasts 2 mths after opening. Serve chilled to time-travel to DOU.

Taylor's Port ★★→★★★★ Historic Port brand, FLADGATE's jewel in the crown. Pioneered LBV, dry WHITE PORT. Impressive range of top Port wines. VINTAGE PORTS 63' 66' 70' 77' 94' 97' 00' 03' 07' 11' 16'. In non-declared yrs: single QUINTAS (Terra Feita, *Vargellas*), new Sentinel's. Rare, splendid *Vargellas Vinha Velha* from 70-yr-old+ vines. Outstanding *Tawny range* (some from stocks of reputable Krohn brand), esp 20-, 30-, 40-yr-old, 50-yr-old Golden Age, 1863' single-harvest, Scion, Kingsman Edition (average 90 yrs old); new VERY VERY OLD PORT, a luscious, decadent liquid treasure.

Textura Dão ★★→★★★ Recent family-owned Serra da Estrela estate; v.gd bio range (vibrant, complex Pura w); v.gd Textura da Estrela (r/w); gd value Encoberta, Pretexto (r/w).

Vadio Bair ★★★ Fine, consistent BAGA-focused boutique project. Classic *Estate label* and Grande Vadio v.gd.

Vale D. Maria, Quinta do Dou, Port ★★→★★★ Fine DOU range: v.gd *estate label*, single-vyd Vinha do Rio, *Vinha da Francisca*, new top, rare cellar-release Vinha do Moinho. Oak-aged whites gd, esp Vinha do Martim; Dou Superior range gd value. Try Ports: LBV, RES, VINTAGE PORT, VERY OLD TAWNY. AVELEDA owned.

Vale Meão, Quinta do Dou ★★★ Historic, family-run estate. Fine range incl sought-after eponymous top red; v.gd single-vyd varietal range Monte Meão, esp Vinha dos Novos; gd-value Meandro (r/w); gd VINTAGE PORT.

Vallado, Quinta do Dou ★★→★★★ Régua-based firm. Top-notch: old-vine Coroa, Granja, 100-yr-old-vine Adelaide red. Value: RES (r/w), organic DOU Superior. Port: thrilling, pre-phylloxera 1888 VERY OLD TAWNY; v.gd 10-, 20-, 30-, 40-, 50-yr-old TAWNY. Striking hotel/winery.

Valle Pradinhos Trás M ★★→★★★ Historic, family-owned estate just n of DOU; v.gd, consistent quality range (r/w RES, Grande RES).

Van Zellers & Co Dou, Port ★★★ Van Zeller's family project, now focus after sale of VALE D MARIA. Top: CV – Curriculum Vitae (r/w). Also v.gd: VZ (r/w). Port: superb stylish COLHEITA range 34 35 40 50 76, v.gd 10-, 20-, 30-, 40-, 50-yr-old TAWNY.

Vasques de Carvalho Dou, Port ★★★→★★★★ Boutique firm, est 2012 from inherited family cellars, stock, vyds. Liquid gold: fine, pricey, stylish *10-, 20-, 30-, 40-, 50-yr-old Tawny* and WHITE PORT; gd vintage and DOU range. Charming GAIA tasting room.

Verdelho Mad Classic MAD grape. Sweeter than SERCIAL and drier than BUAL. Versatile: gd with hard cheese, unique fusion with Japanese food. Popular in Mad table wine.

Vértice Dou ★★★→★★★★ Portugal's best fizz, ages well; v.gd-value Gouveio, *Millésime*. Pricey, high-altitude, 84-mth-aged PINOT N. Co-owned by SYMINGTON

Wine tourism in the Douro

Scenic beauty, terraced vyds, wine tastings, vyd tours and river cruises. What's not to like? Favourites have a ★. **Visit & Taste** ★ Bomfim, ★ CARVALHEIRA, CRASTO, La Rosa, ★ NIEPOORT, ★ NOVAL, PACHECA, ★ QUINTA NOVA, Roêda, Seixo, WINE & SOUL. **Stay** ★ Casa do Rio, Gricha, Octant, ★ Quinta Nova, S Bernardo, ★ Six Senses, S Luiz, Tedo, ★ Ventozelo, Wine House Hotel. **Eat** ★ Bomfim 1896, ★ Castas e Pratos, DOC, Seixo, Toca da Raposa, ★ Ventozelo. **Boat** multi-day river cruises from Porto stopping at various QUINTAS or Régua-based tour. On a budget: take the **train** for a unique perspective.

Very Very Old Tawny Port ★★★★ Bottled treasures, best ethereal. Wood-aged for decades (min 80 yrs). Top: 1900, 1910 (ANDRESEN), 1918 (POÇAS), 5G (WINE & SOUL), Carvalhas Memories (RCV), Coronation, Ne Oublie (GRAHAM'S), Scion, VV (NIEPOORT), VVOT (TAYLOR'S).

Vesuvio, Quinta do Dou, Port ★★★ →★★★★ Magnificent, historic SYMINGTON-owned riverside QUINTA, book to visit. Fruit-driven DOU range: classy old-vine estate red; gd-value second label Pombal. Port still foot-trodden, on par with best, esp 100-yr-old-vines *Capela*.

Olive oil is a national treasure: cooking ingredient, skincare secret and heart's best friend.

Vicentino Alen ★★ ALEN Atlantic-coast pioneer, making gd-value mineral, saline range: ALVARINHO, ARINTO, SAUV BL, PINOT N, SYRAH, entry-level label.

Vinhas Velhas Old vines. Sought-after national treasure. Age and meaning vary by region, only regulated in DOU – min 40-yr-old vyds, min four-variety field blend, low yield.

Vinho Verde ★ →★★★ Portugal's most exported wines, known for spritzy freshness, increasingly for quality. Borders Galicia/Spain. Top ALVARINHO: *Anselmo Mendes*, ★★ Barão do Hospital, *Luis Seabra*, MÁRCIO LOPES, *Regueiro*, ★★ *Santiago*, SOALHEIRO. Top bio LOUREIRO: AMEAL, ★★ Aphros. Top Avesso: ★★ bio *A&D*, ★★ Covela. Also try: ★ Azevedo, ★★ Casa de Cello, ★★ Casa de Vilacetinho. Large brands with cheap, off-dry, slightly fizzy wines: Adega de Monção, Adega Ponte da Barca, Casal Garcia, Gazela, Muralhas. Influx of new players: ESPORÃO, FALUA, FLADGATE, GRANVINHOS, SYMINGTON, WINESTONE.

Vintage Port Port Prestigious, one of the world's greatest classics. Aged patiently in bottle after 2 yrs in wood. Old vintages 27' 45' 63' 66' 70' 77' are ethereal, a sweet treat when young. Made in v. finest yrs (aka "classic" or "declared" yrs), increasingly made back-to-back due to precision viticulture and winemaking. Underrated *Single-quinta VPs* made in non-declared yrs: Bomfim, Senhora da Ribeira (DOW'S), Guimaraens, Panascal (FONSECA), Malvedos (GRAHAM'S). Rare, superlative *special editions*: Capela (VESUVIO), Sērikos (CROFT), Stone Terraces (GRAHAM'S), Vinha da Pisca (NIEPOORT), Vinha Velha (TAYLOR'S). Throws deposit, always decant. Serve at red-wine temperature.

Viúva Gomes Lis ★★★ Historic C19 estate. Baeta family bringing subregion back. Blend of trad, modernity on phylloxera-resistant sandy soils. Classic *estate label* v.gd: Ramisco (r), MALVASIA de Colares (w). Decades-old vintages still in shops. Experimental, low-intervention *Pirata* range.

Warre's Port ★★★→★★★★ Underrated SYMINGTON-owned historic Port brand. Rich, long-ageing VINTAGE esp limited-edition VINHAS VELHAS, v.gd unfiltered LBV, elegant single-QUINTA Cavadinha, racy *20-yr-old Tawny Otima*.

White Port Port Underrated category, often overshadowed by TAWNY. Undergoing revival with high-quality labels: age-dated 10-, 20-, 30-, 40-, or 50-yr-old v.gd (ANDRESEN, KOPKE, Quevedo, S Leonardo, Vieira de Sousa); superb, rare COLHEITAS (*Dalva, Kopke*). Lágrima is cheap, v. sweet. Best cocktail: refreshing Port & Tonic.

Wine & Soul Dou, Port ★★★→★★★★ Prestigious family-run estate, fine range: complex, iconic Pintas; delicious, elegant, field-blend *Pintas Character*; stunning oak-aged *Guru*; top-notch *Manoella Vinhas Velhas*, Vinha Alecrim, gd-value entry level (r/w); crisp, high-atititude *Vinha do Altar* (w). Elegant Ports. Superlative 100-yrs+ VERY VERY OLD TAWNY 5G.

Winestone Alen, Dou, Lis, Port, Vin Ambitiou new group, owns MONTE DE RAVASQUEIRA (ALEN). New acquisitions: Wiese & Krohn (Port); QUINTA DE PANCAS (LIS); long-term loan of QUINTA do Cotto (DOU) and Paço do Teixeiró (VIN).

PORTUGAL

Switzerland

Abbreviations used in the text:

Aar   Aargau
Gris   Grisons
Luc   Lucerne
Neu   Neuchâtel
Schaff   Schaffhausen
Thur   Thurgau
Tic   Ticino
Val   Valais
Vd   Vaud
Zür   Zürich

Switzerland is something of an island, which is both a blessing and a curse: its wine has retained its uniqueness but has a lot of catching up to do when it comes to international fame. Quantities of the best are tiny. Pinot Noir (from Graubünden or Neuchâtel), Petite Arvine, Cornalin or Syrah (from Valais), Chasselas (from Lauvaux) are only known to insiders – even within Switzerland it is difficult to get hold of them. Swiss specialities fall into a category of their own, best found by visiting the growers *in situ*. Bonne chance! It is worth it.

Recent vintages

2024 Frost, mildew. What was left has gd quality.
2023 Another rollercoaster: rain at harvest, hail in Tic.
2022 Warm and dry yr, generally gd quantity, quality.
2021 Frost, hail, mildew: tiny crop. Lighter wines, sound quality, v.gd whites.
2020 Early, small, 20–40% less: uneven flowering, drought, v.gd quality.
2019 Rain at harvest time, esp in e; Vd and Val better.
Earlier fine vintages: 18 17 15 09 05 90, (Pinot N) 13 10, (Dézaley) 99 97.

Adank, Hansruedi Gris ★★★ Young Patrick A makes delicate PINOT N (Spondis); Brut Nature, one of country's best.
Aigle Vd ★→★★★ Popular CHASSELAS AOC, best from Plantour hill on moraine soil.
AOC Equivalent of France's appellation contrôlée; 62 AOCs countrywide.
Auvernier, Ch d' Neu ★★→★★★ Important estate (60 ha), typical NEU CHARD,

CHASSELAS, OEIL-DE-PERDRIX, PINOT N (single-vyd Les Argiles 15' 18'). Kairos series of special vinifications, eg. No 3 (20 Chasselas, rich, subtle).

Bachtobel, Schlossgut Thur ★★★ Family estate (since 1784): refined PINOT N labelled 1–4 (higher number = better quality), gd SAUV BL, Mousseux Extra Brut.

Bad Osterfingen Schaff ★★★ Historic spa (est 1472), now restaurant, wine estate. Michael Meyer's PINOTS BL/N v. fine food matches.

Badoux, Henri Vd ★★ AIGLE Les Murailles (classic lizard label) most popular Swiss brand. Ambitious Lettres de Noblesse series (barrel-aged YVORNE).

Uninvited guest in Ticino's Sottoceneri: Japanese beetle loves maize, soya, grapes.

Baumann, Ruedi Schaff ★★★ Family estate; PINOT N (Ann Mee, R, ZWAA).

Bern Capital and canton, wine villages on Lake Biel and Lake Thun. Top growers: Andrey, Johanniterkeller, Keller am See, Krebs & Steiner, Schlössli, Schott (bio).

Besse, Gérald Val ★★★ Sarah B converted excellent family estate to organic. One of many SPÉCIALITÉS in steep terraces up to 600m (1969ft) is *Ermitage Les Serpentines* 15 16 17 18 19 20 (MARSANNE on granite soils, planted 1945).

Blass, Cantina Tic ★★→★★★ Up-and-coming; low- (but not no-) sulphur MERLOT: foot-trodden, juicy Vittorio; Regina more trad; CAB FR Pietro, peppery.

Bonvin Val ★★→★★★ Old name of VAL, intriguing local grapes: *Nobles Cépages* series (eg. HEIDA, PETITE ARVINE, SYRAH).

Bovard, Louis Vd ★★→★★★★ Keeper of the grail in DÉZALEY (La Médinette 99' 00' 05' 07' 11' 12' 15' 16 17 18' 19 20 21 22); other AOCs equally reliable. Doyen Louis-Philippe B, now in his 90s, joined by Fabio Bongulielmi.

Calamin Vd ★★★ GRAND CRU of LAVAUX, 16 ha of deep calcareous soils on a landslide, CHASSELAS tarter than nearby DÉZALEY.

Chablais Vd ★★→★★★★ Wine region at upper end of Lake Geneva around AIGLE and YVORNE. Name is from Latin *caput lacis*, head of the lake.

Chappaz, Marie-Thérèse Val ★★★→★★★★★ Small bio estate. Tiny quantities of nobly sweet Ermitage (MARSANNE), Petite ARVINE 06' 07' 15' 18. In 2020, 54 litres of "grain par grain" in essencia style (*see* Hungary).

Colombe, Dom La Vd ★★→★★★ At FÉCHY; bio. Age-worthy CHASSELAS Brez, terracotta-aged field-blend white (Curzilles), SAVAGNIN Amédée.

Constantin, Thierry Val ★★★ Passionate grower, 7 ha of steep slopes, top SYRAH Anastasi (ex-L'Odalisque).

Corbassière, Cave Val ★★→★★★ SPÉCIALITÉS from VAL: L'Effervescence (PINOT N sp).

Cortaillod Neu PINOT N stronghold on shores of Lake Neuchâtel, eponymous low-yielding local clone. Best: PORRET.

Côte, La Vd ★→★★★ A breadbasket of CHASSELAS: 2000 ha w of Lausanne on Lake Geneva, v. variable quality. Villages incl FÉCHY, Mont-sur-Rolle, Morges.

Cruchon Vd ★★★ In LA CÔTE, bio, led by Catherine C. Many SPÉCIALITÉS: PINOT N from local SERVAGNIN 18' 19' 20', Raissennaz 10' 13' 15' 17'.

Devinière, Dom de la Gen ★★→★★★ Organic family estate. Age-worthy: CHASSELAS, PINOT N, finesse; CAB SAUV, purity. Free series (no sulphur).

Dézaley Vd ★★★ LAVAUX GRAND CRU on steep slopes of Lake Geneva, 54 ha; planted in C12 by Cistercian monks. Potent CHASSELAS develops with age (7 yrs+). Best: DUBOIS, DUBOUX, *Fonjallaz*, LEYVRAZ, *Louis Bovard*, MONACHON, Ville de Lausanne.

Dôle Val ★→★★ VAL's answer to Burgundy's Passetoutgrains: PINOT N plus GAMAY for light, quaffable red.

Donatsch Gris ★★★ Martin D made name for spectacular auction results (PINOT N Res Privée). Local Completer SPÉCIALITÉ.

Dubois, Frères Vd ★★→★★★ Age-worthy, silky DÉZALEY-Marsens Vase No 4; fine Epesses Braise d'Enfer.

Duboux, Blaise Vd ★★★ Family estate in LAVAUX. Rich, mineral CALAMIN, DÉZALEY.

Dutruy, Frères Vd ★★→★★★ Fine organic estate in LA CÔTE, LAVAUX, incl DÉZALEY, rare local red Plant Robez. Top old-vines-blend Les Romaines Res GAMAY.

Féchy Vd ★→★★★ Famous though unreliable AOC of LA CÔTE, mainly CHASSELAS.

Fendant Val ★→★★★ Full VAL CHASSELAS; balsamic scent, ideal for fondue or raclette.

Fläsch Gris ★★★→★★★★ Village of Bündner Herrschaft, PINOT N from schist, limestone. Try ADANK, Hermann, Marugg families, HÖRLER. Top **Gantenbein**.

Switzerland has 0.4% of Europe's surface, but 6% of its drinkable water.

Flétri / Mi-flétri Late-harvested grapes for sweet/slightly sweet wine.

Fromm, Georg Gris ★★★ Top bio grower in MALANS: light-coloured, subtle, age-worthy single-vyd PINOT N (Fidler, Michel, Schöpfi, Selvenen, Spielmann).

Gantenbein Gris ★★★★ Star growers Daniel and Martha G in FLÄSCH. PINOT N is famous, but CHARD (tiny quantity) even more intriguing.

Geneva Gen 1400 ha of vines remote from the lake (vyds belong mainly to VD): Balisiers, Clos des Pins, GRAND'COUR, LA DEVINIÈRE, Les Hutins, Novelle.

Germanier, Jean-René Val ★★→★★★ Reliable FENDANT Les Terrasses, SYRAH Cayas, local AMIGNE from schist at Vétroz (dr/sw).

Gialdi Tic ★★→★★★ Prime producer in TIC. Bought-in grapes from small producers in mtn-altitude vyds: top MERLOT Sassi Grossi 11 12 13' 14 15 16' 18' 19 20' (no 21).

Glacier, Vin du (Gletscherwein) Val ★★★ A sort of Alpine "Sherry" from rare Rèze grape of Val d'Anniviers, aged in larch casks. Taste at Grimentz town hall.

Grain Noble ConfidenCiel Val Quality label for authentic sweet wines. Berries must be concentrated on vine.

Grand'Cour, Dom Gen ★★★ Leading estate of GENEVA, 25 varieties on 15 ha, outstanding CABS FR/SAUV blend Grand'Cour 03' 05 07 09 13' 15' 16' 17 18' 19'.

Grand Cru Val, Vd Inconsistent term, used in VAL and VD, sometimes linked to specific varieties or restricted yields, or to designations like clos, ch, abbaye. Only few are classifications of a vyd site (eg. CALAMIN, DÉZALEY).

Grisons (Graubünden) A mtn canton, PINOT N king. Famous Bündner Herrschaft: four villages (FLÄSCH, Jenins, Maienfeld, MALANS): 6000 inhabitants, 329 growers.

Hammel, Maison Val, Vd ★→★★★★ Merchant with 15 doms. Dom de Crochet Cuvée Charles Auguste SYRAH/CABS SAUV/FR 06' 09 10 11' 12 13' 15 16' 17 18' 19.

Herter Zür ★★→★★★ PINOT N expert nr Zürich: fragrant Grimbart, dense Ruprecht.

Hörler, Silas Gris ★★→★★★ New at FLÄSCH: powerful, oaked CHARD Valäris, spicy PINOT N Carsilias.

Hubervini ★★→★★★ Family estate (7 ha): MERLOT/CAB FR Montagna Magica.

Jet Zür ★★★ New on Lake Zürich: barrel-fermented Räuschling, PINOT N, orange.

Kartause Ittingen Thur ★→★★★ Former Carthusian monastery, owned (beautifully restored) by Canton of Thurgau. Fine PINOTS N/GR Kirchwingert.

Kastanienbaum, Weingut Luc ★★→★★★ Formerly Weinbau Ottiger. Now Kevin Studer, Denis Koch prove inner Switzerland wine-growing: PINOT N **Rosenau**.

Lavaux Vd ★★→★★★★ UNESCO World Heritage Site, 30 km steep s-facing terraces e of Lausanne. Uniquely rich, mineral CHASSELAS. GRANDS CRUS CALAMIN, DÉZALEY, several village AOCs.

Leyvraz, Pierre-Luc Vd ★★★→★★★★ Perfectionist at LAVAUX, now joined by André Bélard; terroir-led ST-SAPHORIN Les Blassinges, age-worthy DÉZALEY.

Litwan, Tom Aar ★★★ Grower at Schinznach, 5 ha, bio: CHARD (Büel, Wanne), single-vyd PINOT N (Auf der Mauer, Chalofe, Rüeget).

Lüthi Weinbau Zür ★★★ Small, perfectionists: age-worthy PINOT N, MÜLLER-T (labelled RIES x Madeleine Royale).

Maison Carrée, La Neu ★★★ Family estate, est 1827, 10 ha, bio; v. trad winemaking incl old wooden press, esp delicately scented PINOT N.

Malans Gris ★★→★★★★ Village in Bündner Herrschaft. Top PINOT N: DONATSCH,

FROMM, Liesch, Studach, WEGELIN. Late-ripening, age-worthy local Completer (Giani Boner has ungrafted vines).

Maye, Simon & Fils Val ★★★ Raphaël M's SYRAH Vieilles Vignes 05 09 10' 11 12 13 15' 16' 17 18', plus excellent SPÉCIALITÉS (eg. Païen).

Mercier, Denis Val ★★★→★★★★ Meticulous vyd management; aromatic, top FENDANT, DÔLE, SYRAH, rare CORNALIN 08' 09' 10' 11' 12 13' 15' 16 17 18' 19 20'.

Monachon, Pierre Vd ★★★ Crisp, mineral, v. reliable DÉZALEY Les Côtes Dessus, ST-SAPHORIN Les Manchettes 14 15' 18' 21' 22.

Mont d'Or, Dom du Val ★★→★★★★ Emblematic VAL estate, schist soils, SCHENK owned. Nobly sweet JOHANNISBERG Saint-Martin 06' 09' 11' 15' 16 20; v.gd dry wines (RIES Amphytrion).

Montimbert, Dom Vd ★★→★★★ Small, fine Lavaux estate; precise old-vine PINOT GR, refined PINOT N.

Montmollin, Dom de Neu ★★→★★★ Old name in NEU, organic: PINOT N (Vieille Vigne Auvernier La Pierre).

Morcote, Castello di Tic ★★★ Castle ruin and eponymous 14-ha winery; 3rd-generation Gaby Gianini made bio, top Riserva 17 18' 19' 20'.

Neuchâtel ★→★★★ 606 ha around city and lake on calcareous soil. Slightly sparkling CHASSELAS, exquisite local CORTAILLOD. Try CH D'AUVERNIER, Dom de Chambleau, Kuntzer, LA MAISON CARRÉE, PORRET, TATASCIORE.

Oeil de perdrix "Partridge's eye": PINOT N rosé, originally from NEU, now elsewhere.

Pircher Zür ★★★→★★★★ Gianmarco Ofner continues work of retired Urs P: complex PINOT N Stadtberger Barrique 05' 06' 08 10 15' 16' 17 18' 19' 20'; planted RIES.

Porret Neu ★★→★★★★★ Leading family at CORTAILLOD; Burgundian approach to CHARD, PINOT N (Cuvée Elisa).

Provins Val ★→★★★ Co-op with 4000+ members, largest producer, 1500 ha, 34 varieties. Sound entry-level, gd oak-aged Maître de Chais range. Les Titans series aged at altitude: zero evaporation in barrel, v. slow development.

Riehen, Weingut Bas ★★→★★★★ Boutique winery; Hanspeter Ziereisen (*see* Germany) with merchants Jacqueline and Urs Ullrich: CHARD, PINOT N.

Rouvinez Vins Val ★→★★★ A VAL giant at Sierre; after success of cuvées La Trémaille (w) and Le Tourmentin (r), huge takeovers: BONVIN (2009), Imesch (2003), Caves Orsat (1998).

Ruch, Markus Schaff ★★★ Excellent, ultra-rare PINOT N from Hallau (Buck, Chölle old vines, Haalde), Gächlingen (Schlemmweg); 3.5 ha. Amphora MÜLLER-T, Cidre.

St Jodern Kellerei Val ★★→★★★ VISPERTERMINEN CO-OP: ungrafted old-vines **Heida Veritas** 09' 10 15 16 17 18' 21'.

St-Saphorin Vd ★→★★★ Neighbour AOC of DÉZALEY, lighter but equally delicate. Try LEYVRAZ, MONACHON.

Swiss best buys

Can there be such a thing as a bargain in a high-wage country like Switzerland? It depends. If you look at it from a domestic perspective, many PINOT N from cantons of SCHAFF, NEU, or from Zürcher Weinland (area distant from city of ZÜRICH and lake) cost less than national average (without necessarily compromising on quality); gd FENDANT, DÔLE (emphasis on gd) are usually attractively priced, as are AOCs in the neighbourhood of GRAND CRU DÉZALEY (Epesses, Lavaux, ST-SAPHORIN, or Villette). Export is a different picture: even the cheapest Swiss wine is expensive abroad. Here it is the top wines that can compete: compared to prices in Burgundy, even the best and most expensive Swiss Pinot N seem to be fairly priced.

> **Wine regions**
> Switzerland has six major wine regions: VAL, VD, GENEVA, TIC, Trois Lacs (NEU, Bienne/BER, VULLY/Fribourg) and German Switzerland (Aar, GRIS, SCHAFF, St Gallen, Thur, ZÜR and some smaller wine cantons).

San Giorgio, Tenuta Tic ★★★ Family estate, 7 ha; fine Bx blend Arco Tondo, MERLOT Crescendo.

Schaffhausen ★→★★★ A flood of cheap supermarket wines, but also top growers: BAD OSTERFINGEN, BAUMANN, RUCH, Stamm.

Schenk SA Vd ★→★★★ Wine giant with worldwide activities, based in Rolle, founded 1893. Sound wines (esp VD, VAL); substantial exports.

Schwarzenbach, Hermann Zür ★★★ Family estate on Lake Zürich. Local Räuschling a 3rd of vyd: single-vyd Seehalden 15' 17' 18' 19' 20 21' 23, plus other SPÉCIALITÉS.

Servagnin Vd ★★→★★★ PINOT N clone (said to be brought to LA CÔTE by Marie de Bourgogne in 1420). Now own AOC (stricter than Morges AOC).

Spécialités / Spezialitäten Minor (quantity) grapes make some of best Swiss wines, eg. GEWURZ, PINOT GR, Räuschling, or Completer in German Switzerland; Bondola in TIC; Cornalin, Humagne (Bl/N), or JOHANNISBERG, MARSANNE, SYRAH in VAL.

Stevens, Adrien Tic ★★→★★★ Mineral CHARD Erbaluce, fruity Pensiere senza Pensatore, Blu di Notte MERLOT; organic.

Stucky-Hügin Tic ★★★→★★★★ MERLOT pioneer. Best: Conte di Luna (Merlot/ CAB SAUV), Soma (Merlot/CAB FR), Temenos (Completer/SAUV BL).

Tatasciore, Jacques Neu ★★★ Powerful (and rare) NEU PINOT N.

Ticino ★→★★★★ Italian-speaking. Taut MERLOT (leading grape since 1948): Agriloro, CASTELLO DI MORCOTE, Chiericati, Delea, GIALDI, HUBER, Kopp von der Crone Visini, Pelossi, STUCKY, Tamborini, Valsangiacomo, Vinattieri, ZÜNDEL.

Trécord, Dom de Vd Small family estate at Ollon, glorious Rés de la Famille: lemon cream spiked with herbs.

Tscharner, von Fri ★★★ Family estate at Reichenau Castle; tannin-laden PINOT N Gian-Battista 05 06' 09' 13' 15' 16' 17 18' 19'. New wines less trad in style.

Valais (Wallis) Largest wine canton, in dry, sunny upper Rhône V. Best MARSANNE, SYRAH rival French legends. Many exquisite local varieties.

Vaud (Waadt) On shores of Lake Geneva, where CHASSELAS gives most complex terroir expression. Many fine family estates: Bolle, HAMMEL, Obrist, SCHENK.

Visperterminen Val ★→★★★ Upper VAL vyds, esp for HEIDA. One of highest vyds in Europe (Riben at 1000m/3281ft+): Chanton, ST JODERN KELLEREI.

Vully, Mont Fri, VD ★→★★★★ AOC on shores of Lake Murten. Split Fribourg (116 ha) and VD (46 ha). Try Ch de Praz, Chervet, Cru de l'Hôpital, Javet & Javet, Petit Ch.

Wegelin Gris ★★★ Peter W handed over to long-time employees; brilliant Frassa CHARD, Bothmarhalde, Weisstorkel PINOT N.

Wolfer Thur ★★→★★★ Fine family estate at Weinfelden; fresh, tense PINOT N.

Yvorne Vd ★★→★★★ CHABLAIS village with vyds on detritus of 1584 avalanche: BADOUX, Ch Maison Blanche, Commune d'Yvorne, Dom de l'Ovaille.

Zündel, Christian Tic ★★★→★★★★ Small, bio, elegant: MERLOT/CAB SAUV Orizzonte 16' 17 18' 19'; single-vyd Merlots Al Ronco, Sass, Villa.

Zürich Largest city and wine-growing canton in German Switzerland, 610 ha. Mainly BLAUBURGUNDER: Bechtel, Besson-Strasser, JET, E Meier, Gehring, HERTER, LÜTHI, PIRCHER, SCHWARZENBACH, Staatskellerei, Zahner.

Zürichsee Dynamic AOC uniting vyds of ZÜR and Schwyz on shores of Lake Zürich.

Zur Linde, Weingut Aar ★★★ Photographer Michel Jaussi renovated listed building in Linn; dense PINOT N.

Zwaa Schaff ★★★ Collaboration between: BAUMANN (calcareous, deep soil) and BAD OSTERFINGEN (light, gravelly). Age-worthy PINOT N and PINOT BL/CHARD.

Austria

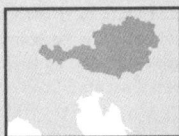

Abbreviations used in the text:

Burgen	Burgenland
Carn	Carnuntum
Kamp	Kamptal
Krems	Kremstal
Nied	Niederösterreich
Stei	Steiermark
S Stei	Südsteiermark
Therm	Thermenregion
Trais	Traisental
V Stei	Vulkanland Steiermark
Wach	Wachau
Wag	Wagram
Wein	Weinviertel
W Stei	Weststeiermark

Every year confirms the quality of Austria's whites, with some reds at the same level. Why? That magic balance of site and vine, plus good viticulture. Organic and biodynamic vineyards are common; natural wines (in a good way) are widespread, and there are some excellent orange wines. Grüner Veltliner works at all levels. Leithaberg DAC and Styria have outstanding Pinot Blanc and Chardonnay; Styria also has Sauvignon Blanc with character beyond green fruit. For reds, Blaufränkisch is the star, capable of real complexity and elegance – especially now the vogue for oak has diminished. DAC? Austria's quality classification: a pyramid with regional wines at the bottom, village wines in the middle and single vineyards at the top, distinguished by the word "Ried" (vineyard) on the label. Drinkers outside Austria might not focus on DAC, but it indicates a complete turnaround in outlook: the site is now the crucial factor.

Recent vintages

2024 Frost, hail, drought in e; rain; ripe grapes; moderate acidity. Stei v.gd.
2023 Variable: Stei wet, Burgen dry, Nied ideal, all perfect autumn, v.gd quality.
2022 Hot, dry summer, changeable spring/autumn: v. ripe wines, less acidity.
2021 Changeable summer, ideal autumn: balanced, ripe wines, gd acidity.
2020 Some disease pressure, some hail. Balanced and classic.
2019 Dream vintage boasting both ripeness and freshness.

Achs, Paul Burgen ★★★★ 19' 20 21 22 23 Polished CHARD and dense, spicy BLAUFRÄNKISCH, both with international touch. Excellent PINOT N.

Altenburger, Markus Burgen ★★★ 16 17 19 20 21' 22' 23' BLAUFRÄNKISCH: mineral RIED Gritschenberg, balanced Spätfüllung. Methode O (sp), fermenting must used for starting 2nd fermentation. Lean, juicy CHARD Vom Kalk.

Alzinger Wach ★★★★ 19' 20 21' 22' 23 Elegance to the max. Clear-cut, long-lived RIES and GRÜNER V. Iconic Ries Steinertal.

Latest trend: ageing wine in casks of local stone. Takes terroir to the limit.

Ambrositsch, Jutta Vienna ★★★ 19' 20 21' 22 23 Delicious field blends. BLAUFRÄNKISCH Hetfleisch with WACHTER-WIESLER, pét-nat WELSCHRIESLING with STRAKA. Great HEURIGE in VIENNA: Buschenschank in Residence open c.10 weekends/yr.

Angerhof-Tschida Burgen ★★★★ 19 21' 22 Hans Tschida in ILLMITZ. Crystalline TBA and BA (*see* Germany) from aromatic grapes such as SCHEUREBE. Rare Eiswein 20.

Beck, Judith Burgen ★★★ 19 20 21' 22' 23' 24 Makes bio, complex BLAUFRÄNKISCH, PINOT N and ZWEIGELT. Beck Ink Zweigelt/ST-LAURENT, Hunny Bunny is lighter Blaufränkisch, Cherry Bomb Zweigelt – clue in name; v.gd natural Bambule!, field-blend Koreaa.

Braunstein, Birgit Burgen ★★★★ 19' 20' 21' 22 23 24 Fine-boned CHARD Felsenstein, skin-fermented PINOT BL Brigid, dark-berried BLAUFRÄNKISCH RIED Thenau.

Bründlmayer, Willi Kamp ★★★★ 19 20 21' 22' 23 Iconic producer, now organic: GRÜNER V Lamm, RIES, esp Alte Reben, Heiligenstein. Five styles of Sekt. More elegant than ever. Francophile reds.

Burgenland Region bordering Hungary. Warmer than NIED; red BLAUFRÄNKISCH, ZWEIGELT prevalent, whites catching up with PINOT BL, CHARD, WELSCHRIESLING and GRÜNER V. Shallow Neusiedlersee, eg. at Rust and in SEEWINKEL, created ideal botrytis conditions, drought a problem.

Carnuntum Nied Region e of VIENNA, accomplished fresh reds, esp ZWEIGELT and cuvées. Look for BLAUFRÄNKISCH from Spitzerberg. Try Artner, Auer, Glatzer, Kellerkünstler, Netzl, Taferner, Weiberwirtschaft Wiederstein.

Christ, Rainer Vienna ★★★ 19 20 21 22 23 24 Top name from Bisamberg. Chewy PINOT BL Der Vollmondwein; GRÜNER V Bruch; elegant Wiener GEMISCHTER SATZ Petershof; intense, herbaceous SHIRAZ. Charming HEURIGE.

DAC (Districtus Austriae Controllatus) Provenance- and quality-based appellation system for regional typicity; 18 in all; 13 have hierarchy of Regional, Ort (village), RIED (cru) – CARN, KAMP, KREMS, Leithaberg, Rosalia, S STEI, Therm, Trais, V STEI, WACH, WAG, WIENER GEMISCHTER SATZ, W STEI. Eisenberg has no village category. RUSTER AUSBRUCH is exclusively sweet. Mittelburgenland, Neusiedlersee, WEIN all just Res and Regional.

Diwald, Martin Krems ★★★ 19 20 21' 22' 23' 24 Organic since 1976, upward-moving since Martin took over; refined GRÜNER V, rare Frühroter Veltliner.

Domäne Wachau Wach ★★★★ 19 20 21' 22' 23' 24 World-class co-op, trend-setting. GRÜNER V, RIES Achleiten, Kellerberg, Singerriedel a tasting must. SMARAGD Ries Brandstatt, Grüner V Kirnberg. Experimental Backstage wines.

Ebner-Ebenauer Wein ★★★★ 19' 20 21' 22' 23' 24 Driving force in WEIN, esp fizz. Elegance, finesse, depth. Single-vyd GRÜNER V and old-vine PINOT N, ST-LAURENT.

Edlmoser Vienna ★★★★ 19' 20 21 22 23 24 Leading winery in S VIENNA. Refined, mineral white, esp RIES and WIENER GEMISCHTER SATZ, powerful red. Try PINOT BL RIED Himmel at superb HEURIGE.

Erste Lage Single-vyd quality designation of ÖTW wineries.

Federspiel Wach VINEA WACHAU middle category of ripeness, min 11.5%, max 12.5% abv. Understated, gastronomic, as age-worthy as SMARAGD; gd value.

Feiler-Artinger Burgen ★★★★ 19 20' 21 22 23 24 Intuitive bio maker, complex white, fine-boned red, stellar RUSTER AUSBRUCH in historic Baroque house in Rust.

Fischer V Stei ★★ 20 21 22' 23' 24 Siblings Claudia, Bernhard, Klaus. Pure wines from mainly volcanic soils. Try excellent fine-boned CHARD (Morillon) Ried Schemming and St Anna (Ortswein). Vibrant, tense RIES Stradenberg.

Frischengruber, Weingärtnerei Wach ★★★ 19 20 21 22' 23 24 Hero of s bank of Danube with RIES and GRÜNER V Kreuzberg in refined, cool style.

Fritsch, Weinlaubenhof Wag ★★★★ 19' 20 21 22' 23' 24 Fine-tuned in all colours; bio. Sublime RIES Mordthal, juicy ROTER VELTLINER, elegant GRÜNER V both Steinberg and Schlossberg, PINOT N Ruppertsthal (Ortswein).

Fritz, Josef Wag ★★★ 19 20' 21' 22' 23' 24 Leading producer of delicate ROTER VELTLINER, sophisticated spiciness, longevity. Two sparkling, rosé and Blanc de Noir, worth trying. Restaurant Himmelreich belongs to family.

Fuchs-Steinklammer Vienna ★★ 21 22 23' 24 Vibrant and juicy field blends in trad and natural styles. Crisp, fresh WIENER GEMISCHTER SATZ; Jesuit from aromatic grapes; fine tangy appeal; super dry, lively Natural Gemischter Satz rosé and rare red version.

Gesellmann Burgen ★★★★ 17 19 20' 21' 22 23 24 Elegance, power in BLAUFRÄNKISCH Hochberg or Creitzer. Fine-boned PINOT N Siglos.

Geyerhof Krems ★★★★ 19 20 21' 22' 23 Historic estate. Super-bio credentials since 1988. Wonderful GRÜNER V Steinleithn, RIES, notable entry-level Stockwerk.

Gindl, Michael Wein ★★★ 19 20' 21' 22' 23 Bio. Barrels from own forest, horses in vyds. Delicate Flora: RIES/SCHEUREBE/YELLOW MUSCAT; creamy, exotic GRÜNER V Buteo; dark-berried, super-dry pét-nat Bubbles (r) Roesler/PINOT N.

Grabenwerkstatt Wach ★★★★ 20' 21 22 23' In cool SPITZER GRABEN; bio. Elegant, exquisite RIES, old vines: Brandstatt, Kalkofen, Trenning. GRÜNER V Schön.

Graf Hardegg Wein ★★★ 20 21 22' 23' 24 Back to former glory, trad with twist. Notable VIOGNIER fizz, full-bodied Grosse Res (CHARD/PINOT N). RIED Steinbügel.

Grassl, Philipp Carn ★★★★ 19 20 21' 22 23 Regional leader. Remarkable CHARD Höflein, Alte Reben WELSCHRIESLING. Impressive ZWEIGELT Schüttenberg.

Groiss, Ingrid Wein ★★★ 19' 20 21' 22 23' 24 Revives old vyds, specializes in GEMISCHTER SATZ, peppery GRÜNER V. Lovely RIES RES Auf der Henne.

Gross S Stei ★★★★ 19 20 21' 22 23 24' Father Alois renowned for age-worthy SAUV BL, rich PINOT BL. Sons Johannes, Michael refined style. Michael left 2018 to run Vino Gross (*see* Slovenia). Several famous RIED: Nussberg, Sulz, Perz.

Gsellmann, Andreas Burgen ★★★ 19' 20 21' 22' 23' 24 Master of TRAMINER; bio, blends of unusual varieties. Pét-nat rosé OMG ("Oh My Gsellmann"), salty Zu Tisch (r/w), PINOT BL Másik (amphora), BLAUFRÄNKISCH Gabarinza.

Gut Oggau Burgen ★★★ 19 20' 21 22 23' Mouthwatering wines, bio estate. Most are blends; sense of Pannonian place. New Eugenie (w).

Hareter, Thomas & Claudia Burgen ★★★ 19 20 21' 22' 23' 24 Detailed winemaking. Fresh varietal Lovely Creatures; precise single-vyd WELSCHRIESLING, PINOT BL, BLAUFRÄNKISCH, PINOT N. Well-balanced blends; bio; taste all.

All wines labelled Kamptal must be organic, or at least sustainable, from 2025.

Harkamp S Stei ★★★★ 19' 20 21 22 23 Fascinating, delicate sparkling and pét-nats too. Among top three in Austria, best in STEI; try all. Favourite fizz: Zero, Solera.

Heinrich, Gernot & Heike Burgen ★★★★ 19' 20 21' 22 23' Made name with BLAUFRÄNKISCH and cuvées; now focus on natural, any colour. Try all: Freyheit, Blaufränkisch Out of the Dark and classic CHARD Leithaberg.

Herrenhof Lamprecht V Stei ★★★ 19 20 21' 22 23' 24' Complex, mineral field blends. Best: Altsteirischer Mischsatz Schrammelberg from 95-yr-old vines. Adorable FURMINT Vom Sandstein. Try any from Buchertberg.

Heuriger New wine. **Heurige:** inn; growers serve own wines, local food – integral to Austrian culture. Also called Buschenschank outside VIENNA.

Hirsch Kamp ★★★★ 19' 20 21' 22' 23' 24 Better every yr; lean RIES of finesse, esp pristine Heiligenstein-Rotfels; complex GRÜNER V from Heiligenstein, Lamm.

Hirtzberger, Franz Wach ★★★★ 19' 20 21' 22 23' 24 Elegance replaced opulence. Single-vyd RIES, GRÜNER V (Honivogl, Singerriedel). Outstanding Ries Hochrain.

Högl Wach ★★★★ 19 20 21 22 23' 24 Small winery in SPITZER GRABEN, introverted father and son team: marvellous, elegant RIES, esp Brandstatt, Bruck; bold GRÜNER V, esp Schön. Impressive steep terraces behind winery.

Huber, Markus Trais ★★★ 19 20' 21 22 23 Emblematic of fine-boned Trais style from limestone with GRÜNER V, RIES. Citrus brilliance, radiance, slenderness.

Hugl, Christina Kamp ★★★ 18 19' 20 21' 22 23' Terroir-driven vyds in WEIN, KAMP, WACHAU. Three GRÜNER V (sp), each terroir: lean, opulent, in-between.

Jaunegg, Daniel S Stei ★★★ 19 20 21' 22 23' Intensely mineral PINOT GR Knily, tangerine-zesty CHARD Muri. Varietal Sand & Schotter.

Jurtschitsch Kamp ★★★★ 19 20 21' 22' 23 Bio; better than ever. Stellar interpretations of RIES Heiligenstein-Rotfels, Heiligenstein-Steinwand, GRÜNER V Loiserberg, all 22'. Also sophisticated fizz, pét-nats.

Kamptal Nied DAC. RIES, GRÜNER V; now also PINOTS BL/GR, CHARD. Rounder style, lower hills, minerality, precision (gd sp). Top vyds: Heiligenstein, Käferberg, Lamm, Loiserberg, Seeberg. Try Allram, Aichinger, Arndorfer, Hiedler, Rabl, Steininger (for sp).

KMW Klosterneuburger (viticultural research station) Mostwaage (must weight) – Austrian unit of sugar content of juice in grams sugar/1000g must. 1° KMW = 4.86° Oechsle (*see* Germany). 20° Brix = 83° Oechsle.

Knoll, Emmerich Wach ★★★★ 19' 20 21' 22 23' Famous for long-lived wines, esp Vinothekfüllung bottlings. Crystalline pure RIES, GRÜNER V RIED Schütt.

Kögl, Tamara S Stei ★★★ 19 20 21' 22' 23 24' Gorgeous, mineral wines, great hospitality: idyllic Buschenschank (inn), rooms. Iconic WELSCHRIESLING Alte Reben, all pét-nats, precise CHARD, rich PINOT GR; bio.

Kolfok Burgen ★★★ 19 20 21' 22' 23 Elegant, mineral. GRÜNER V Vulkan Alte Reben, WELSCHRIESLING, Nolens Volens, intense PINOT BL Muschelkalk Alte Reben.

Kollwentz Römerhof Burgen ★★★★ 19' 20' 21' 22' 23' 24 Quality fanatic (r/w/ sw). Iconic power-blend Steinzeiler (r), mainly BLAUFRÄNKISCH, some CAB SAUV/ ZWEIGELT. Fine-boned CHARD quartet Neusatz, Katterstein, Tatschler, Gloria.

Kopfensteiner Burgen ★★★ 18 19' 20 21' 22 Top Eisenberg name, wines sold with age. Graceful BLAUFRÄNKISCH Eisenberg DAC, RIED Saybritz.

Kracher Burgen ★★★★ 13 17 18 19 20' 21' 22 Brilliant, complex, botrytized. Library releases of sweet 10/15/20/25 yrs later. Rarity: Eiswein 23'.

Kremstal DAC. Top for authentic GRÜNER V, RIES. Try Buchegger, Nigl, Philipp Bründlmayer, Thiery-Weber, Vorspannhof Mayer, Zöller.

Lackner Tinnacher S Stei ★★★★ 19' 20 21' 22' 23 24 Precise, mineral. PINOT BL, RIED Eckberg; SAUV BL, Ried Welles RES 19'; Ried Steinbach key vyd.

Lesehof Stagård Krems ★★★★ 19 20 21' 22' 23' 24 Bold, electric RIES from single vyd to experimental Steinzeug; bio. Try Ries Steiner Hund, also GRÜNER V Stein (village wine), ravishing entry-level Urban.R and Ries Handwerk.

Lichtenberger González Burgen ★★★ 18 19 20 21' 22' 23' Leithaberg. Some wines renamed for legal reasons. Look now for refined Edel Brunn (formerly Edelgraben), round, balanced GRÜNER V (Mira Brunn, Sauspitz).

Loimer, Fred Kamp ★★★★ 19' 20 21' 22' 23 24 Individualistic bio producer of long standing. Famed for GRÜNER V, RIES, esp single vyds Seeberg, Steinmassl. Increasingly elegant PINOT N and *lovely sparkling* NV, Vintage, plus Grosse RES (sp) Langenlois or Grosse Res Gumpoldskirchen.

Lorenz, Michi S Stei ★★★ 19' 20' 21' 22' 23' 24 Ambassador of Sausal's schist. Great aromatic varietals, never loud, but precise, structured. Smoky SAUV BL Schist Happens, noble MUSKATELLER Aura M, and then the rest.

Macherndl, Erich Wach ★★★ 18 19' 20' 21' 22' 23 24 Organic. Classic, plus skin-fermented, min-sulphur, unfiltered Pulp Fiction.

Malat Krems ★★★★ 19 20 21' 22' 23' Clean-cut, concentrated RIES, GRÜNER V. Pioneering PINOT N. Three top sp. Family hotel.

Mantlerhof Krems ★★★ 19' 20 21 22' 23' Long-lasting wines from loess soils; bio pioneer. Long-time expertise with ROTER VELTLINER: Reisenthal, Ungut. Rare top-class SYLVANER. Also spicy RIES Zehetnerin from gravel, sand and loess.

Markowitsch, Gerhard & Johanna Carn ★★★★ 19' 20 21' 22 23' 24 Father and daughter. Powerful but not overpowering RIED Rosenberg (ZWEIGELT/MERLOT/BLAUFRÄNKISCH); convincing, dark-cherried Zweigelt Ried Kirchweingarten. Fresh pét-nats and skin-contact wines by Johanna, solo, labelled JoMa.

Moric Burgen ★★★★ 15 16 17 18 19' 20 21' 22' 23 Cult producer, rebellious mastermind of focused, deservedly famed BLAUFRÄNKISCH: try any. Three top RIED: Kircherg, Maissner, Schwemmer. Co-founder of Reimagine group, focus on varied BURGEN terroirs, esp for white, eg. GRÜNER V St Georgen.

Muhr, Dorli Carn ★★★★ 17 18 19' 20' 21' 22' 23 Silky, fine-boned BLAUFRÄNKISCH. Revived limestone slopes of Spitzerberg. Also excellent: SYRAH.

Müller Klöch V Stei ★★★ 19 20 21' 22' 23' 24 Proves that trad GEWÜRZ doesn't need residual sugar. Gelber TRAMINER RIED Seindl, Gewürz Ried Hochwarth.

Muster, Sepp S Stei ★★★ 18 19 20 21' 22 23' Fine-boned, complex, long-lasting; bio. Salty Graf SAUV BL (old vines), skin-fermented Sauv Bl Gräfin, elegant Sgaminegg (old vines, Sauv Bl/CHARD), Rosé vom Opok blend and mineral, floral Sauv Bl Coprivus by son Elias.

Neumayer Trais ★★★★ 19' 20 21' 22' 23 Doyen in limestone-dominated Trais. Precise, crystalline GRÜNER V (Zwirch), RIES (Rothenbart). Renowned for Wein vom Stein.

Neumeister V Stei ★★★★ 19' 20 21' 22' 23 World-class SAUV BL and Pinots. Try Sauv Bl ALTE REBEN, MORILLON Moarfeitl and PINOT BL Klausen. Also notable PINOTS GR/N.

Niederösterreich (Lower Austria) Region incl over 60% of Austria's vyds. Three climate zones: cooler Danube area in w (KAMP, KREM, Trais, WACH, WAG), WEIN (ne) and CARN, THERM (e, s), dry and warm (Pannonian influence).

Nikolaihof Wach ★★★★ 13 15 17 19' 20 21' 22' 23 One of world's 1st bio wine estates. Today run by son Nikolaus Saahs. Exemplary, pure, textured GRÜNER V, RIES; look for late-release Vinothek. Try any grape, any vintage.

Nittnaus, Anita & Hans Burgen ★★★★ 19 20' 21' 22' 23' Bio pioneers. Famous

AUSTRIA

The search for value

Reds in general more expensive than whites, and WACH more expensive than WEIN. The terraced vyds of Wach are mainly worked by hand, and wines are high quality, eg. DOMÄNE WACHAU. In S STEI too, mechanization is difficult, so costs are higher. Look for lesser known names with gd vyds: RIED Achleiten (Wach) or Ried Kranachberg (S Stei). Village wines combine respectable quality with a sense of place. For GRÜNER V with ageing potential, Wein is top (RÜCKER, WEINRIEDER); for PINOT BL, Leithaberg DAC in BURGEN (PRIELER Haidsatz). For long-lived, complex CHARDS: NITTNAUS Bergschmallister. For Pinots: V STEI and S Stei. For food-friendly reds: HARETER, GSELLMANN. Wines from local red grapes cost more than international ones. In general, v. few wines exceed €100/bottle.

Comondor (r blend). Precise single-vyd CHARD Bergschmallister, Freudshofer; BLAUFRÄNKISCH Jungenberg, Lange Ohn. New FURMINT Tannenberg. Next generation doing own alternative thing in family winery: Manila.

Ott, Bernhard Wag ★★★★ 18 19' 20 21' 22' 23 Iconic, bio: salty, savoury, long-lived GRÜNER V, esp RIED Rosenberg, Spiegel. Fass 4 is cult.

ÖTW (Österreichische Traditionsweingüter) Carn, Kamp, Krems, Therm, Trais, Vienna, Wag, Wein Association of 90 top growers in eight areas. WEIN with 13 growers joined recently. Prominent emblem on bottles. *See* ERSTE LAGE.

There are 32 vyds called Goldberg in Austria. Gold in them thar hills.

Pichler, FX Wach ★★★★ 19' 20 21' 22' 23 Legendary estate, long-lived GRÜNER V, RIES; top WACH sites. Has left VINEA WACHAU but adopted Wach DAC.

Pichler, Rudi Wach ★★★★ 19' 20 21' 22' 23 Magnificent RIES from crus Hochrain, Kirchweg; GRÜNER V from Achleiten, Hochrain.

Pichler-Krutzler Wach ★★★★ 19' 20 21' 22' Thrilling RIES Kellerberg, Loibenberg. GRÜNER V outstanding: der Wand, Pfaffenberg Alte Reben. Organic.

Pittnauer, Gerhard & Brigitte Burgen ★★★★ 19 20' 21' 22' 23' 24 Gracefully ageing BLAUFRÄNKISCH, PINOT N, ST-LAURENT. Serious skin-fermented wines, fresh pétnats. Perfect Day, Red Pitt, Rosé Dogma... expect the unexpected.

Ploder-Rosenberg V Stei ★★★ 17 18' 19' 20' 21 22 23' Natural, v.gd, 75% Piwi (*see* Grapes) plus CHARD PINOT GR, SAUV BL. Clean-cut blend Vivas (w) and Linea.

Prager Wach ★★★★ 19' 20 21' 22 23 Toni Bodenstein, philosopher-winemaker, son Martin. Family passion RIES: 60% of all vyds. Also GRÜNER V Stockkultur.

Preisinger, Claus Burgen ★★★★ 19' 20' 21' 22' 23' 24 Experimental; bio; classic BLAUFRÄNKISCH, PINOT N, ZWEIGELT and PINOT BL, GRÜNER V, also crown-capped fizzy Puszta Libre (r). Erdeluftgrasundreben. Co-fermented Grüner V/apples/quince: Sunny Cide Up.

Prieler Burgen ★★★★ 19' 20' 21' 22' 23' 24 Tightly textured BLAUFRÄNKISCH, needs bottle-age, esp Goldberg, Marienthal; compelling, age-worthy PINOT BL Leithaberg, eg. Alte Reben, Haidsatz, Seeberg, Steinweingarten.

Proidl Krems ★★★ 19 20 21' 22 23' 24 Reliably brilliant GRÜNER V, RIES, both from Ehrenfels vyd. Even better since son Patrick joined. Try library Ries releases.

Reserve (Res) Still wines must have min 13% abv plus longer ageing in winery. SEKT AUSTRIA Res is trad method, 18 mths on lees.

Ried Cru, or single vyd. *See* riedenkarten.at.

Riedmüller, Michaela Carn ★★ 19 20 21' 22' 23 Experimental; impressive results. Elegant BLAUFRÄNKISCH RIED Braunsberg, complex NEUBURGER Down to Earth, fine-boned GRÜNER V.

Rücker, Elisabeth Wein ★★★ 19 20' 21' 22' 23 24 Low-intervention, bio. Two-thirds planted 1955–80. Textbook GRÜNER V Innere Berge, long, intense; subtle CHARD Alte Reben; two complex WELSCHRIESLINGS.

Ruster Ausbruch DAC. Historic botrytized sweet, from Baroque town of Rust, BURGEN. Best: FEILER-ARTINGER, SCHRÖCK, TRIEBAUMER, WENZEL.

Sabathi, Erwin S Stei ★★★★ 17 18 19 20 21' 22' 23 Elegant, profound, age-worthy CHARD, SAUV BL; best site Pössnitzberg; Chard Pössnitzberger Kapelle v.gd.

Sabathi, Hannes S Stei ★★★★ 19 20 21' 22' 23' 24 Single-vyd SAUV BL Kranachberg. New CHARD RIED Graf Woracziczky, Supanek Hube. Falter Ego from Graz.

Salomon-Undhof Krems ★★★★ 19 20 21' 22' 23' 24 Consistent wines; elegant and lean GRÜNER V, RIES, single vyds Pfaffenberg, Wachtberg. RIES Steiner Kögl 22', Kögl 23'.

Sattlerhof S Stei ★★★★ 19' 20' 21' 22' 23' 24 Effortlessly brilliant; bio. Top crus Kranachberg, Sernauberg, monopole Pfarrweingarten. Alter Kranachberg SAUV BL 22', also standout village Sauv Bl Gamlitz.

Sausal S Stei Subregion of mainly schist with some limestone and vyds up to 600m (1969ft). Small enclave, with extraordinarily elegant RIES, SAUV BL, also BLAUFRÄNKISCH, PINOT N.

Scharl, Josef V Stei ★★ 19' 20' 21 22 23' Passion for PINOT; experiments with Muscaris & Co (Piwi; *see* Grapes). RIED Schemming, Souvignier Gris Brut RES, Muscaris Klassik, Scharlemanje PINOT N Res.

Schauer S Stei ★★★ 19 20 21' 22' 23' 24 Light-bodied but consistently profound whites from schisty SAUSAL: RIES, SAUV BL, esp notable PINOT BL Höchtemmel.

Schloss Esterházy Burgen 19' 20' 21' 22' 23' Serious, well balanced, refined; based on Leithaberg, follows Burgundy hierarchy. Central grape BLAUFRÄNKISCH, also PINOT BL, FURMINT, GRÜNER V. Organic from 23. Elegant fizz from Blaufränkisch: Brut NV, Rosé RES, Grosse Res Blanc de Noirs.

Schloss Gobelsburg Kamp ★★★★ 19' 20 21' 22' 23' Cistercian-founded estate, run by Michael Moosbrugger; exquisite GRÜNER V, RIES worth ageing. Tradition series and single vyds Gaisberg, Grub, Heiligenstein, Lamm, Renner. Fine sparkling. Also elegant PINOT N, ZWEIGELT. Detail, complexity.

Schnabel – Ermihof S Stei ★★★★ 18 19 20 21' 22' 23' Beautifully stubborn producer in SAUSAL; natural reds and whites ageing gracefully. Fine-boned BLAUFRÄNKISCH, elegant PINOT N, crus Hochegg, Koregg and Kreuzegg.

Schödl Family Wein ★★★ 19 20 21 22' 23' 24 Siblings Leonhard, Mathias, Viktoria. Went from organic to bio and to (often) natural; fine-tuned, clean, precise. Reddish Bloody MUSCAT with jasmine florals, spicy Grün Grün Grüner, cool-site GRÜNER V Steinberg, fragrant Blanc des Blancs NV.

Schröck, Heidi Burgen ★★★★ 19 20 21 22 23 Doyenne of RUSTER AUSBRUCH, also on dry mission, esp FURMINT. Working with twin sons Georg and Johannes.

Schuster, Rosi Burgen ★★★★ 19' 20 21 22' 23 Formerly bold reds, now all about purity. Elegance, focus on FURMINT, BLAUFRÄNKISCH, ST-LAURENT and GRÜNER V, esp ravishing Aus den Dörfern (r/w) and Dorfkultur (r/w).

Seewinkel Burgen Region e of Neusiedlersee; was ideal for botrytis, but small salt lakes almost dry until refilled 2024.

Sekt Austria PDO for best fizz. Entry-level Sekt Austria, 9 mths; RES, 18 mths; Grosse Res, 36 mths min on lees (trad method mandatory for both Res). Most producers exceed min time, esp for Grosse Res.

Smaragd Wach Ripest category of VINEA WACHAU, min 12.5% abv but can exceed 14%; dry, potent, age-worthy. In past, often botrytis-influenced but dry.

Spitzer Graben Wach Cool side valley nr Spitz. Steepest terraces, v. dry, meagre soils, excellent NEUBURGER, RIES. Interesting, off-beaten-track wineries: GRABENWERKSTATT, Martin Muthenthaler, VEYDER-MALBERG.

Stadlmann Therm ★★★★ 19' 20 21' 22' 23' Exemplary, clear-cut ZIERFANDLER/ROTGIPFLER, esp single vyds Mandelhöh, Tagelsteiner. Subtle, poetic PINOT BL.

Steiermark (Styria) Most s region; aromatic, expressive dry whites, esp SAUV BL and Pinots. *See* S STEI, V STEI, W STEI.

Steinfeder Wach Lightest VINEA WACHAU category for dry wines, max 11.5% abv. Difficult to produce in warming conditions, barely exported.

South-facing slopes? No, thanks. All want e-, w-, even n-facing now. Climate change.

Stift Göttweig ★★★ 19' 20 21' 22 23 24 Prominent hilltop Benedictine abbey surrounded by vyds; crystalline GRÜNER V Gottschelle, RIES Pfaffenberg.

Straka, Thomas Burgen ★★★ 19' 20' 21' 22' 23 24 Experiments with WELSCHRIESLING. Beautifully spiced Rechnitz, herbaceous FURMINT.

Strehn, Pia Burgen ★★ 19 20 21' 22 23' 24 Passion for BLAUFRÄNKISCH rosé, blends. All styles from easy to powerful, from still to bubbles. All dry, but Sushi Rosé with residual sugar, inspired by Japanese food. Also worth a sip: CAB FR.

Südsteiermark DAC. Region close to Slovenian border, famed for elegant, aromatic CHARD here also called MORILLON, MUSKATELLER, SAUV BL from breathtakingly steep slopes. Try Ewald Zweytick, Landesweingut Silberberg (wine-grower's school), Primus am Grassnitzberg, Warga-Hack.

Tement S Stei ★★★★ 12 13 18' 19 20' 21 22 23' Incredible subtlety, age-worthiness, esp MORILLON, SAUV BL. Top sites: Grassnitzberg, Zieregg. Zieregg RES Sauv Bl, top yrs only. Now bio, run by bros Armin and Stefan T.

Foot-treading is trendy again. Perfect for silky tannins in Blaufränkisch, Zweigelt.

Thermenregion Nied DAC (since vintage 2023). Spa region s of VIENNA. Rich, elegant, rare ROTGIPFLER, ZIERFANDLER; historic PINOT N and ST-LAURENT hotspot. Try Alphart, Alphart am Mühlbach, Gebeshuber, Hartl, Reinisch.

Tinhof, Erwin Burgen ★★★ 19' 20 21 22' 23 24 Below-radar but exquisite bio Leithaberg estate. Passion for PINOT BL, NEUBURGER, esp RIED Golden Erd (vintages back to 12). ST-LAURENT Feiersteig and village wines Eisenstadt (r/w).

Trapl, Johannes Carn ★★★ 18 19' 20' 21' 22 23 Wunderkind with expressive, site-specific reds. Floral BLAUFRÄNKISCH (Spitzerberg), PINOT-esque ZWEIGELT.

Triebaumer, Ernst Burgen ★★★★ 18 19' 20 21 22 23 Iconic Rust producer; bio. Try BLAUFRÄNKISCH legend Mariental, also as late release (from 13 eg.). "Nothing added" Urwerk.

Tschida, Christian Burgen ★★★★ 18 19' 20' 21' 22' 23 No interest in compromise, min intervention. Cult in natural-wine circles. Notable range Himmel auf Erden, elegant, subtle, but don't expect continuity in names or styles. Try any.

Umathum, Josef Burgen ★★★★ 19' 20' 21' 22 23 Originally famous for reds, ZWEIGELT and ST-LAURENT; today bio legend, all colours. Try Austria's best Zweigelt: single-vyd Hallebühl, also BLAUFRÄNKISCH Kirschgarten, Cuvée Rosa rosé. Beautiful Brut Nature (sp).

Velich, Heinz ★★★★ 19 20 21 22' 23 Both CHARDS Darscho, Tiglat legends with depth. Less oak now. Try any vintage, the older the better.

Veyder-Malberg Wach ★★★★ 19' 20 21' 22' 23 Terroir fanatic. Precise, even austere. Old vines up to 70 yrs, steep terraces in SPITZER GRABEN and other WACH. Try GRÜNER V, RIES. Also orange Grüner V Alter.Native.

Vienna (Wien) 131 wineries, 588 ha vyds within city borders. Wine ancient trad, now quality focus. Local field blend enshrined as WIENER GEMISCHTER SATZ DAC. *Heurigen among vines; visit a must.* Recommended: Fuhrgassl-Huber, Hajszan-Neumann, Rotes Haus. Best crus: Bisamberg, Maurerberg and Nussberg with its renowned subsites Preussen and Rosengartl.

Vinea Wachau Wach Quality growers' association. Ripeness scale for dry WACH white: FEDERSPIEL, SMARAGD, STEINFEDER. Exists parallel to official Wach DAC.

Vitikultur Moser Krems ★★★★ 19' 20' 21' 22 23' Was called Sepp Moser. Grower since 1848, family ties with Lenz Moser. Run by Nikolaus M and daughter Kathi. Early bio adopter. Exemplary GRÜNER V, also RIES, long-lived CHARD.

Vulkanland Steiermark DAC. Was famous for GEWÜRZ from Klöch. Now renowned for CHARD, all Pinots, SAUV BL. Best: Frauwallner, Krispel, Neue Heimat, PLODER-ROSENBERG, SCHARL, Winkler-Hermaden.

Wachau DAC. Danube region; world repute, age-worthy GRÜNER V and RIES. VINEA WACHAU classification. Try Johann Donabaum, MACHERNDL, Muthenthaler, Tegernseerhof. Note newcomers: PAX, Wabi-Sabi.

Wachter-Wiesler, Weingut Burgen ★★★ 19 20' 21' 22' 23 Fine-boned, elegant, silky BLAUFRÄNKISCH with a twist, from iron clay and green schist of Eisenberg DAC. Great ageing potential. Also entry-level Handgemenge (r/w/rosé).

Wagram DAC (GRÜNER V, RIES, ROTER VELTLINER); w of VIENNA. Deep loess, spicy Grüner V. Best: FRITSCH, JOSEF FRITZ, Leth, Nimmervoll, OTT.

Warnung, Matthias Kamp ★★ 19 20 21 22' 23' Fresh, elegant and intense: Matthias W focuses on craftsmanship and low intervention. Compact GRÜNER V Potatoland, Feldstück RIES, blend Wild Bunch 6th Gear (r/w).

Weingut Stadt Krems Krems ★★★ 19' 20 21' 22 23' 24 Brilliant municipal estate, 31 ha within city limits. GRÜNER V, RIES slightly riper, rounder than WACH, crystalline, expressive at top level; gd single vyds, value entry-level.

Weinrieder Wein ★★★★ 15' 16' 17' 18 19 20' 21 22 23 Was famous for Eiswein, rare now. Fabulous complex RIES and polished GRÜNER V, dry to TBA (*see* Germany).

Weinviertel DAC. Country's largest region, GRÜNER V in classic, RES, Grosse Res versions. Region once slaked VIENNA's thirst, now quality counts. Base wine for Viennese Sekt houses like Schlumberger, home of excellent fizz by EBNER-EBENAUER, SCHÖDL FAMILY and ZUSCHMANN-SCHÖFMANN. For still wines try Christoph Bauer, Dürnberg, Faber-Köchl, Fidesser, Gruber-Röschitz, Neustifter, Obenaus, Uibl.

Wellanschitz Burgen ★★★ 19' 20 21 22' 23 Family winery; profound, complex wines from BLAUFRÄNKISCH grown in mica schist. Try Blaufränkisch Sonnensteig. *See also* KOLFOK, solo wine project run by son Stefan W.

Weninger, Franz Burgen ★★★★ 19' 20 21' 22' 23 Expressive, seductive, terroir BLAUFRÄNKISCH, single-vyds Hochäcker, Kirchholz. Brilliant FURMINT.

Wenzel, Michael Burgen ★★★★ 19 20' 21' 22' 23' 24 A quiet man, who speaks loudly through his excellent natural wines (r/w, sometimes sw). Makes a lot of shades of FURMINT.

Weststeiermark DAC. Super-crisp rosé Schilcher from Blauer Wildbacher grape (r). Different styles: trad rosé, rare sweet, modernist fizz, natural and orange. Try Lex Langmann, Jöbstl, from natural-wines expert Franz Strohmeier.

Wiener Gemischter Satz VIENNA DAC. Historic white field blends. Complex. Fuchs-Steinklammer, Fuhrgassl-Huber, Hajszan-Neumann, Mayer am Pfarrplatz, Peter Uhler. Gemischter Satz/Mischsatz elsewhere (*see* GROISS).

Wieninger, Fritz Vienna ★★★★ 19' 20' 21' 22' 23' 24 Mastermind behind quality renaissance; bio. Exemplary WIENER GEMISCHTER SATZ Nussberg, Rosengartl. Great PINOT N. Also runs experimental winery Hajszan-Neumann.

Wohlmuth S Stei ★★★★ 19 20 21 22' 23' 24 200-yr trad. Subtle, dazzling CHARD, RIES, SAUV BL, esp from single vyds Edelschuh, Gola, Hochsteinriegl; gd reds. Recultivating Ries in steepest terraces: try RIED Dr. Wunsch.

Zillinger, Herbert Wein ★★★★ 19 20 21' 22' 23' 24 Splendid, complex GRÜNER V; bio. Try Kalkvogel, Hirschenreyn, entry-level Neuland. Also WELSCHRIESLING Alte Reben, GEWÜRZ Profund, Toast Hawai 22, Springbreak Rosé.

Zillinger, Johannes Wein ★★★ 19 20 21' 22' 23 Organic pioneer, today bio; min intervention in cellar. Velue: well-defined varietals. Parcellaire: fresh blends of similar site, character eg. cooler parcels, grown on limestone. Revolution: everyday drinking.

Zuschmann-Schöfmann ★★★★ 19' 20 21' 22' 23' 24 Couple with focus on excellent trad-method fizz and pét-nats. Entry-level GRÜNER V SEKT AUSTRIA of exceptional quality. Also RIES Grosse RES Ralessen, Rosé Brut Res. Try all

---

Green or greenish

Roughly a quarter (24%) of Austria's vyd is organic, and 14% of that – or 3% of the total surface – is bio. Another 27% is certified sustainable – always a vague term, but Sustainable Austria takes into account the reduction of greenhouse gases in transport, responsible use of resources, production processes, treatment of vyd workers and so on. Was criticism of green-washing, because label was v. easy to obtain, but has got stricter.

AUSTRIA

England

Single-estate wines are the norm, and run the gamut from brilliant to a bit dismal. The further you go from the warm, dry southeast, the more likely you are to find non-classic grapes like Bacchus, Faber, Huxelrebe, Madeleine Angevine, Ortega, Phoenix, Seyval Blanc, Siegerrebe, Solaris, Regent, Rondo; but I confess I am seldom a fan. (Breaky Bottom's lovely Seyval Bl is the outstanding exception.) It's hard to beat sparkling Chardonnay, Pinot Noir and Meunier grown in a good site. Still wines can be good, if expensive for the quality, and making the more screechingly aromatic non-classic grapes as orange wines often works very well and produces unexpected subtlety. Try also low-intervention artisanal wines, natural or almost – a growing and good sector. Abbreviations: Berkshire (Berks), Buckinghamshire (Bucks), Cornwall (Corn), East/West Sussex (E/W Sx), Essex (Esx), Hampshire (Hants), Herefordshire (Her), Oxfordshire (Oxon), Wiltshire (Wt).

All Angels Berks ★★★ Classic, fine, mineral; elegance and tension. Long ageing on lees a feature here, and makes huge difference. Long Aged bottling has even longer, for great depth.

Ambriel W Sx ★★ Small, ambitious; delicacy and depth. Lovely Blanc de Blancs.

Artelium E Sx ★★ Elegant, mineral, savoury. Try Curator's Cuvée, Blanc de Blancs, Makers Rosé; still PINOTS GR/N.

Balfour Kent ★★ Rosé is flagship; much focus on still, done well. New ALBARIÑO.

Beare Green Surrey Naturalish, interesting, taut. Still CHARD, PINOT N. Dio BACCHUS shows how well this variety responds to skin contact.

Beaulieu 58 Hants New, still, promising, esp GEWURZ. Made by WHARIE EXPERIENCE.

Blackbook Urban winery, bought-in grapes, vinified in S London; min intervention, small lots, so see what it has. Innovative, interesting.

Black Chalk Hants ★★ Wines of tension and purity. Back on form.

Bluestone Wt ★★ Bluestone as in Stonehenge. Fine, pure, poised fizz. New, and getting it right from the word go.

Breaky Bottom E Sx ★★★★ Fabulous wines, tiny vyd, eccentric owner. Richness, tension; layered flavours. Probably best SEYVAL BL in world (a small contest, true, but terrific wine).

Bride Valley Dorset New local owners. Wine focused on fruit, not lees character.

Camel Valley Corn ★★ Lots of fruit, easy-drinking, attractive wines from one of 1st wave of English vyds.

Candover Brook Hants ★★ Slightly smoky, textbook chalkland acidity; elegant, taut. Delicate rosé. Made at HAMBLEDON.

Chapel Down Kent One of largest producers. Wine is somewhat improved, fresher. ★★ Rich Kit's Coty Coeur de Cuvée.

Rondo grape adds colour; might be a touch in Pinot Noir for that reason.

Coates & Seely Hants ★★★★ As gd as ever. Lovely Blanc de Blancs, detailed, precise, with gd depth and complexity. Top: La Perfide (saline, brioche Blanc de Noirs).

Coolhurst W Sx On the light side for the price. But ambitious: watch.

Cottonworth Hants Length and depth gd here. Best: Classic Cuvée.

Court Garden E Sx Family-owned, on the Downs. Rich, elegant style.

Danbury Ridge Esx ★★★ New solstice fizz, multi-vintage, to add to concentrated CHARD, ripe PINOT N. Rich, powerful style – still wine with bubbles rather than usual English apéritif style; v. ripe site.

Denbies Surrey Hotel, restaurant, tours, concerts, art shows. Wines okay, could be better. Solaris Orange gd, crunchy, fresh.

Digby Hants, Kent, W Sx ★★★ Lovely mineral wines; owners love greensand and the tension it gives. Beginning to acquire vyds. Tasting room in Arundel is worth a visit.

Everflyht E Sx Excellent start; fine, salty, tight wines. Much investment. Vines still young, and wines need bottle-age. Late Release has gd depth.

Evremond, Dom Kent Champagne Taittinger's much-heralded UK outpost; 1st release detailed, precise, delicate. A credit to time spent getting it right.

Climate in Essex's Crouch Valley similar to that of Burgundy c.25 years ago.

Exton Park Hants ★★★ NV is called RB (Res Blend): graceful, gd depth, plus richness of res wines to balance acidity. Cuvée M Isaac, elegant power, saline.

Folc ★★ Only still pink, and they do it well. Grapes from local growers, and Provence rosé is target style. Pronounced "folk".

Grange, The Hants ★★★ Small; a must-buy at Grange Opera. Classic lemon-shortbread notes; gd still Pink and The Pink fizz.

Gusbourne Kent, W Sx ★★★★ Splendid wines, incl excellent single vyds and v. expensive 51°N. Weight and richness throughout: gd still PINOT N, when possible. New restaurant v.gd.

Gutter & Stars ★★ Cambridge urban winery in a windmill; innovative small lots from local grapes.

Hambledon Vineyard Hants ★★★ New owners Berry Bros and Symington Group (*see* Portugal) should give firm footing. Superb rich, saline Première Cuvée. New restaurant 2025 aiming high.

Harrow & Hope Bucks ★★★ Getting better and better; gd weight, confident style. Blanc de Blancs, Brut Rosé v.gd.

Hart of Gold Her ★★ Made at RIDGEVIEW; lemony, biscuity; attractive. Also vyds in Maury (*see* France): The Dom of the Bee.

Hattingley Valley Hants ★★★ One of best, and goes on improving. Top Blanc de Blancs. Ripe baked-apple style with lovely balance; Classic Res, seductive.

Henners E Sx ★★ Lovely. Sleek, elegant fizz, pretty still. Structured wines.

Herbert Hall Kent ★★ Tiny vyd in Kent apple-and-hop country, wines precise; v.gd limited-edition Kirsty's Blanc de Blancs.

Highweald W Sx Lovely poise and layered complexity; toasty Rosé; gd weight. From Sx High Weald clay and greensand.

Hoffmann & Rathbone E Sx ★★ Firm, well-made wines from bought-in fruit.

Hugo, Dom Wt Family farm; bio, individual, can be startling. Saline, poised and uncompromising. I love it.

Hundred Hills Oxon ★★★ Big investment, well spent: energetic, concentrated, characterful wines, many different cuvées.

Langham Wine Estate Dorset★★★ *Corallian Classic Cuvée*, expensive, gd still PINOT N; Zig Zag Col Fondo (Pinot N/CHARD/PINOT M) v.gd.

Leckford Estate Hants Waitrose's own estate, vinified by RIDGEVIEW. Nicely mature, gd fruit, straightforward.

Leonardslee W Sx Making a gd start. Lots of investment, beautiful property bought for the estate more than for wine potential, so a happy accident.

Litmus Project of DENBIES winemaker John Worontschak. Fruit from all over: v.gd still Orange BACCHUS, excellent still *white Pinot N*, improves for 10 yrs+.

Nyetimber W Sx ★★★★ Deserves reputation. Round, deep, elegant. Super-pricey 1086. Fine Tillington.

Oastbrook E Sx ★★ Still wines v.gd, concentration across board: CHARD, white PINOTS N/BL/GR; impressive red PINOT N.

Plumpton College E Sx ★★ UK's only wine college; attractive wines (as they should be), made by students. Still wines pretty, sparkling better.

Pommery England Hants ★★ Layered, elegant. Offshoot of Pommery Champagne (*see* France), making wines at least as gd as in Champagne.

Raimes Hants ★★ Tense, fresh style; gd fruit. Made at HATTINGLEY V.

Rathfinny E Sx ★★★ Chalk in excelsis from the S Downs: tight, taut, precise, needs bottle-age. Big operation, huge investment, gd tourism and restaurant. Blanc de Noirs is best wine.

Rice, Emma ★★★ Winemaker behind much top English fizz at last has own label. Two wines, same blend, different lees ageing – taste totally different. Both elegant, rich, excellent.

Ridgeview E Sx ★★ A little more solid than most contemporary English fizz: focused on weight, breadth. Big range.

Riverview Esx Crouch V ripeness in still CHARD, PINOT N, plus elegance.

Roebuck W Sx ★★ Getting better and better; v.gd Blanc de Noirs, rich, focused.

Sandridge Barton Devon ★★ Used to be called Sharpham. Excellent Figgie Daniel Col Fondo from Madeleine Angevine. Wild Ferment PINOT GR.

Simpsons Kent ★★ Q Class still range has lots of oak – oak is a favourite flavour here. Still and sparkling both gd, esp Classic Cuvée (sp).

Squerryes Kent Rich, autolytic character, ripe and focused. Vintage Brut weighty.

Sugrue South Downs E Sx ★★★★ UK's best, for character, depth, aliveness. Tiny operation but now new vyds and winery; wines complex, long, layered. Wine names ditto, esp 1st still: rich, succulent CHARD, known as Bonkers.

Tidebrook E Sx Still wines, lightish, well made: CHARD, PINOTS N/GR all appealing. Impressive start. Offshoot of Jordan Wine Estate (*see* S Africa).

Trotton W Sx Spectacular Sparkling (that's the brand, not a description) elegant, fine, well made; gd still BACCHUS/PINOT GR.

Vagabond ★★ Urban winery, still wines. Innovative, experimental. Skin-contact BACCHUS, assured Night Tripper, min intervention, ambient yeast, no fining, light filtration occasionally. Steel and old oak.

Westwell Kent ★★★ Pure, taut, fine Pelegrim fizz; still wines adventurous, experimental; trying amphorae, pét-nat, Col Fondo, orange, min intervention. Worth seeking out.

Weyborne Surrey ★★→★★★ Stylish newcomer: wines unfold on palate. Citrus, tense style; rounder, brioche-like Oriana. Plus gd demi-sec that winemaker recommends with delicate cheese like Chaource.

Wharie Experience, The Hants Small range artisanal low-intervention still: esp BACCHUS Orange.

Wiston W Sx ★★★★ Steely, chalk-grown wines of perfect poise, elegance, precision. Even better if put away for a couple of yrs. Chalk, v.gd restaurant, uses local ingredients; lovely place to visit and walk.

Wyfold Oxon ★★ Nicely elegant wines from Laithwaite-owned vyd. Same family has Windsor Great Park Vyd, from – well, yes.

Keep still

England is a sparkling country beginning to make still. It's difficult to make both to the same standard from the same place: still needs more ripeness, concentration, structure and can be heavy if made into sparkling. Equally, wines perfect for sparkling are too light for still. But still brings cash in quicker: sparkling needs long ageing and deep pockets. Pét-nat is cheaper to produce and is often gd. Still rosé is usually pretty; vermouth (esp Albury) can be delicious.

Scandinavia

Scandinavia's wine scene has grown over the past two decades to more than 1000 producers. Most are hobbyist, but commercial wineries now exist in Denmark, Sweden and Norway. Although at the limits of viable viticulture, the best sites and disease-resistant hybrids, such as Solaris, Muscaris and Rondo (copper use is banned in Scandinavia), make sparkling, white, rosé, orange and reds. Certain *Vitis vinifera* are also successful, such as Frühburgunder (aka Pinot Noir Précoce) for light reds. Norway's production is tiny but growing. KP Keller's (*see* Germany) Riesling/Pinot Noir is a hope in future summers.

DENMARK

In recent yrs, Danish vyd plantings (c.175 ha) have grown. Vines are predominantly found on Jutland and Zealand; also on Funen and Bornholm. Long coastlines, bays and straits provide moderating effects, and recent hot summers have aided still-wine production; vyd soils are sand and loam.

Barfod Vin ★★→★★★ Regenerative, bio. Try Solaris, Souvignier Gr, Cabernet Cantor.

Drudgaard ★★→★★★ Delicious natural wine and cider from Funen.

Klitgaard Vin ★★→★★★ Started in 2005 as a hobby; bio, some of country's most celebrated. Try Pet Not (FRÜHBURGUNDER/Ortega).

Njord ★★★→★★★★ On sandy hills of W Zealand, Sune Albertsen makes arguably Scandinavia's finest wines. Focus on organic FRÜHBURGUNDER (like fine PINOT N).

Sønderstrand Vin ★★→★★★ On Jutland's w coast, newcomers make v.gd organic whites; also grow flowers.

Stokkebye Vingård ★★★ On Funen, organic, excellent sparkling, Stella (L'ACADIE BL/ Johanniter), Stella Mary (PINOT N).

Vejrhøj Vingård ★★→★★★ Some of Denmark's most delicious white, sparkling and rosé hybrids. Collaborates with Copenhagen's iconic Fiskebar to create no-sulphur Nøgen (Naked) cuvées for the restaurant.

Vexebo Vin ★★→★★★ Tasty organic natural wines and ciders just n of Copenhagen.

Weirdloose Overdrive ★★→★★★ Creative natural wines, ciders, co-ferments and a veg farm on ancient grasslands of Særløse Overdrev.

Try co-fermented wine/cider (apples, pears, quince) from Sweden's Fruktstereo and Denmark's Æblerov.

SWEDEN

Most vyds are in the sw; with similar varieties and climate to its neighbour. Plantings are growing quickly, at c.200 ha; soils are sand, gravel to clay, and even some limestone on Gotland and in Öland.

Flädie Mat & Vingård ★★ Organic, fruity hybrid wines; try elegantly oaked Midnattssol (Solaris).

Flyinge Vingård ★★ Bright, zesty, organic Solaris.

Hällåkra Vingård ★★→★★★ Organic, natural Five Generations; orange Cuvée Anna.

Jesper Friberg ★★★ On e coast of Skåne, talented winemaker, experience with natural methods (Lapierre in Beaujolais, L'Anglore in Rhône). Striking wines.

Kullabergs Vingård ★★→★★★ From Cape Kullaberg; classy. Try aromatic Lyckeri.

Thora Vingård ★★→★★★ In Bjäre peninsula; organic Solaris (try Pure), also PINOT GR, FRÜHBURGUNDER, PINOT N. Restaurant on-site.

Vingården i Klagshamn ★★→★★★ Pioneer on w coast of Skåne; precise wines. Textur is complex macerated Solaris.

Central & Southeast Europe

More heavily shaded areas are the wine-growing regions.

Prague ○
CZECHIA
SLOVAKIA
Bratislava ○
Danube
Budapest ○
MOLDOVA
Ljubljana ○
Drava
HUNGARY
ROMANIA
Chişinău ○
SLOVENIA
Zagreb ○
Olt
Prut
CROATIA
Timişoara ○
BOSNIA-
HERZEGOVINA
Sava
Belgrade ○
Danube
Bucharest ○
Danube
Split ○
Sarajevo ○
SERBIA
Adriatic Sea
MONTENEGRO
Varna ○
Dubrovnik ○
Podgorica ○
KOSOVO
Sofia ○
Black Sea
BULGARIA
Plovdiv ○
Skopje ○
NORTH
MACEDONIA
Tirana ○
ALBANIA

Abbreviations used in the text:

Bal	Balaton		
Cri & Mar	Crişana & Maramureş		
Cro Up	Croatian Uplands		
Dalm	Dalmatia		
Dan P	Danubian Plain	Pos	Posavje
Dob	Dobrogea	Prim	Primorje
Is & Kv	Istria & Kvarner	Sl & CD	Slavonia & Croatian Danube
Mold	Moldovan Hills	Thr L	Thracian Lowlands
Mun	Muntenia & Oltenia Hills	Tok	Tokaj
N/S Pann	North/South Pannonia	Trnsyl	Transylvania
Pod	Podravje	U Hun	Upper Hungary

ALBANIA

This country has a distinctive wine culture with 8400 ha and an ancient history back to Illyrian times (c.800 BCE). It's undergoing a quality revolution but is still catching up with its neighbours, helped by a busy tourist industry. It has a mild Mediterranean climate, with most vineyards at altitude (up to 1000m/3281ft) and a raft of unique grapes led by Shesh i Zi (Black Shesh), Shesh i Bardhë (White Shesh), Kallmet (aka Kadarka), Debinë e Bardhë, Pulës, Serina, Vlosh and Vranac.

First Wild River National Park in Europe: Albania's Vjosa River

BOSNIA & HERZEGOVINA

A small but improving wine country with most of its vineyards on the hot, stony, karst hills of Herzegovina around Mostar and the Neretva River; just a handful are in the north. Local white grape Žilavka is capable of good quality, but juicy Blatina and inky Trnjak also show promise. Not much exported, but watch Begić, Domano, Imperial Vineyards, Jungić, Matić, Nuić, Tvrdoš Monastery, Vilinka, Vinarija Čitluk (Teuta only).

Andrija, Podrumi ★→★★ Modern family winery with long trad. Try Žilavka, can age remarkably well; also SYRAH.

Brkić ★→★★ Three generations; bio principles. Žilavka (fresh to orange Mjesečar).

Carska Vina ★★ Father-and-son winery for bright, pure examples of local grapes plus blends with international varieties. Try David, Gregorius, Sophia.

Škegro Family Winery ★★ Terraced vyds up to a century old; v.gd Blatina, Trnjak, Žilavka (fresh, orange). Krš for fresh wines, Carsus for aged styles.

Vino Milas ★★ Family winery; age-worthy Blatina Res, v.gd Žilavka Premium.

Vukoje 1982, Podrumi ★→★★ Historic vyd plus restaurant nr Trebinje. Try VRANAC, Žilavka, incl vyd-selection Carsko Vino.

BULGARIA

Today's industry in Bulgaria is buzzing with higher quality than ever and a real focus on regional identity and local grapes. There's plenty of amazing history to see too. Several great wine events/festivals, wine bars and restaurants now add to the new concept of wine as culture.

The bagpipe is a traditional Bulgarian instrument, called gayda.

Alexandra Estate Thr L ★★ VERMENTINO (w) and *qvevri* styles, rosé, red varietals, age-worthy Res.

Angel's Estate Thr L ★★ Part of Purcari Wineries Group (*see* Moldova). Stallion range for rich supple red blends; Deneb for v.gd varietals esp CAB FR, rosé; great-value Angels range.

Bessa Valley Thr L ★★★ One of 1st true estates, French consultancy. Try Enira, v.gd SYRAH and Enira Res, excellent *Grande Cuvée*.

Better Half Thr L ★★ Intriguing, small-batch wines from amphorae and concrete eggs. Unusual varieties: Malagouzia, MISKET, NEBBIOLO.

Bononia Dan P ★★ Historic brewery building-turned-winery, close to Danube. Well-made, bright DIMYAT/VERMENTINO, Vrachanski MISKET; gd GAMZA, Istar CAB FR.

Borovitsa Dan P ★★★ Back on form; small-parcel wines from nw. Top: age-worthy Dux. Canyon Park MRV, Cuvée Bella Rada (RKATSITELI), Great Terroirs (old-vine versions of GAMZA), Maxxima Res, Sensum.

Boyar, Dom Thr L ★→★★★ Large modern winery, dramatic painted tanks. Reliable entry-point ranges Bolgaré, Deer Point; mid-range Elements, Quantum. Top: single-vyd Solitaire (MERLOT). Boutique Korten cellar: Grand Vintage, Natura.

Bratanov Thr L ★★ Low-intervention family estate in SAKAR. Try 3 Blend (r/w); *sur lie* CHARD, benchmark Tamianka (MUSCAT); v.gd CAB FR, RUBIN Private Res, SYRAH.

Burgozone Dan P ★★ Significant family estate close to Danube for well-made wines. Try Collection Tamianka, old-vine GAMZA plus flagships Eva, Iris Creation.

Clos Bibliothèque Dan P ★★★ New super-premium estate in ne. Expensive but glorious single vyds, esp CHARD, PINOT N, SYRAH and even amphora DIMYAT.

Copsa, Ch Thr L ★★ In heart of Rose V, producing one of best MISKET Cherven called AXL. Also gd SAUV BL and improving reds.

Dragomir Thr L ★★→★★★ Big, bold reds with RUBIN as star grape, esp in long-lived Pitos, Res. Fruity unoaked Sarva range (DIMYAT, MAVRUD, Rubin) gd.

Georgiev / Milkov ★★→★★★ Parcels from old vines, local grapes, made by two top winemakers. Exciting versions of MAVRUD, RUBIN, funky Mavrud pét-nat, Pink Side of Rubin, Why Not MISKET, Pamid-based light red Mixtape.

Haralambievi Dan P ★★ Family winery in n, Royal Rouge CAB FR, RUBIN, crisp whites.

Katarzyna Thr L ★★ Supple, ripe, well-made wines. Flagship Res impresses, also Cheval MAVRUD, 16 Harvests MERLOT, Encore SYRAH.

Logodaj Thr L ★★ STRUMA winery for super-ripe reds; esp Nobile Early MELNIK, v.gd rosé, fine bottle-fermented *Satin*.

Medi Valley Thr L ★★→★★★ Owns vyds at 550m (1804ft) nr Rila Monastery; v.gd reds, esp Great Bulgarian, Incanto Black, MELNIK 55; fine VIOGNIER.

Menada, Dom Thr L ★ Large producer. Tcherga blends, Barrique Point reds.

Midalidare Estate Thr L ★★→★★★ Immaculate boutique winery. Some of country's best *trad-method sparkling*, plus v.gd reds, esp Grand Vintage.

Minkov Brothers Thr L ★→★★ Large but consistent winery, esp premium Oak Tree and v.gd Enoteca. Cycle is solid entry-point range.

Miroglio, Edoardo Thr L ★★★ Significant Italian/Bulgarian estate. Excellent trad-method fizz: possibly best in country. Flagship red is impressive Soli Invicto; v.gd Elenovo Res range, fruit-forward Prometheus MAVRUD. Passion for PINOT N (Heritage, Blanc de Noir [sic], Soli).

Odessos Dan P ★★ Garage project of two bros, with international experience. Old-vine parcels: RIES, DIMYAT, CAB FR, SYRAH and Claret dark rosé.

Orbelia Thr L ★★ Family winery in STRUMA V; v.gd Via Aristotelis range, also Estate Res, esp MELNIK. Fun pét-nat from Sandanski MISKET.

Rossidi Thr L ★★→★★★ Pioneering winery nr Sliven. Top concrete-egg-fermented CHARD; v.gd MAVRUD, RUBIN, excellent SYRAH.

Rumelia Thr L ★★ MAVRUD specialist, v.gd: Rumelia Res, Erelia, unoaked Merul.

Sakar Dynamic region in se; working together. New joint Birds of Sakar project, each winery has own bird on label, donates to Bulgarian bird protection society.

Salla Estate Dan P ★★ Try SAUV BL, RIES, Vrachanski MISKET, TRAMINER, CAB FR.

Santa Sarah Thr L ★★→★★★ Quality pioneer, now 40 ha nr Pomorie. Best known for Bin Series, Zar Simeon reds. Flagship: Privat.

Stephan Pirev Wines ★★→★★★ Personal project of respected winemaker. Eager v.gd, esp CHARD, SYRAH, Red Blend.

Struma Valley Thr L Dramatic wine region surrounded by mtns: don't miss the sand pyramids and quaint historic town of Melnik. Focus on local grapes: MELNIK 55, Sandanski MISKET, Shiroka Melnik (aka Broadleafed Melnik). Look for: Aya Estate (esp Ayano Shiroka Melnik), Bottled Opinions, Damianitza (Redark, Volcano), Damyanov (Broadleafed Melnik, Keratsuda Orange), Kapatovo (PETIT VERDOT, GRENACHE/MOURVÈDRE/SHIRAZ), Libera (Hotovo, Melnik 55, Orange Keratsuda), Mihovi (Keratsuda), Rupel, Uva Nestum, Via Verde (Expressions Sandanski Misket), Zlaten Rozhen.

Tohun Dan P ★★ Precise, refreshing whites, rosé: Barrique CHARD, Greus range.

Tsarev Brod Dan P ★★ Innovative estate in n. Try Amber CHARD, Evmolpia (r/rosé), rare local Gergana (still, sp), pét-nat RIES, SAUV BL Res. Ries Icewine v.gd.

Villa Melnik Thr L ★★ Family estate, focus on local grapes, esp MAVRUD, MELNIK. Rare Varieties label, esp Melnik Jubilee, Ruen. Impressive Aplauz Res.

Vinex Slavyantsi Thr L ★ Fair for Life-certified for supporting local ethnic community. Reliable well-priced varietals, blends, esp Leva brand.

Yamantiev's Thr L ★→★★ Sound, commercial Kaba Gayda, SHIRAZ. Excellent *Marble Land (r)*, Yamantiev's Grand Res CAB SAUV.

Zagreus Thr L ★★ Organic vyd, MAVRUD in all styles: complex Vinica from semi-dried grapes, Santimenti is fun natural version. Three Generations (r) gd.

Zelanos Thr L ★★ Pristine winery/wines. Try fresh (Red) MISKET, PINOT GR, elegant Z premium wines esp CAB FR, PINOT N, SYRAH.

CROATIA

Tourism, and the food and wine consumption that comes with it, is still hugely important to wineries along Croatia's vast coastline and islands. Exports are growing, so there's more chance of finding Croatian wines elsewhere, but the country is still a net importer of cheap stuff that undercuts local production, so tourists should take note. At least 95 indigenous varieties have recently been identified, many still rare but being replanted. Local grapes rule in terms of area planted: Graševina, Malvazija Istarska and Plavac Mali are the top three.

Ante Sladić Dalm ★★ Next-generation family winery; v.gd local grapes, esp Lasina, Oya Noya Debit, Plavina.

Antunović Sl & CD ★★ Female winemaker-owner, now with son, at Erdut on Danube. Elegant, age-worthy Tradition GRAŠEVINA, gd CHARD *sur lie.*

Arman, Marijan Is & Kv ★★ Family estate for consistent fresh MALVAZIJA and always impressive G Cru from selected plot. Also gd TERAN.

Badel 1862 ★ Largest, oldest producer in Croatia. Best: Korlat Supreme, SYRAH. Owns Benkovac, Duravar, Ivan Dolac.

Benvenuti Is & Kv ★★★ Family winery run by two bros. One of best producers of TERAN, esp Santa Elisabetta, superb San Salvatore MUŠKAT. Try Livio in best yrs (named after late father), consistent classic range (Caldierosso r).

BIBIch Dalm ★★→★★★ Family estate from C15. Flagship Bas de Bas; excellent R6 blend, local Debit.

Bire Dalm ★★→★★★ Family estate specializing in rare Grk grape, esp single-vyd Defora from Lumbarda on Korčula.

Boškinac Dalm ★★→★★★ Top boutique hotel and winery on Pag Island: impressive Cuvée (r). Superb Ocu (rare Gegić w).

Bura-Mrgudić Dalm ★★ Weighty, trad, but gd Bura PLAVAC MALI. Modern Benmosche DINGAČ, ZIN.

Cattunar Is & Kv ★★ Hilltop winery notable for MALVAZIJA from ISTRIA's four different soils, plus late-harvest Collina.

Clai Is & Kv ★★ Organic, skin-contact, natural. Try MALVAZIJAS Baracija, Sv Jakov Malvazija; Ottocento blends.

Coronica Is & Kv ★★→★★★ Pioneer of quality TERAN. Age-worthy benchmark Gran Teran; v.gd Gran MALVAZIJA, fresh DYA version.

Croatian Uplands Međimurje is coolest, focus on vibrant Pušipel (aka FURMINT), expressive SAUV BL: *Cmrečnjak*, DK Vina, Horvat, Jakopić, Kocijan, Kopjar, Lovrec, Preiner, Štampar. Moslavina is notable for mineral-fresh Škrlet (Florijanović, Košutić, Romić, Voštinić Klasnić). Plešivica for great fizz, precise Sauv Bl, RIES, orange/amphora wines, esp Griffin Ivančić, *Korak*, *Šember*, TOMAC.

Dalmatia Sunny rocky coastline and islands from Zadar to Dubrovnik. Divided into N Dalm, The Hinterland, s-central Dalm. Unique varieties, exciting producers.

Damjanić Is & Kv ★★→★★★ New winery, taken wines to next level; v.gd Borgonja (aka BLAUFRÄNKISCH), Clemente (r/w), Justina MALVAZIJA.

Dingač Dalm Croatia's 1st PDO since 1962 for weighty reds from PLAVAC MALI, on steep sea-facing slopes of Pelješac peninsula. Try Benmosche, BURA-MRGUDIĆ,

Crna Ovca, KIRIDŽIJA, Korta Katarina, Madirazza, SAINTS HILLS, Skaramuča, Vinarija Dingač.

Enjingi, Ivan Sl & CD ★★ Legendary natural-wine maker in SLAVONIA. Noted for GRAŠEVINA, long-lived Venje.

Enosophia Sl & CD ★→★★ Ambitious recently renovated cellar in Slavonia. Best: Miraz (v.gd CAB FR, Frankovka), also Trs No. 5 GRAŠEVINA.

Oldest clue of cheese-making: 7200-yr-old fermented milk traces in Dalmatian pot.

Fakin Is & Kv ★★★ "Fakin good wines" is winery motto – young winemaker delivers just that. Exciting top labels La Prima MALVAZIJA, Il Primo TERAN. Also fresh Malvazija, latest release Teran.

Galić Sl & CD ★★★ Space-age winery: refined CHARD, Crno 9, GRAŠEVINA, PINOT N.

Grabovac Dalm ★★→★★★ Family winery in hinterland of DALM impressing with Kujundzuša, Modro Jezero Ris, Trnjak.

Gracin Dalm ★★→★★★ Professor Leo G pioneered revival of BABIĆ: complex, herby, elegant. Also as sweet PROŠEK and in v.gd Kontra blend made with KIRIDŽIJA.

Grgić Dalm ★★ Trad PLAVAC MALI, typical POŠIP on Pelješac peninsula, founded by Miljenko "Mike" Grgich of Judgement of Paris fame (RIP 2023).

Hvar Dalm Island with UNESCO listing for Stari Grad Plain and its vyd *chora*, dating to C4 BCE. Noted for PLAVAC MALI (Carić, PZ Svirče, TOMIĆ, ZLATAN OTOK).

Iločki Podrumi Sl & CD ★→★★★ Historic cellar from 1450. GRAŠEVINA specialist, also gd TRAMINAC. Try Premium, Principovac, Sofija labels.

Istria Adriatic peninsula, more a country within a country, also noted for great olive oil, truffles. Versatile local MALVAZIJA Istarska is main grape and red TERAN. Best (without own entry): Banko Mario, Bastian, Cossetto, *Degrassi*, Deklić, Dobrovac, Dom Koquelicot, Franković, Ferenac, Ipša, Kadum, Meneghetti (excellent Val Gambelara, Red, White), *Milan Budinski (Omo)*, Misal Peršurić (sp), Novacco, Piquentum, Radovan, *Rossi*, Roxanich, San Tommaso, Sosich, Trapan, Veralda (organic, v.gd REFOSCO), Vivoda, Zigante.

Kabola Is & Kv ★★★→★★★★ Immaculate organic estate, wines to match. MALVAZIJA as fizz, young wine, cask-aged Unica and superb Amfora (also a TERAN).

Kiridžija Dalm ★★ Modern DINGAČ, PLAVAC MALI v.gd; Kontra JV with GRACIN.

Komarna Dalm Newest wine region since 2013: all organic, on precipitous slopes by sea. Try Rizman, SAINTS HILLS Sv Roko, Volarević. Watch Deak, Terra Madre too.

Korta Katarina Dalm ★★ US roots; luxury hotel on Pelješac overlooking Korčula; gd POŠIP, weighty PLAVAC MALI (Reuben's Res).

Kozlović Is & Kv ★★★→★★★★ Stunning family winery and pioneer of modern winemaking in region continues to raise standards. Benchmark entry-point MALVAZIJA, TERAN; superb Santa Lucia selections.

Krajančić Dalm ★★→★★★ Owner Luka is guru for all styles of POŠIP (try 1214 Statut, Intrada, Opera, Sur Lie), now joined by excellent PLAVAC MALI (esp Zaglav).

Krauthaker Sl & CD ★★★ Pioneer and GRAŠEVINA specialist from Kutjevo: as (dr/sw/vyd-selection) Mitrovac. Also Zelenac (aka ROTGIPFLER).

Kutjevo Cellars Sl & CD ★★ Large producer, cellar from 1232; gd-value, consistent GRAŠEVINA main focus. Also premium De Gotho, Vinkomir, lovely Icewine.

Kvarner Is & Kv Bay and islands off ISTRIAN coast. White Žlahtina is main focus from fizz to PROŠEK (Ivan Katunar, Katunar Winery, Pavlomir, Šipun) and revived Sansigot red (Grand Village, Ivan Katunar, Katunar).

Laguna, Vina Is & Kv ★★→★★★ Signficant winery at Poreč on *terra rossa*, new winemaker. Vina Laguna for gd-value varietals, premium Festigia range for better vyd selections, esp MALVAZIJA; gd Blanc de Moi (sp).

Markus Fine Wines ★★★ Ambitious new project, planting on Šolta. Canadian investor, top winemakers. Superb POŠIP, old-vine BABIĆ, Fetivi (r), Maraština (w).

Matošević Is & Kv ★★★ Benchmark, age-worthy MALVAZIJA: Alba, Alba Antiqua, Alba Robinia (in acacia). Grimalda vyd selections v.gd.

Medea Is & Kv ★→★★ Largest of small ISTRIAN wineries. Consistent varietals, excellent top vyd selections: Montiron MALVAZIJA, *Punta Greca Merlot.*

Pilato Is & Kv ★★ Consistently gd family winery; v.gd MALVAZIJA, esp ★★★ *sur lie.*

Prošek Dalm A trad sweet wine, from sun-dried local grapes on coast (1st mention 1556). Can't be confused with Italy's Prosecco, in spite of frequent legal battles.

Rossi Is & Kv ★★ Family winery run by three bros for consistent fresh MALVAZIJA ISTARSKA, v.gd Templara selections.

Saints Hills Dalm, Is & Kv ★★→★★★ Two estates in DALM, ISTRIA. Consultant Michel Rolland (*see* France): Nevina (w), Posh POŠIP, Pape (r), Sv Roko PLAVAC MALI, one of best DINGAČ .

Slavonia / Croatian Danube This e wine region is heartland of GRAŠEVINA. Mostly whites planted, improving reds. Try Adzić, *Antunović*, Belje, ENJINGI, ENOSOPHIA, Erdutski Vinogradi, GALIĆ, Jakovac, Kast, KRAUTHAKER, KUTJEVO, Royal Hill, Sontacchi, Zlatno Brdo. Slavonia also famous for its oak.

Stina Dalm ★★ Dramatic steep vyds on Brač Island. PLAVAC MALI (Majstor label, top Remek Djelo). Also v.gd POŠIP, Tribidrag, Vugava.

Testament Dalm ★★→★★★ Organic estate in historic area at Šibenik: v.gd POŠIP, BABIĆ, Tribidrag. Fun Dalmatian Dog (r/w). Sister winery is Black Island on Korčula (Merga Victa Pošip).

Tomac Cro Up ★★★ Family winery and amphora pioneer nr Zagreb, bio: excellent *qvevri* wines, plus Rockstar RIES (trad-method sp).

Tomaz Is & Kv ★★ Family winery pushing boundaries in ISTRIA: complex MALVAZIJA Sesto Senso; impressive Barbarossa TERAN.

Tomić Dalm ★★ Bold wines from leading personality on HVAR; organic Caplar Illyricum; gd reds (esp Plavac Barrique); PROŠEK Hectorovich (sw).

Zlatan Otok Dalm ★★ Famous family winery from HVAR with vyds also at Makarska, Šibenik. Noted for ripe reds, gd DYA POŠIP.

Zure Dalm ★★★ Specialist in Grk from Lumbarda on Korčula. Try Grk Bartul, Reventon *sur lie*, Quinta Essentia (sp). Also PLAVAC MALI, POŠIP, Rebellion.

CZECHIA

Should wine face excise duty, unusual in producer countries? Ministers seeking new sources of revenue frequently raise this question, especially as most wine is imported. The answer is still no. But for how long? Don't hold your breath. Two regions: Bohemia (Boh) and Moravia (Mor).

Martinmas feast sees release of young wines (Svatomartinské) on 11 Nov each year.

Baloun Winery Mor ★★★ Radomil B est 1991; specializes in no-nonsense drinkable wines: award-winning MERLOT.

Hartman, Jiří Mor ★★ Small producer of burgundian-style (r/w) in picturesque cellar settlement typical of Slovácko area. Also v.gd RIES, WELSCHRIESLING.

Lobkowicz, Bettina Boh ★★→★★★ Swiss-born ex-princess produces admirable PINOT N Barrique Selection, trad-method Blanc de Noirs Brut and Sekt Bettina Lobkowicz Brut. Also PINOTS BL/GR, RIES, TRAMINER, Saphira; v.gd-value entry-level "LL" label (r/w/rosé).

Naturvini Mor ★★ Patrik Staško makes aromatic PÁLAVA (TRAMINER x MÜLLER-T), expressive PINOT GR, WELSCHRIESLING from foot of Pálava Hills, 90% bio.

Nepraš & Co Mor ★★★ Architect Radek N produces vibrant Maidenstein PINOT BL, RIES, SAUV BL. Also opulent Gravettien Grande Cuvée CAB SAUV/MERLOT.

Porta Bohemica Boh ★★ Outstanding Frühroter Veltliner, RIES. Try also interesting blends Charpin (CHARD/PINOT N), natural MüVé.

Springer, Jaroslav Mor ★★★ Jaroslav S and son Tomáš make remarkable single-vyd Záhřebenské CHARD, PINOT N. Flagship burgundy-style Roučí Pinot N.

Stávek, Richard Mor ★★→★★★ Dedicated terroirist. Best sites: Kolberg, Odměry, Špigle-Bočky, Veselý. Orange, pét-nat hits in Japan, US (NY).

Štěpán Maňák Winery Mor ★★→★★★ Štěpán M with wife Helena in Slovácko subregion, est 1992; 25 ha, 35 vinifera varieties plus a host of Piwis (*see* Grapes).

Vican Mor ★★★ Film producer Tomáš V est his Farma Pálava 2015. Accent on WELSCHRIESLING, RIES from Mušlov, PINOT N from Kienberg vyds. Top: Karel Roden Edition, Cuvée Jupiter, Kvevri House range. Try also SYLVANER from Kotel, Yellow MUSCADELLE or bone-dry orange TRAMINER from Nesyt.

Wilomenna Boh ★★→★★★ Boutique family winery on volcanic Central-Boh Uplands nw of Prague; CHARD, RIES, SAUV BL. Unusual varieties (Rubinet), blends (Provocateur, Rozmarné Cuvée JM), trad-method Sekt Wilomenna Brut.

Zilvar Boh ★★→★★★ Boutique winery, est 2015, on steep slate slopes overlooking Vltava and Prague zoo. Focus on RIES, PINOT N.

HUNGARY

Volcanic wines are a hot topic in wine right now, and Hungary has around two-thirds volcanic bedrock, especially north of Lake Balaton and in the northeast regions of Mátra, Eger and Tokaji, giving vibrancy and liveliness to the wines. Local grapes are in the ascendency – Furmint has a place on any serious international wine list now, but Olaszrizling reigns supreme as the Hungarian white favourite. Reds continue to become fresher and more refined, with smarter oak if at all: Cabernet Franc, Kadarka and Kékfrankos are showing the way.

Aszú Tok Noble rot, extreme shrivelling define Aszú berries – always picked one by one. Resulting sweet wine might be world's best thanks to balance of sweetness and vibrant acidity, incredibly long-lived too. Most label as 5-PUTTONYOS (min 120g/l sugar) or sweeter, richer 6-Puttonyos (min 150g/l sugar, often higher).

Balassa Tok ★★★→★★★★ Small personal winery for superb dry FURMINT, esp Mézes-Mály, Szent Tamás, plus gorgeous Villő ASZÚ, lovely SZAMORODNI. Fruity estate Furmint gd value, and possibly TOK's only RIES.

Balaton Dynamic region around Hungary's inland sea, new pyramid of quality: community brand Balaton-bor is entry point; Hegy-bor is next level up (mtn wine); dűlő for top crus. Volcanic n shore suits Hungarian favourite OLASZRIZLING, plus new plantings of old varieties FURMINT, KADARKA, KEKFRANKOS, KÉKNYELŰ. Around Badascony and Szent György-hegy: 2HA, Borbély, Buttne, Földi Bálint, GILVESY, Laposa, Nyári, Sabar, Szászi, Szeremley, Ujvári, ValiBor, Villa Sandahl, VILLA TOLNAY. Balatonfüred-Csopak n of lake: Dobosi, FIGULA, Homola, Jasdi, Liszkay, St Donát, organic ZELNA. Balaton Uplands and Zala, try Bussay, Káli Kövek, Pálffy. Balatonboglár on s shore (riper): Budjosó, GARAMVÁRI, Ikon, Kislaki, KONYÁRI, bio Kristinus, Légli plus giant TÖRLEY.

Barta Tok ★★★→★★★★ Highest vyd in region, plus beautifully renovated Rákóczi mansion. Super-elegant wines, esp Öreg Király FURMINT, HÁRSLEVELŰ and fun entry-point Egy-Kis. Glorious SZAMORODNI, superb ASZÚ.

Béres Tok ★★→★★★ Beautiful estate; family created popular remedy, Béres drops. Rich ASZÚ, gd dry, esp Diókút HÁRSLEVELŰ, Lőcse FURMINT.

Bikavér ★→★★★ "Bull's Blood". PDO in EGER and SZEKSZÁRD, unique bottles – best are some of Hungary's top reds. Oak-aged, based on KÉKFRANKOS, min four varieties. Szekszárd requires min 5% KADARKA: Eszterbauer, HEIMANN, Markvart, Mészáros, Schieber, SEBESTYÉN, Szeleshát, TAKLER, Tüske, Vesztergombi, VIDA. Eger: Superior, Grand Superior for restricted yield, longer ageing. Best Egri

Bikavér: BOLYKI, Bukolyi Marcell, Csutorás, GÁL TIBOR, Grof Buttler, KOVÁCS NIMRÓD, ST ANDREA, Tóth Ferenc, Thummerer.

Bock, József S Pann ★★→★★★ Bold VILLÁNY reds: Capella, Ermitage, Royal Cuvée, CAB FR selection.

Bolyki N Hun ★★ Dramatic winery in a quarry in EGER, great labels, appealing juiciness: v.gd Egri Csillag, Meta Tema, rosé and BIKAVÉR.

Danube (Duna) Duna Largest region on Great Plain, lighter wines. Three districts: Csongrád, Hajós-Baja (Koch), Kunság (Frittmann, Font, Gedeon, Szentpéteri); incl PDOs Monor, Soltvadkert.

Degenfeld, Gróf Tok ★★→★★★ Stunning castle hotel, organic vyds. Try Terézia HÁRSLEVELŰ, Zomborka FURMINT, excellent barrel-select ASZÚ.

Demeter, Zoltán Tok ★★★★ Legendary winemaker with passion for old vines, excellent vyd selections. Pioneer of PEZSGŐ (sp) in TOK and one of best. Fine SZAMORODNIS Anett, Eszter; superb ASZÚ.

Dereszla, Ch Tok ★★→★★★ Consistent gd-value producer for dry FURMINT, ASZÚ, reliable PEZSGŐ. Also try flor-aged dry SZAMORODNI Experience. Excellent bistro.

Disznókő Tok ★★★★ Dramatic estate. Superb, elegant, long-lived sweet wines, one of v. few to make ASZÚ every yr. Wonderful *Kapi* cru in top yrs; v.gd 1413 SZAMORODNI, plus complex dry Szamorodni. Consistent, gd-value dry FURMINT.

Dobogó Tok ★★★ Superb family winery. Benchmark ASZÚ 6-PUTTONYOS, excellent long-lived late-harvest *Mylitta*; dry FURMINT, esp Úrágya vyd selection.

Dűlő Named single vyd or cru. Increasing emphasis on vyd selections in TOK for dry and sweet. Top dűlő in TOKAJ incl Betsek, Bomboly, Király, Mézes-Mály, Nyúlászó, Szent Tamás, Úrágya, Urbán. Dűlő selections also increasing in BAL, EGER, SZEKSZÁRD, VILLÁNY.

Eger N Hun The s-facing slopes of Bükk Mtns. Reds do well here, esp Egri BIKAVÉR, KÉKFRANKOS, PINOT N, SYRAH plus fragrant fresh whites, esp Egri Csillag ("Star of Eger", dr w Carpathian-grape blend). Try Bukolyi, Csutorás, Gróf Buttler, Kaló Imre (natural), Marcell Bukolyi, Petrény, Thummerer, Tóth Ferenc.

Essencia / Eszencia Tok Rare, pricey, free-run trickle of syrup from ASZÚ grapes, min 450g/l residual sugar, barely ferments. Reputed to raise the dead.

Etyek-Buda N Pann Rolling limestone hills, increasing emphasis on gd fizz, plus expressive, crisp white (esp SAUV BL), decent PINOT N. Top: ETYEKI KÚRIA, HARASZTHY, Hernyák, Kertész, Nyakas, Rókusfalvy, TÖRLEY Sparkling Cellar.

Etyeki Kúria N Pann ★★ Top ETYEK-BUDA winery, noted for SAUV BL, elegant reds (esp Red, PINOT N). Winemaker Meresz Sandor also has natural project; try *Zenit*.

Figula Bal ★★★ Leading family winery in BAL, v.gd selections of OLASZRIZLING, esp Gella, Öreghegy, Söskut, Száka. Excellent vyd blends: Köves, Szilénusz.

Gál Tibor N Hun ★★ Appealing Egri Csillag, fine KADARKA, gd Pajardos BIKAVÉR Grand Superior.

Garamvári Bal ★★ Leading PEZSGŐ specialist, esp FURMINT Brut, Evolution Rosé; gd Garamvári varietals; top is Sinai-hegy CAB FR. Lellei label for great-value varietals.

Gere, Attila S Pann ★★★→★★★★ Standard-setting family winery in VILLÁNY: Attila Cuvée, Kopar, *Solus Merlot*, *Villányi Fr Csillag-völgy* (CAB FR). Also gd varietals plus rare historic Fekete-Járdovány.

Hungarian is the most gender-neutral language: all get same pronouns at birth.

Gilvesy Bal ★★ Canadian-Hungarian returned to roots, vyds on Szent-Gyorgy-Hegy volcano. Low-intervention FURMINT, OLASZRIZLING, RIES and blends (try St George) v.gd.

Gizella Tok ★★★★ Gloriously gd wines from tiny family estate worked by horse. Delicious dry HÁRSLEVELŰ, superb SZAMORODNI, wonderful ASZÚ.

Grand Tokaj Tok ★→★★ Largest winery in TOK. Look for Grand Tokaj label guided by highly regarded Karoly Áts. Late-harvest Arany Késői is appealing, stylish dry FURMINT Kővágó, v.gd ASZÚ, esp Szarvas.

Haraszthy N Hun ★★ Beautiful ETYEK-BUDA estate for expressive SAUV BL, aromatic Sir Irsai (w/rosé), complex The Champ (sp).

Heimann S Pann ★★★ Family winery in SZEKSZÁRD: gd VIOGNIER, plush MERLOT, flagship is Barbár blend. Next-generation Heimann & Fiai offshoot, local grapes, natural ferments (superb vyd selections: KADARKA, KÉKFRANKOS, juicy BIKAVÉR).

Hétszőlő Tok ★★★ Historic cellar and organic vyd on TOKAJ Hill itself. Try elegant Kis-Garai FURMINT, fine ASZÚ.

Heumann S Pann ★★★ German/Swiss-owned estate in Siklós part of VILLÁNY making great Kékfrankos Res, impressive *Cab Fr La Trinitá*, top Terra Tartaro blend, delicious rosé, classy SYRAH.

Hilltop Winery N Pann ★★ In Neszmély. Reliable well-made, gd-value varietals; gd Kamocsay Premium range (CHARD, Ihlet Cuvée).

Holdvölgy Tok ★★→★★★ Super-modern winery in MÁD, TOK's youngest winemaker. Complex, dry Vision, Expression, plus v.gd Eloquence SZAMORODNI.

Juliet Victor Tok ★★★ Ambitious investment by family of founder of Wizz Air. Excellent vyd FURMINTS, superb rich SZAMORODNI, ASZÚ.

Kikelet ★★★ Lovely, ageable HÁRSLEVELŰ and elegant FURMINT vyd selections from a tiny family cellar owned by French winemaker and her Hungarian husband.

Királyudvar Tok ★★★ Pioneering private winery in old royal cellars at Tarcal, bio. FURMINT Sec, Henye PEZSGŐ, Cuvée Ilona (late-harvest), flagship Lapis ASZÚ.

Konyári Bal ★★→★★★ Pioneering estate s of lake, son of founder in charge. Try Loliense (r/w), Jánoshegy KÉKFRANKOS, MERLOT Sessio, age-worthy Páva.

Every June, Tisza River blooms with unique mating dance of millions of Tisza mayfly.

Kovács Nimród Winery N Hun ★★→★★★ In heart of EGER. Try Battonage CHARD, Sky FURMINT, Rhapsody BIKAVÉR, Blues KÉKFRANKOS, 777 PINOT N, NJK.

Kreinbacher Bal ★★→★★★ Standard-setting producer of PEZSGŐ, based in SOMLÓ, always FURMINT in blend; v.gd Classic Brut, superb Prestige Brut. Also gd still: Öreg Tokék, Selection FURMINT, HÁRSLEVELŰ.

Mád Tok Historic village surrounded by top vyds, with protected origin/quality scheme. Leading: Árvay, Áts (family project of Karoly Áts, also of GRAND TOKAJ), BARTA, Budaházy, Demetervin (Mád FURMINT, Úrágya DŰLŐ), HOLDVÖLGY, JULIET VICTOR, Lenkey (unique, long-aged, complex), Mád Hill, Orosz Gabor, Pelle (Szent Tamas Furmint, PEZSGŐ), ROYAL TOKAJI, SZEPSY, Tokaj Classic.

Mad Wine Tok ★★ Sizeable winery in MÁD (with bistro) selling under Mád label. Try Mád Moser FURMINT MM5 and MM55, jointly with Lenz Moser (Austria).

Malatinszky S Pann ★★★ Organic VILLÁNY cellar. Barrel-fermented Maghari impresses, plus long-lived Kúria CAB FR, v.gd Rozé, Serena.

Mátra N Hun ★→★★ Overlooked volcanic region for lively whites, gd rosé, elegant reds. Try Balint, Benedek (gd PINOT N, KÉKFRANKOS), Centurio (esp Diós, Liberty), Dubicz, Gábor Karner, NAG (try Föld és Ég range), Nagygombos (rosé).

Mór N Pann Small region, fiery EZERJÓ; CHARD, OLASZRIZLING; ★★ *Csetvei Winery*.

Oremus Tok ★★★→★★★★ Part of Vega Sicilia (*see* Spain) stable: dry FURMINT Mandolás better than ever. Also fine, elegant SZAMORODNI, ASZÚ.

Pajzos-Tokaj Tok ★★→★★★ Notable French-founded estate. Fruit-driven New Age varietals, T range for estate selections, Selection label from cooler Megyer vyd. Fantastic flor-aged dry SZAMORODNI, excellent ASZÚ.

Pannonhalma N Pann ★★ 800-yr-old abbey. Look for top Hemina blends plus v.gd SAUV BL. Tricollis blends gd entry point.

Patricius Tok ★★→★★★ Steely, vibrant dry FURMINTS, esp Sajgo vyd; gd PEZSGŐ, appealing Katinka late-harvest; superb long-lived ASZÚ.

Pezsgő Hungarian for sparkling; growing trend. PDO TOK must be bottle-fermented.

Puttonyos (Putts) Sweetness indication for TOK ASZÚ, min 120g/l sugar for 5 Puttonyos, 150g/l for 6 Puttonyos. Was the number of 25-kg *puttonyos* or hods of Aszú grapes added to each 136-litre barrel (*gönci*) of base wine. Now more about stylistic balance of sweetness, acidity.

Royal Tokaji Wine Co Tok ★★★→★★★★ MÁD winery leading rebirth of TOK. (Hugh Johnson was co-founder 1990.) New focus on FURMINT only for v.gd ASZÚ, esp excellent 6-PUTTONYOS single vyd. Blue label is benchmark 5-Puttonyos. Look for small parcels of By Appointment, plus consistent Late Harvest and dry.

St Andrea N Hun ★★★★ Standard-setting BIKAVÉR one of Hungary's v. best wines (fruity Áldás, single-vyd Hangács, barrel-selection *Merengő*, flagship *Nagy-Eged-Hegy*, *Agapé selection*). Also gd Egri Csillag (w): Napbor, Örökké. FURMINT-based Mária is white flagship.

Sauska S Pann, Tok ★★★→★★★★ Returning expat, superb winery in VILLÁNY and new space-age PEZSGŐ cellar in TOK. Champenois consultant Régis Camus. Reds always impress, esp CAB FR, Cuvée 7, Cuvée 5. Consistent dry FURMINT, plus complex vyd selections Birsalmás, Medve; excellent precise fizz.

Sebestyén S Pann ★★ Brother-and-sister team in SZEKSZÁRD, gd vyd BIKAVÉR (esp Görögszó, Ivan-völgy), appealing KADARKA

Somló Bal Dramatic extinct volcano; firm, mineral white, esp Juhfark (sheep's tail). Small wineries dominate. Try Fehérvári, Fekete, Kancellar, *Kolonics*, KREINBACHER, Royal Somló, Somlói Apátsági, Somlói Vándor, Spiegelberg, Tornai.

Sopron N Pann Across the lake from Burgenland (*see* Austria). Fine reds, esp signature KÉKFRANKOS on old schist rocks. Try exemplary bio WENINGER. Also: organic Steigler, Taschner, Vincellér.

Szamorodni Tok Name of Polish origin for TOK made from whole bunches, partial botrytis or less shrivelled berries. Gaining popularity: more authentically Tok than late-harvest. *Édes* (sweet) is min 65g/l sugar (usually sweeter), 6 mths' oak ageing. Try BALASSA, BARTA, Bott, DEMETER ZOLTÁN, Demetervin, GIZELLA, HOLDVÖLGY, JULIET VICTOR, KIKELET, Kvaszinger, Maison aux Pois, OREMUS, Pelle, SZEPSY, TOKAJ-NOBILIS. Best dry (*szaraz*) versions flor-aged like Sherry, try Breitenbach, CH DERESZLA, Disznókő, Hársanyi, *Pajzos*, ROYAL TOKAJI, *Tinon*.

Szekszárd S Pann Famous for rich reds, increasing focus on vyd selections of elegant BIKAVÉR, KÉKFRANKOS, reviving lighter KADARKA. Try Bodri, Dúzsi, Eszterbauer, Fritz, HEIMANN, Lajver, Markvárt, SEBESTYÉN, Szent Gaál, TAKLER, Tüske, VESZTERGOMBI, VIDA.

Szepsy Tok ★★★★ Quality in a different league. Now guided by István Jnr, with focus on complex, terroir-selected dry FURMINT (esp Bányász, Percze, Szent Tamás, Urbán), though don't ignore v.gd estate Furmint. Gorgeous sweet SZAMORODNI and superb ASZÚ, incl recent single-vyd releases.

Takler S Pann ★★ Next-generation family estate in SZEKSZÁRD. New focus on DŰLŐ selections, esp Szenta, Gurovica KÉKFRANKOS, Görögszó CAB SAUV. Consistent gd-value BIKAVÉR Heritage.

Teleki S Pann ★→★★ Rebranded largest winery in VILLÁNY after historic founder and industry hero Zsigmund T who developed grafting to save vines after phylloxera. Try varietals, more serious Kővilla.

Tinon, Samuel Tok ★★★ Frenchman in TOK since 1991. Long-ageing, complex ASZÚ in more trad style, with long maceration, oak-ageing; gd vyd-selected FURMINT. Wonderful, flor-aged dry *Szamorodni*.

Tokaj-Nobilis Tok ★★★ Fine, small organic estate run by Sarolta Bárdos (Hungary's winemaker of year 2024). Excellent dry Barakonyi, Rány FURMINTS, v.gd ASZÚ, Benchmark for Furmint PEZSGŐ.

Tokaj / Tokaji Tokaj is the town and region; Tokaji the wine. Recommend (without own entry): Árvay, Áts, Bardon, Basilicus, Bodrog Borműhely, Bott Pince, Breitenbach, Budaházy, Carpinus, Demetervin, Erzsébet, Espák, Füleky, Harsányi, Karádi-Berger, Kvaszinger, Lenkey, Maison aux Pois, Orosz Gábor, Pelle, Pendits, Peter, Présello, Sanzon, Szarka, Szóló, TR, Zsirai.

"In the grape fields of Tokaj, you dripped sweet nectar": national anthem, 3rd verse.

Törley ★→★★ Reliable, gd-value DYA international and local varieties (labels incl Chapel Hill, St Stephen's Crown, Talisman); György-Villa for better selections. Major fizz producer (esp Gala, Hungaria, Törley labels), v.gd classic-method François, based on history of sparkling back to 1886.

Tornai Bal ★★ Signficant SOMLÓ estate; gd-value entry-level varietals. Excellent, weighty, mineral Top Selection FURMINT, HÁRSLEVELŰ, Juhfark.

Tűzkő S Pann ★★ Antinori-owned estate; gd CAB FR, KÉKFRANKOS, MERLOT, TRAMINI.

Vesztergombi ★★→★★★ Family SZEKSZÁRD estate impressing with next generation at helm. Look for Alpha, BIKAVÉR, Kétvölgy KÉKFRANKOS.

Vida S Pann ★★→★★★ Multi-generation family winery in SZEKSZÁRD. Wonderful *Bonsai (100-yr-old vine) Kadarka*, Hidaspetre KÉKFRANKOS, La Vida, gd BIKAVÉR.

Villány S Pann Most s region. Serious ripe Bx varieties, esp top-performing CAB FR – labelled Villányi Franc with rules for premium and super-premium. Juicy KÉKFRANKOS, PORTUGIESER. High quality (without own entry): Bakonyi, Gere Tamás & Zsolt, Günzer Tamás, Hummel, Jackfall, Jammertal, Kiss Gabor, Koch Csaba, Lelovits, Maul Zsolt, Polgar, Riczu, Ruppert, Streit-Zagonyi, Tiffán, Wassmann (bio).

Villa Tolnay Bal ★★ Swiss-owned organic estate on volcanic basalt slopes for expressive, refined wines. Try FURMINT, GRÜNER V, OLASZRIZLING, RIES.

Vylyan S Pann ★★→★★★ Red specialist in VILLÁNY for fruity Classicus range, new-wave amphora Variáció, more serious premium KÉKFRANKOS, Montenuovo, rare Csóka, top vyd selections (Mandulás CAB FR), plus flagship Duennium Cuvée.

Weninger N Hun ★★★ Standard-setting bio winery in SOPRON run by Austrian Franz W Jnr. Superb single-vyd *Steiner Kékfrankos*; try Frettner CAB FR, Rózsa too.

Zelna Bal ★★ Organic small family winery with handy wine bar n of Balaton lake. Focus is v.gd OLASZRIZLING, plus gd fizz and KÉKFRANKOS.

MALTA

M alta and Gozo's unique native grapes (and 20 internationals), varied geology, hot/dry climate (irrigation is fundamental), phylloxera-resistance, bush-farmed old vines and passionate winemakers are reviving 2000 years of winemaking tradition. Natives Girgentina (nuanced, high-acid whites redolent of lemon, crisp pear and Granny Smith apple) and Gellewza (rosés and light-bodied reds) are often blended for greater structure (the usual suspects: CHARD/SYRAH). Also good idiosyncratic Syrah and savoury MERLOT (oak alert!); SANGIOVESE and VERMENTINO have fans too. The 800 ha are (maybe?) best for reds, especially in the clay-rich soils of the south, but locals prefer whites, given the heat. Three appellations: DOK Malta, DOK Gozo and IGT Maltese Islands (wines of both). In Malta, try Delicata (Gellewza Medina, Gellewza Frizzante), Mar Casar (natural wines), Marsovin (Cassar of Malta traditional fizz), Antinori-owned Meridiana (good Vermentino Astarte), Zafrana. In Gozo, try Bacchus, Ta'Betta (founded by a couple of Cambridge graduates), Ta'Mena, Tal-Massar. Best are boutique wines, hard to find outside of the archipelago. Source carefully: seasonal tourist demand is such that grapes and must are also imported from Italy to make wine, but then that's not Maltese wine.

MONTENEGRO

Inky-dark Vranac dominates this small Adriatic country with 2561 ha under vine. Likely origin of Vranac and its probable parent Kratošija (aka Zinfandel) first mentioned in Budva statute, early 1400s. With 90% of the country's wine production and the leader in viticultural research, 13-Jul Plantaže boasts a 2310-ha single vyd (maybe Europe's largest). Quality is generally gd, esp Vranac (Pro Corde, v.gd Stari Podrum). Small wineries sell mostly at home, plenty of tourists help drink most wine locally. Look for Keković, Lipovac, Priča, Rupice, Savina, Sjekloča.

NORTH MACEDONIA

Officially the Republic of North Macedonia. Most vineyards are in the central Vardar River valley and Vranec [sic] dominates with 10,800 ha out of a total 28,000 ha; this is the warmest and driest part of Balkans, with a continental-meets-Mediterranean climate. There is an increasing emphasis on quality bottled wine and showcasing terroir, and a new association for small producers (under 30,000 litres) shows lots of dynamism, especially with indigenous Stanušina grape – try Eros, Kartal, Maksimilian, Paradžik, Peshkov, Sarika, Winecellar Popovi.

Bovin ★→★★ The 1st private winery of new era. Powerful oaky wines, esp A'gupka, My Way. Classic collection, fruitier/more drinkable.

Ezimit ★→★★ Large modern winery, beautiful vyds. Well-made, gd-value varietals.

Imako Vino ★→★★ One of largest estates in N Macedonia, own vyds, competent winemaking. Majestic label, decent value; top Constellation reds v.gd.

Kamnik, Ch ★★→★★★ On 550m (1804ft) hill nr Skopje; 1st proper small estate. Consistently high quality; rich, concentrated: v.gd 10 Barrels, Cuvée Prestige, Terroir Grand Res. Wines repay ageing.

Lazar ★★ Small personal winery; v.gd Erigon reds, also GRASEVINA Special Edition, appealing Pearl frizzante Charmat.

Popov ★→★★ Private estate; one of best Kratošjias; gd CARMENÈRE, Dom Vrsnik (w).

Tikveš ★→★★★ Oldest Balkan winery (since 1885); quality pioneer with French-trained winemaker. Big brands: Alexandria, T'ga za Jug. Better label: Luda Mara. Excellent vyd selections: Babuna, *Barovo*, Bela Voda. Also owns Dom Lepovo.

Venec ★→★★ Founded 1956; focus now on quality. Try Koria Temjanika, Kratoshija Single Block, VRANEC Orle, plus selected Disan range.

ROMANIA

By far the largest wine producer in E Europe, most wine is drunk at home. Food and wine culture is developing strongly in larger cities – Bucharest, Cluj-Napoca, Iași and Timișoara – which all repay visiting. Quality is improving; styles incl sparkling, orange and diverse reds.

Aramic, Crama Ban ★→★★ Family estate, 80 ha nr Timișoara, Italian consultants: FETEASCĂ ALBĂ, Piatra Soarelui SAUV BL, FETEASCĂ NEAGRĂ (oaked and not).

Averești, Domeniile Mold ★★ Large estate, focus on local grapes: Busuioacă and only producer of Zghihară. Look for Diamond, Nativus labels.

Avincis Mun ★★→★★★ Stunning historic mansion, dramatic hilltop winery in DRĂGĂȘANI. New impressive Alutus, v.gd orange wine. Benchmark Crâmpoșie Selecționată (still, sp); Negru de Drăgășani; Cuvées Alexis, Grandiflora, Petit.

Balla Géza Cri & Mar ★★→★★★ Consistently gd family estate. Top Stone Wine from vyds up to 400m (1312ft) on Miniș Hills (CAB FR, Cadarca, FETEASCĂ NEAGRĂ, FURMINT). Also try Clarus (sp) from Cadarca, fruity Kolna label esp Mustoasă.

Banat Dynamic region in w. Try Agape Artă & Natură, CRAMA ARAMIC, CRAMELE RECAŞ, Petro Vaselo, Thesaurus.

Bauer Winery Mun ★★★→★★★★★ Top low-intervention winery of Oliver and Raluca B (also at PRINCE ŞTIRBEY). Limited-edition old-vine batches: CAB SAUV, FETEASCĂ NEAGRĂ, PETIT VERDOT, Novac (rosé), CRÂMPOŞIE (s/sw), SVS (SAUVIGNONASSE).

Bogdan, Domeniul Dob ★★ Ambitious bio vyd (Romania's 1ST) in DOBROGEA, Stéphane Derenoncourt consults (*see* France). Try Cuvée Experience blends, Patrar and rich super-smart Primordial as tribute to late Philippe Cambié.

Budureasca Mun ★→★★ Modern DEALU MARE estate, British winemaker. Best labels: Noble 5, Origini, Vine-in-Flames export range. Look for PINOT N, SHIRAZ, TĂMÂIOASĂ ROMÂNEASCĂ.

Caii de la Letea Dob ★→★★ Large winery in Sarica Niculiţel inspired by wild horses of Letea. ALIGOTÉ is emblem, also gd FETEASCĂ NEAGRĂ, rosé, multi-vintage Quintessence Res. Shares ownership with Crama de Matei (DEALU MARE).

Corcova Roy & Dâmboviceanu Mun ★★ Renovated historic royal cellar, superb vyds. New Lady Asquith (w); FETEASCĂ NEAGRĂ, SYRAH, age-worthy Cuvee Racoveanu.

Cotnari, Casa de Vinuri Mold ★★ Only Romanian producer using only local varieties. Excellent long-lees-aged fizz from Frâncuşă, Grasă de Cotnari. Naiv label for gd modern examples of local grapes: Busuioacă, FETEASCĂ ALBĂ, Grasă. Top Colocviu range for selected vyd whites. Vladoianu FETEASCĂ NEAGRĂ v.gd.

Cotnari Winery Mold ★ Dominant large producer in DOC of same name. Mostly dry and semi-dry whites from local grapes. Aged sweet Collection can impress.

Romanian Henri Coanda developed first aircraft jet engine in 1910.

Crişana & Maramureş Cooler region in nw. Look for BALLA GÉZA, Carastelec (v.gd Carassia bottle-fermented sp), Darabont Family (esp Urme), organic NACHBIL, Weingut Edgar Brutler (orange, pét-nat).

Dagon Mun ★★→★★★ Small, impressive quality-focused vyd. Best: Clearstone FETEASCĂ ALBĂ, Sandridge old-vine FETEASCĂ NEAGRĂ.

DAR1892 Mun ★→★★ Domeniile Alexandrion Rhein 1892; 255 ha in DEALU MARE, long history of gd trad fizz under Rhein & Cie Ltd (1892). Also top Hyperion.

Davino Winery Mun ★★★★ One of Romania's v. best, in DEALU MARE. Focus on blends: age-worthy Dom Ceptura, Flamboyant, Rezerva, Revelatio (w). FETEASCĂ NEAGRĂ, FETEASCĂ ALBĂ under Valahica label v.gd. Entry-level Faurar, great value.

Dealu Mare / Dealul Mare Mun Means "Big Hill"; regarded as Romania's Tuscany. Top: AURELIA VISINESCU, BUDUREASCA, Crama Mierla Alba, DAGON, DAVINO, DEMATEI, Domeniile Franco-Române, Gramofon, LACERTA, LICORNA, SERVE, VIILE METAMORFOSIS.

DeMatei, Crama Mun ★★ Notable 92-ha estate in DEALU MARE; serious reds under Migala, Patima, Prince Matei labels.

Dobrogea Sunny Black Sea region. Try Alcovin-Macin (Curtea Regala), Alira (rosé, SAUV BL, MERLOT), BOGDAN, CAII DE LA LETEA, Dropia (BĂBEASCĂ NEAGRĂ), Gabai, Histria (v.gd Ammos, Nikolaos CAB SAUV, rosé), La Sapata (bio, Băbească Neagră), Rasova (Imperfect, Sur Mer), Vladoi (Alb Cuvée, Anca Maria TĂMÂIOASĂ).

DOC Romanian term for PDO: 40 registered. Sub-categories incl DOC-CMD: harvest at full maturity. DOC-CT: late harvest. DOC-CIB: noble harvest. PGI is vin cu indicatie geografică, or simply IG.

Drăgăşani Mun OLTENIA plateau and hills. Unique grapes: Crâmpoşie Selecţionată, Negru de Drăgăşani, Novac. Dynamic wineries: AVINCIS, BAUER, PRINCE ŞTIRBEY.

Gîrboiu ★→★★ Family estate in one of Europe's most tectonically active areas; names reflect this. Special focus on rare indigenous Şarba, try Bacanta, Petite Helene, top red blend Constantin.

Gramma Mold ★★ Bright, fresh wines, esp ALIGOTÉ from family winery close to Iaşi.

Jidvei Trnsyl ★→★★ Romania's largest single vyd, 2500 ha+. Best: Owner's Choice (with Marc Dworkin of Bulgaria's Bessa V); Eiswein and Extra Brut (sp).

LacertA Mun ★★ Estate in DEALU MARE: gd Cuvée IX (r), Cuvée X (w), SHIRAZ.

Licorna Wine House Mun ★★ Small DEALU MARE estate. Try Serafim for local grapes, Bon Viveur for international blends. Anno top selection.

Liliac Trnsyl ★★★ Impeccable Austrian-owned estate in heart of TRNSYL; *liliac* means bat. Crisp fine whites, elegant reds, v.gd orange CHARD, delicious sweet Nectar, Icewine with Kracher (*see* Austria).

Metamorfosis, Viile Mun ★★ DEALU MARE estate, part of Antinori group (*see* Italy), Italian winemaker. Top: rich, bold Cantvs Primvs, esp MERLOT; v.gd Colțul Pietrei SAUV BL, SYRAH, Via Marchizului Negru de DRĂGĂȘANI, PINOT N; reliable entry-point Villa Metamorfosis range.

Moldovan Hills Largest ne region. Fresh white, rosé; refined red: AVEREȘTI, GRAMMA, GÎRBOIU, Hermeziu (Busuioacă de Bohotin), Strunga (FETEASCĂS ALBĂ/NEAGRĂ).

Muntenia & Oltenia Hills Major region in S. DOC areas: DEALU MARE, Dealurile Olteniei, DRĂGĂȘANI, Pietroasa, Sâmburești (Ch Valvis), Stefanești, Vanju Mare.

Nachbil Cri & Mar ★★ Organic producer in Satu Mare. Try almost extinct Grünspitz in amphora, BLAUFRÄNKISCH, fresh juicy MERLOT, v.gd SYRAH Res.

Oltenia Up-and-coming region in overlooked sw: Catleya, CORCOVA, CRAMA OPRIȘOR, Domeniul Coroanei Segarcea, Mosia Galicia Mare.

Oprișor, Crama Mun ★★→★★★ Consistent German-owned winery; La Cetate range, v.gd Crama Oprișor CAB SAUV, Jiana Rosé, Rusalca Alba; top *Smerenie* (r).

Petro Vaselo Ban ★★ Organic vyd in BANAT; fizz focus from Charmat Bendis to serious Kotys; fruity basics then Melgris, Otarnita, Ovas; top experimental PV.

Prince Știrbey Mun ★★★→★★★★ Pioneering top-quality estate in DRĂGĂȘANI, just celebrated 20th yr. Local variety main focus: precise, vibrant dry whites, esp Crâmpoșie Selecționată, FETEASCĂ REGALĂ, TĂMÂIOASĂ. Impressive local reds (Negru de Drăgășani, Novac), fine complex sparkling.

Recaș, Cramele Ban ★★→★★★ Large, consistent and v. successful winery, part British-owned with long-standing Australian and Spanish winemakers. Leading both export and home market. Multiple labels, incl entry-point Calusari, Paparuda, Schwaben Wein, Wildflower. Mid-range: Implicit, Regno Recaș, Selene, Sole, Solo Quinta. Excellent La Stejari, flagship *Cuvée Uberland* (r).

Serve Mun ★★★★ As 1st private winery, continues vision of founder Count Guy de Poix: v.gd Terra Romana, Cuvée Clemence (w), Cuvée Sissi rosé, FETEASCĂ NEAGRĂ. Top: *Guy de Poix Fetească Neagră*. Iconic *Cuvée Charlotte* back on form.

Tohani Mun ★★ Large winery with S African winemaker; bright fruity Siel label, flagship is Apogeum old-vine FETEASCĂ NEAGRĂ.

Transylvania Cool mtn plateau encircled by Carpathians, great wildlife. Crisp whites; increasingly lighter, elegant reds. Worth trying (without own entry): Jelna (Navicella r), La Salina (Issa label for gd NEUBERGER, RIES, PINOT N), Lechburg.

Villa Vinèa Trnsyl ★★ Stylish wines from cool hilly vyd nr Târnave. Top: Diamant, GEWURZ, FETEASCĂ REGALĂ, RUBIN.

Vișinescu, Aurelia Mun ★★ Female-led DEALU MARE estate, gd Artisan label for local grapes. Top brand: Anima, esp *Feto Negre* from selected FETEASCĂ NEAGRĂ, new flagship Signature.

SERBIA

A progressive wine country, fast catching up on its neighbours, with 20,000 ha and over 500 wineries. Grapes mix international and revived locals like white Bagrina, Grašac, Morava and red Probus and Prokupac.

Serbia has Europe's largest desert (Deliblato Sands), deepest gorge (Djerdap Gorge).

ROMANIA / SERBIA

Aleksandrović ★★→★★★ One of pioneers of new private era. Trijumf (sp), Serbia's best trad-method fizz. Also v.gd Prokupac, Regent, Trijumf Gold, Vozd.

Aleksić ★★ Pretty Žuti Cvet Tamjanika; v.gd Amanet VRANAC, Biser (trad-method sp).

Bikicki ★★ Try natural, orange: Cu (PINOT GR), Moma (TRAMINER), S/O (SAUV BL).

Budimir ★→★★ Grandpa B is legendary figure. Noted for aromatic Tamjanika, long-lived, old-vine Prokupac Boje Lila.

Čokot (aka Radovan) ★★→★★★ Highest winery/vyd in Župa. Prokupac specialist: easier-drinking Experiment, benchmark Radovan.

Deurić ★★ FRUŠKA GORA estate for v.gd Aksiom, Probus, *Severna Morava* blends. Attractive trad-method fizz.

Djoković ★★ Family winery of famous tennis player and his uncle. Refined, precise wines: CHARD, SYRAH so far.

Doja ★★ Modern family winery in s, specializing in Prokupac, from rescued old clones. Flagship: Breg range.

Erdevik ★★ Serbia's oldest winery (1826), overlooks Danube. Reinvented as quality producer (2015). Controversial labels but v.gd wines: *Geronimo Grašac*, Ominbus Lector CHARD; plus bold, rich Stifler's Mom SYRAH, Grand Trianon (r blend).

Fruška Gora Dramatic hill and national park close to Danube, birthplace of Serbian wines in Roman times. Dynamic region with many exciting producers (without own entries): Belo Brdo, Chichateau, Đurđić, Frug, Fruškogorski Vinogradi, Kiš, Kovačević, Milanović, Trivanović, Veritas Cuković, Verkat, Vinum.

Ivanović ★★→★★★ "Gaga" I (RIP) was key in revival of Prokupac. Now run by son and daughter; v.gd Prokupac, rosé, No. 1/2 (CAB SAUV/MERLOT/Prokupac).

Matalj ★★→★★★ Pioneering winery in historic Negotin. Great vyd-selection CAB SAUV Kremen Kamen, Zemna. Also v.gd Bagrina, Bukovski Cuvée.

Matijašević ★★→★★★ Quality-focused estate; great Sovinoa SAUV BL; v.gd Belina (Smederevka), Čukundeda Prokupac, Tri Doline MERLOT.

Radovanović ★★ The 1st private winery of new era (1990); speciality CAB SAUV Res; gd RIES, oaky CHARD.

Šapat ★★→★★★ Small estate. Super-elegant wines: Atila CHARD, SAUV BL, plus pretty Bianca, Šu-Šu rosé. Forthcoming CAB SAUV, TEROLDEGO show huge promise.

Šumadija Hilly volcanic region at centre of quality revival, early 1990s. Worth trying (without own entry): Despotika, Tarpoš.

TemeT ★★→★★★ All styles v.gd, from fizz to terroir-selection reds: Beli Kamen, Ergo, Tri Morave, all recommended.

Vinčić ★★★ Tiny boutique winery, 50-yr-old vines on FRUŠKA GORA, fabulous Grašac.

Virtus ★→★★ Main estate in Mlava region. Flagships MARSELAN, PINOT GR, Prokupac; esp Credo blends best yrs.

Vojvodina Autonomous province covering N Serbia, also PGI. FRUŠKA GORA is most important subregion, but also incl Subotica, S Banat. Worth trying (without own entries): Drasković, Oskar Maurer (natural wines, notable 1880-planted KADARKA), Rjnak, Tonković (Kadarka).

Zvonko Bogdan ★★→★★★ Dramatic winery on Hungarian border. Elegant Eclater (sp); gd PINOT BL, Cuvée No. 1 (r). Icon Campana Albus/Rubimus in top yrs.

Wines of Kosovo

Western Balkan economy with partial recognition as independent, but crucially not by Serbia. Two sets of wine laws: Kosovo's own and Serbia's. Around 2500 ha under wine grapes, 64% red; 37 wineries. Bodrumi i Vjetër (Old Cellar), Stone Castle dominate; smaller Kosova, Labi Wine, Lakicević, Sefa improving. Vranç (aka VRANAC) most planted red, plus GAMAY, Prokupac; whites led by Smederevka (aka DIMIAT), WELSCHRIESLING.

SLOVAKIA

European varieties dominate, alongside international staples. Six wine regions: Central Slovakia (C Slo), Eastern Slovakia (E Slo), Lesser Carpathians (L Car), Nitra (Nit), Southern Slovakia (S Slo), Tokaj (Tok).

Slovenský Grob centre of goose-feasting: 45 restaurants serve nothing but.

Belá, Ch S Slo ★★★ Fine Mosel-style RIES by joint Egon Müller (*see* Germany) and Miroslav Petrech venture; Alibernet (ALICANTE BOUSCHET X CAB SAUV), PINOT N.

Dudo, Miroslav L Car ★★★ CAB SAUV; unusual crosses Devín, Dunaj, MUSCAT Ottonel, popular Naše Cuvée blend (w).

Elesko L Car ★★ Unique concept in Modra, wine capital of Lesser Carpathians, combining ultra-modern facilities with gastronomy, featuring art gallery with Warhol originals. Elegant modern wines exclusively from own grapes.

Fedor Malík & Sons L Car ★★★ Family winery, mainly whites. Red crosses Hron, Rudava; blends Sahral Noir, Petit Sahral, Hrom (Thunder); Modragne fizz.

J&J Ostrožovič Tok ★★★ Pure dry FURMINT, Lipovina (HÁRSLEVELŰ) and Yellow Muscadelle plus admirable Tok styles ranging from Samorodné (Szamorodni) to Tokajský výber (Aszú) 3–6 Putňový (Puttonyos). Esencia (Eszencia) yr 2000.

Karpatská Perla L Car ★★→★★★ Laco Šebo specializes in zesty RIES (Kramáre, Suchý Vrch single vyds), quaffable GRÜNER V (Ingle, Noviny).

Magula L Car ★★★ Family facility with bio principles: GRÜNER V, WELSCHRIESLING. Exquisite Frankovka (BLAUFRÄNKISCH) grown on loess in single-vyd Rosenberg.

Mavín – Martin Pomfy L Car ★★→★★★ Founded 2001, family-run. Organic.

Múrani Víno Čajkov Nit ★★→★★★ Doctor Jaromír M est 1993, 15 ha volcanic soils.

Pivnica Brhlovce Nit ★★→★★★ Artisanal production, volcanic wines, troglodyte dwellings, est 2011 by photographer Ján Záborský. Try youthful Pesecká Leánka (FETEASCĂ REGALĂ) Happiness: fruit and hardy earthiness.

SLOVENIA

Small but beautiful (wines and scenery), Slovenia's wine regions are all within easy reach of the capital. Quality is higher than ever, with increasing emphasis on a sense of place through clear regional distinctions, vineyard selections and more refined winemaking. A picture of consistently good big wineries and often exciting smaller family estates.

Slovenia has at least 10,000 known caves – mind your step.

Albiana Pos ★★ Lovely family vyds in DOLENJSKA: try fizz, esp rosé. Also gd SILVANER, MODRA FRANKINJA Alto.

Batič Prim ★★ VIPAVA estate; bio; three ranges – Classic, Selekcija, Angel for top selections. Try Marlon for pioneering blend of 20 fungus-resistant grapes.

Bjana Prim ★★★→★★★★ One of country's v. best trad-method PENINA producers in BRDA. Top Cuvée Prestige Extra Brut; v.gd Blanc de Noirs/Blancs, Rosé Brut.

Brda Prim Top-quality region of hilly terraced vyds. Worth trying (without own entry): Benedetič, Blažič, Bužinel, Dobuje, Domačija Bizjak, Emeran Reya Organic Winery, Iaquin, Klincc, Kristančič, Medot, Moro, Mulit, Nebó, Ronk, Schumacher Wines, Zalatel, Zanut.

Burja Prim ★★★→★★★★ Bio VIPAVA estate. Try Overture, Petite Burja for local whites. Main range is v.gd: Burja Bela, Burja N (PINOT N), Burja Reddo; excellent vyd selections in top yrs.

Dolenjska & Bizeljsko Sremič Pos Improving regions, moving on from trad sharp red Cviček. Try ALBIANA, Dular, FRELIH, Klet Krško (Turn Classic, Premium), Kobal, Kozinc (v.gd sp Nord, Zara, Blanc de Noirs; Selekcija still wines). Local Žametovka/Žametna Crnina proving great for fizz: *Dom Slapšak*, Frelih, Kozinc.

Dolfo Prim ★★→★★★ Family winery in BRDA: v.gd Spirito PENINA, consistent fresh, mineral REBULA. Serious Gredič, Res labels.

Dveri-Pax Pod ★★→★★★ Historic Benedictine-owned estate nr Maribor. Bright precise whites; v.gd old-vine selections, esp FURMINT Ilovci, SAUV BL Vajgen, plus age-worthy BLAUFRÄNKISCH, excellent *Furmint Penina*.

Erzetič Prim ★★ Family winery, organic. Superb Orbis range, aged in five woods.

Ferdinand Prim ★★★→★★★★ Hilltop estate. Superb cross-border Sinefinis (sp, with Gradis'ciutta, Italy), excellent Epoca (r/w), impressive long-skin-contact Brutus.

Frelih Pos ★★ Mother/daughter team making v.gd SILVANER, MODRA FRANKINJA, PENINA; modern interpretation of trad Cviček.

Frešer Pod ★★ Organic, 7th generation: PINOT N, Markus RIES, LAŠKI RIZLING.

Gašper Prim ★★★ Impressive brand of Gašper Čarman with KLET BRDA: excellent CAB FR; v.gd MALVAZIJA, REBULA Selekcija; Markisa rosé; Bonita; fruity Palamida.

Gross, Vino Pod ★★ Low-intervention terroir wines from steep terraces. Try Colles (SAUV BL), Gorca, Iglič (FURMINT), Korže; impressive Furmint Brut Natur.

Guerila Prim ★★ Pioneering bio estate in VIPAVA: v.gd MALVASIA, Pinela, Zelen; BARBERA, CAB FR; Retro blends.

Herga Pod ★★ Former Kupljen estate reinvented by leading winemaker Mitja H. On gd track: CHARD, PINOT GR, SAUV BL, PINOT N.

Hiša Joannes Protner Pod ★★ Passionate about RIES, gd CHARD, PENINA, PINOT N; Natura (w) from bio estate.

Istenič Pos ★★ Pioneering fizz specialist. Try Prestige Extra Brut, Gourmet Rosé, No. 1 Brut, Rare Brut Natur.

Istria (Slovenska Istra) The Slovenian part of the peninsula; main grapes: MALVAZIJA, REFOŠK. Best: Bordon, Brič, Korenika & Moškon (bio), MonteMoro, Pucer z Vrha, Rodica (organic), SANTOMAS, Steras (superb Epulon, Saurin Malvazija), VINAKOPER, Zaro.

Jakončič Prim ★★★ In BRDA: v.gd Carolina range, skin-contact Uvaia PINOT GR.

Jermann Prim Silvio J (of Jermann Italy fame) has invested in personal project in BRDA; possibly Slovenia's highest vyd being planted. Watch.

Kabaj Prim ★★★ French-led BRDA estate; complex skin-contact whites, bold reds.

Klet Brda Prim ★★→★★★ Slovenia's largest co-op continues to set quality, environmental standards. Fresh Quercus range v.gd, unoaked Krasno. Bagueri vyd selections excellent, esp REBULA. Impressive De Baguer range incl superb flagship A+ (r/w), single-vyd MERLOT, Rebula. Produces v.gd Schumacher wines.

Kobal Pod ★★ Boutique winery in HALOŽE: v.gd fruit-focused white-label range; more structured black label and Bajta for long skin contact and pét-nat.

Kogl Pod ★★ Historic estate nr Ormož (1542). Appealing fresh Mea Culpa whites, more complex Magna Domenica.

Krapež, Vina Prim ★★ Organic, low-intervention VIPAVA estate. Appealing, spicy, herby flagship Lapor Belo (w); try also Lapor Rdeče, MERLOT.

Kras Prim Most noted for TERAN PDO made from REFOŠK, also gd MALVASIA, Vitovska. Try Čotar, Marko Fon, Štoka, Vinakras.

Kristančič Prim ★★ Family estate in BRDA: Cristatus PENINA, excellent top Pavó.

Neanderthal flute, 55,000 years old, found in cave; made from a cave bear femur.

Marjan Simčič, Dom Prim ★★★★ Benchmark classic varietal range, v.gd cru selection from older vines, selected plots. Superb single-vyd old-vine Opoka range, esp wonderful CHARD, SAUV VERT, MERLOT, PINOT N Breg. Superb Unico M as new red flagship, Leonardo (sw) consistently glorious.

Marof Pod ★★→★★★ No-compromise estate. Grand Vin for vyd selections: Bodonci SAUV BL, Kramarovci CHARD, Mačkovci Frankinja. Also v.gd Goričko varietals.

Movia Prim ★★★→★★★★ Charismatic Aleš Kristančič with son Lan; bio. Excellent

> **Rebula: the future?**
> BRDA and VIPAVA's most important native grape, a Cinderella story of
> rising from ashes. It copes well with climate extremes. It's fussy, though:
> it only turns golden and offers quality and complexity on steep, stony,
> well-drained marl slopes. On damp plains, it stays green and mean.

Veliko range, esp Belo (w), showstopping *Puro Rosé (sp)*, *Rdeče (r)*. New Kapovolto (sp). Also admired for long-macerated orange Lunar.

Pasji Rep Prim ★★ Next-generation bio VIPAVA estate. Try local Zelen, Moser (w field blend), esp lovely MERLOT Breg, plus Jebatschin Merlot/CAB FR.

Penina Name for quality sparkling, Charmat or trad method.

Podravje Largest region, incl ŠTAJERSKA SLOVENIJA and Prekmurje. Best for vibrant, dry whites, esp FURMINT, Laški, SAUV BL; lighter reds.

Posavje Region in se covering DOLENJSKA, Bizeljsko-Sremič, Bela Krajina (Metlika, Prus, Šturm, ŠUKLJE). Focus building on v.gd fresh fizz, elegant MODRA FRANKINJA. Izbor (sw) can be excellent: great acidity.

Primorje / Primorska Region in w covering Slovenian BRDA, ISTRIA, KRAS, VIPAVA.

Puklavec Family Wines Pod ★★→★★★ Large family winery, consistent expressive whites in Puklavec & Friends and Jeruzalem Ormož ranges; v.gd Seven Numbers label, amazing archive wines. Also Instinct winery in N Macedonia.

Pullus (Ptujska Klet) Pod ★→★★ Reliable Pullus label; G range, sweets impress.

Radgonske Gorice Pod ★→★★ Historic sparkling cellar, top-selling Srebrna (silver) PENINA. Classic-method Selection Brut, long-aged Millesimé CHARD gd.

Santomas Prim ★★→★★★ Benchmark producer of REFOŠK, from organic grapes. Mezzo Forte (r), SYRAH v.gd.

Ščurek Prim ★★★ Family estate in BRDA, five sons; gd varietal entry-point wines. Superb *Rebula Up*, attractive Stara Brajda (r/w), gd Zero Brut PENINA.

Simčič, Edi Prim ★★★★ Beautiful family winery and standard-setter in BRDA. Excellent Fojana, Kozana vyd selections and some of country's top reds, esp barrel-selection Kolos, Kozana MERLOT. Classic range, Lex blends v.gd.

Štajerska Slovenija Pod Major region in e, incl important districts of Haloze, Ljutomer-Ormož, Maribor. New winery association. Crisp, vibrant whites, elegant lighter reds and top sweet. Try Dom Ciringa, Doppler, Familija, FREŠER, Gaube, Horvat, Jaunik, Meum, M-Simply Good Wines, Miro, Roka, Sanctum, SiSi Druzovič, Statera, Valdhuber, Zlati Grič.

Steyer Pod ★★ TRAMINER specialist in ŠTAJERSKA, esp Vaneja.

Šuklje ★★→★★★ Exemplary small family estate, with terroir focus in Bela Krajina: Lozice SAUV BL, Lodorna and excellent Vrbanjka MODRA FRANKINJA.

Sutor Prim ★★★→★★★★ Excellent small producer from VIPAVA. Lovely Sutor White, fine CHARD, elegant MERLOT-based red.

Tilia Prim ★★→★★★ Tagline is "House of Pinot", reflecting passion for PINOT N in all styles, from refined sparkling via juicy estate to top age-worthy selections. Expressive Sunshine whites, appealing Rubido red blend.

Verus Pod ★★★ Fine, beautifully made, vibrant whites: v.gd FURMINT, PINOT GR, refined RIES, aromatic SAUV BL. Great value too.

Vicomte de Noüe-Marinič, Dom Prim ★★→★★★ Burgundy meets BRDA (Jeanne Leflaive connection): CHARD, REBULA, PINOT N impress from historic cru vyds.

Vinakoper Prim ★★ Large ISTRIAN winery, local-grape focus: MALVAZIJA, REFOŠK. Try Capo d'Istria, Capris, Rex Fuscus labels.

Vipava Prim Dramatic valley noted for Burja wind in PRIM. Try Benčina, Bizjak, Fedora, Ferjančič, JNK, Koglot, Lepa Vida, Lisjak, Marc, Miška, Mlečnik, Poljšak, Saksida, Štokelj, Vina Ušaj Ussai, Wipach. Promising newcomer Grof.

Vipava 1894 Prim ★→★★ Large winery in VIPAVA. Lanthieri range, Terase MALVAZIJA.

Greece

Greek wine-growers were playing around with mountainous vineyards before it was cool. They were cultivating old vines before there were any initiatives about them, or much interest. They vinified rare grape varieties back at a time when this was considered a serious disadvantage. They knew how to handle warm climates and craft delicious wines brimming with freshness before climate change was on anybody's radar. It seems that the words that are on everybody's lips have been key features of Greek wine for millennia. Abbreviations: Aegean Islands (Aeg), Attica (Att), Central Greece (C Gr), Ionian Islands (Ion), Macedonia (Mac), Peloponnese (Pelop), Thessaloniki (Thess).

Aivalis Pelop ★★★ NEMEA tiny producer, cult following, esp for "4" and Armakas reds but whites are not far off. Full, new-oak style.

Akrathos Mac ★★ Rising star from just off Mt Athos. Doesn't rush to release wines to market: 4-yr-old ASSYRTIKO, possibly most SANTORINI-like on the mainland.

Alpha Estate Mac ★★★→★★★★ Largest vyd owner in Greece, leading KTIMA, defining AMYNTEO, but now has foothold in SANTORINI too. Barba Yiannis XINOMAVRO from century-old vines is star for many.

Amynteo Mac (POP) Captivating, elegant XINOMAVRO (r/rosé/sp) from coolest Greek POP, at 600m (1968ft)+ altitude. Many new players kicking in: KARAMOLEGOS, NICO LAZARIDI.

Anhydrous Aeg ★★★ Fine SANTORINI producer, from man who created AVANTIS in Evia. Icon is, well, pretty iconic.

Aoton Att ★★ While others try to revive the image of excellent, clean, correct but fine SAVATIANO, Aoton produces some of the most offbeat examples around. Try bold, full RETSINA.

Argyros Aeg ★★★★ Top SANTORINI producer, largest vyd owner on island; prices beyond reasonable. VINSANTOS out of this world; Evdemon, Gerontampelo, Monsignori all dreamy ASSYRTIKOS.

Avantis C Gr ★★★ Boutique winery in Evia. Top: Agios Chronos (SYRAH/VIOGNIER), Collection SYRAH. On rich side.

Averoff Epir, Mac ★★→★★★★ Historic Katogi a popular range, punching above its weight. Rossiu di Munte (firm, reserved) from 1000m (3281ft)+, one of highest vyds in Europe, while Inima wines all about fruit.

Biblia Chora Mac ★★★ Superb KTIMA. Ovilos (r/w) rivals Bx in style at third of the price. Sister wineries in Pelop (Dyo Ipsi), SANTORINI (Mikra Thira), GOUMENISSA (Mikro Ktima) and NAOUSSA (in the making).

Boutari ★→★★ Historic brand under new ownership; more focus on volume and value; gd Greek varietals.

Yields on Santorini are among the lowest on earth: c.15 hl/ha.

Carras, Dom Mac ★★ Historic estate at Halkidiki, recently changed hands, again; Ch Carras always a benchmark.

Cephalonia Ion Island famous for mineral, floral ROBOLA (w) and getting famous for dry, herbaceous, tannic MAVRODAPHNE (r). Many excellent growers; for many the next SANTORINI.

Dalamara Mac ★★★→★★★★ Prodigious producer in NAOUSSA, at top of XINOMAVRO game. Ethereal, dazzlingly complex reds to keep for decades.

Diamantakos Mac ★★→★★★★ Another hidden jewel in NAOUSSA: XINOMAVRO, modern yet lean; Preknadi (w) a curiosity that has to be tasted (*see also* p.10).

Dougos C Gr ★★★ Ambassador for RAPSANI. Reds are broad and top-class, like Old Vines or MAVROTRAGANO, yet Tourtoura is v. elegant.

Douloufakis Crete ★★★ VIDIANO pioneer, but do not miss Liatiko. Several styles, all round and expressive, from sparkling to amphora. Try spicy Liatiko Grande Res.

Economou, Ktima Crete ★★★★ One of great artisans of Greece; unicorn status. Recently more oxidative in style, not for faint-hearted. Labyrinthine aromatics.

Gaia Aeg, Pelop ★★★ Exquisite range from NEMEA, SANTORINI. **Gaia Estate** is top Nemea, ditto for flinty Ammonite Santorini. Lean whites, more opulent reds.

Keep a good Savatiano for 5 years; taste blind against a Hunter Valley Semillon.

Gentilini Ion ★★★ Historic CEPHALONIA winery, incl *steely Robola*, esp R24. Benchmark dry MAVRODAPHNE Eclipse (r) is v. precise, tannic, imposing.

Gerovassiliou, Ktima Mac ★★★ Trendsetter on repeat. Practically created MALAGOUSIA genre (smooth, peachy). Museum (r/w) too gd to spit. BIBLIA CHORA link.

Goumenissa Mac ★★→★★★ (POP) Excellent XINOMAVRO/Negoska (r), rounder than NAOUSSA. Try Chatzyvaritis (lean), Ligas (wild), Mikro KTIMA (polished), TATSIS (full-on natural).

Hatzidakis Aeg ★★★ Legend of SANTORINI; 2nd generation now in charge. Louros, Nyhteri, Rambelia, Skytali all impeccable, less oxidative than in past.

Karamolegos Aeg ★★★ SANTORINI winery, excellent restaurant on top. Rare Louroi, Pappas, Pyritis: complex, broad-shouldered. Investing in AMYNTEO.

Karanika Mac ★★★ Best sparklings in Greece; mainly ASSYRTIKO/XINOMAVRO. Must-buy razor-sharp Cuvée Prestige and Extra Cuvée de Res.

Karydas, Ktima Mac ★★★ Tiny vyd in NAOUSSA, crafting uplifting, herbaceous, age-worthy XINOMAVRO. Hidden jewel, crazy value. Syllektiko has a touch of CAB SAUV.

Katsaros, Ktima Thess ★★★ Tiny enterprise on Mt Olympus. KTIMA (r) nods at Bx and ages well. Buttery Stella CHARD is California-like, while Valos XINOMAVRO tastes like warm vintage NAOUSSA.

Kechris ★★→★★★★ ASSYRTIKO-based The Tear of the Pine, possibly *world's best Retsina*: full of zing, just a note of pine perfume. Fantastic wine, no kidding.

Kir-Yianni Mac ★★→★★★ NAOUSSA and AMYNTEO originally, now owns SIGALAS in SANTORINI. Reds increasingly lean towards the silk rather than towards the silt.

Ktima "Estate" in Greek; equivalent of Weingut or bodega.

Lafazanis Pelop ★★ Large but always reliable producer; wineries in Messinia and NEMEA. Fresh whites, juicy reds, never missing a bit.

Lazaridi, Costa Att, Mac ★★★ KTIMA in Drama and Att. Top: Cava Amethystos CAB FR. Michel Rolland (*see* France) consults, and you can taste it. Plantings in high Drama promising: try minty MALAGOUSIA.

Lazaridi, Nico Mac ★→★★★ Originally from Drama. Vast range, v. strong on value labels. However, Magiko Vouno (r) is a timeless Bx lookalike.

Lyrarakis Crete ★★★ *Single-vyd versions* extraordinary, and introduce rare Dafni, Melissaki, Plyto grapes. All about texture and detail, not about flavour acrobatics.

Malvasia Four POPS recreating the medieval "Malmsey". Not MALVASIA, but local varieties. POPs are Monemvassia-M in Laconia, M of Paros and M Chandakas-Candia, M of Sitia (from Crete). Lush but never cloying. Still quite rare.

Manoussakis Crete ★★★ Initially Rhône-inspired, now focusing on Greek varieties: ASSYRTIKO, full MUSCAT of Spinas, VIDIANO, silky Romeiko (r). Opulent and ripe.

Mantinia Pelop (POP) High-altitude, cool mtn plateau. Crisp, lifted, almost Germanic whites from *Moschofilero*. Excellent fizz next big thing.

Mercouri Pelop ★★ Greece's most beautiful, must-visit KTIMA on w coast. MAVRODAPHNE/REFOSCO, full of finesse; Foloi (w), RODITIS at its finest.

Mitravelas Pelop ★★→★★★ Producer in NEMEA, making quality strides recently. If you can have a bottle of Old Vines, why bother with most Super Tuscans?

Monemvassia Winery – Tsimbidi Pelop ★★→★★★ Only producer of POP MALVASIA-Monemvassia (sw) and godfather of Kydonitsa: for lovers of soft, textured whites.

Mylonas Att ★★→★★★ Young Stamatis M stubbornly crafts fine SAVATIANO, a grape bad-mouthed by many. Subtle complexity and balanced extraction.

Naoussa Mac ★★★→★★★★ (POP) Breathtaking XINOMAVRO bringing spices, herbs, sun-dried tomato in the glass. Best on par in quality, style (but not in price) with Barolo: firm, linear, otherworldly. Top: DALAMARAS, KARYDAS, KIR-YIANNI, THIMIOPOULOS, many others. Age for 10 yrs++.

Nemea Pelop ★★→★★★ (POP) AGIORGITIKO reds. Try Driopi from TSELEPOS (French-inspired), AIVALIS (New World-style), GAIA (pristine), Ieropoulos (oak), MITRAVELAS (modern), PALYVOS (fruit-focused), PAPAÏOANNOU (classic), SKOURAS (polished). Nemea Lions is a new category: look for extract, ageing potential.

Oeno P ★★★★ New venture of Paris Sigalas, founder of KTIMA SIGALAS. Premier Cru prices, but Grand Cru quality. ASSYRTIKO at its elegant grandest.

Palyvos Pelop ★★→★★★ KTIMA in NEMEA making big-framed, age-worthy reds with AGIORGITIKO and French varieties, from SYRAH to VIOGNIER. Light, fresh whites.

Panagiotopoulos Pelop ★★ Reputable producer in Messinia. Specializes in CAB SAUV, v. trad, but gives trad a gd name.

Papagiannakos Att ★★→★★★ Original mouthpiece of SAVATIANO, Vassilis P shows dry-farmed old vines of Att can produce grace, vivacity. Solid fruit, broad texture.

Papaioannou Pelop ★★★ Legend of NEMEA. Top: Microclima, Palea Klimata (old vines), Terroir. Foursquare, trad reds that keep for ages. Don't be scared by oak: fruit will prevail.

Pavlidis Mac ★★★ KTIMA in Drama. Thema (w) ASSYRTIKO/SAUV BL, bestseller; Alma, layered premium rosé. Emphasis range has more extract, higher ripeness.

POP Greek equivalent of France's AOP. Many top wines belong here, many not.

Rapsani C Gr XINOMAVRO-based POP on Mt Olympus – the (dr) Nectar the gods feasted on. DOUGOS is leader. Softer than NAOUSSA.

Retsina New-wave Retsinas (GAIA, KECHRIS, natural-style Kamara) have freshness, character – impeccable food wine, great alternative to Fino Sherry. If you don't mind oak flavours, why not pine?

Samos Aeg ★★→★★★ (POP) Island famed for benchmark sweet MUSCAT BL. Main producer is co-op; fortified Anthemis and sun-dried Nectar are steals. New producers emerging: Kostaki, Nopera, producing mainly dry wines.

Santorini Aeg ★★★→★★★★ Dramatic, windy volcanic island with white (dr/sw) wines to match, from century-old gnarled vines. Luscious VINSANTO, salty, **bone-dry** Assyrtiko. Even with prices rising given huge tourism/land-grab pressure, cheapest ★★★★ whites around, age 20 yrs. Not a single average producer here.

Santo Wines Aeg ★★→★★★ Successful SANTORINI co-op. Kontarades, entry-level ASSYRTIKO a wonderful intro. Lovely veranda next to winery is place to be.

Sclavos Ion ★★★ Brilliant mind studying terroir of CEPHALONIA; bio. Master of MAVRODAPHNE: top Orgion ("orgies"), Sclavos ("slave"). Go figure...

Semeli C Gr, Pelop ★★ Vast range, gd value. Main focus on NEMEA (try Grand Res) and MANTINIA (esp Thea). Soft, approachable style.

VFM – Greek Style

With the notable exception of SANTORINI, Greece can offer some of the most surreal value for money in the world. Whites like creamy SAVATIANO, minty MALAGOUSIA or a bold ASSYRTIKO from the mainland can be a 3rd of the price of a moderately gd SANCERRE. AGIORGITIKO from NEMEA, XINOMAVRO from the n, or Liatiko and Kotsifali from Crete can be Cru Bourgeois quality (not style) but Bx Supérieur (*see* France) in price.

> **The fall, the rise and the fall of the pinkies**
> When Greeks decided to move upmarket with bottled wine in the 90s, the pink stuff was for the old guys. Then, in 2015 or so, Provence-style rosés became all the rage, and producers rushed to make more of it. In the past 3 yrs, consumers have gone off it, leaving vast surpluses in cellars and restaurant fridges. A shame, because these wines are better than ever. Try rosés from AGIORGITIKO (velvety), XINOMAVRO (crisper), MERLOT (pure fruit), SYRAH (structured). Some blend in MALAGOUSIA for aromatic lift.

Sigalas Aeg ★★★★ Original winery of Paris S, now in v. able hands of KIR-YIANNI. Kavalieros, Nychteri out of this world; marble-statue-like beauty in full range.

Silva Daskalaki Winery Crete ★★→★★★ Woman based in Heraklion, crafting bio Liatiko, VIDIANO with great sensitivity, depth, richness.

Skouras Pelop ★★★ Ever-evolving KTIMA. Lean, wild-yeast Salto MOSCHOFILERO. Megas Oenos a fine-boned classic. Try solera-aged Labyrinth, complex Peplo rosé. Recently invested in MANTINIA.

Tatsis Mac ★★★ Natural-movement leader in GOUMENISSA. Yes, wines might be cloudy and wild, but they're also defined and delicious.

Tetramythos Pelop ★★★ From the amazing terroir of Aigialia, a pillar of the natural-wine community. If you try only one of that kind, let it be this. Mavro Kalavritino (r) smells like the surrounding hills on a summer's day.

Theopetra Thess ★★ Tsililis family makes one of greatest Tsipouros brandies in Greece, but do not miss the wines. Copybook expressions of the varieties used, full of fruit, clarity.

Thimiopoulos Mac ★★★★ Superstar producer in NAOUSSA and RAPSANI (Terra Petra). XINOMAVRO at most delicious best. Single-vyd range is breathtaking, can shame Barolos, esp ultra-focused Kaiafas.

T-Oinos Aeg ★★★★ From Tinos island, what many consider Greece's finest. ASSYRTIKO and MAVROTRAGANO, beyond bold and of epic proportions, with prices to match, esp Rare. Stéphane Derenoncourt (*see* France) consults.

Tour Melas, La C Gr ★★★★ Top-drawer KTIMA in Achinos. Idylle rosé rules the market. Convincingly Médoc-like La Tour Melas and Palies Rizes both top, with eye-popping prices. Amazing B&B.

Troupis Pelop ★★ Redefining MOSCHOFILERO: Hoof & Lur is natural style, but old-style natural, not hipster. Delicious.

Tselepos Pelop ★★★ Leader in MANTINIA, NEMEA (Driopi) and SANTORINI (Canava Chrysou). Not a dull wine. Don't forgo CAB SAUV, MERLOT, velvety masterpieces.

Vassaltis Aeg ★★★ Small establishment in SANTORINI. Quirky Plethora lives where Santorini and Amontillado meet.

Vinsanto Aeg ★★★★ Sun-dried, cask-aged luscious but highly acidic ASSYRTIKO and Aidani from SANTORINI that can age forever. Insanely low yields. DOA (Drink Oldest Available).

Volcanic Slopes (Pure) Aeg ★★★★ Single-wine winery, tiny, sister project to ARGYROS. Pure: Greek wine at v. finest, crystalline clarity, dazzling structure; v. rare.

Voyatzis, Ktima Mac ★★ Long-standing but now ex-winemaker of BOUTARI, back in his home base, in Velventos. Quiet-genius stuff here. Spicy, herby Tsapournakos grown here, thought to be a rare variety, turns out to be CAB FR.

Vriniotis C Gr ★★ At the n tip of Evia, Konstantinos V specializes in Vradiano grape (rich, MOURVÈDRE-like), Wild Fermentation labels (ASSYRTIKO is exotic but steely).

Wine Art (Techni Oinou) Mac ★★ Family venture in Drama, making significant strides in popularity, with fresh, crisp Plano ASSYRTIKO and MALAGOUSIA.

Zafeirakis Thess ★★★ Carrying the LIMNIONA flag with grace. Several versions of this amazing red grape, rather burgundian in style. Try Young Vines for 1st taste.

Eastern Mediterranean, North Africa & Eastern Levant

EASTERN MEDITERRANEAN

It has been a violent year in the Levant. Wineries have been in the front line. Wine folk are peaceful types who just want to grow wine and spread a little joy. Let's hope the winemakers of the region can hold hands, spread the goodwill and shed light where there is darkness.

CYPRUS

For a country that is on the edge of being too hot and dry to grow grapes well, recent extreme weather has been a real challenge – giving problems with pollinations and yield. Increased emphasis on the benefits of altitude (vyds up to 1500m/4921ft) can be seen through a new club called Vines Above Clouds, for owners of vyds over 800m (2625ft). It seems local drinkers are finally appreciating local wineries and indigenous varieties – a gradual but real switch that helps support the ancient vines on this phylloxera-free island.

Oldest known perfume in world found on Cyprus, made around 4000 years ago.

Aes Ambelis ★→★★ Family winery for sound varietals. Try floral/spicy Morokanella, more trad fortified COMMANDARIA.

Argyrides Winery ★★→★★★ Stunning 5th-generation winery in 200-yr-old house, run by one of Cyprus's few women winemaker-owners. Standard-setting *Maratheftiko*, plus v.gd VIOGNIER, MERLOT/CAB SAUV, MOURVÈDRE.

Commandaria Rich, sweet PDO; sun-dried XYNISTERI and/or MAVRO; mentioned by Hesiod in 800 BCE, may be oldest wine in continuous production. Try modern unfortified versions from small producers: *Kyperounda, Tsiakkas, Zambartas*. More trad fortifieds: AES AMBELIS, St Barnabas (KAMANTERENA), St John (KEO).

Constantinou ★→★★ Family winery; dry reds, esp SHIRAZ, best.

Ezousa ★→★★ Small winery focussing on terroir wines, gd XYNISTERI.

Kamanterena (SODAP) ★ Was a co-op. Recently re-opened for v. limited production.

KEO ★ Large drinks group and brewer with winery; trad-style St John COMMANDARIA.

Kyperounda ★★→★★★ *Petritis* showcases ageability of XYNISTERI; terroir releases from East and West vyds. Entry-level Andessitis (r), new easy-drinking MARATHEFTIKO. Excellent own-vyd *Epos* (W, CHARD; r, CAB SAUV, SYRAH). Modern COMMANDARIA.

Makarounas ★★ Promising young organic winery with experimental approach. Try zesty Vasilissa, Promara from amphora, juicy Yiannoudi.

Tsiakkas ★★→★★★ Exemplary, high vyds, organic, focus on local grapes. Try (w) *Promara*, XYNISTERI, elegant Exelixis; (r) v.gd Vamvakada (aka MARATHEFTIKO); fine Mouklas MAVRO; excellent *Yiannoudi*; new red flagship Anagennisis blend of local varieties. Fantastic, fruity, modern COMMANDARIA.

Vasilikon, K&K Winery ★★ Family winery; consistent XYNISTERI, juicy Ayios Onoufrios (r), long-lived Methy. New Xynisteri, floral Vasilissa, complex LEFKADA.

Vlassides ★★→★★★ Family winery, quality pioneer, famous for SHIRAZ. New emphasis on local varieties, esp excellent Alátes XYNISTERI, *Óroman* based on Yiannoudi. Winery flagship is Artion, entry point is fruit-driven Grifos range.

Vouni Panayia ★→★★ Family winery all about local grapes, limited batches: Alina XYNISTERI, MARATHEFTIKO, Morokanella, Promara, Spourtiko.

Zambartas ★★→★★★ Family winery, Australia-trained winemaker-owner. Single-vyd range v.gd: Margelina (100-yr vines), XYNISTERI, Promara, top SHIRAZ/LEFKADA, Not Orange rosé MARATHEFTIKO. Superb long-aged Melusine COMMANDARIA.

ISRAEL

The vyds and wineries of N Israel have been under attack for over 12 mths; 40% of Israeli wine is in the Galilee and Golan. Though vyds were lost, they managed to harvest in 2024 and bravely continued the winemaking cycle.

Deep-sea Canaanite shipwreck discovered 2024, with intact amphorae, 3300 yrs old.

1848 ★★ Family vintners since 1848. Juicy SYRAH, v.gd CAB FR, plush Argaman.

Abaya ★★ Natural *terroiriste*. Complex to gluggable CARIGNANS. Funky COLOMBARD.

Agur ★★★ Rejuvenated. Edgy, well-crafted wines with tone, texture.

Ahat ★★ Quality *garagiste*. Superb CHENIN BL, complex ROUSSANNE/VIOGNIER, rosé.

Barkan ★→★★ Giant owned by largest brewery. Platinum sturdy CAB SAUV. Cherryberry Argaman. Gold popular label. Segal Whole Cluster SYRAH.

Carmel ★→★★ Historic, est by Rothschild 1882. Largest winery. Big brands: Selected, Private Collection. Top wines: Carmel Signature series.

Castel, Dom du Jud ★★★★ Great consistency at highest level over three decades. Pioneer of Judean Hills. Prestige Grand Vin always delivers. "C" Blanc (CHARD) ages beautifully. Petit Castel great value. Persistent rosé. La Vie (r/w) entry level.

Clos de Gat ★★→★★★ Powerful SYRAH, MERLOT. Mid-price Harel label sweet spot.

Cremisan ★→★★ Palestinian winery. Monastery est 1885, pioneer of local varieties. Other Palestinian wines: Kassis promising vigneron. Philokalia natural, artisan.

Dalton ★→★★★ Galilee pioneer. English-Israeli family. Vibrant Majestic CARIGNAN, mouthfilling PETITE SIRAH, minerally CHENIN BL; gd Family Collection SHIRAZ.

Feldstein ★★★ Innovative. Wines with verve, freshness. Excellent CAB SAUV, ROUSSANNE, complex Gilgamesh, gd Dabouki.

Flam ★★★→★★★★ Flam bros offer style, quality. Beautiful Judean Hills vyd on ancient terraces. Elegant, age-worthy Bx blend Noble, classy CAB SAUV. Fruitforward SYRAH. Classico great value. Fragrant SAUV BL/CHARD. Crisp rosé.

Galil Mountain ★→★★★ Upper Galilee. Bold PETIT VERDOT; gd prestige Yiron.

Golan, Ch ★★→★★★ Geshem v.gd Med blends. Favourful SAUV BL with texture.

Gva'ot ★★→★★★ Fruity Bittuni. Flagship Masada has v.gd ageability.

Jezreel Valley ★→★★★ Excellent Argaman, CARIGNAN. Value Alfa. Flagship Icon.

Lahat ★★★ Rhône ranger. Focus on SYRAH, ROUSSANNE. Makes white like red and vice versa, uses amphorae. Charming GSM; ageable white.

Lewinsohn ★★★ Owner MW, creative winemaker. Garage de Papa: elegant CHARD, fragrant rosé, sensual SYRAH blend. Whole Cluster *Petite Sirah*, bursts with fruit.

Margalit ★★→★★★ Best with Bx varieties. White from CHARD with local variety.

Mia Luce ★★★ *Garagiste*. Vivid SYRAH, floral MARSELAN, crisp COLOMBARD.

Mika ★★ Steely white blend; crunchy GRENACHE; prestige Outback.

Odem Mountain ★→★★ High elevation in N Golan; gd Volcanic CHARD, CAB SAUV.

Oryah, Ya'acov ★★★ Creative artisan. Pioneer of orange wines. Always experimenting.

Pelter ★★ Popular brand. Light, fragrant SAUV BL, Matar ★→★★ kosher.

Pinto ★→★★ Desert wines. Lean CHENIN BL, CHARD. Spicy SHIRAZ.

Psagot ★→★★★ Fast-growing. Peak succulent Med blend; gd VIOGNIER.

Ramat Negev ★→★★ Desert pioneer. Neve Midbar (w), Ramon (r) gd.

Razi'el ★★★ Ben Zaken family (CASTEL). Gastro rosé; fine, focused Med blend. Handcrafted trad-method fizz. New ROUSSANNE/VIOGNIER.

Recanati ★★★ Complex old-vine CARIGNAN. Juicy SYRAH. Value Yasmin, Jonathan.

Sea Horse ★★→★★★ Idiosyncratic. Complex Antoine. Alluring Oz. Age-worthy Elul.

Shiloh ★★→★★★ Robust CAB SAUV; MERLOT. Honi v. drinkable. Prestige Mosaic.

Shvo ★★★ Non-interventionist, true vigneron. Super-rustic chewy red, rare Gershon SAUV BL, fresh BARBERA, characterful rosé.

Sphera ★★★★ Whites only. Intense cool-climate White Concept varietals. Well-defined First Page blend. Complex, rare White Signature (SEM), gd for ageing. Delicate, rare trad-method fizz.

Tabor ★→★★ Ecological vyds. Whites best, esp ROUSSANNE, SAUV BL; gd CHENIN BL.

Tel ★★ Exquisite RIES, fresh GRENACHE, herbaceous CAB FR from N Golan.

Teperberg ★→★★★ Legacy CAB FR, PETITE SIRAH excellent; v. drinkable GSM.

Tulip ★★ Works with adults with special needs; gd SYRAH, SAUV BL. Maia, Med style.

Tura ★→★★ Central Mtns. Full-flavoured Mountain Peak, fleshy MERLOT.

Tzora ★★★★ MW leader in white awakening and terroir-led, precision winemaking. Beautiful high-altitude Shoresh vyd. Intensity, balance, elegance. Fine, mineral Shoresh Bl; Judean Hills (r/w) top value. Graceful Misty Hills (CAB SAUV/SYRAH).

UnderDog Rising star. Mineral SEM; crisp rosé; quaffable Snunit (r).

Vitkin ★★→★★★★ ABC icebreaker. Quality CARIGNAN pioneer. Quality PETITE SIRAH. Floral PINOT N. Crunchy GRENACHE. Value entry-level (r/w/rosé).

Vortman ★★ Passionate vigneron; N Coastal; v.gd COLOMBARD, CARIGNAN.

Yarden-Golan Heights ★★→★★★★ Cutting-edge viticulture. Consistency over decades. Approachable Hermon, gd QPR Gamla, premier Yarden, prestige Katzrin. New, edgy Lava.

Yatir ★★★→★★★★ Desert winery, forest vyds. Beguiling Med blend. Velvet prestige Yatir Forest (r). Value Mt Amasa. Less expensive Darom.

LEBANON

More ultra-boutique winemakers emerge. They work at v. high altitudes (2000m/6562ft+) using native Asmi N, Aswad Karesh, Jouzani, Marini, Meksassi, Merwah and Obeideh grapes, complementing "heritage" Rhône varieties CARIGNAN, CINSAULT and GRENACHE – challenging the perception of international blends as the typical Lebanese style – along with crisp, elegant CHARD, SAUV BL, VIOGNIER.

Wines from Byblos, esp Bybline, were considered Grand Cru of ancient world.

Coteaux du Liban ★★ CINSAULT blend and varietal crunchy rosé, plus old-vine Cinsault, Obeideh, VIOGNIER varietals. Young, dynamic winemaking couple. Look for Ayn range developed for export markets.

Couvent Rouge ★★★ Remote, E Bekaa winery dedicated to swapping cannabis fields for vyds. Range of easy-drinkers (r/w/rosé), posher oaked VIOGNIER, SYRAH, plus fun white and rosé pét-nat, both with local Obeideh.

Heritage, Ch Hefty Family Res CAB SAUV/SYRAH; Plaisir du Vin; nine-variety, Cinsault-led blend Nine. Plus SAUV BL, VIOGNIER, MUSCAT Blanc de Blancs.

Ixsir ★★→★★★ High vyds across Lebanon; stony SYRAH-based blends, floral whites and prestige El red. The Altitudes range and Grande Res Rosé excellent. Cemented Batroun's status as Lebanon's 2nd region.

Karam Wines ★★★ Family-run; S Lebanon's 1st winery. Extensive range: Meksassi (w), ALBARIÑO; SEM/SAUV BL/VIOGNIER Cloud 9 a bestseller. Value Maison (r), TOURIGA N. CAB/SYRAH/MERLOT St John more polished.

Kefraya, Ch ★★→★★★★ Innovative; long-serving French winemaker. Les Exceptions varietals; Aswad Karesh (r), SAPERAVI in amphorae; complex *Comte de M*, oaky Comtesse de Blancs, famous Blanc de Blancs, easy-drinking Les Breteches (r/w/rosé).

Ksara, Ch ★★★→★★★★★ Icons: Ch and Res du Couvent (est 1857). More innovative now: old-vine CARIGNAN, Merwah. Consistent, v.gd value. Blanc de Blancs, outstanding CHARD. Sunset "adult" rosé. Superb Cuveé du Printemps (r). Back catalogue to rival Ch MUSAR.

Marsyas, Ch ★★★ Powerful flagship CAB/SYRAH, thrilling CHARD/SAUV BL. Diffusion range B-Qa de Marsyas. Satyr range (no-oak Cab, Sauv Bl). Owns complex ★★★ Dom Bargylus, Syria, miracle wines, age-worthy (esp Bargylus w, Jabal r).

Massaya ★★ Terraces de Baalbeck: refined GSM. Entry-level Les Colombiers v.gd value. Cap Est (r) from E Bekaa vyds on Anti-Lebanon Mtns. Punchy rosé, elegant white from high altitude in 2nd winery in Mt Lebanon. Ramzi Ghosn, owner-winemaker with high-profile Châteauneuf and St-Émilion partners.

Mersel Natural wines and pét-nat; reviving ancient Jouzani, Marini, plus Merwah, Obeideh, often in amphorae; CINSAULT. Winery is also incubator for at least three micro-producers: Dar Richi, Heya, Love Letter. Destined for cult status.

Cinsault, Carignan, Grenache brought to Bekaa V from Algeria by Jesuits in 1850s.

Musar, Ch ★★★→★★★★ 02 03 05' 10 11 12 13 14 15 16 17 *Unique recognizable style*. Best after 15–20 yrs in bottle. Flagship red still most famous, but Obeideh/ Merwah (w) arguably more interesting; ages indefinitely. Second label: Hochar (r) now higher profile. Musar Jeune is softer, easy-drinking.

Oumsiyat, Ch Mt Lebanon winery; no-nonsense, easy-drinking Bx/Rhône blends and varietals; also ASSYRTIKO, Obeidy [sic].

St Thomas, Ch ★→★★★ Old Bekaa arak producers and grape farmers. Les Gourmets "cadet" range of red (aromatic CINSAULT), white, rosé. Textured Obaidy [sic] and muscular, high-altitude PINOT N. Vintage "Chateau" wines ageing well.

Sept ★★★ Pioneer *garagiste* winemaker, former rugby league player. Skin-contact Merwah, Obeideh; min-contact varietals VIOGNIER, GRENACHE, haunting SYRAH.

Tourelles, Dom des ★★→★★★★ Winery (C19) now run by French-trained Faouzi Issa. Blockbuster SYRAH, gd Marquis des Beys (r/w). Outstanding old-vine CARIGNAN, CINSAULT, Obeideh/Merwah, skin-contact Merwah; top classic range (r/w/rosé).

Vignes du Marje, Les New to S Lebanon, on sea-facing 800m (2625ft) slopes. Five wines (r/w/rosé) from SAUV BL, VIOGNIER, CAB, MERLOT, SYRAH, TEMPRANILLO.

Wardy, Dom ★★ Varietal pioneer: SAUV BL, VIOGNIER, CINSAULT, Obeideh. Also trad French blends, incl outstanding, easy-drinking red. J-B Soula consults.

TURKEY

New emphasis to preserve indigenous varieties and protect old vines. A country with unlimited potential, where the authorities make it so difficult.

Buzbag ★ Main brand since 40s. Rustic ÖKÜZGÖZÜ/BOĞAZKERE (Kayra). Better now.

Chamlija ★★→★★★★ Reviving aromatic Papaskarasi grape; v.gd CABS SAUV/FR.

Corvus ★→★★ Bozcaada island. Intense, oaky New World style.

Doluca ★→★★ Three generations. Villa Doluca gd value. Sarafin noble varieties.

Kalpak ★★→★★★★ Deep, rich, full-bodied Bx blends; min intervention.

Kavaklidere ★→★★★ Largest winery. Elegant Pendore Harmonie. Rich ÖKÜZGÖZÜ.

Kayra ★→★★ Plush ÖKÜZGÖZÜ, tannic BOĞAZKERE. Fresh NARINCE. Diageo-owned.

Likya ★→★★ Revives lost varieties, vibrant Fersun; gd PINOT N.

Pasaeli ★→★★ Innovative champion of local varieties. Cherry-berry Karasakiz.

Sevilen ★→★★ Large winery offering value; SAUV BL, SYRAH best.

Suvla ★→★★ Full-bodied Bx blend Sur; fruity SYRAH backed by oak.

Urla ★★ Big-spend winery. NERO D'AVOLA/Karasi is concentrated, spicy.

Notable names in North Africa & Eastern Levant
Jordan Zumot (Saint George). **Morocco** Amal, ★★ Baccari (Première de Baccari), Castel Group, ★ Celliers de Meknès (Ch Roslane), La Ferme Rouge, ★→★★ Ouled Thaleb (*Tandem/Syrocco*), ★→★★ Val d'Argan (Orian r), Zouina. **Syria** ★★★ *Bargylus*. **Tunisia** Neferis.

Asia & Black Sea & Caucasus

ASIA

China Ningxia, the "Bordeaux of China", would rather forget the 2024 vintage. Over 20 continuous days in Sept it was deluged by 160mm (6in) of rain. (Annual average rainfall is less than 200mm/8in.) The vyds of nw Gansu Province had much the same. Meanwhile Xiangning County, Shanxi, produced one of the best vintages since 2013. China continues courtship with PETIT MANSENG: it delivers aromatics, intense fruit and gravity-defying acidity. Usually sweet, but innovative wineries are turning out medium, even dry expressions. It is a natural partner with spicy mala Szechuan food, the most popular cuisine with China's 1.4 billion population. Taila Winery's Vendange Tardive is gd; also Dom Franco Chinois and Longting, and Lafite's Dom de Long Dai planted Petit Manseng plus CHENIN BL, CHARD in 2024; RIES also performs well, incl Ningxia's Dom du 1er Juin and Xinjiang's Silk Road. China's best unoaked Chard is Jiabeilan Baby Feet by multi-award-winning winemaker Zhang Jing. Pernod Ricard's Helan Mtn Res, while oaked, is fine and elegant.

China has three times as much land under vine as Australia.

As for red Bx blends, Long Dai commands eye-watering prices, as does Ao Yun from Moët-Hennessy. China's own Jiabeilan Res is as gd. Also try Grace Vyd, Kanaan Winery, Li Family, Rongzi, Silver Heights, Tiansai and Xige Estate. CoPower Jade Fei Tswei and Ch Chanson make excellent CAB FR. As for MARSELAN, the best are unoaked. Jiabeilan Baby Feet is pristinely fruit-driven; Ch Kings, Jade Vyd, Tiansai also worthy; Ch Rongzi produces a head-turning Amarone-style red (see Italy).

Koshu grapes often have paper hats over each bunch: keeps rain off.

India Most of the wine drunk in India is local, and imported wine is heavily taxed, but it's still a relatively small industry. Rich reds are the local taste: the climate might not suit that style, but the air-con does. Quality continues to improve. Sula Vyds is the biggest and has a tourist-friendly winery in Nashik: try Dindori Res, The Source GRENACHE Rosé, oaked SAUV BL. Also try Fratelli, Grover Zamper (Bx styles), KRSMA, M/S Akluj, Vallonné, plus Chandon and York fizz. Main regions: Andhra Pradesh, Karnataka, Maharashtra states.

Japan Renowned for its ski fields, Hokkaido has added PINOT N to its attractions. The De Montille (see France) & Hokkaido Project has planted some 10 ha of Pinot N and CHARD and released a promising inaugural 23 Pinot. Camel Farm continues to dazzle with BLAUFRÄNKISCH. Over in Yamanashi, Keiichi Shiina's return (after 16 yrs at Ch Lagrange, Bx) to Suntory has been a game-changer; he has produced the best Bx blend since Japanese winemaking began some 150 yrs ago. Called Tomi No Oka, the 21 is excellent and the 23 even better. Japan's finest bottle-fermented fizz remains Grace Blanc de Blancs Chard. Yamanashi-based Grace is also the benchmark for KOSHU, from screwcap entry-level to single-vyd Cuvée Misawa (1st subregional Koshu, from Akeno). Best Koshu are without oak or have just a pinch of wood: Aruga Branca, Ch Mars, Dom Hide, Haramo, Huggy Wine, Kurambon, L'Orient, Lumiere, Manns Wines, Marquis, Morita Koshu Winery, Sanwa Shurui, Soryu and Suntory's single-vyd Tomi No Oka.

BLACK SEA & CAUCASUS

Ukraine mourns significant losses caused by the war, but wine production continues, including new investments. The Caucasus countries, while clinging to their millennia-old wine heritage, are starting to diverge. Georgia and Armenia prioritize their local grape varieties. The wines – made with long skin macerations and vinified in amphorae – find international success among niche wine drinkers and millennials. Azerbaijan, known for brandy, is unexpectedly embracing Italian grapes. Moldova delivers value-driven wines, striving for a higher level. Uzbekistan and Kazakhstan have their own tiny production.

Armenia Shares with Georgia the ancient trad of using amphorae, known here as *karas*. Red Areni is the signature grape, among 31 native grapes cultivated; others incl (w) Voskeat, (r) Akhtanak, Karmrahyut. Phylloxera-free vyds at high altitude up to 1800m (5906ft) are common. Try Armenia Wine and Hin Areni, or boutique ArmAs, Frunz, Keush (sp), Noa, Old Bridge, Tushpa, Van Ardi, Voskeni, Voskevaz, v.gd Zorah. The brandy is also gd.

Georgia Proudly holds *qvevri* as its contribution to world winemaking. Buried in the ground, enormous clay vessels are used for skin-macerated fermentation and ageing of whites and reds. The practice has continued unbroken for 8000 yrs: new experiments involve temp control, different sizes and rosé wines. Ancient methods co-exist with modern production. Of 500 indigenous varieties, around 40 are in commercial use. Acidic white RKATSITELI is most common: it has prompted the phenomenon of orange/amber wines. Red star SAPERAVI is great in full-bodied, tannic, age-worthy wines. White Chinuri, Kisi, Mtsvane of note. Kakheti region is the powerhouse for production; Kartli is on the rise. Better known names: Badagoni, Ch Mukhrani, Jakeli, Khareba, Marani, Papari V, Shumi Winery, Tbilvino, Teliani V, Tsinandali Estate, Vazisubani Estate.

Moldova Neighbouring Ukraine and Romania, Moldova has more vyds than S Africa. Backed by long history and fame in tsarist Russia, it now makes approachable wines offering value at all price levels. International grapes dominate, but worth seeking local: (w) FETEASCĂS ALBĂ/REGALĂ, Viorica, (r) FETEASCĂ NEAGRĂ, Rară Neagră. Try unusual red blend Negru de Purcari (CAB SAUV/SAPERAVI/Rară Neagră) and Icewine. Leading producers: Cricova (sp), Mileştii Mici, Purcari Winery, both with great limestone cellars. Also try Asconi, Castel Mimi, Ch Vartely, Et Cetera, Fautor, Gitana, Lion Gri, Vinăria Bostavan, Vinăria din Vale.

Russia Russian wine must comprise one-fifth of restaurant wine lists, but the choices are limited. Natural conditions best in sw by Black Sea and River Kuban. Harsh climate in Don V requires vines to be buried in winter. Reds better than whites. Indigenous tannic Krasnostop has est itself as the signature red grape, also Sibirkovy (w) and Tsimliansky (w) can be gd. Most winemaking is about international grapes, esp Aligoté, Chard, Ries and red Bx varieties. At the time of writing, Russia is under international sanctions.

Ukraine Only half of the pre-war 46,000 ha of vyds are in use, others destroyed or mined. Stretching from the Black Sea to Carpathian Mtns and Kyiv, winemaking is concentrated in Odesa and Zakarpattia. Local Odesa Black of note, otherwise mostly international and Georgian grapes. Russian-invaded Crimea accounts for premium wines, esp Oleg Repin, Uppa Winery. Thanks to climate change, new vyds in n. Try Beykush Winery, Big Wines (est during war), Bolgrad, Esse, Guliev Wines, *Kolonist*, Stoic, Satera, Shabo, Veles, Villa Tinta. Fizz has important heritage: ArtWinery, Novy Svet, Odessavinprom, Zolotaya Balka. Historic fortified styles have niche too: Ch Chizay, Koktebel, Massandra, Solnechnaya Dolina.

United States

NORTH COAST
BRITISH COLUMBIA
WASHINGTON
OREGON
IDAHO
NEVADA
CALIFORNIA
COLORADO
ARIZONA
NEW MEXICO
BAJA CALIFORNIA
CANADA
ONTARIO
USA
MISSOURI
OKLAHOMA
TEXAS
MEXICO
WISCONSIN
MICHIGAN
OHIO
NOVA SCOTIA
VERMONT
MASSACHUSETTS
RHODE ISLAND
NEW YORK
NEW JERSEY
PENNSYLVANIA
MARYLAND
VIRGINIA
NORTH CAROLINA
GEORGIA

Mendocino Sierra Foothills
Redwood Valley
Anderson Valley
Clear Lake
Clear Lake
Sonoma Coast
Northern Sonoma
Sonoma Valley
Napa Valley
Carneros
Coombsville/Oak Knoll
Clarksburg
Sacramento
Lodi
El Dorado
Shenandoah Valley
Amador
Calaveras
Sacramento
Lake Tahoe
NEVADA
San Francisco
Livermore Valley
Santa Clara Valley
Santa Cruz Mountains
Monterey
Salinas
CENTRAL VALLEY
San Joaquin
Fresno
Carmel Valley
Santa Lucia Highlands
Arroyo Seco
San Lucas
CENTRAL COAST
Pacific Ocean
Paso Robles
CALIFORNIA
San Luis Obispo
Edna Valley/Arroyo Grande Valley
Santa Maria Valley
Santa Barbara
Sta Rita Hills
Santa Ynez Valley
Santa Barbara
Los Angeles

Abbreviations used in the text (*see also* principal viticultural areas pp.264, 286, 294):

Arroyo GV	Arroyo Grande Valley, CA
Clark	Clarksburg, CA
Coomb	Coombsville, CA
H Can	Happy Canyon, CA
Mad	Madera, CA
Oak K	Oak Knoll, CA
PNW	Pacific Northwest, CA
San LO	San Luis Obispo, CA
Santa Cz Mts	Santa Cruz Mountains, CA
Son	Sonoma, CA
Tem	Temecula, CA

Where is US wine going now? In every possible direction, is the answer. In California, the engine of US wine, sales are down, quite dramatically. In the east, and perhaps in California too, drinkers and growers are looking anew at hybrids, those crossings of vinifera and native American vines regarded since phylloxera as inferior to, you know, real vinifera. But around the world there's a willingness to move away from traditional flavours: orange wines, new ciders, wines that blend grapes with other fruit; so why not Chambourcin, Marquette and Catawba? Lovers of Pinot Noir, Syrah and the Cabernets might think of several reasons why not; and the quality of these, and other "noble" varieties, is superb – better than ever. Regional characteristics, from Oregon to Sonoma, add interest; and there's good value to be found too.

American Viticultural Areas

With no production rules or trad to protect, AVAs are only loosely comparable to appellations contrôlées. Administered by the US government's TTB, they are instead guides to location – and climate, soil, market – and are a wine-minded alternative to state or county labels. Whether a region within a state or a traits-based overlap such as high-toned Columbia Gorge shared by WA and OR, or NY, PA, OH's cool, water-tempered Lake Erie, there are 276 est AVAs – and a steady queue of applied and pending. Most (154) are in CA, which boasts a wealth of nested AVA subregions, some hyperfocused, like Napa V's Stags Leap District. While an AVA label indicates a min higher standard at the federal level (state and county labels mean min 75% provenance, AVA promises min 85%), some have stricter rules: OR famously demands 100% for state labels, 95% for its AVAs. The AVA approval standards are rigorous: petitions must show distinguishing features verifiable on US Geological Survey maps, and how they affect viticulture inside vs outside the petitioned zone – whose proposed name must be one historically applied to the area. The TTB says AVAs allow "producers to better describe the origin of their wines and... consumers to better identify wines". Some even translate to higher prices.

Arizona (AZ)

High-desert climate allows gd ripening: Sonoita and Verde V limestone-based; Willcox volcanic-based. Best varieties: Iberian, Med, Bx; MALVASIA leads white. Wineries: **Arizona Stronghold** ★★★ two ranges, everyday Provisioner, top Arizona Stronghold. Tuscan blend Mangus (r) v.gd. **Bodega Pierce** grown in Willcox AVA; Malvasia (w), PINOT N rosé. **Caduceus Cellars** ★★★ consistent quality leader with Nagual del Sensei SAGRANTINO top; also v.gd Dos Ladrones (w), Primer Paso (r). Owned, along with sibling winery MERKIN VYDS, by musician Maynard James Keenan. **Callaghan Vyds** ★★★ excellent Iberian and Bx styles; flagship Caitlin's PETIT VERDOT/CAB SAUV (r), La Osa TANNAT/Cab Sauv (r). **Ch Tumbleweed** ★★ old vyds; single-vyd Cimarron Vyd MONTEPULCIANO and Deep Sky Vyd MALBEC stand out. **Cove Mesa Vyd** large range led by Malvasia (w). **Dos Cabezas WineWorks** emphasis on blends; La Montaña (r), Meskeoli (w). **Javelina Leap Vyd & Winery** SYRAH, TEMPRANILLO, ZIN signatures. **Merkin Vyds** ★★★ known for Chupacabra line. **Page Springs Cellars** Rhône specialist, esp Syrah Clone series and single-vyd ROUSSANNE. **Pillsbury Wine Company** ★★ owned by film-maker Sam Pillsbury; estate-grown, wild-yeast Rhône varieties; SHIRAZ-based Guns and Kisses (r). **Rune Wines** low-intervention winemaking, mainly Rhône varieties; graphic, illustrated labels. **Sand-Reckoner** ★★ dry aromatic Malvasia, rich Tempranillo.

California (CA)

Today, industry panic is over a steep decline in wine consumption (down 8% in the last year) among Americans, the chief consumers of CA wine. After four solid harvests in a row, now some grapes are going unpicked for lack of demand. It's a demand problem that Europe has been coping with for a while. If you're a home winemaker who knows a grower, you could probably dial your neighbour up and pick some grapes for your home brew for free. It has been decades since that was the case. Vineyard land is currently overpriced in CA, and wine is considered more of an aspirational luxury here than an everyday dinner accompaniment, the way it is in France, Spain, or Italy. Maybe CA winemakers overcomplicate wine production to justify a higher price tag. An intersting tale (pun intended) often wags the dog to justify an overpriced product. The natural-wine corner of the business continues to churn out half-competent weirdness that alternately embraces and alienates large younger cohorts, who are increasingly wine-shy. What seems to be missing is simple, honest, affordable, well-made wine for younger consumers. In conditions of oversupply there may be savvy winemakers who can step in and develop the next-gen "Two Buck Chuck" that revives populist interest in CA wine. Those who still appreciate gd wine will enjoy some really gd deals in the next few yrs. Same for winemakers with an opportunistic production plan. Let's hope those latter two meet in the middle.

Recent vintages

CA is too diverse for simple summaries. There can certainly be differences between the N, Central and S thirds of the state, but no "bad" vintages in over a decade. Recent relief from drought and autumn fires is welcome indeed.

2024 Classic; v. warm summer buffeted by moderate spring/autumn with compacted, frenetic harvest.

2023 Light crop, but v. high quality after long, cool season. Late, great harvest.

2022 Spring frosts = smaller crop; state-wide Sept heatwave not ideal, but expect concentration, high quality.

2021 Small crop but high quality; v. impressive wines emerging across board.

2020 Small crop: great whites. Fire issues, but some early picked wines v.gd.

2019 Solid harvest. Minor late losses in Alex V to fires, smoke taint.

2018 Bumper crop of great quality, but smoke issues in Lake County.

2017 Wildfires in Napa, Son after most grapes picked; quality mostly v.gd.

2016 Gd quality: reds/whites show great freshness, charm.

Principal viticultural areas

There are well over 100 AVAs in CA. Below are the key players.

Alexander Valley (Alex V) Son. Warm region in upper Son. Best known for gd Zin, Cab Sauv on hillsides.

Amador County (Am Co) Warm Sierra County with wealth of old-vine Zin; Rhône grapes also flourish.

Anderson Valley (And V) Mend. Pacific fog and winds follow Navarro River inland. Superb Pinot N, Chard, sparkling, v.gd Ries, Gewurz, some stellar Syrah.

Atlas Peak E Napa. Exceptional Cab Sauv, Merlot.

Calistoga (Cal) Warmer n end of Napa V. Red-wine territory esp Cab Sauv.

Carneros (Car) Napa, Son. Cool AVA at n tip of SF Bay; gd Pinot N, Chard; Merlot, Syrah, Cab Sauv on warmer sites, v.gd sparkling.

Coombsville (Coomb) Napa. Cool region nr SF Bay; top Cab Sauv in Bx style.

Diamond Mountain Napa. High-elevation vines, outstanding Cab Sauv.

Dry Creek Valley (Dry CV) Son. Top Zin, gd Sauv Bl; gd hillside Cab Sauv, Zin.

Edna Valley (Edna V) San LO. Cool Pacific winds; v.gd Chard.

El Dorado County (El Dor Co) High-altitude inland area surrounding Placerville. Some real talent emerging with Rhône grapes, Zin, Cab and more.

Howell Mountain Napa. Briary Napa Cab Sauv from steep, volcanic hillsides.

Livermore Valley (Liv V) Suburban, gravelly, warm region e of SF, gd potential.

Mendocino County (Mend) Large county n of Son County, incl warm Red V and cool And V.

Mendocino Ridge (Mend Rdg) Emerging region in Mend, dictated by elevation over 365m (1198ft). Cool, above fog, lean soils.

Monterey County (Mont) Big ranches in Salinas V: affordable Chard, Pinot N in cool, windy conditions. Carmel V bit warmer, Arroyo Seco moderate.

Mount Veeder Napa. High mtn vyds for gd Chard, Cab Sauv.

Napa Valley Cab Sauv, Merlot, Cab Fr. Look to sub-AVAs for meaningful terroir-based wines, and mtn areas for most complex, age-worthy.

Oakville (Oak) Napa. Prime Cab Sauv territory on gravelly bench.

Paso Robles (P Rob) San LO. Popular with visitors. Reds: Rhône, Bx varieties.

Pritchard Hill (P Hill) E Napa. Elevated, woodsy, prime terrritory for Cab Sauv.

Red Hills of Lake County (R Hills) N extension of Mayacama range; great Cab Sauv country.

Redwood Valley (Red V) Mend. Warmer inland region; gd Zin, Cab Sauv, Sauv Bl.

Russian River Valley (RRV) Son. Pacific fog lingers; Pinot N, Chard, gd Zin on benchland.

Rutherford (Ruth) Napa. Outstanding Cab Sauv, esp hillside vyds.

Saint Helena (St H) Napa. Lovely balanced Cab Sauv.

Santa Barbara County (Santa B) County n of LA; transverse valleys, several notable subzones, cool and warm.

Santa Lucia Highlands (Santa LH) Mont. Higher elevation, s-facing hillsides, great Pinot N, Syrah, Rhônes.

Santa Maria Valley (Santa MV) Santa B. Coastal cool; gd Pinot N, Chard, Viognier.

Sta Rita Hills (Sta RH) Santa B. Excellent Pinot N.

Santa Ynez (Santa Ynz) Santa B. Rhônes (r/w), Chard, Sauv Bl best bet.

Sierra Foothills (Sierra Fhills) El Dor Co, Am Co, Calaveras County. All improving.

Sonoma Coast (Son Coast) A v. cool climate; edgy Pinot N, Chard, Syrah.

Sonoma Valley (Son V) Note Son V is area within Son County; gd Chard, v.gd Zin, excellent Cab Sauv from Son Mtn sub-AVA.

Spring Mountain Napa. Elevated Cab Sauv, complex soil mixes and exposures.

Stags Leap (Stags L) Napa. Classic red, black-fruited Cab Sauv; v.gd Merlot.

West Sonoma Coast (W Son Coast) Exceptionally cool, marine-influenced parts of Son Coast: Chard, Pinot N, Syrah.

Acorn RRV ★★→★★★ Preserving CA heritage making lively co-fermented field blends from historic Alegria vyd, featuring ZIN plus 17 other mixed black grapes.

Acumen Napa ★★★→★★★★ Pedigreed, hillside Atlas Peak Cabs (mostly) from volcanic terroir; winemaker Phillip Titus (CHAPPELLET). Not cheap, but legit, and age-worthy. I do love *Mountainside* SAUV BL, CAB SAUV.

Alban Edna V ★★★→★★★★ John A explored potential of Rhône varieties in CA's Central Coast in mid-80s, in Shangri-La moderate clime of EDNA V, s of P ROB. Handmade, low-intervention wines that occasionally go sideways, but more often are profound, distinctive, thrilling. Benchmark Reva SYRAH named for his mother.

Andrew Murray Vineyards Santa Y ★★★ SYRAH leads Rhône pack, but white VIOGNIER, ROUSSANNE, fresh GRENACHE BL hits too.

Anthill Farms Son Coast ★★★ Three hard-working WILLIAMS-SELYEM alumni: lively, ethereal cool-climate PINOT N, SYRAH, old-vine, head-trained CHARD from coastal SON COAST, AND V. Great-value And V Pinot N. Serious up-and-comer.

Aperture Son ★★★→★★★★ Winemaker Jesse Katz been on steep trajectory for two decades, now controls more land and facilities, finally his own brand. One to watch. Excellent Bx-inspired reds.

A Rafanelli Winery Dry CV ★★★→★★★★ Generations of family wisdom shows. Steadily producing superb ZIN-based reds in arguably ideal terroir for CA Zin.

Auteur Son V ★★★★ Ken Juhasz's articulate wines can tell stories. Try SON COAST CHARD, notably flinty, reductive burgundian style, hints of lemon, apricot. Constellation of star CHARD, PINOT N vyds up and down the coast, from Ferrington vyd (MEND) to Crown's Gap (Son Coast), all with sense of place. Definitely brand to watch; tasting room in Sonoma.

Aventure, L' P Rob ★★★→★★★★ Shifted from MERLOT-driven Bx blends to more Rhône-style blends in recent yrs. Chloé red blend, named after proprietor Stephan Asseo's daughter, stands out for freshness, vivaciousness. Terrific wines; visitors love relatively new tasting room.

Barnett Spring Mtn ★★★ Under-the-radar mtn-top gem managed by David Tate, who also makes CHARD, PINOT N from SON V. Screaming gd wines across board, towering views, plus 1st-rate NAPA V CAB SAUV – all well worth drive up mtn. Make an appt.

Fog line in Napa is c.427m (1400ft). Different climates below and above.

Barra Red V ★★★ Arguably no wine-growers more salt-of-the-earth than Charlie (RIP 2019) and Martha Barra. Family farms 50 acres of organic grapes in RED V and makes loveliest, most delicious, sun-kissed CA wines imaginable without an ounce of pretence. Second label Girasole (organic) source of great values.

Beaulieu Vineyard (BV) Napa V, Ruth ★★★→★★★★ Iconic Georges de Latour Private Res CAB SAUV is back on fine form; spin-off branded wines are serviceable down the line. Rebounding.

Beckmen Vineyards Santa B ★★★ Exceptional, Rhône-inspired; innovative family winery firmly committed to bio agriculture. Affordable, excellent Cuvée le Bec red blend popular nationwide.

Bedrock Wine Co Son V ★★★ Morgan Peterson's label, paean to historic ZIN vyds, old techniques. Wisdom of ages seen through clear young eyes and claret-style Zins.

Bella Union St H ★★★ NAPA off-shoot of FAR NIENTE now around a decade old; brand named after an old brothel-casino in Deadwood. Focus on younger generations with requisite Napa CAB SAUV, plus red/white blends at moderately high prices; ST H tasting-room fees bargain for area. It's all about gettin' younger sinners through the saloon doors...

Beringer Napa ★★→★★★★ Private Res CAB SAUV, single-vyd Cabs iconic, age-worthy artistically combining mtn and valley fruit. Historic ST H location well worth a visit. CHARD better than ever.

Berryessa Gap Winery Central V ★★→★★★ Refreshingly unpretentious, affordable spectrum of wines made by Nicole Salengo nr Winters in Yolo County. Mostly neutral oak, bright, sunny fruit, and great varietal character in BARBERA, PETITE SIRAH, TEMPRANILLO. Well worth trying. Also L'Apéro Les Trois apéritif wines infused with locally grown fruit.

Bevan Cellars N Coast ★★★★ Boutique brand (mostly sold by subscription) from Russell B, collector-turned-winemaker. Exceptional wines from select sites in NAPA, SON. Age-worthy Tin Box CAB SAUV (Napa V), Dry Stack SAUV BL (Bennet V, Son) exceptional nectar from an oddball Italian clone.

B Kosuge Wines Son ★★★ Ex-SAINTSBURY winemaker Byron K devotes himself to subtle, refined PINOT N from N Coast. SON COAST Pinot N, sublime, well priced. Meditative wines coming mostly from CAR and S Coast.

Blue Farm Son ★★★★ Anne Moller-Racke's next act, piloting PINOT N-driven project in SON from CAR to Fort Ross-Seaview – 1st-rate farming, 1st-rate wines, a few tasty whites on side.

Bogle Central V, Lodi ★★ Solid, under-$15, grocery-store, family-owned brand delivers ever-reliable varietal wines from Lodi, Clark and now more coastal zones, all aged in barriques without oak flavour additives. Respect!

Boisset Collection Napa V, Son ★★★ Ambitious portfolio of sustainably farmed estates and brands assembled by Burgundy-born *boulevardier* Jean-Charles Boisset (*see* France): historic BUENA VISTA, DELOACH, Lyeth, Wattle Creek (SON COUNTY); JCB and Raymond (NAPA V), excellent quality across board.

Bokisch Vineyards Lodi ★★★ Visionary champion of Iberian varieties in warm Lodi region; great TEMPRANILLO plus superb ALBARIÑO, GRACIANO, flirty Rosado.

Bond Oak ★★★★ Allocated, members-only, Oak-based exclusive affair owned by Bill H (HARLAN ESTATE). Excellent CAB SAUV. Recommended if you're looking to spend c.$900–1000 on a bottle of wine. Those determined to re-sell/speculate may be kicked off waiting list (though those rules may relax soon).

Bonny Doon Mont ★★★ You can't not love Randall Grahm, Willy Wonka envisioner of everything plausible in CA wine. Everything he makes is pretty gd. His art of the presentation is unmatched. Enthusiastically recommend his wonderful wines with ridiculous backstories.

Brewer-Clifton Santa B ★★★★ Steve B makes appreciably nerdy, cool-climate wines balancing locale's rich latitude with whole-cluster fermentation and no new oak. 3D CHARD is immersive.

Buena Vista Son V ★★→★★★★ Historic winery, est 1857, bedazzled by owner Jean-Charles BOISSET (DELOACH, Raymond Vyds) with period-costume tours, lights and animatronics straight outta Disneyland. Try The Count's Selection SYRAH.

Calera ★★★→★★★★ Josh Jensen sought limestone and altitude for PINOT N, CHARD on Mt Harlan. Sold to The Duckhorn Portfolio in 2017, wines still outstanding. Everyone should try epic Jensen Pinot N once in their life – represents CA wine history in a bottle and does not disappoint.

Carneros, Domaine Car ★★★→★★★★ Taittinger (*see* France) outpost, led by women (currently Remi Cohen), for decades executes one of best Blanc de Blancs sparkling in CA, Le Rêve. Other bubblies and PINOT N also superb.

Cattleya RRV ★★★★ Colombian-born Bibiana González Ravé, with mad CV making wine in Europe and US at 1st-tier wineries, stakes her own claim in CA with ultra-premium CHARD, PINOT N, SYRAH from N CA premium sites, coveted overseas even at high prices; 2nd-tier Alma de Cattleya wines also deliver resonant, unpretentious, bargain Pinot N; sublime Chard. Don't overlook.

Caymus Napa V ★★★ Popular NAPA status brand. Special Selection CAB SAUV, esp iconic, but on rich, sappy end of current style spectrum. Conundrum off-dry white blend deserves note for innovation.

Insurance cost for wine estates has quintupled. Risk of fire and/or smoke taint.

Chanin Wines Santa B, Sta RH ★★★ Low-input SANTA B winery making accurate, mineral CHARD, focused PINOT N and peppery, varietal SYRAH from Schlock Family vyd. Becoming influential.

Chappellet Napa V ★★★★ Rugged P HILL property has delivered savoury, age-worthy, madrone scrub-laced CAB SAUV for decades. Signature-series Cab Sauv is flat-out killer and beats any NAPA rival for value. Dry CHENIN BL, tangy treat if a bit spendy. Also owns formidable PINOT N, CHARD-themed Sonoma-Loeb brand.

Chimney Rock Stags L ★★★→★★★★ Latina winemaker Elizabeth Vianna elevated

> **Warmth suits whites**
> This might seem counterintuitive, but as warming increases, unfamiliar white wines might start showing up on your radar more often. Consider the Greek varieties ASSYRTIKO and MOSCHOFILERO, 1st vinified by New Clairvaux Monastery and Winery in CA, that have won best white wine in show at the California State Wine Competition for the last two consecutive yrs. St Amant, based in Lodi, produces a superb VERDELHO from SIERRA FHILLS for a bargain price. There should be more Assyrtiko planted in Central Valley. Also look to MASSICAN for a vivacious parade of lesser-known Italian varieties, often blended.

Terlato property to next level. Relatively affordable Elevage Bx blend glowing introduction to brand.

Cline Car Stalwart family operation delivers on affordable varietal offerings, with some exotic, old-vine, single-vyd ZIN and Rhône bottles. Eucalypt-inflected Small Berry MOURVÈDRE from Big Break vyd hyper-cool.

Constellation Brands ★→★★★ Publicly traded major wine/beer/spirits company owns famed ROBERT MONDAVI brand, Meiomi, The Prisoner, Woodbridge and many more inernational brands. Lately re-focusing on beer and cannabis products, but still a big dipper in the wine biz.

Continuum Napa V, St H ★★★★ Tim Mondavi est his bona fides with 2nd-generation, top-tier P HILL estate making impeccable CAB SAUV. Second label: Novicium, from younger vines.

Corison Napa V ★★★ Cathy C stays on course, producing elegant NAPA V CAB SAUV; was often an outlier but has proven her strength with ever-focused age-worthy Kronos vyd Cab Sauv.

Covenant Napa V ★★★ Professional wine-writer, saxophonist-turned-winemaker Jeff Morgan makes CA's best kosher wines (Hagafen also deserves shout-out), sourced from terrific sites in NAPA V, SON V and beyond.

Crema, La ★★→★★★ Mostly grocery-store CHARD, PINOT N label from JACKSON FAMILY worth noting as relatively high-quality value proposition, but brand becoming a bit scattered, sourcing from CA Central Coast, SON COAST, OR. Wines pretty gd for the money.

Cuvaison Car ★★★ Quiet historic property, making great wine yr after yr. Top marks to CHARD, PINOT N from CAR estate; gd CAB SAUV, SYRAH, from MT VEEDER. Single Block bottlings: lovely rosé, slinky, sexy Méthode Béton SAUV BL.

Dalla Valle Oak ★★★★ A 1st-rate hillside estate transitioning to 2nd generation. Maya CAB SAUV is legendary, eponymous Cab Sauv a cult wine, Dalle Valle Collina edition *the best* younger-vine, relatively affordable entry to luxury NAPA Cab. Get some.

Daou P Rob ★★★ Ambitious estate sold to Australia's Treasury Estates for whopping $900m price tag. Makes fine CAB SAUV from elevated w-side P ROB.

Dashe Cellars Dry CV, N Coast ★★★ RIDGE veteran Mike D makes tasteful, affordable and balanced DRY CV and ALEX V ZIN from urban winery in Alameda, CA. Terrific old-vine CARIGNANE, zesty GRENACHE rosé leaning natural, but sound.

Davis Bynum RRV ★★★ Acquisition by Rodney Strong proved fruitful for this RRV stalwart. Superb SAUV BL might even outshine fine CHARD, PINOT N.

DeLoach Winery Son ★★★ Flamboyant Jean-Charles BOISSET saw gd value in progressive organic, bio-oriented winery making great CHARD, PINOT N. Solid down-to-earth investment, if not his sexiest.

Denner P Rob ★★★ Well-farmed Templeton Gap estate making fine Rhône-inspired reds and more, acquired 2022 by E&J GALLO. Ditch Digger red blend a personal fave and a loose translation of my last name (*see* Contributors list).

Diamond Creek Napa V ★★★★ Extraordinary longevity of CAB SAUV from iconic sites like Volcanic Hill and Gravelly Meadow makes some of most coveted, collectable wines of NAPA V.

Dominus Estate Napa V ★★★★ Moueix-owned (*see* France). Herzog de Meuron-designed winery is epic, but not open to hoi polloi. Gravelly terroir in cool S NAPA is indisputably great. Second label: Napanook also great. You can buy the wine, but you can't pet the vines.

Drew Family And V, Mend ★★★→★★★★ A MEND RDG visionary making minimalist, savage PINOT N from AND V and higher up hills. Look for estate Field Selections Pinot N from Mend Rdg, SYRAH from coastal Valenti vyd. Hunt these down.

Dry Creek Vineyard Dry CV ★★★ Standard-bearer on its A-game. Trustworthy, Loire-inspired, grassy FUMÉ BL and other SAUV BL always delicious, CHENIN BL and all reds better than ever; great stop nr Healdsburg. What's not to love? ZIN/Bx-blend Mariner also better than ever.

Duckhorn Vineyards Napa V ★★★→★★★★ Crowd-pleasing, ultra-consistent CAB SAUV, MERLOT, incl legendary Three Palms vyd famed for MERLOT, gd SAUV BL. Second label Decoy hugely successful, excellent value. Bought recently by private equity firm Butterfly in a 2B deal. The Duckhorn Portfolio also owns CALERA, GOLDENEYE (AND V), KOSTA BROWNE, Migration brand (N Coast CHARD, PINOT N), SONOMA-CUTRER and Canvasback (WA).

Dunn Howell Mtn ★★★★ Hard-ass cowboy Randy D, famed for his likewise hard-ass, age-worthy wines that made HOWELL MTN famous, passed production torch to son Mike, who has tidied up some brett issues; 1st-class NAPA CAB SAUV to hold for long term. Epic potential. Watch.

Dutton-Goldfield RRV ★★★ Classical cool-climate CA CHARD, PINOT N from RRV-based powerhouse grower; not super-edgy or risky, maybe a gd thing.

Eberle P Rob ★★→★★★ Former Penn State footballer is literally a giant of Central Coast wine history and one of 1st to explore potential of SYRAH in P ROB. Dependable, classically proportioned wines.

Edmunds St John Sierra Fhills ★★★ Energy over power: motto of Berkeley *garagiste* Steve E. Bone-Jolly GAMAY (EL DOR CO) a perfect introduction.

Emeritus RRV ★★★→★★★★ Emergent estate, three home dry-farmed (!) vyds making focused, structured PINOT N under supervision of gifted winemaker Dave Lattin. Hallberg Ranch bottlings exquisite, singular in style.

Etude Car ★★★ Ever-trustworthy brand that always succeeded at making great CAB SAUV, PINOT N under same roof, using same attentive techniques. Now owned by TWE (*see* Australia), but legacy stays true. Pinot N Rosé to die for.

Far Niente Napa V ★★★→★★★★ Pioneer of generous CAB SAUV, CHARD. Hedonism with soul. Dolce: celebrated dessert wine. Also Nickel & Nickel single-vyd Cabs.

Farrell, Gary RRV ★★★ Namesake founder long gone, but wines still terrific despite a few ownership changes, much thanks to winemaker Theresa Heredia, Farrell's hand-picked successor. Basic RRV CHARD beams brightly, Hallberg and Fort Ross single-vyd PINOT N among top offerings.

Flowers Son Coast ★★★→★★★★ Pioneer next to Pacific now owned by Huneeus Vintners; CHARD, PINOT N remain great illustrations of that climate, elevation.

Foppiano Son ★★→★★★ Honest RRV wines loaded with sunny fruit and little pretence. Note PETITE SIRAH, SAUV BL.

Fort Ross Vineyard Son Coast ★★★ Dazzling high-elevation estate, a stone's throw from Pacific; zesty CHARD, terrific, savoury PINOT N, surprisingly gd PINOTAGE (!).

Foursight And V ★★★ Family operation making consistent PINOT N, a few whites and bubbly nr Boonville. Tireless promoters of region, and wines deliver. Zero New Oak Pinot N sees only used barrels.

Foxen Santa MV ★★★ Homey Foxen Canyon winery, founded 1985, with steady hand for PINOT N; try Block 8 from Bien Nacido Vyd. Intriguing, cool-climate Heritage SYRAH from home estate.

Freeman ★★★ A v. strong SON COAST CHARD, PINOT N contender delivering consistently delicious, elegant cool-climate coastal CA wines. Ken and Akiko F arrived 2001 and deserve some credit for pioneering drive towards cold end of west coast. If you visit, pack a jacket.

Freemark Abbey Napa V ★★★ Classic name claimed by JACKSON FAMILY in 2006, improved. Great-value single-vyd Bosché, Sycamore CAB SAUV bottlings.

Frog's Leap Ruth ★★★ John Williams is a pioneer of bio viticulture in CA. He coaxes best out of NAPA V floor with elegant CHARD, refreshing SAUV BL, supple, juicy CAB SAUV, MERLOT and brambly ZIN.

Gallo, E&J ★→★★★ Biggest wine company in world, titan in under-$20 sector with dozens of major CA brands, incl Apothic, Barefoot, Louis Martini. Recent buys: Black Box, Clos du Bois, ROMBAUER, Jayson, RAVENSWOOD. Gallo of Sonoma makes excellent wines from owned vyds; lately been buying boutique brands like DENNER, MASSICAN.

Gentleman Farmer Napa V ★★★→★★★★ Jeff and Joey offer depth of human hospitality unequalled in NAPA V. Making great wine (with Jerome Chéry), they can cook, and will make group bookings feel right at home. Hard to put a price on this kind of warmth. Get there.

Gloria Ferrer Car ★★★ Exceptional CA bubbly. Toast to decades-long team of owners, growers, winemakers that made this Freixenet-owned venture extraordinary. All wines v.gd, Vintage Royal Cuvée best.

On social media, a glass of wine can't compete with a craft cocktail.

Goldeneye And V ★★★→★★★★ Well-conceived and managed estate winery with three principal vyds. PINOT N on ripe side, but undeniably delicious, esp The Narrows vyd. Bubbly also special, and visitors welcome.

Green & Red Napa V ★★★ Back-to-the-land hippie winery, founded in early 70s by Jay Heminway, still cranks out mouthwatering SAUV BL and some killer ZIN, one custom-blended for Chez Panisse in Berkeley.

Greenwood Ridge And V ★★★ Recharge your EV at cosy octagonal redwood tasting room in Philo; array of well-made wines, esp PINOT N, ZIN. Vintage CA spirit at its best.

Gundlach Bundschu Son V ★★★ Terrific wines, welcoming vibe, popular tasting destination, with adventurous cool Huichica Fest music concerts for hipster set. Best: GEWURZ, CAB SAUV, MERLOT.

Hall Napa V ★★★→★★★★ Glitzy ST H winery makes great NAPA CAB SAUV, but bewildering variety of selections. Signature offering best, velvety SAUV BL, MERLOT among best in CA. Also owns coastal CHARD, PINOT N brand Walt.

Halter Ranch P Rob ★★→★★★ Boasting 200 acres+ of sustainably farmed vyds on P ROB's w-side, Halter reckons large as premium grower and winery in AVA. Solid CAB SAUV, SYRAH. PICPOUL a sprightly surprise.

Hanzell Son V ★★★ Pinot pioneer of 50s still making CHARD, PINOT N from estate vines. Both reward cellar time. Mineral Chard still thrilling. Sebella Chard (young vines) all bright, crisp fruit.

Harlan Estate Napa V ★★★★ Concentrated, robust CAB SAUV from W Oakville bench, cult Cab with long waiting list from Meadowood Resort owner Bill H. Resort rebuilding after 2020 fires, but vyds intact. Wines made by Cory Empting.

Harney Lane Lodi ★★★ Family-owned with a century+ of grape-growing under belt. Old-vine ZIN from Home Ranch and Lizzy James vyds the stars, but ALBARIÑO, TEMPRANILLO also impress as Iberian grapes gain momentum in Lodi.

Hartford Family Son Coast ★★★ Winemaker Jeff Stewart is quietly killing it at this

JACKSON FAMILY winery, with small batches of CHARD, PINOT N, ZIN from sites up and down N Coast. Taut Seascape Chard, subtle Fog Dance Pinot N (Green V).

HdV Wines Car ★★★ A gem: fine complex CHARD with honed edge; PINOT N from Larry Hyde with Aubert de Villaine of DRC (*see* France); v.gd CAB SAUV, SYRAH.

Hendry Oak K ★★★ Classic, soulful, minimalist wines, est 1939. Note brambly, distinctive CAB SAUV, ZIN (try Block 28) from cool pocket. Never disappointing.

Hirsch Son Coast ★★★→★★★★ Edgy, influential; nervy, high-acid, moderately oaked CHARD, PINOT N nr Fort Ross. In ideal yrs excellent produce.

Hobo Son V ★★★ Tough to classify these min-intervention wines. Kenny Likitprakong is skateboarder-turned-winemaker grinding margins of CA wine: refreshing, expressive from grapes culled from gd sources in SON COUNTY, Sta Cruz Mts. Pure, fresh fruit with DIY punk attitude. Value tasting in Sta Rosa.

Hope Family P Rob ★★★ Visionary Austin H bangs out some fine Rhône reds from Templeton Gap and CAB SAUV under his eponymous label, plus affordable Liberty School varietals, complex Treana brand blends. Experienced, dependable.

House of Brown Napa V ★★★ NAPA's Brown Estate 2nd-generation spin-off; fruit-driven, youthful, naturalish wines. On-point rosé, juicy, chillable blend of CAB SAUV/PINOT N/TEMPRANILLO from Lodi. Timely, youth-oriented, Black-owned label with legit experience and chops. Watch.

Hundred Acre Napa V ★★★★ NAPA V Jayson Woodbridge schooled by some great consultants, forged excellent CAB SAUV brand through many legal battles as civil plaintiff and (petty) criminal defendant. Maybe all publicity is gd publicity. The Diplomat (r blend) resonates. Make love, not war.

Inglenook Oak ★★★ Director FF Coppola's legendary estate. Rubicon CAB SAUV is flagship proprietary red; v.gd CHARD, MERLOT. Showpiece mansion is spectacular, popular with international visitors.

Jackson Family Wines ★★→★★★★ Visionary, continually expanding privately held company, massive vyd owner in CA and beyond, with remarkable empire of stellar properties. Holdings focus on elevated sites, high-quality terroir. Owns popular Kendall-Jackson brand plus ritzier BREWER-CLIFTON, Cardinale, Copain, Edmeades, FREEMARK ABBEY, HARTFORD FAMILY, LA CREMA, La Jota, Lokoya, MAGGY HAWK, Matanzas Creek, Murphy Goode, Siduri, VÉRITÉ. Jackson Estate series great for N Coast mtn CAB SAUV. Uniformly high-quality wines.

Jessie's Grove Lodi ★★→★★★★ Deep roots in Lodi, est 1868, home to some seriously old ZIN vines. Boss Greg Burns knows Zin inside out: it shows in fine, generous wines. The Westwind Zin is potent; also ALBARIÑO, VERMENTINO.

Jordan Alex V ★★★ Showcase estate generates elegant, balanced, Bx-faithful CAB SAUV for devoted following; CHARD, now sourced from RRV, delivers lemony, mouthwatering panache.

Joseph Phelps Vineyards Napa V ★★★★ Insignia Bx blend a CA benchmark luxury wine. NAPA V CAB SAUV and Hyde Vyd SYRAH dazzle. Freestone coastal wines also worth a gander.

Keenan Spring Mtn ★★★ Just one of many reliably rocksteady mtn wineries in NAPA V. CAB SAUV is age-worthy, but don't sleep on structured MERLOT.

Keller Estate Son Coast ★★★ One more eg. of balanced, elegant CA wine from cool coastal regions; CHARD, La Cruz vyd PINOT N from Petaluma Gap delightful.

Kistler Vineyards RRV ★★★→★★★★ Style of CHARD, PINOT N adapted over time, wines only improved. Decadent, but balanced, nutty Les Noisetiers CHARD from SON V, exceptional.

Kornell, Paula Napa V ★★★→★★★★ This 2nd-gen bubbly specialist brings the party with outstanding CA fizz: 1st-rate Brut and Brut Blanc de Noirs. Seek.

Kosta Browne Son Coast ★★★★ Top-notch, moon-shot PINOT N, CHARD, under The Duckhorn Portfolio umbrella, making world-class wines at world-class

> **Bordeaux blends at decent prices**
> A lot of people probably associate elevated Bx-blend wines with NAPA V,
> but you can buy thrilling examples in P ROB and SON County. In Napa V,
> arguably BEVAN CELLARS Ontogeny is the "it" wine from Napa for a
> Benjamin. More frugal shoppers opt for J LOHR Cuvée Pau, Cuvée Pom
> (P Rob). CH ST JEAN Cinque Cépages is legend, RODNEY STRONG Symmetry
> is excellent (Son). MIRAFLORES Meritage from EL DOR CO also formidable.

prices. Keefer Ranch Pinot insanely gd, and don't sleep on flinty Chards
(One Sixteen). They ain't cheap.

Kutch N Coast ★★★→★★★★ Jamie K produces some prime coastal PINOT N.
Currently developing a home ranch, he sources from other top sites outside
textbook locales. Delivers consistently, like McDougall Ranch Pinot N (vyd
at c.305m/1000ft), precise, expressive, special wines.

Ladera Napa V ★★★ Brand has been through some changes, but hillside Napa
CAB SAUVS, SAUV BL from NZ winemaker still damn gd.

Lang & Reed Mend, Napa ★★★ If you're interested in CA CAB FR, start here. John
Skupny's wines capture perfume, litheness of variety, with NAPA generosity. Also
delicious MEND CHENIN BL.

Larkmead Napa V ★★★★ Family-owned, extraordinary gravelly property in CAL
survived winemaking transition well. Latest CAB SAUVS tense, mineral, precise as
ever. Not thought of as a cult Cab, but maybe that should change.

Leoness Tem ★★→★★★ Favourite in SoCal's Temecula, where weddings and other
wine-tourism jaunts seem to drive most traffic. There *is* some gd wine, and gd
food while you're at it too. Leoness is an example.

Lindquist Family – Verdad Arroyo G, Arroyo Seco ★★★ Rhône Ranger Bob L's pivot
toward Spain, incl authentic-ish ALBARIÑO, TEMPRANILLO from bio Sawyer
Lindquist vyd in nearby EDNA V. *Muy bueno.*

Littorai And V, Son Coast ★★★★ Burgundy-trained maestro Ted Lemon's N Coast
CHARD, PINOT N are nervy, coastal and seeking global audience. Small lots, but all
sleek, exciting. Thrilling Cerise, Savoy, Wendling Vyd offerings.

Lohr, J P Rob ★★→★★★ Arguably among best value in CA, from CAB SAUV to MERLOT
to SYRAH. Everything under $20 is well worth it. Cuvée Pau and Cuvée St E pay
homage to Bx. Don't miss seductive, floral Beaujolais-like Wildflower Valdiguié.

Lone Madrone P Rob ★★★→★★★★ Personal/family venture of accomplished TABLAS
CREEK winemaker Neil Collins. Naturally focused on Rhône varieties with some
ZIN liaisons, organic and delving into terroir of Adelaida Hills. Labels could use
some work, but no arguing with the wines.

Long Meadow Ranch Napa V ★★★→★★★★ Smart, holistic vision, incl destination
winery with restaurant, cattle on organic farm. Supple, age-worthy, fresh CAB
SAUV has reached ★★★★ status; lively Graves-style SAUV BL.

Lucia Santa LH ★★★ Access to great vyds and 2nd-generation knowledge has
positioned Jeff Pisoni well. Impressive CHARD, PINOT N. Central Coast, SANTA LH
brand to watch. Juicy Lucy GAMAY, delicious.

Macchia Lodi ★★★ One of Lodi's most accomplished winemakers, Tim Holdener
vacuums up medals in blind tastings yr after yr. Speciality is balanced old-vine
ZIN, but also interesting SANGIOVESE, TEROLDEGO; PETITE SIRAH v.gd.

MacRostie RRV, Son Coast ★★★ Tasting room a post-modern beauty; minimalist
screwcapped wines 1st rate. Lovely PINOT N, SYRAH; SON COAST CHARD a delight.
Get on the bus.

Maggy Hawk And V ★★★ Copain alumna Sarah Wuethrich heads JACKSON FAMILY
team crafting great CHARD, PINOT N in deep end (cold part) of AND v. Don't just
drink it, visit new tasting room.

Massican Napa V ★★★ Only whites from ex-LARKMEAD wiz Dan Petroski. Recently sold to E&J GALLO; Dan stays on for now. Direct wines, some complexity, vivacious Med styles. California Vino Bianco modestly priced but expertly crafted; SAUV BL, fragrant, delightful. Annia (Tocai FRIULANO/RIBOLLA GIALLA/CHARD) creative, well executed.

Masút Mend ★★★ Newish elevated Eagle Peak property, run by Ben and Jake Fetzer, shines. Estate PINOT N ethereal. Will inspire others to explore area.

Matthiasson Napa V ★★★ Mostly certified organic vyd sources in NAPA, making trendy, relatively low-alc CAB SAUV, REFOSCO, VERMENTINO; v. hip.

Mauritson Dry CV ★★★ Clay M, 6th-generation grower, captains extraordinary holdings in elevated Rockpile district; wines only got better under his two decades. ZIN is flagship, of course; CAB SAUV, SAUV BL also excellent.

Mayacamas Mt Veeder ★★★→★★★★ For many yrs, I've wavered over this venerable, stern, rocky estate. Previous iterations could be brutal, coarse, but more polished recent CAB SAUV is civilized, displaying class of mtn Mayacama range terroir. All coming into focus as Mt Veeder warms. Watch.

Medlock Ames Son ★★★ Winery on Bell Mtn with reliably delicious, bio, round, mostly Bx-style reds made under respected consultant Jean Hoefliger. Sharp wines, labels, Healdsburg tasting room. Classy.

Melka Napa V, Son V ★★★★ Jewel-box holding of great NAPA consultant Philippe M and wife Cherie, comprises hillside properties in CAL (Napa V) and Knights V (SON). Limited, pricey, coveted. Mostly CAB SAUV, Bx blends, stellar MERLOT.

"I tried some of my older wines, and they were horrible. Now I'm adding sulphur," said a recovering natural-wine maker.

Michael Mondavi Family Napa V ★★★→★★★★ This Mondavi scion might be best known for his Folio import biz, but he makes great wines too. The M CAB SAUV from ATLAS PEAK is killer. Animo Cab Sauv, SAUV BL also formidable.

Miraflores Sierra Fhills ★★★ Marco Cappelli left NAPA V to set up in Sierra Mtns; vinifies sublime, broad array from estate and region he rightly believes in.

Mi Sueno Napa V ★★★ Rolando started dishwashing at a NAPA resort, worked his way up at wineries. Lorena's family worked vyds, bought property. Together they make excellent wine, every bit as gd as story.

Montelena, Ch Napa V ★★★ Epic, elevated, historic Mayacamas castle property with sublime grounds so worth a visit. CAB SAUV can be a bit wild, CHARD shocked world at 1978 Judgement of Paris tasting.

Morgan Santa LH ★★★→★★★★ Dan M Lee's organically farmed ranch overdelivers with killer CHARD, PINOT N across board. Double L vyd offerings top charts.

Mount Eden Vineyards Santa Cz Mts ★★★→★★★★ Gorgeous vistas from high vyd, one of CA's 1st boutique wineries, with Burgundian clones dating back to Martin Ray days. Taut, mineral CAB SAUV, PINOT N, stunning CHARD since 1945. Inspired by Burgundy, but pure rugged CA character.

Nalle Dry CV ★★★ Refined craftsmanship-level ZIN, impeccable, elegant claret-style reds. Great family-owned stop nr Healdsburg.

Navarro And V ★★★ Long-time cool-climate N CA outpost reliably delivers fresh, affordable, minimalist, delicious GEWURZ, PINOT N and everything in between. Wine-club subscription you won't regret.

New Clairvaux Central V ★★★ NAPA scion Aimée Sunseri makes impressive hot-climate whites and reds at remote Franciscan monastery nr Chico. The ASSYRTIKO is fruity, electric; PETITE SIRAH polished, smooth.

Obsidian Ridge Lake ★★★ Star of Lake County extension of Mayacamas mtn range. Super CAB SAUV, SYRAH from hillside vyds, volcanic soils scattered with glassy obsidian. Half Mile Cab 1st-rate. Also owns Poseidon brand from CAR.

Opus One Oak ★★★★ Mouton Rothschild family-controlled (*see* Bordeaux) CAB SAUV estate always intended to glamour international markets, and it still does.

O'Shaughnessy Howell Mtn ★★★★ Outstanding elevated outpost atop HOWELL MTN putting out stellar CAB SAUV that's built to last. Worth seeking out.

Patz & Hall N Coast ★★★★ James H one of CA's most thoughtful winemakers; culls fruit from top vyds from Central Coast to MEND. Style is generous, tasteful, super-reliable. Zio Tony *Chard* v. special, lemony, electric, opulent.

Paul Hobbs Wines N Coast ★★★→★★★★ Hugely influential winemaker since 90s, working in CA and a lot in S America. Terroir-expressive single-vyd CHARD, CAB SAUV, PINOT N, SYRAH always impressive. Don't sleep on these wines.

Pax Mend, Son ★★★ Cult-level New World SYRAH from coastal and hillside sites since 2000 for less than cult-follower prices. Fresh TROUSSEAU Gr and GAMAY also available at The Barlow tasting room in Sebastopol.

Peay Vineyards Son Coast ★★★→★★★★ Standout brand from coldest, elevated zones. Finesse-driven CHARD, PINOT N, SYRAH superb. Second label: Cep, v.gd, esp rosé. Weightless, ethereal wines that reckon international appreciation.

Pedroncelli Dry CV ★★★ CA wine at its most exuberant, glowing, unpretentious. Grown on superb terroir, gently made, beautiful without makeup: SAUV BL, CAB SAUV, ZIN all singing in harmony and v. reasonably priced. Unsurprising sales are on upswing; CA wine needs more of this.

Pelle, La Napa V ★★★→★★★★ Founded 2016, talented team with rising star Maayan Koschitsky as winemaker seeking to control more vyds in NAPA V and SANTA B, likely soon. Napa V CAB SAUV, opulent blend of grapes from COOMB, OAK, Oak Knoll, ST H. Work in progress.

Philip Togni Vineyard Spring Mtn ★★★ No bling, just beauty, and long life.

Pine Ridge Napa V ★★★ Outstanding CAB SAUV from several vyds. Estate STAGS L bottling, silky, graceful. Lively CHENIN BL/VIOGNIER innovative classic.

Pisoni Family Vineyards Santa LH ★★★ A 2nd-generation Central Coast PINOT N legend, with refined Pinot N, CHARD. Cheeky second label Lucy incl exceptional CA GAMAY, refreshing Pico Blanco, white blend of PINOTS GR/BL.

Presqu'ile Santa MV ★★★ Cool-climate estate with ocean views and lovely SANTA MV PINOT N aged in neutral barrels; spicy, slightly gamey SYRAH.

Pride Mountain Napa V, Spring Mtn ★★★→★★★★ Epic Mayacamas mtn-top estate straddles NAPA V/SON border. Superb, bold CAB SAUV; amazing MERLOT. Tasting appointments required and worth the drive up. Call ahead.

Quintessa Ruth ★★★★ Well-conceived, gorgeous, single-wine estate owned by Chilean international wine wizard Augustin Huneeus. That one red Bx blend is special and justifies three-figure price.

Quivira Dry CV ★★★→★★★★ Bio property of Pete and Terri Kight, helmed by accomplished winemaker Hugh Chappelle, sells estimable SAUV BL, ZIN with integrity, balance.

Qupé Santa B ★★★ One of original Central Coast SYRAH champions; Bien Nacido offerings still outstanding and CC Syrah still impressive despite departure of founder Bob LINDQUIST. The trad continues so far.

Declining domestic wine drinking tough for wineries, but gold rush for drinkers.

Radio-Coteau Son Coast ★★★ Notable new-wave PINOT N, serious coastal SYRAH and old-vine, dry-farmed ZIN. Bulletproof CHARD, Zin, but Pinot N steals show. Veg gardens, cider orchard, goats, chickens, honeybees and cats gild the lily.

Ramey Son ★★★→★★★★ Influential David R delivers flinty, reductive burgundian-style whites in his Hyde, Ritchie and RRV CHARD. Reds gd, but his Chards should be *de rigueur* tasting at UC Davis winemaking school.

Rancho Sisquoc Santa MV ★★→★★★★ Rustic tasting room and historic chapel deliver satisfying spectrum of Bx styles and great visitor experience, with outstanding CHARD, CAB FR, PINOT N.

Ravenswood ★★★ CONSTELLATION-owned, but single-vyd ZIN still from remarkable sites like Bedrock, Old Hill, Teldeschi. "No wimpy wines" motto still applies.

Red Car Son Coast ★★★ Hip brand with colourful label making precise CHARD, lacy, fruit-forward PINOT N and killer rosé.

Rhys Santa Cz Mts ★★★→★★★★ Up-and-coming brand; focus on high-elevation PINOT N, CHARD from Sta Cruz Mts and AND V, some exciting vyds in its quiver. Given rugged terrain and wildfire possibility, will this brave venture end in even greater kudos or tragedy. Great wines; wishing tremendous success.

CA's oldest vineyard is Sausal Ranch Century, planted 1870s. Owned by Silver Oak.

Ridge N Coast, Santa Cz Mts ★★★★ Hi, natty wine kids! Ridge represents decades of natural winemaking with min additives, local oak and 1st-class terroir in Monte Bello CAB SAUV, one of greatest, most age-worthy Cabs in CA. Also a champ of ingredient labelling and transparency. Watch and learn.

Rivers-Marie Napa V ★★★→★★★★ Private label of acclaimed vintner and consultant Thomas Rivers Brown (Schrader) and partner Genevieve Marie Welsh features superb varietals. Reservations required at Hwy 128 tasting room in CAL. Wicked Herb Lamb CAB SAUV.

Robert Mondavi Winery ★★→★★★ Once iconic, now a corporate concern. Top wines still pretty gd; everything in between mostly okay.

Robledo Family Son V ★★★→★★★★ Along with, and related to, MI SUEÑO, among 1st estate wineries founded by Mexican vyd workers. Luis and his sons came to US in 40s as *braceros* and worked way up from fields. American Dream, now 4th generation. Delicious, rare, claret-style NAPA V TEMPRANILLO.

Rodney Strong Vineyards Son ★★★ Strong indeed, across board; 14 vyds producing sinewy coastal CHARD, PINOT N, citrus SAUV BL, super ALEX V CAB SAUV from Alexander's Crown, Rockaway vyds.

Roederer Estate And V ★★★★ Adventurous Champagne Roederer venture brought glamour to AND V fizz. Finesse off charts, esp luxury cuvée L'Ermitage. Also makes Scharffenberger now. Dom Anderson PINOT N also among best of AVA.

Rombauer Napa V ★★★ Buttery CHARD is calling card, but sunny MERLOT, CAB SAUV also deliver juicy CA fruit.

St Jean, Ch Son V ★★★ Solid on all fronts, but consensus flagship for decades has been Cinq Cépages: five Bx varieties. Classic nectarine-rich Robert Young CHARD.

St Supery Ruth ★★★→★★★★ Stalwart, estate-grown certified Napa Green wines from RUTH. Dollarhide Estate SAUV BL is legendary, but some Bx blends that inspired this estate still seem relevant, value. Try Dollarhide Estate CAB SAUV, Elu Bx blend.

Saintsbury Car ★★★ Regional pioneer and benchmark still making exciting, highly relevant PINOT N, CHARD, yummy Vincent Vin Gr of Pinot N rosé. Lee vyd Swan clone Pinot is vibrant, velvet.

Sandhi Sta RH ★★★ Former sommelier Raj Parr's visionary SANTA B winery producing Burgundy-inspired low-alc wines with balance, restraint. Not an easy feat at this latitude.

Sandlands Napa V ★★★→★★★★ Tegan Passalacqua rescues ancient and sandy pre-phylloxera vyds from CA; boutique small batches of ultra-premium wine.

Saracina Mend ★★→★★★ Beautiful, sustainably farmed estate owned by Taub family. Wide range of solid, wholesome wines. Try the Soul of Mendocino co-ferment red. Best yet to come, methinks.

Saxum P Rob ★★★ Famed for opulent, heady Rhône-inspired reds – perhaps a bit too heady for some. James Berry Vyd blend is flagship.

Scherrer RRV ★★★ Fred S makes structured SON wines from PINOT N to CAB SAUV and ZIN, all built to last and matured for extra yr or two. Hallberg Ranch PINOT N, finessed Sasha SYRAH standouts.

Schramsberg Napa V ★★★★ A 2nd-gen CA bubbly specialist not afraid to compete with Champagne, and keeps up well. Memorable tours of historic caves by reservation. Classic Blanc de Blancs.

Scribe Son ★★★ Hipster gentleman-farmer aesthetic seduces younger set. Tasting room (SON) pours well-made esoterica like SYLVANER, ST-LAURENT and exceptional Van der Kamp PINOT N, aged in neutral oak.

Sea Smoke Sta RH ★★★ Cultish, high-end, opulent PINOT N and excellent bubbly made in strictly estate-driven model, with incredible continuity of leadership, talent. Luscious wines, but drink them while they're fresh.

Shafer Vineyards Napa V, Stags L ★★★→★★★★ Solid brand, widely respected. Hillside Select CAB SAUV a lavish CA classic; Relentless SYRAH/PETITE SIRAH blend an artful in-house invention. One Point Five, beautiful Cab Sauv for money.

Shannon Ridge Lake ★★→★★★ Grand, undulating, high-elevation estate overlooks Clear Lake. Terrific reds and whites from PETITE SIRAH to SAUV BL, esp Res series. Great value. Second label: Vigilance, a big seller.

Shenandoah Vineyards / Sobon Estate Amador ★★★ Green-leaning scientists/ engineers got SIERRA FHILLS endeavour going in late 70s, still makes some of best ZIN and more in EL DOR CO. Charging station for your EV while you taste.

Sky Mt Veeder ★★★ Comeback kid: stunning estate planted atop Mt Veeder, red volcanic soil at 640m (2100ft), rebuilding after fire in 2017. Sustainably grown and handmade in small fermentations, old-vine ZIN is name of game, but elevated SYRAH merits mention. Great visit (book) if you don't mind a drive.

Smith-Madrone Napa V ★★★→★★★★ Indie old-school outpost founded by Smith bros in 1971 atop SPRING MTN, featuring Euro-inspired, balanced CAB SAUV and exotic, trend-eschewing old-vine RIES. Worth a visit.

Smith-Story And V, Son V ★★★ Always hustling, shared-dream couple makes plucky, v.gd wines and sometimes German RIES from where Eric cut his winemaking teeth. Sometimes the story is everything.

Sojourn Son ★★★ Angelina Mondavi-owned, single-vyd N Coast project; top NAPA V CAB SAUV (Oakville Ranch) and PINOT N (Gap's Crown) SON COAST shine bright.

Sonoma-Cutrer Vineyards Son ★★★ Big, successful RRV brand now sold to The Duckhorn Portfolio; SON COAST CHARD still impresses major audience.

Spottswoode St H ★★★★ Five-star, sublime estate always chasing perfection with every sustainable/organic/bio bona fide ever invented. Estate Cabs thrilling with modest alc. Second wine: Lyndenhurst, superb, value CAB SAUV. Spottswoode SAUV BL always zesty, immaculate. Stand and clap.

Staglin Family Vineyard Ruth ★★★★ Refined CAB SAUV from 2nd-generation, family-owned estate on RUTH Benchlands. Always impressive, and a leader, never just another cow in the herd.

Stag's Leap Wine Cellars Stags L ★★★ Founder sold to Ste Michelle Wine Estates (WA), gd to see quality held. Flagship CAB SAUV (top Cask 23, Fay, SLV).

Stags' Leap Winery Stags L ★★★→★★★★ Oft confused with STAG'S LEAP WINE CELLARS, historic estate est by Carl Doumani excels in its own right. Been kicked around like a waterlogged football lately, but some terrific winemakers (latest Ludovic Dervin) have it on track. Try The Leap estate CAB SAUV. Tastings (book), well worth it.

Steven Kent Winery ★★★ SK Mirassou is hands-down the best winemaker in LIV V, lately zeroing-in on area's great potential for CAB FR. L'Autre Côte best.

Storybook Mountain Napa V ★★★ Dr Jerry Seps's fairytale CAL estate makes some of most stylish, classically proportioned ZIN in CA. Classic Eastern Exposures.

Tablas Creek P Rob ★★★→★★★★ When it comes to Rhône and Med varieties, nobody does it better; makes me feel sad for rest. Enlightened regenerative farming begets glorious, well-edited red/white (latter rare in P ROB); CA elite. A wine club worth joining.

Talbott Mont ★★★ Lavish, classy, v. well-made CHARD, PINOT N, esp Sleepy Hollow (SANTA LH), Diamond T (Carmel V), opulence, grace. Second label Kali Hart, killer Central Coast wines with sense of place, price tough to beat.

Terre Rouge / Easton Sierra Fhills ★★★ Exceptional red producer in AM CO sporting Rhône and ZIN offerings with equal aplomb. Affordable Tête-à-Tête red blend a steal, Ascent SYRAH reliably special.

Three Sticks Son ★★★→★★★★ Billy "Three Sticks" Price III is major player in SON COAST; interests in Durell and Gap's Crown vyds, GARY FARRELL, KISTLER and other brands. Connected, solid N Coast CHARD and PINOT N done well by N CA native Ryan Prichard.

Three Wine Clark ★★★ Long-time CLINE winemaker Matt C's latest brand has tasting room in Clarksburg, but he continues to work magic with ancient, own-rooted ancient vyds in Oakley (Contra Costa Co). Early CA varieties like CARIGNAN, MATARO, ZIN are in Three's wheelhouse.

Toulouse ★★★ Dark horse from Philo, CA, making excellent PINOT N, terrific GEWURZ, Valdigué. Founded in 2002 by Oakland Fire Dept captain and flight-attendant wife. Sustainably farmed too.

Trefethen Family Vineyards Oak K ★★★ Underappreciated winery in cool Oak Knoll deserves more credit; CHARD, delicious dry RIES, elegant CAB SAUV, MERLOT.

Trinchero Family Estates Napa V ★→★★★ Bewildering slew of labels, incl mass-market Sutter Home; esp pleasing CAB SAUV under Napa Wine Co label.

Turkovich Central V ★★ Impressive Yolo County operation over Vaca range from NAPA, min coastal influence; tight, fresh wines from warm-climate grapes that fit the bill. Try The Boss – racy, clean, powerful blend of PETITE SIRAH, PETIT VERDOT and more. Great prices.

Turley Wine Cellars Amador ★★★★ Brilliant CA ZINS from over 40 vyd sites, some ancient vyds, many field-blend fermentations scattered across CA. True CA treasures, Hayne vyd in ST H perhaps most famed of portfolio. Tegan Pessalaqua presiding. Zin may be out of fashion, but Turley not so.

Turnbull Oak ★★★ Outstanding entry-level estate CAB SAUV. Black-label estate Cab also thrilling with gravelly kick, and don't sleep on luscious, tropical SAUV BL.

Vérité Son ★★★★ Luxury SON hillside Mayacamas mtn estate helmed by long-time Jess Jackson *copain* Pierre Seillan and daughter Hélène for five decades now. Age-worthy Bx blends, incl MERLOT-driven La Muse and CAB SAUV-led La Joie among top wines. Tastings (by reserve) pricey.

Seeking value in California wine

In recent decades, the price of vyds has escalated rapidly in CA, and wine seems like more of an indulgence than an average meal accompaniment. To me, a "value" wine is soundly made, has a sense of place and a hint of personality. In CA, that will run you $20 25 retail. If a glass of the same costs you $14–20 in a restaurant, maybe that's not unreasonable. For penny pinchers, BOGLE is still value, with its Lodi/Clarksville wines often under $15 a bottle. I can't argue with KENDALL-JACKSON's offerings in the under-$20 range. There are still some long-time grower-winemakers like PEDRONCELLI (DRY CV) committed to value; FOPPIANO and RODNEY STRONG (both SON) likewise. Decoy and Raeburn (CHARD, PINOT N) from Son and J LOHR (P ROB) deliver gd bang for the buck.

Vineyard 29 Napa V ★★★→★★★★ Top winemaker Philippe MELKA's fingerprints all over gorgeous CAB SAUV at maturing estate venture; gd but oaky SAUV BL.

Volker Eisele Family Estate Napa V ★★★ Special site tucked way back in Chiles V continues to overdeliver with CAB SAUV and more. Looking for an adventure?

Williams-Selyem RRV ★★★ Legendary SON PINOT N since 70s; handcrafted, low intervention, with loyal following. Rochioli vyd (RRV) put N CA PINOT N on map.

Witching Stick And V ★★★ Ambitious winery with working-class sensibilities making sound, world-class wines. Invested in prime terroir at right time and did the work. Try Valenti vyd wines; forgive klutzy website.

Zaca Mesa Santa B ★★★ OG Rhône-variety leader planted SYRAH in 1978, delivering boss wines for five decades. Z red blend graceful, affordable.

Colorado (CO)

Cool-climate varieties best, experimentation with hybrids though vinifera grown extensively. Two AVAs: Grand V more Bx, Rhône varieties; West Elks cooler, more Alsace, Burgundy. **Alfred Eames** ★ historic producer; Carmine (r) lauded. **Bookcliff Vineyards** ★★★ new owners taking to new heights; oft-awarded, top producer of French grapes: SYRAH, CAB SAUV, MALBEC, MERLOT. **Carboy** ★★ four wineries, tasting rooms; splashy new Grand Cuvée (sp CHENIN BL). **Carlson** history of fruit and sweet wines; gd dry GEWURZ, LEMBERGER and St Vincent (r) hybrid. **Colterris** ★★★ top bottlings of Bx-style Cab Sauv, Merlot; red blend; signature Coral White Cab Sauv. **Jack Rabbit Hill Farm** ★ only certified bio winery in state; elegant PINOTS N/M, Alsace whites. **Plum Creek Winery** Bx-style reds; gd CHARD, pét-nat. **Qutori Wines** ★ Cab Sauv, Syrah; outstanding Merlot. **Sauvage Spectrum** ★★ quality Italian, Bx-style reds; Malbec, TEROLDEGO lead. **Snowy Peaks** ★★ v. high-altitude; Rhône, Bx styles; hybrids; try Rhône blend Élevé (r), MUSCAT (sw). **Stone Cottage Cellars** high-elevation, Alsace specialist, racy GEWURZ, PINOT GR. **Sutcliff Vyds** outlier in frontier area Four Corners, Bx varieties. **The Storm Cellar** focus on high-elevation white and (best) rosé. **Veraison Vyds and Winery** estate Perle Blanche Chard from Dijon clones.

Georgia (GA)

Two AVAs in N Georgia: Bx styles, CHARD, PETIT MANSENG, PINOT N, unusual hybrids. **Ch Élan** Mameli light red blend is star. **Cloudland** Lomanto, PETIT VERDOT. **Crane Creek** hybrid focus, try Enotah (Chardonel fermented in Hungarian oak), Hellbender Norton/CAB FR/Chambourcin. **Frogtown Cellars** awarded Bravado SANGIOVESE/TANNAT. **Sharp Mtn** GEWURZ, Sangiovese. **Stonewall Creek** focus on Petit Manseng (incl amber) and Traminette. **Three Sisters** 100% GA grapes; AVA range Vidal Bl, Cab Fr. **Tiger Mtn** Petit Manseng, TOURIGA N. **Wolf Mtn** awarded Blanc de Blancs range. **Yonah Mtn Vyds** Marian's Meritage is co-ferment MERLOT-led Bx, fruit wine (trad blackberry), some v.gd.

Idaho (ID)

Frontier underdog region; mere 65 wineries, 526 ha. Age of exploration in Snake River Valley and beyond. Resulting wines have richness, structure from warm days, cool nights. SYRAH, VIOGNIER already clear standouts.

Cinder Wines Snake RV ★★ Melanie Krause (ex-Ch Ste Michelle, *see* WA) makes velvety SYRAH, stainless VIOGNIER. Valentina standout Bx blend.

Colter's Creek ★★ Benchmark producer in Lewis-Clark V destroyed by fire (2024), now closed. Find SYRAH, Rhône-style blends while you can.

Huston Vineyards Snake RV ★ Chicken Dinner RIES blend a surprising delight. MALBEC pure, varietally correct.

Rivaura ★★ Lewis-Clark V estate, with highly regarded consulting winemaker. One to watch, esp SYRAH.

Ste Chapelle Snake RV ★ ID's founding winery (1975), also largest. Focus on sweet whites, soft reds. Well-priced quaffers.

Sawtooth Winery Snake RV ★ One of ID's oldest, est 1987. Now owned by WA's Precept. Makes tasty estate RIES, SYRAH, TEMPRANILLO.

Maryland (MD)

Mid-Atlantic, emerging e-coast star. Launched post-Prohibition by reporter P Wagner, a hybrids fan; focus now on classical styles, pét-nats, meticulous attention to local terroirs; E Shore sandy soils, hills of Garrett and Allegheny mtns, blue-crab-rich Chesapeake Bay checks freezing winters, stifling summers. Reliable ripeners SAUV BL, MERLOT, PETIT VERDOT; also ALBARIÑO, CHARD, CHENIN BL; top hybrids incl Vidal Bl, Vignoles. New state law says grow more grapes.

Multi-vintage blends popular in eastern states: called soleras, but just blends.

Black Ankle ★★★ Setting MD viti-vini standards since 08: spontaneous ferment, dry-farmed. Barrel-ferment CHARD, plus ALBARIÑO (tense Sur, softer Norte), SAUV BL, MOURVÈDRE. New: ageable CAB SAUV; red blend Tela; trad-method rosé; SYRAH 22. Piedmont: Chard-led 23 (other yrs GRÜNER V) blend incl Sauv Bl, co-ferment, 6 mths' oak. Library wines incl unforgettable Bx-style Crumbling Rock, Estate (15 to 22), Slate (#10 latest, 22); Albariño, Chard. New in 2025: trad-method rosé.

Old Westminster ★★★ Family farm, spontaneous-ferment cult wines. Earthy amphora-vinified PINOT BL; MALBEC 36 mths in French oak; elevated PETIT VERDOT and CAB SAUV (both Cool Ridge vyd), single-vyd CAB FR 30 mths' élevage. Red blends – Anthem (Cab Fr/Petit Verdot); Origins (Cabs/CHARMBOURCIN) – expression of e climate; white-blend Salt, *sur lie*, meditative. Taut, beguiling ALBARIÑO among best in e. Serious pricey pét-nats: CHARD, Cab Fr.

Philosophy ★★★ Top local fruit, plus own vyd. High-altitude ALBARIÑO, CHARD, Chambourcin, CAB FR, PETIT VERDOT. Premium wines raised in Baltimore's The Wine Collective: floral Cab Fr; pithy VIOGNIER; meaty, cherry Femme N aged red, complex elegance. New MUSCAT pét-nat, Chambourcin rosé.

Other good estates Big Cork (CAB FR; CHENIN BL Brut), Boordy (1st bonded winery, mid-C20 by P Wagner), Bordeleau, Catoctin Breeze, Crow, Dodon, Elk Run, Linganore (Bx-style, ageable; SAPERAVI), Lowe Vyd (BARBERA novello, serious MALBEC), Port of Leonardtown (in s, aged Chambourcin, Bx-style), Sugarloaf Mtn, Windridge.

Michigan (MI)

The n-midwest, 196 producers. "Third Coast" on huge Lake Michigan (LM Shores AVA), glacial hills, nearby **Good Harbor** awarded ALBARIÑO, v.gd Blanc de Blancs/ Noirs, KERNER. Sustainability project collaboration with NY State. Pinots, CHARD, GEWURZ, RIES; CAB FR, MERLOT, TEROLDEGO; hybrids (top Petite Pearl, Vignoles; Itasca, slowly) and cherries (Ch Chantal's gd Cerise Noir, 80/20% PINOT N/ Montmorency cherry; rcs AUXERROIS). Leelanau and Old Mission Peninsula AVAs since 80s, still top: **Mari** Chard, Ries, MALVASIA BIANCA, Cabs, SYRAH, Italian reds SANGIOVESE to REFOSCO; **Black Star** Gewurz, Pinot N (several), GAMAY, Nouveau Marquette, trad-method fizz; **Brys Estate** Ries, gd Merlot, Cab Fr braving cold Traverse City; **Ciccone** (1998, by Madonna's dad) PINOTS BL/GR, DOLCETTO; **Mawby** Blanc de Blancs, de Noirs, rosé (sp); **Neu Cellars**, Ries, Pinot N 18-mth pét-nat, spontaneous ferment; **Talismøn** Brut (incl Res wine to 93), Vignoles; **Verterra** awarded whites; Pinot Gr, Merlot Res. Also try **Filkins Vyd**'s peppery Syrah; **Left Foot Charly** BLAUFRÄNKISCH; **Lemon Creek**'s dark-fruit SHIRAZ;

Modales Pinot N, long-ferment Ries, El Suelo (r blend, incl ALICANTE, native yeasts); **St Julian** Braganini, esp Cab Fr; **WaterFire** min-intervention GRÜNER V, Kerner (blend, also plus Gewurz), SIP certified.

Missouri (MO)

Official state grape Norton (r) one of best US hybrids along with Vignoles (w) and Chambourcin (r). Wineries incl: **Adam Puchta** oldest continuously owned family farm winery in US; fortifieds, heady dry Res Vignoles (w). **Augusta Winery** Chambourcin, Chardonel. **Hermannhof** rich, structured Norton can age; try Chardonel, Vignoles (w). **Les Bourgeois** Chardonel, Norton. **Noboleis Vyds** juicy Chambourcin, oak-aged VIDAL. **Röbller Vyd** ★★ structured Le Trompier N (r), rich Vignoles Res, both capable of ageing. **Stone Hill** ★★ complex lauded Norton, v.gd Chardonel, SEYVAL BL, Vidal. **TerraVox** ★★ champion of hybrid and native varieties; top dry/fortified Norton.

Nevada (NV)

Most wineries import grapes from CA or make flavoured/fruit wines. Hybrid Frontenac (r) is star of wineries making NV wines. **Artesian Cellars** ★ Pahrump V, Battle Born range, NV grapes, vinifera: v.gd, dry crisp RIES; oak-aged, textured SEM.

New England

NE Atlantic, six states (*see also* Vermont) n of NYC sharing hybrids (Cayuga, Petite Pearl, St Croix), fruit (esp apples, blueberries) and mixed wines, and vinifera (CHARD, CAB FR, Pinots, RIES) across cold-climate terrains. Three share SE New England AVA, cool Atlantic climate moderated by Gulf Stream. **Connecticut** small, growing; Hopkins Vyd, Lake Waramaug; experimental station at UConn. **Massachusetts** Martha's Vyd AVA; Concord created here 1849; many fruit wines, some v.gd. Alfalfa Farm CAB SAUV, awarded blueberry wine. Black Birch Cab Fr, Traminette. Glendale Ridge Cab Fr, Corot N, VIDAL BL. Westport Rivers farm, forest, GRÜNER V, PINOT N, Blanc de Blancs, 36 mths. Willow Spring Léon Millot Res. **Rhode Island** smallest state, faces North Fork (*see also* NY) across cold-tempering Sound. Carolyn's Sakonnet GEWURZ, blends Cab Fr/Chancellor. Diamond Hill synthetics-free farm, barrel-aged Pinot N. Greenvale min-touch family estate. Mulberry Vyds Pinot Gr, SYRAH. Newport Gewurz, Bx style. Sakonnet River v.gd Chard, natural-ferment PINOT GR *ramato* (*see* Grapes), smart-oak MERLOT. Verde biology-prof-turned-farmer on lake, Cab Fr-led blend Surveyor, awarded St Croix. Also **Maine** ne-most state, small growers, warming. Bulet and RAS both make excellent blueberry fizz. Oyster River natural, orange Chard, Frontenac Gr rosé. **New Hampshire** elevation; sandy loam nr coast. NOK Vino St Croix/Sabervois, Marquette field blend, or with L'Acadie Bl; incl 1969 vyd.

New Jersey (NJ)

70 wineries, some among best in E US; four AVAs. Rutgers University studies say akin to Bx, esp Médoc. Four hardiness zones; growing seasons getting drier, for now. Stretches s–n along Atlantic: Italian varieties in gravelly maritime Outer Coast Plain (incl Cape May); bucolic central NJ, soft hills, new focus on agritourism, and quality; limestone, granite Warren Hills in n for elegant GEWURZ, GRÜNER V, RIES, BLAUFRÄNKISCH, PINOT N, SYRAH. Try also Almathea, Bellview, Cedar Rose, Meadowbrook (ex-UNIONVILLE winemaker; CAB FR, rosés), Sharrott, White Horse (owns historic Chaddsford winery, PA), Working Dog.

Alba ★★★ Limestone, granite in Warren Hills AVA. One of largest PINOT N plantings on E Coast. Burgundy aspiration, incl earthy Grand Res (best vintages 24 mths' barrique); excellent CHARD (oldest plants, Dijon clone), gd GEWURZ, RIES (also in aromatic field-blend GTR, w), Heritage CAB FR, PINOT GR. New fizz: Ries; Blanc de Blancs soon.

Auburn Road ★★ Barrel-ferment CHARD Res; Bx style with Chambourcin backbone (Eidolón), and without (Gaia); PETIT VERDOT.

Beneduce Vineyards ★★★ Family estate, polyculture farm incl heritage Warthog hard red winter wheat, flour for sale. BLAUFRÄNKISCH, CAB FR, PINOT N (spicy, cool fruit). Intermezzo GEWURZ (dr). Super Tuscan-inspired Mangione; Chambrusco Chambourcin, Modena style; pét-nats incl Blaufränkisch, Gewurz. Acqua Pazza (piquette but Italian, honey-ferment). BARBERA, DOLCETTO planted.

Hawk Haven ★★★ Cape May Peninsula; glacial, river quartz; ocean air. Complex, structured CAB SAUV, v.gd CAB FR, MERLOT; dry RIES is Meyer lemon-plush. Steely ALBARIÑO. Flagship Q, lasting Bx. Fizz technology, quality focus, incl precise Blanc de Noirs; could incl US-rare serious Charmat soon.

Mount Salem **★★★** Small, distinguished estate, with Austrian varieties (mostly). Burgundy methods to match Pattenburg gravel-loam terroir: masterful Matthias (BLAUFRÄNKISCH, ST-LAURENT, ZWEIGELT 21 23 24); barrel-fermented, *sur-lie* CHARD, GRÜNER V; BARBERA (vines from Italy); CAB FR. Wild ferments. Exploring San Marco hybrid, testing NJ resilience, or weather changes.

Unionville ★★★ Single-vyd burgundy takes: CHARDS (v.gd Pheasant Hill Vyd 23), serious pét-nat too; PINOT N. Savoury CAB FR (with Chambourcin, no malolactic). Sourland Ridge Red (Bx style, powerful 23). Rhone-ish VIOGNIER 23, Mistral Rouge SYRAH, v.gd fanciful Hunterdon Mistral Blanc (MARSANNE/ROUSSANE/ Viognier), also as 10 yrs+ library wines.

William Heritage **★★★** Outer Coastal Plain AVA. Single-vyd Chambourcin Res; chewy complex Blanc de Noirs, top Blanc de Blancs; co-ferment GRENACHE/ SYRAH rosé, Provence style; CHARD, vibrant French/Austrian oak (ferment/age) ; citrus SAUV BL Res, short maceration; three-site co-ferment CAB FR; cool maritime Bx-inspired Norman's Vyd CABS Fr/SAUV, 10 yrs+.

NJ town repealed Prohibition no-alc law; 20 wine-shop-free towns to go.

New Mexico (NM)

Oldest wine-growing region in US. High-altitude vyds, moderate warm climate. **Black Mesa ★★** MONTEPULCIANO, PETITE SIRAH; off-dry Abiquiu (w), Traminette/ SEYVAL BL. **DH Lescombes Family Vyds** Bx focus; also Italian, Rhône. **Embudo Valley Vyds** gd French, Italian varieties. **Gruet ★★** historic producer of trad-method fizz, now mostly US grapes. **La Chiripada ★** oldest NM winery, signature CAB SAUV, bright, crisp Kabinett-style RIES (*see* Germany). **Luna Rossa Winery** v.gd range of Italian varieties; VERMENTINO, plus Res AGLIANICO, NEBBIOLO. **Noisy Water ★★** farms historic cool-climate Engle Vyd; large range; Ruidoso Bubbly, skin-fermented CHENIN BL, Res; Cab Sauv all excellent. **Vivác ★★** top French vines with PINOT M starring.

New York (NY)

Almost 500 confident, devoted producers; wines world-class, playful. Wide-ranging cool-climate (changes: earlier budding, later frosts, sudden heavy rains, dry spells, early harvest) vinifera experience; 150 yrs of native and French-American hybrids, a culture of experimentation keep US's 3rd-largest producer innovative, as do statewide sustainability and export programmes. Winters are freezing, but lakes, rivers and the ocean are moderating influences. Look for BLAUFRÄNKISCH, CAB FR, PINOT N, SYRAH, RIES, GEWURZ, RKATSITELI, SAPERAVI, notable dry hybrids and natives, top trad sparkling, single-site bottles. AVAs total 11, incl Finger Lakes (Finger L), sunlight hours equal Napa's in fewer days; Hudson River Region (Hudson RR), complex soils, microclimates; Lake Erie, cooler spring, warm ripening autumns; Long Island (Long I), maritime, bio pioneer, some decades-old, own-rooted, in sandy soils, sub-AVA North Fork (N Fork), warmer, for longer than Hamptons; Niagara Escarpment (Niag).

NY's first commercial vinifera: 1959 Finger Lakes Pinot N, Chard, released 1960.

21 Brix ★★ Estate on Lake Erie with 1st-rate CHARD, GEWURZ, GRÜNER V, RIES; aromatic BLAUFRÄNKISCH, CAB SAUV; v.gd PINOT N. Serious Noiret. VIDAL Icewine.

Anthony Road Finger L ★★★ Seneca Lake; v.gd RIES incl barrel-ferm, trad-method, top natural-ferment Art Series (library too). Vignoles, v. serious, incl Martini-Becraft Selection, worth price. Textbook Finger L PINOT N, CAB FR.

Apollo's Praise Finger L ★★★ New, from Seneca Lake winemakers Kelby James Russell (RED NEWT) and Julia Rose Hoyle (HOSMER); 1st vintage 23. Single-vyd CHARD, GRÜNER V, RIES (dr), CAB FR, barrel-ferment SCHEUREBE.

Arrowhead Spring Vineyards ★★★ Sustainable never-herbicide estate (est 2006) in Niag limestone. Top PINOT N, Bx blends. CAB FR (Res too), SYRAH (13% abv, cool-climate acidity). Linear CHARD, VIOGNER (plus barrel-aged).

Atwater Finger L ★★ Seneca Lake. Emphasis on aromatic whites: GEWURZ, PINOT GR (skin-contact), RIES, Vignoles. BARBERA, BLAUFRÄNKISCH, CAB FR, Corot N.

Bedell Long I ★★★ Pre-eminent estate; Long I-sustainability (LISW) leader. Native yeasts, maritime climate, powerful, saline wines: Musée (MERLOT/PETIT VERDOT/MALBEC) top; Taste Red (base SYRAH/Merlot), Gallery 21 (CHARD/VIOGNER); v.gd CAB FR; rare Long I MELON DE BOURGOGNE, VERDEJO. Small Batch wine club: old-vine GEWURZ, Chard. Director's *Sun, Sea, Soil, Wine* book is N Fork masterclass.

Bloomer Creek Finger L ★★★ Wild-ferment, Finger L natural-wine styles pioneer. Three bio-minded sites: Auten GEWURZ, RIES; Cayuga PINOT N; Morehouse Rd CHARD. Co-ferments gd, also skin-fermented whites.

Boundary Breaks Finger L ★★★ Germanic RIES, ageable, several styles. Ovid Line pleases all; refreshing Icewine. Earthy early-pick GEWURZ. The Harmonic: gd cool Bx blend, MERLOT-led.

Channing Daughters Long I ★★★ Estate famed for beachy terroir via experiments: natural ferment, Italian varieties. Textured, ageable FRIULANO; cool-maritime LAGREIN; Ramato PINOT GR (*see* Grapes); REFOSCO; CHARDS (single-vyd Hamptons, no-oak blend, L'Enfant Sauvage). Single-site floral PETIT VERDOT. Research is CAB SAUV-led, earthy, tart fruit. Local-aromatics vermouth. Watch new MERLOT (Sculpture Garden adds TEROLDEGO/BLAUFRÄNKISCH). Library blends (r/w).

Damiani Finger L ★★ E Seneca Lake. Fruit from Cayuga, Keuka Lake too. Brut voted best in NY 2024, Blanc de Noirs. Sole e Terra (r); single-vyd GEWURZ, Lemberger (best yrs); Little Lotus Flower (w); Vignoles (w, age 3–5 yrs).

Dear Native Grapes ★★ Small estate vyd, plus sourcing. Big project: pre-Prohibition

---

History in the glass

Pre-Prohibition wines are modish again: local, authentic, sustainable, historical. Vastly improved viti and vini skills help. Look for hybrids: early-C19 (Catawba, Delaware, Diamond, Elvira), in Hudson Valley, NY (Clinton, Dutchess, Iona); turn-of-century French-US (Chambourcin, SEYVAL BL, Vignoles); C20 Geneva, NY (Noiret, Traminette) and MN (Frontenac, Marquette); C21 US (Itasca, Louise Swenson, TBD) and se native muscadines (Noble, Magnolia). Bountiful lessons in e history: in fruit wines from trad blackberries or NJ-invented blueberries, or in grape co-ferments with old apple varieties, or native pawpaws.

native cultivars (CATAWBA, Isabella), MN hybrids (Petite Pearl), new US species (*Vitis aestivalis*). Try Steuben pét-nat, barrel-aged Delaware (or Catawba); field-blends Diana Duchess, Empire State, Iona (from specialist Steve Casscles).

Element Winery Finger L ★★★ Smart, exploratory use of difficult climate: magical, necessary blends like co-ferment PINOT N/SYRAH/GRENACHE; releases only when ready. Library incl 10-yr+ CAB FR, GAMAY. Two more ranges: young fresh In Our Element; Can't Stop/Won't Stop blend. Colloquial: estate, tiny quantities by plot; trad-method NV Brut. New experiments: Petites ARVINE/MANSENG, VERDOT.

Fjord Hudson RR ★★★ Sustainable; benchmark ALBARIÑO in e. Top spontaneous-ferment CAB FR, GAMAY; v.gd CHARD Icewine; ageable MERLOT, also in serious blend with BLAUFRÄNKISH/Cab Fr. Field blend: SAPERAVI/Blaufränkish/Cab Fr.

Floral Terranes Long I ★★★ Fruit from N Fork, wild ferment in garage for concentrated, wild, moody wines (<13% abv). Textured skin-contact RIES; barrel-ferment/raised. Delicious slow-evolve CAB FR, MERLOT (also co-ferment). Library if you can find: earthy CAB SAUV, ferocious PETIT VERDOT. Ciders, most yrs.

Forge Cellars Finger L ★★★ E Seneca Lake. Precise single-site RIES, single-vyd PINOT N (Tango Oaks, cool-climate classic; Leidenfrost, lifted power).

Fox Run Finger L ★★★ Range of RIES v.gd; rare Res CAB FR, LEMBERGER; CAB SAUV; MERLOT. Winemaker Peter Bell mentored many of Finger L's greatest.

Frank, Dr Konstantin Finger L ★★★ Founder of vinifera in Finger L and e, winery on Keuka Lake. Flagship: Lena Res 20 (Bx blend). Many RIES. Rare Siberian/N China AMUR 22, rustic elegance. BLAUFRÄNKISCH 22. Amber RKATSITELI. Old Vines PINOT N (1958 vyd); CAB FR (50-yr+ vines). SAPERAVI, robust, sells out. Masterful trad-method: Ries Brut Nature (30 mths+), Keuka Lake Blanc de Blanc [sic] (CHARD); Blanc de Noirs 19; Brut Natures 20 21, Rosé 21.

Hermann J Wiemer Finger L ★★★ Top US RIES name, many bottlings, some single vyd, Res. Top e nursery. Experimental Julia vyd incl rare SCHIOPPETTINO, PETITE ARVINE, FURMINT. Fine GEWURZ (vines among NY's oldest), CAB FR (single vyd), PINOT N, superlative fizz, some 10 yrs+ tirage. Owns Standing Stone (SAPERAVI; Blanc de Blancs, 1974 vyd; old-vine Ries); gd CAB SAUV, Pinot N. Testing NEBBIOLO.

Hickory Hollow Finger L ★★★ Seneca Lake. Lauded low-intervention: CHARD, RIES (incl 10-yr+ solera), GEWURZ, PINOT BL (Extra Brut too), MERLOT. Winemaker's Nathan K range: library Ries, neutral-oak CAB FR, PINOT N. Chëpika bottles: Catawba, Delaware fine pét-nat.

Hillick & Hobbs ★★ Napa winemaker Paul Hobbs's RIES, in hometown cool-climate Finger L of course. Two fine bottlings: Estate, *sur lies* (library too); Lower Terrace (barrel-ferment, puncheon-raised, natural yeast).

Hosmer Finger L ★★★ On Cayuga Lake, vyd est 1972; RIES, incl limited bottlings. Also CHARD, CAB FR; 80s PINOT N vines, some for Blanc de Noirs.

Keuka Lake Vineyards Finger L ★★★ Vivacious RIES, incl Falling Man (from steep slopes), Evergreen Lek vyd (planted 1999); v.gd CAB FR. Hybrids incl Vignoles (gd pét-nat), cult Alsatian Léon Millot.

Lakewood Vineyards Finger L ★★★ A 3rd-generation estate; gd Res CAB FR; everyday bottle too. Impressive GEWURZ, PINOTS GR/N, multiple RIES.

Hudson Valley? Cab Fr? A marriage made in heaven. In the vineyard, anyway.

Liten Buffel ★★★ Estate in Niag, two PINOT N, PINOT GR Ramato (*see* Grapes), RIES (whole-cluster; also skin-contact). Co-ferment BLAUFRÄNKSICH/SAUV BL. Wild yeasts in neutral oak, no filtering, no sulphur. Noble rot some yrs.

Macari Long I, North F ★★★ Clifftop estate focused on plot, massal selection, bio. Horses cult PETIT VERDOT pét-nat. SAUV BL: clean, grassy Katherine's Field; concrete Lifeforce (perfumed CAB FR too). Breakwater CHARD: Burgundy method shows off Long I quality. Top yrs Alexandra (woodsy CAB SAUV-led Bx blend),

Bergen Road (elegant Merlot-led Bx blend); 21 22. Ethereal, structured PINOT N, savoury Cab Fr, herbal MERLOT (incl library, 20 yrs+).

McCall Long I, North F ★★★ Top Long I-terroir PINOT N since 07, various clones, incl single vyd, Res, rosé, library bottles; gd CAB FR, SAUV BL; red Bx blends. Also French-origin Charolais cattle.

Milea Hudson RR ★★ Rolling, foggy hills; CAB FR (Sang's vyd). Solid BLAUFRÄNKISCH. Heritage Project (restoration-minded old hybrids): VIDAL BL (incl barrel ferment/raised); Baco N/Marcheal Foch/Palmer (little known); CHAMBOURCIN. Started Hudson V Projects with goal of top trad-method wines; PINOT N red too.

Millbrook Hudson RR ★★★ Estate 1st to grow vinifera in Hudson V: CHARD, RIES, PINOT N. Single-vyd Tocai (FRIULANO), CAB FR. Acidity lets reds age a few yrs.

Osmote North F ★★ Seneca Lake. Estate and Finger L/Long I-sourced. CAB FR, also rosé; gd RIES. Equal focus on hybrids: v.gd pét-nat, Cayuga (w, NY hybrid), DeChaunac (r, French-US hybrid, also still wines), Melody (w, NY hybrid).

Paumanok Long I ★★★ Complex cool-climate North F wines; spontaneous ferments, low sulphur. In best yrs only, ageable, occasional library: Assemblage (Bx varieties, 21 22); Grand Vintage (umami MERLOT, herbal CAB FR, 21 22, no 23, top 24); v.gd Minimalist (savoury CHENIN BL, vyd planted 1982; floral Cab Fr; earthy CAB SAUV). Tuthills Lane Cab Sauv, Apollo Drive PETIT VERDOT; 22. New: trad-method Rosé de Pinot 21. Owns/makes Palmer Vyds: Old Roots Merlot, CHARD; Res (Bx-style blend 15 still fresh); Cab Fr; v. exciting ALBARIÑO, SAUV BL.

Ravines Finger L ★★★ Seneca Lake. Inspired RIES: single-vyd Argetsinger, Falls 16, White Springs. SAUV BL, concentrated top GEWURZ. Flagship Argetsinger PINOT N; Limestone Springs vyd CAB FR; MERLOT, Bx style. New: GAMAY on Keuka Lake.

Red Newt Finger L ★★★ Renowned RIES, top US quality. Terroir focus, incl Seneca Lake crus. Viridescens, Bx style from best sites. Elegant GEWURZ, GRÜNER V, PINOT GR. Single-vyd CAB FR, PINOT N, SYRAH. Bistro, local produce.

Red Tail Ridge Finger L ★★★ Seneca Lake. Wild ferment; super CHARD, RIES; elegant BLAUFRÄNKISCH, LAGREIN, v.gd PINOT N (also pét-nat), ZWEIGELT. TEROLDEGO sells out. Sparkling: Blanc de Noirs, pét-nats, Sekt 19, Blanc de Blanc [sic] 19; Perpétuelle Change, takes on NV Champagne, Cuvee #4 (19–22, released 24).

Shaw Vineyard Finger L ★★★ On Seneca Lake, quieter w side. Focus on Res: full-bodied CAB SAUV, MERLOT, PINOT N; clear-cut GEWURZ, RIES on fine lees; barrel-aged Ries too. Orange, blends incl Gewurz, PINOT GR, SAUV BL.

Sheldrake Point Finger L ★★ W Cayuga Lake. Exuberant cool-climate GAMAY; fresh, earthy Bx blends; RIES; single-plot PINOT GR, MUSCAT Ottonel; MERLOT, also v.gd rosé; CAB FR, also trad-method fizz. Unwooded CHARD. Experimental Beta bottles: Lambrusco-like Rouge Éclat, Blanc de Cab Fr, bravely acid-driven RIES.

Silver Thread Finger L ★★★ Small-batch cellar blends; CHARD 40-yr+ vines (also Blanc de Blancs 21), single-vyds (incl 1973-planted Doyle Fournier) RIES (plus Aravelle/Caguya blend), off-dry GEWURZ; LEMBERGER, ageable Cabs/MERLOT; bio. Terroir-convinced: vyd soils match surrounding forest's, solar-powered, vegan.

Sparkling Pointe Long I ★★★ Convincing *fizz*; French winemaker, Champagne grapes, loam soil. Single-vyd Boisseau Blanc de Blancs, 5-yr tirage. Pink Cuvée Cynthia Blanc de Noirs (three PINOT N clones/PINOT M). Creamy, floral Topaz Impérial Brut Rosé (CHARD, Pinots N/M). Solid Brut (Nature too), Blanc de Blancs. Cuvée Carnaval lets MUSCAT (w), MERLOT (r/rosé) into mix.

Suhru & Lieb Long I ★★★ NY maritime. Union of two top estates, some of Long I's oldest vines, largest PINOT BL plot in US. Mostly varietals: glacial-soil SHIRAZ 10 yrs+, age-worthy CAB FR, MALBEC, PETIT VERDOT, TEROLDEGO; rich SAUV BL (MACARI-grown), PINOT GR; takes La Crescent seriously, rich acidity. Ember (Bx blend 21), Estate Meritage, hold both 10+ yrs; trad-method Pinot Bl Brut.

World-class dry, fruity East Coast ciders: Eden Cider Co, Eve's, Sylvan (perry too).

Thirsty Owl Finger L ★★★ W Cayuga Lake. RIES and Finger L-rare MALBEC, plus CAB SAUV, PINOT N, SYRAH (among NY best), planted over 20 yrs ago. Dock for boats.

Usonia Finger L ★★ Cayuga Lake. Estate (CAB FR, RIES, hybrids, co-planted 2023), plus sourced (incl SHAW VYD). Responding to climate change with eg. Geneva White #2, skin-contact GRÜNER V; one bio Cab Fr plot. New Suns (estate Cab Fr).

Weis Vineyards Finger L ★★ Keuka Lake. Winemaker trained in Mosel; v.gd RIES from dry to sweet, incl from limestone, from slate, and TBA-style bottlings; also new NY hybrid Aravelle. Awarded GRÜNER V, BLAUFRÄNKISCH, ZWEIGELT (r/rosé).

Whitecliff Hudson RR ★★ Vegan, site-, soils-driven, incl Olana slope for v.gd barrel-aged CAB FR, GAMAY. PINOT N from limestone ridge. Robust RIES, stony CHARD (also fizz). Serious hybrids: Noiret-led reds, Traminette, VIDAL Bl whites.

Wölffer Estate Long I ★★★ Premier S Fork estate, rosé range (1st set off Hamptons craze) topped by focused, creamy Grandioso. White Horse range: Christian's Cuvée MERLOT, PINOT N; Bx-blend Fatalis Fatum; perfumed Pinot N Landius; rich Antonov SAUV BL; Noblesse Oblige luminous vintage rosé fizz. Limited-release Cellar Series: Merlot rosé, TOCAI. Gold Label CAB FR, Classic Red Blend gd value. Leader in 0% abv wines, red blend by osmosis, gd fruit, no warmth; pink sparkling. Experimenting: massal-planted TREBBIANO Toscano.

North Carolina (NC)

Six AVAs, Atlantic coast to Piedmont foothills to Blue Ridge Mtns. Hurdles: humidity, late-season hurricanes; some heavy oak; but steady growth of serious inventive producers (2024 storm ruined natural-wines leader **plēb**, return hopeful), excellent CAB FR, PETIT MANSENG, TANNAT. In the e: **Cypress Bend** (dr, native muscadine wines), **Sanctuary Vyds** (TEMPRANILLO, SYRAH/Tannat co-ferment). In hilly central NC: **Mountain Books** (incl NC oak barrels), **Parker-Binns**; est Yadkin V AVA, once tobacco plots, dairy farms, try **Jones Von Drehle**, **Junius Lindsay** (new: ROUSSANNE), **Shelton**, **Stony Knoll**; Italy focus in Swan Creek AVA, esp **Raffaldini** (top *appassimento* skills, new 3-yr cycle for r; v.gd MONTEPULCIANO, incl Grande Riserva blend, premium Patrimonio, SAGRANTINO, SANGIOVESE, VERMENTINO), **Sotrio** (v.gd FIANO, TEROLDEGO), plus **Dynamis** (luxury focused on CAB SAUV). In mtns: new steep, tiny Crest of the Blue Ridge AVA, try **Burntshirt**, **Euda** (Cabs Fr/Sauv, gd SAUV BL). **Marked Tree** (herbal Cab Fr), **Souther Williams**, **Stone Ashe**. NC Fine Wines lifts wine (and food, NC-style bbq reputed US best) grown in state.

Ohio (OH)

Midwest; Lake Erie moderates continental winters; 300+ wineries, five AVAs in rich glacial Great Lake-making soils, river valley to Appalachian mtns to Lake Erie islands; C19 fame as Wine Belt (esp Catawba), learning new ways since mid-C20. Look for OQW logo on bottles: min 90% OH-grown. **Debonné** since 70s. Family-run **Ferrante** Grand River Valley AVA DOLCETTO, PINOT N, gd CHARD, RIES. **Laurentia** concrete-tank whites. **Markko** Lake Erie Chard, CAB SAUV, Pinot N;

followed NY's Dr Frank to launch Ohioan vinifera in 70s. **M Cellars** RKATSITELI, Bx style. Site-focus **Vermillion V** granite, clay Cabs; sandstone, loam ARNEIS, MALBEC; limestone LEMBERGER, Moscato Giallo, Pinot N (compost soil).

Oklahoma (OK)

One AVA shared with MO and AR: Ozark Mtn. Hybrids most important, with Chambourcin top variety. **Bois d'Arc** concentration on sweet. **C&H Vyd** grower for other wineries making small quantities of quality sweet (from winery only). **Clauren Ridge** gd Rhône-style reds and CAB FR. **Pecan Creek Winery** excellent Barrel Res Chambourcin, estate CAB SAUV. **Sabatia** ★★ Steve Sneed crafts some of best wines in OK: top SEYVAL BL (w), Chambourcin (r); v.gd rosé. **Shakespeare Wine Company** well-regarded hybrid reds; literary inspired labels.

Oregon (OR)

Cooler and wetter than CA, OR is nonetheless a Med climate, with only the winters seeing heavy rains; 18,600 ha of vyds stretch across 23 AVAs and make nearly every style of wine. While 1143 producers make a bit of everything, OR is best known for its high-quality PINOT N coming out of WILL V. These wines now compete with the best of Burgundy and CA. In the past decade, consumer demand for Chard and trad-method sparkling has increased rapidly, with production growing to meet it. However, these wines still see more limited export than Pinot N and are best found by visiting the wineries.

Principal viticultural areas

Columbia Gorge (Col G) is split between WA and OR. Experimentation, variety, sustainable viticulture.
Rocks District of Milton-Freewater (Walla Walla V [Walla]) entirely in OR, producing dense, age-worthy Syrahs and sapid Grenaches.
Southern Oregon (S OR) warmest growing region, encompasses much of W OR, s of Will V: s sub-AVA Rogue V (Rog V) incl Applegate (App V); n sub-AVA Umpqua V (Um V) incl Elkton OR and Red Hill Douglas County. Rhône and Spanish varieties best. Quality is spottier than Will V but future promising.
Willamette Valley (Will V) sub-AVAs Chehalem Mts (Ch Mts), Dundee Hills (Dun H), Eola-Amity Hills (E-A Hills), Laurelwood District (LD), Lower Long Tom, McMinnville (McM), Mt Pisgah, Polk County, Ribbon Ridge (Rib R), Tualatin Hills, Van Duzer Corridor (Van DC), Yamhill-Carlton (Y-Car). Pinots Bl/Gr, Ries and Gamay excel; beautiful Chard; Pinot N remains star.

Recent vintages

2024 Relatively mild season with long, dry autumn. Projected gd quality.
2023 Warm. Heatwave at véraison reduced yield. Gd quality.
2022 Cool growing season, small, reduced yield; v.gd bright, fresh wines.
2021 Hot, dry; concentrated, balanced acidities. Outstanding wines.
2020 Wildfires: widespread smoke taint in Will V. S OR less so; Rog V esp gd.
2019 What used to be classic: cool, wet = elegant, restrained. Age-worthy.
2018 Hot, dry; deeply coloured, concentrated, age-worthy; S OR smoke issues.
2017 Bumper crop of excellent quality; Col G smoke issues.
2016 Warm; balanced wines, moderate alc.

00 **(Double Zero)** Will V ★★★ Highly lauded label sourcing from v. prestigious vyds to make v. expensive wines.
Abacela Um V ★★★ US's 1st TEMPRANILLO: Fiesta, Barrel Select, South East Block Res, Paramour increasing quality. Classic Private Selection ALBARIÑO.

Abbott Claim E-A Hills, Y-Car ★★★★ Antony Beck owner (*see* Graham Beck, S Africa). Organic, dry-farmed. Flinty CHARD, impeccably balanced PINOT N. Age-worthy.

Adelsheim Chehalem Mtns, Rib R ★★→★★★ Classic, fruity, lightly oaked Breaking Ground PINOT N, Staking Claim CHARD reliably gd value, well distributed.

Analemma Col G ★★★ With 15 bio, estate-grown varieties; seek floral GODELLO, fresh, energetic MENCÍA, TROUSSEAU, GRENACHE.

Antica Terra Will V ★★★★ Spicy, age-worthy PINOT N. Opulent, golden, tannic CHARD. Tasting experiences here lauded.

Antiquum Farm Will V ★★★★ Grazing-based regenerative viticulture. All estate fruit. Concentrated, complex, expressive PINOTS GR/N with beautiful fine tannins.

Archery Summit Dun H, E-A Hills ★★→★★★ Owned by Crimson Wine Group. Rich, structured Summit and Arcus PINOT N age-worthy. New tasting room.

Argyle Will V ★★ Owned by Distinguished Vyds; zesty trad-method sparklings.

Arterberry Maresh Dun H ★★★ One of oldest estates in WILL V, much dry-farmed, own-rooted. Delicate, red-fruit, earthy PINOT N: Maresh Vyd, Old Vines, Weber.

A to Z Wineworks OR ★ Owned by WA's Ste Michelle Wine Estates. Value-priced, soundly made, fruit-forward wines.

Audeant Will V ★★★★ Concentrated, age-worthy, single-vyd PINOT N, outstanding, balanced, toasty CHARD.

Ayoub Dun H ★★★ Elegant; balanced oak. Top estate PINOT N, fun new CAB FR.

Beaux Frères Rib R ★★★ Majority-owned by Champagne Henriot (*see* France). Mikey Etzel still in charge of winemaking. Stars remain estate bottlings, esp elegant, earthy Belles Soeurs PINOT N.

Beckham, AD Chehalem Mtns ★★★ Thoughtfully farmed estate wines; native yeasts, unfined, min sulphites. Perhaps only winery in world where production of terracotta vessels for fermenting is on-site (also sells to other wineries).

Bergström Will V ★★★★ Estate fruit (100%) since 2020. Organic; elegant, powerful wines. Sigrid CHARD v. age-worthy, La Spirale and Le Pre du Col PINOT N.

Bethel Heights E-A Hills ★★★ Now run by 2nd generation (est 70s). Precise, focused PINOT N with layered fruit.

Big Table Farm Will V ★★★★ Holistic farm with animals, vegetables, wine. Complex, concentrated, esp Elusive Queen CHARD, SYRAH, all single-vyd PINOT N.

Brick House Rib R ★★★★ All bio farming; all native ferments. Hands-on, family winemaking team. Excellent Cascadia CHARD, Les Dijonnais PINOT N.

Brooks E-A Hills ★★★ Family estate, bio wines. Exceptional perfumed RIES (dr to sw; up to 20 cuvées; try Ara, Bois Joli, Estate). Also v.gd fruity Rastaban PINOT N.

Cameron Dun H, Rib R ★★★★ One of OR's best-kept secrets. Opulent yet age-worthy CHARD, esp Clos Electrique. Structured, age-worthy PINOT N, esp Arley's Leap. Entry DUN H cuvées gd value. Fun NEBBIOLO from RIB R.

Carriere, JK Will V ★★★ St Dolores Estate on Parrett Mtn: one of least recognized, most promising areas in WILL V. Exquisitely balanced, nuanced, earthy PINOT N from estate and from purchased fruit; v. age-worthy.

Corollary Wines Will V ★★★ Elevated trad-method sparkling.

Crowley Wines Will V ★★★ Tyson C makes classic, graceful CHARD, PINOT N; WILL V blends gd value.

Pinot N is 70%+ of planted vineyard in Will V – higher proportion than Burgundy.

David Hill Vineyards & Winery Tua ★★★ Planted 1966. Organic; Alsace varieties; classic Blackjack (original-vine PINOT N). Discovery Series experimental, natural.

De Ponte Cellars Dun H ★★★★ Beautiful classic PINOT N, fresh MELON DE BOURGOGNE.

Divio, Dom Will V ★★★ Bruno Corneaux pays homage to Burgundian heritage making classic CHARD, PINOT N, bright ALIGOTÉ, juicy Passetoutgrain.

Drouhin Oregon, Dom Dun H, E-A Hills ★★★ Drouhin family-owned (*see* France), made by Véronique Boss-D. Restrained Arthur CHARD, Laurène PINOT N v.gd, firm, best aged. Sister label Roserock in E-A HILLS.

Élevée Winegrowers Will V ★★★ Exploration of sub-AVAs of WILL V with single-vyd sources. Classic, structured, showcase terroir.

Elk Cove Will V ★★→★★★ Family-owned, 400 acres, dry-farmed, some own-rooted, 1st vintage 1977. Single-vyd PINOT N more complex, dark-fruited than entry levels, Clay Court, outstanding Five Mtn and Mt Richmond; v.gd PINOTS BL/GR.

Et Fille Will V ★★★ Family-owned/operated; small estate plot and six sustainably farmed vyds in WILL V. Top age-worthy PINOT N: Gabriella, Palmer Creek best.

Evening Land E-A Hills ★★★ Label that revolutionized OR CHARD. Precise, mineral La Source and Summum Chard, earthy PINOT N with nuanced oak.

Evesham Wood Will V ★★★ Incredible value, age-worthy and complex PINOT N made from all dry-farmed vyds: Le Puits Sec best.

Eyrie Vineyards, The Dun H ★★★★ Dry-farmed, organic, no-till, min-intervention winemaking. Oldest producer in WILL V, original vines planted 1965. Elegant, age-worthy, low-alc. Incredible library releases; CHARD, Daphne, PINOT GR, Sisters, original South Block PINOT N bottlings textural wonders.

Flâneur Wines Will V ★★★ Excellent-value entry-level CHARD, PINOT N. More structured Cuvée Constantin, La Belle Promenade.

Goodfellow Will V ★★★ Sources fruit from dry-farmed vyds. Complex, concentrated yet elegant; Durant CHARD, Lewman PINOT GR, Heritage Whistling Ridge PINOT N.

Gran Moraine Will V ★★★ Part of Jackson Family Wines OR (*see* CA), specializing in trad-method sparkling, restrained CHARD, bright structured PINOT N.

Hamilton Russell Oregon Will V ★★★ Anthony and Olive HR invested in OR to complement S African wines. Elegant CHARD, restrained, structured PINOT N.

Hope Well Wine E-A Hills ★★★ Regenerative-warrior Mimi Casteel; top CHENIN BL.

Hundred Suns Will V ★★★ Firm, vibrant PINOT N, age-worthy structure.

Johan Van D ★★★ Dry-farmed, bio, no-till estate vyd. Owned by Mini Banks, also of Cowhorn. Unique CHARD, PINOTS GR/N, KERNER, BLAUFRÄNKISCH. Skin-contact wines deeply flavoured, resonant.

Kelley Fox Will V ★★★★ Beautifully energetic, elegant wines from PINOTS N/BL, CHARD, GRÜNER V, also blueberries. Mirabai esp gd value.

Ken Wright Cellars Will V ★★★ Single-vyd bottlings from 13 sites in WILL V. Tightly wound, challenging young, lovely with age.

King Estate Will V ★★ Now largest bio producer in US. Still family-owned. Appley PINOT GR core of portfolio, a dozen PINOT N, fruity CHARD, GEWURZ, SAUV BL, fizz.

Lavinea Will V ★★★ Owned by EVENING LAND alumni Isabelle Meunier and Greg Ralston. Entire portfolio of lithe, fine-boned PINOT N.

Lemelson Chehalem Mtns, Dun H, Y-Car ★★★ Family-owned, organic estate growing PINOTS N/GR, CHARD, RIES. Rich, textured wines, often oak-forward.

Lingua Franca E-A Hills ★★★ Stylish CHARD (Bunker Hill, Estate, Sisters), balanced PINOT N (Mimi's Mind, The Plow). Now owned by Constellation Brands (*see* CA).

Loop de Loop Col G, Will V ★★★ Organic, dry-farmed, no-till. Ethereal, red-fruited, spicy PINOT N, bright, fresh CAB FR.

Love & Squalor ★★★ Decidedly superior RIES, GAMAY. Great value.

Deep Roots Coalition: group of producers making wine from dry-farmed vineyards.

Martin Woods Winery Will V ★★★ Talented winemaker Evan Martin sources from myriad AVAs. Excellent earthy GAMAY, PINOT N, SYRAH. Cracklingly energetic CHARD, RIES manage to outperform reds.

Morgen Long Will V ★★★★ CHARD specialist. Laser-focused acid, mineral, citrus, well-integrated oak. Incredibly ageable. Seven Springs, X Omni standouts.

Nicolas-Jay Will V ★★★ More Burgundians in OR: Jean-Nicolas Méo of Dom Méo-Camuzet (*see* France) and music entrepreneur Jay Boberg. Bold, structured Momtazi, concentrated Own-Rooted PINOT N.

Patricia Green Cellars Will V ★★★ Excellent, red-fruited, moderate-weight, single-vyd PINOT N. Estate Bonshaw Block, Estate Etzel Block, Mysterious, Notorious superb. Rare OR SAUV BL.

Perkins Harter E-A Hills ★★★ Lightweight, balanced, wet-earth, cherry-fruit PINOT N and fresh, floral, toasty CHARD from Bracken estate vyd.

Ponzi Lau ★★→★★★ Owned by Champagne Bollinger (*see* France). Avellana CHARD, Aurora PINOT N v.gd. Fruit-forward Classico, Tavola Pinot N gd value.

Purple Hands Will V ★★★ Family-owned, dry-farmed, organic estate vyds making ripe, rich yet fresh CHARD, PINOT N.

Résonance Will V ★★★ Jadot's (*see* France) OR project. Découverte CHARD, Estate PINOT N best, most age-worthy. Need vigorous decant when young.

Rex Hill Will V ★★ Owned by WA's Ste Michelle Wine Estates. B Corp (*see* box, opposite). Rich CHARD, Bumptious, red-fruited, oak-forward PINOT N.

Ribbon Ridge Winery Rib R ★★★ Ridgecrest label gd-value, textural wines: GRÜNER V, RIES, GAMAY, PINOTS GR/N. Aged Pinot N from RIB R label outstanding, elegant.

Rose & Arrow Will V ★★★ Micro-production; age-worthy PINOT N from winemaker Felipe Ramirez and terroir consultant Pedro Parra. Second label: Alit, v.gd value if you subscribe. 2021 not as impressive as prior vintages.

Sequitur Rib R ★★★ Another project from BEAUX FRÈRES' Etzel family (vyds border); focused, fine CHARD, PINOT N. Labels, names change annually.

Serene, Dom Dun H ★★★ Full, oaky, rich, polished CHARD, PINOT N. Thriving hospitality programme in Bend, Portland, WILL V, often pouring library vintages.

Shea Wine Cellars Y-Car ★★★ One of most lauded vyds in all of OR; own-estate CHARD, PINOT N in richly fruited, oak-forward style.

Sokol Blosser Will V ★★→★★★ Family-owned, organic, historic producer run by 2nd generation. Estate and Orchard Block PINOT N, structure, length. Evolution early-drinking value.

Somers, JC Will V ★★★ Small-production, dry-farmed, focused, elegant PINOT N, beautiful Bx-esque, lightly oaked SAUV BL.

Soter Will V ★★★★ Tony S, CA legend, shines with balanced, age-worthy CHARD, PINOT N, bubbly. Estate-grown Mineral Springs Ranch, all bio, has best portfolio. Planet Oregon for value.

Stoller Will V ★★ Larger production, enjoyable, earlier-drinking CHARD, PINOT N.

Tan Fruit Will V ★★★★ Jim Maresh (ARTERBERRY MARESH) CHARD project, sourcing vyd designates around WILL v. Eyrie, Oak Grove, Fairview incredibly different but all v.gd.

Thomas Dun H ★★★★ Best-kept secret in WILL v; one man, 4 acres, dry-farmed PINOT N; one wine, one release/yr in early Nov. No visits. Buy at a handful of small retail locations in OR, and A&B Vintners in UK. Ethereal wine that is always expressive of the vintage.

Troon App V ★★→★★★ The 2nd regenerative organic vyd in US. Excellent textural Estate VERMENTINO, SYRAH (Siskiyou best). Rest of portfolio tends towards funky light reds, orange (Glou Glou GRENACHE, Kubli Bench Amber).

Tumwater Vineyard Will V ★★★ Fresh mineral CHARD, red-fruited PINOT N, both with subtle well-integrated oak.

Twill Will V ★★★ Small-production fresh CHARD, pure PINOT N, peppery SYRAH from dry-farmed vyds.

Walter Scott E-A Hills ★★★★ Family-owned, focused on vyd sources. Precise, linear, buzz-worthy CHARD. Earthy, balanced PINOT N, well-integrated oak. GAMAY also excellent. Freedom Hill, Sojourner, X-Novo vyds top list. Age-worthy.

Willamette Valley Vineyards Rocks, Will V ★★ Many shareholder/owners; extensive vyds, mostly value CHARD, PINOT N, premium Elton. Rocks District now home to Maison Bleue, Pambrun.

Winderlea Will V ★★★ Vibrant single-vyd PINOT N. Legacy, Weber, fizz v.gd; all bio.

Pennsylvania (PA)

Mid-Atlantic, continental climate, humidity; 1st commercial vines (Alexander, native) in US, end of C18. Now: ALBARIÑO v.gd, esp **Galen Glen**; GRÜNER V, PINOT N, Bx varieties; many Italians, BARBERA to FIANO. Lake Erie-softened nw. Milder in se: **Va La** cult Avondale field blends, incl Rondinella, CORVINA, 11 NEBBIOLO clones, funky rosato; **Vox Vineti** Nebbiolo, sell-out rosé (five early pick r blend, barrel-fermented), orange SEM/SAUV BL. Central Lehigh V: **Galen Glen** windy, 305m (1000ft) up; **Stone Cellar** range from oldest vines; Grüner V, gd sparkling; **Stony Run** v.gd Brut, plush Albariño, library Cabs, Chambourcin. Try also **Allegro**, reliable since 70s; **Armstrong Vyd** CAB FR; **Fero Vyds** bright LEMBERGER, celebrated SAPERAVI; **Karamoor** MERLOT; **Mazza** Lake Erie TEROLDEGO; **Mural City Cellars** Philly urban winery, serious natural style, incl Bx-inspired PA Merlot/Cab Fr/PETIT VERDOT/NJ Chambourcin, figgy, citrus Phinato vermouth; **Penns Woods** Sauv Bl, Pinot N, Chambourcin Res; **Presque Isle** early vinifera PA winery, DORNFELDER; **Vynecrest**; **Waltz** Cab Fr; **Wayvine** gd barrique-aged native Carmine (also rosé and Merlot blend). Local sommeliers' favourite: **Binah Winery** Blanc de Blancs.

Philly urban wineries: Mural City; Camuna; Pray Tell. Local grapes, city tastes.

Texas (TX)

Texas Hill Country (THC) and Texas High Plains (THP) major AVAs; THC has subregions, THP does not. Other regions outside AVAs incl N TX, nr Dallas, and E TX towards Louisiana. Portuguese and Med varieties best in THP. Rhône and Bx varieties best in THC. Hybrids excel in E TX.

Ab Astris ★★ Textured, refined. Elegant Narra TANNAT, esp elegant. Avignon blend (r), homage to Châteauneuf (*see* France). Souzão great, rarely seen as varietal.

Adega Vinho Specialist in Iberian and Rhône varieties in refreshing style. CHARD well regarded; TEMPRANILLO excellent; TOURIGA N and blends also v.gd.

Becker Vineyards ★★ Historic property with visitor centre and lavender fields. Bold, ripe, oaky Bx and Rhône styles; Claret is oft-awarded favourite; try various CAB SAUV bottlings; Prairie Rôtie is a signature.

Bending Branch Winery ★★★ Big reds and lesser-known grapes here. Known for superlative TANNAT in a couple of bottlings; also v.gd Iberian and Med: PETITE SIRAH, SAGRANTINO, Souzão.

Duchman Family Winery ★★★★ Benchmark Italian stars here from older vyds:

Oswald Vyd MONTEPULCIANO is signature, v.gd AGLIANICO, SANGIOVESE; crisp, refreshing, textured TREBBIANO, VERMENTINO.

Enoch's Stomp ★ Superb fortifieds from Blanc du Bois and Lenoir in NE TX, outside AVAs. Light Portejas perennial award winner. Also v.gd orange Villard Blanc, red Norton.

Fall Creek Vineyards ★★ Several ranges: super-premium ExTerra range; Classics: CHENIN BL, SAUV BL. Blends perform well here.

Frio Canyon Vineyard ★ Tim Leach crafts benchmark MOURVÈDRE along with signature FCV Cuvée red blend.

Haak Winery ★★★ Age-worthy vintage Madeira-style Blanc du Bois and Jacquez are classic, world-class. Dry herb-and-citrus Blanc du Bois also v.gd.

Heath Family Brands Owns several brands; try Heath fizz. Owns Kuhlman Cellars (Rhône, Bx r blends) and Invention Vyds (awarded SANGIOVESE).

Hilmy Cellars ★★ One of largest vyds in Hill Country. Rhône, Bx reds, plus TEMPRANILLO. Excellent stainless-steel Tejas Bl ROUSSANNE/MARSANNE (w), v.gd inky AGLIANICO, PETIT VERDOT, structured Tempranillo.

Kerrville Hills ★★★ John Rivenburgh produces leathery TANNAT, supple PICPOUL Bl, plus varietal Souzão and TEROLDEGO; all v.gd.

Lewis Wines ★★★★ Focus on single-vyd Iberian varieties, esp leading TEMPRANILLO, v.gd crisp CHENIN BL; experimenting with carbonic reds. Try two different vyd bottlings of Tempranillo and MOURVÈDRE.

If you want 100% TX grapes in your glass, buy an AVA, county or vineyard wine.

Llano Estacado ★★ Consistently excellent full-bodied 1836 (r/w); Super Tuscan-styled Viviana (r/w) also gd.

Lost Draw Cellars ★★★ Same group as William Chris Vyds. Sparkling PINOT M. Numerous styles of rosé. Compare single-vyd or THC/THP bottlings of MOURVÈDRE, SANGIOVESE, TEMPRANILLO.

McPherson Cellars ★★★ Pioneering TX wine family. Restrained, balanced Iberian, Rhônes, plus heritage-vyd SANGIOVESE. Age-worthy ROUSSANNE Res. Crisp PICPOUL Bl. Excellent varietal ALICANTE BOUSCHET, CARIGNAN, CINSAULT. Try Block Selection special bottlings.

Messina Hof Winery ★★ Bold, oaky. SAGRANTINO pioneer; CAB FR consistent award-winner. Range of sweet.

Pedernales Cellars ★★★ Rhône, Spanish grapes, structured style. Benchmark VIOGNIER, TEMPRANILLO. GSM excellent. Co-founder Julie Kuhlken's PhD in philosophy shows in thoughtful, meditative wines that can age.

Perissos Vineyard and Winery Italian focus, plus Spanish. Big reds, incl excellent AGLIANICO, TEMPRANILLO, ever-evolving Racker's Blend. Doro Collection of special bottlings each yr.

Signor Vineyards Planted 2015, 1st vintage 2017. Estate-vyd MALBEC, MOURVÈDRE, SANGIOVESE, TANNAT, all v.gd.

Spicewood Vineyards ★★★★ Sibling winery to RON YATES. Estate-grown wines of finesse, elegance, vibrancy. Outstanding signature Good Guy field blend (r); taut, textured The Independence Bx blend (r); upfront El Guey (r); refined Battle of Toro TOURIGA N/TEMPRANILLO.

Valley Mills Vineyards Located in Waco between Dallas and Austin; excellent MOURVÈDRE, v.gd TEMPRANILLO.

Wedding Oak ★ Leading AGLIANICO producer. Outstanding Castanet CINSAULT rosé. Excellent flagship Tioja TEMPRANILLO blend. Big, oak-aged ROUSSANNE. Red Blend, Tempranillo v.gd.

Westcave Cellars Winery and brewery; consistently benchmark CAB FR. Compare estate-vyd THC CAB SAUV. Big NEBBIOLO, rich PETIT VERDOT also gd.

William Chris Vineyards ★★★★ Terroir-expressive. Best-in-class single-vyd bottlings of MOURVÈDRE. Flagship Hunter (r) also v.gd. Distinctive Jacquez fortified. LOST DRAW CELLARS same group.

Wine for the People ★★ Rae Wilson's reputation began with brand Dandy Rosé but has expanded to encompass excellent range of La Valentía reds, incl CARIGNAN, CINSAULT, GRENACHE.

Wright, Ch In Texas Davis Mountains AVA, W TX. Living Water Vyd MALBEC is star. Heraldic red blend, VIOGNIER also v.gd. Closed at time of writing; future unclear.

Yates, Ron ★★★ Single-vyd Friesen red blend best. Farmhouse Vyds rosé also v.gd. Focus on Rhône, Spanish, Italian varieties.

Vermont (VT)

In the ne, 28 producers, 92 acres. Thought/quality leader of the six NEW ENGLAND states. With mtns, harsh winters, brief sunny summers, frost, hail, humidity, new flash floods and landslides, those who dare plant vyds share fruit: hybrids like Frontenac N, La Crescent plus vinifera in extreme n terroirs. Masterful apple-grape blends. Lots bio-farmed, natural-thinking, like pioneers **La Garagista** (top Marquette, skins also used for w-grapes rosé; Brianna with other hybrid skins, r/w; Frontenac, La Crescent) with many collaborators/mentees, incl **Iapetus** weighty L'Acadie Bl; Marquette still blends, pét-nats; Antecedent rare VT-grown RIES, 24-yr-old vines; Petite Pearl. **La Montanuela** fizz-focused. **Shelburne Vyds** Marquette Res; owns top Eden cider. **Ellison Estate** beguiling St Croix, also in blends. **Lincoln Peak** incl nouveau Marquette. **Stella 14** by MS, spontaneous-ferm Frontenacs N/Bl, Marquette. **Kalchē Wine** co-op: social values, gd wine.

Virginia (VA)

Mid-Atlantic/s-continental climate. Challenges: humidity, spring frost, winter freeze, harvest-time hurricanes, downy mildew, black rot; wide grower knowledge-sharing helps, so do recent rain-free ripening seasons. A little MERLOT in many reds, planting on heights, esp Shenandoah V foothills (least humid of e) and Blue Ridge slopes. Elegant outcomes statewide in classical (CAB FR, Merlot, PETIT VERDOT; stars of central and s) and experimental (hardy, rich, high-acid PETIT MANSENG sings in dr or sw; NEBBIOLO, TANNAT gaining ground); CAB SAUV; VIOGNIER favoured too. Serious about hybrids, incl Traminette, Norton, new VA types being worked out now.

Eastern trend for juicy, easy reds: nouveau/novello releases, Barbera to Marquette.

Ankida Ridge ★★★ Top, ageable, precise PINOT N: rare, possibly best in VA; rosé too. Steep, ancient-granite slopes up to 590m (1800ft) in Blue Ridge Mtns; CHARD; Brut; thoughtful GAMAY, incl nouveau. Farm incl chickens, Katahdin sheep.

Barboursville ★★★ In Monticello: rolling hills, cattle, inn, Zonin family-owned. Mainstays PETIT VERDOT, varietal or for best-vintage blend Octagon, decades ageable. White Nascent: VIOGNER/VERMENTINO (also as varietal Res)/FALANGHINA's oiliness. Monticello ideal CAB FR Res, 99 still energetic. Paxxito is luscious VIDAL/MUSCAT Ottonel *appassimento*. Blanc de Noirs from PINOT M. Italian focus incl NEBBIOLO Res age 10 yrs+, FIANO Res, plush BARBERA.

Blenheim ★★ In hilly Charlottesville, elegant wines, <13% abv; raised in French/US/Hungarian oak. Earthy estate ALBARIÑO, GRÜNER V; round ROUSSANNE; pithy RKATSITELI (80s vines); local-sourced Monticello CAB FR, PETIT VERDOT; Painted White Loire blend, labels by founder/musician Dave Matthews. Base of Oenoverse club, an access and wine-education initiative.

Cana Vineyards ★★ Rosé-serious. N VA farmland; CABS SAUV/FR, MERLOT. Unité Res (Bx-style r). Also MALBEC, TEMPRANILLO.

Capstone Vineyards ★★ High-altitude, LINDEN neighbour; CHARD, CHENIN BL, plus Bx blend estate-bottled since 2023.

Cave Ridge ★★ Shenandoah V. Red Silk, vintage-reflecting CAB FR in noteworthy yrs with special labels. Awarded Fossil Hills Res is Cabs, PETITE VERDOT (library wines). Oak-raised Chambourcin.

Norton Network: 22 VA producers of Norton, C19 hybrid grown by Daniel Norton.

Early Mountain ★★★ Champions VA winemaking. Made name with rich, earthy Bx-style Eluvium. Rise in best yrs: 19 21 22, incl TANNAT. Single-site CAB FR: Quaker Run is lush; try 21 22 (CHARD too). Elegant, age-worthy PETIT MANSENG. White-blend Intention in Petit Manseng best yrs. Top tourist facilities.

Glen Manor Vineyards ★★ Historic farm, 5th generation. Vines on steep rocky slopes in Blue Ridge Mtns 305m (1000ft)+ up. Began with SAUV BL, now joined by rich CAB FR from 20–30-yr-old vines; off-dry PETITS MANSENG/VERDOT.

King Family Vineyards ★★★ Mountain Plains, best lots by yr. Structured whites (CHARD, PETIT MANSENG, VIOGNER); complex reds (Bx style). MERLOT-based Meritage worth waiting for (library wines too); peppery red-fruit CAB FR (concrete/oak); top tiny-production *vin de paille*-style Petit Manseng. Experimental Small-Batch Series, incl co-ferment PETITS VERDOT/Manseng. SAVAGNIN planted 2020. French winemaker's own Dom Finot, natural yeast, no sulphites: single-vyd Petit Verdot rosé, Cab Fr, TANNAT.

Linden ★★★★ A mtn estate founded in 80s by early believer in site over fruit; classic methods, grapes, ageing in mind; now responding to more erratic weather with experimental Wabi Sabi: PETIT MANSENG, SEM, 80s-planted VIDAL Bl. Small production, three high-altitude dry-farmed sites, ageable: lively single-vyd CHARD, VA benchmark; vivacious SAUV BL, 7 yrs+; savoury PETIT VERDOT; elegant, complex Bx-style reds often require ageing; also Claret. Some library wines; vertical pours in tasting room.

Lost Mountain ★★★★ Was RdV: new French owners, same MW winemaker. Named after flagship wine: elegant, powerful CAB SAUV-led Lost Mountain (VA's 1st $100 wine) from granite hillside (complex MERLOT-led Rendezvous is too). New projects: ALBARIÑO, SEM, PETIT MANSENG.

Midland ★★★ Old family farm, limestone soils 400m (1312ft) up. Sharp, rich no-dosage Rosé Brut 19. Benchmark CHARD, long spontaneous oak-ferment; peppery BLAUFRÄNKISCH (incl as CAB FR/Noiret blend); structured Cab Fr; top PETIT MANSENG; RIES. New high plantings incl resistant MERLOT Kanthus. Family's custom-crush Common Wealth is also VA-wine co-op, think tank, tasting room for like-minded producers. Winemaker makes *Lightwell Survey* too, bold co-ferments: earthy Cab Fr/Petit Manseng; astounding Ries-assisted Petit Manseng; rosé (co-ferment Chambourcin/Petit Manseng), three white hybrids.

Pollak ★★ Estate fruit, looks to France for VA understanding, international style: big earthy PETIT VERDOT; hefty ageable Meritage; creamy PINOT GR; lush, spicy VIOGNIER; heftier CABS FR/SAUV, MERLOT. NEBBIOLO now planted.

Ramiiisol ★★★ Monticello AVA in Blue Ridge Mtns foothills. No-expense-spared CAB FR, holistic-terroir focus incl iron-rich granite gneiss parcels, forest, top Italian cooperages. Complex lasting vintages, 16–20 ethereal, wild site blends; single-vyd trials. MONTEPULCIANO as v.gd rosato inspired by Cerasuolo (*see* Italy).

Rausse, Gabriele / Vino dal Bosco ★★★ Two labels, small, quality estate nr Monticello, one of VA's 1st planters and son; NE Italian sensibility, French technology. Single-vyd CAB FR Res (sulphur-free too), MALBEC; ROUSSANNE Res, GRÜNER V Res. Blanc de Noirs, *méthode ancestrale* CHASSELAS, PINOT N, amphora-raised Cabernet Dorsa, VA-grown, v. rare in US (also in Rosato blend).

Stinson ★★ Small producer in Blue Ridge Mtns. Estate (SAUV BL to PETIT VERDOT) plus sourced VA fruit; v.gd wait-for-it Meritage, acidity-driven ripe fruit; oak-raised CAB FR, TANNAT; Blanc de MOURVÈDRE.

Veritas ★★★ Solid estate, steep forest vyds. Ageable PETIT MANSENG, restrained SAUV BL. Long-macerated Bx-style Monticello Res (dark fruit, leather, acidity), complex PETIT VERDOT, concentrated, floral CAB FR (age 10 yrs+), St-Émilion-inspired Claret; CHARD (oak or no). Scintilla trad-method (up to 5 yrs on lees). Momentarious range is vintage one-offs.

Walsh ★★ In VA-wine stronghold Loudoun County. Site-specific SAUV BL, incl Loire-inspired. Terroir-driven CHENIN BL, PETIT MANSENG. Twin Notch vyd: red blend; single-vyd TANNAT (long maceration, for ageing), Cabs, MERLOT (granite mtn site).

Washington (WA)

Washington is the 2nd-largest wine producer in the US but sits in CA's massive shadow. The wines mix New World ripeness with Old World structure, providing immediate enjoyment and profound ageability. There's also exceptional value to be had across all prices. The catch? Limited production makes many wines hard to find but well worth seeking out.

Principal viticultural areas

Columbia Valley (Col V) Huge AVA in central and E WA, with a touch in OR. High-quality Cab Sauv, Merlot, Ries, Chard, Syrah. Key sub-divisions incl Yakima Valley (Yak V), Red Mtn, Walla AVAs.

Red Mountain (Red Mtn) Sub-AVA of Col V and Yak V. Hot region known for Cabs and Bx blends.

Walla Walla Valley (Walla) Sub-AVA of Col V with own identity and vines in WA and OR. Home of important boutique brands and prestige labels. Syrah, Cab Sauv and Merlot.

Yakima Valley (Yak V) Sub-AVA of Col V. Focus on Merlot, Syrah, Ries.

WA all about variety (with 100+), growing everything from Algianico to Zinfandel.

Abeja Col V, Walla ★★★ WALLA winery; high-quality COL V CHARD, CAB SAUV. Beekeeper's Blend gd value.

Airfield Yak V ★ All estate fruit, providing high quality-to-price wines across entry, Res tiers. Lone Birch value.

Amavi Walla ★★ All estate wines with v.gd WALLA SEM, CAB SAUV, SYRAH.

Andrew Will Col V, HH Hills, Yak V ★★★★ 10' 12' 14' 16 18 Winemaker (2nd generation) Will Carmada focuses on reserved, age-worthy style. Sorella flagship.

Avennia Col V, Yak V ★★★ 10 12' 14' 16' 18' 21 Benchmark Woodinville producer focuses on old vines, earlier picking. Sestina Bx blend top. Gravura Bx blend v.gd value. Lydian value label.

Baer Winery Col V ★★★ Woodinville stalwart dedicated to luscious Stillwater Creek Vyd red blends. MERLOT-based Ursa consistent standout.

Betz Family Col V ★★★→★★★★ 10 12' 14' 16' 18' 19 21 One of Woodinville's founding wineries; top-quality Bx, Rhône styles for 25 yrs+. All of note. Père de Famille CAB SAUV flagship. SUNU label (OR). Recently purchased by Ackley Brands (WA).

Browne Family Col V ★ Brand from wine giant Precept. CAB SAUV the highlight.

Cadence Red Mtn ★★★ 10' 12' 14 16' 17' 19' 21 Focus on Bx blends from estate vyd. Immortal wines with emphasis on structure, class. All standouts that punch well above their weight. Coda from declassified barrels exceptional value.

Cairdeas Col V ★★★ Rhône specialist making everything from plush, pleasurable blends to rarely seen varieties. Diffraction value label.

Canvasback Red Mtn ★★ Napa's The Duckhorn Portfolio WA brand: v.gd CAB SAUV.

Cayuse Walla ★★★★ 10 11 12' 14 16' 19 21 Vigneron Christophe Baron planting in cobblestone soils helped put WALLA on map. Cult, mailing list-only, with yrs-long wait. Stratospheric scores, steep prices on secondary market, but worth it. Sister wineries Hors Categorie, Horsepower, No Girls also top quality. Double Lucky v.gd value.

Charles Smith Wines Col V ★★ Eponymous winemaker spun off brand to wine-giant Constellation before The Wine Group (both CA) took over in 2022, Ackley Brands (WA) in 2024. Focus on value RIES, CAB SAUV, MERLOT.

Put one foot in France and another in CA and you'll be right where WA wine stands.

Col Solare Red Mtn ★★★→★★★★ 10 12' 14 18 Started as RED MTN partnership between CH STE MICHELLE and Antinori (*see* Italy). Antinori took full ownership 2023. CAB SAUV, complexity, longevity.

Columbia Crest Col V ★★→★★★ Sister winery to CH STE MICHELLE, all about quality, value. Well-priced, v.gd Grand Estates label; Res wines cut above, esp CAB SAUV.

Columbia Winery Col V ★ One of WA's founding wineries, now owned by (WA) Ackley Brands. Value, grocery-store wines.

Corliss Col V ★★★→★★★★ 08' 10 12' 14 16 18 Cult producer, extended ageing in barrel/bottle in classic style. Sister winery Tranche focuses on Blue Mtn fruit. Secret Squirrel value brand.

Côte Bonneville Yak V ★★★ Estate wines from DuBrul, highly regarded vyd; 2nd-generation winery. Extended bottle-age before release, with focus on sophistication. *Train Station* v.gd value.

DeLille Col V, Red Mtn ★★★ 10' 12' 14' 16 18 19 21 Among Woodinville's founding wineries, 30 yrs in 2022. High-end Bx, Rhône styles; D2, Four Flags v.gd value. Chaleur Bl often state's best white. Métier entry-level offerings.

Devison Walla ★★★ Attention-getting wines with voice, incl state's best SAUV BL, MALBEC, ROSÉ. Above the Flood outrageously gd Rhône blend.

Dossier Col V ★★★ Joint winery from Seattle businessman and a former NFL player. Focus on sophisticated hedonism.

Doubleback Walla ★★★→★★★★★ 10' 12 16 18 21 Ex-footballer Drew Bledsoe's winery isn't a vanity project; classy, elegant WALLA CAB SAUV. Bledsoe Family sister winery. Bledsoe-McDaniels OR PINOT and WA SYRAH project.

Dunham Walla ★★ Long-time WALLA producer of v.gd CAB SAUV, SYRAH, mixing fruit and barrel. Three-Legged Red, Trutina gd value.

Dusted Valley Walla ★★ Focus on COL V, WALLA, from value Boomtown to high-end single-vyd offerings. Stained Tooth SYRAH consistent standout.

Echolands Walla ★★★ Lower alc, food-friendly Bx styles, SYRAH, GRENACHE.

Figgins Walla ★★★★ 08 10 12 14 16 18 21 Winemaker Chris F (LEONETTI; 2nd generation) focuses on single vyd in Upper Mill Creek. Big, structured Bx blends. Patience/decanting required.

Foolhardy Walla ★★★ Swoon-worthy, food-friendly wines show region they're grown. Try CAB SAUV, SAUV BL.

Force Majeure Red Mtn ★★★→★★★★ Todd Alexander left Napa's Bryant Family Vyd to take reins at all-estate winery using RED MTN, WALLA fruit. Big, bold style. Among best in state.

Gård Col V ★★★ Winemaker Matías Kúsulas breathes new life into this winery; expansive lineup of estate wines from Royal Slope and beyond. Focused, flavourful. All hit high marks.

Gorman Col V, Red Mtn ★★★ Hedonism: rich, ripe wines. Evil Twin CAB SAUV/ SYRAH calling card. Devil You Know/Don't v.gd value. Ashan CHARD project.

Gramercy Walla ★★★ 10 12' 13 16 18 19 Founded by sommelier, emphasis on lower-alc/oak, higher-acid, food-friendly wines. Speciality earthy SYRAH, herby CAB SAUV. John Lewis Res Syrah consistent standout. Lower East cheaper label.

Grosgrain Walla ★★ Champion of underdog varieties: fruity LEMBERGER (sp).

Guardian Col V ★★★ One of Woodinville's original "Grape Killers", wines in bold style. Newsprint less pricey label.

H3 Col V ★ Spin-off from COLUMBIA CREST. Value CAB, MERLOT, Red Blend.

Januik Col V ★★★ 10 12' 18 19 21 Consistent quality, value Bx varieties and blends. Some of state's best CHARD. Son Andrew has eponymous label.

Washington breaks estate model, with wineries rarely co-located with vineyard.

J Bookwalter Winery Col V ★★★ Long-time producer of hedonistic, old-vine red blends. Readers v.gd value.

Kevin White Winery Yak V ★★★ Micro-producer of high-quality, pure, outrageous-value Rhône-style wines. The trick? Getting them before they're gone.

Kiona Red Mtn ★★ A 3rd-generation winery, 1st to plant on RED MTN and still one of the largest growers. Estate LEMBERGER v.gd.

K Vintners Col V, Walla ★★★ Founder Charles Smith made his name with cattle brand-style black-and-white labels, cultish, single-vyd SYRAH, Syrah/CAB SAUV blends. CHARD-focused sister winery. Also CasaSmith, Substance, ViNo.

Latta Col V ★★★ Ex-K VINTNERS winemaker Andrew L; stunning, pure single-vyd GRENACHE, MALBEC, MOURVÈDRE, SYRAH. Latta Latta v.gd value. Disruption, Kind Stranger side projects, value.

L'Ecole No 41 Walla ★★★ 10 12' 14 16 18 21 One of WALLA's founding wineries. Superb-value COL V wines, incl MERLOT. Higher-tier Walla offerings. Ferguson flagship Bx blend. CHENIN BL, SEM v.gd value.

Leonetti Walla ★★★★ 08 10' 12' 14 18 19 Well-deserved cult status; WALLA's founding winery. Steep prices for all-estate, cellar-worthy CAB SAUV, MERLOT, SANGIOVESE; Res Bx-blend flagship.

Liminal Red Mtn ★★★★ New cult producer of high-elevation, intense RED MTN reds and whites that demand attention.

Long Shadows Walla ★★★→★★★★ Brings globally famous winemakers to WA to make one wine each. Feather Cab by Randy Dunn (Napa). Poet's Leap RIES one of best in state. All worth seeking.

Luke Col V ★★ Producer of well-priced Wahluke reds that way overdeliver.

Mark Ryan Winery Red Mtn, Yak V ★★★ Original Woodinville "Grape Killer" known for big, bold style. But there's refinement too. Dissident v.gd value. MERLOT-based Long Haul, Dead Horse CAB SAUV standout. Lonely Heart Cab top Res. Second label: Board Track Racer, gd value.

Matthews Col V ★★★ Long-time Woodinville brand recently re-envisioned with new winemaking team. Attention getting results.

Northstar Walla ★★★ When MERLOT was WA's guiding star, this producer helped lead way. Decades later, it still does. CH STE MICHELLE sister winery.

Novelty Hill Col V ★★★ Focus on fruit from Stillwater Creek Vyd. Outstanding value across portfolio, esp CHARD, CAB SAUV.

Owen Roe Yak V ★★★ Long-time producer of YAK V CAB SAUV, SYRAH and Bx blends emphasizing restraint.

Pacific Rim Col V ★★ Oceans of tasty, inexpensive, eloquent Dry to Sweet and Organic. For more depth, single-vyd releases.

Passing Time Col V ★★★→★★★★ Former pro quarterbacks Dan Marino and Damon Huard focus on appellation-specific CAB SAUV. Winemaker Chris Peterson (AVENNIA). Horse Heaven Hills tops. Quickly earning cult status.

Pepper Bridge Walla ★★★ Estate wines, Bx style, from top WALLA sites. Structured, classy. Time in cellar required. SAUV BL v.gd.

Prospice Col V ★★★ One of most exciting entrants of past decade, making reserved wines with a sense of place.

Pursued by Bear Col V ★★★ Project from actor Kyle MacLachlan makes delicious, age-worthy CAB SAUV, SYRAH.

Quilceda Creek Col V ★★★★ 04' 07 10 12' 14' 16' 18' 21 Flagship producer of WA, CAB SAUV known for richness, layering, ageing potential. One of most lauded in world. Sold by allocation. Buy if you can find it – and if you can afford to.

Reininger Walla ★★ Long-time producer of tasty WALLA reds. Second label: Helix.

Reynvaan Family Walla ★★★ 10' 11 12' 14 16 18 21 Wait-list winery focusing on estate vyds in Rocks District, Blue Mtn foothills. Reds get raves – deservedly so – but don't miss whites.

Ste Michelle, Ch Col V ★★→★★★ State's founding winery offers gd value (r/w), plus estate offerings and higher-end Res. World's largest RIES producer, dry and off-dry COL V exceptional value.

Savage Grace Yak V ★★ Producer of low-oak, low-alc, low-intervention, single-vyd wines with something to say.

Saviah Walla ★★★ Long-time producer of estate wines in reserved style. High quality:value ratio The Jack label gd value.

Seven Hills Winery Walla ★★★ 10 12' 14 16 18 21 One of WALLA's founding wineries, now owned by CA's Crimson Wine Group. MERLOT v.gd value.

Sleight of Hand Walla ★★★ Audiophile Trey Busch focuses on Bx blends, Rhône styles. Seek Funkadelic SYRAH from Rocks District. Renegade cheaper label.

Sparkman Red Mtn, Yak V ★★★ Woodinville "Grape Killer" producer, focus on power, diversity, making 24+ wines. Ruby Leigh, Stella Mae Bx blends consistent standouts. Kingpin top CAB SAUV.

Spring Valley Walla ★★★ CH STE MICHELLE property focusing on estate reds. Uriah MERLOT Bx blend the headliner, showing class.

Syncline Col V ★★★ Columbia Gorge, focus on fresh, pure Rhône styles. Subduction Red v.gd value. Sparkling GRÜNER V insider wine. PICPOUL consistent standout.

The Walls Walla ★★★ Former Pride (Napa) winemaker Sally Johnson Blum now in charge. Opulent RED MTN, WALLA reds.

Trothe HH Hills ★★★→★★★★ 19 20' 21 New producer reaching for brass ring of cult status. Quality is stratospheric. So are prices.

Two Vintners Col V ★★★ Some of WA's best Rhône styles; COL V SYRAH and GRENACHE v.gd value.

Valdemar Walla ★★★ WALLA outpost for Spain's Bodegas Valdemar. Huge investments in vyd, winery.

Valo Col V ★★★ Grower-winemaker Matías Kúsulas focuses on Royal Slope AVA's Conner Lee vyd. Classically styled. Massalto, his playground. Winery on way up.

Walla Walla Vintners Walla ★★ Long-time producer: luscious CABS FR/SAUV, MERLOT.

Waterbrook Walla ★ One of state's oldest wineries, now owned by wine-giant Precept; focus on value.

WeatherEye Red Mtn ★★★★ New cult micro-producer; eponymous vyd on top, n side of Red Mtn. Todd Alexander (FORCE MAJEURE) crafts bold wines with spectacular results. Seek out.

Woodward Canyon Walla ★★★★ 07 10 12' 14 16 18 21 Founding WALLA producer; 2nd generation in charge. Focus on Bx styles: CHARD among best in state; Old Vines CAB SAUV.

WT Vintners Yak V ★★★ Sommelier-winemaker Jeff Lindsay-Thorsen picks earlier, pulls back oak on single-vyd GRÜNER V, GRENACHE, SYRAH.

Wisconsin (WI)

Vibrant, dynamic industry. Look for locally grown, cold-hardy hybrids such as white Brianna, Frontenac Gr, St Pepin. **American Wine Project** pét-nat, piquette recommended. Historic **Wollersheim Winery** v.gd estate wines.

Mexico

If you expect big, bold reds from Mexico, you won't be disappointed.
Not much gets exported. Baja California, with its maritime-influenced
Mediterranean climate, produces more than 75%, and subregion Valle
de Guadalupe has the most wineries. Other states – including historic
Coahuila and high-altitude areas of Zacatecas, Aguascalientes,
Guanajuato and Querétaro – are making great strides in quality.
Vineyards tend to be at high altitude and have cool nights.

Adobe Guadalupe ★★★★ Destination winery and inn. Any of Archangel wines recommended, with Serafiel (CAB/SYRAH) top. Jardín Secreto blend (TEMPRANILLO-based) expresses a signature grape of the region.

Bichi ★★ Known for crazy "naked" labels, natural winemaking, min-intervention, old organic dry-farmed vyds. Pet Mex pét-nat (unknown grape), Listan (MISSION).

Bruma Valle de Guadalupe Winery and luxury destination resort in Valle de Guadalupe. Try Plan B (r), a GSM/NEBBIOLO blend.

Carrodilla, Finca La Organic/bio. Rich, ripe, luxury-priced. Best: Canto de Luna (r/w). Varietal CAB SAUV, SHIRAZ, TEMPRANILLO, CHENIN BL all gd.

Casa de Piedra ★★★ Modern winery/winemaking; 1st project of prolific Hugo d'Acosta. Vino de Piedra CAB SAUV/TEMPRANILLO oaky, structured, age-worthy modern classic Mexican.

Casa Vieja, La Hand-destemming, natural yeasts, no sulphur, no oak flavours; 120 yrs old+, ungrafted Mission (PAÍS), skin-contact PALOMINO most interesting.

Corona del Valle Winery/restaurant destination in Valle de Guadalupe. TEMPRANILLO/NEBBIOLO top rated. Varietal Tempranillo and CAB SAUV also gd.

Cuna de Tierra In Dolores Hidalgo, Guanajuato. Architecturally significant, award-winning winery and wines. NEBBIOLO, SYRAH, MALBEC stand out.

Henri Lurton, Bodegas ★★ France's Lurton family. Refined yet sturdy CAB SAUV, CARMENÈRE. Try inky PETITE SIRAH, elegant NEBBIOLO. Winemaker is ex-Ch Brane-Cantenac (*see* Bordeaux).

LA Cetto Italian heritage. Exported, well known abroad. High-altitude, juicy, value: Res Privada range (NEBBIOLO, PETITE SIRAH). CHENIN BL largest production.

Lomita, Hacienda La Renowned for winery, restaurant and murals. Organic; CHENIN BL/SAUV BL shines, award-winning Tinto de la Hacienda (r).

Mina Penelope Winemaker Verónica Santiago at helm, one of growing number of women making wine here. Cutting-edge amber and rosé offerings. Reds with NEBBIOLO focus. Julio 14 (SYRAH-driven GMS blend) is signature.

Monte Xanic ★★★ The 1st modern premium winery, excellent CAB SAUV, v.gd MERLOT. Fresh whites from SAUV BL, unoaked CHARD, CHENIN BL. Elegant high-elevation PINOT N. Top: Calixa blend (r), NEBBIOLO Limitada.

Paralelo ★★ Created by Hugo d'Acosta to explore terroir. Wines made in same way from different locations. Ensamble Colina (hillside vines); Arenal (old river bed).

San Miguel, Viñedo Largest winery in Guanajuato nr San Miguel de Allende. Top is Latiendo (MALBEC/SYRAH/MERLOT); also gd Malbec Res and CAB SAUV.

Tres Valles ★★ Grapes sourced from three subregions: Valle de San Vicente Ferrer, Valle de San Antonio de las Minas and Valle de Guadalupe. Big, jammy Kuwal blend is top red. TEMPRANILLO, SANGIOVESE, MERLOT all gd.

Vena Cava ★★★ Wine/dining/architecture destination featuring reclaimed fishing boats. Value in organic wines. Recommend: CAB SAUV, SAUV BL, TEMPRANILLO.

Vinaltura ★ In Querétaro: high-altitude vyds, high desert climate. Terruño blends excel: Bajio (MERLOT/MALBEC/TEMPRANILLO), Blanco (French/German varieties).

Canada

Canada is hitting its stride and getting attention for robust reds from Okanagan Valley, elegant whites and reds from elsewhere in British Columbia and throughout Ontario, plus racy whites and sparkling wines from Nova Scotia. But the moderating effects of water in most regions are no match for the disastrous cold snaps that have hit British Columbia in particular in recent years. The long-term viability of some regions is in question, while Canadian wines as a whole are doing well in domestic and their small export markets.

Ontario

Cool climate influenced by lakes Ontario and Erie. Key varieties: CHARD, RIES, CAB FR, GAMAY, PINOT N. Three geographical indications (GIs): Niagara Peninsula (Niag), most important, has two regional and ten sub-appellations; Prince Edward County (PEC); Lake Erie North Shore (LENS) with one sub-appellation. More and more wineries opening outside appellations.

2027 Cellars Niag ★★ Founded 2007 but wines available from 2020; v. well-made range (r/w), esp CHARD, CAB FR, GAMAY. Note Wismer-Foxcroft Cab Fr.

Bachelder Niag ★★★★ Thomas B made wine in Burgundy, OR, knows Niag inside and out. Stunning vyd- and parcel-specific CHARD, GAMAY, PINOT N.

Cave Spring Niag ★★★ RIES pioneer in Niag: nervy dry Ries (incl old vines), within impressive range (r/w/sp) and Icewine.

Clos Jordanne Niag ★★★★ Owned by Arterra, new winery 2024. Modelled on Burgundy; only CHARD, PINOT N. Several tiers; highlight: Le Grand Clos.

Closson Chase Niag ★★ Early (1998) PEC winery specializing in elegant CHARD, PINOT N. Note Grande Cuvée tier.

Flat Rock Cellars Niag ★★ Gravity-fed winery with various tiers of stylish CHARD, RIES, PINOT N. Highlights: Gravity Pinot N, Nadja's Vyd Ries.

Henry of Pelham Niag ★★ Pioneer in Niag, with notable generous reds: Speck Family Res, Bin 106 Baco Noir. Fine fizz: racy Cuvée Catharine Carte Blanche Blanc de Blancs.

Vineyard-covered Pelee Island in Lake Erie on same latitude as CA/OR border.

Hidden Bench Niag ★★★★ Superb wines, with strengths in elegant CHARD, CAB FR, PINOT N. Highlights: Terroir Caché (r blend), Tête de Cuvée Chard.

Keint-He PEC ★ Small winery, focus on well-defined single-vyd CHARD, PINOT N: Greer Road Chard, Little Creek The Ridge Pinot N.

Lailey Stonebridge Niag ★★ Merger of two wineries with Lailey vyds planted in 70s. Delicious range, esp CHARD, CAB FR. Standout Stonebridge SAUV BL Res 20, slightly botrytized.

Leaning Post Niag ★★ Wide portfolio, incl clone-specific CHARD, single-vyd PINOT N. Notable: rich, textured Senchuk Vyd Pinot N.

Malivoire Niag ★★ Brainchild of movie SFX director Martin Malivoire. Outstanding small-lot CHARD, GAMAY, PINOT N: Moira Chard, Courtney Gamay.

Pearl Morissette Niag ★★★★ Original, pure CHARD, RIES, CAB FR, PINOT N. Highlights: Irrévérence (aromatic w blend), Madeline Cab Fr. Superb on-site restaurant.

Queylus, Dom Niag ★★★ Québec-owned, organic. Fine, sculpted CHARD, CAB FR, MERLOT, PINOT N. Top tiers: Rés du Domaine, La Grande Rés.

Southbrook Vineyards Niag ★★ Organic, bio: biodiverse, with chickens, sheep. Juicy wines (r/w/sp): Triomphe CAB FR, Poetica red blend.

> **On the bench**
> Many of Canada's sub-appellations (4 of 11 in Ok V, 4 of 10 in Niag) are named after benches, such as Naramata Bench (Ok V), and Beamsville Bench (Niag). In geographical terms, a bench is a long, narrow, flat or gently inclined strip of land with steeper slopes above and below it – essentially a piece of land protruding from a cliff, ending with its own cliff-face. Benches often provide protected, well-drained conditions for vyds.

Stanners Vineyard PEC ★★★ *Garagiste* with juicy CHARD, PINOT GR, PINOT N: Cuivré Pinot Gr, Narrow Rows Pinot N.

Stratus Niag ★★★ Elegant blends (Stratus White, Red), top-tier White Label range from micro-sites; Charles Baker, same property, makes bright-acid RIES.

Tawse Niag ★★★ Organic, vyd-specific, elegant CHARD, RIES, PINOT N: Robyn's Block Chard, Limestone Spark! Ries. Partner in Maison Marchand-Tawse, Burgundy.

Thirty Bench Niag ★★★ Early boutique winery with exciting single-vyd, some old-vine RIES, CHARD, PINOT N, CAB FR. Highest tier: Small Lot series.

Traill Estate PEC ★★ Small, innovative: juicy edgy CAB FR, CHARD, PINOT N, plus orange, natural, pét-nat. Juicy Red (five varieties) esp appealing.

Two Sisters Niag ★★★ Destination winery strong on flavourful CAB FR and other Bx-style reds. Highlight: Blanc de Franc (sp).

Vineland Estates Niag ★★ Founded 1979 by Mosel's Weis family to grow RIES: Elevation St Urban Ries. Now many clone-specific, pure (r/w), CAB FR (try Res).

British Columbia (BC)

Cool and warm-climate regions. Key varieties: MERLOT, PINOT N, PINOT GR, CHARD, CAB SAUV, CAB FR, RIES, SYRAH. Nine GIs incl: Okanagan Valley (Ok V), most important by far, with 11 sub-appellations (more due); Similkameen Valley (Sim V); Vancouver Island (Van I) with one sub-appellation. Cold snaps cut harvest by 50–60% in 2023 and almost 100% in 2024.

1 Mill Road Ok V ★★ New small winery to watch, esp fine, elegant CHARD (East Kelowna Slopes), PINOT N (Black Pine).

Blue Grouse Van I ★★ Small, owned by California's Jackson Family; v.gd bright, crisp CHARD, PINOT GR, PINOT N. Outstanding Res Pinot N.

Blue Mountain Winery Ok V ★★★★ Well-est, stellar reputation across board, esp bright fizz, elegant CHARD, PINOT N. Highlight: Gravel Force Block 14 Pinot N.

CedarCreek Ok V ★★★ Highly regarded producer of stylish single-vyd CHARD, PINOT N, esp Platinum tier and Aspect Collection.

CheckMate Ok V ★★★ Part of Mark Anthony Group; chess-themed range of rich CHARD, MERLOT only: Fool's Mate Chard, Silent Bishop Merlot. Opulent facilities.

Haywire Ok V ★★ Lovely lively wines, esp PINOT GR, GAMAY, PINOT N. Standout: Secrest Mtn Vyd Gamay, Pinot N.

Little Engine Ok V ★★ Focus on rich, structured CHARD, PINOT N. Note Platinum Tier, esp Chard, CAB FR, Pinot N.

Martin's Lane Winery Ok V ★★★★ Top-notch range of elegant single-vyd PINOT N, RIES from sites throughout Ok V. Stellar: Fritzi's Vyd Pinot N. Some wines club members only. All sell out quickly.

Meyer Family Vineyards Ok V ★★★ Impressive range of structured vyd-specific, small-lot CHARD, PINOT N. Outstanding Micro Cuvée tier.

Mission Hill Family Estate Ok V ★★★ Spectacular architecture. Large portfolio classic styles; fine top tiers: Oculus (elegant r blend), Perpetua CHARD.

Nicol Vineyard Ok V ★★★ Pioneering Naramata Bench winery, specialist in generous, structured SYRAH (esp Old Vines), but also fine CAB FR, PINOT N.

Osoyoos Larose Ok V ★★★★ French-owned; Bx-style reds, planted 1998, produces elegant, cellar-worthy Grand Vin, second wine Pétales d'Osoyoos.

Painted Rock Ok V ★★ On Skaha Lake, strong portfolio: robust Bx blend, CAB FR, CHARD, SYRAH. Top Red Icon (five-variety Bx blend). Older vintages available.

Phantom Creek Ok V ★★★ Destination winery. Fine estate, single-vyd textbook CABS SAUV/FR, SYRAH; whites from Sim V. Top: Kobau Vyd Cuvée (r blend).

Poplar Grove Ok V ★★ Early (1993) winery, stylish portfolio (r/w/rosé), many reserved for club members. Note Legacy (r blend), North Block SYRAH.

Quails' Gate Ok V ★★ Pioneer (1989) with strengths in balanced, layered CHARD, PINOT N. Top tier: Stewart Family Res.

Roche Wines Ok V ★★★ Founded by couple with Bx roots (Ch Les Carmes Haut-Brion); stunning Bx blends (esp Château tier) and succulent PINOT N (esp Vig Len's Cuvée).

Tantalus Ok V ★★ Old (70s/80s) CHARD, PINOT N, RIES vines produce gorgeous still and sparkling. Note Old Vines Ries, Ries Brut, Res Pinot N.

Tightrope Winery Ok V ★ NZ-trained owners produce attractive range of flavourful, balanced wines; note BARBERA, SYRAH.

Unsworth Vineyards Van I ★ Owned by members of California's Jackson family. Bright, stylish wines (r/w/sp); highlights incl Cuvée de l'Île (PINOT N sp), Saison Vyd Pinot N.

Vieux Pin, Le Ok V ★★★ Specialist in fine, serious SYRAH, also VIOGNIER, CAB FR. Outstanding Equinoxe Syrah and Old Vine Cab Fr.

Nova Scotia & Québec

Nova Scotia Small cool-climate region of about 20 wineries on Atlantic coast. Hybrids and vinifera, notable for crisp white (Tidal Bay) and bubbly. Benjamin Bridge ★★ top-notch vibrant fizz (trad method/pét-nat): Brut Rés (CHARD, PINOT N), Nova 7 (off-dr from hybrids). Blomidon Estate ★ on Bay of Fundy makes high-acid still red/white, racy fizz from hybrids/vinifera: Cuvée L'Acadie Brut Rés. Lightfoot & Wolfville ★ organic and bio, Annapolis V: bright high-acid, esp RIES, Pinot N, Chard; reliable Terroir Series.

Île d'Orléans (12 wineries) in St Lawrence River called Isle de Bacchus in 1500s: wild vines.

Québec Cold climate, becoming cool in the s thanks to warming temps. Varieties mainly hybrid, with slowly increasing vinifera, esp CHARD, PINOT N. Many small wineries, some v. promising thanks to growing expertise and site/variety matching. Les Bacchantes ★ gd fruit, racy acidity (r/w); note M1 juicy citrus fizz (VIDAL). Les Pervenches ★ small emerging organic producer, crisp Chard, juicy Pinot N. Léon Courville ★ well-made, structured wines from hybrids and vinifera; planted from 90s. Vignoble de l'Orpailleur ★ well est; reliable, gd quality, hybrids and vinifera.

"International-domestic"

Ontario and BC allow blends of their wines with outside wine as long as they are labelled not with a provincial GI but with some variation on "international-Canadian blend". (For yrs, the ambiguous term "Cellared in Canada" was used.) Mainly produced by large corporate wineries, these blends are confusing to consumers because the labels look much the same as those on Canadian wines. The poor 2024 harvest in BC led many producers to import grapes or wine from Ontario and the US for blending, simply so that they had some wine to sell.

South America

CHILE

Aco	Aconcagua
Bío	Bío-Bío
Cach	Cachapoal
Casa	Casablanca
Cho	Choapa
Col	Colchagua
Coq	Coquimbo
Cur	Curicó
Elq	Elqui
Ita	Itata
Ley	Leyda
Lim	Limarí
Mai	Maipo
Mal	Malleco
Mau	Maule
Rap	Rapel
San A	San Antonio

Abbreviations
used in the text:

ARGENTINA

Cata	Catamarca
La R	La Rioja
Luján	Luján de Cuyo
Men	Mendoza
Neu	Neuquén
Pat	Patagonia
Río N	Río Negro
Sal	Salta
San J	San Juan
Uco	Uco Valley

CHILE

The post-pandemic crisis has seen Chile's vineyards shrink (down to 138,000 ha at the latest count), but while there may be fewer today, there is still enormous diversity and range. Vineyards span almost the length of the country – from the top, on the border with Peru, via the Atacama Desert, and through the arid regions with starry skies in the north, where salty coastal Sauvignon Blanc and meaty Syrah thrive. In the central chunk, the Andes frame the eastern edge and make top Cabernet Sauvignon territory, while the cool Pacific Ocean runs along the west, ideal for crisp Chardonnay and crunchy Pinot Noir. Vines are widely spread between both frontiers, and this is prime Carmenère country. As you make your way further south, the vines get older and shorter: there are treasure troves of old-vine Carignan, País, Moscatel and Semillon in Maule, Itata and Bío-Bío. Just when you thought you might have reached the end, you come to Malleco. Here, overlooking snowcapped volcanoes, Riesling has found a home. Vines have even made it down to the watery, cool-climate archipelago of Chiloe, where penguins outnumber people.

Recent vintages

Too diverse to generalize, but overall 22 18 most exciting of decade; 24 21 v.gd and cool, while 23 20 19 17 hotter.

Aconcagua One of Chile's historic regions that made its red blends famous; n of Santiago, spanning Costa to Andes. Rich reds towards mtns, fresh whites by sea.

Almaule Mau Association championing fresh, juicy old-vine PAÍS from MAU. The soul (Alma) of Maule = Almaule

Almaviva Mai ★★★★ Luxury Bx blend (r) by Mouton Rothschild (*see* Bordeaux). Doing what Puente Alto (MAI) does best: age-worthy, complex. Second label: Epu.

A Los Viñateros Bravos Ita ★★★ ITATA-champion Leo Erazo and familia. Top CINSAULT, PAÍS and old-vine white, orange blends.

Altaïr Wines Rap ★★★→★★★★ Sophisticated CACH label by SAN PEDRO. Winemaker Gabriel Mustakis makes smooth, seductive Bx blends (incl second label, Sideral).

Antiyal Mai ★★★ Alvaro Espinoza was integral to discovery of CARMENÈRE over 30 yrs ago; champions spicy style today and elegant CAB SAUV from bio MAI label.

Apaltagua Col ★★ Everyday, reliable wines from all over Chile, incl rarer white Rhône blends.

Aquitania, Viña Mai, Mal ★★★ Heart in MAI, soul in MAL; this family winery spans two regions and diverse wines, from rich CAB SAUV (try Lazuli) to racy fizz.

Arboleda, Viña Aco ★★ Bright ACO coastal wines from ERRÁZURIZ: top-value CHARD, SAUV BL and juicy Brisas blend.

Baettig, Vinos Mal, Mau ★★★ Stylish CHARD, PINOT N from deep-s MAL; vibrant CAB SAUV from old-vine MAU from one of Chile's best.

Bío-Bío Heartland of old vines, savoury wines; new generation pours in new energy, style. Excellent old-vine PAÍS, CINSAULT, and new-vine RIES, SAUV BL, PINOT N.

Bouchon Mau ★★→★★★ Estate specializing in old-vine whites (Granito SEM), fresh PAÍS, juicy Med blends. Owned by UNDURRAGA.

Caliboro Mau ★★★ Javier Rousseau now heads up this handsome estate, focusing on regenerative viticulture, bright PAÍS, and rescuing native-born varieties (soon to harvest 1st Caliboro grapes) from plethora of old vines.

Calyptra Cach ★★→★★★★ Mountain wines: brooding CAB SAUV, striking SAUV BL, host of gd stickies. Now in MEN too.

Carmen, Viña Casa, Col, Mai ★★→★★★★ ANA MARÍA CUMSILLE now holds reins at this MAI-based winery, with vibrant wines from all over Chile. DO range is top stuff, as are modern Bx-styles Delanz, Gold.

Casablanca Pioneering coastal region is Chile's largest (5000 ha+), from v. cool to nicely warm zones – goes some way to explain growing range, from zippy SAUV BL to fragrant MERLOT and inky SYRAH. Bustling wine route worth a visit.

Casa Marín San A ★★★→★★★★ Felipe M has taken driving seat from matriarch María Luz M. Cipreses, one of Chile's top SAUV BL, but also top RIES, CHARD, SYRAH. All cool climate, just 4 km from ocean.

Casas del Bosque Casa, Mai ★★→★★★★ Popular CASA winery with top restaurant, neat gd-value portfolio of coastal whites, reds, sparkling (Bo).

Casa Silva Col, S Regions ★★→★★★ Family winery in Los Lingues, with trad, rich mtn reds, fresh Col-coast whites. Plush CARMENÈRE; most exciting are RIES and sparkling from Lago Ranco in Osorno.

Clos Apalta Col ★★★★ Iconic, silky Bx blend, lion's share CARMENÈRE. Andrea Leon is winemaker; bio estate (part of LAPOSTOLLE).

> ## Chile's sweet spot
> Chile was made for brilliant value. The almost ideal climate, plentiful land, diverse conditions and relatively cheap labour help too. Chile overdelivers compared to many international counterparts – look for smart CAB SAUV, or mouthwatering coastal SAUV BL. Exceptional value-for-money brands incl CONO SUR 20 Barrels, ERRÁZURIZ Aco Costa, MIGUEL TORRES Cordillera, MONTES Outer Limits, UNDURRAGA Terroir Hunter.

Clos des Fous Cach, Casa, S Regions ★★→★★★ Taking terroirs from n to v. far s, refreshing range shows off-beat Chile at best: RIES, CHARD, PINOT N all v.gd. Mr Chile is cool new PAÍS/CINSAULT/CARIGNAN blend.

Concha y Toro Central V ★→★★★★ Powerhouse of Chilean wine with history stretching back to 1883. Diverse range with highlights in MAI being top Bx-blend labels Don Melchor and Gravas (CAB SAUV, SYRAH); in LIM Amelia PINOT N; in CASA Terruñyo SAUV BL. Marques de Casa Concha v.gd mid-range, Casillero del Diablo reliable entry-level. *See also* ALMAVIVA, TRIVENTO (Argentina).

Cono Sur Bío, Casa, Col ★★→★★★ Reliable producer making benchmark styles of most main varieties around Chile. Excellent value for PINOT N esp, ranging from everyday Bicicleta to top-shelf Ocio. Centinela, new Blanc de Blancs bubbly.

Cousiño Macul Mai ★★→★★★ Stalwart since 1856, esp CAB SAUV (Lota), appetizing Isadora Sauv Gr. Gota de Luna is tasty outlier, SAUV BL from MAL.

Cumsille, Ana María Ita ★★★ Celebrated grower of dry-farmed s, Ana María makes juicy, vibrant, supple old-vine CARIGNAN, CINSAULT, MALBEC.

Elqui Pisco stars and SYRAH. One of prettiest valleys in Chile and runs gamut of fresh coastal whites to meaty mtn reds.

Emiliana Bío, Casa, Rap ★★→★★★ Chile's bio leader: bright, juicy wines under hand of Noelia Orts. Based in COL but with vyds all over, incl new acquisition in LIM. Top red blends: Coyam, Gê.

Errázuriz Aco, Casa ★★→★★★★ Top ACO estate and family winery (*see also* SEÑA, VIÑA ARBOLEDA, VIÑEDO CHADWICK), diverse but reliable portfolio from fresh Costa wines to rich mtn blends. World-class Las Pizarras CHARD; Kai, silky CARMENÈRE; Don Maximiano, a Chilean classic. Now under tutelage of Emily Faulconer.

Falernia, Viña Elq ★★ Early ELQ pioneer; enjoyable everyday pours. Start with PEDRO XIMÉNEZ with local goats' cheese, and *appassimento*-style CARMENÈRE to finish.

Garcés Silva, Viña San A ★★→★★★ One of leaders in Ley, selling grapes to some of best and making own smart portfolio too. Excellent SAUV BL, SYRAH, Garden Blend range gd fun too.

Haras de Pirque Mai ★★→★★★ Antinori's (*see* Italy) outpost looks like a horseshoe from above, but wines far from barnyard. Polished, classy Bx-style reds.

Henríquez, Roberto Bío ★★★ Lo-fi, artisanal wines from one of ITA and BÍO's new generation stars. Earthy, delicious SEM, CINSAULT, PAÍS and more.

Itata So many delicious wines, yet still suffering low investment and worryingly frequent wildfires. Perhaps because this is a region of growers with vyds but few wineries? Winemakers come to snap up excellent old-vine MUSCAT, CINSAULT, PAÍS and more.

Koyle Col, Ita ★★→★★★ Toti Undurraga is a leader in Chile's growing bio scene; fresh, juicy, fragrant COL, ITATA wines. Hunt down Cerro Basalto.

Laberinto Mau ★★★→★★★★ One of most exciting yet under-the-radar projects in Chile. Mountainous, volcanic MAU under Rafael Tirado. Exceptional RIES, SAUV BL, PINOT N, blends.

Lapostolle Cach, Casa, Col ★★→★★★ Luxury Apalta estate, winery and hotel; classic, structured Bx varieties, and Provence-style rosé.

Leyda, Viña Col, Mai, San A ★★→★★★ It took an 8-km pipeline to bring water to this region when Viña Leyda pioneered 1st vyds. Major investment, but worth it: today Ley is one of Chile's best coastal regions, this a leading winery. Top-value CHARD, SAUV BL, PINOT N, SYRAH. Charming RIES.

Limarí Drought is a challenge in this region but cool coastal wines are a strength. Top CHARD, PINOT N.

Longaví Ita, Mau ★★★ Christian Sepúlveda and Bouchon family make brilliant BIO, ITA, MAU: fresh, vibrant CARIGNAN, CINSAULT, PAÍS; superb old-vine CHENIN BL.

Luis Felipe Edwards Central V ★★ One of Chile's biggest, still family-owned. Based in COL, but vyds all over and plethora of gd-value labels.

Maipo Heartland of top CAB SAUV influenced by Andes – river gravels, cool nights, warm and sunny days. Excellent Bx blends too, and spicy CARMENÈRE. Home to Chile's longest-running wineries.

Malleco Southerly region with small (100 ha) vyds in quantity, but high quality. Excellent CHARD, PINOT N, and gd RIES. Volcanic, moderate climate, dry farmed.

Martino, De Cach, Casa, Elq, Ita, Mai, Mau ★★→★★★★ MAIPO-based and -focused producer, bringing old-school, elegant Bx-style reds back into fashion, plus steely SEM. Also old vines in ITA for juicy *tinaja*.

Matetic Casa, San A ★★★→★★★★ Top SAN A and CASA producer, excellence across ranges and price points. SYRAH some of Chile's best, esp black-label Matetic. Beautiful bio estates.

Maule Chile's old-vine heartland, head-trained and dry-farmed. Particularly gd for SEM, CARIGNAN (*see* VIGNO), PAÍS, but also some excellent MALBEC and Bx blends.

Montes Casa, Col, Cur, Ley ★★→★★★★ Aurelio M Snr changed image of Chilean wine with this pioneering winery; Aurelio Jnr continues legacy. Stunning winery in Apalta, but vyds from coast to deep s. *Folly Syrah* top stuff, Outer Limits more playful range.

MontGras Col, Ley, Mai ★★→★★★★ A trad COL winery becoming much more exciting under new winemaking team. Handcrafted range is engaging stuff, classy Intriga CAB SAUV (MAI).

Montsecano Casa ★★★ PINOT N specialist in CASA, with niche, sought-after production. Try newer CHARD, MALBEC too.

Morandé Casa, Mai, Mau ★★→★★★ Ricardo Baettig makes solid lineup of classic and off-beat wines. Highlights: VIGNO CARIGNAN, LIM SYRAH and mature Brut Nature bubbles.

Neyen Col ★★★ Planted 1890 in Apalta, v. old vines make rich, silky CAB SAUV, CARMENÈRE. Special edition MALBEC.

Odfjell Cur, Mai, Mau ★→★★★ Classic lineup of bio juicy reds, embracing Bx varieties in MAI and Med varieties in MAU; v.gd CARIGNAN (*see* VIGNO).

Pedro Parra y Familia Ita ★★→★★★ Fresh, sometimes funky, range from top terroir expert with focus on ITA old vines. Fragrant PAÍS, top cru CINSAULT.

Pérez Cruz, Viña Mai ★★→★★★ Alto MAI winery; reliable lineup of Bx-style reds, juicy GRENACHE. Worth trying COT.

Pisco Chile's elixir of choice. Clear, aromatic brandy from handful of white varieties. Top is served pure, chilled, but most is diluted and sweetened in a classic Sour.

There are 86 vine varieties now grown in Chile: 49 red, 37 white.

Polkura Col ★★→★★★ Indie producer Sven Bruchfeld has strong following for his rich, warming COL reds. Top SYRAH.

PS García Ita, Mal, Mau ★★→★★★ Plenty of personality in Felipe G's colourful portfolio covering Chile's range of climates, varieties. Facundo, a favourite, age-worthy CARIGNAN blend.

Quebrada de Macul, Viña Mai ★★→★★★ Classy CAB SAUV and Bx blends from prime terroir. Domus Aurea, Viña Peñalolén labels.

Rapel Rather useless catch-all appellation to cover vast, diverse COL, CACH regions.

RE, Bodegas Casa ★★★ Family winery by Pablo Morande, father and son; vines in MAU too. Quirky blends, orange wines, structured reds, complex sparkling.

Requingua, Viña ★★ Large, consistent, gd-value player in Central V, try CARIGNAN.

Reta Lim, Mau ★★★→★★★★ Marcelo Retamal's own brand with small production, extremely age-worthy CHARD, PINOT N (LIM); delicious old-vine MALBEC (MAU).

San Antonio San A Just to s of CASA, but notably cooler. Granite coastal region making excellent CHARD, SAUV BL, SYRAH, PINOT N. Subregion Ley best known.

San Pedro Cur ★→★★★ One of Chile's biggest with huge range from n to s, cheap to pricey. Cabo de Hornos CAB SAUV at top is gd stuff; 1865 range offers gems incl top SYRAH (ELQ), social project in MAL made by Mapuche (Tayu PINOT N). *See also* ALTAÏR, TARAPACÁ; LA CELIA in Argentina.

Santa Carolina, Viña Mai ★★→★★★ Still going strong (est 1875); vyds around Chile. Classy Luis Pereira CAB SAUV, silky Herencia CARMENÈRE. El Pacto, fun new range.

Santa Rita Mai ★★→★★★★ Mammoth winery but with plenty of smaller, interesting wines, incl Chile's original icon *Casa Real Cab Sauv*. Floresta is a highlight; top vibrant SEM blend (Apalta) and peppery CAB FR (Col).

Seña Aco ★★★★ Lovely estate in ACO tucked into hills; top sumptuous, poised Bx blend, vibrant second label Rocas. Owned by ERRÁZURIZ.

Tabalí Lim ★★→★★★★ Top producer in LIM with Chile's most striking coastal vyd, Talinay. Laser-sharp whites, savoury PINOT N (try Pai), bolder SYRAH.

Chile has 2000+ volcanoes, incl 500 still active: plenty of volcanic soil for vines.

Tarapacá, Viña Casa, Ley, Mai ★★ Isla de Maipo winery and producer, part of SAN PEDRO. Classic range covering all major bases, reliable if a little predictable.

Torres, Miguel Cur ★★→★★★★ Reliable entry ranges from Spain's Torres family make up most of production. Expressive, interesting Cordillera range (Osorno SAUV BL to LIM CHARD). Unique labels incl Los Inqueitos MALBEC, Millapoa PAÍS hidden gems. Manso de Velasco is centenarian CAB SAUV.

Undurraga Casa, Ley, Lim, Mai ★★→★★★★ Rafael Urrejola is one of Chile's top winemakers; Terroir Hunter range offers benchmark Chilean varieties from all over country. Increasingly exciting Icons: Pirque's Altazor CAB SAUV, Trama PINOT N (SAN A), excellent Red Field Blend.

Valdivieso Cur, San A ★→★★★ Big in the bubble business; mainly everyday Charmat. Caballo Loco is where winemaker Brett Jackson lets his hair down.

Vascos, Los Rap ★★ From Lafite Rothschild (*see* Bordeaux), based in Col. New Primo releases incl SEM, PINOT N, moving away from trad Bx styles that dominates rest.

Ventisquero, Viña Casa, Col, Mai ★→★★★ Large, Col-based, covers some of Chile's most extreme terroirs, from Huasco in Atacama Desert to Chile Chico in Chilean Pat. Ranges: Grey (solid), Tara (fun, natural). Luscious Pangea SYRAH.

Veramonte Casa, Col ★★ González Byass (*see* Spain) runs large CASA estate offering bright if simple range of classics.

Vigno Mau One of most exciting associations to come out of New World, championing old-vine, dry-farmed CARIGNAN. Age-worthy, delicious wines from 12+ wineries.

Vik Cach ★★→★★★ Beautiful estate, state-of-the-art winery, just other side of Apalta hill. Top Vik red blend; several other labels incl vibrant rosé. Makes own Champagne (yes, in Champagne) too.

Villard Casa, Mai ★★→★★★ Large CASA estate making v.gd range of coastal classics, plus more adventurous wines in JCV label. Ramato PINOT GR anyone?

Viñedo Chadwick Mai ★★★★ One of most elegant CAB SAUVS in New World, from prime terroir in Puente Alto, where ERRÁZURIZ owner Eduardo Chadwick planted vines on father's polo field.

Viu Manent Casa, Col ★★ Producer in Col, est as MALBEC specialist, but makes so much more. Easy to enjoy.

von Siebenthal, Viña Aco ★★→★★★ Mauro von S has been making structured, age-worthy reds for over two decades. Don't miss velvety VIOGNIER.

ARGENTINA

Seventh largest in the world, Argentina's wine industry is mammoth and has been for over a century. The dry, sunny climate certainly helps, and making wine along the corridor of the Andes mountains is, for many winemakers, an absolute dream. The only major challenges here are the occasional frost, and hailstones that can be as big as golf balls. The rocky economy is a bit of a challenge too. Nevertheless, Argentina is turning out the best wines in its history – increasingly elegant, fresh and focused. Malbec rules the roost, accounting for a fifth of plantings, and although it might be vast in quantity, there is also a vast range of styles. From the chiselled finesse of Altamira and Gualtallary in the Uco Valley, to the rich concentration of old vines in Lunlunta, Maipú, or the wild spicy streak that Jujuy and Salta give – there's a Malbec for most tastes. Good news for white-wine lovers too though, Argentina's vino blanco is booming: with waxy Semillon, star-bright Sauvignon Blanc, exotic Torrontés and precise Chardonnay as the emerging stars.

Achaval Ferrer Men ★★→★★★ Specialist in old-vine MALBEC; trio of top single vyds. New Quimera (w blend), joins host of varietals, incl CARMENÈRE.

Alandes Men ★★★ Sumptuous Paradox blends are highlight (esp SEM/SAUV BL) in exclusive label from Karim Mussi.

Alpasión Men ★★ Smart set of wines from large estate in Las Chacayes, Uco. Best: CAB FR, PETIT VERDOT.

Alta Vista Men ★→★★★ French-owned winery in Luján; vyds span Argentina. Single-site MALBEC and more. TORRONTÉS always a highlight.

Altocedro Men ★★→★★★ La Consulta vyd brand by Karim Mussi; classic reds, focus on TEMPRANILLO too. Polished, understated.

Altos las Hormigas Men ★★★→★★★★ Consistent and exciting, hard combination to achieve. Cru MALBEC Jardín De Hormigas, one of country's best. Also fab SEM, BONARDA, CAB FR.

Argento Men ★★→★★★ Leading organic producer; balanced, fruity wines. All v.gd value, esp Single Vyd CHARD, CAB FR, MALBEC.

Atamisque Men ★→★★★ Serbal is one of best value ranges on offer in Uco today, and climbing scale is even more rewarding (CHARD, CAB FR, MERLOT).

Bemberg Estate Wines ★★★ Crème de la crème from family that owns PEÑAFLOR. Terroir-specific wines from all over Argentina. Expensive, age-worthy.

Benegas Men ★★→★★★ Historic winery on border of Luján and Maipú; some v. old vines. Intense, age-worthy reds. Pioneer of CAB FR, champion of SANGIOVESE.

Bianchi, Bodegas Men ★→★★ Rapidly growing presence in Uco, still leader in San Rafael. Rather classic portfolio. IV Generación more contemporary.

Bosca, Luigi Men ★★→★★★ Name/producer of note in Luján, part of revived focus on DOC (denomination of controlled origin). Try Finca Las Nobles MALBEC.

Bressia Men ★★→★★★ Renowned winemaker Walter B's family winery. Complex red Bx blends are forte, but Monteagrelo offers younger drinking varietals.

Cadus Men ★★→★★★ Stylish premium winery, sister of NIETO SENETINER, mainly Uco and Luján fruit. Winemaker Santiago Mayorga makes excellent single-vyd range, classy CHARD highlight.

Callia San J ★→★★ Simple but enjoyable everyday wines from large producer.

Canale, Bodegas Humberto Río N ★→★★★ One of pioneers, still making impressively diverse portfolio for this s region. Excellent old-vine RIES, MALBEC.

Cara Sur San J ★★ Pancho Bugallo and Sebastian ZUCCARDI make juicy, vibrant old-vine wines in beautiful region of Barreal, high in the Andes. Speciality is Criolla Chica and mtn BONARDA.

Caro Men ★★★ Long standing partnership between the Rothschild and CATENA dynasties. Top blend is luscious, silky. Second and third labels, Amancaya and Aruma, more easy-drinking.

Casarena Men ★★→★★★ Luján champion focusing on single-site expressions at top end. Excellent for CAB SAUV, CAB FR.

Catena Zapata, Bodega Men ★★→★★★★ One of 1st to push premium in Argentina, still at top of game. Striking CHARD, layered MALBEC from Adrianna vyd in Gualtallary are top (try White Bones/Stones, River). Alamos is weekday brand. *See also* CARO.

Chacra Río N ★★★→★★★★ Old vines of PINOT N 1st attracted Italy's Piero Incisa della Rocchetta to RÍO N; now mouthwatering CHARD, Trousseau too.

Chandon Men ★→★★ Ignited bubble industry in S America in late C20, still major producer of everyday fizz, plus step-up Baron B. *See* TERRAZAS DE LOS ANDES.

Cheval des Andes Men ★★★★ Two vyds (Uco, Luján) come together to make one wine. Owned by Cheval Blanc team (*see* Bordeaux) aiming to make top growth with rich MALBEC/CAB SAUV blend.

Clos de los Siete Men ★★ Biggest Bx investment in Uco, bringing together renowned vignerons from France in collective adventure. In addition to individual wineries (BODEGA ROLLAND, CUVELIER LOS ANDES, DIAMANDES, MONTEVIEJO), one wine (big Bx blend) made for whole group.

Cobos, Viña Men ★★★ One of Argentina's 1st flying winemakers, who eventually stayed. Paul Hobbs's winery makes bold CHARD, CAB SAUV, MALBEC.

Colomé, Bodega Sal ★★→★★★ One of highest-altitude estates in world, creeping to over 3100m (10,170ft) for brooding Altura Maxima MALBEC. Powerful, to age.

Cruzat Men ★★★ Range of sparkling, pink to orange; top Millesime.

Cuvelier Los Andes Men ★★→★★★ Master of Bx blends, chiselled, structured from organic Uco estate (also bio). Cuvée Nature is fresher (carbonic maceration).

Decero, Finca Men ★★ Agrelo producer: firm, dense Bx reds. Top velvety Amano.

DiamAndes Men ★★ Bonnie family's (Malartic Lagravière, *see* Bx) Uco outpost; v.gd VIOGNIER, CAB SAUV.

Doña Paula Men ★★ SANTA RITA owned, headed by Chilean winemaker Toti Undurraga. Plenty of gd value (RIES); fun sparkling SAUV BL.

Durigutti Men ★★→★★★★ Pablo and Hector D championing Luján since 2002. Exciting Las Compuertas range, clutch of fresh, fragrant, contemporary wines (excellent MALBEC 5 Suelos).

El Enemigo Wines Men ★★→★★★★ Exciting, ever-growing range from Ale Vigil and Adrianna CATENA; flor-aged TORRONTÉS, spicy CAB FR excellent GARNACHA.

El Esteco Sal ★★→★★★ Solid portfolio from PEÑAFLOR; floral TORRONTÉS, peppery CAB SAUV. Old Vines label is top stuff.

El Porvenir de Cafayate Sal ★★→★★★ One of top names in region, offering charming reds, whites and now orange. Alto Los Cuises MALBEC, elegant game-changer for n.

Escala Humana Men ★★★ "Human scale" wines by Germán Masera and family; highlight forgotten old vines in Uco. Excellent SEM, spicy CAB SAUV, surprising orange MALVASIA.

Estancia Uspallata Men ★★→★★★ Highest vyd in MEN, towering at 2000m (6560ft) deep in middle of Andes. Unique terrain: floral, fragrant, fresh MALBEC, PINOT N by Colo Sejanovich.

Etchart Sal ★→★★ Historic winery, popular locally: gd-value TORRONTÉS, MALBEC.

Fabre Montmayou Men, Río N ★★→★★★ Classic range of Bx varieties. MERLOT from Patagonia is particularly gd.

Fin del Mundo, Bodega Del Neu ★→★★ Reliable brand; intense CAB FR; organic.

Flichman, Finca Men ★★ Founded 1910, owned by Sogrape (*see* Portugal) since 1998; gd value, covers classic MEN bases. Dedicado CHARD increasingly refined.

Kaikén Men ★★→★★★ Champion of Las Compuertas (old-vine MALBEC); fresher styles from Uco and beyond. Reliable CABS FR/SAUV. MONTES owned (*see* Chile).

La Anita, Finca Men ★★ In heart of Luján's wine route; family winery focuses on warming reds (PETIT VERDOT, SYRAH).

La Celia, Finca Men ★★ Founded 1890, Uco's 1st major estate. Winemaker Andrea Ferreyra steers wines in increasingly fragrant, fresh style. Often top value.

Masi Tupungato Men ★★ Italians in MEN, certainly don't hide their Italian accent: gd PINOT GRIGIO/TORRONTÉS, must-try *ripasso*-style MALBEC/CORVINA.

Matervini Men ★★★ Santiago ACHÁVAL and Roberto Cipresso's label of terroir-driven reds. Bold, age-worthy, often from pioneering vyds hidden in mtns.

Mendel Men ★★★ Handsome collection of wines by legendary Roberto de la Motta; CHENIN BL, SEM need bottle-age, reds are pure class.

Mendoza Powerhouse of Argentine wine, but also some of continent's finest. Regions are diverse: from hot Lavalle desert, to Winkler I in upper parts of Uco. MALBEC most planted; increasingly gd CHARD, CAB FR, GARNACHA.

Winery restaurants in Mendoza get most Michelin stars and recommendations.

Michelini i Mufatto Men ★★★ Gerardo Michelini, Andrea Mufatto and son Manu make small but thoughtful Uco portfolio with son Manu. Low intervention, large-format oak, savoury verve. Excellent old-vine CHENIN BL, SEM.

Mil Suelos Men ★★→★★★ "A thousand soils", apt name for family of labels by terroir-expert Colo Sejanovich: v.gd Buscado Vivo o Muerto, Manos Negras, TeHo, Tinto Negro, ZaHa. Top CHARD, MARSANNE, CAB FR, MALBEC.

Monteviejo Men ★★→★★★ Classy Bx blends, varietals in Campo de los Andes, Uco, made by Jose Mournier. Part of CLOS DE LOS SIETE tribe.

Moras, Finca Las San J ★→★★ Stalwart with popular local following: gd-value SYRAH, BONARDA. Top Sagrado Pedernal; Pedrito PX Sherry style a revelation.

Neuquén Pat Gateway to Pat, but rather warm. Neighbours older RÍO N; offers rich reds and dinosaur fossils.

Nieto Senetiner, Bodegas Men ★→★★★ Leader in fizz and still for the masses: gd-value, reliable Benjamin; top ranges more sophistication (single-vyd BONARDA).

Noemia Pat ★★★→★★★★ Naunced, sophisticated old-vine RÍO N reds; top Bx blends, supple MALBEC by Hans Vinding Diers.

Norton, Bodega Men ★→★★★ Large winery in heart of Perdriel but vyds extend to Uco. Plenty of everyday, but Lote Negro blend, Lote single-vyd MALBEC special.

Onofri Wines Men ★★→★★★ Boutique label by sommelier Mariana Onofri and family. Excellent white blend, lively Pedro Giménez, spicy CAB FR.

Otronia Pat ★★★→★★★★ One of most exciting portfolios in S America, under hand of Juan Pablo Murgia and Alberto Antonini. Extreme Pat at 45°S, so cool climate: savoury CHARD, elegant MALBEC, oily TORRONTÉS, mouthwatering bubbles.

Passionate Wine Men ★★→★★★ Matías Michelini revolutionized Uco scene a decade ago; still offers extreme, lean style but with more polish, precision today. Agua de Roca SAUV BL is killer.

Pelleriti, Marcelo Men ★★→★★★ Renowned for classic touch in the cellar, Marcelo favours ageable CAB FR, MALBEC.

Peñaflor Men ★→★★★ Argentina's largest: enormous stable of brands incl EL ESTECO, FINCA LAS MORAS, Mascota, Navarro Correas, Santa Ana, Suter, TRAPICHE.

Per Se Men ★★→★★★ Focused on single vyd in Gualtallary Monasterio, overlooking old monastery; passion project of Edy del Popolo and David Bonomi. Chalky, tense, mouthwatering CAB FR, MALBEC.

Piatelli Sal ★★ Two wineries in distinctive terroirs: MEN, Cafayate. Both offer firm reds, fragrant whites.

Piedra Negra Men ★→★★★ Francois Lurton's outpost in Uco. Bold, structured reds (MALBEC often blended with COT) best known, but one of biggest draws is excellent, oily Sauvignon Vert white blend Corte Friulano.

Pulenta Estate Men ★★→★★★ Eduardo and Hugo P's Agrelo winery, with vyds in Uco too. Classy reds (CAB FR), but latest crush is unctuous Palma Carola (SEM/VIOGNIER/CHARD).

Renacer Men ★★ Chilean-owned, but in MEN since 2003. Wide range, versatile for pairings in winery restaurant. Calling-card, Amarone-style MALBEC.

Riccitelli, Matias Men ★★★→★★★★ Star, with superb portfolio of racy whites (SAUV BL from La Carrera is electric) from Uco; old vines from RÍO N; juicy, elegant reds from MEN.

Riglos Men ★★ Stalwart in Gualtallary; firm reds with penchant for CABS FR/SAUV.

Riojana, La La R ★ One of Argentina's largest co-ops with 400+ growers in La R. Best for everyday TORRONTÉS.

Río Negro Southerly region, still losing ground, but wealth of old vines worth saving and potential for new. Mild, riverside setting ideal for RIES, SEM, MALBEC, PINOT N, also old-vine Trousseau.

Rolland, Bodega Men ★★★ Michel R's (*see* France) wine baby in Uco; winemaker Rodolfo Vallebella manages. Perfumed SAUV BL, intense MALBEC.

Ruca Malen Men ★★→★★★ Winemaker Agus Hanna brought Ruca Malen back to life with re-energized vibrant portfolio (r/w): excellent SAUV BL/SEM, GARNACHA.

Rutini Men ★★→★★★ Mariano di Paolo heads up trad estate, making top wines in Uco. Antologia blends special.

Salentein, Bodegas Men ★★→★★★ Pioneer in San Pablo; Dutch-owned estate one of most attractive in valley. Portillo is gd value, but Single Vyd range is where excitement is (SAUV BL).

Salta Lion's share of vines in Calchaquí valleys fall in Salta province. High altitude, mountainous, filled with most exuberant TORRONTÉS. Also v.gd MALBEC, TANNAT.

San Juan Major wine region, just n of MEN. Not as well known as neighbour, but turns out lots of gd-value everyday wines (TORRONTÉS, BONARDA, MALBEC, SYRAH). Top-quality regions: Calingasta, Pedernal.

San Pedro de Yacochuya Sal ★★★ Intense high-altitude wines from Michel ROLLAND and ETCHART. Heady MALBEC from old (100 yrs+) vines.

Santa Julia Men ★★ Everyday, v.gd value from ZUCCARDI; growing natural brand.

Schroeder, Familia Neu ★★ PINOT N specialist; plenty of MALBEC too. A dinosaur species was named after Schroeder (*Panamericansaurus schroederi*) after fossils found in cellar.

Sophenia, Finca Men ★★→★★★ One of 1st to settle in Gualtallary; always been hot on top SAUV BL. Also v.gd age-worthy Bx-style reds; *Antisynthesis Field Blend* fresher alternative.

Susana Balbo Wines Men ★★→★★★★ The "Queen of Torrontés" is also a master of reds. Hard to go wrong with anything from Susana's impressive portfolio. Signature White Blend (TORRONTÉS/SAUV BL/SEM) one of Argentina's best.

Tapiz Men ★★→★★★ Family winery with particularly exciting estate in San Pablo, Uco. Alta CAB FR, top-value highlight; Notas de Jean Claude MERLOT, sumptuous.

Terrazas de los Andes Men ★★→★★★ Fine-wine sister of CHANDON, making host of classic varieties. Single-vyd MALBECS fresher in recent yrs, and continue going upwards: now with vines at 1650m (5413ft) in Gualtallary.

> **Put your money where your Malbec is**
> When it comes to the best value from Argentina, you can't go wrong with Malbec – a variety producers here have been honing for decades, and one that has taken the world by storm. For that sweet-spot price you can get some seriously gd stuff from ALTOS LAS HORMIGAS Meteora, ARGENTO Single Vineyard, MATIAS RICCITELLI Vineyard Selection, SUSANA BALBO WINES Benmarco, ZUCCARDI Poligonos.

Tikal / Alma Negra / Animal / Stella Crintina Men ★★→★★★ Ernesto Catena and wife Joanna have handful of organic, bio projects, mostly in Uco. Diverse range: red, orange, white, fizz. Joanna makes kombucha too.

Toso, Pascual Men ★★→★★★ A Maipú icon: silky, concentrated reds from old vines.

Trapiche Men ★→★★★ Flagship winery of PEÑAFLOR with huge host of labels; excellent blends (CAB FR/MALBEC; SYRAH/VIOGNIER) under Iscay. Mostly in MEN, but Costa y Pampa (ALBARIÑO, SAUV BL) from Buenos Aires coast.

Trivento Men ★→★★ CONCA Y TORO-owned: large volumes of everyday wine, incl supermarket hit White MALBEC. Top Eolo Malbec (old vines in Luján).

Ver Sacrum ★★★ One of most radical and uncommon portfolios in Argentina. GARNACHA, MENCÍA, NEBBIOLO focus: no MALBEC! Fragrant, lively, evocative wines from Edu Soler in Uco.

Vines of Mendoza / Winemaker's Village Men ★★ Beautiful hotel and vyd estate in Los Chacayes with some 250 owners; micro-vinifications from 600-ha vyd. Winemaker's Village incl Corazon del Sol, Gimenez Riili, Super Uco.

Zorzal Men ★★→★★★ Refreshing wines in Gualtallary, v.gd SAUV BL, CAB FR and PINOT N. Vibrant Eggo range.

Zuccardi Men ★★→★★★★ Sebastian Z is one of Argentina's top winemakers, continues to grow in flair and prestige in family winery in Uco. MALBECS on austere side, concrete and freshness win over oak and ripe fruit. Brilliant for mineral CHARD (try Fosil), waxy SEM, racy reds.

BRAZIL

One of the few wine countries that keeps growing, Brazil is still on the rise. And the wines are getting better too. The heartland of Rio Grande do Sul is still best for bubbles but also has some stellar Cabernet Sauvignon coming from Campanha on the border of Uruguay. The high-altitude region of Santa Catarina is where the country's best Sauvignon Blanc is. And if you are looking for meaty, smoky Syrah, look no further than the winter-harvest wines of Serra da Mantiqueira.

Aurora ★→★★ Mammoth co-op with hundreds of families, turning out lots of juice and everyday wines.

Casa Valduga ★★→★★★ Family winery in the heart of Vale dos Vinhedos wine route; brilliant bubbles, enjoyable reds.

Cave Geisse ★★★ Showing potential of Brazil's trad-method bubbly, still at top of game. Excellent Brut Nature; fun sparkling orange.

Era dos Ventos ★★★ Luiz Henrique Zanini is a poet and winemaker; each bottle of his exclusive, lo-fi wines comes with a poem instead of a tasting note. Heartfelt, delicious wines.

Guaspari ★★→★★★ Stunning estate in Serra da Mantiqueira (in São Paulo state); v.gd winter-harvest SYRAH.

Lidio Carraro ★★ One of leading family wineries in Rio Grande do Sul making host of gd wines (fun NEBBIOLO).

Miolo ★→★★★ Large operation; big, diverse range; quality focus. Lote 43 v.gd.

Pizzato ★→★★★ One of top producers in Vale dos Vinhedos; v.gd quality across board. Fun unfiltered bubbly, bright SEM, juicy reds.

Salton ★→★★ One of most important brands in Brazil; long history, wide-reaching portfolio (still and sp). Plenty of Prosecco-style, but Lucia Canei is top fizz.

URUGUAY

The "Switzerland of South America", or so the moniker goes. Not only because of its political neutrality but its affluent society too. Uruguay is an oasis of calm and financial stability in a turbulent continent. Perhaps that's why so many investors from Brazil and Argentina are increasingly setting up wineries here. Or perhaps it is because of the charming lifestyle, moderate coastal climate and diverse array of ancient soils that make for interesting wine regions. Tannat is very much king, but fresh Albariño, peppery Cabernet Franc, juicy Marselan and savoury Pinot Noir are highlights too.

Alto de la Ballena ★→★★★ Charming family winery, modern-day pioneer of Maldonado. Old-school nuance: spicy CAB FR, savoury SYRAH, TANNAT/VIOGNIER.

Bouza ★★→★★★ Leading family producer; two wineries, four terroirs, two excellent restaurants. Try ALBARIÑO, RIES, PINOT N, also classic TANNAT, TEMPRANILLO.

Cerro Chapeu, Bodega ★★→★★★ Family winery in Rivera, on n border with Brazil. Excellent range of Castel Pujol Folklore wines, incl MANSENG N.

Cerro del Toro ★★→★★★ Fresh wines from vyds overlooking Atlantic Ocean: ALBARIÑO, Fósiles de Mar CHARD, vibrant TANNAT.

Deicas, Familia ★→★★★★ Santiago D fast becoming one of Uruguay's best – from adventurous natural wines (Bizarra Extravaganza) to effortlessly classy Cru range (ALBARIÑO). Extreme Vyds a highlight, and Santiago would know as Uruguay's only winemaker experienced in all its terroirs.

Garzón, Bodega ★★→★★★★ Uruguay's most impressive estate; flying flag for Maldonado around world. Consistent, reliable range, most exciting wines at top. Underrated gem CAB FR, but all v.gd.

Pablo Fallabrino Wines ★★ Expect the unexpected with Pablo – from orange and pét-nat to Barolo Chinato-style sweet.

Pisano ★→★★★ Multi-generational family winery in Progreso, heart of Canelones. Top age-worthy reds: RPF TANNAT; but bestseller in France is PINOT N.

Progreso, Viña ★★→★★★ Gabriel Pisano's own label from Canelones; zesty ALBARIÑO, lively SANGIOVESE, v.gd TANNAT.

Proyecto Nakkal ★★ Cool kids: low abv, low intervention. Doing it well: lively pét-nat, juicy amphora wines, gluggable Nakcool. Even TANNAT, but not as you know it.

OTHER SOUTH AMERICAN WINES

Bolivia It takes guts, grit and a bag of coca leaves to travel around at these high altitudes, but Bolivia is a rewarding wine country for the adventurous. Whether exploring the gnarly old vines of the Cinti V (try Cepa de Oro, Jardin Oculto) or the big, bold reds of Tarija (Aranjuez, Kohlberg, Kuhlmann), or perhaps the fragrant whites of the Santa Cruz Vs (Vinos 1750), these wines are quite unlike anything else. Certainly not polished or perfect, but definitely memorable.

Peru The lost empire of wine in S America: Peru's history overshadows its present, but Peru's winemakers are working hard on a revival. There's an exciting natural-wine scene in the coastal regions (Bodega Murga, Mimo), plus more classic styles (Intipalka, Tacama, Vista Alegre). Perhaps most exciting of all, though, are the high-altitude mtn vyds of Apu, just a stone's throw from Machu Picchu... a brave attempt to reclaim Peru's wine empire?

Australia

SOUTH AUSTRALIA

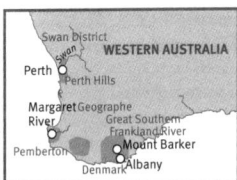

NEW SOUTH WALES Upper Hunter

Darling

Mudgee

Clare Valley

Riverland Mildura Big Rivers Griffith Orange Lower Hunter

Sydney

Cowra

Barossa/Eden Valleys Murrumbidgee

Adelaide Adelaide Hills Murray River Riverina Canberra Southern Highlands

McLaren Vale/Langhorne Creek Murray

Kangaroo Island **VICTORIA** Rutherglen Beechworth/Alpine/King Valleys

Grampians Pyrenees Goulburn Valley

Coonawarra Bendigo/Heathcote/Macedon

Melbourne Yarra Valley

Indian Ocean Geelong Mornington Peninsula

Gippsland

Swan District **WESTERN AUSTRALIA**

Perth Perth Hills **TASMANIA**

Margaret River Geographe

Great Southern Hobart

Frankland River

Pemberton Mount Barker

Denmark Albany

It's sacrilegious to state "drink less" in a wine book. Of course there's a proviso: buy better, drink better. We always want something delicious, but imagine having a bottle that's exceptional too – enjoyed a couple of times a week, not daily. No lecture here, but what is wine about? It's many things: history and culture, sure; farming and community, definitely. It's also about joy – coming to the table with good food and wine, friends and/or family. Australia does that so well, and yet, as with all wine-producing countries, it churns out plenty of generic, boring booze; they are not recommended here. But Australia is also making the best examples of varieties or styles to date in all regions;

take your pick. A good bottle will be more expensive, but it doesn't need to be prohibitive. Consider other tiers from leading producers: Garagiste's Le Stagiare, Hoddles Creek Estate's Wickham Road, Wynns Black Label, Xanadu's Vineworks – the list goes on. A bit of homework is required, but the starting point is in your hands: this book. Happy discoveries and drinking, folks.

Recent vintages

New South Wales (NSW)
2024 Early vintage, low yields; v.gd Hunt V (r). Frost Can, top made v.gd (r/w).
2023 Cool, wet, disease pressure, low yields, yet Hunt V has excellent Shiraz.
2022 La Niña strikes. Heavy rain, not much heat. Difficult vintage.
2021 Heavy rain, some disease pressure. Whites generally gd, choose wisely.
2020 Hot, fire-affected yr with all manner of challenges.
2019 Hot, with just enough rain for generous whites/reds.

Victoria (Vic)
2024 Unseasonally wet/humid, then heat. Low yields, whites gd (Yarra V, Mor P).
2023 Challenging, flooding ne. Some fine (r/w). Yields down in Yarra V, Mor P.
2022 Cool, often wet, low yields. High acidity, v.gd whites, esp Yarra V.
2021 Stark contrast to 20. Many calling it season of elegance, balance; gd yields.
2020 Fire-affected in ne and generally challenging. Yields down.
2019 Compressed season, but wines (r/w) look vibrant.

South Australia (SA)
2024 Dry, some frost, low yields; quality Bar V (r), Clare V Ries.
2023 La Niña in force; wet, cool, lower yields. Clare V v.gd Ries.
2022 Cool, long ripening; v.gd overall. McLaren V solid (r/w).
2021 Said to be nr perfect. Bar V outstanding, Clare V exceptional (r/w).
2020 Hard/tragic yr, but Ries and reds look promising. Seriously low yields.
2019 Exceptionally low yields should produce concentrated wines.

Western Australia (WA)
2024 Warm/dry, v. early season, yields down but Marg R, Gt S v.gd (r/w).
2023 Cool spring, mild conditions. Marg R, Gt S v.gd (r/w).
2022 Excellent in Marg R but low yields, esp Chard.
2021 Challenging due to late-season rain but ultimately rewarding.
2020 Early, low-yield, high-concentration yr.
2019 Cool vintage, the kind to sort the wheat from the chaff.

Accolade Wines Owned by global investment firm Carlyle Group. Hardys, HOUGHTON, KATNOOK, PETALUMA, ST HALLETT. Continues to sell off assets.

Adams, Tim Clare V ★★ Family-owned, v.gd RIES, solid CAB SAUV/MALBEC, SHIRAZ.

Adelaide Hills SA Diverse region in the Mt Lofty ranges, 70 km long, cool: up to 650m (2132ft). Two official subregions: Lenswood, Piccadilly V. CHARD, SAUV BL, GRÜNER V; SHIRAZ over PINOT N, sparkling. Try ASHTON HILLS, DEVIATION ROAD, HAHNDORF HILL, HENSCHKE, JERICHO, SHAW & SMITH, SIDEWOOD ESTATE.

Adelina Clare V ★★★ Family-owned, organic, great vyds; exellent RIES, GRENACHE, MATARO, NEBBIOLO, SHIRAZ.

Agricola Vintners Bar V Star of next-generation BAR V, Callum Powell (son of Dave P ex-Torbreck) sourcing excellent fruit from est and/or old vyds ie. Ashbrook 1864; poised, rich yet refined SHIRAZ. Watch.

Alkina Wine Estate Bar V ★★ Argentinian-owned. No expense spared; est 50s site, now bio; concrete tanks, eggs, *qvevri*, older oak. Compelling GRENACHE, SHIRAZ.

Alkoomi Fra R ★★ Large-scale, family-owned; go-to v.gd RIES, regionally expressive CABS SAUV/FR, SHIRAZ.

All Saints Estate Ruth ★★★★ Rating for exceptional fortifieds, esp Museum MUSCAT, MUSCADELLE, average age 100-yrs+ solera. Table wines fair.

Alpine Valleys Vic Foothills of Victorian Alps. Growers of cool-climate red/white, esp Italian varieties; superb TEMPRANILLO. Stars: BILLY BUTTON, MAYFORD.

Andrew Thomas Hun V ★★ Old-vine SEM; SHIRAZ. A HUN V game-changer, esp with more elegant expressions of SHIRAZ.

Angove's SA ★★→★★★ Family business, founded 1886. Keenly priced across range; MCL V site organic with focus on premium and single-vyd GRENACHE, SHIRAZ.

Aravina Estate Marg R ★★ Formerly Amberley Estate, est vyds, v. cool altitude; only ARINTO in MARG R, v.gd GRENACHE, TEMPRANILLO, plus classic CHARD, CHENIN BL, CAB SAUV.

Arenberg, d' McL V ★★ Some kooky names (eg. The Cenosilicaphobic Cat SAGRANTINO), but wines solid, incl v.gd GRENACHE, SHIRAZ.

A Rodda Beech ★★ Excellent CHARDS from est vyds; *Tempranillo* grown at high altitude can be a beauty.

Ashton Hills Ad H ★★ Distinctive PINOT N 23' 20' 21 22 23 from 30-yr-old+ vyds; tiptop CHARD, RIES.

Baileys of Glenrowan NE Vic ★★ Historic property/vyds, organic; excellent Durif, SHIRAZ, fabulous fortified MUSCAT (★★★★), TOPAQUE. Owned by CASELLA.

Balnaves of Coonawarra SA ★★ Family-owned COONW champion. Rich CHARD, full Tally CAB SAUV flagship, v.gd spicy SHIRAZ. "Joven-style" (*see* Spain) Cab gd.

Bannockburn Vic ★★★ (CHARD) 19 21' 22 23 (PINOT N) 18' 19' 21 22 23 Family-owned, pioneers of GEELONG, quality never wavers. Outrageously gd structured Chard, complex PINOT N, RIES, SAUV BL.

Barossa Valley SA Bastion of v. old-vine CAB SAUV, GRENACHE, MOURVÈDRE, SHIRAZ. Expect richness, but new brigade shaking things up. ELDERTON, GRANT BURGE, HENTLEY FARM, JOHN DUVAL, LANGMEIL, PETER LEHMANN, ROCKFORD, RUGGABELLUS, ST HALLETT, SALTRAM, SAMI-ODI, SEPPELTSFIELD, SPINIFEX, TEUSNER and YALUMBA.

Barry, Jim Clare V ★★★ RIES rules thanks to top vyds and lots of them. LoosenBarry Wolta Wolta a collaboration with Mosel mogul Ernst Loosen (*see* Germany). Reds solid: age-worthy Armagh SHIRAZ. Also Oz's only ASSYRTIKO.

Bass Phillip Gippsland ★★★→★★★★ (PINOT N) 20' 21' 22' 23 Tiny amounts of distinctive Pinot N; CHARD v.gd, delightful GEWURZ, GAMAY. Burgundian J-M Fourrier (*see* France) leads winemaking.

Battle of Bosworth McL V Organic, gd folk caring for land/wine, top value. SHIRAZ leads many offerings.

Beechworth NE Vic Spectacular rocky region in highlands; CHARD, SHIRAZ best, but NEBBIOLO makes statement. Try A RODDA, DOMENICA, FIGHTING GULLY ROAD, GIACONDA, SAVATERRE, SCHMÖLZER & BROWN, SENTIO, SORRENBERG.

Bekkers McL V ★★★ Emmanuelle and Toby B focus on organic GRENACHE, SYRAH.

Bellebone Tas ★★★ Queen of Bubbles, Natalie Fryar (ex-Jansz) showcases "pristine fruit power and elegance of Tasmania" with Blanc de Blancs, rosé and more.

Bellwether Coonw ★★ A love of CAB SAUV kept winemaker Sue Bell in COONW, turning Glen Roy 1868 shearing shed into boutique winery, cellar door and more. CHARD from TAS v.gd, sources Italian varieties too.

Bendigo Vic Hot central Vic region. Balgownie Estate, PASSING CLOUDS, SUTTON GRANGE. Home of rich CAB SAUV, SHIRAZ.

Best's Great Western Gra ★★★ Superstar, in best yrs flagship Thomson Family SHIRAZ

17' 19' 20' 21 22 from 120-yr-old vines; *v.gd mid-weight reds*; exceptional old-vine PINOT M; excellent RIES. History, great people, worth drive from Melbourne.

Billy Button Alpine V ★★ Umpteen varieties/styles: alas, small quantities. Italian varietals (rare SCHIOPPETTINO); CHARD, SAPERAVI, SHIRAZ and more. Delicious.

Bindi Mac ★★★★ Outstanding single-block CHARD, PINOT N 20' 21' 22' 23. Small production, high-density-vyd Block 8 jewel in crown.

World's oldest Grenache and Sem, planted 1848 Barossa V; custodian Cirillo family.

Bleasdale Lang C ★★→★★★ Historic winery est 1850. Fabulous fortifieds and top CAB SAUV, MALBEC, SHIRAZ, plus gd-value range. Ever reliable.

Bondar McL V ★★ Modern yet thoughtful producer of excellent GRENACHE, SHIRAZ, also Italian varieties; v.gd AD H CHARD.

Bortoli, De Griffith, Yarra V ★→★★★ (Noble SEM) Sauternes-style from irrigated region Griffith; YARRA V for cool-climate, quality CHARD, PINOT N, SHIRAZ. Loads of styles, range of prices yet serious player.

Brave New Wine Marg R ★★ Natural wines, loaded with personality; capable of v. high highs, so to speak; CHARD, GEWURZ, SHIRAZ can all be excellent.

Bremerton Lang C ★★ Family-owned/run; stars rich CAB SAUV, MALBEC, SHIRAZ, but CHARD, FIANO no slouches.

Brokenwood Beech, Hun V ★★★→★★★★ (ILR Res SEM) 11' 14' 15 17' 18' (Graveyard SHIRAZ) 14' 17' 18' 19' 21 22 Both HUN V classics. High-quality, gd-value *Cricket Pitch* Sem/SAUV BL. Suite of excellent CHARD, SHIRAZ, TEMPRANILLO from BEECH.

Brown Brothers King V, Tas, Yarra V ★→★★ Crowd-pleaser and top producer by volume of Prosecco variety; premium Patricia range, fizz esp excellent. Innocent Bystander (YARRA V), Devil's Corner/Tamar Ridge (TAS) savvy acquisitions.

Calabria Family Wines Bar V, Riverina ★★→★★★ Family-owned, large-scale, incl excellent BAR V; bought historic MCWILLIAM'S in 2021 (not MOUNT PLEASANT), plus fruit from CAN DISTRICT, TUMBARUMBA. Great wines, all price points incl top.

Campbells Ruth ★★ Reds rule, rich and big Durif, SHIRAZ but unique fortifieds are king: Merchant Prince Rare *Muscat*, Isabella Rare TOPAQUE (★★★★).

Canberra District NSW High-end, cool-climate, quality-driven. CLONAKILLA top; also COLLECTOR, MOUNT MAJURA, NICK O'LEARY, RAVENSWORTH.

Cape Mentelle Marg R ★★ Region's pioneering producer; CHARD promising, SAUV BL/SEM appealing, CAB SAUV often the highlight.

Casella Riverina Through Yellow Tail budget range came an empire. Owns heritage brands BAILEYS OF GLENROWAN, Brand's of Coonawarra, MORRIS, PETER LEHMANN.

Chalmers Hea, Murray D ★→★★ Grower, vine-nursery specialist, focus on Italian varieties. Range of diverse wines: gd FIANO, VERMENTINO.

Chambers Rosewood NE Vic With MORRIS, greatest maker of fortified TOPAQUE (★★★★), *Muscat*.

Chandon Australia Yarra V ★★→★★★ Cool-climate fizz and table wine. Owned by LVMH. Known in UK as Green Point. NV cuvées in best-ever shape.

Chapel Hill McL V ★★ Solid performer in MCL V. These days, GRENACHE (esp old vines), SHIRAZ lead show, but CAB SAUV ever a solid back-up.

Charlotte Dalton Wines Ad H ★★ Breath of fresh air. Classic varieties CHARD, SHIRAZ, but also v.gd Lang C FIANO.

Chatto Tas ★★★ Young vyd, yet some v. fine PINOT N. Fragrance, layers of flavours, beautiful tannins, delicious.

Clarendon Hills McL V ★★★ Powerful, rich reds; think GRENACHE, SHIRAZ; retain depth, savouriness, freshness. Built for cellaring; always decant.

Clare Valley SA Bucolic, high-quality region 142 km n of Adelaide. Top RIES. Unique CAB SAUV, gumleaf-scented SHIRAZ. Try JIM BARRY, GROSSET, KILIKANOON, MOUNT HORROCKS, PIKES, WINES BY KT, but WENDOUREE jewel in crown.

Clonakilla Can ★★★★ (SHIRAZ/VIOGNIER) 15′ 16′ 18′ 19′ 21′ 22′ 23 Regional legend/ superstar. Shiraz/Viognier put on vinous map, but elegant SYRAH often shines brighter. Outstanding RIES, Viognier.

Clyde Park Vic ★★ Single-vyd CHARD, PINOT N v.gd form. SHIRAZ turning heads.

Cobaw Ridge Mac ★★★ Family-owned. Cool-climate, compelling CHARD, SYRAH. Some *qvevri*, amphorae used; bio: super-fine PINOT N, finest LAGREIN in Oz.

Coldstream Hills Yarra V ★★→★★★ Excellent CHARD; PINOT N to drink young, *Res and single vyd to age*. Part of TWE.

Collector Can ★★★ Alex McKay weaves magic: top CHARD (TUMBARUMBA), fine RIES, Shiraz (CAN), host of delicious Italian varieties.

Coonawarra SA Home to some of Australia's finest, most distinctive CAB SAUV, and certainly its richest red soil (on limestone), excellent SHIRAZ too. WYNNS leads pack; BALNAVES, BELLWETHER, KATNOOK, Lindeman's, MAJELLA, YALUMBA all solid.

Coriole McL V ★★★ (Lloyd Res SHIRAZ) 15′ 16′ 18′ 19 20 21 from 100-yr-old+ vines. Pioneer of FIANO, PIQUEPOUL, NEGROAMARO, NERO D'AVOLA, SANGIOVESE v.gd.

Corymbia Marg R, Swan V ★★★ Superstar owner-winemakers. Textural CHENIN BL, elegant CAB SAUV (MARG V); impressive TEMPRANILLO/MALBEC (SWAN V).

Craiglee Sunbury ★★★ (SHIRAZ) 16′ 17′ 18′ 19 20′ 21 22 Salt-of-the-earth producer on historic farm. Rich CHARD, distinctive, fragrant, peppery Shiraz.

Crawford River Henty ★★★ Outstanding RIES producer. Cool/cold, scintillatingly dry, intense. Highly age-worthy.

Crittenden Estate Mor P ★★→★★★ Focus on v.gd CHARD, PINOTS GR/N; Cri de Coeur Sous Voile SAVAGNIN excellent *vin jaune* style.

Cullen Wines Marg R ★★★★ (CHARD) 20′ 21′ 22 23 (CAB SAUV) 18′ 19′ 20′ 21′ 22′ A bio advocate. Kevin John Chard, Diana Madeline and Vanya Cab Sauvs expressing place; long-lived reds.

Dal Zotto King V ★★ "Prosecco" pioneer, many styles, incl excellent Col Fondo. Italian lineup morphs into fresh, lively or structured, detailed. Legendary patriarch has best name: Otto Dal Zotto.

Dappled Yarra V ★★★ Top-flight/value, elegant-but-complex CHARD, PINOT N.

Deep Woods Estate Marg R ★★★★ Styles/varieties from ALBARIÑO, frisky rosé to succulent SHIRAZ; CHARD, CAB SAUV steal limelight. Star of burgeoning FOGARTY GROUP juggernaut.

Delamere Tas ★★★ At Pipers Brook vyd, Fran Austin, Shane Holloway make high-end CHARD, PINOT N but also exquisite fizz. Boutique. Unique. Stylish.

Deviation Road Ad H ★★★ Family vyd. Kate Laurie the fizz queen also sources growers' fruit, constantly fine-tuning styles; top Beltana Blanc de Blancs.

Devil's Lair Marg R ★★★ Finely tuned CHARD, complex CAB SAUV (top-tier 9th Chamber), new excellent SYRAH. Winemakers give love but owned and therefore largely hidden/ignored by TWE.

Dirty Three Wines Gippsland ★★→★★★ Name relates to vyds where Marcus Satchell (aka Mr Gippsland) sources fruit; MENCÍA, REFOSCO, TEROLDEGO planted; cracking CHARD, PINOT N (All The Dirts, Magic Dirt, 100% whole-bunch fermented).

Domenica Beech ★★★ Excellent producer with est vyds. Textural MARSANNE. Exuberant, spicy SHIRAZ, but NEBBIOLO shines.

Rotundone, black-pepper molecule, also found in Syrah, first found in... grass.

Dormilona Marg R, Swan V Winery in hip industrial area. Josephine Perry's diverse, delicious range, personality+; eye on sustainability.

Dr Edge Tas ★★★ Leading light of Oz, Peter Dredge, in TAS: compelling CHARD, PINOT N. Also in Oregon.

Eden Valley SA Climatically cooler cousin of neighbour BAR v. Hilly region; RIES, SHIRAZ from HENSCHKE, Max & Me, PEWSEY VALE, TORZI MATTHEWS and more.

Elanto Ambitious project: Oz's largest high-density vyd, 10.6 ha with 11,111 vines/ha, only CHARD, PINOT N; 1st vintage 23 v.gd, but 24 outstanding. Watch.

Elderton Bar V ★★★ Family-owned/run. Old vines; opulent CAB SAUV, SHIRAZ built to last. Something for everyone, incl v.gd RIES.

Eldorado Road Beech ★★★ Small, family-owned; old-vine SHIRAZ (1890s); powerful reds (Durif, blends). Arguably Oz's finest NERO D'AVOLA. Distinctive wines.

Eldridge Mor P ★★→★★★ Owned by enthusiasts who appointed ex-GIANT STEPS' Steve Flamsteed to help. Expect CHARD, GAMAY, PINOT N to be better than ever.

Entropy Wine Gippsland ★★→★★★ New name turning heads with thoughtful winemaking, sourcing v.gd fruit. Textural SAUV BL/SEM, wonderfully expressive PINOT N, peppery SYRAH and more, crafted by Ryan Ponsford.

Eperosa Bar V ★★★ Organic off-grid winery, 6th-generation BAR V vigneron. Magnolia (1896 SHIRAZ) and Krondorf (1903 GRENACHE) vyds. Respectful of past with nod to future; flavoursome, detailed wines.

Faber Vineyards Swan V ★★ Guru of WA winemaking, John Griffiths redefines what's possible for SWAN V SHIRAZ. Polished power. Fortifieds always a highlight.

Fighting Gully Road Beech ★★★ Lauded producer, plus fruit from ALPINE V. Outstanding CHARD, AGLIANICO, SANGIOVESE, SYRAH, TEMPRANILLO. New plantings of VERDICCHIO, GRENACHE are v. promising. Oz's only PETITE ARVINE.

Flametree Marg R ★★→★★★ No vyds but sources excellent CHARD, CAB SAUV, esp for SRS (subregional series); v.gd SHIRAZ surprise late entry.

Flowstone Marg R ★★★ Partners/veterans bring whimsy, class to diverse range. Top CHARD, CAB SAUV Queen of the Earth; Moonmilk blends.

Forest Hill Vineyard Gt Southern ★★★ Regional pioneer est 1st commercial vyd 1965; RIES the hero, Block 1 the star; v.gd MALBEC, SHIRAZ, outstanding CAB SAUV.

Frankland Estate Fra R ★★★ RIES royalty 20' 21' 22' 23 24, outstanding organic vyd, Isolation Ridge (most remote in WA), range of styles. Medium-bodied CABS FR/ SAUV, SYRAH, impressive GRÜNER V, MOURVÈDRE.

Fraser Gallop Estate Marg R ★★ Rich yet stylish CHARD, SEM/SAUV BL, CAB SAUV. Reliable on all levels.

Freycinet Tas ★★★ Pioneer family winery on TAS e coast; v.gd CHARD, outstanding RIES, fragrant PINOT N 18' 19' 20' 21' 22 23, Radenti (sp).

Garagiste Mor P ★★★ Tiny; outstanding CHARD, PINOTS GR/N. Quality from vyd care, run but not owned by winemaker Barnaby Flanders. Impressive.

Geelong Vic Region w of Melbourne, maritime, dry climate. Leaders: BANNOCKBURN, LETHBRIDGE, OAKDENE, PROVENANCE, WINE BY FARR.

Gembrook Hill Yarra V ★★★ Cool site on upper reaches of Yarra River: CHARD par excellence, fine-boned PINOT N. Excellent gin a sideline.

Gemtree Vineyards McL V ★★ Rich SHIRAZ, TEMPRANILLO and other exotica, linked by quality; bio/organic.

Great Southern value

If one region offers outstanding value, it is GT S. Diversity comes via subregions Albany, Denmark, Fra R, Mount Barker and Porongurup. The 1st commercial vyd, planted 1965, is still going strong: FOREST HILL; the famed Block 1 RIES from original plantings, is a steal. Ries rules, and none has done more to promote it than FRANKLAND ESTATE: fabulous range, incl *foudre* for texture, off-dry, plus pristine and racy. And reds? Spicy, inky, ferruginous SHIRAZ is a highlight (SWINNEY'S SYRAH); excellent bush-vine GRENACHE too. Not just varietals but cool blends are on form at LA VIOLETTA, with Ye-Ye Rouge a juicy, drink-now combo of PINOTS N/M plus Syrah. The eclectic range is all value – bargains, really.

Gentle Folk Ad H ★★ Marine scientists turned vignerons, in natural-wine scene; top CHARD, PINOT N, SYRAH. Viti/regenerative expert Dr Dylan Grigg advises.

Giaconda Beech ★★★★ Stellar NEBBIOLO, PINOT N, SHIRAZ; CHARD 18' 19' 21' 22' 23.

Giant Steps Yarra V ★★★ 18' 19' 20' 21' 22' 23 (24) Top single-vyd CHARD, PINOT N, SHIRAZ. Jackson Family-owned (*see* US).

Glaetzer-Dixon Tas ★★→★★★ Nick G turned SA wine-family history on head by relocating to cool TAS. Euro-style RIES, autumnal PINOT N, Rhôney SHIRAZ.

Goulburn Valley Vic Warm region in mid-Vic taking in Nagambie Lakes. Full reds, distinct whites: MARSANNE, CAB SAUV, SHIRAZ. MITCHELTON, TAHBILK flag-bearers.

Grampians Vic Temperate region in NW Vic; excellent RIES, distinct peppery SHIRAZ (and sp). MOUNT LANGI GHIRAN head and shoulders above all.

Granite Belt Qld High-altitude, (relatively) cool, improbable region just n of Qld/NSW border. Spicy SHIRAZ, rich SEM (Boireann, Golden Grove, Ridgemill Estate). Plus Italian varieties.

Grant Burge Bar V ★★ Smooth red and white from best grapes of large vyd holdings. ACCOLADE-owned.

Great Southern WA Remote cool area at bottom left corner of Oz; Albany, Denmark, Fra R, Mount Barker, Porongurup official subregions; 1st-class RIES, CAB SAUV, SHIRAZ. *Style, quality, value here.*

Grosset Clare V ★★→★★★ (RIES) 21' 22 23 24 Nervy, acid-driven Ries in youth, many styles incl high-end G110 from one clone, organic site. Appealing FIANO; distinctive *Gaia* 19' 20 21' 22, mainly CAB SAUV.

Gundog Estate Hun V ★ Aspirational SEM, SHIRAZ from CAN, HUN V.

Hahndorf Hill Ad H ★★★ Made GRÜNER V its own, consistently richly spiced, textured; interest, experimentation across range; plus intriguing Austrian reds.

Hardys SA ★★ Historic company, but glory days long gone, ACCOLADE-owned; CHARD, SHIRAZ often excellent despite lack of company direction.

Heathcote Vic 500-million-yr-old Cambrian geology, calcium-rich, red soils can produce compelling reds, esp SHIRAZ, but Italian varieties flourishing. JASPER HILL, PAUL OSICKA, TAR & ROSES, Whistling Eagle, WILD DUCK CREEK.

Helm Can Pioneer of RIES all styles; and yes, even Ries Rosé.

Henschke Eden V ★★★★ (SHIRAZ) 05' 09' 10' 14' 15' 16' 17 18' 19, 20 21 (CAB SAUV) 12' 15' 16' 17 18 19 21 Oz wine royalty, 150-yr-old family business; masterpiece is Hill of Grace, site and wine (Shiraz) with v.gd single-vyd Cab Sauv Cyril Henschke. Red blends gd, whites also from AD H, incl GRÜNER V.

Hentley Farm Bar V ★★★ Gutsy SHIRAZ, flavour, tannins, power, concentration. Built for long haul.

Hewitson Bar V ★★ (*Old Garden Mourvèdre*) 17' 18' 19 20 21 Old Garden planted 1853, making it world's oldest MOURVÈDRE; v.gd SHIRAZ, range of prices.

Hickinbotham Clarendon Vineyard McL V ★★★★ Dry-grown SHIRAZ, CAB SAUV planted 1971 (Jackson Family-owned, *see* US); separate business to YANGARRA but same philosophy: organic, respect for land. Excellent suite of wines.

Hoddles Creek Estate Yarra V ★★★ Family-owned/run: outstanding cool-climate CHARD, PINOT N, esp top-tier single blocks. Quality high, value too.

Hoosegg Orange ★★→★★★ Veteran Philip Shaw made Rosemount a roaring success in Southcorp days, now TWE. Eponymous label run by sons, this the nest egg: excellent boutique CHARD, CABS SAUV/FR and more.

Houghton Marg R Brand with ACCOLADE, shadow of former self. Fruit from GT S, MARG R, wines made in latter. ★★★★ for Jack Mann CAB SAUV; credit to winemaker Courtney Treacher for dedication.

House of Arras Tas ★★★★ Most prestigious fizz house in Oz, all credit to winemaker Ed Carr. Key is magic confluence of tannins, ageing on lees and acidity. EJ Carr Late Disgorged the pinnacle. Bought by Handpicked Wines 2023.

Howard Park WA ★★→★★★ With v.gd RIES from GT S, plus MARG R CHARD and CAB SAUV. *MadFish* can be gd value. Marchand & Burch, family collaboration with Burgundian vigneron Pascal Marchand.

Hugh Hamilton Wines McL V ★★ All-rounder, quirky names: The Larrikin CAB/ SHIRAZ, The Mongrel SANGIOVESE; SAPERAVI a speciality, several styles incl powerful Oddball the Great.

Quirkily good match: Vegemite/Marmite cheese toasty + aged fizz. Umami heaven.

Hunter Valley NSW Historic region 250 km n of Sydney. Unique SEM can be steely in youth, elixir with age; mid-weight, earthy SHIRAZ. Try ANDREW THOMAS, BROKENWOOD, MOUNT PLEASANT, SILKMAN, *Tyrrell's*.

Jacob's Creek Bar V ★ Mostly focused on uninspiring but reliable wines; solid RIES.

Jasper Hill Hea ★★ Emily's Paddock SHIRAZ/CAB FR, Georgia's Paddock Shiraz intense. Much-needed vyd work on-going; run by 2nd generation.

Jericho Ad H, McL V ★★ Careful fruit selection, skilled winemaking, modern, tasty wines: FIANO, GRENACHE, SHIRAZ, TEMPRANILLO.

John Duval Wines Bar V ★★★ John D (ex-PENFOLDS) Grange) makes *delicious Rhôney reds* of great intensity, character. Son (2nd generation) Tim works with dad.

Joshua Cooper Wines Mac ★★★ Son of COBAW RIDGE founders, uber-talented with love of Oz wine history. Site in MAC, sources fruit within and outside region. Outstanding CHARD, PINOT N, teases best from BENDIGO CAB SAUV 1970 plantings.

Juniper Marg R With est sites: glubbable Nouveau (r blend), FIANO, plus single-vyd CHARD, CAB SAUV. Ever reliable. Higher Plane 2nd tier: drink-now, fun styles.

Kalleske Bar V ★★ Old family farm makes captivating single-vyd SHIRAZ; all intensely flavoured; bio/organic.

Katnook Estate Coonw ★→★★ (Odyssey CAB SAUV) **14' 15'** 19 21 Pricey icons Odyssey, Prodigy SHIRAZ. Big wines in need of restrained love. ACCOLADE-owned.

Kay Brothers McL V Old-school/trad family winery, wonderful history: 1892 SHIRAZ in top Block 6; v.gd GRENACHE, MATARO, plus fortifieds.

Kilikanoon Clare V ★★ Top performers: RIES, SHIRAZ. Luscious, generous, well made. Chinese investment group-owned.

King Valley Vic Altitude range 155–860m (509–2821ft) has big impact stylistically. Noted for Italian varieties. Quality from BROWN BROTHERS, Chrismont, DAL ZOTTO, PIZZINI (esp).

Kirrihill Clare V ★★ RIES, CAB SAUV, SHIRAZ v.gd, often at excellent prices.

Knappstein Wines Clare V ★ Always reliable RIES, SHIRAZ, CAB SAUV; gd value.

Kooyong Mor P ★★★ PINOT N, *excellent Chard* of detail, structure; PINOT GR of charm. High-quality single vyds.

Lake Breeze Lang C ★★★ Family-owned, salt of the earth: excellent, regionally distinct CAB SAUV, SHIRAZ; few producers do mid-level so consistently well.

Lake's Folly Hun V ★★★ (CHARD) **20' 21'** 22 23 (Cab blend) **18'** 19' 20 21 22 Pioneer of HUN V CAB SAUV, now part of FOGARTY GROUP. Still a beacon of quality, character.

Lambert, Luke Yarra V ★★ Focus only on NEBBIOLO at new estate vyd, yet to produce. Until then, v.gd cool CHARD, PINOT N, SYRAH.

Langmeil Bar V ★★ Custodian of some of world's oldest SHIRAZ vines (planted mid-1800s) and other ancient vyds. Big CAB SAUV, GRENACHE, Shiraz. Much loved.

Larry Cherubino Wines Fra R, Marg R ★★★ Outstanding CHARD, RIES, SAUV BL, SHIRAZ; classy CAB SAUV. Lots of labels, and polish. Takes best Fra R, MARG R fruit.

LAS Vino Marg R ★★★ Nic Peterkin is grandson of Kevin and Diana CULLEN, and son of PIERRO founder Mike. A trailblazer, experimenter, yet fastidious producer of outstanding CHARD, CHENIN BL, CAB SAUV.

Leeuwin Estate Marg R ★★★★ Iconic. Age-worthy Art Series CHARD 18' 19' 20' 21' 22. Solid RIES, SAUV BL; v.gd *Cab Sauv*.

Leo Buring Bar V ★★ Gets lost in TWE empire, still v.gd. RIES rules; Leonay top label *ages superbly.*

Lethbridge Vic ★★ Estate wines; bio, v.gd: CHARD, PINOT N, with regional RIES, SHIRAZ. Dabbles in Italian (r/w). Always interesting.

Limestone Coast Zone SA Important, increasingly diverse region, incl COONW, Mt Benson, Mt Gambier, PADTHAWAY, Robe, WRATTONBULLY.

Living Roots Ad H ★★ Sebastian Hardy and wife Colleen also make wine in Finger Lakes (*see* US). Focus on mid-weight reds: AD H SHIRAZ, MCL V GRENACHE.

Lowboi Denmark ★★ Guy Lyons (FOREST HILL) and wife Nicola bought est site in Porongurup Range. Fine CHARD, RIES, gorgeous GRÜNER V (Forest Hill fruit).

Lowestoft Tas ★★★ Part of expanding FOGARTY GROUP; est vyd nr Hobart, excellent CHARD, PINOT N, terrific fizz.

LS Merchants Marg R ★★→★★★ Motto: gd wine, fun times. Delicious, drink-now blends; also excel in classy, regional CHARD, CAB SAUV, plus Fra R RIES, SHIRAZ.

Macedon and Sunbury Vic Adjacent regions: Macedon high elevation, cool for CHARD, PINOT N; Sunbury, nr Melbourne airport, for SHIRAZ. Try BINDI, COBAW RIDGE, CRAIGLEE, JOSHUA COOPER.

Mac Forbes Yarra V ★★★ Savvy Mac Forbes is obsessed with wines of place, ie. single-site CHARD, PINOT N. Also smitten with NEBBIOLO.

McHenry Hohnen Marg R ★★→★★★ More detail, class in past few yrs; winemaker Jacopo Dalli Cani teases out best from CHARD, CAB SAUV, plus surprise, SHIRAZ.

McLaren Vale SA Outstanding, diverse region nr Adelaide. Centre of Italian varieties FIANO, VERMENTINO to NERO D'AVOLA, SANGIOVESE, plus weighty, rich or elegant reds, esp SHIRAZ, but dry-grown, old-bush-vine GRENACHE today's hero. Stars: BEKKERS, BONDAR, CORIOLE, Hither & Yon, JERICHO, OLIVER'S TARANGA VYDS, SC PANNELL, THISTLEDOWN, WIRRA WIRRA, YANGARRA.

McWilliam's SE Aus ★★ Historic producer, owned by CALABRIA FAMILY, quality focus guaranteed (*see* MOUNT PLEASANT).

Main Ridge Estate Mor P ★★★ Pioneer of region, sold 2015 with owners respecting its history while cementing its future. Full, rich CHARD, distinctive PINOT N. Small quantities.

Majella Coonw ★★ Archetypal CAB SAUV, SHIRAZ (also top sp). Value at every level.

Margaret River WA Maritime region s of Perth. Arguably finest CHARD, CAB SAUV in Oz. Try CAPE MENTELLE, CORYMBIA, CULLEN, DEEP WOODS, FLAMETREE, FRASER GALLOP, LAS VINO, LEEUWIN, LS MERCHANTS, MOSS WOOD, PIERRO, TRIPE ISCARIOT, VASSE FELIX, VOYAGER, WINDOWS ESTATE, WOODLANDS and more. Premium location of bush, beaches, surfing.

Mayford NE Vic ★★★ Tiny, exquisite vyd in hidden valley. Put ALPINE V region on map. CHARD, SHIRAZ and Oz's finest TEMPRANILLO.

Meerea Park Hun V ★★ Age-worthy SEM, SHIRAZ often as single-vyd expressions.

Mike Press Wines Ad H ★ Reliable, affordable: SAUV BL, CAB SAUV, SHIRAZ.

Ministry of Clouds McL V Diversity, difference, refinement define terrific selections: MCL V reds, AD H CHARD, plus cool-altitude PICPOUL, MENCÍA.

Mitchelton Goulburn V ★★ Stalwart RIES, CAB SAUV, SHIRAZ; speciality *Marsanne*, ROUSSANNE. Fancy new hotel set among fabulous river red gums.

Marri blossom keeps birds off Margaret R grapes: flowers nr vintage, nectar is nicer.

MMAD McL V ★★★★ SHAW & SMITH/TOLPUDDLE make single vyds from Blewitt Springs in separate business: outstanding CHENIN B, GRENACHE, SHIRAZ.

Montalto Mor P ★★→★★★ Focus on single-vyd CHARD, PINOT N highlights best of MORN P. Fab cellar door, restaurant; sculptures dotted through vyd.

Moorilla Estate Tas ★★ Pioneer nr Hobart on Derwent River; CHARD, RIES, PINOT N; v.gd restaurant, extraordinary art gallery (MONA). Also owns nearby Dom A.

Moorooduc Estate Mor P ★★→★★★ Solid performer of region's best varieties: CHARD, PINOTS N/GR.

Moppity Vineyards ★ Value CAB SAUV, SHIRAZ (Hilltops); fine CHARD (TUMBARUMBA).

Mornington Peninsula Vic Stunning coastal area se of Melbourne; cool, maritime climate noted for CHARD, PINOTS GR/N. Playground for wealthy. ELANTO, ELDRIDGE, GARAGISTE, KOOYONG, MAIN RIDGE, MONTALTO, MOOROODUC, PARINGA, RARE HARE WINES, STONIER, TEN MINUTES BY TRACTOR, YABBY LAKE and more.

Light bottles reduce greenhouse gas emissions 20%: Margaret R voluntary charter.

Morris NE Vic ★★★★ In RUTH; 5th-generation David M at helm; CASELLA-owned. Arguably Oz's finest fortifieds, *Muscats*, TOPAQUES.

Moss Wood Marg R ★★★ Most opulent MARG R reds. Star: CAB SAUV 18' 19' 20 21. Rich, full CHARD bucks regional trend, gd SEM.

Mount Horrocks Clare V ★★ Racy RIES, SEM, CAB SAUV, SHIRAZ in gd shape. Note NERO D'AVOLA.

Mount Langi Ghiran Gra ★★★★ Peppery, *Rhône-like Shiraz* (excellent Langi) 14' 15' 17' 18' 19' 21. Estate-grown RIES, on special patch of dirt, v.gd.

Mount Majura Can ★★ Leading TEMPRANILLO producer plus other Iberian varieties; CHARD, SHIRAZ gd; excellent RIES.

Mount Mary Yarra V ★★★★ Goes from strength to strength. Known for Bx blend Quintet 19' 20' 21' 22' 23 and Triolet (w), yet CHARD, PINOT N outstanding. Rhône varieties latest additions, made by Sam Middleton, grandson of founder.

Mount Pleasant Hun V ★★★★ Owned by Medich. One of the most important names in Oz wine thanks to history, single-vyd SEM (esp *Lovedale*) and Maurice O'Shea SHIRAZ. Old vyds, great sites, sensational wines.

Mudgee NSW Region nw of Sydney. Full CHARD, textural RIES, fine SEM, earthy reds. Quality gd with Robert Stein Vyd riding high, but more heroes needed.

Mulline Geelong ★★→★★★ Rhymes with divine, so too the wines; collaboration between friends. Fruit from GEELONG, top single-vyd CHARD, PINOT N, SYRAH. Focus on organic, eco business. Winner all round.

Ngeringa Ad H ★★ Perfumed NEBBIOLO, PINOT N, SHIRAZ; savoury rosé; bio, holistic farming incl extensive veg and fruit trees, free-range livestock.

Nocturne ★★★ Marg R All about MARG R subregions; limited volumes CHARD, CAB SAUV, v.gd rosé. Side hustle of Julian Langworthy (DEEP WOODS).

Oakdene Geelong Notable fizz, CHARD, PINOT N and more; best enjoyed at winery restaurant.

Oakridge Yarra V ★★★★ Leading producer of CHARD, plus excellent PINOT N, SHIRAZ, and CAB SAUV. Multiple single-vyd releases.

O'Leary, Nick Can ★★→★★★ One of younger generation leading charge with racy and/or textural RIES, spicy SHIRAZ, super TEMPRANILLO; TUMBARUMBA CHARD.

O'Leary Walker Clare V ★★ Pure CLARE V RIES, solid CAB SAUV, big, bolshie MCL V SHIRAZ. Value all round.

Oliver's Taranga Vineyards McL V ★★ A 6th-generation grower supplying top producers (eg. PENFOLDS); GRENACHE, SHIRAZ v.gd. Trailblazer Corrina Wright, 1st family winemaker, esp Italian, Spanish vines: FIANO, MENCÍA highlights.

Onannon Mor P Creative side hustle for friends Will Byron (ex-STONIER), Sam Middleton (MOUNT MARY) and Kaspar Hermann (ROCHFORD): CHARD, PINOT N, different sites/techniques. Super-smart.

Orange NSW Cool-climate, high-elevation region. Lively SHIRAZ (when ripe), but best suited to aromatic whites esp RIES, also CHARD; v.gd fizz, naturally.

Ossa Wines Tas ★★ New, exciting player: CHARD, GRÜNER V, PINOT N, fizz. Watch.

Padthaway SA Rarely mentioned these days, but important region: v.gd CHARD, CAB SAUV, SHIRAZ. Soil salinity on-going issue.

Pannell, SC McL V ★★★★ Trailblazer. Intuitive winemaking, gd vyds. Midas touch with GRENACHE, SHIRAZ, plus AGLIANICO, NEBBIOLO under Protero label. Dabbles with Spanish varieties.

Paringa Estate Mor P ★★ Big, rich PINOT N, SHIRAZ; same with CHARD.

Parker Coonawarra Estate Coonw ★★ In gd yrs full, age-worthy, tannic CAB SAUV of authority, distinction.

Passing Clouds Bendigo ★★ Down-to-earth folk; reliable, robust reds, esp CAB SAUV (often a showstopper), SHIRAZ. Mac CHARD has verve.

Patrick Sullivan Wines Gippsland ★★★ Smart winemaker obsessed with CHARD. New planting will be highest-density Chard in Oz. Farms other sites (with WILLIAM DOWNIE); Ada River and Bullswamp Chards outstanding, plus PINOT N.

Paul Osicka Wines Hea ★★★ Family-owned/run. Vines dating back to 50s. Both character/flavour writ large. Small-scale, low-profile, high-impact; quality CAB SAUV, SHIRAZ.

Paxton McL V ★ Prominent organic/bio grower-producer: note GRENACHE, SHIRAZ.

Pemberton WA Region between MARG R and GT S; PINOT N, SHIRAZ matched to CHARD, RIES. Fizz usually steals limelight.

Penfolds ★★★★ (Grange) 96 06' 08' 10' 14' 17' 18' 19' 20 (CAB SAUV Bin 707) 15 18 19 21 22 Oz's most famous (r) brand. So many Bins, so many wines: now incl Bx, Champagne, California, China. Exceptional CHARD Bin A and *Yattarna* personally, consistently, two finest in the range; v.gd RIES.

Penley Estate Coonw ★★→★★★ Owned by sisters Ang and Bec Tolley; star winemaker Kate Goodman. Cellar door in MCL V, but CAB SAUV rules; diverse styles, all excellent from experimental Project wines, ie. whole-bunch Cab Sauv (it works), to high-end, structured Helios. COONW business for sale 2025.

Petaluma Ad H ★→★★ Croser (sp) can be v.gd, plus gd RIES, SHIRAZ (AD H) and CAB SAUV (COONW).

Peter Lehmann Wines Bar V ★★ Well priced overall, incl easy RIES. Rich, structured Stonewell SHIRAZ among many others. Part of CASELLA.

Pewsey Vale Eden V ★★ Most recognizable RIES brand and done well. Value with several styles, incl Museum release The Contours grown on beautiful tiered vyd.

Pfeiffer Ruth Historic winery, built 1885, family-owned with 2nd-generation Jen P caring for all plus precious fortifieds (★★★★ for Rare MUSCAT and Topaque, aka MUSCADELLE).

Pierro Marg R ★★★ Rich, distinct CHARD 20' 21 22 23, with loyal fanbase; gd SEM/SAUV BL and tiptop Bx blend.

Fortifying value

Oz wine history was built on fortifeds, but now they're less than 2% of production. We drink differently today. That means they are exceptional value. The level of skill and the time they need to evolve require a life's commitment. Thankfully, the younger generation in Australia's fortified capital, RUTH, is ensuring these nectars survive. Jen PFEIFFER is a master of styles, her aperas (formerly "Sherries"; EU directive) are special: love Seriously Nutty Medium Dry. At CAMPBELLS, Jane C continues her family's trad beautifully; so too, 6th-generation Stephen CHAMBERS, while 5th-generation David MORRIS is the torchbearer. The pinnacle is Morris's Old Premium Rare Muscat or Topaque (formerly Tokay; EU directive) or Tawny. Classification of styles is via a tiered system that starts with Ruth (average age of base wine 3–5 yrs) to most complex Rare (20 yrs old+, but many are 70 yrs+). Underpriced, unique, utterly decadent.

Pikes Clare V Excellent winery restaurant, even better RIES, esp flagship The Merle, v.gd CAB SAUV and more.

Pipers Brook Tas ★★ Cool-area pioneer; gd RIES 21' 22 23 24; PINOT N variable; *restrained Chard and sp* from Tamar V. Second label: Ninth Island. Owned by Belgian Kreglinger family.

Pizzini King V ★★ Pioneer of Italian varieties: NEBBIOLO, SANGIOVESE (all styles, authentic). Wonderful family.

Place of Changing Winds Mac ★★★ Powerful, rich CHARD, PINOT N, grown on high-density vyds. Also Rhône-style SHIRAZ from HEA fruit.

Pooley Tas ★★★→★★★★ Historic, impressive property c.1832 in Coal River V. Some of TAS's – nay, some of Oz's – finest RIES; CHARD, PINOT N. Distinctive wines.

Primo Estate SA ★★ Joe Grilli's many successes: rich MCL V SHIRAZ, tangy COLOMBARD, potent Joseph CAB SAUV/MERLOT, complex NEBBIOLO, Shiraz (sp).

Printhie Orange Super-cool wines in super-cool region. Fab fizz, fine CHARD.

Provenance Geelong ★★★ Top CHARD from GEELONG and around; SHIRAZ red star.

Punch Yarra V ★★★ Lovely Lance family ran Diamond Valley for decades. Retained close-planted PINOT N vyd when it sold: can make beautiful, age-worthy wines.

Pyrenees Vic Central Vic region; rich, often minty reds. Blue Pyrenees, Dog Rock, Mitchell Harris, Summerfield, TALTARNI leading players; happy hunting ground for assorted small producers.

Quealy Mor P PINOT GR pioneer. Tom McCarthy, 2nd generation, leads organic estate: complex CHARD, PINOT N; and yes, v.gd Pinot Gr; skin-contact FRIULANO.

Rare Hare Wines Mor P ★★ Was Willow Creek until 2022. Impressive CHARD, PINOT N. Power, poise.

Ravensworth Can ★★★ Innovative producer, brilliant classic styles eg. SHIRAZ/ VIOGNIER, plus skin-contact whites and Italian varieties too, outstanding RIES. Texture a big part, no surprise as winemaker Bryan Martin is ex-chef.

Rieslingfreak Clare V, Eden V ★★→★★★ Apt name: John Hughes only makes RIES. Winemaker wife Belinda (ex-GRANT BURGE) also at helm.

Riverina NSW Large-volume irrigated zone centred on Griffith.

Robert Oatley Wines Mudgee ★★→★★★ Three brands: everyday Signature Series, single vyds with Finisterre, best barrels for The Pennant. Fruit from MARG R, GT S, MCL V. Reliable, gd value, can be excellent.

Robert Stein Vineyard Mudgee ★★★ Regional stalwart: young Jacob S carrying torch for brilliant RIES (all styles), plus cool CAB SAUV, SHIRAZ.

Rochford Yarra V ★★→★★★ Main outdoor entertainment venue in YARRA V makes complex CHARD, CAB SAUV, PINOT N of note.

Rockford Bar V ★★★ Various old low-yielding vyds; reds best; iconic Basket Press SHIRAZ and noted *sparkling Black Shiraz*.

Ruggabellus Bar V ★★★ Modern iteration of BAR V, savoury, even lighter-framed. Old oak, wild yeast, whole bunches/stems. Blends of CINSAULT/GRENACHE/ MATARO/SHIRAZ. Compelling.

Rutherglen and Glenrowan NE Vic Two regions in warm NE Vic, both offer rich reds, outstanding fortifieds. ALL SAINTS, BAILEYS OF GLENROWAN, CAMPBELLS, MORRIS, SCION, TAMINICK CELLARS.

Marron, largest crayfish in West Oz, perfect poached, best with Chard or Ries.

St Hallett Bar V ★★ Star: SHIRAZ (Old Block 18' 19' 20); rest of range is smooth, sound, stylish. ACCOLADE-owned.

Salomon Estate S Fleurieu Austrian legend Bert S (*see* Austria): fragrant VIOGNIER, CAB SAUV, SYRAH.

Saltram Bar V ★★ Value Mamre Brook (CAB SAUV, SHIRAZ) and No.1 Shiraz leaders. Main claim to fame is ubiquitous Pepperjack Shiraz.

Sami-Odi Bar V ★★★ Fraser and Andrea McKinley are BAR V avant-garde. Hand-crafted, tiny quantities, benchmark Shiraz/SYRAH; est sites, uber-cool labels.

Savaterre Beech ★★★ Star: full-bodied CHARD 19' 21' 22 23. Meaty PINOT N 18' 19' 21 22; close-planted SAGRANTINO, SHIRAZ.

Schmolzer & Brown Beech ★★ Estate vyd, Thorley, highest in BEECH. Scintillating CHARD, perfumed PINOT N, spicy SYRAH, excellent RIES, NEBBIOLO to watch.

Scion Ruth ★★ Fresh, vibrant approach to region's stalwarts SHIRAZ and Durif.

Scorpo Wines Mor P Top producer, refined CHARD, PINOTS GR/N, mainstays of region. Skin-contact Pinot Gr reflecting Italian heritage of Paul S.

Sentio Beech ★★★ Chris Catlow picks eyes out of various cool-climate regions incl MAC for compelling CHARD, PINOT N, SHIRAZ.

Seppelt Gra ★★★ Historic in name only, owned by TWE. St Peter's SHIRAZ 18' 19' 20 21 22. Excellent CHARD, RIES. Lost its way when business gutted; some love now with winemaker Clare Dry. Here's hoping.

Seppeltsfield Bar V ★★★→★★★★ National Trust Heritage Winery owned by Warren Randall. Fortified stocks back to 1878. A must-visit.

Serrat Yarra V ★★ Micro-vyd of noted winemaker Tom Carson (YABBY LAKE) and wife Nadège; CHARD, PINOT N, SHIRAZ/VIOGNIER and Rhône varieties.

Seville Estate Yarra V ★★★ YARRA V pioneer, still solid. Excellent CHARD 20' 21' 22 23, SHIRAZ, structured PINOT N.

Shaw & Smith Ad H ★★★ Savvy outfit: complex CHARD; crisp, *harmonious Sauv Bl*; and, surpassing both, *Shiraz*. PINOT N v.gd.

Sidewood Estate Ad H ★★ Cidery, winery, snazzy restaurant, cellar door with v.gd wines in tow. Fizz a feature, cool CHARD, SHIRAZ too.

Silkman Hun V ★★★ Star: takes best of region – CHARD, SEM, SHIRAZ – and turns into best wines.

Sinapius Tas Special, high-density site, wonderful CHARD, PINOT N. GRÜNER V, GAMAY too. Drinkability writ large.

Singlefile Denmark Lovely property/cellar door in remote area; sourcing fruit across region incl MARG R; gd value, gd wines.

Sittella Swan V Heady fortifeds, fizz, table wines; vyds in MARG R keep this family-owned business at top of game.

Snake + Herring Marg R Two friends, Tony (Snake) Davis winemaker, Redmond (Herring) Sweeney marketing, make fun wines eg. Bizarre Love Triangle PINOT GR; classy CHARD, CAB SAUV; sourcing fruit across the state.

Sorrenberg Beech ★★★★ No fuss, but highest quality; CHARD, SAUV BL/SEM, Oz's finest GAMAY, Bx blend. Ultimate "in the know" winery; legend owner-winemaker Barry Morey.

Southern NSW Zone NSW Cool-climate zone incl CAN, Gundagai, Hilltops, TUMBARUMBA. Scintillating CHARD, pure RIES, savoury SHIRAZ.

Spinifex Bar V ★★★ Reds dominate, attention to detail in winemaking. Spicy GRENACHE, rich MATARO, SHIRAZ. Single vyds of note.

Stargazer Tas ★★★ Boutique enterprise of Samantha Connew (ex-WIRRA WIRRA). Refined CHARD, RIES, PINOT N; Tupelo, Alsace-style blend.

Stefano Lubiana S Tas ★★★ Beautiful bio vyds on banks of Derwent River. Stamped with quality from fizz to outstanding CHARD, PINOT N, plus Italian, Austrian varieties. Osteria Vista restaurant Italian to the core.

Stella Bella Marg R ★★→★★★ Solid performer across range of styles, prices. Top CHARD, CAB SAUV called Luminosa often illuminating.

Stoney Rise Tas ★★ Cricket champ-turned-winemaker Joe Holyman crafts compelling CHARD, PINOT N; v.gd GRÜNER V, RIES.

Stonier Wines Mor P Pioneering CHARD, PINOT N. Re-energized with new owners (2022). Co-owner Julian Grounds (ex-Craggy Range, *see* NZ) winemaker (2024).

Sunbury Vic *See* MACEDON AND SUNBURY.

Sutton Grange Bendigo ★★ Noteworthy SYRAH; Rosé rocks; FIANO, AGLIANICO, SANGIOVESE more than a sideshow.

Swan Valley WA Vines 1st planted 1829, 25 mins n of Perth. Star: CHENIN BL; also SHIRAZ, GRENACHE, fortifieds.

Swinney Fra R ★★★ Grower for decades, now excellent own-label RIES, GRENACHE, SHIRAZ, TEMPRANILLO. Top-tier Farvie; by WA winemaking royalty Rob Mann.

Tahbilk Nagambie ★★ Oldest family-owned winery in Vic, original 1860s estate/cellar door still going strong. Best: old-vine (1927) *Marsanne* 08' 12' 13' 15' 16 17 18. Res CAB SAUV, SHIRAZ can be v.gd. Rare 1860 Vines Shiraz.

Taltarni Pyrenees ★★ Built to age; CAB SAUV, SHIRAZ in gd shape; v.gd fizz.

Taminick Cellars Glenrowan ★ Booth family has farmed this tough patch since 1914. Fair amount of character accumulated along way.

Tapanappa SA ★★→★★★ WRATTONBULLY collaboration between Brian Croser, Bollinger and J-M Cazes of Pauillac (*see* France). Splendid CHARD, CAB SAUV blend, MERLOT, SHIRAZ. Surprising *Pinot N* from Fleurieu Peninsula.

Tar & Roses Hea ★★ Inspired by Med varieties and others. SANGIOVESE, SHIRAZ to NEBBIOLO all gd. Modern success story.

TarraWarra Estate Yarra V ★★→★★★ Great Res: Chard 20' 21' 22', Pinot N 18' 19 21. Plus Rhône, Italian varieties: BARBERA a delight. Sarah Fagan (ex-DE BORTOLI) joined 2023. Home to TarraWarra Museum of Art.

Tasmania Cold island, hot reputation. Envy of many mainlanders and strong presence ie. TOLDPUDDLE (SHAW & SMITH). Outstanding fizz, CHARD, PINOT GR, RIES, SAUV BL, PINOT N.

Taylors Wines Clare V ★→★★ Large scale, family-owned. Solid RIES, CAB SAUV, SHIRAZ. Umpteen labels, keen to enter luxury market with flagship The Legacy Cab Sauv, v.gd but eye-watering A$1000 (c.£500), matching PENFOLDS Grange price without its history. Ambitious. Exports as Wakefield Wines.

Ten Minutes by Tractor Mor P ★★→★★★ Top-notch wines, top-notch restaurant. Focus on single-vyd CHARD, PINOT N.

Terre à Terre Ad H ★★★ Xavier Bizot (son of late Christian B, Bollinger, *see* France) and wife, Lucy Croser (daughter of Brian C) making mark. Labels incl Down to Earth and Daosa, v.gd fizz; close-planted vyd at WRATTONBULLY.

Teusner Bar V ★★ Old vines, clever winemaking, pure fruit flavours. Leads a BAR V trend towards "more wood, no good".

Thistledown Ad H ★★★★ MWs Giles Cooke and Fergal Tynan champion MCL V old-vine GRENACHE. Quirky names: Cunning Plan, Sands of Time, She's Electric, all tiptop. Plus SHIRAZ BAR V.

Tolpuddle Tas ★★★★ SHAW & SMITH own this outstanding 1988-planted vyd in Coal River V: CHARD powerful, PINOT N superb. Demand outstrips supply.

Topaque Vic Ho-hum replacement name for iconic RUTH fortified "Tokay", directive of EU.

Torbreck Bar V ★★→★★★ Dedicated to (often old-vine) Rhône varieties led by GRENACHE, SHIRAZ. Ultimate expression of rich, sweet, high-alc style.

Torzi Matthews Eden V ★★→★★★ Aromatic, stylish, big-hearted SHIRAZ. Value RIES, SANGIOVESE. Incredible consistency yr-on-yr.

tripe.Iscariot Marg R ★★ Kooky name, compelling wines. Highlights greatness of CHENIN BL, yet excels in region's finest grapes, CHARD, CAB SAUV.

Tumbarumba NSW Cool-climate region tucked into the Australian Alps. Sites at 500–800m (1640–2625ft); CHARD the out-and-out star; v.gd sparkling base.

Turkey Flat Bar V ★★★ Top producer of rich rosé, GRENACHE, SHIRAZ from 150-yr-old vyd. Controlled alc/oak. Single-vyd wines. Old but modern.

TWE (Treasury Wine Estates) Aussie wine behemoth. COLDSTREAM HILLS, DEVIL'S LAIR, PENFOLDS, Rosemount, SALTRAM, WYNNS COONAWARRA among them. Currently off-loading Lindeman's and WOLF BLASS.

Two Hands Bar V ★★★ Big reds, lots of them. They've turned volume down a fraction; glory of fruit seems all the clearer.

Tyrrell's Hun V ★★→★★★★ Family-owned/run, a gem. Benchmark SEM Vat 1 16' 17' 18' 19' 21 22' 23, plus individual vyd or subregional renditions. *Vat 47* 15' 17' 18' 22 23, Oz's 1st CHARD, continues to defy climatic odds. Outstanding old-vine 4 Acres SHIRAZ, Vat 9 SHIRAZ.

Vasse Felix Marg R ★★★→★★★★ Excellent, flinty CHARD, esp Heytesbury 19' 20' 21' 22' 23. Elegant CAB SAUV 18' 19' 20' 21, top-tier Tom Cullity exceptional. Diversity throughout incl Idée Fixe (sp).

Vickery Clare V Legacy of Oz's greatest RIES master, late John V, lives on. Zeeda Kilm crafting gorgeous "rizza", also from EDEN V.

Violetta, La Denmark Quirky names: Das Sakrileg RIES, Fric Frac CAB FR; reflecting quirky personality of winemaker Andrew Hoadley. Don't be fooled: delicious, fascinating wines; fruit from GT S.

Voyager Estate Marg R ★★★ Organic viticulture; range of styles/prices from value Coastal to top-tier MJW CHARD, CAB SAUV. Tim Shand (ex-Punt Road, Vic) shaking things up, positively.

Wanderer, The Yarra V ★★★ Exceptionally fine-boned PINOT N, equally fine CHARD, SAUV BL plus fizz. Excellent gin too, more than a side project.

Wantirna Estate Yarra V ★★★ Flies under radar for a regional pioneer. Worth seeking out. Lovely wines from Bx blend, PINOT N to CHARD, and cute labels via renowned Oz cartoonist and artist Michael Leunig.

Wendouree Clare V ★★★★ DRC of Australia (*see* France). Old vines, commitment to quality, history. Long-lived reds now veering towards more refined, elegant CAB SAUV, MALBEC, MATARO, SHIRAZ. Demand outstrips supply. Respect.

West Cape Howe Mt Barker ★→★★ Affordable, flavoursome reds, yet RIES the star. Solid options.

Wild Duck Creek Hea ★★ Super-concentrated, high-octane reds, mostly CAB SAUV, MALBEC, SHIRAZ. Yet vigour, freshness somehow kept intact.

Art with your wine?
Want to visit Australian wineries with impressive art galleries? Try MARG R: VASSE FELIX showcases rolling exhibitions and its own extensive collection, esp of Indigenous art; nearby LEEUWIN hangs the original works that feature on its Art Series labels. TAS: MOORILLA is overshadowed by MONA (Museum of Old and New Art), the largest privately funded museum in s hemisphere. YARRA V: TARRAWARRA is dedicated to modern Oz art from 50s on. Pt Leo Estate (MOR P) has impressive sculpture garden. Award for most flamboyant space/collection goes to D'ARENBERG's The Cube (MCL V).

William Downie Gippsland ★★★ Whip-smart farmer, leader of local avant-garde, dedicated to PINOT N: Bull Swamp, Camp Hill Pinot N, organic, minuscule quantities. Always compelling, always thoughtful, cool labels.

Windows Estate Marg R Bush property, handgrown/made, superb CHARD, CAB SAUV, SYRAH. Family-run, eco conscious, organic, beautiful people. A must-visit.

Wine By Farr Geelong ★★★→★★★★ Pioneers of close-planted vyds in dry, windy Moorabool V; est 1994. PINOT N the star off individual blocks labelled Côte Vyd, Farrside, Sangreal, Tout Près. Impressive CHARD, VIOGNIER, SHIRAZ.

Wines by KT Clare V Kerri Thompson, queen of CLARE V RIES; from pristine, off-dry to textural, wild ferment, plus tiptop reds.

Wirra Wirra McL V ★★ High-quality, concentrated, in flashy livery. The Angelus CAB SAUV named Dead Ringer outside Australia.

Wolf Blass Bar V ★ Not what it was when WB himself led the orchestra. Now churns out big volumes. Another brand being off-loaded by TWE.

Woodlands Marg R ★★★ 40-yr-old+ CAB SAUV among top vyds in Wilyabrup, plus younger but v.gd plantings of other Bx-style reds. ★★★★ for flagship Cab Sauv, name changes each yr, honouring a family or friend.

Wrattonbully SA Important growing region in LIMESTONE COAST ZONE; profile lifted by activity of Peppertree, TAPANAPPA, TERRE À TERRE.

Wynns Coonawarra Estate Coonw ★★★★ (SHIRAZ) 17' 18' 19' 20' 21 22 (CAB SAUV) 15' 16' 18' 19' 20' 21 22 Legendary yet largest producer in region; excellent vyds; TWE-owned. Fair CHARD, RIES; stars Cab Sauv, Shiraz, esp Black Label and pinnacle *John Riddoch*, plus single vyd. Long-lived propositions. Quality attributed to long-time winemaker Sue Hodder, who credits her team, as great leaders do.

Most expensive grapes in Oz, 2024: from Tas, average A\$3674 (c.£1790)/tonne.

Xanadu Wines Marg R ★★★→★★★★ 18' 19' 20' 21' 22 23 Super-fine CHARD, single-vyd and Res CAB SAUV stars. Range of styles, SYRAH a highlight, and price points, all excellent. Classy winemaking thanks to Glenn Goodall accessing best fruit.

Yabby Lake Mor P, Tas ★★★ Made name with CHARD, PINOT N and boosted with single-site releases; spice-shot SYRAH adds to reputation. Now TAS vyd too.

Yalumba Bar V, SA ★★★ Oldest family-owned winery in Oz, with eye on quality as much as affordability. Powerhouse of reds: The Caley, benchmark CAB/SHIRAZ. Flies flag for country's finest VIOGNIER, The Virgilius.

Yangarra Estate McL V ★★★★ Exquisite GRENACHE thanks to cherished vyds, incl 1946 old bush vines; bio. Respectful winemaking, pushing boundaries with long-skin-contact ROUSSANNE of such beauty. Excellent SHIRAZ, blends and more. Dress-circle producer.

Yarra Valley Vic Cool, high-end region NE of Melbourne. Emphasis on CHARD, PINOT N, SHIRAZ and elegant CAB SAUV. Try COLDSTREAM HILLS, DE BORTOLI, DOM CHANDON, GEMBROOK HILL, GIANT STEPS, HODDLES CREEK, MAC FORBES, MOUNT MARY, OAKRIDGE, PUNCH, ROCHFORD, SERRAT, SEVILLE, TARRAWARRA, WANTIRNA, YARRA YERING, YERINGBERG, YERING STATION – a formidable lineup.

Yarra Yering Yarra V ★★★★ (Dry Reds) 19' 20' 21' 22' 23 One-of-a-kind YARRA V pioneer. Powerful PINOT N; deep, refined CAB SAUV (Dry Red No.1); SHIRAZ (Dry Red No.2); CHARD morphed into magnificence of late. Absolute upper echelon (r/w). Winemaker Sarah Crowe winning many accolades.

Yeringberg Yarra V ★★★★ (MARSANNE/ROUSSANNE) 20' 21' 22' 23 (BX blend) 18' 19' 20' 21 22' 23 Historic estate (1862) still with founding Swiss family. Small quantities, v. high-quality CHARD, MARSANNE, CAB SAUV, PINOT N.

Yering Station / Yarrabank Yarra V ★★ Site of Vic's 1st vyd; replanted after 80-yr gap. Snazzy table wines (Res CHARD, PINOT N, SHIRAZ VIOGNIER). Yarrabank (sp), joint venture with Champagne Devaux (see France).

New Zealand

Abbreviations used in the text:

Auck	Auckland
B of P	Bay of Plenty
Cant	Canterbury
Gis	Gisborne
Hawk	Hawke's Bay
Hend	Henderson
Marl	Marlborough
Mart	Martinborough
Nel	Nelson
N/C Ot	North/Central Otago
Nlnd	Northland
Waih	Waiheke Island
Waip	Waipara Valley
Wair	Wairarapa

Map labels: Northland; Auckland; Auckland; Waiheke Island; Waikato; Bay of Plenty; Gisborne; Hawke's Bay; Nelson; Nelson; Wairarapa (incl Martinborough); Marlborough; Wellington; Blenheim; Waipara Valley; Canterbury; Christchurch; North Otago (incl Waitaki Valley); Central Otago; Dunedin; *Tasman Sea*; *Pacific Ocean*

N ew Zealand's ticket to international wine renown, Marlborough Sauvignon Blanc, remains popular and profitable for now. That's why the world's three largest wine companies have a stake in the region. But Marlborough is now at a crossroads. A fear that a number of the industrial-scale producers are threatening the well-being of brand Marlborough has triggered a response by many of the region's quality-focused players, mostly smaller wineries. More than 50 of them have banded together to form Appellation Marlborough Wine (AMW), whose membership must adhere to strict quality criteria. Meanwhile, around the country, high-end producers of Pinot Noir, Chardonnay and Syrah – some of whom have vines and experience going back decades – are doing outstanding work. Chardonnay, especially, is having a moment, with more being planted, especially in the South Island.

Recent vintages

2024 Small in quantity, exceptionally high in quality across country.

2023 A yr of two islands. Intense rain cancelled some top reds in Hawk/Marl. Dry, mostly warm in s.

2022 Record crop. Marl/Hawk. wet/cold, hit quality. C Ot: clean, ripe Pinot N.

2021 Marl: small (frost), but flavour-packed. Hawk: warmer, drier than usual, esp gd Chard, Syrah.

Accolade Wines Australian, owns MUD HOUSE, recently purchased Pernod Ricard's NZ wine holdings (mainly BRANCOTT ESTATE, CHURCH ROAD, STONELEIGH brands).

Akarua C Ot ★★★ Most s outpost of Edmond de Rothschild Heritage (France) empire; CHARD, PINOT N (*Akarua* means "two vines" in Māori) grown in Bannockburn. Complex The Siren Pinot N; crowd-pleasing Chard.

Allan Scott Marl ★★ Long-est, family-owned Wairau V producer, extensive estate vyds. Estate range gd value, fresh, racy (PINOT GR, RIES, SAUV BL). With Steytler family "Stellenbosch + Marlborough" Sauv Bl: rare, gd-value S Africa/NZ blend.

Alpha Domus Hawk ★★→★★★ Family-owned; Bridge Pa Triangle, est 1989; organic. Outstanding Bx blends and SYRAH. Richer-style CHARD and VIOGNIER.

Amisfield C Ot ★★★ Known for top-notch, innovative restaurant and cellar door, nr Queenstown. All wine estate-grown in Pisa, Cromwell Basin; organic. Quality across range, esp RIES, dark brooding PINOT N (esp RKV Res).

Amoise Hawk ★★★ Excellent new natural producer, zero-zero, fruit from proven sites. Delightful, mouthwatering CHENIN BL from Two Terraces vyd.

Astrolabe Marl ★★→★★★ Family-owned, est 1996. Fine quality across range, discerningly sourced fruit from diverse sites. Elegant, much-admired SAUV BL (AWATERE V), statement CHENIN BL from Wrekin Vyd.

Ata Rangi Mart ★★★★ Internationally renowned, pioneering PINOT N specialist. Proudly family-owned. Estate Pinot ages well: 13' 14' 15 16' 19' 20' 21' 22. More recent single vyds: impressive Kotinga Pinot, Masters CHARD and Pinot.

Auckland NZ's largest city (n, warm, humid). Diverse region with history, today 0.7% vyd area (not expanding) but 12% of wineries, almost all small players. Oldest district: W Auckland (incl Henderson, Huapai, Kumeu) clay soils, pioneered by Croatians, CHARD the hero, esp KUMEU RIVER. Newer districts (since 80s): Clevedon, Matakana and WAIH (island known for tourism, weddings, wealthy residents); intense Bx blends and flavoursome SYRAH.

Auntsfield Marl ★★★ Sloping s-valleys site was home to 1st MARL vines, C19. Original "hobbit hole" cellar now a museum. Family-owned/operated. Textural SAUV BL, dark savoury PINOT N.

Awatere Valley Marl Sited se of WAIRAU, Awatere is that valley's younger, cooler (literally), wilder sibling. Name means fast-flowing river. Wineries are sparse, but vyd area is greater than HAWK. Loam over alluvial soils, ocean winds and big diurnal temp range. Harvest starts later than Wairau. Awatere SAUV BL typically lean, incisive acidity, greener flavour spectrum. Key component in regional blends of MARL Sauv Bl. Also vibrant PINOT GR, lighter, racier, red-fruit PINOT N.

Babich Hend ★★→★★★ Oldest family-owned winery in NZ (1916); HQ in Henderson, but vyds, winemaking in HAWK, MARL. Largest seller: Marl SAUV BL. Irongate site in GIMBLETT GRAVELS produces single-vyd CHARD, Bx blends of quality, incl flagship red The Patriarch.

Good buy to all that

Finding the best-value NZ wine is a variety-by-variety proposition. In the case of that most Kiwi of styles, MARL SAUV BL, don't go for the cheapest. Opt for a wine produced by a member of Appellation Marlborough Wine (AMW), all of whom must abide by strict quality standards. The AMW mark is increasingly displayed on the necks of bottles. For PINOT N, it becomes trickier. You don't encounter much evidence of the sensitive growing this grape demands at low prices. Among the handful of Pinots offering remarkable value are MARTINBOROUGH VYD Te Tera (WAIR), Peregrine Saddleback (C OT), SERESIN Momo (Marl). With HAWK Bx blends and SYRAH, there is value to be found in the shallows, at around Sauv Bl prices, but it is v. vintage-dependent. Among recent vintages, 24 is your friend here. A value-hunter's paradise is CHARD, as quality has been on the up but prices not so much. For great value, try DOG POINT, GREYWACKE (Marl); Greenhough Hope Vyd (Nelson); CHURCH ROAD, ELEPHANT HILL, Tony Bish Wines (Hawk); KUMEU RIVER Chard (AUCK).

Barrowman, Ashleigh Marl ★★★ New producer uses organic fruit from selected vyds, hands-off winemaking. Delightful Queen of Cups CHENIN BL; crisp The Magician CHARD.

Bell Hill Cant ★★★★ Fascinating; boutique producer near Waikari; CHARD (grace, tension), PINOT N (multi-faceted, energetic) only in high-density, organic vyd.

Bilancia Hawk ★★★→★★★★ Top estate founded/owned by Lorraine Leheny and Warren Gibson. La Collina SYRAH, one of NZ's finest, grown on slope above GIMBLETT GRAVELS. Vivid, outstanding single-vyd CHARDS; Uvaggio, intriguing white field blend.

Abel Pinot Noir clone (Ata Rangi etc.) arrived hidden in a gumboot in 70s. Tut tut...

Blackenbrook Nel ★★ Boutique; Schwarzenbach family from Switzerland; gd value across range, esp generous MONTEPULCIANO, handsome PINOT N.

Black Estate Cant ★★→★★★ Small, organic estate. Limestone-rich sites and hands-off winemaking. One of NZ's best winery restaurants, locavore approach. Best: Home Block CHARD, CHENIN BL; Damsteep PINOT N. Age-worthy wines.

Blank Canvas Marl ★★★ Quality-focused boutique label. All small-batch, single-vyd, several regions. Excellent Reed Vyd CHARD; textural Tano Chard; savoury Escaroth PINOT N.

Borthwick Wair ★★→★★★ Farming family started growing wine in 90s; 27-ha vyd in Gladstone, mostly SAUV BL, PINOT N.

Brancott Estate Marl ★→★★★ Sold 2024, to ACCOLADE WINES. Was Montana, rebranded by Pernod 2007. Big exporter of Marl SAUV BL. Quality, value Letter Series range.

Brookfields Hawk ★★→★★★ Boutique, family-owned (1937), guided by old Bay hand Peter Robertson. Reds typically ripe, robust; richer CHARD.

Burn Cottage C Ot ★★★→★★★★ American owner has best name in NZ wine – Marquis Sauvage. Cult label. Basin-shaped, bio site in Pisa, plus vyd in Bannockburn. Ethereal PINOT N; fascinating RIES/GRÜNER V.

Cambridge Road Mart ★★→★★★★ Singular, idiosyncratic producer on MART terrace. Range incl pét-nats, field blends. Latest project: 100-yr-old barrels made from native totara wood to imbue wines with *wairua* (spirit of place).

Canterbury 64 producers, most in relatively warm N CANT district. Best known for savoury PINOT N, increasingly sophisticated CHARD, aromatic RIES; SAUV BL heavily planted, but often minor component in other regions' wines.

Carrick C Ot ★★★ Owned by Cleland family, est player on Bannockburn's Cairnmuir Road. Farmed organically. Fine CHARD, reliably intense PINOT N.

Catalina Sounds Marl ★★→★★★ Australian-owned, est 2005. Top: estate-grown Sound of White single-vyd, barrel-fermented CHARD, SAUV BL.

Central Otago Most s (and scenic) region, with as close to a continental climate as NZ gets. Vines grown in Alpine river valleys, most in Cromwell Basin. Collegial wine-growing culture and astute marketing made PINOT N the hero grape, giving region a global reputation; top have depth, structural finesse, among NZ's best; CHARD on rise, quality and quantity. Also trad-method sparkling.

Chard Farm C Ot ★★ Pioneering Gibbston winery. Hair raising home vyd on ledge above bungee gorge. Most vyds now in Cromwell Basin. Top: series of single-vyd PINOT NS. Popular second label: Rabbit Ranch.

Church Road Hawk ★★ ★★★★ Recently sold by Pernod Ricard to ACCOLADE. Historic, est 1896 by former Catholic lay brother Bartholomew Steinmetz. Strong rep for quality across multi-tiered range. McDonalds Series gd value (CHARD, SYRAH). Grand Res Chard typically intense, flinty. Prestige range, featuring Bx blends, named Tom after mid-C20 owner-winemaker Tom McDonald.

Churton Marl ★★ Superb, elevated, bio-farmed Waihopai V site. Elegant SAUV BL, expressive PINOT N (The Abyss). Innovative Natural State range. Several other producers source Churton-grown fruit.

Clearview Hawk ★★→★★★ Family-owned/operated (est 1986). Stony Te Awanga home vyd, plus fruit from other HAWK sites. Big local following for brassy, rich, old-school CHARD. Big, powerful Bx blends.

Clos Henri Marl ★★★ Sancerre's own corner of MARL; est by Henri Bourgeois (*see* France). Organic. Two compelling expressions of single-vyd SAUV BL, one grown on stony soils, the other on clay. Taut, delightful PINOT N. Second label: Estate range. Excellent Blanc de Noirs.

Cloudy Bay Marl ★★★ NZ's most successful global luxury brand, regardless of product. Owned by LVMH. Despite large volume, SAUV BL maintains prestigious reputation. Te Koko, barrel-fermented "supercharged" vintage Sauv Bl. Pelorus NV, quality trad-method fizz.

Coal Pit C Ot ★★→★★★ Quality SAUV BL, PINOT N estate-grown on elevated Gibbston site. Recent addition: Bannockburn Pinot N.

Collaboration Hawk ★★★ Boutique, quality-driven, est by owner-winemaker Julianne Brogden. Sources fruit from several HAWK vyds. Argent CAB SAUV often fresh, lively; Arulent CHARD lean, graceful.

Constellation New Zealand Auck ★→★★ NZ outpost of global wine titan of same name. Large volume player, mostly MARL SAUV BL under mass-market labels KIM CRAWFORD, SELAKS.

Craggy Range Hawk ★★★→★★★★ Glamorous, Napa-esque cellar door; est 1999 by Australian Peabody family. Quality across range. Top Prestige collection.

Čuvar Hawk ★★→★★★ Name means "guardian" in Croatian. New venture by octogenarian founder of VILLA MARIA, Sir George Fistonich; vyds in HAWK, MARL. Ranges: excellent-value Iris; smart single-vyd Guardians.

Decibel Hawk ★★ Estate est in 2009 by US-born Daniel Brennan, former rock-band manager. Fruit sourced from organic vyds in HAWK and WAIR. Broad varietal range. Signature: inky dark, silky, flavoursome Decibel MALBEC.

Deep Down Marl ★★→★★★ Organic, single-vyd, hands-off: CHARD, SAUV BL, PINOT N.

Delegat Auck ★★ Publicly listed but still mostly family-owned; est 1947 by Croatian Delegat family. Ambitious, outward-looking, growth built on stunningly successful OYSTER BAY SAUV BL. Producer of mid-range, smart-value wines.

Delta Marl ★★→★★★ Owned by St Clair; HAWK, MARL wines consistently gd value.

Destiny Bay Waih ★★→★★★ Boutique operation, sloping vyd, exclusively high-priced Bx blends. French, US oak-aged. Approachable wines.

Deutz Auck ★★★ Champagne house lends name to ACCOLADE-owned MARL fizz since 1988; gd value, esp Brut NV (min 2 ys on lees), strong local following.

Dog Point Marl ★★★ By MARL vets Ivan Sutherland and James Healy (est 2004). Largest organic vyd in NZ. Elegant flinty whites, PINOT N with depth, harmony.

Domaine-Thomson C Ot ★★→★★★ Small, family-owned, organic. PINOT N vyds in Lowburn and Gevrey-Chambertin (*see* France). Typically dark, muscular style; 2nd-tier Explorer gd value.

Why aren't there more Cloudy Bays in Marl? Brand-building not an NZ strength.

Dry River Mart ★★★ Boutique, well-nurtured brand built around top-quality aromatics and PINOT N (est 1979). Now owned by neighbouring LUNA ESTATE. Ravishingly textural GEWURZ, PINOT GR; Pinot N, depth, structure.

Eaton Wines Marl ★★★ Vastly experienced Mike E and sons craft wines from selected sites. Speciality SAUV BL (bottle-aged 2 yrs before release). Captivating Forte Definition Sauv Bl.

Elephant Hill Hawk ★★→★★★ German family-owned. Elegance, restraint in wines (esp CHARD, SYRAH) and cellar-door architecture. Coastal and inland vyds.

> **Chardonnay: quality all over down under**
> The presence of CHARD in the Kiwi varietal firmament is both glittering and ubiquitous. A recent rising tide of sensitively made, excellent examples has affected almost every region, from the far n with quality-focused THE LANDING, to C OT where there are now several, esp Felton Road, Prophet's Rock. The starkest example of the grape's reputation for not being fussy about the "where", but rather the "who" and "how", is KUMEU RIVER. The producer of arguably NZ's finest Chard does so from its base in W Auckland, a region that, despite being an early bastion of NZ wine, lost both lustre and vyds as the industry drifted to less humid, cooler and generally more hospitable points s from the 80s on.

Escarpment Mart ★★★ One of 1st wineries at Te Muna, e of Martinborough township (est 1998). Organic. Owned by Torbreck (*see* Australia). Classy Kupe PINOT N, plus fascinating old-vine, single-vyd Pinot N from different sites.

Esk Valley Hawk ★★→★★★★ Brand owned by INDEVIN. Estate wines consistently gd value. Innovative Artisanal Collection: excellent ALBARIÑO, CHENIN BL, GRENACHE, TEMPRANILLO. Flagship, MALBEC-influenced Heipipi The Terraces.

Esses Marl ★★★ Family-owned, boutique fizz specialist based on Kaikoura coast, s of MARL. Quality-driven, min 3 yrs on lees. Outstanding Essential Brut NV, plus several distinctive vintage cuvées.

Felton Road C Ot ★★★★ Pre-eminent brand with international following. English owner Nigel Greening v. involved in business; bio, terroir-driven approach. Multiple expressions of PINOT N, incl nuanced Blocks 3 and 5 from home vyd and extrovert Cornish Point. Classy CHARD, RIES.

Foley Wines Auck NZ arm of US billionaire Bill Foley's empire, incl MT DIFFICULTY (C OT); Clifford Bay, Dashwood, Goldwater, GROVE MILL, VAVASOUR (MARL); MARTINBOROUGH VYD, TE KAIRANGA (MART).

Folium Marl Small, owned/run by Japanese-born Takaki Okada. Organic, dry-farmed. Distinctive SAUV BL. Impressive CHARD, PINOT N.

Forrest Marl ★★→★★★ Family-owned; 2nd-generation Beth F current GM/winemaker. Broad, multi-tiered range, fruit sourced from several regions, known for quality/value, innovation. Low-alc The Doctors' highly successful.

Framingham Marl ★★→★★★ One of NZ's top RIES producers. Multiple styles, using some of oldest Ries vines in MARL. Organic; owned by Sogrape (*see* Portugal).

Fromm Marl ★★★ Regional standout. Known for meticulous organic viticulture, wines with detail, depth. Swiss-owned. Impressive CHARD, PINOT N; elegant SYRAH in gd vintages.

Gibbston Valley C Ot ★★★ The 1st Gibbston winery, est 1981. Popular to visit; alfresco dining, hillside cellar. Most vyds in Bendigo. Organic. Exciting range of single-vyd PINOT N (China Terrace, old-vine Glenlee); China Terrace CHARD.

Giesen Cant ★★→★★★ Large player, est by three German bros, now huge producer of MARL SAUV Bl. Having great success with zero-alc range. Top-quality Clayvin CHARD, PINOT N, SYRAH.

Gimblett Gravels Hawk An 800-ha and former riverbed w of Hastings, since 2001 defined, marketed as HAWK subregion. Stony, low-fertility soils. Each bottle carries "G" spot branding. Renowned for SYRAH, MERLOT-dominant Bx blends. Top wines are world-class: 13' 14' 15' 18 19' 20' 21'.

Gisborne Once a centre of the NZ industry, today 5th-largest region; gd sunshine hours, often rainy around harvest; fertile, alluvial soils. Strong reputation for CHARD, though most plantings now SAUV BL; ALBARIÑO, GEWURZ can be excellent.

Gladstone Vineyard Wair ★★ Strong presence in N WAIR, now owned by Singapore-based family. SAUV BL, VIOGNIER, PINOT N gd. Other N Wair labels made here.

Grasshopper Rock C Ot ★★ Small Alexandra producer, single-vyd PINOT N focus. Stony, n-facing site, named after rare local grasshopper. Dark-fruited, svelte.

Greenhough Nel ★★★ Family-owned, experienced, a NELSON gem (est 1979). Thoughtful CHARD, PINOT BL, RIES, PINOT N. Best: old-vine Hope Vyd.

Greystone Waip ★★★ Exciting, innovative, organic. Most vyds on limestone-rich slopes. Delightful CHARD (Erin's Block), structured PINOT N, elegant SYRAH.

Greywacke Marl ★★★ Standout label created/owned by founding Cloudy Bay winemaker Kevin Judd. Flinty CHARD, one of MARL's best. Joyous PINOT N. Delightful, barrel-fermented Wild SAUV BL.

Grove Mill Marl ★★ Part of FOLEY FAMILY WINES. Small, gd-value range.

Hāhā Hawk, Marl ★→★★ Name means "catch your breath" in Māori. Multi-region focus, easy-drinking wines.

Halcyon Days Hawk ★★→★★★ Innovative natural wines. Zero-zero. Grapes from two organic HAWK vyds. Broad, exciting range: pét-nat CHENIN BL, SANGIOVESE.

Hans Herzog Marl ★★★ Intriguing boutique label, est/run by Swiss couple. Meticulous viticulture, low-cropping, organic, broad quirky varietal range, incl BLAUFRÄNKISCH, LAGREIN, MONTEPULCIANO. Textural VIOGNIER; impressive Grandezza, NZ's 1st "Super Tuscan".

Hawke's Bay Largest North I region. Has history, many attractions for wine tourists. Dry, sunny, diverse soils. Star CHARD (ripe, full), SYRAH (aromatic, elegant). Excellent Bx blends in gd yrs: **19' 20' 21'** 24. SAUV BL plantings increased recently. *See also* GIMBLETT GRAVELS.

Helio Hawk ★★→★★★ Set up 2019 as HAWK CHARD specialist. Fine MART PINOT N and Hawk SYRAH. Impressive Haumoana-grown Chard, with more single-vyd Chards planned.

Hunter's Marl ★★ →★★★ Respected label, owned/run by Jane H since 1987. Vibrant SAUV BL, gd-value Estate CHARD, funky Offshoot Chard. Successful MiruMiru bubbles programme, esp vintage.

Indevin Marl ★★ Largest grower/producer of NZ wine, NZ-owned; 4000 ha in GIS, HAWK, MARL. Major supplier of own brands for overseas markets: Dulcét, ESK V, Left Field, Thornbury, VIDAL, VILLA MARIA.

Invivo Auck ★★ Marketing-savvy label known for celebrity endorsements, notably Graham Norton, Sarah Jessica Parker. Vivid SAUV BL (MARL), plus styles from other regions, countries.

Jackson Estate Marl ★★→★★★ Old MARL campaigner, now owned by NZ-based Benton Wine Group. Top wines: crisp Stich SAUV BL; engaging Vintage Widow PINOT N. Attractive cellar door on Jackson's Road.

Johanneshof Marl ★★→★★★ Boutique winery with hillside vyd "off-Wairau" on Picton road. Handcrafted, outstanding GEWURZ, distinctive trad-method sparkling.

Jules Taylor Wines Marl ★★→★★★ Named after owner-winemaker, a former MARL Girls' College head girl. Strength across range (GRÜNER V, SAUV BL). Organic PINOT N from Wrekin vyd fruit.

The Māorification of NZ wine

More so than any other field of NZ agriculture, wine is embracing aspects of Māori culture. This is most obvious in language use. You'll often see the word *kaitiakitanga* (guardianship) on winery websites instead of "care for the land" or "sustainability practices". *Tūrangawaewae* (place to stand) is increasingly used as a substitute for "terroir". But the influence goes deeper than words. Māori attitudes, values, practices are being taken on board, such as adopting the lunar calendar (*maramataka*), which represents an early S Pacific version of bio.

Kim Crawford Wines Hawk ★→★★ Owned by CONSTELLATION NZ. Mostly classic, pungent SAUV BL, majority sold in US.

Kumeu River Auck ★★★★ Top-rank CHARD producer, strong international reputation (est 1944); still owned/run by Brajkovich family, originally from Croatia. Several single-vyd expressions (refined Hunting Hill, bold Maté's), both clay sites close to winery. Recent expansion to HAWK with elevated Rays Road (Chard, PINOT N).

"Un petit vin blanc léger... délicieux," Dumont d'Urville, 1840. NZ's 1st tasting note?

Landing, The Nlnd ★★→★★★ Stunningly beautiful coastal site nr Kerikeri, US-based Kiwis Peter and Sue Cooper est 2007; CHARD, SYRAH among region's best, 1st vintages of SANGIOVESE, MONTEPULCIANO show great potential.

Lawson's Dry Hills Marl ★★→★★★ Trusted label, 1st planted 1982, super-consistent quality across range. Was leader in screwcap revolution. Top old-vine GEWURZ.

Leveret Mills Reef B of P ★★ Fruit sourced from multiple regions. Easy-drinking Estate selection: gd-value MERLOT/CAB SAUV. Top Elspeth range from HAWK (CHARD, Cabs Sauv/FR, Merlot, SYRAH, fizz).

Lindauer Auck ★→★★ Excellent value trad-method sparkling. Once big in UK, now mostly sold in NZ. Owned by Lion brewery. Brut NV Blanc de Blancs, Rosé.

Loveblock Marl ★★→★★★ Ex-owners of KIM CRAWFORD, Kim and Erica C est, with sustainable, hands-off philosophy. Estate vyd in AWATERE V, partly organic. Textural, terroir-driven wines across range.

Luna Estate Mart ★★→★★★ Locally owned; several sites in and around MART. Owns DRY RIVER. Quality across ranges. Eclipse range CHARD, PINOT N impressive.

Mahi Marl ★★→★★★ Name means "work" in Māori; est/run by experienced Brian Bicknell. Thoughtful, hands-off winemaking with expressive, textural wines: single-vyd Twin Valleys CHARD, Boundary Farm SAUV BL.

Man O' War Auck ★★→★★★ Largest producer on WAIH. Owned by NZ rich-list Spencer family, heirs to loo-paper fortune. Multiple steep, hair-raising island vyds on loam-clay soils. Extroverted styles: Valhalla CHARD, Dreadnought SYRAH. Popular PINOT GR grown on neighbouring island.

Marisco Marl ★★ Large Waihopai V-based producer. Several brands: Leefield Station, The Craft Series, The Kings Series, The Ned; SAUV BL the mainstay.

Marlborough NZ's largest region by far, centred on two sheltered river valleys at the top of S Island, WAIRAU V and AWATERE V; 1st SAUV BL planted 1975. Constant growth ever since, only tailing off recently. Diurnal range – hot sunny days, cold nights – one of keys to success. Gravel and silt on valley floors ideal for aromatic whites; clay hillsides in Wairau V suited to CHARD, PINOT N; Sauv Bl dominant. Classic Marl style: intense, crisp, pungent, leafy. More producers making barrel-fermented, less "manufactured" Sauv Bl styles; Chard the big improver: leaner, racier than HAWK. Some of NZ's best GEWURZ, RIES. Pinot N plantings in decline, despite some excellent expressions. Some quality trad-method fizz: watch.

Martinborough Wair Subregion in S WAIR, NZ's "Burgundian" village, where a PINOT N culture took hold in early 80s. Most wineries clustered around township on free-draining river terrace. Cold s winds reduce yields; warm dry summers, reliable autumns. Popular destination for Wellington day-trippers. Excellent CHARD, RIES, but best known for savoury-edged, elegantly structured Pinot N.

Martinborough Vineyard Mart ★★★ Pioneering winery that helped put MART PINOT N on map in 80s, now owned by US billionaire Bill Foley. Outstanding CHARD, RIES, old-vine Home Block Pinot N. Te Tera ("The Other") range gd value.

Matawhero Gis ★★ Legendary in 80s for GEWURZ and idiosyncratic owner Denis Irwin. New ownership. Well-made, accessible range.

Maude C Ot ★★→★★★ Enquiring, quality-driven husband-and-wife winemaking team. Range of refined, structured single-vyd PINOT N. Old-vine RIES a highlight.

Millton Gis ★★→★★★ NZ's 1st bio producer, renowned for long-lived CHENIN BL. Intriguing Libiamo and Crazy By Nature ranges more natural-leaning. Top: single-vyd Clos de Ste Anne, only in gd vintages.

Misha's Vineyard C Ot ★★→★★★ Challenging, sloping site above Lake Dunstan. Quality across range: Limelight RIES (s/sw), High Note PINOT N.

30% of C Ot's vineyards certified organic, highest proportion of any NZ region.

Mission Hawk ★★→★★★★ NZ's oldest winery, est 1851, still owned by Catholic Society of Mary. Large producer; vyds in MARL, plus HAWK; gd-value Estate range. Top: Huchet, named after NZ's 1st trained winemaker.

Mondillo C Ot ★★→★★★ Boutique Bendigo label. Opulent PINOT N; intense, off-dry RIES; honeyed, fresh Nina Late Harvest Ries.

Mount Edward C Ot ★★→★★★ Quality-driven, boutique, organic producer, Gibbston-based but most vyds in Cromwell Basin. Delightful CHARD, fine single-vyd PINOT N plus rare, popular GAMAY.

Mount Riley Marl ★★ Family-owned, mid-sized, named after highest peak on n side of WAIRAU V. Dependable quality, gd value (ALBARIÑO). Top: 17 Valley CHARD.

Mt Beautiful Cant ★★ Large vyd in Cheviot hills, an outlier well n of WAIP. Approachable, attractive wines.

Mt Difficulty C Ot ★★★ Popular brand based in Bannockburn, now owned by US billionaire Bill Foley. Restaurant perched above vines a favoured lunch spot. Best known for spicy PINOT N, esp estate label, gd-value Roaring Meg (named after a famous Gold Rush party girl). Easy-drinking CHARD, RIES.

Mud House Cant ★★→★★★ ACCOLADE WINES owned, featuring wines grown in several S Island regions. Impressive Waipara Hills brand. Excellent value across range, esp single-vyd C OT PINOT N, Waipara Hills RIES.

Nautilus Marl ★★→★★★ Medium-sized, well-regarded player owned by S Smith & Sons (see Yalumba, Australia). Known for crisp, flavoursome aromatic whites, quality trad-method fizz (min 3 yrs lees).

Nelson Small region w of MARL, wetter but equally sunny. Two distinct terroirs: rolling Moutere Hills with clay soils (CHARD, PINOT N) and silty Waimea plains (aromatic whites). Delightful Chard, vivid PINOT GR, savoury Pinot N. Large SAUV BL plantings, most of it trucked to Marl for blending.

Neudorf Nel ★★★→★★★★ Family-owned label in Upper Moutere on old hippie commune site. Regional flagship with international reputation. Organic. Famous for CHARD: elegant old-vine Home Block Moutere, more extroverted Rosie's Block. Bold Moutere PINOT N, textured ALBARIÑO, PINOT GR.

No 1 Family Estate Marl ★★→★★★ Fizz specialist est by Champenois Daniel Le Brun (no longer owns label). Best known for citrus CHARD-based NV (2 yrs on lees), toasty Res Blanc de Blancs (5 yrs+ on lees).

Nobilo Marl ★→★★ Since 2020 owned by E&J Gallo (see US). Known for high-volume SAUV BL production: top Icon label grown in AWATERE V.

North Canterbury Cant Dominant CANT subregion, n of Christchurch, centred on Waipara V. Gravel on flats, richer clay and limestone on e hills; incl wineries on limestone-rich sites to w nr Waikari. The Nor'wester, a hot dry wind, devigorates vines. Stars: CHARD, RIES, PINOT N. Tight-knit culture of quality producers.

Novum Marl ★★★ Small; deep knowledge of region. Identifies small vyd pockets of top grapes, from "sites within sites"; sells most direct. Svelte CHARD, PINOT N.

Oyster Bay Marl ★★ Core brand of DELEGAT. Hugely successful around the world, esp SAUV BL. Flavoursome, gd value, easy drinking.

Palliser Mart ★★→★★★ One of region's earliest, largest; popular, attractive cellar door. Quality multi-tiered range. Pencarrow, gd value. Top single vyds. Smart, value estate range: CHARD, RIES, PINOT N. Excellent vintage fizz The Griffin.

Pask Hawk ★★→★★★ Owned by NZ-based Benton Wine Group; 1st winery on GIMBLETT GRAVELS. Stylish new cellar door. Top Declaration: fine CHARD, SYRAH.

Passage Rock Waih ★★→★★★ Located e side of WAIH. Popular restaurant, cellar door. Award-winning, bold, oak-seasoned styles: SYRAH, Bx blends.

Pegasus Bay Waip ★★→★★★★ Family-owned, renowned, pioneering N CANT label. Flinty CHARD, complex PINOT N; multiple RIES; 2nd-tier Main Divide top value.

Peregrine C Ot ★★→★★★ Gibbston winery building an architectural gem. Organic. Quality across range: structured PINOT N; approachable whites; 2nd-tier Saddleback range excellent value.

Poppies Mart Former Dry River winemaker Poppy Hammond and viticulturist husband Shayne (est 2012). Well-patronized cellar door/lunch spot where nearly all wine is sold. Broad range of approchable varietals made from grower fruit. Dry, moreish rosé a big hit. L'Elu PINOT N one of NZ's most expensive.

Prophet's Rock C Ot ★★★→★★★★ Boutique, much-admired Bendigo producer. Organic. Elevated home vyd. Excellent Alsace-style PINOT GR and RIES. Deep PINOT N. Top tier: Cuvée aux Antipodes (with Burgundy's François Millet).

Puriri Hills Auck ★★★→★★★★ Small estate in Clevedon subregion dedicated to high-quality MERLOT-dominant Bx blends. Earthy Estate wine; res Harmonie du Soir complex, oaky. Top: bold Pope.

Pyramid Valley Cant ★★★→★★★★ Legendary limestone-rich, amphitheatre-like site nr Waikari, now owned by SMITH & SHETH CRU; bio. Excellent CHARD, PINOT N. Other wines from around N CANT.

Quartz Reef C Ot ★★★ Pioneer of rugged, warm Bendigo subregion; bio. Half made into classy fizz. Stylish CHARD, harmonious PINOT N.

Radburnd Cellars Hawk ★★→★★★ Experienced HAWK winemaker Kate R's personal project. Small parcels of fruit sourced from around region. Three well-crafted wines: CHARD, MERLOT/CAB SAUV, SYRAH.

Rapaura Springs Marl ★★ Always overdelivers on quality for Classic range CHARD, SAUV BL, PINOT N. Rohe ("territory") offers subregional expressions.

Rewa, Dom C Ot ★★★ Boutique, est 2010 by NZ-French Fourbet family. Organic vyd in Pisa subregion. Elegant CHARD, lively PINOT GR, ripe PINOT N.

Rippon Vineyard C Ot ★★★★ Pioneering family-owned estate beside Lake Wanaka; NZ's most ravishing vyd vista; bio. Age-worthy PINOT N of stature, grace, esp old-vine Tinker's Field, Emma's Block. Compelling RIES (dr).

Rockburn C Ot ★★→★★★ Experienced Cromwell-based producer; vyds in Lowburn, Gibbston (and cellar door). Vivid CHARD, off-dry PINOT GR, textural estate PINOT N.

Rock Ferry Marl ★★★ Family-owned, organic; ten varieties in C OT, MARL vyds (NEBBIOLO, TEMPRANILLO). Seductive C OT PINOT N. Excellent fizz.

Sacred Hill Hawk ★★→★★★ Multi-region player owned by low-profile NZ Poulter family (est 1986). Multi-tiered range: easy-drinking orange to Special Selection with acclaimed Riflemans CHARD, Brokenstone MERLOT, Deerstalkers SYRAH.

Saint Clair Marl ★★→★★★ Family-owned, range of nine racy, pungent SAUV BL. Small-parcel Pioneer Block reliably intense, vibrant. Owns DELTA, Lake Chalice.

Seifried Estate Nel ★★ Still family-owned/run, Herman and Agnes S est 1973; now region's largest winery. Top Aotea range: CHARD, PINOT N. Winemaker Collection: delectable GEWURZ, botrytized RIES. NZ's only Wurzer, ZWEIGELT.

SUV: around these parts means Pinot Gris... Suburban Utility Vino.

Selaks Marl ★→★★ Pioneering Croatian label, now CONSTELLATION NZ supermarket brand. Easy-drinking ranges. Some made with cheaper Australian grapes.

Seresin Marl ★★→★★★ Cinematographer Michael S set-up; organic since 2003. Thoughtful wines: Marama SAUV BL, complex Res CHARD, Rachel PINOT N; 2nd-tier Momo fantastic value.

Sileni Hawk ★★ Large player, now part of NZ-owned Booster Wine Group; HAWK estate vyds in warm Bridge Pa triangle and cooler inland sites. Imposing reds in Grand Res range; Cellar Selection MARL SAUV BL gd value.

Smith & Sheth Cru Hawk ★★★ Partnership of US billionaire Brian Sheth and Kiwi wine veteran Steve Smith. Self-styled "contemporary négociants": single vyds from selected sites. Outstanding CHARD, charming Cantera (CABS SAUV/FR/ TEMPRANILLO), stylish Omahu SYRAH. *See also* PYRAMID V.

Spy Valley Marl ★★→★★★ Named after neighbouring Five Eye satellite dish, now dismantled. Quality across range: dependable SAUV BL, rich GEWURZ, textural PINOT N, approachable PINOT N. Top: Envoy.

Starborough Family Estates Marl ★★ Family-owned vyds in AWATERE V, WAIRAU V. Zesty SAUV BL, PINOT GR.

Stonecroft Hawk, Marl ★★ Small organic label with history, now owned by Fistonich Family Vyds. Two vyds in GIMBLETT GRAVELS, incl NZ's oldest SYRAH vines. Luscious GEWURZ, harmonioius Syrah; NZ's only ZIN.

Stoneleigh Marl ★★ Now part of ACCOLADE. Based on warm, stony Rapaura vyds. Huge-selling flinty, juicy SAUV BL. Sustainability trumpeted, though not organic. Top: Raupara Series, generous, refined.

Stonyridge Waih ★★★→★★★★ Boutique winery with cult following est 1982 by the flamboyant Stephen White. Since 2022 majority-owned by Singaporean company. Popular vyd restaurant. Five-variety Bx blend Larose; bold Luna Negra MALBEC; dense SYRAH-based Pilgrim.

Te Kairanga Mart ★★→★★★ One of MART's oldest, largest; owned by FOLEY WINES. Excellent new restaurant/cellar door The Runholder. Estate range CHARD, RIES, PINOT N gd value; John Martin Pinot N outstanding.

Te Mata Hawk ★★★→★★★★★ A *taonga* (treasure) of NZ wine, family-owned/run, located below Te Mata Peak. Collectable MERLOT-dominant Bx blend Coleraine 13' 14' 15' 16 17 18 19' 20' 21'. Lower-priced, fresher Awatea CABS/MERLOT also classy, as are flinty Cape Crest Sauv Bl, Bullnose SYRAH; gd-value Estate tier.

Te Pā Marl ★★→★★★ Owned by Māori family, roots in MARL. Home vyd on Wairau Bar, close to sea. Pungent SAUV BL vibrant PINOT GR; 2nd-tier Pā Road gd value.

Terra Sancta C Ot ★★→★★★ Bannockburn's 1st vyd; family-owned. Several excellent PINOT N: old-vine Slapjack Block, Jackson's Block, gd-value Mysterious Diggings. Takes rosé seriously, Special Release First Vines Rosé NZ's most expensive.

Te Whare Rā Marl ★★ TWR on label. Boutique, family-owned, organic, one of oldest vyds in MARL. Quality-focused: elegant RIES, deft Toru (GEWURZ/RIES/ PINOT GR), outstanding PINOT N from Clayvin Vyd.

Thousand Gods, A Marl ★★★ Bright new natural star. Zero-zero. Fruit grown on bio Churton vyd. Top: exciting Flos PINOT N, ethereal Love Letters rosé.

Tiki Marl ★★ Owned by McKean family with proud Māori heritage. Extensive vyds

---

Passing the torch

The generation of Kiwi wine pioneers who built the industry almost from scratch in the 80s has been moving towards the exit. Where there is no built-in succession arrangement, their wineries are sold. This has meant that some labels, and even vyds, have been lost. But what's exciting is that there are green shoots appearing around the country as a new generation emerges. Some adhere to conventional production; others embrace a more hands-off, natural philosophy. Most can't afford vyds and buy their fruit from growers with whom they have developed close relationships. They are making great contributions to the richness and texture of NZ wine.

in MARL, N CANT. Approachable, fruit-forward, esp N Cant SAUV BL, PINOT N. Stylish Hariata NV fizz; 2nd tier, Maui.

Tohu Marl, Nel ★★ World's 1st Māori-owned winery. Rewa Blanc de Blancs, Rosé. AWATERE V SAUV BL, RIES. Top: Whenua Awa Single-Vyd CHARD, PINOT N.

Trinity Hill Hawk ★★→★★★★ Extensive vyds in GIMBLETT GRAVELS. Excellent quality/value: CHARD, SYRAH, Bx blend The Gimblett, only NZ "port" styles using trad Portuguese grapes. Homage Syrah a NZ classic **14′ 15′ 16 17 18′ 19′** 20′ 21′.

Māori word Te Wa, meaning area or region, sounds very like "terroir".

Two Paddocks C Ot ★★ Owned by hard-working actor Sir Sam Neill; vyds in Alexandra, Bannockburn. Organic. PINOT N mainstay: vivacious main label, resonant single-vyd The Fusilier (Bannockburn). Drink-young Picnic range.

Two Rivers Marl ★★→★★★ Family-owned, with vyds in WAIRAU V, AWATERE V (hence Two Rivers). Best known for two-valley SAUV BL blend Convergence, restrained Island of Beauty rosé (dr); 2nd-tier Black Cottage v.gd value.

Valli C Ot ★★★ Label created by Grant Taylor, ex-GIBBSTON V winemaker, now runs wine bar in WAITAKI V. Subregional differences in PINOT N highlighted with four versions. Excellent quality; Waitaki V CHARD outstanding.

Vavasour Marl ★★ Owned by US billionaire Bill Foley, was 1st AWATERE V label (est 1986). Epitomizes Awatere V style: high-wire acidity PINOT GR, SAUV BL; elegant CHARD; red fruit PINOT N. Top: Papa (mudstone) wines, well made, complex.

Vidal Hawk ★★ Under INDEVIN ownership, est 1905. Top tiers dropped, leaves standard, Res ranges for supermarkets: gd-value HAWK CHARD, MERLOT/CAB.

Villa Maria Auck ★★→★★★ Recently acquired by INDEVIN to "spearhead" aim of becoming "leading NZ global wine business". Entry-level Private Bin, great-value Cellar Selection, Single Vineyard, Res (regional character). Distinguished Icon.

Waiheke Island Sun-kissed isle in Hauraki Gulf where day visits, weddings and lazy holidays comprise key market for local wineries. Pricey wines because (a) they're expensive to make, and (b) wealthy people flock to Waih. Fragrant Bx blends (esp Onetangi district clay soils) and more recently bold SYRAH.

Waimea Nel ★★ One of region's largest. Now part of NZ-owned Booster Wine Group. Breezy, fresh whites (RIES, SAUV BL); 2nd tier, Spinyback.

Wairarapa At the base of N Island, similar latitude to MARL. NZ's 7th-largest wine region. Centred around MART, but across large river valley. Driest, coolest region in N Island. Exposed to cold s winds, reducing yields. Farmer William Beetham and his French wife planted 1st PINOT N in 1890s; after long hiatus, grape returned in 80s to great acclaim. Also strong in CHARD, RIES, PINOT GR, SAUV BL.

Wairau Valley Marl Marl Centre is a vine-filled flood plain surrounded by sheltering ranges. Wairau means "many waters". Three important side valleys called Southern Valleys: Brancott, Omaka, Waihopai; SAUV BL thrives on flat alluvial valley floor; most PINOT N planted on clay-based, n-facing slopes. Recent planting in upper Wairau V. Biggest town Blenheim gateway to 30+ cellar doors.

Waitaki Valley Small, beautiful subregion in N Ot. Limestone the big attraction, but climate marginal, frost-prone; CHARD, PINOT GR, PINOT N excellent in top vintages. Big potential for bubbles.

Whitehaven Marl ★★ Part-owned by Gallo (*see* US). Mostly SAUV BL, exported to US. Pristine whites, stylish PINOT N. Top: Greg (after winery co-founder G White).

Wither Hills Marl ★★ Big producer owned by Lion brewery. Dependable standard SAUV BL, but other gems incl single vyds Rarangi RIES, Calrossie PINOT N.

Yealands Marl ★★ Vast vyd (c.1000 ha, NZ's largest) on rolling coastal AWATERE V site, est 2008. High profile for sustainability, but not organic. Zesty SAUV BL.

Zephyr Marl ★★→★★★ Organic family vyd in lower WAIRAU V, bounded by Opawa River. Principled winemaking. Quality across range (CHARD, GEWURZ, RIES).

South Africa

"Regenerative" is the word on everyone's lips, as more wine-growers convert to the belief that not only is greatness born in the vineyard (as opposed to the cellar), it's actually born in the soil. Hence the concerted focus on understanding the current health of the earth, and using the wealth of available tools to improve it. Like swearing off chemicals where possible, and bringing in cattle, sheep and/or goats to provide natural nutrients, and ducks and other natural predators to control vineyard pests. Also establishing effective cover crops and managing them with the necessary attention and precision. Dovetailing with this work is a greater emphasis and urgency around climate change. Figuring out, for example, not only which hardier grape varieties to plant where, but also which particular rootstocks to use, to save the most water while making the vines as resilient and long-lived as possible. All this effort is directed at protecting and building on the gains that have been made over the past few decades in creating wines that are compelling and delicious young yet have longevity. Snappier Sauvignons, sexier Syrahs, more curvaceous Cabernets. And gains made in recognizing the sleeping beauty in the ubiquitous, workhorse grape, Chenin Blanc, and allowing it to bloom; reviving rundown vineyards and letting their quiet authority shine; restoring the dignity of yesteryear's varieties like Cinsault, so a new generation of wine-lovers can admire their timeless allure.

Recent vintages

2024 Variable; let producer track record guide buying/cellaring decisions.
2023 Cool kick-off for whites and early reds, wet 2nd half needed steady nerves.
2022 Smaller crop, but slow ripening built flavour while preserving freshness.
2021 Late but bountiful, gd early rains, cool conditions. Much excitement (r/w).
2020 A humdinger: exceptional structure, intensity, verve, with moderate alc.

AA Badenhorst Family Wines Swa ★★→★★★★ With subtle, savoury-edged releases from Med and heritage grapes, accenting site, old vines, wild yeasts et al., prime mover Adi B helped revolutionize SA's wine aesthetic and approach from mid-2000s. Portfolio-pruning sees half-dozen varietal CHENIN BL reduced to single bottling, named Grensloos, with pair of CINSAULTS, solo PALOMINO, and Red/White blends retained. Secateurs label remains byword for value.

Alheit Vineyards W Cape ★★★★ Chris and Suzaan A in 2010s brought a novel, explorer's approach to the avant-garde by seeking out distinctive CHENIN BL pockets on Cape coast to vinify with min intervention alongside profound multi-site Cartology. Latterly also SEM. Mostly old vyds, but Hereafter Here – younger-vine, fruitier Chenin Bl from recently acquired SWA farm – as exciting.

Alto Wine Estate Stell ★★★ Neighbour and sibling to ERNIE ELS and STELLENZICHT WINES in orbit of Baron Hans von Staff-Reitzenstein. Produces reds exclusively, incl occasional "Port". Rouge (BX/SHIRAZ), value-priced industry institution.

Anthonij Rupert Wyne W Cape ★→★★★★ Wide, impressive portfolio honours owner and international businessman Johann R's late brother. Some exceptional 3rd-party vyds (in acclaimed Cape of Good Hope collection) but mostly own parcels, incl newly released CINSAULT from old bush vines in SWA. Upcyclable Protea range, eye/pocket-pleaser.

Anysbos Bot R ★★★ Heyns family's pair of blends, GRENACHE N- and CHENIN BL-led, now joined by varietal SYRAH, its aroma hinting more at berry and lily than the anise in brand name. Winemaker Marelise Niemann also crafts her admired Momento label (mostly GRENACHE BL and N) on-site.

Babylonstoren W Cape ★★→★★★★ Media tycoon Koos Bekker and wife Karen Roos's reinvigorated wine-and-lifestyle farm nr PAARL with newly opened interactive replica of a pre-industrial country village. Wine lineup led by plush, long-haul-styled Bx blend Nebukadnesar. The Newt in Somerset is sibling property in UK.

Bartho Eksteen Estate Wine W Cape ★★★→★★★★ At Eksteen clan's boutique farm in HEM V, Bartho (CWG member) and son Pieter Willem make elegant SAUV BL, SYRAH. Also run academy named Wijnskool, with own namesake label, for aspiring vintners, hence pedagogy-themed wine names. Pieter and Argentinian wife Sol make steak-friendly MALBEC from WELL under Yerden Eksteen brand.

Bartinney Private Cellar W Cape ★★→★★★★ Rose and Michael Jordaan's trio of ventures: Bartinney boutique winery on steep STELL slopes of Simonsberg, with classic CHARD, CAB SAUV; sweeping Plaisir estate on warmer PAARL side of mtn, hitting its stride esp with Grand Plaisir Red/White (cedary Bx r and peachy Chard); and lifestyle brand Noble Savage led by juicy bargain Cab Sauv/SHIRAZ.

Beaumont Family Wines Cape SC ★★★→★★★★ Excellent Bot R familial estate with old-time ambience and gnarly vines. Much smoother-complexioned son Sebastian handmakes characterful wines incl superlative CHENIN BL, more recent New Baby (w blend). Matriarch Jayne B's namesake label features CHARD, PINOT N from small parcels beside working antique watermill.

Beck, Graham W Cape ★★→★★★★ A-list CAP CLASSIQUE specialist nr ROB with portfolio that ticks boxes for all sparkling styles, water white to salmon-hued. Delicious, often stellar surprises in Artisan Collection, eg. new savoury/herbal PINOT M, one of handful of solo bottlings of that grape.

BEE (Black Economic Empowerment) Initiative aimed at increasing wine-industry ownership and participation by previously disadvantaged groups.

Bored with food-and-wine pairing? Try music-and-wine at Black Elephant Vintners.

Beeslaar Wines W Cape ★★★★ Masterclass in refined PINOTAGE and, now, mineral CHARD, by ex-KANONKOP winemaker Abrie B and family. Thrilling eg. of trad approach with modern tweaks like ceramic vessels for portion of the white.

Bellingham W Cape ★★→★★★ Enduring DGB brand with v.gd fruit-driven limited releases The Bernard Series and newer The Founders, homage to vivacious World War Two-era couple, Pod and Fredagh Podlashuk, who revived FRAN home-farm Belle en Champ, and championed SHIRAZ at the Cape.

Benguela Cove Lagoon Wine Estate Wlk B ★★★ Penny Streeter OBE's cellar, vyds and destination on Bot R lagoon. Top: Catalina SEM, Wild At Heart CAB SAUV, experimental/cellar-door-only bottlings under Vinography flag. Johann Fourie also crafts Penny's UK wines (Leonardslee, Mannings Heath), plus those of Terra Loci, a new, separate brand he owns with partners.

Beyerskloof W Cape ★★→★★★★ PINOTAGE champion nr STELL: 11 fruit-forward versions of the grape (12, incl spirit for "Port"), soloists, blends and blush. Equally fine CAB SAUV named Eerste Ry for 1st vines planted 1988/9 by co-founder Beyers Truter.

Boekenhoutskloof Winery W Cape ★→★★★★ Among SA's most important producers, for quality and volume, based in FRAN. Enviable consistency 40 yrs+ under Boekenhoutskloof and Porcupine Ridge labels, later The Wolftrap range and standalone ventures in HEM, SWA (*see* CAP MARITIME, PORSELEINBERG).

Bon Courage Estate W Cape ★→★★★ Bruwer family nr ROB with stylish Brut CAP CLASSIQUE trio, aromatic desserts (MUSCAT, RIES) in broad range.

Boplaas Family Vineyards W Cape ★→★★★ Carel Nel and family at CDORP, known for "Port" and deep-flavoured table wines of Portuguese grapes (r/w).

Boschendal Wines W Cape ★→★★★ Evergreen DGB brand on hospitable C17 estate nr FRAN. Fruit-forward Bx/Rhône (r/w) blends, CHARD, SAUV BL, SHIRAZ, various tiers of CAP CLASSIQUE.

Boschkloof Wines W Cape ★★★→★★★★ Acclaimed Reenen Borman in STELL with, eg. stellar Epilogue SYRAH under Boschkloof and Kottabos labels. With partners, notable Saga Vyds bottlings, (unoaked) reds (silky Syrah from Stell, new piquant BARBERA from BRE) both labelled Sons of Sugarland; whites (CHENIN BL, blend) branded Patatsfontein after source farm in unsung area Montagu.

Botanica Wines Cit, Stell ★★→★★★ On wine- and flower-growing home farm nr STELL, American Ginny Povall crafts excellent eg. succulent CAB FR, newer perfumed ALBARIÑO, draws on old w-coast bush vines for superlative, rich yet refined Mary Delany CHENIN BL.

Bouchard Finlayson Cape SC ★★★→★★★★ Family-owned HEM pioneer, with v. fine expressions of CHARD (unoaked version among SA's best), PINOT N.

Breedekloof Breede River V DISTRICT (c.12,650 ha); trad bulk, entry-level focus, lately lifted by new generation, often working with heritage vines, esp CHENIN BL.

Brookdale Estate Paarl ★→★★★ Dynamic, UK-owned, advised by eminent Duncan SAVAGE. Refined old-vine CHENIN BL; pair of white blends: Bradbourne, featuring rare PIQUEPOUL BL, and Sixteen, from 16 interplanted varieties.

Bruce Jack Wines W Cape ★★→★★★ From home base nr Napier on s coast, multi-tasking Bruce J makes varietals, blends, bubbly from unusual grapes for estate label The Drift. Collaborates with others for namesake international brand. Mary Le Bow (r blend) and VIOGNIER, both US oak-scented, and newer range Ghost in the Machine, incl lemony version of heirloom grape CLAIRETTE BL. Also owns boutique brand The Berrio, starring racy SAUV BL from Africa's windblown tip.

Buitenverwachting W Cape ★★→★★★ Family farm in CONST with lovely trad feel yet modern, forthright wines, exported as Bayten; CHARD, SAUV BL, Bx-style reds, varying mix of Ltd Releases; 1st in area with own-vine CHENIN BL.

Calitzdorp In KL K DISTRICT (c.200 ha), similar climate to Douro V (*see* Portugal), known for "Port" and latterly unfortified Port-grape wines (r/w).

Cap classique Bottle-fermented sparkling still officially known as "méthode cap classique" but producers urging use of shortened version. Major success: labels have more than doubled the past decade, to 400+.

Cape Blend Usually red with a significant PINOTAGE component; occasionally a CHENIN BL blend, or simply wine with "Cape character".

Cape Coast Umbrella appellation ("OVERARCHING REGION" in officialese) for Coast (w and central) and CAPE SC regions.

Capensis W Cape ★★★→★★★★ Starry venture in STELL owned by US Jackson Family's Barbara Banke, specializing in sophisticated, lengthily bottle-aged CHARD, multi-site and single-vyd. *See also* DALKEITH.

Cape Point Vineyards W Cape ★★→★★★★ Acclaimed family winery nr tip of CAPE TOWN peninsula. Cellarable Isliedh (Bx-style w), recent Elixirr (CHARD/SAUV BL).

Cape Rock Wines W Cape ★★→★★★ Willie Brand and son Gavin among OLI R's top boutique growers. Creative, strikingly packaged varietals, blends (r/w) featuring rarities eg. CARIGNAN, VERMENTINO.

Cape South Coast Cool-climate REGION (c.2640 ha) comprising DISTRICTS of Cape Agulhas, ELG, Lower Duivenhoks River, Overberg, Plettenberg Bay, Swellendam, WLK B, plus stand-alone WARDS Herbertsdale, Napier, Stilbaai E. *See also* CAPE COAST.

Cape Town Coast DISTRICT (c.2570 ha) covering namesake city, its peninsula WARDS, CONST and Hout B, plus nearby wards DURBANVILLE and Philadelphia.

Cape West Coast Only subregion; incl DARLING and Lutzville V DISTRICTS, plus Bamboes B and Lamberts B WARDS. *See also* CAPE COAST.

Cap Maritime Cape SC ★★★ Classy CHARD, PINOT N specialist in UP HEM owned by BOEKENHOUTSKLOOF, looking to build on enviable track record as own young vyds come on-stream.

Catherine Marshall Wines W Cape ★★★ Cool-climate (chiefly ELG) specialist Cathy M focused on CHENIN BL, SAUV BL, PINOT N and dry, mineral RIES.

Cederberg Tiny (98 ha) free-standing WARD in Cederberg Mtns, with some of the remotest, highest vyds (950–1100m/3117–3609ft), mostly CHENIN BL, SHIRAZ. Main producers: CEDERBERG PRIVATE CELLAR, Driehoek. Newer Kromrivier makes a chewy version of rare-in-SA TEMPRANILLO.

Cederberg Private Cellar W Cape ★★→★★★★ Nieuwoudt family; among highest (CED) and most s (ELIM) vyds. Make mostly varietals and bubbly, incl exceptional CWG SHIRAZ. David N shareholder in exciting newer Escape Wines in WLK B.

"Restraint" takes on new meaning at The Garajeest: name of a new scent.

Central Orange River DISTRICT (c.1720 ha) in N CAPE GU. Hot, dry, irrigated; trad white (most is Sultana for dried/table grapes) and fortified, but major producer ORANGE RIVER CELLARS pushing envelope with eg. SHIRAZ.

Certified Heritage Vineyard *See* OLD VINE PROJECT.

Chamonix Wine Farm Fran, Stell ★★→★★★ Norwegian-owned top cellar/vyds overlooking FRAN, also sourcing grapes from STELL. Age-worthy CHARD, PINOT N, Bx varietals/blends (r/w).

Charles Fox Cap Classique Wines Elg ★★★ A trad-method bubbly house founded by 1964 Olympics swimmer and wife Zelda, with eight classic, delicious Bruts (w/rosé), most vintage-dated, many featuring rarely seen (Pinot) MEUNIER.

Coastal Region Largest REGION (c.43,200 ha); incl ocean-influenced CAPE TOWN, DARLING, Lutzville V, STELL and SWA DISTRICTS, plus Bamboes B and Lamberts B WARDS. Also incl non-maritime FRAN, PAARL, TUL, WELL districts.

Colmant Cap Classique & Champagne W Cape ★★★→★★★★ Sparkling house at FRAN, founded by Belgian Colmant family, now owned by compatriots, the Boones. Brut Nature and trio of Brut (w/rosé), all NV and excellent.

Constantia CAPE TOWN WARD (415 ha), est 1685 on cool Constantiaberg slopes; SA's 1st and most historically famous growing area, still a pace-setter.

Constantia Glen Const ★★★→★★★★ Waibel family-owned model of consistency, quality on upper Constantiaberg. Trio of Bx blends (r/w), solo SAUV BL.

Constantia Uitsig W Cape ★★→★★★ Prime vyds, cellar and multi-faceted cellar door in CONST. Estate and wider-sourced Ex Oppido ranges (mostly w, some sp).

Creation Wines W Cape ★★★→★★★★★ Buzzy, inventive cellar door and bold wines vie for attention/awards at scenic estate in HEM RDG, part-owned by Martin family. Standouts: CHARD, PINOT N, incl versions by daughter and son.

Crystallum W Cape ★★★→★★★★ Always impressive and satisfying CHARD, PINOT N from cool sites, mostly ELA, HEM, vinified at GABRIËLSKLOOF by Peter-Allan Finlayson, brand co-owner with brother Andrew.

CWG (Cape Winemakers Guild) Independent, invitation-only association of 41 top growers. Stages a benchmarking annual auction of limited premium bottlings.

Of wine sold in SA, including imports, barely a third is in traditional glass.

Dalkeith Stell, Swa ★★★ Pair of fine, textured CHENIN BL, and new peppery SYRAH, all single site and named after watering hole in the Kgalagadi Transfrontier Park. Siblings to CAPENSIS CHARD trio in Cape portfolio of US Jackson Family.

Darling DISTRICT (c.2500 ha) around this w-coast town. Best vyds in hilly Groenekloof WARD. Most fruit goes into 3rd-party brands, some spectacular.

David & Nadia Swa ★★★★ Quietly arresting sextet of CHENIN BL (single- and multi-site, latter incl newer CWG bottling), blends (r/w) and GRENACHE N, mostly from heritage vyds, by Sadie husband and wife on Paardeberg Mtn-side.

David Finlayson Wines W Cape ★★→★★★ Expressive, fruity wines, incl mostly old-vine Camino Africana series, by 3rd-generation vintner David F nr STELL.

De Grendel Wines W Cape ★★★ Sir De Villiers Graaff's Table Mtn-facing venture in DURBANVILLE draws on own and far-flung contracted vyds, notably elevated Ceres Plateau and maritime ELIM. New CHARD Blanc de Blancs, Lady Gaedry, expands CAP CLASSIQUE offering.

De Kleine Wijn Wine-grower Wynand Grobler and wife Anya based on steep-sloped property (formerly known as Tulbagh Mtn Vyds), where they craft Rhône-style TMV Estate Blend from own vines, source widely for extensive range of playfully named, seriously conceived wines eg. FRAN SEM Debutant White from ancient site.

De Krans Wines W Cape ★→★★★ Nel family at CDORP noted for "Port" styles and fortified MUSCAT. Success with robust unfortified (r/w) from Portuguese grapes.

Delaire Graff Estate W Cape ★★→★★★★ UK diamond merchant Laurence Graff's eyrie vyds, winery and visitor venue in STELL's Banhoek V. Glittering portfolio incl consistently superior, single-vyd Terraced Block Res CHARD and convincing, fruit-cakey Cape Vintage "Port" from SWA grapes.

Delheim Coast ★→★★★ Eco-minded family venture high on Simonsberg Mtn nr STELL. PINOTAGE (powerful single-block, charming rosé), cellar-worthy Grand Res (Bx-style r), ever-scintillating botrytis RIES from heritage vines.

DeMorgenzon W Cape ★★→★★★★ Gorgeous music-themed family winery on STELL hilltop with high notes with Res CHARD, CHENIN BL (incl vine-selected The Divas), Maestro Bx and Rhône blends (r/w); DMZ stylish early drinkers.

De Trafford Wines Elg, Stell ★★★→★★★★ Trafford family's boutique venture on saddle between STELL and Helderberg mtns, reputed for unabashedly bold wines, eg. Bx-style/SHIRAZ Elevation 393, CAB SAUV (incl newer version from Belfield vyd in ELG), SYRAH, CHENIN BL (dr/sw). *See also* SIJNN.

DGB W Cape Long-est producer/wholesaler in WELL/FRAN. Owns/controls high-end brands Backsberg, BELLINGHAM, BOSCHENDAL, Fryer's Cove, Old Road. Also easy-drinking labels, eg. newer Vineyard Friends, some export-only.

Diemersdal Estate W Cape ★→★★★ DURBANVILLE Louw family excelling with confident, full-fruited site/row/style-specific CHARD, SAUV BL (incl new local 1ST, The Globe, fermented in glass sphere), CAB SAUV, PINOTAGE and SA's only commercial GRÜNER V.

District *See* GU.

Dorrance Wines W Cape ★★→★★★★ French family boutique, with cellar in CAPE TOWN city-heritage building. Delicate, consistently excellent CHARD, CHENIN BL, SYRAH, newer PINOT N.

Durbanville Sea breezy WARD (1350 ha) on Tygerberg Hills in CAPE TOWN DISTRICT, best known for SAUV BL and whites generally.

Durbanville Hills Dur ★→★★★ Area pioneer, owned by HEINEKEN BEVERAGES, local growers, staff, noted for generous, fruit-focused styling and fair prices. Excellent pinnacle Bx-style blends (r/w), Tangram; ubiquitous entry-level SAUV BL.

Eagles' Nest Const ★★★ Constantiaberg mtn-side winery, lately German-owned, with reliably superior VIOGNIER, MERLOT, SHIRAZ. Also vibrant SAUV BL.

Elgin Cool-climate DISTRICT (c.730 ha) recognized for CHARD, SAUV BL, PINOT N. Exciting CHENIN BL, RIES, SYRAH, CAP CLASSIQUE. Mostly family boutiques.

Elim Windswept WARD (c.150 ha) in most S DISTRICT, Cape Agulhas, producing aromatic white blends, SAUV BL, SYRAH. Grape source for majors and boutiques.

Ernie Els Wines W Cape ★→★★★★ Star golfer's wine venture nr STELL, centred on CAB SAUV: four cellar-worthy tiers, earlier-ready Big Easy line. Co-owner Baron Hans von Staff-Reitzenstein also owns eminent STELLENZICHT WINES and ALTO.

Estate wine Grown, made and bottled on "units registered for the production of estate wine". Not a quality designation.

Fairview W Cape ★→★★★★ Back family's caprine-themed wine-and-cheese venture on panoramic Paarl Mtn farm, sourcing on-site and more widely for cornucopia of varietal, blended, single-vyd and fizzy bottlings under Fairview, Goats Do Roam, La Capra, Spice Route and Klein Amoskuil labels. Bustling, multi-faceted cellar-door experience, incl famous goat herd and tower.

FirstCape Vineyards W Cape ★→★★ Huge export venture involving four Breede River V cellars. Mostly entry-level wines in multiple ranges.

Flagstone Winery W Cape ★→★★★ Accolade Wines' high-end winery at Somerset W, sourcing widely for plush-fruited PINOTAGE, Bx style (w), SAUV BL et al. Mid-tier Fish Hoek, entry-level Kumala sibling brands.

Fleur du Cap W Cape ★→★★★ HEINEKEN BEVERAGES premium label, with opulent headliner Laszlo (Bx r blend) and v.gd Series Privée Unfiltered CHARD, MERLOT.

Foundry, The Piek, Stell, V Pa ★★★→★★★★ Among 1st to focus on the Rhône (r/w) in 2000. Cellar and most of its source vyds in PAARL's V Pa for elegantly crafted single-variety bottlings under Foundry and newer Geographica labels.

Franschhoek Huguenot-founded DISTRICT (1170 ha) known for CHARD, SEM, CAB SAUV and CAP CLASSIQUE. Home to some of SA's oldest farms and vines.

Free State Province and GU. Aptly named Mile High Vyds sole producer (under The Bald Ibis label) in viticulturally challenging e highlands.

Gabriëlskloof W Cape ★★→★★★ CWG member and CRYSTALLUM co-owner Peter-Allan Finlayson makes this lauded range in the family cellar nr Bot R, with emphasis on CHENIN BL (incl new aromatic Era René), CAB FR and site/technique-based expressions of SYRAH.

Glenelly Estate Stell ★★★→★★★★ "Retirement" venture in STELL of Bx eminence May-Eliane de Lencquesaing, run by grandson Nicolas Bureau. Glossy flagships Lady May (Bx-style r), Res CHARD and Bx style/SHIRAZ. Remarkable glass collection at cellar door.

Groot Constantia Estate Const ★★★ Magnet attracting 450,000 visitors to beautifully preserved farmstead and SA's longest-producing cellar. Suitably eminent wines, esp MUSCAT DE FRONTIGNAN Grand Constance helping restore CONST dessert to C18 glory.

GU (geographical unit) Largest of the WO demarcations: FREE STATE, KWAZULU-NATAL, LIMPOPO and new NORTH EAST, plus E, N, W Cape – last three constitute the OVERARCHING GU known as Greater Cape. Other WO appellations (in descending size): overarching region, REGION, subregion, DISTRICT and WARD.

Hamilton Russell Vineyards Hem V ★★★→★★★★ The 1st to succeed with Burgundy grapes in cool S Cape in early 80s at Hermanus: long-lived CHARD, elegant PINOT N. Sibling Southern Right focus on SAUV BL, PINOTAGE, ditto Ashbourne label, only here SAUV BL joined by other white grapes. Stand-alone employee brand Tesselaarsdal, made at/by HRV, comprises CHARD, PINOT N exclusively.

Hartenberg Estate W Cape ★★→★★★ Welcoming, eco-minded family farm nr STELL with tiers of SHIRAZ/Syrah; fine Bx-style red, CHARD, RIES (dr/s/sw/botrytis).

Heineken Beverages SA's biggest drinks company, a 2023 merger of Distell, Namibia Breweries and Heineken SA, headquartered in upcountry Sandton. Owns or has interests in many wine brands, spanning styles/quality scales. *See* DURBANVILLE HILLS, FLEUR DU CAP, JC LE ROUX, NEDERBURG WINES.

Hemel-en-Aarde Trio of cool-climate WARDS (Hem V, Up Hem, Hem Rdg) in WLK B DISTRICT, producing outstanding CHARD, SAUV BL, PINOT N.

Iona Vineyards Elg ★★→★★★ Family winery atop cool, breezy ridge nr ocean, co-owned by staff; excels with taut, mineral CHARD, SAUV BL, PINOT N. Also v. fine SYRAH under Wines of Brocha label. Well-priced lifestyle brand Sophie.

JC le Roux, The House of W Cape ★→★★ The 1st specialist fizz producer in 80s, now HEINEKEN BEVERAGES-owned with must-visit brand home nr STELL. Scintilla CAP CLASSIQUE; sugar-dabbed carbonated sparklers, some trendily de-alc and/or sold in alu-cans.

Value: a SA speciality

South Africa's growers often wish they could charge a cent or two more for their wines. But for consumers there's gd value across the spectrum, from large-volume producers focused on price points to high-end boutiques with a handful of labels. There are also hybrids: small, upper-echelon ventures with pocket-pleasing brands in big quantities. Here are some names to look for: BOEKENHOUTSKLOOF (The Wolftrap and Porcupine Ridge), Darling Cellars, Daschbosch, Du Toitskloof, FAIRVIEW (Goats Do Roam), KANONKOP ESTATE (Kadette), KEN FORRESTER (Petit), KLEINE ZALZE, LA MOTTE, Leopard's Leap, NEDERBURG, Perdeberg Winery, ROBERTSON WINERY, Rooiberg Winery, RUSTENBERG WINES, SPIER, STELLENBOSCH VYDS, STELLENRUST, VILLIERA. The ultimate test for gd value in SA has to be PINOT N, and here standouts incl Elgin Vintners, Haute Cabrière, Julien Schaal, KRUGER FAMILY WINES, La Vierge, MULDERBOSCH VYDS, OAK VALLEY ESTATE, PAUL CLÜVER FAMILY WINES and newcomer Lenuzza Vyds.

Joostenberg Wines Paarl ★★→★★★ Organic family business with flavoursome SYRAH, CHENIN BL (incl sw botrytis) et al. Honours forebears via Myburgh Bros lineup. Also partners with STARK-CONDÉ in revitalized STELL estate Lievland, and in volume, value brand MAN Family Wines.

Jordan Wine Estate W Cape ★★→★★★★ Family venture nr STELL, admired for consistency, quality, value, from entry Chameleon to stellar CWG bottlings. Recently joined hands with leading conservation winery, Painted Wolf, to strengthen sustainability efforts.

Mini-boom in wines with antique plane names: Catalina, Harvard, Shackleton.

Kaapzicht Wine Estate Stell ★→★★★ Steytler family; charmingly packaged portfolio of boldly fruited wines, featuring eg. SA's 2nd-oldest CHENIN BL.

Kanonkop Estate Coast ★★★→★★★★ "First Growth" status since early 70s; classically styled, long-lived senior wines, Paul Sauer (Bx-style r), CAB SAUV and PINOTAGE (regular and old-vine Black Label), and latterly second label, Kadette. Recently acquired organic STELL neighbour Ladybird Vyds is now officially merged with larger estate, and cellarmaster appointed chief winemaker, after departure of long-time Kanonkop helmsman Abrie Beeslaar (see BEESLAAR WINES).

Kara-Tara W Cape See STARK-CONDÉ WINES.

Keermont Vineyards Stell ★★★ Wraith family estate; terraced vyds (Cape rarity) in cleft between Helderberg and STELL Mtns. Intense CHENIN BL, SHIRAZ et al. by CWG member Alex Starey. Neighbour/grape supplier to A-league DE TRAFFORD.

Keet Wines Stell ★★★★ Having named his debut wine First Verse, applauded owner-winemaker Chris K since 2009 resisted all temptations to add to single, beautifully crafted, classically inspired, New World-styled Bx red blend.

Ken Forrester Wines W Cape ★→★★★ With French AdVini partners, STELL vintner and restaurateur Ken F tireless champion of Med grapes and CHENIN BL (dr/sp/ off-dry/botrytis), lately via creative/experimental collection The Misfits. Petit range is quintessence of quaffing.

Kershaw Wines W Cape ★★★→★★★★★ UK-born MW Richard K's exceptional, refined portfolio is headed by Clonal Selection, featuring ELG's standout varieties CHARD, PINOT N, SYRAH. Constituent sites showcased in Deconstructed collection, while GPS and Smuggler's Boot ranges spotlight other prime Cape areas and new techniques, respectively.

Klein Constantia Estate W Cape ★★→★★★★ Iconic mtn-side property focused on SAUV BL and luscious, cellar-worthy non-botrytis MUSCAT DE FRONTIGNAN Vin de Constance, convincing recreation of legendary CONST sweet wine and restorative of C18. Sibling winery, Anwilka (r) in STELL.

Kleine Zalze Wines W Cape ★→★★★★ A STELL star, majority-owned by France's AdVini. Family Res, Vyd Selection and new Heritage Vyds collections shine brightest; lab range Project Z tinkers spectacularly; Cellar Selection overachieves. Stand-alone BEE venture Visio Vintners uplifts staff.

Klein Karoo REGION (c.1900 ha), mostly semi-arid and known for fortified, esp "port" style in CDORP. Revived old vines feature in some premium terroir labels eg. Le Sueur by ex-DE KRANS winemaker Louis van der Riet.

Krone W Cape ★★★ Made at Twee Jonge Gezellen estate in TUL. Krone label houses collection of elegant, vintage-dated CAP CLASSIQUE (dr/off-dry) inspired by French grower-Champagne movement; sibling still-wine range TJG features pair of widely sourced aromatic blends (r/w).

Kruger Family Wines W Cape ★★→★★★ From recently completed facilities in Somerset W, Johan K ranges far and wide for his and wife Sophie's extensive portfolio of site-specific wines; CHARD, PINOT N and old vines at core. Much of output is exclusive to Naked Wines (UK, US).

KwaZulu-Natal Province and GU on e coast; not-ideal tropical climate nr ocean; central plateau and, further n, Drakensberg foothills more propitious but no cakewalk. Abingdon Estate, Cathedral Peak, Highgate only producers.

KWV W Cape ★→★★★ Formerly national wine co-op and controlling body; today one of largest producers/exporters, based in PAARL. Close to a dozen labels, headed by serially decorated The Mentors.

La Motte W Cape ★★→★★★ Elegant estate, winery, cellar door at FRAN owned by Koegelenberg-Rupert family. Classically constructed varietals, blends. Neighbour-sibling Leopard's Leap emphasizes food side of wine match.

Leeu Passant *See* MULLINEUX.

Le Lude Cap Classique W Cape ★★★→★★★★ Celebrated family-owned sparkling house in FRAN. Elegant offering: Agrafe CHARD/PINOT N, 1st locally to undergo 2nd ferment under cork.

Le Riche Wines Stell ★★★→★★★★ Fine, modern-classic boutique CAB SAUV Richesse (varietal and heritage blend with CINSAULT) by Christo LR and siblings. Recent series of fascinating deconstructions showcase and honour long-term growers' Cab Sauv sites.

Limpopo Most n province and GU in wo system.

Lowerland Pri ★★★ Meaning "Verdant Land", part of large family agribusiness in Prieska WARD beside Orange R. Area's most exciting winery, grapes vinified in PAARL by Lukas VL of VAN LOGGERENBERG WINES. Latest is rarity: blush TANNAT.

Per capita wine consumption dipped 2023, 7.57 litres; still beat 20-yr average 7.06.

Meerlust Estate Stell ★★★ Myburgh family-owned since 1756; vyds and cellar lie in S STELL, landscape more undulating, reminiscent of Bx, than mountainous. Cue French-inspired classics led by elegant Rubicon, among SA's 1st Bx-style reds.

Méthode cap classique *See* CAP CLASSIQUE.

Miles Mossop Wines Coast ★★★→★★★★ CWG member Miles M's polished bottlings, most named after his family. Latterly wider sourcing, same top quality.

Morgenster Estate Stell ★★★ Historic farm nr Somerset W developed into prime wine-and-olive estate in early 90s by late Italian industrialist Giulio Bertrand; children continue Old World varieties, styling, with packaging updates.

Mulderbosch Vineyards W Cape ★→★★★ Reputed US-owned STELL winery and welcoming cellar door with modern, amply fruited CHENIN BL, CAB FR, pair of Bx-style reds, newer cherry-earthy PINOT N.

Mullineux & Leeu Passant W Cape ★★★→★★★★ Chris M and US-born wife Andrea transform SWA CHENIN BL, SYRAH and handful of compatible varieties into ambrosial soil-specific varietals, blends, CWG bottlings and *vin de paille*. Leeu Passant portfolio (FRAN), from mostly venerable vines plus some own younger ones, as sublime. Also v.gd Great Heart, with new PINOT N from cool-climate Ceres, owned and made by staff.

Mvemve Raats Stell ★★★★ Mzokhona Mvemve, 1st qualified Black winemaker, and Bruwer Raats (RAATS FAMILY) select barrels for forthright, best-of-vintage Bx blend named MR de Compostella.

Nederburg Wines W Cape ★→★★★★ One of SA's biggest (2m cases) and best-loved brands, PAARL-based, HEINEKEN BEVERAGES-owned. Top ranges: Two Centuries, Heritage Heroes, Manor House, many purse-pleasers and wine-list fixtures.

Neil Ellis Wines W Cape ★★→★★★★ Pioneer STELL négociant now majority-owned by VAN LOVEREN. Sources mostly cooler-grown parcels locally and around w CAPE for masterly site expressions.

Newton Johnson Vineyards Cape SC ★★★→★★★★ Family cellar in UP HEM, acclaimed CHARD, PINOT N; SA's 1st commercial ALBARIÑO also superb.

Northern Cape (N Cape) Largest province and GU in wo scheme; with a new

REGION, Karoo-Hoogland. Semi-arid to arid, with temp extremes. *See also* SUTHERLAND-KAROO.

North West Province, new GU and neighbour to LIMPOPO, FREE STATE, N CAPE. Continental climate, summer rain; mostly flat grassland with Magaliesberg Mtns in ne; s border is Vaal R.

Oak Valley Estate Cape SC ★★★→★★★★ Extensive family agribusiness in ELG. Tabula Rasa: exceptional, fine-boned, single-clone bottlings of CHARD, PINOT N.

Old Vine Project Pioneering initiative aided by businessman-vintner Johann Rupert (ANTHONIJ RUPERT) to locate, catalogue, preserve SA's old vyd blocks (35 yrs+), currently totalling 4870 ha. Certified Heritage Vyd seal on bottle shows planting date.

Olifantsberg Family Vineyards Bre ★★→★★★★ Dutch-owned mtn-side venture draws on own and area vines for restrained Rhône-style (r/w), CHENIN BL, PINOTAGE.

Olifants River REGION on w coast (c.5600 ha). Warm valley floors gd for organics; higher, cooler sites in Citrusdal Mtn DISTRICT and its WARD, Pie, produce some of SA's finest wines.

Opstal Estate W Cape ★→★★★ One of BRE's quality leaders, family-owned, in mtn amphitheatre. Old-vine CHENIN BL, SEM; newer v. fine, floral VERDELHO.

Orange River Cellars N Cape ★→★★★ Vast operation with c.140 grower-owners and 1100-ha vyd on Orange R banks. Increasingly impressive Res bottlings complement trad speciality, sweet fortified MUSCAT.

Overarching GU / region *See* GU.

Paarl DISTRICT (c.8400 ha) around historic namesake town with WARDS Agter Paarl, Sim-P, V Pa. Diverse styles, approaches; best results from Med vines (r/w), CHENIN BL, CAB SAUV, PINOTAGE.

Paul Clüver Family Wines Elg ★★→★★★ Area pioneer, family-owned/run; elegant CHARD, PINOT N; convincing RIES (wood-touched semi-dry, unoaked botrytis).

Porseleinberg Swa ★★★★ BOEKENHOUTSKLOOF's organic vyds/cellar; only one wine, superb SYRAH. Handcrafted, incl front label printed on-site by winemaker.

Raats Family Wines Stell ★★★→★★★★ Exquisite CHENIN BL (oaked and not), CAB FR, esp CWG and new, partly wooded Vlag ("Flag"). Bruwer R and cousin Gavin Bruwer Slabbert also join forces to unearth vinous gems as Bruwer Vintners Vine Exploration Co. *See also* MVEMVE RAATS.

Radford Dale W Cape ★★→★★★ Thoughtful, dynamic STELL venture (Australian, French, SA and UK shareholders). Land of Hope, Radford Dale, Thirst, Vinum, Winery of Good Hope brands, restrainedly New World in style. Organic vyd/ cellar in ELG. Viticulturist Edouard Labeye has own namesake GRENACHES BL/N.

Rall Wines Coast ★★★→★★★★ Owner-winemaker and consultant Donovan R has outstanding track record since late 2000s. Initial SWA blends (r/w) since joined by Med varietals (r/w) and CHENIN BL showing same flavoursome understatement. Also vinifies Callender Peak wines (w) from vines (some ungrafted, v. rare) on snowy Ceres Plateau.

Region *See* GU.

Restless River Wines Wlk B ★★★→★★★★ Wessels and Fourie families' small, thoughtfully run vyd/cellar in UP HEM, as successful with area calling cards CHARD, PINOT N as scarcely planted CAB SAUV, all showing cool-climate minerality.

Reyneke Wines W Cape ★→★★★★ Leading bio producer nr STELL. Beguiling CHENIN BL, SAUV BL, CAB SAUV, SYRAH; characterful Vinehugger easy-sippers (r/w/rosé).

Robertson Valley Low-rainfall inland DISTRICT with most WARDS (14); c.12,700 ha; lime soils; historically gd CAP CLASSIQUE, CHARD, desserts; more recently SAUV BL, CAB SAUV, SHIRAZ.

Robertson Winery Rob ★→★★★ Consistency, value throughout extended portfolio. Best: Constitution Rd CHARD, SHIRAZ.

Rogge Cloof ★★★ Gerntholtz family venture; some of SA's highest, remotest vyds, at 1500m (4921ft) in N CAPE. Current releases, perfumed SYRAH, delicate CHARD, labelled De Knolle Fonteyn after original Kanolfontein site. Wines from 2nd parcel, at Rogge Cloof, will follow. All made by Johan K of KRUGER FAMILY WINES.

Roodekrantz Wines Paarl, Stell, Swa ★★→★★★ Subtly thrilling collection of mostly CHENIN BL from old-vine grapes rescued from big-brand anonymity. Equally satisfying sibling lineup named Fuselage inspired by cellar's location on family owners' private airfield nr WELL.

Sign of the times: total vines 10 yrs ago, 296 million. Total vines now, 262 million.

Rustenberg Wines Stell ★→★★★★ Barlow family on Simonsberg Mtn nr STELL; gracefulness of cellar complex, gardens and vyds reflected in portfolio based on French classics.

Rust en Vrede Wine Estate W Cape ★→★★★★ Historic STELL farm/winery; powerful, polished reds. Sibling brands owned by Jean Engelbrecht: Afrikaans (trendy CAB SAUV/CINSAULT heritage blend et al.); Cirrus (PINOT N expressing elevated Ceres Plateau terroir); Donkiesbaai (from Pie, v.gd CHENIN BL dr, *vin de paille*); Guardian Peak (fruit-forward, easy-drinking); Stell Res (mostly solo bottlings of varieties associated with region), both cellar doors for non-estate wines.

Sadie Family Wines Piek, Stell, Swa ★★★★ Iconic portfolio by revered Eben S. Signature Series: SYRAH blend Columella, multi-variety Palladius (w), both Cape benchmarks. Magnificent District Series (previously Old Vine Series), pure, detailed, age-worthy, celebrating heritage, site.

Sakkie Mouton Family Wines W Cape ★★★→★★★★ Working from Vredendal on w coast, young Izak "Sakkie" M burst on scene with stunning, pared-back and unforgettably named CHENIN BL, Revenge of the Crayfish. Follows up with more great wines/names eg. Dawn of the Salty Tongues SYRAH, some featuring heritage and rare varieties like ASSYRTIKO, all intended to showcase and champion fruit of area, specifically cool, maritime Koekenaap ward.

Saronsberg Cellar W Cape ★★→★★★ Family estate in TUL. Awarded SHIRAZ and Bx/Rhône blends/varietals, incl rare solo ROUSSANNE, bracing CHARD CAP CLASSIQUE.

Savage Wines W Cape ★★★→★★★★ CWG member Duncan S ranges far and wide from Cape Town city base: thrilling, understated wines (mostly Med varieties, CHENIN BL). Assistant Banele Vakele's fine own-label Tembela Wines (r/w).

Shannon Vineyards Elg ★★★→★★★★ Top MERLOT, also v.gd PINOT N; SAUV BL, SEM, Bx-style white showing area's elegance, freshness. Grown by siblings James and Stuart Downes, vinified by NEWTON JOHNSON.

Sijnn Mal ★★★→★★★★ Pronounced "Sane", DE TRAFFORD co-owner David T and partners' pioneer maritime venture on stony promontory overlooking the Breede R. Distinctive, aromatic blends and Varietal Series with solo bottling of ultra-rare TINTA AMARELA.

Silverthorn Wines Rob ★★★→★★★★ Distinguished collection of special-occasion CAP CLASSIQUE (w/rosé) crafted in ROB by CWG member John Loubser. All Brut, mostly CHARD, some PINOT N and, unusually, SHIRAZ and area speciality COLOMBARD.

Simonsig Family Vineyards W Cape ★→★★★★ Malan family nr STELL admired for unwavering quality; 1st with CAP CLASSIQUE in 70s, original Brut since joined by sweeter, equally delicious celebrators. Boundary-pushing Med (r/w) blends under stand-alone label The Grapesmith.

Solms-Delta Wine Company W Cape ★→★★★ Ambitious early 2000s wine-growing, land restitution and community-upliftment venture nr FRAN recently revitalized by US national Tommy Hall. Fruity fizz from SHIRAZ named Cape Jazz joins serious-yet-swiggable pair of Rhône blends (r/w) in rebooted lineup.

Spier W Cape ★→★★★★ Major winery and tourist magnet nr STELL. Flagship ranges: 21 Gables, Creative Block, Frans K Smit (honouring cellarmaster, a CWG member); expanding organic lines; pocket-pleasing Signature with rare ALBARIÑO. All fruit-focused, carefully made, mostly vegan.

Stark-Condé Wines W Cape ★★★→★★★★ Reputed US-born boutique vintner José Condé in STELL's postcard Jonkershoek V. Intensity, freshness in CAB SAUV, SYRAH; differentiation/excitement via rarities: field blend (w) and terraced vyd (CHENIN BL). Younger, wider-sourced brand Kara-Tara showcases Burgundy varieties, notably knockout Res PINOT N from Overberg. *See* JOOSTENBERG.

Steenberg Vineyards W Cape ★★→★★★ GRAHAM BECK's CONST winery, vyds, chic cellar door; glossy SAUV BL/SEM, SAUV BL (still/sp); CAP CLASSIQUE, rare NEBBIOLO.

Stellenbosch Instagrammable university town, demarcated wine DISTRICT (c.11,800 ha) and heart of wine industry (Napa of SA); all tourist facilities and many top estates tucked into mtn valleys and foothills. Heartland of CAB SAUV and powerful reds generally, also major success with CHARD, CHENIN BL, white blends et al.

Stellenbosch Vineyards Stell ★→★★★ French-owned, big-volume winery with impressive, fruit-centred limited releases incl savoury CHENIN BL and only bottling of SA-developed white grape Therona.

Stellenrust Stell ★→★★★★ Family winery with wide portfolio from trio of own prime STELL sites. Headliner range of magnificent barrel-fermented old-vine CHENIN BL. Partly wider-sourced ArtiSons lineup pushes envelope with eg. white CINSAULT The Albatross.

Stellenzicht Wines Coast ★★→★★★ Famous Helderberg Mtn cellar and vyds rejuvenated by Baron Hans von Staff-Reitzenstein, also owner of neighbour ALTO and long-time partner in nearby ERNIE ELS. Powerful but not blockbusting CHARD and CAB SAUV, SYRAH (solo, blended).

Storm Wines Hem Rdg, Hem V, U Hem ★★★→★★★★ PINOT N and CHARD specialist Hannes S uniquely expresses three HEM wards in one portfolio with precision, sensitivity. Free-standing label Wild Air spotlights HEM V SAUV BL on shale soil.

Super Single Vineyards W Cape ★★★ Boutique vintner Daniel de Waal, on venerable Canettevallei family wine-and-lavender estate in STELL, sources in area and further afield for mostly varietal wines, incl excellent SYRAH from extreme vyds nr Sutherland, SA's coldest town.

Sutherland-Karoo High-altitude DISTRICT in viticulturally challenging N CAPE, at 1450m (4757ft), not to be confused with separate, distant KL K. Only 5 ha under vine, chiefly CHARD, PINOT N, SHIRAZ, nr Sutherland town, known for bitter cold and stargazing. *See* ROGGE CLOOF, SUPER SINGLE VYDS.

Swartland COASTAL DISTRICT; profound influence on wine-growing since early 2000s through innovators, eg. SADIE FAMILY. Around 9400 ha of mostly shy-bearing, unirrigated bush vines producing concentrated, distinctive, fresh wines.

Testalonga Swa ★★→★★★ Range name El Bandito says it all: Craig Hawkins's natural vinifications defy convention; much respected and loved nonetheless. Earlier/easier Baby Bandito label for hipsters-in-training.

The little can that could: sales of tinned wine soared 720% in 2023.

Thelema Mountain Vineyards W Cape ★★→★★★★ STELL pioneer of SA's modern wine revival, still beacon of quality, consistency (and touch of hedonism, per Rabelais-inspired brand name). Complementary flavours from ELG vyds.

Thorne & Daughters Wines W Cape ★★★→★★★★ Bot R vintners John Thorne Seccombe and wife Tasha's wines, some from v. old vines and heirloom grapes, cerebral yet sensual, expressed with marvellous clarity and refinement.

Tokara W Cape ★★→★★★★ Wine, food, art showcase nr STELL; vyds also in ELG. Elegant Director's Res blends (r/w); gorgeous new Res CHENIN BL *vin de paille*; impressive new Ltd Release Simonsberg CAB SAUV from gravelly mtn site.

Trizanne Signature Wines Cape SC ★→★★★★ Female soloists like Trizanne Barnard still rare. Avid surfer sources from mostly COAST vyds for seriously gd boutique CHARD, SAUV BL (solo/blend), SYRAH. Dawn Patrol brand mostly export.

Tulbagh Inland DISTRICT (855 ha) historically associated with white and CAP CLASSIQUE, latterly also red, esp PINOTAGE, SHIRAZ, some sweet styles.

Tulbagh Mountain Vineyards Tul *See* DE KLEINE WIJN.

Uva Mira Mountain Vineyards Stell ★★★ Helderberg Mtn eyrie vyds/cellar owned by Toby Venter. Leashed power in CHARD, SAUV BL, SYRAH et al.

Van Loggerenberg Wines W Cape ★★→★★★★ PAARL-based Lukas VL star of light-styled, new-wave scene. Top: CHENIN BL, CAB FR; affordable range Break a Leg features v.gd rosé CINSAULT. Crafts also-excellent LOWERLAND, Michaella Wines and most of Carinus Family portfolios.

Van Loveren Family Vineyards Rob ★→★★★ Based in ROB, multiple cellar doors to welcome wine-lovers, dynamic VL claims to be Africa's leading family-owned private wine business, producing c.2m cases p.a. Easy-drinking, often sweeter styles, epitomized by Four Cousins labels (named for quartet of Retief men who run it), recent major push into premium markets has seen younger Survivor brand, and venerable NEIL ELLIS, join family.

Vergelegen Wines Stell ★★★→★★★★ Resources company Anglo-American's historic mansion and gardens, stylish cellar door at Somerset W. Leashed power in wines from classic French varieties. Deserved WWF-SA Conservation Champion.

SA's first vintage, 1659, was long before most people had even heard of the Médoc.

Vilafonté W Cape ★★★ Founded by California's Zelma Long and Phil Freese, and local eminence Mike Ratcliffe. Trio of luxurious red blends, vinified in STELL.

Villiera Wines W Cape ★★→★★★ Respected STELL winery and eco leader founded by Grier family, now in French hands. Exceptional quality/value ratio, esp in famed CAP CLASSIQUE range, featuring thrilling new flagship CHARD Brut, Pithos.

Vondeling V Pa ★→★★★ UK-owned, sustainability-focused estate nr PAARL. Eclectic offering covers everything from Bx-style red to pét-nat to vine-dried MUSCAT (sw).

Walker Bay Prestigious maritime DISTRICT (c.1000 ha) with standout CHARD, SAUV BL, PINOT N, SHIRAZ in Bot R, HEM, Springfontein Rim, Stanford Foothills, Sunday's Glen WARDS.

Ward *See* GU.

Warwick Wine Estate W Cape ★→★★★★ US-owned tourist drawcard on STELL fringe. Classic French varieties, incl standout CAB FR, plus PINOTAGE yield rich yet harmonious, fresh wines.

Waterford Estate W Cape ★→★★★ Ord family's Tuscany-inspired winery nr STELL, with suave, multi-faceted flagship red blend The Jem, one of several themed winetasting options at stylish courtyard cellar door. Winemaker Mark le Roux's freewheeling namesake brand worth a try.

Waterkloof W Cape ★→★★★ British wine merchant Paul Boutinot's organic vyds, cellar on exposed hilltop nr Somerset W. New range, Beeskamp ("Cattle Camp"), underscores importance of farm animals in aiding winery's sustainability drive.

Wellington Warm-climate DISTRICT (c.3700 ha) bordering PAARL and SWA. Growing reputation for CHENIN BL, CINSAULT, PINOTAGE, SHIRAZ, red blends.

Western Cape (W Cape) Most s province and dominant GU in wo system, with 85% official appellations.

Worcester Sibling DISTRICT (c.6300 ha) to ROB and BRE in Breede R basin; three new WARDS: Keeromsberg, Moordkuil, Rooikrans. Largely bulk for export, but some fine (family) wines and dynamic grower/BEE-owned Stettyn Family Vyds.

WO (Wine of Origin) "AOP" but without French restrictions. Certifies vintage, variety, area of origin and, on opt-in basis, sustainable production.

The price of wine

—

How much should we be paying for a bottle of wine? That is the subject of the pages that follow. You won't be surprised to know that there is no definitive answer. And if you say, "My definitive answer is how much I can afford," then join the club.

Wine prices have risen. In the UK, an unfriendly tax system makes things worse, but energy prices and labour costs everywhere mean that the wine you paid x for ten years ago now costs $x+y$, and sometimes $x+x$. Sometimes it does look as if producers are taking advantage. But if they are, they are taking advantage of a market that, for the moment, favours them. The market for burgundy, for example, is strong; the market for lawyers is strong; the market for doctors is strong. They earn accordingly. But winemakers can have a year's income removed by a brief frost on an April morning. Or a ten-minute August hailstorm.

One argument I hear a lot is that it doesn't cost any more to make a bottle of, say, First Growth Bordeaux than to make a bottle of Cru Bourgeois. This is not entirely true; but even if it were, the higher the price, the smaller the part played in it by costs. And how many of us would think it right if we were paid the same as somebody below us in the office hierarchy?

I am not arguing for high prices in the pages that follow, nor for cheapness; instead I am trying to show why some wines are more expensive than others, and how we can use that knowledge to buy cleverly.

We all want bargains. There are fewer bargains in wine than there used to be, and they probably cost more than they used to. But equally, the quality is probably better. And hunting down the bargains can take us towards wines we didn't know or hadn't considered. The great thing is to enjoy the hunt.

How is wine priced?

Awine merchant was visiting an affluent Greek resort. Everyone was drinking a particular imported rosé famous for its high price; he ordered the same. He sniffed the wine and said, "I know what this smells of. Profit."

This encapsulates the problem of very expensive wine: a wine that costs £200 (choose your currency; the same point applies to all) does not taste twice as good as one that costs £100. Or four times better than one that costs £50.

Does a £50 wine taste five times better than a £10 wine? Almost certainly not – though I do not know how you would measure such things. But let's pretend we can. At the most basic level, you probably do double the quality by doubling the price. In the UK, with its unfavourable tax regime, the tax per bottle stays the same and therefore the amount you're spending on the actual wine more than doubles. In countries with lower alcohol taxes, you're still getting many more bangs for your bucks.

Double the price again, and the wine should be better again. But twice as good? Hmm. With most wines, quality rises sharply towards a sweet spot of pricing. Then it rises more slowly, and eventually, if the price line on the graph keeps rising, the quality line might rise very slowly indeed.

Let's suppose you are a quality-conscious producer making four wines. The cheapest is your entry-level: it contains grapes from young vines, lesser vineyards, bits and pieces that don't fit into the other wines. You also make quite a lot of it, and you can keep the price down.

The next wine up will have more concentration, be made in smaller quantities and will be aged slightly longer, probably in some very good second- or third-use barrels, and will sell for perhaps double the price. The third wine up will be more prestigious: it may have some new oak and will have enough concentration of fruit not to taste of oak; it will come from your best sites. There will be a lot less of it. It might cost up to double the previous wine.

And the very top wine? Perhaps you only make this in the best years, in tiny quantities. It will be very concentrated but will (we hope) have perfect balance and elegance and will be aged in some very expensive

invisible oak – *see* p.364 for what "invisible oak" means. It will be a wine to lay down for some years. It will cost an arm and a leg.

Where is the sweet spot, where price meets value? Probably the second wine. The cheapest will be made with the same skill as the others; the next one up will have real individuality and style. The most expensive wine is aimed at people who want to spend unlimited amounts on the very rarest. It will be better than your third wine, but the difference in quality will be less than the difference in price.

What if those sweet-spot wines are too expensive for you the consumer, squeezed by taxes/interest rates/energy bills/inflation/aged parents/children (tick all that apply)? Then stick to the entry-level wine; it will be enjoyable and well made. The quality of such wines is better than it was even ten years ago: we are living in a golden age of wine quality.

But we started by talking about rosé. That wine merchant was suggesting that rosé might be cynically profit-driven. Is it?

It is, or can be, a cash cow. It can be made quite quickly and well, for drinking young, and turned out in large quantities. It is the only wine that sells largely on its colour. Rosé cash-flow is the foundation of some wine businesses: make it delicious, make it pretty and make it in quantity – give people what they want, in other words – and watch the profits roll in. But they have to know how to market it – and all rosé is not equally fashionable. The reason that most rosés are pale in colour now is because they need some of the fashionability of Provence rosé to rub off on wines from less modish places.

Which brings me to my next question: what do we want from wine?

Reliability or glamour?

What do we want from wine? It seems like an obvious question, but the answer determines how much we are prepared to pay and where we should be looking.

A drink that tastes nice and gives us a boost? A point in the day that marks the end of work and the beginning of the evening? Something sociable to share with people? Something that enhances a meal? Something that adds to our prestige with other people?

For some consumers, reliability is key. They want a brand they know they will like; and they know they will like it because they bought it last week, and the week before. I regard cars as those consumers regard wine: I really don't care as long as it doesn't let me down. Making wine for those consumers is as serious as making any other wine: no matter the vagaries of climate or supply, it must taste the same and must meet a particular price point in the shops, and that price point must satisfy both the shops and the producer's bean-counters, all of whom want a particular profit margin for a particular quantity. It will be made to that price. Consumers will get exactly what they expect: no bargains, no disappointments.

Readers of this book, by definition, have more curiosity about wine. Some have been hit hard by rising prices: the wines they used to buy are now too expensive to contemplate. They look at other sources and are dismayed because the wines don't taste the same, and the ones they like best are just as expensive as the ones they can no longer afford. What to do?

In the end, you have to adapt. Take Bordeaux. At the top of the Bordeaux tree there are a few dozen wines that are often treated as investment vehicles. At the bottom, there are quantities of wine that cannot find a market at all – hence the vine-uprooting schemes, intended to reduce the production of bulk Bordeaux and Bordeaux Supérieur, unsellable even at cost. In the middle is the sweet spot for drinkers – yet that sweet spot can sometimes feel a bit workaday, a bit lacking in glamour. Bordeaux has always been driven by the glamour of its top wines, but that glamour fades surprisingly fast once you lose sight of the Classed Growths.

Even so, Bordeaux has the virtue of producing a great deal of wine, and if you want the reassurance of that familiar flavour, then there are plenty of Cru Bourgeois and *petits châteaux* to choose from. This is the point at which you are most likely to get what you pay for in terms of quality: you're not paying a premium for fame, but the wines are certainly aspirational and well made. If you go for a Cru Bourgeois or a *petit château*, then pay the most you can, because it will be reflected in the glass. True, Château Peu Célèbre is never going be as exciting as Château Margaux. But it should be good value.

However, value in Bordeaux can be found in different vintages too. Again, it's all about demand; some years are overlooked, some are unreasonably sought after. Mature vintages can be far cheaper than younger ones, because of the rate at which en primeur prices have risen, and are ready to drink: win-win. James Lawther takes the matter in hand on page 112.

In the end, if you want to look elsewhere for claret flavours, you have to be prepared for differences. In California, Cabernet Sauvignon has thicker skins, more tannins; in Australia, richer fruit. Neither, at the top end, is cheap. So, investigate Cabernet Franc – from the Loire, from Hungary and Eastern Europe – or Carmenère. Or Malbec from Argentina. Or Tannat from Uruguay. It won't taste the same as the wine you can't afford any more; it's time for a change. You're about to discover a different world.

What you shouldn't do is trade down in Bordeaux until you hit rock-bottom. Value is not found in rock-bottom prices. There are plenty of people, indeed, for whom the pleasure of wine can only be attained at the very highest prices. What effect have they had on wine pricing? That's what we'll look at next.

Wine as
luxury goods
—

I t's hard to put a precise date on when wine joined the ranks of luxury goods, along with handbags and shoes and art and yachts and diamonds and who knows what else.

It was some time in the 80s or 90s, and it happened gradually, with a few super-expensive Napa Cabernets murmuring the phrase, their reputations and their prices boosted by 100-point scores from US critic Robert Parker. Bordeaux First Growths thought, Well, if they are, we jolly well are too; and so it spread. One wine after another woke up and realized that it too was luxury goods. And once you've decided that, you have to stay there. Nobody wants to be discounted luxury goods. But what does it mean? Just really, really expensive? Or is a resale value implied?

That depends on the market, which is something over which producers have only limited control. Launching a wine at £200 a bottle (again, choose your currency) is one thing; getting people to want it enough for there to be a secondary market is quite another. When you're buying wine, you might start inferring a resale value once you start paying somewhere between £50 and £100 per bottle, though it doesn't necessarily follow. Not all high-priced wines are in demand at auction.

But there are super-high-priced wines everywhere now. Often it's market-making by producers: you launch your brand-new wine at £200, and within weeks you announce that it's on allocation worldwide. These are weasel words. Allocation to whom? How much have you actually released? You don't have to produce any evidence. Some excited and uncritical coverage on social media will help. If the wine is genuinely good, and it should be at that price, then good scores will gradually come in. If your strategy works, then demand will increase over the years to become whatever you said it was in the first place.

If this sounds cynical, then a bit of cynicism is always a useful seasoning in wine. Some of the luxury-goods wines launched in the 90s have become classics and proved their quality; others are just a memory.

Pushing the market doesn't always work. When LVMH bought Château d'Yquem back in 1996, the new owner considered the market price for a case of the wine to be far too low. So he released it at a much higher price, only to find that the market refused to go along. The price had to come down – and this for a wine with a worldwide reputation of long standing. Nobody would dispute that Yquem is luxury goods; it's just that, in spite of its rarity and the extraordinary detail of its production, it can't command the price of an equivalent red.

People buy luxury-goods wines as investments, of course, and that means that a lot gets tucked away in cellars. Producers don't like this: they want people to drink their wines and then buy more. Some producers are now arranging to age their wines themselves and release them to top restaurants worldwide at attractive prices, so that the wines go on lists and on to tables and get talked about and drunk. To stay in demand, a wine has to be visible.

For those who buy and collect in the luxury-goods wine market, those longed-for bottles are not just about flavour – and may not be very much about flavour. Prestige and competitiveness play their parts: it's the lust of acquisition much more than the desire to see what so-and-so has done with the new vintage. When allocations of Grand Cru burgundies go down – because of higher demand or a small harvest – merchants will be answering the telephone to collectors shouting, "Don't you know who I am?" Buying wine at £500 a bottle is not necessarily about buying wonderful flavours and elegance; it can be about buying a place among those who pay £500 a bottle. And no doubt they consider it good value.

Some collectors at this level take pleasure in sharing their wines with friends and colleagues, though presumably only with those who will recognize the label. I'm reminded of a British politician who famously served Krug to his guests. "Did they appreciate the finer points of such wonderful Champagne?" he was asked. He said he had no idea, but they could read.

Good value?

—

I t's extraordinary to think that Yquem cannot reach the astonishing prices commanded by First Growth Bordeaux reds. It's not cheap; but by the standards of equivalent reds, it's underpriced.

So are all Sauternes; so, indeed, are most sweet wines. All, probably. And yet they're rare. Quantities of great sweet wines are always small. If you want bargains, here they are. "Ah," you say, "but I hardly ever drink dessert wines." And that's the answer, of course: they're unfashionable. The demand just isn't there. Their makers love them and want to keep alive the traditions and skills behind them, but it must sometimes seem a thankless task.

The main determinant of wine price is supply and demand, and what lies behind that is fashion. Fashion is what has driven the extraordinary increase in demand for red burgundy, and by extension Pinot Noir from everywhere else; at the beginning of this century it was Cabernet Sauvignon that everybody wanted. Not only was it planted here, there and everywhere, but wines that had nothing to do with Cabernet did their best to taste as if they did – even red burgundy.

Then fashion changed, and the Cabernetization of everything turned to the Pinotization of everything. Look at Grenache: instead of being big and beefy, it's light, pale and delicate. Everything is going Pinot-ish. Fashion and demand pushed up prices of red Bordeaux year after year, and merchants complained that they wouldn't be able to sell the wines. But the producers didn't listen, and the merchants bought them anyway – and sold them. The 2023 vintage, which found much less of a ready market, might be a turning point or it might just be a blip; if the former, then it will suggest that there is a limit to what people will pay. Until then it looked as if there was no limit.

Burgundy is a much smaller region than Bordeaux, and Burgundy vineyards and estates are tiny in comparison. For many years, Burgundy was excellent value compared to Bordeaux, but now the number of buyers piling into the burgundy market is making Bordeaux look relatively cheap. Burgundy is now astonishingly expensive, and rare: a top producer might have just a single barrel of some wines. And if you want anything from Domaine Leroy (assuming you have the slightest chance of getting near it), you'll be paying up to six figures. Per bottle.

At the same time, there are wines that fashion ignores. Sherry, famously, remains astonishingly good value. Wines of considerable age and enormous complexity cost less than a bottle of reasonable Bordeaux. Fino is a classic apéritif for very good reasons, and Amontillado is great with tagines. With aged hard cheese, it's hard to beat Amontillado or Oloroso. The cash-strapped in search of quality should look here first.

Where else? South Africa is good value; so is much of Italy, and Spain too. Central and Eastern Europe are good hunting grounds. Greece too, and Austria. Chile and Argentina also have interest at lower price levels. Germany has some classic Rieslings from excellent producers at very good prices. In France, the southwest, the Loire (where quality has soared) and Languedoc-Roussillon are your starting points. Alsace too. The Rhône? Maybe. But Crozes-Hermitage is also said to be France's most profitable appellation.

If you're in the US, the picture will be different, and US wines will be priced very differently; in the US chapter, and in many other chapters throughout the book this year, there are boxes pointing you towards value hotspots. There's nothing like a bit of insider knowledge.

But as ever, the cheapest price is not the best value. The cheapest is merely the cheapest. Mass production brings costs per bottle down, but mass-produced wines are seldom very interesting and may not be sustainable in the long run. So, without wanting to sound like an accountancy investigation, let's take a look next at what costs are actually incurred in making wine.

Vineyards and the land

—

Afew years ago, a British merchant did a study that found that no wine could cost more than €60 a bottle to make, and most top wines cost no more than €25 – figures that are easy enough to translate into other currencies. A couple of years of high inflation will have pushed them up, but you get the picture.

How much does this matter to us as consumers? How many of us really think, when buying a bottle, What was the production cost of this? Do we examine the quality of the stopper to see if it cost more or less? Do we look at the bottle, the label, the box the bottles came in, to see if they're trimming pennies or splashing the cash?

We pay what we're prepared to pay. And costs (apart from our costs) don't have a lot to do with what we're prepared to pay. Costs might also have little to do with what producers charge. As we've seen, that's more likely to be determined by fashion and demand. No producer of, say, Sauternes, undervalued as it is, will get anywhere by saying, "But it cost me *x* to make! I need you to pay more!"

So, what are these costs? First, of course, there is land, and vineyards. On the prime bits of the Côte d'Or, tiny plots of vines were being offered at the equivalent of €80 million per hectare a couple of years ago. Even if you could sell the wine for €700–800 a bottle, it still wouldn't make a lot of sense. It would take generations to make a profit. And as one burgundy merchant said, they take a long-term view, but not that long.

High prices are not new – back in 1900, 43 ares of the Doctor vineyard in Germany's Bernkastel sold for the equivalent of €3 million – though prices this high are certainly new. In England, with its relatively new wine industry, agricultural land in Essex's tiny Crouch Valley is normally around £8000–9000 per hectare. But if you want precisely the right plots for vineyards, the price might triple. When the first pioneering winemakers went to Gredos in Spain and started sniffing around for old, abandoned vineyards they could bring back to life, prices were not high because the region had been forgotten. But the word got around, and owners raised their prices. Elsewhere in Spain, when Vega Sicilia wanted to buy old vineyards in Toro, it looked using a different name, well aware that if it was known to be looking, prices could rocket in seconds.

If you're a winemaker with family vineyards, the problem of vineyard value doesn't arise – until you come to inherit. If you have Grand Cru vines on the Côte d'Or, how on Earth will you pay the inheritance tax? The answer is, you won't be able to. So, you will have to sell, and there will be one less family company, and another multi-national with deep pockets and a wish for trophy vineyards will take over.

If you're planting new vineyards from scratch, or replanting old ones, then a few years ago (2021 to be precise) the cost of planting a hectare was €25,000–30,000, including preparing the land, planting, stakes, trellising and so on. A vine costs at least €10.

If an aspiring winemaker decides to duck all that and buy grapes from growers, then the price of grapes varies enormously according to region. In Champagne, the price per kilo can be €8 or more, depending on quality, and I remember the CEO of one famous Champagne producer inviting me to the annual lunch he gave for his growers, looking around and saying, "They're all millionaires, you know". Yields are pretty high in Champagne. Elsewhere it might be different. In Toro, for example, some growers are giving up and growing pistachios instead; €0.60 per kilo for Tinta de Toro, rising to €1 for old vines or €0.35 for white grapes, just isn't economical in a hot, dry region where yields are low.

In Sauternes (sorry to keep returning to Sauternes, but it's an extreme case – probably the most expensive wine of all to make – and an extreme wine), let's say it costs around €60 a bottle to make. If, in a good year, you put half your crop into the *grand vin* and half into the second wine, and the cost of making the second wine is around €15, you'll probably sell it to a merchant for maybe €10, and you'll lose on every bottle. But the reputation of your *grand vin* depends on tight selection and on all but the very best lots going into the second wine. Even Tokaji is cheaper to make; the climate is less variable and labour is cheaper. A variable climate is a great driver of costs.

As are splendid new cellars, of course, and we see lots of those, all over the world. Are we, the consumers, ultimately paying for them? Let's look at that next.

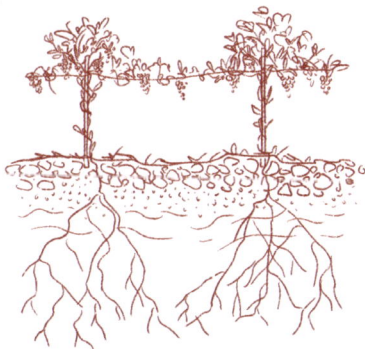

In the winery

—

We looked at the cost of making a bottle of wine just now, and the cost of vineyards. But actually making the stuff is a part of that total cost, and you need some pretty pricey kit. You also need a building to put it in.

You can do it on a shoestring. A cheap, functional shed will do for a building, and you can buy barrels, a press and lots of kit secondhand. That makes a lot of sense for small start-ups. Add winemaking skill and good terroir, and some very good wine can be turned out: not everybody needs or wants the latest gadget or whizzy new experimental container.

But many do. It might be because they have good funding and an experimental turn of mind: winemakers love trying new things. A cellar like this will have amphorae, concrete eggs, a granite egg, a glass Wineglobe (spherical, made of glass, for ageing) or two, barriques from different coopers designed to suit that particular wine, *foudres* from a cooper like Stockinger, where the oak is meant to be invisible on the palate, maybe a GalileOak barrel (it's spherical, and it rotates) – and that's only for ageing the wine. There might be an optical sorting table or two and the latest in presses, all fitted into a gravity-fed winery with climate control and a collection of art on the walls. If the architect was a big name, you could spend – what? – several million on the whole thing, before you start on the art. Producers tend to be coy about those details.

However, it's easy to find out the cost of the ageing containers. A barrique of 225 litres, with the oak chosen to suit your wine, will cost €800 and up, according to what you want. A *foudre* from Stockinger – an Austrian cooperage that is the choice of biodynamic producers seeking purity and oak so refined that tasters will not notice it has been used – is around €22,000; other coopers can be even more expensive. A rotating GalileOak 15-hectolitre barrel, which keeps the lees in suspension and looks great on Instagram, costs around €50,000; a glass Wineglobe – spherical and made of clear glass, as you might guess – comes in different sizes and is priced accordingly, but expect to pay about €3000 or more; amphorae are around €2000 upwards; even stainless-steel tanks start at around €1000, and more if you want lots of bells and whistles. Nowadays, it's all about containers that are so neutral in flavour you wouldn't know they were there, and you can decide on the precise amount of oxidation or reduction you want at each stage. Invisibility is expensive.

"What a lot of nonsense," you might say. "A barrel is a barrel. These are just gimmicks." Sometimes they are. I recall a Champagne producer boasting about a barrel lined with pure gold. That was a gimmick. But clay amphorae, Wineglobes, invisible oak *foudres*, concrete tanks, stainless-steel tanks and barriques all have definite and different effects on flavour. Even ageing sparkling wine under the sea – an experiment started by Veuve Clicquot and copied by others including, in England, Exton Park – affects flavour. The differences are there in the glass. And in an intensely competitive market, something that gives your wine an extra edge of elegance or complexity is worth it. And if it's Instagrammable, that's not a disadvantage.

Winemaking is now so good and reliable at all levels that it's hard (though not impossible) to find badly made wines. Once you've made all the easy improvements, you must embark on the more difficult ones. At the top level, wines are so good that to make them just a tiny bit better costs a fortune. But your competitors are doing it, so you must too.

Economies of scale help, of course. If you're making plenty of wine, investing in a granite egg as an experiment is more affordable than if you're tiny. But however tiny you are, if you're aiming to be seen as top-quality, you need to keep spending.

Ageing wine in the cellar is expensive too, and sparkling-wine makers point to this as one of their big costs. On the other hand, yields for sparkling are usually higher than for still. Production costs from the point at which the grapes arrive in the cellar vary, but you could reckon about £10–12 per bottle; and as one producer said to me, the margin has to be 100%, or why bother? You sell it to a merchant, who also has costs and needs to make a margin, and might have worked extremely hard to source particular wines; and eventually we pick it off the shelf.

When we look at the back label and see the words "oak-aged", we might think it sounds a bit premium. But do we ever think what it really means and what we're paying for? That's what we'll look at next.

The quality of oak

—

Every bottle of wine has a backstory. We can imagine, more or less, the backstory of the grapes – the vineyard, the choice of variety, the weather that year – and, if we want, we can trace all those back further – the history of the region, the reason that those grapes are planted there, the effect of climate change on what we are drinking.

Oak, we tend to think of as new or old, French or American. (Or chips or staves, if we're buying cheap industrial wine.) But oak is far more complex than that, and it is used for much more than the obvious reason of rounding out the wine and adding a note of rich vanilla. The relationship between oak and cooper is as personal as that between winemaker and vineyard; the terroir of a particular patch of forest as individual as the terroir of each parcel of vines.

To discover why some oak tastes one way and some tastes another way, and what we're paying for, let's do a quick dive into the backstory of an oak barrel, starting in the forest.

French forests, owned by the state and intended to produce oak for commercial purposes, are famously well managed. When Gusbourne wanted to make a barrel from its own oak in Kent, it was pretty hard to find enough trees that were straight enough and uniform enough for the job: English oaks tend to be a bit undisciplined in their approach to growth. But a forest managed for timber will have trees growing straight up, with few side branches low down: nodes mean faults in the timber; twists in the trunk mean unsuitability for staves. And even then, coopers don't use the sapwood, the roots or the branches: only the first 2–3m (6.5–10ft) from the ground are suitable for barrels.

Each year, the Office National des Forêts selects plots from each forest for

sale. In each plot, every tree will be different: one tree will have a very tight grain and another, maybe next to it, will have a more open grain. A tight grain, in a barrel, gives slower evolution of wine but more aroma; a more open grain gives more tannin and less aroma. That's the first and most obvious choice for a winemaker.

Every cooper has parts of each forest that it knows well: it might specialize in the northwest of Tronçais, for example. It will know the different plots; even the different trees. And it's grain they focus on. The perfect tree can be expensive, perhaps €1200; too expensive, sometimes, for even the fussiest cooper.

Trees are cut in winter, when the pores are closed. Six cubic metres of wood make one cubic metre of thick staves for *foudres*, if you split the wood into staves. Sawing gives more staves, but they're more liable to leak.

The wood, cut into planks, must be dried. But where? Air-drying, with the wind and rain taking out the astringency of the oak, varies according to where you do it: the maritime climate of Bordeaux has totally different effects than drying in a hotter, drier climate. Even oak air-dried in Burgundy is different. How you stack the planks matters and is shifting with climate change; and oak dried for five years is much more subtle in flavour and develops more micro-flora and bacteria, which act as flavour precursors in wine, than oak dried for two years. And, of course, it costs more.

How you toast the oak in the cooperage, while bending the staves into barrel-shaped curves, is vital: hot and fast is not the same as long and slow. Will your barrel give you vanilla flavours, caramel, coffee, or coconut? The toast that is perfect for Pinot will not be right for Cabernet.

Each cooperage has its own traditions and its own ways. Winemakers and coopers will taste together and choose the wood accordingly. A winemaker in Burgundy might have different coopers for each vineyard. Some winemakers favour particular forests: Champagne Henri Giraud always uses wood from the Argonne Forest and says, of the different plots there, that Châtrices is more angular in its effects on wine; Valmy is more velvety. Other plots in the same forest give generosity, or apricot notes. They maintain that the north-facing part of the tree is different from the south-facing part, and that the wood lower down gives more breadth, while that from higher up gives elegance and finesse. Winemakers who want that degree of detail will go to the forest and chew the wood. Stockinger says that if you chew the wood, you can tell Austrian oak from German, French from Slavonian.

Winemakers pay €800 and more for a barrique because the right one will show off the wine; but a dud barrel is a disaster. Better and better barrels, more perfectly suited to the wine, are one reason why wines are so much sleeker and fresher than they used to be.

Which leads to my final question: can a wine taste expensive?

Can a wine taste expensive?

—

"Taste expensive" rather than just be expensive? The answer is yes. Not all expensive wines taste expensive, though they might (or should) taste complex, characterful and well made with a sense of their origin.

An expensive taste is something other than this. It's a gloss, a polish, a sense of perfection. The traditional way of describing tension in a wine – the tension that gives excitement – is of a person on a tightrope. There's a sense of risk. Wines that taste expensive may not have such a nuance, any more than a Bentley feels risky. Risk in wine might come from exposing the terroir; an expensive-tasting wine will polish up the terroir until all the lumps and bumps are erased. Perfection is expensive tasting. Bordeaux, at the top end, aims at perfection. Burgundy has traditionally preferred to express terroir.

Do I mean that burgundy doesn't taste expensive, even though it is? Sort of, but only sort of. Great burgundy is resonant, complex, detailed; it almost defies description, though yes, I do realize that describing it is part of my job. But you can taste the sun and the rain and the rock in a way that is less clear in great Bordeaux. Latour tastes like Latour; it has tasted like Latour for so long that it is impossible, for most of us, to say why it tastes as it does. If we could taste each individual vat, each individual barrel, we might have more of a clue. In Burgundy, what you taste might be just two or three barrels' worth.

An expensive gloss is not just about site; it comes from process. It comes from optical sorting machines that reject any imperfect berry; it comes from the most precise extraction of tannins and the most expensive oak. Wines with that plutocratic gloss are more likely to be red. Really silky tannins confer a sense of rightness; expensive-tasting wines don't challenge. They're not bland – wine can't be great and bland at the same time – and they should have depth and detail and all those things. But a great Riesling can be difficult to understand; a great white Rhône can be difficult to understand. A plutocratic-tasting red from Chile, or California, or Italy, or Spain, or Australia, or many other places will speak of its origin, but in a language that is instantly recognizable. Wherever you go in the world, you can spot cashmere when you see it.

A little learning ...

A few technical words

Winemaking terms inevitably creep into any discussion of wine styles and changing fashions. Here are the ones we use most in the book.

Acidity This is both fixed and volatile. **Fixed** is mostly tartaric, malic and citric, all from the grape, and lactic and succinic, from fermentation. Acidity may be natural or (in warm climates) added. **Volatile (VA)**, or acetic acid, is formed by bacteria in the presence of oxygen. A touch of VA is common and can add complexity. Too much = vinegar. Total acidity is fixed + VA combined.

Alcohol content (mainly ethyl alcohol) This is expressed as per cent (%) by volume of the total liquid. (Also known as "degrees".) Table wines are usually 12.5–14.5%. Controlling alcohol levels is big challenge of modern viticulture.

Amphora The fermentation vessel of the moment, and the past 7000 yrs. Throw in grapes, return in 6 mths. Risky. *Tinaja* in Spain, *talha* in Portugal.

Barrels Small (225-litre) oak barriques – for fermentation, ageing – are classic, but invisible oak flavours are the fashion now. Bigger barrels give less oak flavour; used barrels are increasingly popular too – same reason. Acacia can be gd for whites: subtle aromatic note.

Biodynamic (bio) Type of viticulture that uses herbal, mineral and ORGANIC preparations in homeopathic quantities, in accordance with the phases of the moon and the movements of the planets. Now mainstream. NB: "bio" in French means organic as well, but in this book it means biodynamic.

Carbonic maceration Whole (red) berries go into closed vat; fermentation starts within each berry. Gives juicy, light style.

Concrete eggs The fermentation vessel of the moment; keeps lees moving. Concrete generally has returned to fashion as part of move away from oak.

Field blend Different varieties planted together, picked and fermented together. Ultra-trendy, and tastes different too.

Malolactic fermentation This occurs after the alcoholic fermentation and changes tart malic acid into softer lactic acid. Can add complexity to red and white alike. Often avoided in hot climates, where natural acidity is low and precious.

Micro-oxygenation This widely used bubbling technique allows controlled contact with oxygen during maturation. Softens flavours, helps to stabilize wine.

Minerality Tasting term to be used with caution: fine as descriptor of chalky/stony flavours. Should not imply actual minerals from soil in wine.

Natural wines Undefined but start by being ORGANIC or BIO, involve minimal intervention in the winery and minimal SULPHUR or none. At best, wonderful; shouldn't be an excuse for faults. Often made in AMPHORAE or CONCRETE EGGS.

Old vines These give deeper flavours. No legal definition: some "vieilles vignes" turn out to be c.30 years. Should be 50+ to be taken seriously.

Orange wines Tannic whites fermented on skins, perhaps in AMPHORAE. Like NATURAL WINES, some good, some not. Excellent with food.

Organic viticulture This prohibits most chemical products in the vineyard; organic wine prohibits added SULPHUR and must be made from organically grown grapes.

Pét-nat (pétillant naturel) Bottled before end of fermentation, which continues in bottle. Slight residual sugar, quite low ALCOHOL. Dead trendy.

pH Not a measure of acidity, but low pH mostly goes with acidity. Wine is normally 2.8–3.8. High pH can be a problem in hot climates. Lower pH gives better colour, helps stop bacterial spoilage and allows more of the SULPHUR to be free and active as a preservative. So, low is good in general.

Residual sugar That which is left after fermentation has ended or been stopped, measured in grams per litre (g/l). A dry wine has almost none.

Sulphur dioxide Added to prevent oxidation and other accidents in winemaking. Some combines with sugars, etc., and is "bound". Only "free" sulphur is effective as a preservative. Trend worldwide is to use less. To use none is brave.